A JOURNAL OF THE PLAGUE YEAR

AUTHORITATIVE TEXT
BACKGROUNDS
CONTEXTS
CRITICISM

W. W. NORTON & COMPANY, INC.
Also Publishes

THE NORTON ANTHOLOGY OF AFRICAN AMERICAN LITERATURE
edited by Henry Louis Gates Jr. and Nellie Y. McKay et al.

THE NORTON ANTHOLOGY OF AMERICAN LITERATURE
edited by Nina Baym et al.

THE NORTON ANTHOLOGY OF CONTEMPORARY FICTION
edited by R. V. Cassill and Joyce Carol Oates

THE NORTON ANTHOLOGY OF ENGLISH LITERATURE
edited by M. H. Abrams and Stephen Greenblatt et al.

THE NORTON ANTHOLOGY OF LITERATURE BY WOMEN
edited by Sandra M. Gilbert and Susan Gubar

THE NORTON ANTHOLOGY OF MODERN POETRY
edited by Richard Ellmann and Robert O'Clair

THE NORTON ANTHOLOGY OF POETRY
edited by Margaret Ferguson, Mary Jo Salter, and Jon Stallworthy

THE NORTON ANTHOLOGY OF SHORT FICTION
edited by R. V. Cassill and Richard Bausch

THE NORTON ANTHOLOGY OF THEORY AND CRITICISM
edited by Vincent B. Leitch et al.

THE NORTON ANTHOLOGY OF WORLD LITERATURE
edited by Sarah Lawall et al.

THE NORTON FACSIMILE OF THE FIRST FOLIO OF SHAKESPEARE
prepared by Charlton Hinman

THE NORTON INTRODUCTION TO LITERATURE
edited by Alison Booth, J. Paul Hunter, and Kelly J. Mays

THE NORTON INTRODUCTION TO THE SHORT NOVEL
edited by Jerome Beaty

THE NORTON READER
edited by Linda H. Peterson, John C. Brereton, and Joan E. Hartman

THE NORTON SAMPLER
edited by Thomas Cooley

THE NORTON SHAKESPEARE, BASED ON THE OXFORD EDITION
edited by Stephen Greenblatt et al.

For a complete list of Norton Critical Editions, visit us at
www.wwnorton.com/college/english/nce.welcome.htm

A NORTON CRITICAL EDITION

Daniel Defoe

A JOURNAL OF THE PLAGUE YEAR

AUTHORITATIVE TEXT
BACKGROUNDS
CONTEXTS
CRITICISM

Edited by

PAULA R. BACKSCHEIDER

AUBURN UNIVERSITY

W · W · NORTON & COMPANY · *New York · London*

Library of Congress Cataloging-in-Publication Data

Defoe, Daniel, 1661?–1731.
A Journal of the plague year : authoritative text, backgrounds,
contexts, criticism / edited by Paula R. Backscheider.
    p.   cm. — (A Norton critical edition)
Includes bibliographical references and index.
1. Plague—England—London—Fiction.   I. Backscheider, Paula R.
                            II. Title.
            PR3404.J6   1992
        823′.5—dc20   91-21599

ISBN 0-393-96188-5

W. W. Norton & Company, Inc., 500 Fifth Avenue, New York, N.Y. 10110
www.wwnorton.com

W. W. Norton & Company Ltd., Castle House, 75/76 Wells Street,
London W1T 3QT

9 0

To My Students

Contents

Criticism   265

Preface

A plague is always a moral as well as biological crisis for a community. It allows no individuals; it makes all people a community and emphasizes human relationships. A New York City doctor remarked of the 1916 polio epidemic, "We have learned very little that is new about the disease, but much that is old about ourselves." His rueful observation could speak for antiquity and for our own time's AIDS epidemic.

When Daniel Defoe wrote A *Journal of the Plague Year,* he believed that his country was in immediate, perhaps inevitable, danger of the kind of visitation of the plague that had struck London and parts of the English nation in 1665, the year he was about five years old. Nearly every issue of the London papers since 1719 had been reporting on the outbreaks and progress of the plague on the Continent. In 1720, two years before the publication of A *Journal,* between forty thousand and sixty thousand people had died in Marseilles, France, alone. Between 1345 and 1720, at least fifty million people had died of bubonic plague in Europe, including an estimated one-third of the population of Europe in the 1348 epidemic. Even today, between 60 and 80 percent of those infected by bubonic plague die.

In 1722 Defoe was a retired businessman, election-opinion sampler, spy, and public poet. We would probably identify his occupation as journalist, for he was controlling or writing for nine newspapers and periodicals. Since his thirtieth birthday he had written some of the most powerful political propaganda of the century and been arrested several times for it. His first novel, *Robinson Crusoe,* had been published only three years earlier, and with it and his other 1722 novels, *Moll Flanders* and *Col. Jack,* he was discovering fiction's power to reach people and to spread his ideas. Defoe would soon say, "Every Man ought . . . to contribute in his Station, to the publick Welfare, and not be afraid or ashamed of doing, or at least, meaning well"; he was, he said, "resolv'd to commit [his ideas] to Paper . . . and leave, at least, a Testimony of my good Will to my Fellow Creatures." A *Journal* and another book published a month earlier, *Due Preparations for the Plague,* were completely in harmony with his vision of his purpose as writer. First, he felt that they were useful books. Much of A *Journal* is an accurate, even researched, rendering of the 1665 plague, but much of it is an idealistic picture of how ministers, health care professionals, city officials, and even individuals should conduct themselves in the time of crisis he feared would come.

Second, *A Journal* is propaganda, but like all Defoe's propaganda it is not mindless support for the government's policies and actions. For instance, although *A Journal* obviously supports the ship quarantine and some of the measures in the 1721 Quarantine Act, it deeply opposes shutting up houses and points relentlessly at the possible consequences of quarantining entire towns. In fact, reactions such as Defoe's helped bring about the Act's repeal and the passage of the drastically altered 1722 Act. Such analytical and independent thinking had made Defoe hated, feared, and distrusted but respected and influential in his lifetime. Defoe's text raises many of the issues with which we are still grappling: the limits of public authority, the rights of the diseased, the government's responsibility to finance health care, and the conflicting pressures of self-preservation and compassion. It also reminds us of how consistent is human nature. Just as Defoe's contemporaries wore charms and brewed preservatives, people in 1916 believed alcohol rubs might keep polio from attacking the spine and periodicals advertised Chinese herbal therapies for AIDS in 1990. Just as Defoe's contemporaries wondered if the plague was a punishment from God, perhaps specifically for post-Restoration revelry, in 1988 Cardinal Siri of Genoa called AIDS "a holy plague to punish sinners" and the Soviet Health Minister termed it "a disease of decadence." Just as the Lord Mayor and the College of Physicians publicized information about the plague, measures for prevention, and resources for treatment and advice, so informational pamphlets, posters, brochures, and even bookmarks and comic books published by public health authorities and private agencies are available to us in a dozen languages.

A Journal has always been recognized as one of Defoe's most artistic works and is one of the most vivid, perenially popular novels in English. It is an excellent introduction to his writing. The novel is filled with the kinds of facts, statistics, and details that the best journalists use to bring to life an event and a people's experience and responses. Defoe's special concerns with how people live, with ethics, with trade, and with civic administration add depth to the vivid accounts of mass death and of individual suffering and heroism. Like a good journalist, too, Defoe has done research. His reading and use of books and pamphlets published as awareness of the continental plague grew provided his alert mind with episodes both representative and bizarre. Some incidents seem to be stories he heard from family and friends who survived the 1665 plague, and others, such as that of the plague piper on our cover, are embellished London folklore.

As I have said in another place, Defoe built beautiful, thematically rich patterns into the novel. The opening pages establish the pattern of severe anxiety followed by complacency, a pattern that is repeated at the end and that mirrors H. F.'s vacillations about whether to go or stay and to shut himself up or walk the streets. The phrase "all the 97 parishes" becomes a refrain, and the regular appearances of the bills of mortality that Defoe uses to integrate individual anecdotes into mass casualties become visual markers. As the months pass and the plague moves from west to east, the patterns in the book come together. The confused deaths of hundreds are punctuated first by anecdotes of people who are not so much individuals as representatives, and, second, by yet sharper moments conveyed in single violent images, such as the scream "O Death! Death! Death!" and the pregnant woman kissed. Underlying all of the action of the book is the fierce struggle between the city officials and a city on the verge of breakdown.

Defoe's narrator is an especially effective artistic creation. Very much a man of his time, H. F. is observer, witness, and fascinated, frightened mortal. He, like his contemporaries in the Royal Society, wants to understand the material world and discover causes. He collects evidence, ponders, sorts, and entertains or rejects hypotheses about the causes of plague, not identified until 1894 as the bacillus *Yersinia pestis*, which is primarily an internal parasite of rodents and carried initially by fleas from the dying animals. He wants to record for posterity the list of brave men and women who stayed in the city to govern, to organize, to minister, and to doctor. He wants to witness—to write a history of what Maximillian E. Novak has called London's "victory of life over death." Like his contemporaries, he is existing at the historical moment when the religious certainty of the sixteenth and seventeenth centuries gave way to modern skepticism and secularism. He believes, therefore, that human beings can make a difference—their actions can slow, perhaps even prevent and eventually cure, the plague. One of his favorite sayings was, "The God that gave me brains will give me bread." That belief in the brains God gave humankind undergirds the modern commitment to progress, and without denying God's existence and power Defoe insists upon the need and responsibility for human action.

Although H. F. is an observer and recorder, a medium through which we see the plague, he is also an individual. He is craven and tries to pull strings when his turn to be an examiner of the ill comes. He is caught in a ludicrous scene when he discovers women raiding his brother's hat warehouse. Men in a tavern jeer at him. Although he strongly condemns the quacks and mountebanks, he is not immune to superstition and uses it as partial justification for his remaining in London. His energy and curiosity compete with his fear and loathing, and he wavers and oscillates. Careful as he has been, he finally declares himself both foolish and lucky.

The material that accompanies the text of Defoe's novel is divided into three sections. The first is made up of documents from 1665 and the early 1720s. Some are Defoe's sources and suggest his dependence on them, his concern for accuracy, and his methods for evoking the year of the great plague. Others contribute to the understanding of how people felt and responded and how the government acted. The next section offers comparative texts united by the theme of a community in crisis. Beginning with the excerpt from Thucydides' description of the epidemic in 430 B.C. and concluding with readings about AIDS, this group includes some of the most famous observers and critics in Western civilization who have seen the metaphoric significance of "plague." As Albert Camus wroted in his *The Plague*, "No longer were there individual destinies; only a collective destiny, made of plague and the emotions shared by all." The final section contains most of the best modern critical essays on the novel. Although these essays are literary analyses, they are somewhat unusual in that Defoe's text has brought each critic to respond in some way to social issues and to contemplate the power and emotional force that literature can have.

The text is the 1722 first edition, the only edition published in Defoe's lifetime. I have corrected obvious typographical errors and modernized the eighteenth-century long "s," which appears very much like an "f." Spelling and punctuation were not standardized in Defoe's time, and I have preserved the irregularities and idiosyncrasies. Reading aloud was a popular recreation and improving activity, and punctuation for many writers was elocutionary rather than syntactical. Defoe's often emphasizes the rhythms present in his text. What Samuel Johnson said of writing his *Dictionary* definitions can be said of my textual annotations: "Things equally easy in themselves, are not all equally easy to any single mind . . . what is obvious is not always known, and what is known is not always present." There is no standard edition of Defoe's works, and only the Oxford World's Classic edition has numerous notes. I would like to acknowledge my debt to those notes, prepared for the 1969 Oxford edition by Louis A. Landa, but my greatest debt is to my students and to those fellow Defoe scholars who contributed to my knowledge and understanding during the time I was writing my biography of Defoe, *Daniel Defoe: His Life*. I am especially grateful to the students in my freshman class who volunteered to divide the book among themselves and list every word that they believed needed explanation.

The idea and the shape of this edition came from my experiences teaching *A Journal of the Plague Year* in three different kinds of classes, and each group of students made a special contribution. In addition to that freshman class, which also found ways to bring the text to life with, for instance, lotteries that made visible how many of them would have died in 1665, I would like to acknowledge a seminar of juniors and seniors who reminded me of how Defoe can still shock and surprise readers and a seminar of graduate students who brought sophisticated representation and culture-studies theory to bear on the text. I am also grateful to the graduate research assistant who contributed in more ways than I can list to this edition. Catherine Loomis was an ingenious, persistent, efficient assistant and, moreover, read with a sharp critical eye. Her special familiarity with the medical literature of the seventeenth and eighteenth centuries served us well. A number of people contributed to the incorporation of modern material, and I owe special thanks to Joseph Cady, Linda Merians, John Roberts, Michelle Brandwein, John Bender, and John Richetti. I am also grateful to my Norton editor, Carol Bemis, who was intrigued with the idea of this edition from the beginning and has been a model of helpfulness.

The Text of
A JOURNAL OF THE
PLAGUE YEAR

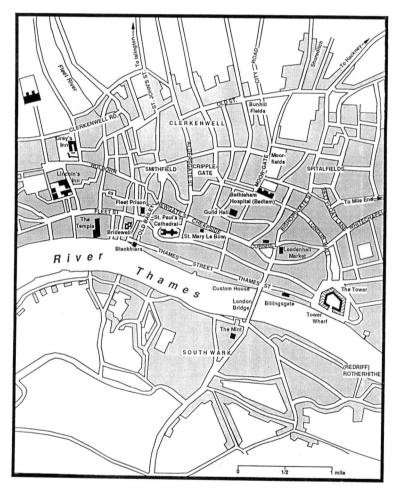

Detail of H. F.'s London

A

JOURNAL

OF THE

Plague Year:

BEING

Obſervations or Memorials,

Of the moſt Remarkable

OCCURRENCES,

As well

PUBLICK *as* PRIVATE,

Which happened in

LONDON

During the laſt

GREAT VISITATION
In 1665.

Written by a CITIZEN who continued all the
while in *London.* Never made publick before

LONDON:

Printed for *E. Nutt* at the *Royal-Exchange*; *J. Roberts*
in *Warwick-Lane*; *A. Dodd* without *Temple-Bar*;
and *J. Graves* in St. *James's-ſtreet.* 1722.

Memoirs of the Plague

It was about the Beginning of *September* 1664, that I, among the Rest of my Neighbours, heard in ordinary Discourse, that the Plague was return'd again in *Holland*; for it had been very violent there, and particularly at *Amsterdam* and *Rotterdam*,[1] in the Year 1663. whether *they say*, it was brought, some said from *Italy*, others from the *Levant* among some Goods, which were brought home by their Turkey Fleet;[2] others said it was brought from *Candia*;[3] others from *Cyprus*. It matter'd not, from whence it come; but all agreed, it was come into *Holland* again.

We had no such thing as printed News Papers in those Days, to spread Rumours and Reports of Things;[4] and to improve them by the Invention of Men, as I have liv'd to see practis'd since. But such things as these were gather'd from the Letters of Merchants, and others, who corresponded abroad, and from them was handed about by Word of Mouth only; so that things did not spread instantly over the whole Nation, as they do now. But it seems that the Government had a true Account of it, and several Counsels were held about Ways to prevent its coming over; but all was kept very private. Hence it was, that this Rumour died off again, and People began to forget it, as a thing we were very little concern'd in, and that we hoped was not true; till the latter End of *November*, or the Beginning of *December* 1664, when two Men, said to be French-men, died of the Plague in *Long Acre*, or rather at the upper End of *Drury Lane*.[5] The Family they were in, endeavour'd to conceal it as much as possible; but as it had gotten some Vent in the Discourse

1. These two Dutch cities were then major world commercial centers and had innumerable transactions with England and Scotland. The general assumption was that plagues began in hot climates, especially in Africa and the Near East, and that goods from Constantinople in Turkey, Alexandria and other Egyptian cities, and southern Greece had carried the disease to Holland. There were 24,148 deaths from it in Amsterdam alone in 1664 (*Considerations on the Nature, Cause, Cure, and Preventing of Pestilences* [London, 1721] 89).

2. The Levant was the territory bordering the eastern shores of the Mediterranean and Aegean seas (Israel, Syria, Lebanon principally). England's Turkey fleet traded in goods from the entire Near East.

3. Crete.

4. The *London Gazette*, the official government paper, was the major source of news in 1664; by 1722 periodical journalism had come of age, and Defoe's pioneering *Review* (begun 1704) had played a major part in its development. The charge of spreading rumors, one often leveled at Defoe, was a common accusation made against political papers, and this sentence gives a hint of Defoe's wry sense of humor.

5. These two streets meet outside the western walls of the City of London and were in the parish of St. Giles-in-the-Fields, Middlesex. The parish was the unit of ecclesiastical and civil government in England from the sixteenth century until 1834. There were ninety-seven parishes within the walls, five in Westminster, sixteen "without" (outside) the walls, and twelve more in Middlesex and Surrey.

of the Neighbourhood, the Secretaries of State[6] gat Knowledge of it. And concerning themselves to inquire about it, in order to be certain of the Truth, two Physicians and a Surgeon were order'd to go to the House, and make Inspection. This they did; and finding evident Tokens[7] of the Sickness upon both the Bodies that were dead, they gave their Opinions publickly, that they died of the Plague: Whereupon it was given in to the Parish Clerk, and he also return'd them to the Hall; and it was printed in the weekly Bill of Mortality[8] in the usual manner, thus,

Plague 2.   *Parishes infected* 1.

The People shew'd a great Concern at this, and began to be allarm'd all over the Town, and the more, because in the last Week in *December* 1664, another Man died in the same House, and of the same Distemper: And then we were easy again for about six Weeks, when none having died with any Marks of Infection, it was said, the Distemper was gone; but after that, I think it was about the 12th of *February*, another died in another House, but in the same Parish, and in the same manner.

This turn'd the Peoples Eyes pretty much towards that End of the Town; and the weekly Bills shewing an Encrease of Burials in St. *Giles's* Parish more than usual, it began to be suspected, that the Plague was among the People at that End of the Town; and that many had died of it, tho' they had taken Care to keep it as much from the Knowledge of the Publick, as possible: This possess'd the Heads of the People very much, and few car'd to go thro' *Drury-Lane*, or the other Streets suspected, unless they had extraordinary Business, that obliged them to it.

This Encrease of the Bills stood thus; the usual Number of Burials in a Week, in the Parishes of St. *Giles's* in the Fields, and St. *Andrew's* Holborn[9] were from 12 to 17 or 19 each few more or less; but from the Time that the Plague first began in St. *Giles's* Parish, it was observ'd, that the ordinary Burials encreased in Number considerably. *For Example,*

From *Dec.* 27th to *Jan.* 3. St. *Giles's*   —16
St. *Andrew's* — 17

6. England had two principal secretaries of state, who were the chief coordinating ministers for the government. Both domestic and foreign affairs were their responsibilities, which were assigned into the northern or southern departments along roughly geographical lines.
7. These dark red spots, occasionally so dark as to appear black, were signs of subcutaneous hemorrhages and usually appeared first on the stomach and chest. A blister appeared at the site of the original fleabite and quickly developed into a gangrenous blackish carbuncle, but the secondary spots were the "tokens." When the lymph nodes of the groin and sometimes the armpits and neck swell and suppurate, blis-
terlike sores called "buboes" form. Paul Slack describes these and other manifestations of the disease in *The Impact of Plague in Tudor and Stuart England* (London: Routledge & Kegan Paul, 1985) 8–10.
8. The parish clerks were responsible for recording all births, marriages, and deaths, with cause of death assigned, in the parish registries and at the Hall of the Company of Parish Clerks. They published the "Bills of Mortality," weekly lists of these deaths compiled by parish and by cause. See pp. 202–5 in this volume.
9. The parish of St. Andrew Holborn in Farringdon Ward, like that of St. Giles-in-the-Fields, was without the walls but in London.

From *Jan.* 3. to—10. St. *Giles's* —12
                       St. *Andrew's*—25

     Jan. 10. to—17. St. *Giles's* —18
                       St. *Andrew's*—18

     Jan. 17. to *Jan.* 24. St. *Giles's* —23
                       St. *Andrew's*—16

     Jan. 24. to—31.   St. *Giles's* —24
                       St. *Andrew's*—15

     Jan. 30. to *Feb.* 7. St. *Giles's* —21
                       St. *Andrew's*—23

     Feb. 7. to—14.   St. *Giles's* —24
     whereof one of the Plague.

The like Encrease of the Bills was observ'd in the Parishes of St. *Brides*, adjoining on one Side of *Holborn* Parish, and in the Parish of St. *James Clarkenwell*, adjoining on the other Side of *Holborn*; in both which Parishes the usual Numbers that died weekly, were from 4 to 6 or 8, whereas at that time they were increas'd, as follows.

From *Dec.* 20. to *Dec.* 27. St. *Brides*— 0
                          St. *James*— 8

     Dec. 27. to *Jan.* 3. St. *Brides*— 6
                          St. *James*— 9

     Jan. 3. to—10.   St. *Brides*—11
                          St. *James*— 7

     Jan. 10. to—17.   St. *Brides*—12
                          St. *James*— 9

     Jan. 17. to—24.   St. *Brides*— 9
                          St. *James*—15

     Jan. 24. to—31.   St. *Brides*— 8
                          St. *James*—12

     Jan. 31. to *Feb.* 7. St. *Brides*—13
                          St. *James*— 5

     Feb. 7. to—14.   St. *Brides*—12
                          St. *James*— 6

Besides this, it was observ'd with great Uneasiness by the People, that the weekly Bills in general encreas'd very much during these Weeks, altho' it was at a Time of the year, when usually the Bills are very moderate.[1]

The usual Number of Burials within the Bills of Mortality for a Week, was from about 240 or thereabouts, to 300. The last was esteem'd a pretty high Bill; but after this we found the Bills successively encreasing, as follows.

			Increased
Dec. the 20. to the 27th,	Buried	291.—	
27. to the 3 Jan.—		349.—	58
January 3. to the 10.	—	394.—	45
10. to the 17.	—	415.—	21
17. to the 24.	—	474.—	59

This last Bill was really frightful, being a higher Number than had been known to have been buried in one Week, since the preceeding Visitation of 1656.[2]

However, all this went off again, and the Weather proving cold, and the Frost which began in *December,* still continuing very severe, even till near the End of *February,* attended with sharp tho' moderate Winds, the Bills decreas'd again, and the City grew healthy, and every body began to look upon the Danger as good as over; only that still the Burials in St. *Giles's* continu'd high: From the Beginning of *April* especially they stood at 25 each Week, till the Week from the 18th to the 25th, when there was buried in St. *Giles's* Parish 30, whereof two of the Plague, and 8 of the Spotted-Feaver, which was look'd upon as the same thing; likewise the Number that died of the Spotted-Feaver in the whole increased, being 8 the Week before, and 12 the Week above-named.

This alarm'd us all again, and terrible Apprehensions were among the People, especially the Weather being now chang'd and growing warm, and the Summer being at Hand: However, the next Week there seem'd to be some Hopes again, the Bills were low, the Number of the Dead in all was but 388, there was none of the Plague, and but four of the Spotted-Feaver.

But the following Week it return'd again, and the Distemper was spread into two or three other Parishes (*viz.*) St. *Andrew's-Holborn,* St. *Clement's-Danes,*[3] and to the great Affliction of the City, one died within the Walls, in the Parish of St. *Mary-Wool-Church,* that is to say, in *Bear-*

1. The highest mortality rates were usually in the autumn according to John Graunt, *Natural and Political Observations made upon the Bills of Mortality* (London, 1662).
2. Either Defoe is referring to the plague in Naples, or this date is a typographical error, either a misreading of his handwriting or a transposition. Graunt lists six plague deaths for that year in England, and Paul Slack does not

cite it as a plague year either (compare 144–64). For 1625 Graunt records 35,417, and 10,400 in 1636, the years with the most plague deaths before 1665, *Reflections on the Weekly Bills of Mortality* (London, 1665).
3. St. Andrew Holborn was without the walls and St. Clement Danes in Westminster. The plague is still well to the west.

binder-lane near the *Stocks-market*;[4] in all there was nine of the Plague, and six of the Spotted-Feaver. It was however upon Inquiry found, that this *Frenchman* who died in *Bearbinder-lane*, was one who having liv'd in *Long-Acre*, near the infected Houses, had removed for fear of the Distemper, not knowing that he was already infected.

This was the beginning of *May*, yet the Weather was temperate, variable and cool enough—and People had still some Hopes: That which encourag'd them was, that the City was healthy, the whole 97 Parishes buried but 54, and we began to hope, that as it was chiefly among the People at that End of the Town, it might go no farther; and the rather, because the next Week which was from the 9th of *May* to the 16th there died but three, of which not one within the whole City or Liberties,[5] and St. *Andrew*'s buried but 15, which was very low: 'Tis true, St. *Giles*'s buried two and thirty, but still as there was but one of the Plague, People began to be easy, the whole Bill also was very low, for the Week before, the Bill was but 347, and the Week above-mentioned but 343: We continued in these Hopes for a few Days, But it was but for a few; for the People were no more to be deceived thus; they searcht the Houses, and found that the Plague was really spread every way, and that many died of it every Day: So that now all our Extenuations[6] abated, and it was no more to be concealed, nay it quickly appeared that the Infection had spread it self beyond all Hopes of Abatement; that in the Parish of St. *Giles*'s, it was gotten into several Streets, and Several Families lay all sick together; And accordingly in the Weekly Bill for the next Week, the thing began to shew it self; there was indeed but 14 set down of the Plague, but this was all Knavery and Collusion, for in St. *Giles*'s Parish they buried 40 in all, whereof it was certain most of them died of the Plague, though they were set down of other Distempers; and though the Number of all the Burials were not increased above 32, and the whole Bill being but 385, yet there was 14 of the Spotted-Feaver, as well as 14 of the Plague; and we took it for granted upon the whole, that there was 50 died that Week of the Plague.

The next Bill was from the 23rd of *May* to the 30th, when the Number of the Plague was 17: But the Burials in St. *Giles*'s were 53, a frightful Number! of whom they set down but 9 of the Plague: But on an Examination more strictly by the Justices of the Peace, and at the Lord Mayor's Request, it was found there were 20 more, who were really dead of the Plague in that Parish, but had been set down of the Spotted-Feaver or other Distempers, besides others concealed.

---

4. Defoe is very particular about locations in London and its suburbs. Here he locates the infected house by parish, by street, and by the nearest landmark. Since houses were not numbered as they are today, prominent buildings, landmarks, and wooden signs with pictures served to locate places.
5. The liberties were between the City walls and the Bars, which were posts, rails, and a chain set up to mark the limits of the liberties. The liberties were within counties but had been granted their own commissions of the peace and were under the city's authority.
6. Representations of the plague as slight or trifling.

But those were trifling Things to what followed immediately after; for now the Weather set in hot, and from the first Week in *June*, the Infection spread in a dreadful Manner, and the Bills rise high, the Articles of the Feaver, Spotted-Feaver, and Teeth, began to swell: For all that could conceal their Distempers, did it to prevent their Neighbours shunning and refusing to converse with them; and also to prevent Authority shutting up their Houses, which though it was not yet practised, yet was threatned, and People were extremely terrify'd at the Thoughts of it.

The Second Week in *June*, the Parish of St. *Giles's*, where still the Weight of the Infection lay, buried 120, whereof though the Bills said but 68 of the Plague; every body said there had been 100 at least, calculating it from the usual Number of Funerals in that Parish as above.

Till this Week the City continued free, there having never any died except that one *Frenchman*, who I mention'd before, within the whole 97 Parishes. Now there died four within the City, one in *Wood-Street*, one in *Fenchurch Street*, and two in *Crooked-lane*; *Southwark*[7] was entirely free, having not one yet died on that Side of the Water.

I liv'd without *Aldgate* about mid-way between *Aldgate Church* and *White-Chappel-Bars*,[8] on the left Hand or North-side of the Street; and as the Distemper had not reach'd to that Side of the City, our Neighbourhood continued very easy: But at the other End of the Town, their Consternation was very great; and the richer sort of People, especially the Nobility and Gentry, from the West-part of the City throng'd out of Town, with their Families and Servants in an unusual Manner; and this was more particularly seen in *White-Chapel*; that is to say, the Broad-Street[9] where I liv'd: Indeed nothing was to be seen but Waggons and Carts, with Goods, Women, Servants, Children, etc. Coaches fill'd with People of the better Sort, and Horsemen attending them, and all hurrying away; then empty Waggons, and Carts appear'd and Spare-horses with Servants, who it was apparent were returning or sent from the Countries to fetch more People: Besides innumerable Numbers of Men on Horseback, some alone, others with Servants, and generally speaking, all loaded with Baggage and fitted out for travelling, as any one might perceive by their Appearance.

This was a very terrible and melancholy Thing to see, and as it was a Sight which I cou'd not but look on from Morning to Night; for indeed there was nothing else of Moment to be seen, it filled me with very

---

7. These deaths showed that at least two more parishes had been infected. Southwark is across the Thames River from London. In Surrey, it was the location of a large part of the greater London population. In his *Tour through the Whole Island of Great Britain*, Defoe said "it might be call'd a long street of about nine miles in lengths."
8. The narrator lives just outside the walls, outside Aldgate, one of the original four Roman gates to the City. Defoe's uncle Henry Foe served his apprenticeship to a London saddler there and lived his entire adult life in the parish. His large house on Well Alley was less than a mile from Defoe's family home. The church is probably St. Botolph, Aldgate, where Defoe was married in 1684 to Mary Tuffley. Many scholars believe that H. F. is Henry Foe.
9. This street ran from the heart of the City's Threadneedle Street by the Royal Exchange north to the walls.

serious Thoughts of the Misery that was coming upon the City, and the unhappy Condition of those that would be left in it.

This Hurry[1] of the People was such for some Weeks, that there was no getting at the Lord-Mayor's Door without exceeding Difficulty; there was such pressing and crouding there to get passes and Certificates of Health, for such as travelled abroad; for without these, there was no being admitted to pass thro' the Towns upon the Road, or to lodge in any Inn: Now as there had none died in the City for all this time, My Lord Mayor gave Certificates of Health[2] without any Difficulty to all those who liv'd in the 97 Parishes, and to those within the Liberties too for a while.

This Hurry, I say, continued some Weeks, that is to say, all the Month of *May* and *June*, and the more because it was rumour'd that an order of the Government was to be issued out, to place Turn-pikes[3] and Barriers on the Road, to prevent Peoples travelling; and that the Towns on the Road, would not suffer People from *London* to pass, for fear of bringing the Infection along with them, though neither of these Rumours had any Foundation, but in the Imagination; especially at first.

I now began to consider seriously with my Self, concerning my own Case, and how I should dispose of my self; that is to say, whether I should resolve to stay in *London*, or shut up my House and flee, as many of my Neighbours did. I have set this particular down so fully, because I know not but it may be of Moment to those who come after me, if they come to be brought to the same Distress, and to the same Manner of making their Choice and therefore I desire this Account may pass with them, rather for a Direction to themselves to act by, than a History of my actings, seeing it may not be of one Farthing[4] value to them to note what became of me.

I had two important things before me; the one was the carrying on my Business and Shop; which was considerable, and in which was embark'd all my Effects in the World; and the other was the Preservation of my Life in so dismal a Calamity as I saw apparently was coming upon the whole City; and which however great it was, my Fears perhaps as well as other Peoples, represented to be much greater than it could be.

The first Consideration was of great Moment to me; my Trade was *a Sadler*,[5] and as my Dealings were chiefly not by a Shop or Chance Trade, but among the Merchants, trading to the *English* Colonies in *America*, so my Effects lay very much in the hands of such. I was a single man 'tis true, but I had a Family of Servants, who I kept at my

---

1. Agitation.
2. These papers declared the bearer free of plague and were similar to the passes the Lord Mayor and secretaries of state routinely issued merchants and travelers in times of domestic unrest.
3. Spiked barriers fixed in or across roads.
4. England's smallest monetary unit; worth one-fourth of one penny.
5. Saddlers make or deal in saddles and other riding equipment; some made or sold equipment for coach horses. The Saddlers Company in London was chartered by Richard II and had the right to search for broken-down and "worthless" saddles and destroy them.

Business, had a House, Shop, and Ware-houses fill'd with Goods; and in short, to leave them all as things in such a Case must be left, that is to say, without any Overseer or Person fit to be trusted with them, had been to hazard the Loss not only of my Trade, but of my Goods, and indeed of all I had in the World.

I had an Elder Brother at the same Time in *London*, and not many Years before come over from *Portugal*;[6] and advising with him, his Answer was in three Words the same that was given in another Case quite different, *(viz.) Master save thy self.*[7] In a Word, he was for my retiring into the Country, as he resolv'd to do himself with his Family; telling me, what he had it seems, heard abroad, that the best Preparation for the Plague was to run away from it. As to my Argument of losing my Trade, my Goods, or Debts, he quite confuted me: He told me the same thing, which I argued for my staying, *(viz) That I would trust God with my Safety and Health,*[8] was the Strongest Repulse to my Pretentions of losing my Trade and my Goods; for, says he, is it not as reasonable that you should trust God with the Chance or Risque of losing your Trade, as that you should stay in so imminent a Point of Danger, and trust him with your Life?

I could not argue that I was in any Strait, as to a Place where to go, having several Friends and Relations in *Northamptonshire*,[9] whence our Family first came from; and particularly, I had an only Sister in *Lincolnshire*,[1] very willing to receive and entertain me.

My Brother, who had already sent his Wife and two Children into *Bedfordshire*, and resolv'd to follow them, press'd my going very earnestly; and I had once resolv'd to comply with his Desires, but at that time could get no Horse: For tho' it is true, all the People did not go out of the City of *London*; yet I may venture to say, that in a manner all the Horses did; for there was hardly a Horse to be bought or hired in the whole City for some Weeks. Once I resolv'd to travel on Foot with one Servant; and as many did, lie at no Inn, but carry a Soldiers Tent with us, and so lie in the Fields, the Weather being very warm, and no Danger from taking cold: I say, as many did, because several did so at last, especially those who had been in the Armies in the War which had not been many Years past; and I must needs say, that speaking of second Causes, had most of the People that travelled, done so, the Plague had

6. A major trading and political ally at that time.
7. Matthew 27.40, Mark 15.30. Defoe, like many people of his time, looked for parallels between his situations and biblical stories. In these verses, passers-by taunt Jesus, "Save thyself, and come down from the cross" (King James version, the translation always quoted by Defoe). Defoe casts himself as Christ and his brother as the secular advisers.
8. Debate over leaving the plague-striken city often centered upon such issues as whether God would judge those who left to be fleeing his

will or exhibiting lack of faith in his mercy.
9. Defoe's father, James Foe, came from Etton, Northamptonshire, an area of gently rolling hills sixty miles northwest of London.
1. Another area quite familiar to Defoe from his merchant days, Lincolnshire was noted for its fine sheep and large coach horses. In Defoe's time a castle built by William the Conqueror was a notable landmark. Both areas had been hard hit by the plagues in the 1630s, and Lincolnshire was a national leader in passing plague-prevention measures.

not been carried into so many Country-Towns and Houses, as it was, to the great Damage, and indeed to the Ruin of abundance of People.

But then my Servant who I had intended to take down with me, deceiv'd me; and being frighted at the Encrease of the Distemper, and not knowing when I should go, he took other Measures, and left me, so I was put off for that Time; and one way or other, I always found that to appoint to go away was always cross'd by some Accident or other, so as to disappoint and put it off again; and this brings in a Story which otherwise might be thought a needless Digression, (*viz,*) about these Disappointments being from Heaven.

I mention this Story also as the best Method I can advise any Person to take in such a Case, especially, if he be one that makes Conscience of his Duty, and would be directed what to do in it, namely, that he should keep his Eye upon the particular Providences which occur at that Time, and look upon them complexly, as they regard one another, and as altogether regard the Question before him, and then I think, he may safely take them for Intimations from Heaven of what is his unquestion'd Duty to do in such a Case;[2] I mean as to going away from, or staying in the Place where we dwell, when visited with an infectious Distemper.

It came very warmly[3] into my Mind, one Morning, as I was musing on this particular thing, that as nothing attended us without the Direction or Permission of Divine Power, so these Disappointments must have something in them extraordinary; and I ought to consider whether it did not evidently point out, or intimate to me, that it was the Will of Heaven I should not go. It immediately follow'd in my Thoughts, that if it really was from God that I should stay, he was able effectually to preserve me in the midst of all the Death and Danger that would surround me; and that if I attempted to secure my self by fleeing from my Habitation, and acted contrary to these Intimations, which I believed to be Divine, it was a kind of flying from God, and that he could cause his Justice to overtake me when and where he thought fit.

These thoughts quite turn'd my Resolutions again, and when I came to discourse with my Brother again I told him, that I enclin'd to stay and take my Lot in that Station in which God had plac'd me; and that it seem'd to be made more especially my Duty, on the Account of what I have said.

My Brother, tho' a very Religious Man himself, laught at all I had suggested about its being an Intimation from Heaven, and told me several Stories of such fool-hardy People, *as he call'd them,* as I was; that I ought indeed to submit to it as a Work of Heaven, if I had been any way disabled by Distempers or Diseases, and that then not being able to go,

---

2. Defoe seems to have set considerable store in what he called "particular Providences," "hints," or "Intimations from Heaven." In his nonfiction as well as his fiction he recommended that people watch carefully for signs and follow their intuitions or feelings about them. See, for instance, his *Serious Reflections during the Life and Surprising Adventures of Robinson Crusoe, with his Vision of the Angelick World.*

3. Strongly, as from "glowing," or aroused feelings.

I ought to acquiesce in the Direction of him, who having been my Maker, had an undisputed Right of Soveraignity in disposing of me; and that then there had been no Difficulty to determine which was the Call of his Providence, and which was not: But that I should take it as an Intimation from Heaven, that I should not go out of Town, only because I could not hire a Horse to go, or my Fellow was run away that was to attend me, was ridiculous, since at the same Time I had my Health and Limbs, and other Servants, and might, with Ease, travel a Day or two on foot, and having a good Certificate of being in perfect Health, might either hire a Horse, or take Post[4] on the Road, as I thought fit.

Then he proceeded to tell me of the mischeivous Consequences which attended the Presumption of the *Turks* and *Mahometans* in *Asia*[5] and in other Places, where he had been (for my Brother being a Merchant, was a few Years before, as I have already observ'd, returned from abroad, coming last from *Lisbon*) and how presuming upon their profess'd predestinating Notions, and of every Man's End being predetermin'd and unalterably before-hand decreed, they would go unconcern'd into infected Places,[6] and converse with infected Persons, by which Means they died at the Rate of Ten or Fifteen Thousand a Week, whereas the *Europeans*, or Christian Merchants, who kept themselves retired and reserv'd, generally escap'd the Contagion.

Upon these Arguments my Brother chang'd my Resolutions again, and I began to resolve to go, and accordingly made all things ready; for in short, the Infection increased round me, and the Bills were risen to almost 700 a-Week, and my Brother told me, he would venture to stay no longer. I desir'd him to let me consider of it but till the next Day, and I would resolve; and as I had already prepar'd every thing as well as I could, as to my Business, and who to entrust my Affairs with, I had little to do but to resolve.

I went Home that Evening greatly oppress'd in my Mind, irresolute, and not knowing what to do; I had set the Evening wholly apart to consider seriously about it, and was all alone; for already People had, as it were by a general Consent, taken up the Custom of not going out of doors after Sun-set, the Reasons I shall have Occasion to say more of by-and-by.

In the Retirement of this Evening I endeavoured to resolve first, what was my Duty to do, and I stated the Arguments with which my Brother

4. Use the horses available at post stations, which allowed travel by relays of horses. It was the fastest way to travel because tired mounts were regularly swapped for fresh ones.
5. One contemporary account describes plague as "the Epidemical Disease of this Country, and the common distemper of the Summer Season." It estimates twelve hundred to thirteen hundred deaths a day from it occurred in the summer of 1661 (Paul Rycaut, *The History of the Turkish Empire from the Year 1623 to the Year 1677* [London, 1680] 81–82). Defoe probably owned this book.
6. Louis Landa notes that by 1665, refusal to fly the plague "had become a 'Turkish Heresy' " (*A Journal of the Plague Year* [Oxford: Oxford UP, 1990] 254n. for p. 11). The Turks took no precautions and believed that plague "was a mercy and a martyrdom sent by God" and that "no Muslim should flee." This "Turkish fatalism" denied the possibilities both of contagion and of appeals for divine mercy (Slack 49–50).

had press'd me to go into the Country, and I set against them the strong Impressions which I had on my Mind for staying; the visible Call I seem'd to have from the particular circumstance of my Calling, and the Care due from me for the Preservation of my Effects, which were, as I might say, my Estate; also the Intimations which I thought I had from Heaven, that to me signify'd a kind of Direction to venture, and it occurr'd to me, that if I had what I might call a Direction to stay, I ought to suppose it contain'd a Promise of being preserved, if I obey'd.

This lay close to me, and my Mind seemed more and more encouraged to stay than ever, and supported with a secret Satisfaction, that I should be kept: Add to this that turning over the Bible, which lay before me, and while my Thoughts were more than ordinarily serious upon the Question, I cry'd out, W E L L, *I know not what to do, Lord direct me!* and the like; and that Juncture I happen'd to stop turning over the Book at the *91st Psalm*, and casting my Eye on the second Verse,[7] I read on to the 7th Verse exclusive; and after that, included the 10th, as follows. *I will say of the Lord, He is my refuge, and my fortress, my God, in him will I trust. Surely he shall deliver thee from the snare of the fowler, and from the noisom pestilence. He shall cover thee with his feathers, and under his wings shalt thou trust: his truth shall be thy shield and buckler. Thou shalt not be afraid for the terror by night, nor for the arrow that flieth by day: Nor for the pestilence that walketh in darkness: nor for the destruction that wasteth at noon-day. A thousand shall fall at thy side, and ten thousand at thy right hand: but it shall not come nigh thee. Only with thine Eyes shalt thou behold and see the reward of the wicked. Because thou hast made the Lord which is my refuge, even the most High, thy habitation: There shall no evil befal thee, neither shall any plague come nigh thy dwelling, &c.*

I scarce need tell the Reader, that from that Moment I resolv'd that I would stay in the Town, and casting my self entirely upon the Goodness and Protection of the Almighty, would not seek any other Shelter whatever; and that as my Times were in his Hands, he was as able to keep me in a Time of the Infection as in a Time of Health; and if he did not think fit to deliver me, still I was in his Hands, and it was meet he should do with me as should seem good to him.

With this Resolution I went to Bed; and I was farther confirm'd in it the next Day, by the Woman being taken ill with whom I had intended to entrust my House and all my Affairs: But I had a farther Obligation laid on me on the same Side; for the next Day I found my self very

---

7. H. F. is practicing "sortes," divination by opening a book at random and then applying an interpretation of the passage to the issue at hand. Usually the works of Virgil, the greatest of Roman poets, who wrote the national epic *The Aeneid* as well as pastoral poetry, were used. Called "bibliomancy" or "sortes Biblicae" when the Bible was used, it was considered an old-fashioned superstition. A legend persisted however, that King Charles I had practiced sortes Virgilianae and touched a verse beginning "But vex'd with rebels and a stubborn race . . ." The passage from Psalm 91 is certainly pertinent with its references to deliverance from the pestilence.

much out of Order also; so that if I would have gone away, I could not, and I continued ill three or four Days, and this intirely determin'd my Stay; so I took leave of my Brother, who went away to *Darking* in *Surry*,[8] and afterwards fetch'd a Round farther into *Buckinghamshire*, or *Bedfordshire*,[9] to a Retreat he had found out there for his Family.

It was a very ill Time to be sick in, for if any one complain'd, it was immediately said he had the Plague; and tho' I had indeed no Symptoms of that Distemper,[1] yet being very ill, both in my Head and in my Stomach, I was not without Apprehension, that I really was infected; but in about three Days I grew better, the third Night I rested well, sweated a little, and was much refresh'd; the Apprehensions of its being the Infection went also quite away with my Illness, and I went about my Business as usual.

These Things however put off all my Thoughts of going into the Country; and my Brother also being gone, I had no more Debate either with him, or with myself, on that Subject.

It was now mid-*July*, and the Plague which had chiefly rag'd at the other End of the Town, and as I said before, in the Parishes of St. *Giles's*, St. *Andrews Holbourn*, and towards *Westminster*, began now to come *Eastward* towards the Part where I liv'd. It was to be observ'd indeed, that it did not come strait on towards us; for the City, that is to say within the Walls, was indifferent healthy still; nor was it got then very much over the Water into *Southwark*; for tho' there died that Week 1268 of all Distempers, whereof it might be suppos'd above 900 died of the Plague; yet there was but 28 in the whole City, within the Walls; and but 19 in *Southwark*, *Lambeth* Parish included; whereas in the Parishes of St. *Giles*, and St. *Martins in the Fields* alone, there died 421.

But we perceiv'd the Infection kept chiefly in the out-Parishes, which being very populous, and fuller also of Poor, the distemper found more to prey upon than in the City, as I shall observe afterward; we perceiv'd I say, the Distemper to draw our Way; (*viz.*) by the Parishes of *Clerken-Well*, *Cripplegate*, *Shoreditch*, and *Bishopsgate*; which last two Parishes joining to *Aldgate*, *White-Chapel*, and *Stepney*,[2] the Infection came at length to spread its utmost Rage and violence in those Parts, even when it abated, at the *Western* Parishes where it began.

It was very strange to observe, that in this particular Week, from the 4th to the 11th of *July*, when, as I have observ'd, there died near 400 of the Plague in the two Parishes of St. *Martin's*, and St. *Giles in the Fields*

<hr>

8. Defoe means Dorking, an area he knew well dating back to childhood visits. The old Roman road ran through it.
9. "Fetch'd a Round Farther" is slang for "tacking," performing a movement, taking a walk. Buckinghamshire, noted for its beechwood forests, and Bedfordshire were prosperous areas that Defoe visited throughout his life. In *A Tour through the Whole Island of Great Brit-*

ain he said that the best market in all of England outside of London was at Bedfordshire.
1. The most common symptoms were buboes and carbuncles, headaches, rapid pulse, high fever, delirium, thirst, and the spots on chest or back. Pneumonic plague caused coughing.
2. Defoe is tracing the progress of the plague from west to east.

only, three died in the Parish of *Aldgate* but four, in the Parish of *White-Chapel* three, in the Parish of *Stepney* but one.

Likewise in the next Week, from the 11th of *July* to the 18th, when the Week's Bill was 1761, yet there died no more of the Plague, on the whole *Southwark* Side of the Water than sixteen.

But this Face of things soon changed, and it began to thicken in *Cripplegate* Parish especially, and in *Clerken-Well*; so that by the second Week in *August*, *Cripplegate* Parish alone, buried eight hundred eighty six,[3] and *Clerken-Well* 155; of the first eight hundred and fifty, might well be reckoned to die of the Plague; and of the last, the Bill it self said, 145 were of the Plague.

During the Month of *July*, and while, as I have observ'd, our Part of the Town seem'd to be spar'd, in Comparison of the *West* part, I went ordinarily about the Streets, as my Business requir'd, and particularly went generally, once in a Day, or in two Days, into the City, to my Brother's House, which he had given me charge of, and to see if it was safe: And having the Key in my Pocket, I used to go into the House, and over most of the Rooms, to see that all was well; for tho' it be something wonderful to tell, that any should have Hearts so hardned, in the midst of such a Calamity, as to rob and steal; yet certain it is, that all Sorts of Villanies, and even Levities and Debaucheries were then practis'd in the Town, as openly as ever, I will not say quite as frequently, because the Numbers of People were many ways lessen'd.

But the City it self began now to be visited too, I mean within the Walls; but the Number of People there were indeed extreamly lessen'd by so great a Multitude having been gone into the Country; and even all this Month of *July* they continu'd to flee, tho' not in such Multitudes as formerly. In *August* indeed, they fled in such a manner, that I began to think, there would be really none but Magistrates and Servants left in the City.

As they fled now out of the City, so I should observe, that the Court[4] removed early, (*viz.*) in the Month of *June*, and went to *Oxford*, where it pleas'd God to preserve them; and the Distemper did not, *as I heard of*, so much as touch them; for which I cannot say, that I ever saw they shew'd any great Token of Thankfulness, and hardly any thing of Reformation, tho' they did not want being told that their crying Vices might, without Breach of Charity, be said to have gone far, in bringing that terrible Judgment upon the whole Nation.[5]

The Face of *London* was now indeed strangely alter'd, I mean the whole Mass of Buildings, City, Liberties, Suburbs, *Westminster, South-*

---

3. Cripplegate parish was extremely hard-hit by the plague. It was Defoe's childhood home, the place of his father's business, and the records of the births of Defoe's two sisters are in the parish registry of St. Giles, Cripplegate. In 1731 Defoe died in the parish, and his death was recorded in the same registry.
4. The royal family and courtiers with their counselors and retinue.
5. Defoe here condemns what he considers to be the immorality of Charles II's notorious Restoration court.

wark and altogether; for as to the particular Part called the City, or within the Walls, that was not yet much infected; but in the whole, the Face of Things, I say, was much alter'd; Sorrow and Sadness sat upon every Face; and tho' some Part were not yet overwhelm'd, yet all look'd deeply concern'd; and as we saw it apparently coming on, so every one look'd on himself, and his Family, as in the utmost Danger: were it possible to represent those Times exactly to those that did not see them, and give the Reader due Ideas of the Horror that every where presented it self, it must make just Impressions upon their Minds, and fill them with Surprize. *London* might well be said to be all in Tears; the Mourners did not go about the Streets indeed, for no Body put on black, or made a formal Dress of Mourning for their nearest Friends; but the Voice of Mourning was truly heard in the Streets; the shrieks of Women and Children at the Windows, and Doors of their Houses, where their dearest Relations were, perhaps dying, or just dead, were so frequent to be heard, as we passed the Streets, that it was enough to pierce the stoutest Heart in the World, to hear them. Tears and Lamentations were seen almost in every House, especially in the first part of the Visitation; for towards the latter End, Mens Hearts were hardned, and Death was so always before their Eyes, that they did not so much concern themselves for the Loss of their Friends, expecting, that themselves should be summoned the next Hour.

Business led me out sometimes to the other End of the Town, even when the Sickness was chiefly there; and as the thing was new to me, as well as to every Body else, it was a most surprising thing, to see those Streets, which were usually so thronged, now grown desolate, and so few People to be seen in them, that if I had been a Stranger, and at a Loss for my Way, I might sometimes have gone the Length of a whole Street, I mean of the by-Streets, and see no Body to direct me, except Watchmen,[6] set at the Doors of such Houses as were shut up; of which I shall speak presently.

One Day, being at that Part of the Town, on some special Business, Curiosity led me to observe things more than usually; and indeed I walk'd a great Way where I had no Business; I went up *Holbourn*, and there the Street was full of People; but they walk'd in the middle of the great Street, neither on one Side or other, because, as I suppose, they would not mingle with any Body that came out of Houses, or meet with Smells and Scents from Houses that might be infected.

The Inns-of-Court[7] were all shut up; nor were very many of the Lawyers in the Temple, or *Lincolns-Inn*, or *Greyes-Inn*,[8] to be seen there.

6. The Lord Mayor and Court of Alderman had ordered the appointment of watchmen for every infected house. They were to prevent anyone entering or leaving the house and to run errands for the family. See pp. 197–98.
7. The four locations for the study and practice of law were the Inner Temple, Middle Temple, Lincoln's Inn, and Gray's Inn.
8. Each of the Inns of Court consisted of a Society; the Temple Society, originally one, had become two separate groups during the time of Henry VI.

Every Body was at peace, there was no Occasion for Lawyers; besides, it being in the Time of the Vacation too, they were generally gone into the Country. Whole Rows of Houses in some Places, were shut close up; the Inhabitants all fled, and only a Watchman or two left.

When I speak of Rows of Houses being shut up, I do not mean shut up by the Magistrates; but that great Numbers of Persons followed the Court, by the Necessity of their Employments, and other Dependencies: and as others retir'd, really frighted with the Distemper, it was a mere desolating of some of the Streets: But the Fright was not yet near so great in the City, abstractly so called; and particularly because, tho' they were at first in a most inexpressible Consternation, yet as I have observ'd, that the Distemper intermitted often at first; so they were as it were, allarm'd, and unallarm'd again, and this several times, till it began to be familiar to them; and that even when it appear'd violent, yet seeing it did not presently spread into the City, or the *East* and *South* Parts, the People began to take Courage, and to be, as I may say, a little hardned: It is true, a vast many People fled, as I have observ'd, yet they were chiefly from the *West* End of the Town; and from that we call the Heart of the City, that is to say, among the wealthiest of the People; and such People as were unincumbred with Trades and Business: But of the rest, the Generality stay'd, and seem'd to abide the worst: So that in the Place we call the Liberties, and in the Suburbs, in *Southwark*, and in the *East* part, such as *Wapping, Ratclif, Stepney, Rotherhith*,[9] and the like, the People generally stay'd, except here and there a few wealthy Families, who, as above, did not depend upon their Business.

It must not be forgot here, that the City and Suburbs were prodigiously full of People, at the time of this Visitation, I mean, at the time that it began; for tho' I have liv'd to see a farther Encrease, and mighty Throngs of People settling in *London*, more than ever, yet we had always a Notion, that the Numbers of People, which the Wars being over, the Armies disbanded, and the Royal Family and the Monarchy being restor'd, had flock'd to *London*, to settle into Business; or to depend upon and attend the Court for Rewards of Services, Preferments, *and the like*, was such, that the Town was computed to have in it above a hundred thousand people more than ever it held before; nay, some took upon them to say, it had twice as many, because all the ruin'd Families of the royal party, flock'd hither: All the old Soldiers set up Trades here, and abundance of Families settled here; again, the Court brought with them a great Flux of Pride, and new Fashions; All People were grown gay and luxurious; and the Joy of the Restoration had brought a vast many Families to *London*.

I often thought, that as *Jerusalem* was besieg'd by the *Romans*, when

9. These townships were suburbs beyond the liberties; all were waterfront towns to the east of London. Wapping was best known as the usual place for hanging pirates. Ratcliffe, Stepney, and Rotherhithe were added to the Bills of Mortality in 1636.

the *Jews* were assembled together, to celebrate the Passover,[1] by which means, an incredible Number of People were surpriz'd there, who would otherwise have been in other Countries: So the Plague entered *London*, when an incredible Increase of People had happened occasionally, by the particular Circumstances above-nam'd: As this Conflux of the People, to a youthful and gay Court, made a great Trade in the City, especially in every thing that belong'd to Fashion and Finery; So it drew by Consequence, a great Number of Work-men, Manufacturers, and the like, being mostly poor People, who depended upon their Labour, And I remember in particular, that in a Representation[2] to my Lord mayor, of the Condition of the Poor, it was estimated, that, there were no less than an Hundred Thousand Ribband Weavers[3] in and about the City; the chiefest Number of whom, lived then in the Parishes of *Shoreditch*, *Stepney*, *White-chapel*, and *Bishopsgate*; that namely, about *Spittle-fields*; that is to say, as *Spittle fields* was then[4]; for it was not so large as now, by one fifth Part.

By this however, the Number of People in the whole may be judg'd of; and indeed, I often wondred, that after the prodigious Numbers of People that went away at first, there was yet so great a Multitude left, as it appear'd there was.

But I must go back again to the Beginning of this Surprizing Time, while the Fears of the People were young, they were encreas'd strangely by several odd Accidents, which put altogether, it was realy a wonder the whole Body of the People did not rise as one Man, and abandon their Dwellings, leaving the Place as a Space of Ground designed by Heaven for an Akeldama,[5] doom'd to be destroy'd from the Face of the Earth; and that all that would be found in it, would perish with it. I shall Name but a few of these Things; but sure they were so many, and so many Wizards and cunning People[6] propagating them, that I have often wonder'd there was any, (Women especially,) left behind.

In the first Place, a blazing Star or Comet appear'd for several Months before the Plague,[7] as there did the Year after another, a little before the Fire;[8] the old Women, and the Phlegmatic Hypocondriac Part of the

---

1. The Emperor Titus attacked in A.D. 70 with four legions and auxiliary troops. The inhabitants of the city forgot their factional differences, bonded together, and fought the Romans with great tenacity. It was August before the Romans took the city and September before they crushed the resistance. Defoe is correct that the Passover pilgrims were trapped inside, shared the starvation and epidemics with the trapped inhabitants, and fought bravely in the city's defense (Martin Noth, *The History of Israel* [New York: Harper and Row, 1960, 441–43]).
2. A formal and serious statement of facts.
3. Ribbon weavers. Defoe exaggerates, perhaps as a sarcastic remark aimed at Restoration luxury and materialism.
4. Londoners often referred to the entire silk-weaving district as "Spittlefields" (or "Spital-

fields"). Defoe knew the area well; for instance, he had been captured by the legal authorities when he hid there in 1703 in the home of a weaver.
5. Hellenized Aramaic for "field of blood," the field bought with Judas's money (Acts 1.19). Formerly called "Potter's Field."
6. Those practicing magic or the occult arts.
7. Defoe is pointing out that people took the comets sighted on December 15, 1664, and April 6, 1665, as portentous omens; they are noted in the *Philosophical Transactions* of the Royal Society.
8. The Great Fire of London began on September 2, 1666; 13,200 houses (90 percent of the City's living accommodations) were destroyed.

other Sex,[9] who I could almost call *old Women* too, remark'd (especially afterward tho' not, till both those Judgments were over,) that those two Comets pass'd directly over the City, and that so very near the Houses, that it was plain, they imported[1] something peculiar to the City alone; that the Comet before the Pestilence, was of a faint, dull, languid Colour, and its Motion very heavy, solemn and slow: But that the Comet before the Fire, was bright and sparkling, or as others said, flaming, and its Motion swift and furious; and that accordingly, One foretold a heavy Judgment, slow but severe, terrible and frightful, as was the Plague; But the other foretold a Stroak, sudden, swift, and fiery as the Conflagration; nay, so particular some People were, that as they look'd upon that Comet preceding the Fire, they fancied that they not only saw it pass swiftly and fiercely, and cou'd perceive the Motion with their Eye, but even they heard it; that it made a rushing mighty Noise, fierce and terrible, tho' at a distance, and but just perceivable.

I saw both the Stars; and I must confess, had so much of the common Notion of such Things in my Head, that I was apt to look upon them, as the Forerunners and Warnings of Gods Judgments; and especially when after the Plague had followed the first, I yet saw another of the like kind; I could not but say, God had not yet sufficiently scourg'd[2] the City.

But I cou'd not at the same Time carry these Things to the heighth that others did, knowing too, that natural Causes are assign'd by the Astronomers for such Things; and that their Motions, and even their Revolutions are calculated, or pretended to be calculated; so that they cannot be so perfectly call'd the Fore-runners, or Fore-tellers, much less the procurers of such Events, as Pestilence, War, Fire, and the like.

But let my Thoughts, and the Thoughts of the Philosophers be, or have been what they will, these Things had a more than ordinary Influence upon the Minds of the common People, and they had almost universal mellancholly Apprehensions of some dreadful Calamity and Judgment coming upon the City; and this principally from the Sight of this Comet, and the little Allarm that was given in *December*, by two People dying at St. *Giles's*, as above.

The Apprehensions of the People, were likewise strangely encreas'd by the Error of the Times; in which, I think, the People, from what Principle I cannot imagine, were more addicted to Prophesies, and Astrological Conjurations, Dreams, and old Wives Tales, than ever they were before or since: Whether this unhappy Temper was originally raised by the Follies of some People who got Money by it; that is to say, by printing Predictions, and Prognostications I know not; but certain it is, Book's frighted them terribly; such as *Lilly's* Almanack, *Gadbury's* Alogical Predictions; Poor *Robin's* Almanack and the like;[3] also several pre-

---

9. So-called because it was thought to be the result of phlegmatic humor, the cold moist, morbid humor. Hypochondria was a form of melancholy at that time.
1. Signified, indicated.

2. Whipped, lashed severely.
3. Three of the best-selling almanacs of the time. Both Defoe and Jonathan Swift satirized the kinds of prophecies such books made. See Swift's *Bickerstaff Papers* (1708–9).

tended religious Books; one entituled, *Come out of her my People, least you be partaker of her Plagues*; another call'd, Fair Warning; another, *Britains* Remembrancer, and many such;[4] all, or most Part of which, foretold directly or covertly the Ruin of the City: Nay, some were so Enthusiastically bold, as to run about the Streets, with their Oral Predictions, pretending they were sent to preach to the City; and One in particular, who like *Jonah to Nenevah*,[5] cry'd in the Streets, *yet forty Days, and L O N D O N shall be destroy'd*. I will not be positive, whether he said yet forty Days, or yet a few Days. Another run about Naked, except a pair of Drawers about his Waste, crying Day and Night; like a Man that *Josephus* mentions, who cry'd, woe to *Jerusalem!* a little before the Destruction of that City:[6] So this poor naked Creature cry'd, *O! the Great, and the Dreadful God!* and said no more, but repeated those Words continually, with a Voice and Countenance full of horror, a swift Pace, and no Body cou'd ever find him to stop, or rest, or take any Sustenance, at least, that ever I cou'd hear of. I met this poor Creature several Times in the Streets, and would have spoke to him, but he would not enter into Speech with me, or any one else; but held on his dismal Cries continually.

These Things terrified the People to the last Degree; and especially when two or three Times, as I have mentioned already, they found one or two in the Bills, dead of the Plague at St. *Giles*.

Next to these publick Things, were the Dreams of old Women: Or, I should say, the Interpretation of old Women upon other Peoples Dreams; and these put abundance of People even out of their Wits: Some heard Voices warning them to be gone, for that there would be such a Plague in *London*, so that the Living would not be able to bury the Dead: Others saw Apparitions in the Air; and I must be allow'd to say of both, I hope with out breach of Charity, that they heard Voices that never spake, and saw Sights that never appear'd; but the Imagination of the People was really turn'd wayward and possess'd: And no Wonder, if they, who were poreing continually[7] at the Clouds, saw Shapes and Figures, Representations and Appearances, which had nothing in them, but Air and Vapour. Here they told us, they saw a Flaming-Sword held in a Hand, coming out of a Cloud, with a Point hanging directly over the City.

---

4. Defoe seems to have constructed this list from memory and his experiences with the London book trade. Several books with "Fair Warning" in the title appeared in the 1660s; only David Lloyd's *Dying and Dead Men's Living Words, or Fair Warnings to a Careless World* (London, 1668) might be identified with Defoe's references. Similarly, John Bell's *London Remembrancer* (London, 1666) or the City's *Remembrancer* records may have been in his mind. The Remembrancer kept all of the City's books as documents were delivered by the Chamberlain and the Town Clerk beginning in 1570.

5. Jonah was sent by God to the City of Ninevah to warn the inhabitants to repent and reform; Defoe modifies the text of Jonah 3.4 for the occasion.

6. Flavius Josephus tells the story of Jesus, the son of Ananus, who was severely beaten and finally concluded to be mad for continually crying out. "Woe, woe to Jerusalem." After seven years, five months of his prophesying, the city was besieged, and he was killed by a stone from a catapult (*The Wars of the Jews*, book 6, chapter 5).

7. Studying continually for signs.

There they saw Herses,[8] and Coffins in the Air, carrying to be buried. And there again, Heaps of dead Bodies lying unburied, and the like; just as the Imagination of the poor terrify'd People furnish'd them with Matter to work upon.

> So Hypocondriac Fancy's represent
> Ships, Armies, Battles, in the Firmament;
> Till steady Eyes, the Exhalations solve,
> And all to its first Matter, Cloud, resolve.[9]

I cou'd fill this Account with the strange Relations, such People gave every Day, of what they had seen; and every one was so positive of their having seen, what they pretended to see, that there was no contradicting them, without Breach of Friendship, or being accounted rude and unmannerly on the one Hand, and prophane[1] and impenetrable on the other. One time before the Plague was begun, (otherwise than as I have said in St. Giles's,) I think it was in *March*, seeing a Crowd of People in the Street, I join'd with them to satisfy my Curiosity, and found them all staring up into the Air, to see what a Woman told them appeared plain to her, which was an Angel cloth'd in white, with a fiery Sword in his Hand, waving it, or brandishing it over his Head. She described every Part of the Figure to the Life; shew'd them the Motion, and the Form; and the poor People came into it so eagerly, and with so much Readiness; Y E S, *I see it all plainly*, says one. *There's the Sword as plain as can be.* Another saw the Angel. One saw his very Face, and cry'd out, What a glorious Creature he was! One saw one thing, and one another. I look'd as earnestly as the rest, but, perhaps, not with so much Willingness to be impos'd upon; and I said indeed, that *I could see nothing*, but a white Cloud, bright on one Side, by the shining of the Sun upon the other Part. The Woman endeavour'd to shew it me, but could not make me confess, that I saw it, which, indeed, if I had, I must have lied: But the Woman turning upon me, look'd in my Face, and fancied I laugh'd; in which her Imagination deceiv'd her too; for I really did not laugh, but was very seriously reflecting how the poor People were terrify'd, by the Force of their own Imagination. However, she turned from me, call'd me prophane Fellow, and a Scoffer; told me, that it was a time of God's Anger, and dreadful Judgments were approaching; and that Despisers, such as I, should *wonder and perish.*[2]

The People about her seem'd disgusted as well as she; and I found there was no perswading them, that I did not laugh at them; and that I

---

8. Hearses, vehicles for transporting the dead.
9. Revision of lines from Defoe's *A New Discovery of an Old Intreague* (1691), his first published poem. Throughout his life Defoe frequently quoted himself.
1. Profane, irreligious and hardened to moral warnings.

2. Landa identifies this phrase as a quotation from Acts 13.41: "Behold, ye despisers, and wonder, and perish: for I work a work in your days, a work which ye shall in no wise believe . . ." There is a misprint in the Oxford note, "wander" for "wonder."

should be rather mobb'd by them, than be able to undeceive them. So
I left them; and this Appearance pass'd for as real, as the Blazing Star it
self.

Another Encounter I had in the open Day also: And this was in going
thro' a narrow Passage from *Petty-France* into *Bishopsgate* Church Yard,
by a Row of Alms-Houses;[3] there are two Church Yards to *Bishopsgate*
Church, or Parish; one we go over to pass from the Place call'd *Petty-
France* into *Bishopsgate* Street, coming out just by the Church Door,
the other is on the side of the narrow Passage, where the Alms-Houses
are on the left; and a Dwarf-wall with a Palisadoe[4] on it, on the right
Hand; and the City Wall on the other Side, more to the right.

In this narrow Passage stands a Man looking thro' between the Palisadoe's into the Burying Place; and as many People as the Narrowness
of the Passage would admit to stop, without hindring the Passage of
others; and he was talking mighty eagerly to them, and pointing now to
one Place, then to another, and affirming, that he saw a Ghost walking
upon such a Grave Stone there; he described the Shape, the Posture,
and the Movement of it so exactly, that it was the greatest Matter of
Amazement to him in the World, that every Body did not see it as well
as he. On a sudden he would cry, *There it is: Now it comes this Way:*
Then, *'Tis turn'd back*; till at length he persuaded the People into so
firm a Belief of it, that one fancied he saw it, and another fancied he
saw it; and thus he came every Day making a strange Hubbub, considering it was in so narrow a Passage, till *Bishopsgate* Clock struck eleven;
and then the Ghost would seem to start; and as if he were call'd away,
disappear'd on a sudden.

I look'd earnestly every way, and at the very Moment, that this man
directed, but could not see the least Appearance of any thing; but so
positive was this poor man, that he gave the People the Vapours[5] in
abundance, and sent them away trembling, and frighted; till at length,
few People, that knew of it, car'd to go thro' that Passage; and hardly any
Body by Night, on any Account whatever.

This Ghost, as the poor Man affirm'd, made Signs to the Houses, and
to the Ground, and to the People, plainly intimating, or else they so
understanding it, that Abundance of the People, should come to be
buried in that Church-Yard; as indeed happen'd: But that he saw such
Aspects, I must acknowledg, I never believ'd; nor could I see any thing
of it my self, tho' I look'd most earnestly to see it, if possible.

These things serve to shew, how far the People were really overcome
with Delusions; and as they had a Notion of the Approach of a Visitation, all their Predictions run upon a most dreadful Plague, which should

---

3. Petty-France, for Petit or Little France, a
part of Bishopsgate parish where a sizable group
of French immigrants had settled. It was outside the Walls. The almshouses were charity
homes maintained for the poor and aged.
4. A small wall with a palisade, or row of stakes,

implanted on it.
5. Medical: A morbid condition caused by
injurious exhalations from the internal organs
of the body, especially the stomach, which
caused depression and nervous disorders (OED).

lay the whole City, and even the Kingdom waste; and should destroy almost all the Nation, both Man and Beast.

To this, as I said before, the Astrologers added Stories of the Conjunctions of Planets in a malignant Manner, and with a mischievous Influence; one of which Conjunctions was to happen, and did happen, in *October*; and the other in *November*; and they filled the Peoples Heads with Predictions on these Signs of the Heavens, intimating, that those Conjunctions foretold Drought, Famine, and Pestilence; in the two first of them however, they were entirely mistaken, For we had no droughty Season; but in the beginning of the Year, a hard Frost, which lasted from *December* almost to *March*; and after that moderate Weather, rather warm than hot, with refreshing Winds, and in short, very seasonable Weather; and also several very great Rains.

Some Endeavors were used to suppress the Printing of such Books as terrify'd the People, and to frighten the dispersers of them, some of whom were taken up, but nothing was done in it, as I am inform'd; The Government being unwilling to exasperate the People, who were, *as I may say*, all out of their Wits already.

Neither can I acquit those Ministers, that in their Sermons, rather sunk, than lifted up the Hearts of their Hearers; many of them no doubt did it for the strengthning the Resolution of the People;[6] and especially for quickning them to Repentance; but it certainly answer'd not their End, at least not in Proportion to the injury it did another Way; and indeed, as God himself thro' the whole Scriptures, rather draws to him by Invitations, and calls to turn to him and live, than drives us by Terror and Amazement; So I must confess, I thought the Ministers should have done also, imitating our blessed Lord and Master in this, that his whole Gospel, is full of Declarations from Heaven of Gods Mercy, and his readiness to receive Penitents, and forgive them; complaining, *ye will not come unto me, that ye may have Life;*[7] and that therefore, his Gospel is called the Gospel of Peace, and the Gospel of Grace.

But we had some good Men, and that of all Persuasions and Opinions, whose Discourses were full of Terror; who spoke nothing but dismal Things; and as they brought the People together with a kind of Horror, sent them away in Tears, prophesying nothing but evil Tidings; terrifying the People with the Apprehensions of being utterly destroy'd, not guiding them, at least not enough, to Cry to Heaven for Mercy.

It was indeed, a Time of very unhappy Breaches among us in matters of Religion: Innumerable Sects, and Divisions, and Separate Opinions prevail'd among the People; the Church of *England* was restor'd indeed with the Restoration of the Monarchy, about four Year before; but the Ministers and Preachers of the Presbyterians, and Independants, and of

6. One of Defoe's lifelong opinions, it can be found in his fiction and nonfiction. He believed firmly that love and mercy, not fear, awakened gratitude and brought people to salvation.
7. John 5.40. Defoe is recommending that the ministers appeal to the people through evidence of God's love and mercy, as Jesus did when he compared himself to John the Baptist and referred the people to his actions as evidence of his love for them.

all the other Sorts of Professions, had begun to gather seperate Societies and erect Altar against Altar,[8] and all those had their Meetings for Worship apart, as they have but not so many then, the Dissenters being not thorowly form'd into a Body as they are since, and those Congregations which were thus gather'd together, were yet but few; and even those that were, the Government did not allow, but endeavor'd to suppress them, and shut up their Meetings.[9]

But the Visitation[1] reconcil'd them again, at least for a Time, and many of the best and most valuable Ministers and Preachers of the Dissenters, were suffer'd to go into the Churches, where the Incumbents were fled away, as many were, not being able to stand it;[2] and the People flockt without Distinction to hear them preach, not much inquiring who or what Opinion they were of: But after the Sickness was over, that Spirit of Charity abated, and every Church being again supply'd with their own Ministers, or others presented, where the Minister was dead, Things return'd to their old Channel again.

One Mischief always introduces another: These Terrors and Apprehensions of the People, led them into a Thousand weak, foolish, and wicked Things, which, they wanted not a Sort of People really wicked, to encourage them to; and this was running about to Fortune tellers, Cunning-men, and Astrologers, to know their Fortune, or, as 'tis vulgarly express'd, to have their Fortunes told them, their Nativities calculated, and the like; and this Folly, presently made the Town swarm with a wicked Generation of Pretenders to Magick, to the *Black Art, as they call'd it*, and I know not what; Nay, to a Thousand worse Dealings with the Devil, than they were really guilty of; and this Trade grew so open, and so generally practised, that it became common to have Signs and Inscriptions set up at Doors; here lives a Fortune-teller; here lives an Astrologer; here you may have your Nativity calculated, and the like; and Fryar *Bacon's* Brazen-Head,[3] which was the usual Sign of these

8. Although Charles II had promised "liberty to tender consciences" at the time of the Restoration, hope for that ended with the Savoy Conference and the passage of the Act of Uniformity in the spring of 1662. A series of Acts of Parliament designed to end religious "dissent" and "protect the nation" from religious groups who might have different ideas about the powers of the monarch and about succession to the throne were passed. Although the voice of H. F. is not that of a Dissenter Nonconformist, Defoe as a Dissenter shows obvious sympathy for the courage of his religious group.
9. Among the acts passed was the Coventicle Act of 1664, which forbade all religious gatherings of five or more people not conducted according to the Church of England liturgy, and the Five Mile Act of 1665, which forbade any who had preached outside the Anglican Church from coming within five miles of any city, corporation, or parliamentary borough.

1. The plague, personified to indicate the action of God to test, try, or even punish his people.
2. Thomas Vincent and others, recorded the Anglican desertion of their parishes. Since the parish was the governing unit responsible for such things as administering the funds for the poor and even appointing supervisors for street maintenance, their absence caused great fear and hardship. See Vincent, *God's Terrible Voice* (London, 1667) 48–52.
3. Roger Bacon (1210/14–94?), inventor of eyeglasses, has been described as the father of English philosophy, but by the seventeenth century the people remembered him for his interest in magic and alchemy. Allegedly he made a brazen head that spoke. Without street numbers and in a time of relatively low literacy, pictorial signs served as guides and advertisements.

Peoples Dwelling, was to be seen almost in every Street, or else the Sign of Mother *Shipton*,[4] or of *Merlin's* Head,[5] and the like.

With what blind, absurd, and ridiculous Stuff, these Oracles of the Devil pleas'd and satisfy'd the People, I really know not; but certain it is, that innumerable Attendants crouded about their Doors every Day; and if but a grave Fellow in a Velvet Jacket, a Band,[6] and a black Cloak, which was the Habit those Quack Conjurers generally went in, was but seen in the Streets, the People would follow them, in Crowds and ask them Questions, as they went along.

I need not mention, what a horrid Delusion this was, or what it tended to; but there was no Remedy for it, till the Plague it self put an End to it all; and I suppose, clear'd the Town of most of those Calculators themselves. One Mischief was, that if the poor People ask'd these mock Astrologers, whether there would be a Plague, or no? they all agreed in the general to answer, *Yes*, for that kept up their Trade; and had the People not been kept in a Fright about that, the Wizards would presently have been rendred useless, and their Craft had been at an end: But they always talked to them of such and such Influences of the Stars, of the Conjunctions of such and such Planets, which must necessarily bring Sickness and Distempers, and consequently the Plague: And some had the Assurance to tell them, the Plague was begun already, which was too true, tho' they that said so, knew nothing of the Matter.

The Ministers, to do them Justice, and Preachers of most Sorts, that were serious and understanding Persons, thundred against these, and other wicked Practises, and exposed the Folly as well as the Wickedness of them together; And the most sober and judicious People despis'd and abhor'd them: But it was impossible to make any Impression upon the midling People,[7] and the working labouring Poor; their Fears were predominant over all their Passions; and they threw away their Money in a most distracted Manner upon those Whymsies. Maid-Servants especially and Men-Servants, were the chief of their Customers; and their Question generally was, after the first demand of, *Will there be a Plague?* I say, the next Question was, *Oh, Sir! for the Lord's Sake, what will*

4. The name affixed to a series of books and lists of prophecies. As in identifying Bacon with a "brazen" idol reminiscent of the golden calf of Exodus 32.1–20, Defoe associates these figures with superstition and evil. Perhaps the most famous "cunning woman" of English folklore, Mother Shipton was allegedly the child of a human mother and the Devil. *The Prophesie of Mother Shipton in the Raigne of King Henry the Eighth* (1641) concludes with the story of a mariner encountering a man sitting on St. James Church hill weeping. The man says, "Ah what a good Citie this was, none in the world comparable to it, and now there is scarce any house that can let us have drinke for our money." This anecdote was interpreted as a prophecy of the plague and fire. Mother Shipton is also the model for many drawings of witches, she was reportedly "big bone'd . . . with great goggling, but sharp and fiery Eyes, her Nose of incredible unproportionable length, having in it many crooks and turnings, adorned with many strange Pimples. . . . Her Chin . . . turning up towards her Mouth" (Robert A. Erickson, *Mother Midnight* [New York: AMS, 1986] 19–20).

5. The magician who guided the destinies of King Arthur. The child of a devil and a virtuous woman, his story first appeared in Geoffrey of Monmouth's *Vita Merlini* (c. 1150).

6. Old-fashioned collar or ruff.

7. Defoe means what modern sociologists would call the lower middle class—shopkeepers, artisans; and tradesmen.

become of me? Will my Mistress keep me, or will she turn me off? Will she stay here, or will she go into the Country? And if she goes into the Country, will she take me with her, or leave me here to be starv'd and undone. And the like of Men-Servants.

The Truth is, the Case of poor Servants was very dismal, as I shall have occasion to mention again by and by; for it was apparent, a prodigious Number of them would be turn'd away, and it was so; and of them abundance perished; and particularly of those that these false Prophets had flattered with Hopes, that they should be continued in their Services, and carried with their Masters and Mistresses into the Country; and had not publick Charity provided for these poor Creatures, whose Number was exceeding great, and in all Cases of this Nature must be so, they would have been in the worst Condition of any People in the City.

These Things agitated the minds of the common People for many Months, while the first Apprehensions, were upon them; and while the Plague, was not, as I may say, yet broken out: But I must also not forget, that the more serious Part of the Inhabitants behav'd after another Manner: The Government encouraged their Devotion, and appointed publick Prayers, and Days of fasting and Humiliation, to make publick Confession of Sin, and implore the Mercy of God, to avert the dreadful Judgment, which hung over their Heads; and it is not to be express'd with what Alacrity the People of all persuasions enbraced the Occasion; how they flock'd to the Churches and Meetings, and they were all so throng'd, that there was often no coming near, no, not to the very Doors of the largest Churches; Also there were daily Prayers appointed Morning and Evening at several Churches, and Days of private praying at other Places; at all which the People attended, I say, with an uncommon Devotion: Several private Families also, as well of one Opinion as of another, kept Family Fasts, to which they admitted their near Relations only: So that in a Word, those People, who were really serious and religious, apply'd themselves in a truly Christian Manner, to the proper Work of Repentance and Humiliation, as a Christian People ought to do.

Again the publick shew'd, that they would bear their Share in these Things; the very Court, which was then Gay and Luxurious, put on a Face of just Concern, for the publick Danger: All the Plays and Interludes,[8] which after the Manner of the *French* Court,[1] had been set up, and began to encrease among us, were forbid to Act;[2] the gaming Tables, publick dancing Rooms, and Music Houses which multiply'd, and began

---

8. Interludes were short plays, common in the fifteenth and sixteenth centuries, but still popular as court performances or as after-dinner entertainments in the Inns of Court and halls of noblemen.
1. Charles II and many of his friends had lived at or in the extended circle of the French court until the Restoration.
2. Public theatrical performances were suspended on June 5, 1665, by the Lord Chamberlain. Although there were performances at Whitehall (the King's Court) beginning October 11, it was December 1666 before the public theaters reopened.

to debauch the Manners of the People, were shut up and suppress'd; and the Jack-puddings, Merry-andrews, Puppet-shows, Rope-dancers,[3] and such like doings, which had bewitch'd the poor common People, shut up their Shops, finding indeed no Trade; for the Minds of the People, were agitated with other Things; and a kind of Sadness and Horror at these Things, sat upon the Countenances, even of the common People; Death was before their Eyes, and every Body began to think of their Graves, not of Mirth and Diversions.

But even those wholesome Reflections, which rightly manag'd, would have most happily led the People to fall upon their Knees, make Confession of their Sins, and look up to their merciful Saviour for Pardon, imploreing his Compassion on them, in such a Time of their Distress; by which, we might have been as a second *Nineveh*,[4] had a quite contrary Extreme in the common People; who ignorant and stupid in their Reflections, as they were brutishly wicked and thoughtless before, were now led by their Fright to extremes of Folly; and as I have said before, that they ran to Conjurers and Witches, and all Sorts of Decievers, to know what should become of them; who fed their Fears, and kept them always alarm'd, and awake, on purpose to delude them, and pick their Pockets: So, they were as mad, upon their running after Quacks, and Mountebanks, and every practising old Woman,[5] for Medicines and Remedies, storeing themselves with such Multitudes of Pills, Potions, and Preservatives, as they were call'd; that they not only spent their Money, but even poison'd themselves before-hand, for fear of the Poison of the Infection, and prepar'd their Bodies for the Plague, instead of preserving them against it. On the other Hand, it is incredible, and scarce to be imagin'd, how the Posts of Houses, and Corners of Streets were plaster'd over with Doctors Bills, and Papers of ignorant Fellows; quacking and tampering in Physick,[6] and inviting the People to come to them for Remedies; which was generally set off, with such flourishes as these, (*viz.*) I N F A L L I B L E preventive Pills against the Plague. N E V E R-F A I L I N G Preservatives against the Infection. S O V-E R A I G N Cordials against the Corruption of the Air.[7] E X A C T Regulations for the Conduct of the Body, in Case of an Infection: Antipestilential Pills. I N C O M P A R A B L E Drink against the Plague, never found out before. An U N I V E R S A L Remedy for the Plague. The O N L Y-T R U E Plague-Water. The R O Y A L-A N T I-

3. These street entertainers were clowns, jugglers, tumblers, jesters. Puppeteers and rope dancers performed in the theaters between acts as well as in the streets. Rope dancers did acrobatic tricks on a rope suspended in the air.
4. See pp. 292–93. Jonah 3.5–10.
5. Fraudulent practitioners of medicine. Quacks usually pretended to an education and had offices; mountebanks hawked their remedies from platforms or ladders in the open streets and often used tricks or juggling to attract a crowd. Women specialized in herbs.
6. *Physick* was the term for "knowledge of the knowable Works of God," especially knowledge of the human body, diseases, and their treatment (OED). Also used to mean medicine.
7. Many suspected the air of carrying the infection, and numerous ways to purify the "corrupt" air were published. See pp. 209–210 in this volume.

D O T E against all Kinds of Infection;[8] and such a Number more that
I cannot reckon up; and if I could, would fill a Book of themselves to set
them down.

Others set up Bills, to summons People to their Lodgings for Directions and Advice in the Case of Infection: These had specious Titles
also, such as these.

> An eminent High-Dutch Physician, newly come over from Holland,
> where he resided during all the Time of the great Plague, last
> Year, in Amsterdam; and cured multitudes of People, that actually
> had the Plague upon them.
> An Italian Gentlewoman just arrived from Naples,[9] having a choice
> Secret to prevent Infection, which she found out by her great
> Experience, and did wonderful Cures with it in the late Plague
> there; wherein there died 20000 in one Day.
> An antient Gentlewoman having practised, with great Success, in
> the late Plague in this City, Anno 1636, gives her advice only to
> the Female Sex. To be spoke with, &c.
> An experienc'd Physician, who has long studied the the Doctrine of
> Antidotes against all Sorts of Poison and Infection, has after 40
> Years Practise, arrived to such Skill, as may, with God's Blessing,
> direct Persons how to prevent their being touch'd by any Conta-
> gious Distemper whatsoever. He directs the Poor gratis.[1]

I take notice of these by way of Specimen: I could give you two or
three Dozen of the like, and yet have abundance left behind. 'Tis sufficient from these to apprise any one, of the Humour of those Times; and
how a Set of Thieves and Pick-pockets, not only robb'd and cheated the
poor People of their Money, but poisoned their Bodies with odious and
fatal preparations; some with Mercury,[2] and some with other things as
bad, perfectly remote from the Thing pretended to; and rather hurtful
than servicable to the Body in case an Infection followed.

I cannot omit a Subtilty of one of those Quack-operators, with which
he gull'd the poor People to croud about him, but did nothing for them
without Money. He had it seems, added to his Bills, which he gave
about the Streets, this Advertisement in Capital Letters, (viz.) He gives
Advice to the Poor for nothing.

Abundance of poor People came to him accordingly, to whom he
made a great many fine Speeches; examin'd them of the State of their

8. These remedies had been openly advertised, even in such semi-official places as Roger
L'Estrange's Newes; the College of Physicians
recommended plague water and gave recipes
for several preventive drugs. See pp. 210–11 in
this volume.
9. The 1656 plague in Naples had been especially devastating. An Account of the Plague at
Naples, reprinted in the 1721 A Collection of
very Valuable and Scarce Pieces Relating to the
Last Plague in the Year 1665, trumpeted "there

died in one Day 20000 Persons" (83).
1. Again these are accurate representations of
advertisements printed in the newspapers and
on handbills and posters.
2. Mercury was a common treatment for
venereal disease, especially syphilis. It was used
as an ointment, a powder (taken internally and
used externally), and as a "vapor." It was also
used for skin diseases. It had no treatment value
and could be fatal if ingested in large enough
quantities.

Health, and of the Constitution of their Bodies, and told them many good things for them to do, which were of no great Moment: But the Issue and Conclusion of all was, that he had a preparation, which if they took such a Quantity of, every Morning, he would pawn his Life, they should never have the Plague, no, tho' they lived in the House with People that were infected: This made the People all resolve to have it; But then the Price of that was *so much*, I think 'twas half-a-Crown:[3] But, Sir, says one poor Woman, I am a poor Alms-Woman, and am kept by the Parish, and your Bills say, you give the Poor your help for nothing. Ay, good Woman, says the Docter, so I do, as I publish'd there. I give my Advice to the Poor for nothing; but not my Physick. Alas, Sir! says she, that is a Snare laid for the Poor then; for you give them your Advice for nothing, that is to say, you advise them gratis, to buy your Physick for their Money; so does every Shop-keeper with his Wares.[4] Here the Woman began to give him ill Words, and stood at his Door all that Day, telling her Tale to all the People that came, till the Doctor finding she turn'd away his Customers; was oblig'd to call her up Stairs again, and give her his Box of Physick for nothing, which, perhaps too was *good for nothing when she had it*.

But to return to the people, whose Confusions fitted them to be impos'd upon by all Sorts of Pretenders, and by every Mountebank. There is no doubt, but these quacking Sort of Fellows rais'd great gains out of the miserable People; for we daily found, the Crouds that ran after them were infinitely greater, and their Doors were more thronged than those of Dr. *Brooks*, Dr. *Upton*, Dr. *Hodges*, Dr. *Berwick*,[5] or any, tho' the most famous Men of the Time: And I was told, that some of them got five Pound a Day by their Physick.

But there was still another Madness beyond all this, which may serve to give an Idea of the distracted humour of the poor People at that Time; and this was their following a worse Sort of Deceivers than any of these; for these petty Thieves only deluded them to pick their Pockets, and get their Money; in which their Wickedness, *whatever it was*, lay chiefly on the Side of the Deceiver's deceiving, not upon the Deceived: But in this Part I am going to mention, it lay chiefly in the People deceiv'd, or equally in both; and this was in wearing Charms, Philters,[6] Exorcisms, Amulets,[7] and I know not what Preparations, to fortify the Body with

3. "Half-a-Crown" is two shillings, sixpence.
4. Defoe loved this kind of tart repartee. His second-earliest-surviving writing, *The Historical Collections*, is a collection of such witty, revealing exchanges.
5. Dr. Brooke (not "Brooks" as it is printed erroneously here) and Dr. Barwick (not Berwick) were among the eight physicians nominated by the Royal College of Physicians to be appointed to the Lord Mayor as special physicians for the plague patients. Their services were paid for by the City, and they would have treated the poor without charge. Dr. Nicholas Upton administered one of the two major London pesthouses, and Nathaniel Hodges remained in London throughout the plague, treated large numbers of patients, and wrote *Loimologia* (see p. 214 in this volume).
6. A magic potion, in ordinary times usually a love potion, often carried in a false jewel worn as a ring or on a necklace.
7. A preservative or charm worn around the neck or wrist. Some were grotesque, as real toads strung on leather thongs threaded through holes bored in their heads.

them against the Plague; as if the Plague was not the Hand of God, but a kind of a Possession of an evil Spirit; and that it was to be kept off with Crossings, Signs of the Zodiac, Papers tied up with so many Knots; and certain Words, or Figures written on them, as particularly the Word *Abracadabra*, form'd in Triangle, or Pyramid, thus.

```
A B R A C A D A B R A
 A B R A C A D A B R       Others had the Jesuits
  A B R A C A D A B           Mark in a Cross.
   A B R A C A D A
    A B R A C A D              I   H
     A B R A C A                  S
      A B R A C
       A B R A             Others nothing but this
        A B R                 Mark thus.[8]
         A B
          A
```

I might spend a great deal of Time in my Exclamations against the Follies, and indeed Wickedness of those things, in a Time of such Danger, in a matter of such Consequences as this, of a National Infection, But my Memorandums of these things relate rather to take notice only of the Fact, and mention that it was so: How the poor People found the Insufficiency of those things, and how many of them were afterwards carried away in the Dead Carts, and thrown into the common Graves of every Parish, with these hellish Charms and Trumpery hanging about their Necks, remains to be spoken of as we go along.

All this was the Effect of the Hurry the People were in, after the first Notion of the Plague being at hand was among them: And which may be said to be from about *Michaelmas*[9] 1664, but more particularly after the two Men died in St. *Giles's*, in the Beginning of *December*. And again, after another Alarm in *February*; for when the Plague evidently spread it self, they soon began to see the Folly of trusting to those unperforming Creatures, who had Gull'd them of their Money, and then their Fears work'd another way, namely, to Amazement and Stupidity, not knowing what Course to take, or what to do, either to help or relieve themselves; but they ran about from one Neighbours House to another; and even in the Streets, from one Door to another with repeated Cries, of, *Lord have Mercy upon us, what shall we do?*

8. Defoe wrote universal histories and books on spirits and apparitions in which he discussed magic signs. Abracadabra dates to the second century and, when written in this triangular arrangement and worn, was said to cure agues. Agues are fevers marked by fits of chills and shivering. The second stands for the Latin phrase "*In Hoc Signo, Vinces,*" meaning "In this sign, conquer"; it is also the abbreviation for IHSOUS, a transcription of the Greek for "Jesus." The third is a printer's "flower."
9. Pronounced "Mik'el mas," September 29 is the feast day for Michael the archangel.

Indeed, the poor People were to be pity'd in one particular Thing, in which they had little or no Relief, and which I Desire to mention with a serious Awe and Reflection; which perhaps, every one that reads this, may not relish: Namely, that whereas Death now began not, *as we may say*, to hover over every ones Head only, but to look into their Houses, and Chambers, and stare in their Faces: Tho' there might be some stupidity, and dullness of the Mind, and there was so, a great deal; yet, there was a great deal of just Alarm, sounded into the very inmost Soul, *if I may so say* of others: Many Consciences were awakened; many hard Hearts melted into Tears; many a penitent Confession was made of Crimes long concealed: would wound the Souls of any Christian, to have heard the dying Groans of many a despairing Creature, and none durst come near to comfort them:[1] Many a Robbery, many a Murder, was then confest aloud, and no Body surviving to Record the Accounts of it.[2] People might be heard even into the Streets as we pass'd along, calling upon God for Mercy, thro' Jesus Christ, *and saying*, I have been a Thief, I have been an Adulterer, I have been a Murderer, and the like; and none durst stop to make the least Inquiry into such Things, or to administer Comfort to the poor Creatures, that in the Anguish both of Soul and Body thus cry'd out. Some of the Ministers did Visit the Sick at first, and for a little while, but it was not to be done; it would have been present Death, to have gone into some Houses: The very buryers of the Dead, who were the hardnedest Creatures in Town, were sometimes beaten back, and so terrify'd, that they durst not go into Houses, where the whole Families were swept away together, and where the Circumstances were more particularly horrible as some were; but this was indeed, at the first Heat of the Distemper.

Time enur'd[3] them to it all; and they ventured every where afterwards, without Hesitation, as I Occasion to mention at large hereafter.

I am supposing now, the Plague to be begun, as I have said, and that the Magistrates begun to take the Condition of the People, into their serious Consideration; what they did as to the Regulation of the Inhabitants, and of infected Families. I shall speak to by it self; but as to the Affair of Health, it is proper to mention it here, that having seen the foolish Humour of the People, in running after Quacks, and Mountebanks, Wizards, and Fortune-tellers, which they did as above, even to Madness. The Lord Mayor, a very sober and religious Gentleman appointed Physicians and Surgeons for Relief of the poor; I mean, the diseased poor; and in particular, order'd the College of Physicians[4] to

1. Vincent contrasts the help and comfort people can draw from neighbors and friends in calamities such as fires to the isolation and loneliness of the plague sufferers (see p. 213). Durst, archaic form of "dared."
2. Camus makes the freedom from fear of arrest one of the central themes in his novel *The Plague*.
3. Inured, hardened, accustomed.
4. Given its charter in 1518 by Henry VIII in response to an outbreak of plague, the Royal College of Physicians had the power to encourage medical education, license physicians who practiced in London and within seven miles of it, and fine violators. At that time only those with seven years of medical study beyond the M.A. degree could be members. Most members of the college fled the 1665 plague (George Clark, A *History of the Royal College of Physicians of London* [Oxford: Clarendon, 1964]).

publish Directions for cheap Remedies, for the Poor, in all the Circumstances of the Distemper. This indeed was one of the most charitable and judicious Things that could be done at that Time; for this drove the People from haunting the Doors of every Disperser of Bills; and from taking down blindly, and without Consideration, Poison for Physick, and Death instead of Life.

This Direction of the Physicians was done by a Consultation of the whole College, and as it was particularly calculated for the use of the Poor; and for cheap Medicines it was made publick, so that every Body might see it;[5] and Copies were given *gratis* to all that desired it: But as it is publick, and to be seen on all Occasions, I need not give the Reader of this, the Trouble of it.

I shall not be supposed to lessen the Authority or Capacity of the Physicians, when, I say, that the Violence of the Distemper, when it came to its Extremity, was like the Fire the next Year; The Fire which consumed what the Plague could not touch, defy'd all the Application of Remedies; the Fire Engines were broken, the Buckets thrown away; and the Power of Man was baffled, and brought to an End; so the Plague defied all Medicine; the very Physicians were seized with it, with their Preservatives in their Mouths; and men went about prescribing to others and telling them what to do, till the Tokens were upon them, and they dropt down dead, destroyed by that very Enemy, they directed others to oppose. This was the Case of several Physicians, even some of them the most eminent; and of several of the most skilful Surgeons; Abundance of Quacks too died, who had the Folly to trust to their own Medicines, which they must needs be conscious to themselves, were good for nothing; and who rather ought, like other Sorts of Thieves, to have run away, sensible of their Guilt, from the Justice that they could not but expect should punish them, as they knew they had deserved.

Not that it is any Derogation from the Labour, or Application of the Physicians, to say, they fell in the common Calamity; nor is it so intended by me; it rather is to their Praise, that they ventured their Lives so far as even to lose them in the Service of Mankind; They endeavoured to do good, and to save the Lives of others; But we were not to expect, that the Physicians could stop God's Judgments, or prevent a Distemper eminently armed from Heaven, from executing the Errand it was sent about,

Doubtless, the Physicians assisted many by their Skill, and by their Prudence and Applications, to the saving of their Lives, and restoring their Health: But it is no lessening their Character, or their Skill, to say, they could not cure those that had the Tokens upon them, or those who were mortally infected before the Physicians were sent for, as was frequently the Case.

It remains to mention now what publick Measures were taken by the Magistrates for the general Safety, and to prevent the spreading of the

5. For an excerpt, see pp. 208–11 in this volume.

Distemper, when it first broke out: I shall have frequent Occasion to speak of their Prudence of the Magistrates, their Charity, the Vigilance for the Poor, and for preserving good Order; furnishing Provisions, and the like, when the Plague was encreased, as it afterwards was. But I am now upon the Order and Regulations[6] they published for the Government of infected Families.

I mention'd above shutting of Houses up; and it is needful to say something particularly to that; for this Part of the History of the Plague is very melancholy; *but the most grievous Story must be told.*

About *June* the Lord Mayor of *London*, and the Court of Aldermen, as I have said, began more particularly to concern themselves for the Regulation of the City.

The Justices of Peace for *Middlesex*, by Direction of the Secretary of State, had begun to shut up Houses in the Parishes of St. *Giles's in the Fields*, St. *Martins*, St. *Clement Danes*, &c. and it was with good Success; for in several Streets, where the Plague broke out, upon strict guarding the Houses that were infected, and taking Care to bury those that died, immediatly after they were known to be dead, the Plague ceased in those Streets. It was also observ'd, that the Plague decreas'd sooner in those Parishes, after they had been visited to the full, than it did in the Parishes of *Bishopsgate*, *Shoreditch*, *Aldgate*, *White-Chappel*, *Stepney*, and others, the early Care taken in that Manner, being a great means to the putting a Cheque to it.

This shutting up of Houses was a method first taken, as I understand, in the Plague, which happened in 1603, at the Coming of King *James* the First to the Crown, and the Power of shutting People up in their own Houses, was granted by Act of Parliament, entitled, *An Act for the charitable Relief and Ordering of Persons infected with the Plague.*[7] On which Act of Parliament, the Lord Mayor and Aldermen of the City of *London*, founded the Order they made at this Time, and which took Place the 1st of *July* 1665, when the Numbers infected within the City, were but few, the last Bill for the 92 Parishes being but four; and some Houses having been shut up in the City, and some sick People being removed to the Pest-House[8] beyond *Bunhill-Fields*,[9] in the Way to *Islington*; I say, by these Means, when there died near one thousand a Week in the Whole, the Number in the City was but 28, and the City was preserv'd more healthy in Proportion, than any other Places all the Time of the Infection.

These Orders of my Lord Mayor's were publish'd, as I have said, the latter End of *June*, and took Place from the first of *July*, and were as follows, (*viz.*)

6. These orders and regulations were passed by the Lord Mayor and Court of Aldermen. For an excerpt, see pp. 197–98 in this volume.
7. I Jac. I, c. 31, renewed an order of 1583 (Landa, 264n. 37.1). Orders for isolating plague sufferers and their families are printed on pp. 197–98.
8. A hospital for people with infectious diseases.
9. The Dissenting burial ground. John Bunyan, Daniel Defoe, and Susannah Wesley are buried there.

ORDERS *Conceived and Published by the* Lord M AY O R *and* Aldermen *of the City of* London, *concerning the Infection of the* Plague *1665.*[1]

WHEREAS in the Reign of our late Sovereign King James,[2] of happy Memory, an Act was made for the charitable Relief and ordering of Persons infected with the Plague; whereby Authority was given to Justices of the Peace, Mayors, Bayliffs[3] and other head Officers, to appoint within their several Limits, Examiners, Searchers, Watchmen, Keepers, and Buriers for the Persons and Places infected, and to minister unto them Oaths for the Performance of their Offices. And the same Statute did also authorize the giving of other Directions, as unto them for the present Necessity should seem good in their Discretions. It is now upon special Consideration, thought very expedient for preventing and avoiding of Infection of Sickness (if it shall so please Almighty God) that these Officers following be appointed, and these Orders hereafter duly observed.

EXAMINERS TO BE APPOINTED IN EVERY PARISH.

FIRST, It is thought requisite, and so ordered, that in every Parish there be one, two, or more Persons of good Sort and Credit, chosen and appointed by the Alderman, his Deputy, and common-Council[4] of every Ward, by the Name of Examiners, to continue in that Office the Space of two Months at least: And if any fit Person so appointed, shall refuse to undertake the same, the said parties so refusing, to be committed to Prison until they shall conform themselves accordingly.

THE EXAMINERS OFFICE.

THAT these Examiners be sworn by the Aldermen, to enquire and learn from time to time what Houses in every Parish be Visited, and what Persons be Sick, and of what Diseases, as near as they can inform themselves; and upon doubt in that Case, to command Restraint of Access, until it appear what the Disease shall prove: And if they find any Person sick of the Infection, to give order to the Constable that the House be shut up; and if the Constable shall be found Remiss or Negligent, to give present Notice thereof to the Alderman of the Ward.

1. Defoe is probably quoting from A *Collection of Very Valuable and Scarce Pieces,* which had been published in 1721.
2. King James I, who reigned from 1603 to 1625.
3. Assistants to the sheriffs with the power to make arrests and execute writs.
4. Common Councilmen were elected each St. Thomas Day (December 21) by the freemen (livery company members who had attained that rank in their companies) of the City. In 1722, there were 234, and they were the legislative body, while the Lord Mayor, Aldermen, and Sheriffs performed the executive and judicial functions.

WATCHMEN.

THAT to every infected House there be appointed two Watchmen, one for every Day, and the other for the Night: And that these Watchmen have a special care that no Person go in or out of such infected Houses, whereof they have the Charge, upon pain of severe Punishment. And the said Watchman to do such further Offices as the sick House shall need and require: and if the Watchmen be sent upon any Business, to lock up the House, and take the Key with him: And the Watchman by Day to attend until ten of the Clock at Night: And the Watchman by Night untill six in the Morning.

SEARCHERS.

THAT there be a special care to appoint Women-Searchers in every Parish, such as are of honest Reputation, and of the best Sort as can be got in this kind: And these to be sworn to make due Search, and true Report to the utmost of their Knowledge, whether the Persons whose Bodies they are appointed to Search, do die of the Infection, or of what other Diseases, as near as they can. And that the Physicians who shall be appointed for Cure and Prevention of the Infection, do call before them the said Searchers, who are, or shall be appointed for the several Parishes under their respective Care; to the end they may consider, whether they are fitly qualified for that Employment; and charge them from time to time as they shall see Cause, if they appear defective in their Duties.

That no Searcher during this time of Visitation, be permitted to use any publick Work or Employment, or keep any Shop or Stall, or be employed as a Landress, or in any other common Employment whatsoever.

CHIRURGEONS. [5]

FOR better assistance of the Searchers, for as much as there hath been heretofore great abuse in misreporting the Disease, to the further spreading of the Infection: It is therefore ordered, that there be chosen and appointed able and discreet Chirurgeons, besides those that do already belong to the *Pest-House*: Amongst whom the City and Liberties to be quartered as the places lie most apt and convenient; and every of these to have one Quarter for his Limit: and the said Chirurgeons in every of their Limits to join with the

---

5. Archaic spelling of "surgeons"; in the early eighteenth century they were members of the Barber Surgeons Guild, a chartered livery company dating from 1462. The guild accepted apprentices, examined, licensed, and trained surgeons, and could fine any nonmembers who practiced within seven miles of London. They could provide external medicine only. Their charter guaranteed them four publically executed bodies a year with which to teach anatomy.

Searchers for the View of the Body, to the end there may be a true
Report made of the Disease.

And further, that the said Chirurgeons shall visit and search such
like Persons as shall either send for them, or be named and directed
unto them, by the Examiners of every Parish, and inform themselves of the Disease of the said Parties.

And for as much as the said Chirurgeons are to be sequestred
from all other Cures, and kept only to this Disease of the Infection;
It is order'd, That every one of the said Chirurgeons shall have
Twelvepence a Body searched by them, to be paid out of the Goods
of the Party searched, if he be able, or otherwise by the Parish.

NURSE-KEEPERS.

IF any Nurse-keeper shall remove her self out of any infected
House before twenty eight Days after the Decease of any Person
dying of the Infection, the House to which the said Nurse-keeper
doth so remove her self, shall be shut up until the said twenty eight
Days be expired.

ORDERS Concerning Infected Houses, and Persons Sick of the Plague.

NOTICE TO BE GIVEN OF THE SICKNESS.

THE Master of every House, as soon as any one in his House
complaineth, either of Botch, or Purple, or Swelling in any
part of his Body, or falleth otherwise dangerously Sick, without
apparent Cause of some other Disease, shall give knowledge thereof
to the Examiner of Health, within two Hours after the said Sign
shall appear.

SEQUESTRATION OF THE SICK.

AS soon as any Man shall be found by this Examiner, Chirurgeon or Searcher to be sick of the Plague, he shall the same
Night be sequestred in the same House, and in case he be so
sequestred, then, though he afterwards die not, the House wherein
he sickned, should be shut up for a Month, after the use of the due
Preservatives taken by the rest.

AIRING THE STUFF.

FOR Sequestration of the Goods and Stuff of the Infection,
their Bedding, and Apparel, and Hangings of Chambers,[6] must
be well aired with Fire, and such Perfumes as are requisite within

---

6. Draperies were hung around beds as well as across windows and walls to hold in heat.

the infected House, before they be taken again to use: This is to be done by the Appointment of the Examiner.

SHUTTING UP OF THE HOUSE.

IF any Person shall have visited any Man, known to be infected of the Plague, or entred willingly into any known infected House, being not allowed: The House wherein he inhabiteth, shall be shut up for certain Days by the Examiners Direction.

NONE TO BE REMOVED OUT OF INFECTED HOUSES, BUT, &C.

ITEM, That none be remov'd out of the House where he falleth sick of the Infection, into any other House in the City, (except it be to the *Pest-House* or a Tent, or unto some such House, which the Owner of the said visited House holdeth in his own Hands, and occupieth by his own Servants) and so as Security be given to the Parish, whither such Remove is made; that the Attendance and Charge about the said visited Persons shall be observed and charged in all the Particularities before expressed, without any Cost of that Parish, to which any such Remove shall happen to be made, and this Remove to be done by Night: And it shall be lawful to any Person that hath two Houses, to remove either his sound or his infected People to his spare House at his choice, so as if he send away first his Sound,[7] he not after send thither the Sick, nor again unto the Sick the Sound. And that the same which he sendeth, be for one Week at the least shut up, and secluded from Company, for fear of some Infection, at the first not appearing.

BURIAL OF THE DEAD.

THAT the Burial of the Dead by this Visitation, be at most convenient Hours, always either before Sun-rising, or after Sun-setting, with the Privity[8] of the Church-wardens or Constable, and not otherwise; and that no Neighbours nor Friends be suffered to accompany the Corps[9] to Church, or to enter the House visited, upon pain of having his House shut up, or be imprisoned.

And that no Corps dying of Infection shall be buried, or remain in any Church in time of Common-Prayer, Sermon, or Lecture. And that no Children be suffered at time of burial of any Corps in any Church, Church-yard, or Burying-place to come near the Corps, Coffin, or Grave. And that all the Graves shall be at least six Foot deep.

And further, all publick Assemblies at other Burials are to be forborn during the Continuance of this Visitation.

---

7. Healthy.
8. Knowledge and approval.

9. Corpse, body. Defoe also spells corpse without the final "e."

NO INFECTED STUFF TO BE UTTERED.

THAT no Clothes, Stuff,[1] Bedding or Garments be suffered to be carried or conveyed out of any infected Houses, and that the Criers and Carriers abroad of Bedding or old Apparel to be sold or pawned, be utterly prohibited and restrained, and no Brokers of Bedding or old Apparel be permitted to make any outward Shew, or hang forth on their Stalls, Shopboards or Windows towards any Street, Lane, Common-way or Passage, any old Bedding or Apparel to be sold, upon pain of Imprisonment. And if any Broker or other Person shall buy any Bedding, Apparel, or other Stuff out of any infected House, within two Months after the Infection hath been there, his House shall be shut up as Infected, and so shall continue shut up twenty Days at the least.

NO PERSON TO BE CONVEYED OUT OF ANY INFECTED HOUSE.

IF any Person visited do fortune[2] by negligent looking unto, or by any other Means, to come, or be conveyed from a Place infected, to any other Place, the Parish from whence such Party hath come or been conveyed, upon notice thereof given, shall at their Charge cause the said Party so visited and escaped, to be carried and brought back again by Night, and the Parties in this case offending, to be punished at the Direction of the Alderman of the Ward; and the House of the Receiver of such visited Person, to be shut up for twenty Days.

EVERY VISITED HOUSE TO BE MARKED.

THAT every House visited, be marked with a red Cross of a Foot long, in the middle of the Door, evident to be seen, and with these usual printed Words, that is to say, *Lord have Mercy upon us*, to be set close over the same Cross, there to continue until lawful opening of the same House.

EVERY VISITED HOUSE TO BE WATCHED.

THAT the Constables see every House shut up, and to be attended with Watchmen, which may keep them in, and minister Necessaries unto them at their own Charges (if they be able,) or at the common Charge, if they be unable: The shutting up to be for the space of four Weeks after all be whole.

That precise Order be taken that the Searchers, Chirurgeons, Keepers and Buriers are not to pass the Streets without holding a red Rod or Wand of three Foot in Length in their Hands, open and evident to be seen, and are not to go into any other House then

---

1. Woven material, especially heavy wool used   2. Happen.
to make clothing.

into their own, or into that whereunto they are directed or sent for; but to forbear and abstain from Company, especially when they have been lately used in any such Business or Attendance.

INMATES

THAT where several Inmates are in one and the same House, and any Person in that House happens to be Infected; no other Person of Family of such House shall be suffered to remove him or themselves without a Certificate from the Examiners of Health of that Parish; or in default thereof, the House whither he or they so remove, shall be shut up as in case of Visitation.

HACKNEY-COACHES.[3]

THAT care be taken of Hackney-Coach-men, that they may not (as some of them have been observed to do) after carrying of infected Persons to the *Pest-House*, and other Places, be admitted to common use, till their Coaches be well aired, and have stood unemploy'd by the Space of five or six Days after such Service.

ORDERS *for Cleaning and Keeping of the Streets Sweet.*

THE STREETS TO BE KEPT CLEAN.

FIRST, it is thought necessary, and so ordered, that every Housholder do cause the Street to be daily prepared before his Door, and so to keep it clean swept all the Week long.

THAT RAKERS TAKE IT FROM OUT THE HOUSES.

THAT the Sweeping and Filth of Houses be daily carry'd away by the Rakers, and that the Raker shall give notice of his coming, by the blowing of a Horn, as hitherto hath been done.

LAYSTALLS[4] TO BE MADE FAR OFF FROM THE CITY.

THAT the Laystalls be removed as far as may be out of the City, and common Passages, and that no Nightman or other be suffered to empty a Vault[5] into any Garden near about the City.

CARE TO BE HAD OF UNWHOLSOME FISH OR FLESH, AND OF MUSTY CORN.

THAT special care be taken, that no stinking Fish, or unwholesome Flesh, or musty Corn, or other corrupt Fruits, of what

3. Coaches available for hire, the equivalent of modern taxi cabs.

4. Places where refuse and dung were dumped.

5. A privy or outhouse.

Sort soever be suffered to be sold about the City, or any part of the same.

That the Brewers and Tippling-houses be looked unto, for musty and unwholsome Casks.

That no Hogs, Dogs, or Cats, or tame Pigeons, or Conies, be suffered to be kept within any part of the City, or any Swine to be, or stray in the Streets or Lanes, but that such Swine be impounded by the Beadle[6] or any other Officer, and the Owner punished according to Act of Common-Council, and that the Dogs be killed by the Dog-killers appointed for that purpose.

ORDERS concerning loose Persons and idle Assemblies.

BEGGERS.

FOrrasmuch as nothing is more complained of, than the Multitude of Rogues and wandring Beggars, that swarm in every place about the City, being a great cause of the spreading of the Infection, and will not be avoided, notwithstanding any Order that have been given to the contrary: It is therefore now ordered, that such Constables, and others, whom this Matter may any way concern, take special care that no wandring Begger be suffered in the Streets of this City, in any fashion or manner, whatsoever, upon the Penalty provided by the Law to be duely and severely executed upon them.

PLAYS.

THAT all Plays, Bear-Baitings, Games, singing of Ballads, Buckler-play,[7] or such like Causes of Assemblies of People, be utterly prohibited, and the Parties offending severely punished by every Alderman in his Ward.

FEASTING PROHIBITED.

THAT all publick Feasting, and particularly by the Companies of this City, and Dinners at Taverns, Alehouses, and other Places of common Entertainment be forborn till further Order and Allowance; and that the Money thereby spared, be preserved and employed for the Benefit and Relief of the Poor visited with the Infection.

6. An inferior parish officer who was appointed to be a parish constable, deliver messages, punish petty offenders, and enforce regulations.
7. Fencing.

TIPLING-HOUSES.

THAT disorderly Tipling in Taverns, Ale-houses, Coffe-houses and Cellars be severely looked unto, as the common Sin of this Time, and greatest occasion of dispersing the Plague. And that no Company or Person be suffered to remain or come into any Tavern, Ale-house, or Coffe-house to drink after nine of the Clock in the Evening, according to the antient Law and Custom of this City, upon the Penalties ordained in that Behalf.

And for the better execution of these Orders, and such other Rules and Directions as upon further consideration shall be found needful; It is ordered and enjoined that the Aldermen, Deputies, and Common-Council-men shall meet together weekly, once, twice, thrice, or oftner, (as cause shall require) at some one general Place accustomed in their respective Wards (being clear from Infection of the Plague) to consult how the said Orders may be duly put in Execution; not intending that any, dwelling in or near Places infected, shall come to the said Meeting whiles their coming may be doubtful. And the said Aldermen, and Deputies, and Common-Council-men in their several Wards may put in Execution any other good Orders that by them at their said Meetings shall be conceived and devised, for Preservation of His Majesty's Subjects from the Infection.

Sir *John Lawrence* } Sir *George Waterman* } Sheriffs.
Lord Mayor.   } Sir *Charles Doe.*   }

I need not say, that these Orders extended only to such Places as were within the Lord Mayor's Jurisdiction; so it is requisite to observe, that the Justices of Peace, within those Parishes, and Places as were called the *Hamlets*, and Out-parts, took the same Method: As I remember, the Orders for shutting up of Houses, did not take Place so soon on our Side, because, as I said before, the Plague did not reach to these Eastern Parts of the Town, at least, nor begin to be very violent, till the beginning of *August*. For Example, the whole Bill, from the 11th to the 18th of *July*, was 1761, yet there dy'd but 71 of the Plague, in all those Parishes we call the *Tower-Hamlets*;[8] and they were as follows.

Algate	14		34		65
Stepney	33	the next	58	and to the	76
White Chappel	21	Week was	48	1st of *Aug.*	79
St. *Kath. Tower*	2	thus.	4	thus.	4
Trin. Minories	1		1		4
	71		145		228

8. The parishes, liberties, and small towns near the Tower of London. Originally they were governed by the Lieutenant of the Tower, which is the most famous fortress in England and was built by William the Conqueror.

It was indeed, coming on a main; for the Burials that same Week,
were in the next adjoining Parishes, thus,

St. *Len. Shorditch*	64	the next Week	84	to the 1*st.*	110
St. *Bot. Bishopsg.*	65	prodigiously en-	105	of *Aug.*	116
St. *Giles Crippl.*	213	creased, as	421	thus.	554
	342		610		780

This shutting up of houses was as first counted a very cruel and
Unchristian Method, and the poor People so confin'd made bitter Lamentations: Complaints of the Severity of it, were also daily brought to my
Lord Mayor, of Houses causelessly, (and some maliciously) shut up: I
cannot say, but upon Enquiry, many that complained so loudly, were
found in a Condition to be continued, and others again Inspection being
made upon the sick Person, and the Sickness not appearing infectious,
or if uncertain, yet, on his being content to be carried to the Pest-House,
were released.

It is true, that the locking up the Doors of Peoples Houses, and setting
a Watchman there Night and Day, to prevent their stirring out, or any
coming to them; when, perhaps, the sound People, in the Family, might
have escaped, if they had been remov'd from the Sick, looked very hard
and cruel; and many People perished in these miserable Confinements,
which 'tis reasonable to believe, would not have been distemper'd if they
had had Liberty, tho' the Plague was in the House; at which the People
were very clamorous and uneasie at first, and several Violences were
committed, and Injuries offered to the Men, who were set to watch the
Houses so shut up; also several People broke out by Force, in many
Places, as I shall observe by and by: But it was a publick Good that
justified the private Mischief; and there was no obtaining the least Mit-
igation, by any Application to Magistrates, or Government, at that Time,
at least, not that I heard of. This put the People upon all Manner of
Stratagem, in order, if possible, to get out, and it would fill a little Volume, to set down the Arts us'd by the People of such Houses, to shut
the Eyes of the Watchmen, who were employ'd, to deceive them, and
to escape, or break out from them; in which frequent Scuffles, and some
Mischief happened; of which by it self.

As I went along *Houndsditch*[9] one Morning, about eight a-Clock,
there was a great Noise; it is true indeed, there was not much Croud,
because People were not very free to gather together, or to stay long
together, when they were there, nor did I stay long there: but the Outcry
was loud enough to prompt my Curiosity, and I call'd to one that look'd
out of a Window, and ask'd what was the Matter.

9. The "City Ditch" had been dug by the Danes
in 1016 so that no one could enter or leave the
City. It had gradually filled up with junk and
filth, including dead dogs (hence perhaps the
modern name), and was paved in 1503. The
seventeenth-century street called Houndsditch
ran through Portsoken and Bishopsgate Ward
Without.

A Watchman, it seems, had been employed to keep his Post at the Door of a House, which was infected, or said to be infected, and was shut up; he had been there all Night for two Nights together as he told his Story, and the Day Watchman had been there one Day. and was now come to relieve him: All this while no Noise had been heard in the House, no Light had been seen; they call'd for nothing, sent him of no Errands, which us'd to be the chief Business of the Watchman; neither had they given him any Disturbance, as he said, from the *Monday* afternoon, when he heard great crying and screaming in the House, which, as he supposed, was occasioned by some of the Family dying just at that Time: it seems the Night before, the Dead-Cart, as it was called, had been stopt there, and a Servant-Maid had been brought down to the Door dead, and the Buriers or Bearers, as they were call'd, put her into the Cart, wrapt only in a green Rug, and carried her away.

The Watchman had knock'd at the Door, it seems, when he heard that Noise and Crying, as above, and no Body answered, a great while; but at last one look'd out and said with an angry quick Tone, and yet a Kind of crying Voice, or a Voice of one that was crying, *What d'ye want, that ye make such a knocking?* He answer'd, *I am the Watchman! how do you do? What is the Matter?* The Person answered, *What is that to you? Stop the Dead-Cart.* This It seems, was about one a-Clock; soon after, *as the Fellow said,* he stopped the Dead-Cart, and then knock'd again, but no Body answer'd: He continued knocking, and the Bellman call'd out several Times, *Bring out your Dead;* but no Body answered, till the Man that drove the Cart being call'd to other Houses, would stay no longer, and drove away.

The Watchman knew not what to make of all this, so he let them alone, till the Morning-Man, or Day Watchman, as they call'd him, came to relieve him, giving him an Account of the Particulars, they knock'd at the Door a great while, but no body answered; and they observ'd, that the Window, or Casement, at which the Person had look'd out, who had answer'd before, continued open, being up two Pair of Stairs.

Upon this, the two Men to satisfy their Curiosity, got a long Ladder, and one of them went up to the Window, and look'd into the Room, where he saw a Woman lying dead upon the Floor, in a dismal Manner, having no Cloaths on her but her Shift:[1] But tho' he call'd aloud, and putting in his long Staff, knock'd hard on the Floor, yet no Body stirr'd or answered; neither could he hear any Noise in the House.

He came down again, upon this, and acquainted his Fellow, who went up also, and finding it just so, they resolv'd to acquaint either the Lord Mayor, or some other Magistrate of it, but did not offer to go in at the Window: the Magistrate it seems, upon the Information of the two Men, ordered the House to be broken open, a Constable, and other

---

1. Undergarment like a chemise.

Persons being appointed to be present, that nothing might be plundred; and accordingly it was so done, when no Body was found in the House, but that young Woman, who having been infected, and past Recovery, the rest had left her to die by her self, and were every one gone, having found some Way to delude the Watchman, and get open the Door, or get out at some Back Door, or over the Tops of the Houses, so that he knew nothing of it; and as to those Crys and Shrieks, which he heard, it was suppos'd, they were the passionate Cries of the Family, at the bitter parting, which, to be sure, it was to them all; this being the Sister to the Mistress of the Family. The Man of the House, his Wife, several Children, and Servants, being all gone and fled, whether sick or sound, that I could never learn; nor, indeed, did I make much Enquiry after it.

Many such escapes were made, out of infected Houses, as particularly, when the Watchman was sent of some Errand; for it was his Business to go of any Errand, that the Family sent him of, that is to say, for Necessaries, such as Food and Physick; to fetch Physicians, if they would come, or Surgeons, or Nurses, or to order the Dead-Cart, and the like; But with this Condition too, that when he went, he was to lock up the Outer-Door of the House, and take the Key away with him; to evade this, and cheat the Watchmen, People got two or three Keys made to their Locks; or they found Ways to unscrew the Locks, such as were screw'd on, and so take off the Lock, being in the Inside of the House, and while they sent away the Watchman to the Market, to the Bakehouse, or for one Trifle or another, open the Door, and go out as often as they pleas'd: But this being found out, the Officers afterwards had Orders to Padlock up the Doors on the Outside, and place Bolts on them as they thought fit.

At another House, as I was inform'd, in the Street next within *Algate*, a whole Family was shut up and lock'd in, because the Maid-Servant was taken sick; the Master of the House had complain'd by his Friends to the next Alderman, and to the Lord Mayor, and had consented to have the Maid carried to the Pest-House, but was refused, so the Door was marked with a red Cross, a Padlock on the Outside, as above, and a Watchman set to keep the Door according to publick Order.

After the Master of the House found there was no Remedy, but that he, his Wife and his Children were to be lockt up with this poor distempered Servant; he call'd to the Watchman, and told him, he must go then and fetch a Nurse for them, to attend this poor Girl, for that it would be certain Death to them all to oblige them to nurse her, and told him plainly, that if he would not do this, the Maid must perish either of the Distemper, or be starv'd for want of Food; for he was resolv'd none of his Family, should go near her; and she lay in the Garret four Story high, where she could not Cry out, or call to any Body for Help.

The Watchman consented to that, and went and fetch'd a Nurse as he was appointed, and brought her to them the same Evening; during this interval, the Master of the House took his Opportunity to break a large Hole thro' his Shop into a Bulk or Stall, where formerly a Cobler had sat, before or under his Shop-window; but the Tenant as may be supposed, at such a dismal Time as that, was dead or remov'd, and so he had the Key in his own keeping; having made his Way into this Stall, which he cou'd not have done, if the Man had been at the Door, the Noise he was obliged to make, being such as would have alarm'd the Watchman; I say, having made his Way into this Stall, he sat still till the Watchman return'd with the Nurse, and all the next Day also; but the Night following, having contriv'd to send the Watchman of another trifling Errand, which as I take it, was to an Apothecary's for a Plaster[2] for the Maid, which he was to stay for the making up, or some other such Errand that might secure his staying some Time; in that Time he conveyed himself, and all his Family out of the House, and left the Nurse and the Watchman to bury the poor Wench; that is, throw her into the Cart, and take care of the House.

I cou'd give a great many such Stories as these, diverting enough, which in the long Course of that dismal Year, I met with, *that is* heard of, and which are very certain to be true, or very near the Truth; that is to say, true in the General, for no Man could at such a Time, learn all the Particulars: There was likewise Violence used with the Watchmen, *as was reported* in abundance of Places; and I believe, that from the Beginning of the Visitation to the End, there was not less than eighteen or twenty of them kill'd, or so wounded as to be taken up for Dead, which was suppos'd to be done by the People in the infected Houses which were shut up, and where they attempted to come out, and were oppos'd.

Nor indeed cou'd less be expected, for here were just so many Prisons in the Town, as there were Houses shut up; and as the People shut up or imprison'd so, were guilty of no Crime, only shut up because miserable, it was really the more intollerable to them.

It had also this Difference; that every Prison, as we may call it, had but one Jaylor; and as he had the whole House to Guard, and that many Houses were so situated, as that they had several Ways out, some more, some less, and some into several Streets; it was impossible for one Man so to Guard all the Passages, as to prevent the escape of People, made desperate by the fright of their Circumstances, by the Resentment of their usage, or by the raging of the Distemper it self; so that they would talk to the Watchman on one Side of the House, while the Family made their escape at another.

For example, in *Coleman-Street*, there are abundance of Alleys, as appears still; a House was shut up in that they call *Whites*-Alley, and this House had a back Window, not a Door into a Court, which had a Passage into Bell-Alley;[3] a Watchman was set by the Constable, at the Door of this House, and there he stood, or his Comrade Night and Day,

---

2. Used in attempts to break the buboes when they rose. Made from leather or cloth, they were soaked in blistering or drying salve and applied to the skin.

3. This is the neighborhood of Defoe's childhood. It was a densely populated area with many small, narrow, winding street and alleys.

while the Family went all away in the Evening, out at that Window into
the Court, and left the poor Fellows warding,[4] and watching, for near a
Fortnight.

Not far from the same Place, they blow'd up a Watchman with Gun-
powder, and burnt the poor Fellow dreadfully, and while he made hidious
Crys, and no Body would venture to come near to help him; the whole
Family that were able to stir, got out at the Windows one Story high;
two that were left Sick, calling out for Help; Care was taken to give them
Nurses to look after them, but the Persons fled were never found, till
after the Plague was abated they return'd, but as nothing cou'd be prov'd,
so nothing could be done to them.

It is to be consider'd too, that as these were Prisons without Barrs and
Bolts, which our common Prisons are furnish'd with, so the People let
themselves down out of their Windows, even in the Face of the Watchman, bringing Swords or Pistols in their Hands, and threatening the
poor Wretch to shoot him, if he stir'd, or call'd for Help.

In other Cases, some had Gardens, and Walls, or Pales between them
and their Neighbours; or Yards, and back-Houses; and these by Friendship and Entreaties, would get leave to get over those Walls, or Pales,
and so go out at their Neighbour's Doors; or by giving Money to their
Servants, get them, to let them thro' in the Night; so that in short, the
shutting up of Houses, was in no wise to be depended upon; neither did
it answer the End at all; serving more to make the People desperate, and
drive them to such Extremities, as that, they would break out at all
Adventures.

And that which was still worse, those that did thus break out, spread
the Infection farther by their wandring about with the Distemper upon
them, in their desperate Circumstances, than they would otherwise have
done; for whoever considers all the Particulars in such Cases must
acknowledge; and we cannot doubt but the Severity of those Confinements, made many People desperate; and made them run out of their
Houses at all Hazards, and with the Plague visibly upon them, not knowing
either whither to go, or what to do, or indeed, what they did; and many
that did so, were driven to dreadful Exigences and Extremeties, and
Perish'd in the Streets or Fields for meer Want, or drop'd down, by the
raging violence of the Fever upon them: Others wandred into the Country, and went forward any Way, as their Desperation guided them, not
knowing whether they went or would go, till faint and tir'd, and not
getting any Relief; the Houses and Villages on the Road, refusing to
admit them to lodge, whether infected or no; they have perish'd by the
Road Side, or gotten into Barns and dy'd there, none daring to come to
them, or relieve them, tho' perhaps not infected, for no Body would
believe them.

On the other Hand, when the Plague at first seiz'd a Family, that is

---

4. Guarding, imprisoning.

to say, when any one Body of the Family, had gone out, and unwarily or otherwise catch'd the Distemper and brought it Home, it was certainly known by the Family, before it was known to the Officers, who, as you will see by the Order, were appointed to examine into the Circumstances of all sick Persons, when they heard of their being sick.

In this Interval, between their being taken Sick, and the Examiners coming, the Master of the House had Leisure and Liberty to remove himself, or all his Family, if he knew whether[5] to go, and many did so: But the great disaster was, that many did thus, after they were really infected themselves, and so carry'd the Disease into the Houses of those who were so Hospitable as to receive them, which it must be confess'd was very cruel and ungrateful.

And this was in Part, the Reason of the general Notion, or scandal rather, which went about of the Temper of People infected; Namely, that they did not take the least care, or make any Scruple of infecting others; tho' I cannot say, but there might be some Truth in it too, but not so general as was reported. What natural Reason could be given, for so wicked a Thing, at a Time, when they might conclude themselves just going to appear at the Barr of Divine Justice, I know not: I am very well satisfy'd, that it cannot be reconcil'd to Religion and Principle, any more than it can be to Generosity and Humanity; but I may speak of that again.

I am speaking now of People made desperate, by the Apprehensions of their being shut up, and their breaking out by Stratagem or Force, either before or after they were shut up, whose Misery was not lessen'd, when they were out, but sadly encreased: On the other Hand, many that thus got away, had Retreats to go to, and other Houses, where they lock'd themselves up, and kept hid till the Plague was over; and many Families foreseeing the Approach of the Distemper, laid up Stores of Provisions, sufficient for their whole Families, and shut themselves up, and that so entirely, that they were neither seen or heard of, till the Infection was quite ceased, and then came abroad Sound and Well: I might recollect several such as these, and give you the Particular of their Management; for doubtless, it was the most effectual secure Step that cou'd be taken for such, whose Circumstance would not admit them to remove, or who had not Retreats abroad proper for the Case; for in being thus shut up, they were as if they had been a hundred Miles off: Nor do I remember, that any one of those Families miscary'd; among these, several *Dutch* Merchants were particularly remarkable, who kept their Houses like little Garrisons besieged, suffering none to go in or out, or come near them; particularly one in a Court in *Throckmorton* Street, whose House looked into *Drapers Garden*.[6]

But I come back to the Case of Families infected, and shut up by the

5. Probably a misprint for "whither."
6. Again, Defoe's neighborhood. The Drapers' Company garden was large, pleasant, and open to the public; it was within a few blocks of his first home with his wife, Mary.

Magistrates; the Misery of those Families is not to be express'd, and it was generally in such Houses that we heard the most dismal Shrieks and Out-cries of the poor People terrified, and even frighted to Death, by the Sight of the Condition of their dearest Relations, and by the Terror of being imprisoned as they were.

I remember, and while I am writing this Story, I think I hear the very Sound of it, a certain Lady had an only Daughter, a young Maiden about 19 Years old, and who was possessed of a very Considerable Fortune; they were only Lodgers in the House where they were: The young Woman, her Mother, and the Maid, had been abroad on some Occasion, I do not remember what, for the House was not shut up; but about two Hours after they came home, the young Lady complain'd she was not well; in a quarter of an Hour more, she vomited, and had a violent Pain in her Head. Pray God, says her Mother in a terrible Fright, my Child has not the Distemper! The Pain in her Head increasing, her Mother ordered the Bed to be warm'd, and resolved to put her to Bed; and prepared to give her things to sweat, which was the ordinary Remedy to be taken, when the first Apprehensions of the Distemper began.

While the Bed was airing, the Mother undressed the young Woman, and just as she was laid down in the Bed, she looking upon her Body with a Candle, immediately discovered the fatal Tokens on the Inside of her Thighs. Her Mother not being able to contain herself, threw down her Candle, and sriekt out in such a frightful Manner, that it was enough to place Horror upon the stoutest Heart in the World; nor was it one Skream, or one Cry, but the Fright having seiz'd her Spirits, she fainted first, then recovered, then ran all over the House, up the Stairs and down the Stairs, like one distracted, and indeed really was distracted, and continued screching and crying out for several Hours, void of all Sense, or at least, Government of her Senses, and as I was told, never came throughly to herself again: As to the young Maiden, she was a dead Corpse from that Moment; for the Gangren which occasions the Spots had spread [through] her whole Body, and she died in less than two Hours: But still the Mother continued crying out, not knowing any Thing more of her Child, several Hours after she was dead. It is so long ago, that I am not certain, but I think the Mother never recover'd, but died in two or three Weeks after.

This was an extraordinary Case, and I am therefore the more particular in it, because I came so much to the Knowledge of it; but there were innumerable such like Cases; and it was seldom, that the Weekly Bill came in, but there were two or three put in *frighted*,[7] that is, *that may well be call'd*, frighted to Death: But besides those, who were so frighted to die upon the Spot, there were great Numbers frighted to other Extreams, some frighted out of their Senses, some out of their Memory

---

7. Death tallies for these months list "fright" as a cause of death; see p. 205 in this volume for an example.

and some out of their Understanding: But I return to the shutting up of Houses.

As several People, *I say*, got out of their Houses by Stratagem, after they were shut up, so others got out by bribing the Watchmen, and giving them Money to let them go privately out in the Night. I must confess, I thought it at that time, the most innocent Corruption, or Bribery, that any Man could be guilty of; and therefore could not but pity the poor Men, and think it was hard when three of those Watchmen, were publickly whipt thro' the Streets, for suffering People to go out of Houses shut up.

But notwithstanding that Severity, Money prevail'd with the poor Men, and many Families found Means to make Salleys out, and escape that way after they had been shut up; but these were generally such as had some Places to retreat to; and tho' there was no easie passing the Roads any whither, after the first of *August*, yet there were many Ways of retreat, and particularly, as I hinted, some got Tents and set them up in the Fields, carrying Beds, or Straw to lie on, and Provisions to eat, and so liv'd in them as Hermits in a Cell; for no Body would venture to come near them; and several Stories were told of such; some comical, some tragical, some who liv'd like wandring Pilgrims in the Desarts, and escaped by making themselves Exiles in such a Manner as is scarce to be credited, and who yet enjoyed more Liberty than was to be expected in such Cases.

I have by me a Story of two Brothers and their Kinsman, who being Single Men, but that had stay'd in the City too long to get away, and indeed, not knowing where to go to have any Retreat, nor having wherewith to travel far, took a Course for their own Preservation, which, tho' in itself at first, desperate, yet was so natural, that it may be wondred, that no more did so at that Time. They were but of mean Condition, and yet not so very poor, as that they could not furnish themselves with some little Conveniencies, such as might serve to keep Life and Soul together; and finding the Distemper increasing in a terrible Manner, they resolved to shift, as well as they could, and to be gone.

One of them had been a Soldier in the late Wars,[8] and before that in the *Low Countries*,[9] and having been bred to no particular Employment but his Arms; and besides being wounded, and not able to work very hard, had for some Time been employ'd at a Baker's of Sea Bisket *in Wapping*.

The Brother of this Man was a Seaman too, but some how or other, had been hurt of one Leg, that he could not go to Sea, but had work'd for his Living at a Sail Makers in *Wapping*, or there abouts; and being a

---

8. In 1665, the late wars would have been the First Dutch War, 1652–54, and the Spanish War, 1655–59. The Second Dutch War began during the plague, and Defoe's novel mentions it.

9. The lower basin of the Rhine, Meuse, and Scheldt rivers along the North Sea; today the region includes Belgium, Luxembourg, and the Netherlands. "Low countries" is a literal translation of "Netherlands."

good Husband,[1] had laid up some Money, and was the richest of the Three.

The third Man was a Joiner or Carpenter by Trade, a handy Fellow; and he had no Wealth, but his Box, or Basket of Tools, with the Help of which he could at any Time get his Living, such a Time as this excepted, wherever he went, and he liv'd near *Shadwel*.

They all liv'd in *Stepney* Parish, which, as I have said, being the last that was infected, or at least violently, they stay'd there till they evidently saw the Plague was abating at the West Part of the Town, and coming towards the East where they liv'd.

The Story of those three Men, if the Reader will be content to have me give it in their own Persons, without taking upon me to either vouch the Particulars, or answer for any Mistakes. I shall give as distinctly as I can, believing the History will be a very good Pattern for any poor Man to follow, in case the like Publick Desolation should happen here; and if there may be no such Occasion, which God of his infinite Mercy grant us, still the Story may have its Uses so many Ways as that it will, I hope, never be said, that the relating has been unprofitable.

I say all this previous to the History, having yet, for the present, much more to say before I quit my own Part.

I went all the first Part of the Time freely about the Streets, tho' not so freely as to run my self into apparent Danger, except when they dug the great Pit in the Church-Yard of our Parish of *Algate*; a terrible Pit it was, and I could not resist my Curiosity to go and see it; as near as I may judge, it was about 40 Foot in Length, and about 15 or 16 Foot broad; and at the Time I first looked at it, about nine Foot deep; but it was said, they dug it near 20 Foot deep afterwards, in one Part of it, till they could go no deeper for the Water: for they had it seems, dug several large Pits before this, for tho' the Plague was long a-coming to our Parish, yet when it did come, there was no Parish in or about *London*, where it raged with such Violence as in the two Parishes of *Algate* and *White-Chapel*.

I say they had dug several Pits in another Ground, when the Distemper began to spread in our Parish, and especially when the Dead-Carts began to go about, which, was not in our Parish, till the beginning of *August*. Into these Pits they had put perhaps 50 or 60 Bodies each, then they made larger Holes, wherein they buried all that the Cart brought in a Week, which by the middle, to the End of *August*, came to, from 200 to 400 a Week; and they could not well dig them larger, because of the Order of the Magistrates, confining them to leave no Bodies within six Foot of the Surface; and the Water coming on, at about 17 or 18 Foot, they could not well, I say, put more in one Pit; but now at the Beginning of *September*, the Plague raging in a dreadful Manner, and the Number of Burials in our Parish increasing to more than was ever

1. Careful manager.

buried in any Parish about *London*, of no larger Extent, they ordered this dreadful Gulph to be dug; for such it was rather than a Pit.

They had supposed this Pit would have supply'd them for a Month or more, when they dug it, and some blam'd the Church Wardens for suffering such a frightful Thing, telling them they were making Preparations to bury the whole Parish, and the like; but Time made it appear, the Church-Wardens knew the Condition of the Parish better than they did; for the Pit being finished the 4th of *September*, I think, they began to bury in it the 6th, and by the 20, which was just two Weeks they had thrown into it 1114 Bodies, when they were obliged to fill it up, the Bodies being then come to lie within six Foot of the Surface: I doubt not but there may be some antient Persons alive in the Parish, who can justify the Fact of this, and are able to shew even in what Part of the Church-Yard, the Pit lay, better than I can; the Mark of it also was many Years to be seen in the Church-Yard on the Surface lying in Length, Parallel with the Passage which goes by the West Wall of the Church-Yard, out of *Houndsditch*, and turns East again into *White-Chappel*, coming out near the three Nuns Inn. [2]

It was about the 10th of *September*, that my Curiosity led, or rather drove me to go and see this Pit again, when there had been near 400 People buried in it; and I was not content to see it in the Day-time, as I had done before; for then there would have been nothing to have been seen but the loose Earth; for all the Bodies that were thrown in, were immediately covered with Earth, by those they call'd the Buryers, which at other Times were call'd Bearers; [3] but I resolv'd to go in the Night and see some of them thrown in.

There was a strict Order to prevent People coming to those Pits, and that was only to prevent Infection: But after some Time, that Order was more necessary, for People that were Infected, and near their End, and dilirious also, would run to those Pits wrapt in Blankets, or Rugs, and throw themselves in, and as they said, bury themselves: I cannot say, that the Officers suffered any willingly to lie there; but I have heard, that in a great Pit in *Finsbury*, in the Parish of *Cripplegate*, [4] it lying open then to the Fields; for it was not then wall'd about, came and threw themselves in, and expired there, before they threw any Earth upon them; and that when they came to bury others, and found them there, they were quite dead, tho' not cold.

This may serve a little to describe the dreadful Condition of that Day, tho' it is impossible to say any Thing that is able to give a true Idea of it

2. A major stop for coaches, it was across from St. Botolph, Aldgate, where Defoe married. The pit was indeed located there.
3. The buriers worked at the pits, pushing bodies in, arranging them, and covering them first with lime and then earth. The bearers carried infected people to the pesthouses during the day and collected the dead at night.
4. Because there was more open space here, bodies from several other parishes were buried there, too. In *Due Preparations for the Plague* (1720), Defoe says that "about 2,200" were "thrown" into these pits (80).

to those who did not see it, other than this; that it was indeed *very, very, very* dreadful, and such as no Tongue can express.

I got Admittance into the Church-Yard by being acquainted with the Sexton, who attended, who tho' he did not refuse me at all, yet earnestly perswaded me not to go; telling me very seriously, for he was a good religious and sensible Man, that it was indeed, their Business and Duty to venture, and to run all Hazards; and that in it they might hope to be preserv'd; but that I had no apparent Call to it, but my own Curiosity, which he said, he believ'd I would not pretend, was sufficient to justify my running that Hazard. I told him I had been press'd in my Mind to go, and that perhaps it might be an Instructing Sight, that might not be without its Uses. Nay, says the good Man, if you will venture upon that Score, *'Name of God go in*; for depend upon it, 'twill be a Sermon to you, it may be, the best that ever you heard in your Life. 'Tis a speaking Sight, says he, and has a Voice with it, and a loud one, to call us all to Repentance; and with that he opened the Door and said, Go, if you will.

His Discourse had shock'd my Resolution a little, and I stood wavering for a good while; but just at that Interval I saw two Links [5] come over from the End of the *Minories*, [6] and heard the Bell man, [7] and then appear'd a Dead-Cart, *as they call'd it*, coming over the Streets so I could no longer resist my Desire of seeing it, and went in: There was no Body, as I could perceive at first, in the Church-Yard, or going into it, but the Buryers, and the Fellow that drove the Cart, or rather led the Horse and Cart, but when they came up, to the Pit, they saw a Man go to and again, mufled up in a brown Cloak, and making Motions with his Hands, under his Cloak, as if he was in a great Agony; and the Buriers immediately gathered about him, supposing he was one of those poor dilirious, or desperate Creatures, that used to pretend, as I have said, to bury themselves; he said nothing as he walk'd about, but two or three times groaned very deeply, and loud, and sighed as he would break his Heart.

When the Buryers came up to him they soon found he was neither a Person infected and desperate, as I have observed above, or a Person distempered in Mind, but one oppress'd with a dreadful Weight of Grief indeed, having his Wife and several of his Children, all in the Cart, that was just come in with him, and he followed in an Agony and excess of Sorrow. He mourned heartily, as it was easy to see, but with a kind of Masculine Grief, that could not give it self Vent by Tears, and calmly desiring the Buriers to let him alone, said he would only see the Bodies thrown in, and go away, so they left importuning him; but no sooner was the Cart turned round, and the Bodies shot into the Pit promis-

---

5. The torches made with pitch and a heavy hemp or jute wick and carried by link-boys who conducted people through the streets at night.
6. A street between Aldgate and the Tower. It was so named because the Abbey of the Mino-

resses of St. Mary had been there.
7. The Bellman rang a bell to announce the approach of the deadcart, thereby giving people time to bring out their dead or avoid its reputedly contagious cargo.

cuously, which was a Surprize to him, for he at least expected they would have been decently laid in, tho' indeed he was afterwards convinced that was impractible; I say, no sooner did he see the Sight, but he cry'd out aloud unable to contain himself; I could not hear what he said, but he went backward two or three Steps, and fell down in a Swoon: the Buryers ran to him and took him up, and in a little While he came to himself, and they led him away to the *Pye Tavern*[8] over-against the End of *Houndsditch*, where, it seems, the Man was known, and where they took care of him. He look'd into the Pit again, as he went away, but the Buriers had covered the Bodies so immediately with throwing in Earth, that tho' there was Light enough, for there were Lantherns and Candles in them, plac'd all Night round the Sides of the Pit, upon the Heaps of Earth, seven or eight, or perhaps more, yet nothing could be seen.

This was a mournful Scene indeed, and affected me almost as much as the rest; but the other was awful, and full of Terror, the Cart had in it sixteen or seventeen Bodies, some were wrapt up in Linen Sheets, some in Rugs, some little other than naked, or so loose, that what Covering they had, fell from them, in the shooting out of the Cart, and they fell quite naked among the rest; but the Matter was not much to them, or the Indecency much to any one else, seeing they were all dead, and were to be huddled together into the common Grave of Mankind, as we may call it, for here was no Difference made, but Poor and Rich went together; there was no other way of Burials, neither was it possible there should, for Coffins were not to be had for the prodigious Numbers that fell in such a Calamity as this.

It was reported by way of Scandal upon the Buriers, that if any Corpse was delivered to them, decently wound up as we call'd it then, in a Winding Sheet Ty'd over the Head and Feet,[9] which some did, and which was generally of good Linen; I say, it was reported, that the Buriers were so wicked as to strip them in the Cart, and carry them quite naked to the Ground: But as I can not easily credit any thing so vile among Christians, and at a Time so fill'd with Terrors, as that was, I can only relate it and leave it undetermined.

Innumerable Stories also went about of the cruel Behaviours and Practises of Nurses, who tended the Sick, and of their hastening on the Fate of those they tended in their Sickness: But I shall say more of this in its Place.

I was indeed shock'd with this Sight, it almost overwhelm'd me, and I went away with my Heart most afflicted and full of the afflicting Thoughts, such as I cannot describe; just at my going out of the Church,

---

8. Another coach inn, Pye Tavern was unusually large. John Stowe calls it "a fair Inn of recipte of travellers" in his *Remarks on London* (1722). It was diagonally across the street from St. Botolph Aldgate.

9. In 1665, corpses were wrapped in coarse cloth, linen, wool, or even canvas, and tied securely at the top and bottom (later all bodies were required to be buried in wool). Flowers and herbs were sometimes wrapped inside the sheet.

and turning up the Street towards my own house, I saw another Cart with Links, and a Bellman going before, coming out of *Harrow-Alley*, in the *Butcher-Row*,[1] on the other Side of the Way, and being, as I perceived, very full of dead Bodies, it went directly over the Street also toward the Church: I stood a while, but I had no Stomach to go back again to see the same dismal Scene over again, so I went directly Home, where I could not but consider with Thankfulness, the Risque I had run, believing I had gotten no Injury; as indeed I had not.

Here the poor unhappy Gentleman's Grief came into my head again, and indeed I could not but shed Tears in the Reflection upon it, perhaps more than he did himself; but his Case lay so heavy upon my Mind, that I could not prevail with my self, but that I must go out again into the Street, and go to the *Pye-Tavern*, resolving to enquire what became of him.

It was by this Time one a-Clock in the Morning, and yet the poor Gentleman was there; the Truth was, the People of the House knowing him, had entertain'd him, and kept him there all the Night, notwithstanding the Danger of being infected, by him, tho' it appear'd the Man was perfectly sound himself.

It is with Regret, that I take Notice of this Tavern; the People were civil, mannerly, and an obliging Sort of Folks enough, and had till this Time kept their House open, and their Trade going on, tho' not so very publickly as formerly; but there was a dreadful Set of Fellows that used their House, and who in the middle of all this Horror met there every Night, behaved with all the Revelling and roaring extravagances, as is usual for such People to do at other Times, and indeed to such an offensive Degree, that the very Master and Mistress of the House grew first asham'd and then terrify'd at them.

They sat generally, in a Room next the Street, and as they always kept late Hours, so when the Dead-Cart came cross the Street End to go into *Hounds-ditch*, which was in View of the Tavern Windows; they would frequently open the Windows as soon as they heard the Bell, and look out at them; and as they might often hear sad Lamentations of People in the Streets, or at their Windows, as the Carts went along, they would make their impudent Mocks and Jeers at them, especially if they heard the poor People call upon God to have Mercy upon them, as many would do at those Times in their ordinary passing along the Streets.

These Gentlemen being something disturb'd with the Clutter of bringing the poor Gentleman into the House, as above, were first angry, and very high with the Master of the House, for suffering such a Fellow, as they call'd him, to be brought out of the Grave into their House; but being answered, that the Man was a Neighbour, and that he was sound, but overwhelmed with the Calamity of his Family, and the like, they turned their Anger into ridiculing the Man, and his Sorrow for his Wife and

1. In Farringdon Ward Without east of the Minories. Again Defoe is using landmarks near his Uncle Henry's home and the church where he himself married.

Children; taunted him with want of Courage to leap into the great Pit, and go to Heaven, as they jeeringly express'd it, along with them, adding some very profane, and even blasphemous Expressions.

They were at this vile Work when I came back to the House, and as far as I could see, tho' the Man sat still, mute and disconsolate, and their Affronts could not divert his Sorrow, yet he was both griev'd and offended at their Discourse: Upon this, I gently reprov'd them, being well enough acquainted with their Characters, and not unknown in Person to two of them.

They immediately fell upon me with ill Language and Oaths; ask'd me what I did out of my Grave, at such a Time when so many *honester Men* were carried into the Church-Yard? and why I was not at Home saying my Prayers, against the Dead-Cart came for me? and the like.

I was indeed astonished at the Impudence of the Men, tho' not at all discomposed at their Treatment of me; however I kept my Temper; I told them, that tho' I defy'd them, or any Man in the World to tax me with any *Dishonesty*, yet I acknowledg'd, that in this terrible Judgment of God, many better than I was swept away, and carried to their Grave: But to answer their Question directly, the Case was, that I was mercifully preserved by that great God, whose Name they had Blasphemed and taken in vain, by cursing and swearing in a dreadful Manner; and that I believed I was preserv'd in particular, among other Ends, of his Goodness, that I might reprove them for their audacious Boldness, in behaving in such a Manner, and in such an awful Time as this was, especially, for their Jeering and Mocking, at an honest Gentleman, and a Neighbour, for some of them knew him, who they saw was overwhelm'd with Sorrow, for the Breaches [2] which it had pleas'd God to make upon his Family.

I cannot call exactly to Mind the hellish abominable Rallery, [3] which was the Return they made to that Talk of mine, being provoked, it seems, that I was not at all afraid to be free with them; nor if I could remember, would I fill my Account with any of the Words, the horrid Oaths, Curses, and vile Expressions, such, as at that time of the Day, even the worst and ordinariest People in the Street would not use; (for except such hardened Creatures as these, the most wicked wretches that could be found, had at that Time some Terror upon their Minds of the Hand of that Power which could thus, in a Moment destroy them.)

But that which was the worst in all their devillish Language was, that they were not afraid to blaspheme God, and talk Atheistically; making a Jest at my calling the Plague the Hand of God, mocking, and even laughing at the Word Judgment, as if the Providence of God had no Concern in the inflicting such a desolating Stroke; and that the People calling upon God, as they saw the Carts carrying away the dead Bodies was all enthusiastick, [4] absurd, and impertinent.

---

2. Breaks, injurious assaults.
3. Raillery, ridicule.
4. Fanatic, overly pious, emotionally fervent.

Defoe, as a Nonconformist, would have felt this a strongly insulting word. The piety of the Nonconformists was often so stigmatized.

I made them some Reply, such as I thought proper, but which I found was so far from putting a Checque to their horrid Way of speaking, that it made them rail the more, so that I confess it fill'd me with Horror, and a kind of Rage, and I came away, as I told them, lest the Hand of that Judgment which had visited the whole City should glorify his Vengeance upon them, and all that were near them.

They received all Reproof with the utmost Contempt, and made the greatest Mockery that was possible for them to do at me, giving me all the opprobrious insolent Scoffs that they could think of for preaching to them, *as they call'd it*, which indeed, grieved me, rather than angred me; and I went away blessing God, however, in my Mind, that I had not spar'd them, tho' they had insulted me so much.

They continued this wretched Course three or four Days after this, continually mocking and jeering at all that shrew'd themselves religious, or serious, or that were any way touch'd with the Sence of the terrible Judgment of God upon us, and I was inform'd they flouted in the same Manner, at the good People, who, notwithstanding the Contagion, met at the Church, fasted, and prayed to God to remove his Hand from them.

I say, they continued this dreadful Course three or four Days, *I think it was no more*, when one of them, particularly he who ask'd the poor Gentleman *what he did out of his Grave?* was struck from Heaven with the Plague, and died in a most deplorable Manner; and in a Word they were every one of them carried into the great Pit, which I have mentioned above, before it was quite fill'd up, which was not above a Fortnight or thereabout.

These Men were guilty of many extravagances, such as one would think, Human Nature should have trembled at the Thoughts of, at such a Time of general Terror, as was then upon us; and particularly scoffing and mocking at every thing which they happened to see, that was religious among the People, especially at their thronging zealously to the Place of publick Worship, to implore Mercy from Heaven in such a Time of Distress; and this Tavern, where they held their Club, being within View of the Church Door, they had the more particular Occasion for their Atheistical profane Mirth.

But this began to abate a little with them before the Accident, which I have related, happened; for the Infection increased so violently, at this Part of the Town now, that People began to be afraid to come to the Church, at least such Numbers did not resort thither as was usual; many of the Clergymen likewise were Dead, and others gone into the Country; for it really required a steady Courage, and a strong Faith, for a Man not only to venture being in Town as such a Time as this, but likewise to venture to come to Church and perform the Office of a Minister to a Congregation, of whom he had reason to believe many of them, were actually infected with the Plague, and to do this every Day, or twice a Day, as in some Places was done.

It is true, the People shew'd an extraordinary Zeal in these religious Exercises, and as the Church Doors were always open, People would go in single at all Times, whether the Minister was officiating or no, and locking themselves into separate Pews, would be praying to God with great Fervency and Devotion.

Others assembled at Meeting-Houses,[5] every one as their different Opinions in such Things guided, but all were promiscuously the Subject of these Mens Drollery, especially at the Beginning of the Visitation.

It seems they had been check'd for their open insulting Religion in this Manner, by several good People of every perswasion, and that, and the violent raging of the Infection, I suppose, was the Occasion that they had abated much of their Rudeness, for some time before, and were only rous'd by the Spirit of Ribaldry, and Atheism, at the Clamour which was made, when the Gentleman was first brought in there, and perhaps, were agitated by the same Devil, when I took upon me to reprove them; tho' I did it at first with all the Calmness, Temper, and Good-Manners that I could, which, for a while, they insulted me the more for, thinking it had been in fear of their Resentment, tho' afterwards they found the contrary.

I went Home indeed, griev'd and afflicted in my Mind, at the Abominable Wickedness of those Men not doubting, however, that they would be made dreadful Examples of God's Justice; for I look'd upon this dismal Time to be a particular Season of Divine Vengeance, and that God would, on this Occasion, single out the proper Objects, of his Displeasure, in a more especial and remarkable Manner, than at another Time; and that, tho' I did believe that many good People would, and did, fall in the common Calamity, and that it was no certain Rule to judge of the eternal State of any one, by their being distinguish'd in such a Time of general Destruction, neither one Way or other; yet I say, it could not but seem reasonable to believe, that God would not think fit to spare by his Mercy such open declared Enemies, that should insult his Name and Being, defy his Vengeance, and mock at his Worship and Worshipers, at such a Time, no not tho' his Mercy had thought fit to bear with, and spare them at other Times: That this was a Day of Visitation; a Day of God's Anger; and those Words came into my Thought. *Jer. v. 9. Shall I not visit for these things, saith the Lord, and shall not my Soul be avenged [on] such a Nation as this?*[6]

These Things, I say, lay upon my Mind; and I went home very much griev'd and oppress'd with the Horror of these Mens Wickedness, and to think that any thing could be so vile, so hardened, and so notoriously wicked, as to insult God and his Servants, and his Worship, in such a

---

5. Nonconformist places of worship. Church of England, or Anglican, places of worship were called churches.
6. The theme of chapter 5 of Jeremiah is the utter sinfulness of the Israelites that makes it impossible for them to receive God's forgiveness. It begins with Jeremiah's search for even a single good man in Jerusalem; were he to find one, God would pardon the city. None could be found, and the verse Defoe quotes is part of God's message to the people to be delivered by the prophet.

Manner, and at such a Time as this was; when he had, as it were, his Sword drawn in his Hand, on purpose to take Vengeance, not on them only, but on the whole Nation.

I had indeed, been in some Passion at first, with them, tho' it was really raised, not by any Affront they had offered me personally, but by the Horror their blaspheming Tongues fill'd me with; however, I was doubtful in my Thoughts, whether the Resentment I retain'd was not all upon my own private Account, for they had given me a great deal of ill Language too, I mean Personally; but after some Pause, and having a Weight of Grief upon my Mind, I retir'd my self, as soon as I came home, for I slept not that Night, and giving God most humble Thanks for my Preservation in the eminent Danger I had been in, I set my Mind seriously, and with the utmost Earnestness, to pray for those desparate Wretches, that God would pardon them, open their Eyes, and effectually humble them.

By this I not only did my Duty, namely, to pray for those who dispitefully used me,[7] but I fully try'd my own Heart, to my full Satisfaction; that it was not fill'd with any Spirit of Resentment as they had offended me in particular; and I humbly recommend the Method to all those that would know, or be certain, how to distinguish between their real Zeal for the Honour of God, and the Effects of their private Passions and Resentment.

But I must go back here to the particular Incidents which occur to my Thoughts of the Time of the Visitation, and particularly, to the Time of their shutting up Houses, in the first Part of the Sickness; for before the Sickness was come to its Height, People had more Room to make their Observations, than they had afterward: But when it was in the Extremity, there was no such Thing as Communication with one another, as before.

During the shutting up of Houses, as I have said, some Violence was offered to the Watchmen; as to Soldiers, there were none to be found; the few Guards which the King then had, which were nothing like the Number, entertain'd since, were disperss'd, either at *Oxford* with the Court, or in Quarters in the remoter Parts of the Country; small detachments excepted, who did Duty at the Tower, and at *White-Hall*,[8] and these but very few; neither am I positive, that there was any other Guard at the Tower, than the *Warders*, as they call'd them, who stand at the Gate with Gowns and Caps, the same as the Yeomen of the Guard; except the ordinary Gunners, who were 24, and the Officers appointed to look after the Magazine, who were call'd Armourers: as to Train'd-Bands,[9] there was no Possibility of raising any, neither if the Lieuten-

7. Luke 6.28; Matthew 5.44.

8. The palace that became Henry VIII's upon the fall of Cardinal Thomas Wolsey. During Charles II's reign it was the center of royal activity.

9. The City militia who were under the command of the Lord Mayor and Court of Aldermen.

ancy,[1] either of *London* or *Middlesex* had ordered the Drums to beat for the Militia, would any of the Companies, I believe, have drawn together, whatever Risque they had run.

This made the Watchmen be the less regarded, and perhaps, occasioned the greater Violence to be used against them; I mention it on this Score, to observe that the setting Watchmen thus to keep the People in, was (1st) of all, not effectual, but that the People broke out, whether by Force or by Stratagem, even almost as often as they pleas'd: And (2d) that those that did thus break out, were generally People infected, who in their Desperation, running about from one Place to another, valued not who they injur'd, and which perhaps, as I have said, might give Birth to Report, that it was natural to the infected People to desire to infect others, which Report was really false.

And I know it so well, and in so many several Cases, that I could give several Relations of good, pious, and religious People, who, when they have had the Distemper, have been so far from being forward to infect others, that they have forbid their own Family to come near them, in Hopes of their being preserved; and have even died without seeing their nearest Relations, lest they should be instrumental to give them the Distemper, and infect or endanger them: If then there were Cases wherein the infected People were careless of the Injury they did to others, this was certainly one of them, if not the chief, namely, when People, who had the Distemper, had broken out from Houses which were so shut up, and having been driven to Extremities for Provision, or for Entertainment, had endeavoured to conceal their Condition, and have been thereby Instrumental involuntarily to infect others who have been ignorant and unwary.

This is one of the Reasons why I believed then, and do believe still, that the shutting up Houses thus by Force, and restraining, or rather imprisoning People in their own Houses, as is said above, was of little or no Service in the Whole; nay, I am of Opinion, it was rather hurtful, having forc'd those desperate People to wander abroad with the Plague upon them, who would otherwise have died quietly in their Beds.

I remember one Citizen, who having thus broken out of his House in *Aldersgate-Street*, or thereabout, went along the Road to *Islington*, he attempted to have gone in at the *Angel Inn*, and after that, at the *White-Horse*, two Inns known still by the same Signs, but was refused; after which he came to the *Pyed Bull*,[2] an Inn also still continuing the same

1. The monarch gave the commissions of lieutenancy to selected Aldermen and Common Council members. They were then entitled to choose the officers of the trained bands. In times of crisis, they had great power.
2. The road to Islington was the Great North Road, one of the major "king's highways." It ran north from London all the way to the Scot-

tish border near Edinburgh. Defoe traces the citizen's route by familiar landmarks, inns with especially good accommodations for travelers. The Angel had stood for many years in Clerkenwell, and the White Horse was on the south side of Fore Street. The Pyed Bull was in Islington, and legend says that Sir Walter Raleigh once owned it.

Sign; he asked them for Lodging for one Night only, pretending to be going into *Lincolnshire*, and assuring them of his being very sound, and free from the Infection, which also, at that Time, had not reached much that Way.

They told him they had no Lodging that they could spare, but one Bed, up in the Garret, and that they could spare that Bed but for one Night, some Drovers being expected the next Day with Cattle; so, if he would accept of that Lodging, he might have it, which he did; so a Servant was sent up with a Candle with him, to show him the Room; he was very well dress'd, and look'd like a Person not used to lie in a Garret, and when he came to the Room he fech'd[3] a deep Sigh, and said to the Servant, I have seldom lain in such a Lodging as this; however the Servant assuring him again, that they had no better. Well, says he, I must make shift; this is a dreadful Time, but it is but for one Night; so he sat down upon the Bedside, and bad the maid, *I think it was*, fetch him up a Pint of warm Ale; accordingly the Servant went for the Ale; but some Hurry in the House, which perhaps, employed her otherways, put it out of her Head; and she went up no more to him.

The next Morning seeing no Appearance of the Gentleman, some Body in the House asked the Servant that had shewed him up Stairs, what was become of him? She started; Alas says she, I never thought more of him: He bad me carry him some warm Ale, but I forgot; upon which, not the Maid, but some other Person, was sent up to see after him, who coming into the Room found him stark dead, and almost cold, stretch'd out cross the Bed; his Cloths were pulled off, his Jaw fallen, his Eyes open in a most frightful Posture, the Rug of the Bed being grasped hard in one of his Hands; so that it was plain he died soon after the Maid left him, and 'tis probable, had she gone up with the Ale, she had found him dead in a few Minutes after he sat down upon the Bed. The Alarm was great in the House, as any one may suppose, they having been free from the Distemper, till that Disaster, which bringing the Infection to the House, spread it immediately to other Houses round about it. I do not remember how many died in the House it self, but I think the Maid Servant, who went up first with him, fell presently ill by the Fright, and several others; for whereas there died but two in *Islington* of the Plague the Week before, there died 17 the Week after, whereof 14 were of the Plague; this was in the Week from the 11th of *July* to the 18th.

There was one Shift that some Families had, and that not a few, when their Houses happened to be infected, *and that was this*; The Families, who in the first breaking out of the Distemper, fled away into the Country, and had Retreats among their Friends, generally found some or other of their Neighbours or Relations to commit the Charge of those Houses to, for the Safety of the Goods, and the like. Some Houses were

3. Fetched, gave.

indeed, entirely lock'd up, the Doors padlockt, the Windows and Doors having Deal-Boards[4] nail'd over them, and only the Inspection of them committed to the ordinary Watchmen and Parish Officers; but these were but few.

It was thought that there were not less than 10000 Houses forsaken of the Inhabitants in the City and Suburbs, including what was in the Out Parishes, and in Surrey, or the Side of the Water they call'd *Southwark*. This was besides the Numbers of Lodgers, and of particular Persons who were fled out of other Families; so that in all it was computed that about 200000 People were fled and gone in all: But of this I shall speak again: But I mention it here on this Account, namely, that it was a Rule with those who had thus two Houses in their Keeping, or Care, that if any Body was taken sick in a Family, before the Master of the Family let the Examiners, or any other Officer, know of it, he immediately would send all the rest of his Family whether Children or Servants, as it fell out to be, to such other House which he had so in Charge, and then giving Notice of the sick Person to the Examiner, have a Nurse, or Nurses appointed; and have another Person to be shut up in the House with them (which many for Money would do) so to take Charge of the House, in case the Person should die.

This was in many Cases the saving a whole Family, who, if they had been shut up with the sick Person, would inevitably have perished: But on the other Hand, this was another of the Inconveniencies of shutting up Houses; for the Apprehensions and Terror of being shut up, made many run away with the rest of the Family, who, tho' it was not pub-lickly known, and they were not quite sick, had yet the Distemper upon them; and who by having an uninterrupted Liberty to go about, but being obliged still to conceal their Circumstances, or perhaps not know-ing it themselves, gave the Distemper to others, and spread the Infection in a dreadful Manner, as I shall explain farther hereafter.

And here I may be able to make an Observation or two of my own, which may be of use hereafter, to those, into whose Hands this may come, if they should ever see the like dreadful Visitation. (1.) The Infec-tion generally came into the Houses of the Citizens, by the Means of their Servants, who, they were obliged to send up and down the Streets for Necessaries, that is to say, for Food, or Physick, to Bakehouses, Brew-houses, Shops, & c. and who going necessarily thro' the Streets into Shops, Markets, and the like, it was impossible, but that they should one way or other, meet with distempered people, who conveyed the fatal Breath into them, and they brought it Home to the Families, to which they belonged. (2.) It was a great Mistake, that such a great City as this had but one Pest-House; for had there been, instead of one Pest-House *viz.* beyond *Bunhil-Fields*, where, at most, they could receive, perhaps, 200 or 300 People; I say, had there instead of that one been several Pest-

4. Fir or pine boards.

houses, every one able to contain a thousand People without lying two in a Bed, or two Beds in a Room; and had every Master of a Family, as soon as any Servant especially, had been taken sick in his House, been obliged to send them to the next Pest-House, if they were willing, as many were, and had the Examiners done the like among the poor People, when any had been stricken with the Infection; I say, had this been done where the People were willing, (not otherwise) and the Houses not been shut, I am perswaded, and was all the While of that Opinion, that not so many, by several Thousands, had died; for it was observed, and I could give several Instances within the Compass of my own Knowledge, where a Servant had been taken sick, and the Family had either Time to send them out, or retire from the House, and leave the sick Person, *as I have said above*, they had all been preserved; whereas, when upon one, or more, sickning in a Family, the House has been shut up, the whole Family have perished, and the Bearers been oblig'd to go in to fetch out the Dead Bodies, none being able to bring them to the Door; and at last none left to do it.

(3.) This put it out of Question to me, that the Calamity was Spread by Infection, that is to say, by some certain Steams, or Fumes, which the Physicians call *Effluvia*, by the Breath, or by the Sweat, or by the Stench of the Sores of the sick Persons, or some other way, perhaps, beyond even the Reach of the Physicians themselves, which *Effluvia* affected the Sound, who come within certain Distances of the Sick, immediately penetrating the Vital Parts of the said sound Persons, putting their Blood into an immediate ferment, and agitating their Spirits to that Degree which it was found they were agitated; and so those newly infected Persons communicated it in the same Manner to others;[5] and this I shall give some Instances of, that cannot but convince those who seriously consider it; and I cannot but with some Wonder, find some People, now the Contagion is over, talk of its being an immediate Stroke from Heaven, without the Agency of Means, having Commission to strike this and that particular Person, and none other; which I look upon with Contempt, as the Effect of manifest Ignorance and Enthusiasm; likewise the Opinion of others, who talk of infection being carried on by the Air only, by carrying with it vast Numbers of Insects, and invisible Creatures, who enter into the Body with the Breath, or even at the Pores with the Air, and there generate, or emit most accute Poisons, or poisonous Ovae, or Eggs, which mingle themselves with the Blood, and so infect the Body;[6] a Discourse full of learned Simplicity, and manifested to be so by universal Experience; but I shall say more to this Case in its Order.

I must here take farther Notice that Nothing was more fatal to the Inhabitants of this City, than the Supine Negligence of the People them-

---

5. Here H. F. propounds the contagionist view of plague, which conceived of the air as contaminated from the vapors from the bodies and respiration of infected people.
6. H. F. rejects the germ theory, that tiny organisms carried the infection.

selves, who during the long Notice, or Warning they had of the Visitation, yet made no Provision for it, by laying in Store of Provisions, or of
other Necessaries; by which they might have liv'd retir'd, and within
their own Houses, as I have observed, others did, and who were in a
great Measure preserv'd by that Caution; nor were they, after they were
a little hardened to it so shye of conversing with one another, when
actually infected, as they were at first, no tho' they knew it.

I acknowledge I was one of those thoughtless Ones, that had made so
little Provision, that my Servants were obliged to go out of Doors to buy
every Trifle by Penny and Half-penny, just as before it begun, even till
my Experience shewing me the Folly, I began to be wiser so late, that I
had scarce Time to store my self sufficient for our common Subsistence
for a Month.

I had in Family only an antient Woman, that managed the House, a
Maid-Servant, two Apprentices, and my self; and the Plague beginning
to encrease about us, I had many sad Thoughts about what Course I
should take, and how I should act; the many dismal Objects, which
happened everywhere as I went about the Streets, had fill'd my Mind
with a great deal of Horror, for fear of the Distemper it self, which was
indeed, very horrible in itself, and in some more than in others, the
swellings which were generally in the Neck, or Groin, when they grew
hard, and would not break, grew so painful, that it was equal to the most
exquisite Torture; and some not able to bear the Torment threw themselves out at Windows, or shot themselves, or otherwise made themselves away, and I saw several dismal Objects of that Kind: Others unable
to contain themselves, vented their Pain by incessant Roarings, and such
loud and lamentable Cries were to be heard as we walk'd along the
Streets, that would Pierce the very Heart to think of, especially when it
was to be considered, that the same dreadful Scourge might be expected
every Moment to seize upon our selves.

I cannot say, but that now I began to faint in my Resolutions, my
Heart fail'd me very much, and sorely I repented of my Rashness: When
I had been out, and met with such terrible Things as these I have talked
of; I say, I repented my Rashness in venturing to abide in Town: I wish'd
often, that I had not taken upon me to stay, but had gone away with my
Brother and his Family.

Terrified by those frightful Objects, I would retire Home sometimes,
and resolve to go out no more, and perhaps, I would keep those Resolutions for three or four Days, which Time I spent in the most serious
Thankfulness for my Preservation, and the Preservation of my Family,
and the constant Confession of my Sins, giving my self up to God every
Day, and applying to him with Fasting, Humiliation, and Meditation:
Such intervals as I had, I employed in reading Books, and in writing
down my Memorandums of what occurred to me every Day, and out of
which, afterwards, I for most of this Work as it relates to my Observations without Doors: What I wrote of my private Meditations I reserve

for private Use, and desire it may not be made publick on any Account whatever.

I also wrote other Meditations upon Divine Subjects, such as occurred to me at that Time, and were profitable to myself, but not fit for any other View, and therefore I say no more of that.

I had a very good Friend, a Physician, whose Name was *Heath*,[7] who I frequently visited during this dismal Time, and to whose Advice I was very much oblig'd for many Things which he directed me to take, by way of preventing the Infection when I went out, as he found I frequently did, and to hold in my Mouth when I was in the Streets;[8] he also came very often to see me, and as he was a good Christian, as well as a good Physician, his agreeable Conversation was a very great Support to me in the worst of this terrible Time.

It was now the Beginning of *August*, and the Plague grew very violent and terrible in the Place where I liv'd, and Dr. *Heath* coming to visit me, and finding that I ventured so often out in the Streets, earnestly perswaded me to lock my self up and my Family, and not to suffer any of us to go out of Doors; to keep all our Windows fast, Shutters and Curtains close, and never to open them; but first to make a very strong Smoke in the Room, where the Window, or Door was to be opened, with Rozen[9] and Pitch, Brimstone, or Gunpowder, and the like; and we did this for some Time: But as I had not laid in a Store of Provision for such a retreat, it was impossible that we could keep within Doors entirely; however, I attempted, tho' it was so very late, to do something towards it; and first, as I had Convenience both for Brewing and Baking, I went and bought two Sacks of Meal, and for several Weeks, having an Oven, we baked all our own Bread; also I bought Malt, and brew'd as much Beer as all the Casks I had would hold, and which seem'd enough to serve my House for five or six Weeks; also I laid in a Quantity of Salt-butter and *Cheshire* Cheese; but I had no Flesh-meat, and the Plague raged so violently among the Butchers,[1] and Slaughter-Houses, on the other Side of our Street, where they are known to dwell in great Numbers, that it was not advisable, so much as to go over the Street among them.

And here I must observe again, that this Necessity of going out of our Houses to buy Provisions, was in a great Measure the Ruin of the whole City, for the People catch'd the Distemper, on those Occasions, one of

7. This name may be fictitious; no Dr. Heath belonged to the College of Physicians, and he is not listed in such places as *Alumni Oxonienses*. It is possible, however, that Defoe is making a joke. Among Robert Heath's poems is the following: "Love-Self when th' Plague in London reigned sore,/Grown rich himself shuts up and wu'd no more/When most his help was wanted: it seems then/Hee'd not his patients keep as married men/Such is the fearful cowardice of wealth./Though thou with th' Plague would'st nothing ha' to do,/A Plaguy cunning Doctour yet wer't thou" (*Epigrams* [1650] 65). Many scholars believe Defoe used Nathaniel Hodges as his model for "his friend" Dr. Heath. It is also possible that Defoe puns on "health."

8. For a sample of recipes of plague antidotes, see pp. 210–11 in this volume.

9. Resin. For examples of the College of Physicians' recommendations for purifying the air, see pp. 209–10 in this volume.

1. Defoe and his father were members of the Butchers' Company.

another, and even the Provisions themselves were often tainted, at least I have great Reason to believe so; and therefore I cannot say with Satisfaction what I know is repeated with great Assurance, that the Market People, and such as brought Provisions, to Town, were never infected: I am certain, the Butchers of *White-Chapel* where the greatest Part of the Flesh-meat was killed, were dreadfully visited, and that at last to such a Degree, that few of their Shops were kept open, and those that remain'd of them, kill'd their Meat at *Mile-End*,[2] and that Way, and brought it to Market upon Horses.

However, the poor People cou'd not lay up Provisions, and there was a necessity, that they must go to Market to buy, and others to send Servants or their Children; and as this was a Necessity which renew'd it self daily; it brought abundance of unsound People to the Markets, and a great many that went thither Sound, brought Death Home with them.

It is true, People us'd all possible Precaution, when any one bought a Joint of Meat in the Market, they would not take it of the Butchers Hand, but take it off of the Hooks themselves. On the other Hand, the Butcher would not touch the Money, but have it put into a Pot full of Vinegar[3] which he kept for that purpose. The Buyer carry'd always small Money to make up any odd Sum, that they might take no Change. They carry'd Bottles for Scents, and Perfumes in their Hands, and all the Means that could be us'd, were us'd: But then the Poor cou'd not do even these things, and they went at all Hazards.

Innumerable dismal Stories we heard every Day on this very Account: Sometimes a Man or Woman dropt down Dead in the very Markets; for many People that had the Plague upon them, knew nothing of it; till the inward Gangreen had affected their Vitals and they dy'd in a few Moments; this caus'd, that many died frequently in that Manner in the Streets suddainly, without any warning: Others perhaps had Time to go to the next Bulk[4] or Stall; or to any Door, Porch, and just sit down and die, as I have said before.

These Objects were so frequent in the Streets, that when the Plague came to be very raging, On one Side, there was scarce any passing by the Streets, but that several dead Bodies would be lying here and there upon the Ground; on the other hand it is observable, that tho' at first, the People would stop as they went along, and call to the Neighbours to come out on such an Occasion; yet, afterward, no Notice was taken of them; but that, if at any Time we found a Corps lying, go cross the Way, and not come near it; or if in a narrow Lane or Passage, go back again, and seek some other Way to go on the Business we were upon; and in those Cases, the Corps was always left, till the Officers had notice, to come and take them away; or till Night, when the Bearers attending the

---

2. A royal ordinance of 1371 had decreed that meat was to be slaughtered in Stratford, near Mile End, Stepney, rather than in the City; it continued to be a major slaughtering area.

3. Believed to purify and fumigate.

4. Framework projecting from the front of a shop, rather like an awning-covered stall.

Dead-Cart would take them up, and carry them away: Nor did those undaunted Creatures, who performed these Offices, fail to search their Pockets, and sometimes strip off their Cloths, if they were well drest, as sometimes they were, and carry off what they could get.

But to return to the Markets; the Butchers took that Care, that if any Person dy'd in the Market, they had the Officers always at Hand, to take them up upon Hand-barrows, and carry them to the next Church-Yard; and this was so frequent that such were not entred in the weekly Bill, found Dead in the Streets or Fields, as is the Case now; but they went into the general Articles of the great Distemper.

But now the Fury of the Distemper encreased to such a Degree, that even the Markets were but very thinly furnished with Provisions, or frequented with Buyers, compair'd to what they were before; and the Lord-Mayor caused the Country-People who brought Provisions, to be stop'd in the Streets leading into the Town, and to sit down there with their Goods, where they sold what they brought, and went immediately away; and this Encourag'd the Country People greatly to do so, for they sold their Provisions at the very Entrances into the Town, and even in the Fields; as particularly in the Fields beyond *White-Chappel*, in *Spittle-fields*. Note, *Those Streets now called* Spittle-Fields, *were then indeed open Fields*: Also in St. *George's-fields* in *Southwork*, in *Bun-Hill* Fields, and in a great Field, call'd *Wood's-Close* near *Islington*;[5] thither the Lord Mayor, Aldermen, and Magistrates, sent their Officers and Servants to buy for their Families, themselves keeping within Doors as much as possible; and the like did many other People; and after this Method was taken, the Country People came with great chearfulness, and brought Provisions of all Sorts, and very seldom got any harm; which I suppose, added also to that Report of their being Miraculously preserv'd.

As for my little Family, having thus as I have said, laid in a Store of Bread, Butter, Cheese, and Beer, I took my Friend and Physician's Advice, and lock'd my self up, and my Family, and resolv'd to suffer the hardship of Living a few Months without Flesh-Meat, rather than to purchase it at the hazard of our Lives.

But tho' I confin'd my Family, I could not prevail upon my unsatisfy'd Curiosity to stay within entirely my self; and tho' I generally came frighted and terrified Home, yet I cou'd not restrain; only that indeed, I did not do it so frequently as at first.

I had some little Obligations indeed upon me, to go to my Brothers House, which was in *Coleman's-street* Parish,[6] and which he had left to my Care, and I went at first every Day, but afterwards only once, or twice a Week.

In these Walks I had many dismal Scenes before my Eyes, as particularly of Persons falling dead in the Streets, terrible Shrieks and Skreek-

5. These were all large open areas.
6. By 1667, Defoe's family had moved into this parish; his father regularly served as auditor of the St. Stephens parish accounts and in other offices such as churchwarden.

ings of Women, who in their Agonies would throw open their Chamber Windows, and cry out in a dismal Surprising Manner; it is impossible to describe the Variety of Postures, in which the Passions of the Poor People would Express themselves.

Passing thro' *Token-House-Yard* in *Lothbury*,[7] of a sudden a Casement violently opened just over my Head, and a Woman gave three frightful Skreetches, and then cry'd, *Oh! Death, Death, Death!* in a most inimitable Tone, and which struck me with Horror and a Chilness, in my very Blood. There was no Body to be seen in the whole Street, neither did any other Window open; for People had no Curiosity now in any Case; nor could any Body help one another; so I went on to pass into *Bell-Alley*.

Just in *Bell-Alley*, on the right Hand of the Passage, there was a more terrible Cry than that, tho' it was not so directed out at the Window, but the whole Family was in a terrible Fright, and I could hear Women and Children run skreaming about the Rooms like distracted, when a Garret Window opened, and some body from a Window on the other Side the Alley, call'd and ask'd, *What is the Matter?* upon which, from the first Window it was answered, *O Lord, my Old Master has hang'd himself!* The other ask'd again, *Is he quite dead?* and the first answer'd, *Ay, ay, quite dead; quite dead and cold!* This Person was a Merchant, and a Deputy Alderman and very rich. I care not to mention the Name, tho' I knew his Name too, but that would be an Hardship to the Family, which is now flourishing again.

But, this is but one; it is scarce credible what dreadful Cases happened in particular Families every Day; People in the Rage of the Distemper, or in the Torment of their Swellings, which was indeed intollerable, running out of their own Government, raving and distracted, and oftentimes laying violent Hands upon themselves, throwing themselves out at their Windows, shooting themselves, &c. Mothers murthering their own Children, in their Lunacy, some dying of meer Grief, as a Passion, some of meer Fright and Surprize, without any Infection at all; others frighted into Idiotism, and foolish Distractions, some into dispair and Lunacy; others into mellancholy Madness.

The Pain of the Swelling was in particular very violent, and to some intollerable; the Physicians and Surgeons may be said to have tortured many poor Creatures, even to Death. The Swellings in some grew hard, and they apply'd violent drawing Plasters, or Pultices,[8] to break them; and if these did not do, they cut and scarified them in a terrible Manner: In some, those Swellings were made hard, partly by the Force of the Distemper, and partly by their being too violently drawn, and were so hard, that no Instrument could cut them, and then they burnt them

7. Tokenhouse Yard was at the south end of Leadenhall Street where Leadenhall Market now stands. The name came from the location of a mint that coined royal farthing tokens. Lothbury ward is now in the Broadstreet ward.

8. Poultices; soft masses of a compound made with meal or herbs that are spread on muslin, linen, or other cloth and applied to the skin as a counterirritant or for warmth.

with Causticks, so that many died raving mad with the Torment; and some in the very Operation. In these Distresses, some for want of Help to hold them down in their Beds, or to look to them, laid Hands upon themselves, as above. Some broke out into the Streets, perhaps naked, and would run directly down to the River, if they were not stopt by the Watchmen, or other Officers, and plunge themselves into the Water, wherever they found it.

It often pierc'd my very Soul to hear the Groans and Crys of those who were thus tormented, but of the Two, this was counted the most promising Particular in the whole Infection; for, if these Swellings could be brought to a Head, and to break and run, or as the Surgeons call it, to digest, the Patient generally recover'd; whereas those, who like the Gentlewoman's Daughter, were struck with Death at the Beginning, and had the Tokens come out upon them, often went about indifferent easy, till a little before they died, and some till the Moment they dropt down, as in Appoplexies and Epelepsies, is often the Case; such would be taken suddenly very sick, and would run to a Bench or Bulk, or any convenient Place that offer'd itself, or to their own Houses, if possible, *as I mentioned before*, and there sit down, grow faint and die. This kind of dying was much the same, as it was with those who die of common Mortifications, who die swooning, and as it were, go away in a Dream; such as died thus, had very little Notice of their being infected at all, till the Gangreen was spread thro' their whole Body; nor could Physicians themselves, know certainly how it was with them, till they opened their Breasts, or other Parts of their Body, and saw the Tokens.

We had at this Time a great many frightful Stories told us of Nurses and Watchmen, who looked after the dying People, *that is to say*, hir'd Nurses, who attended infected People, using them barbarously, starving them, smothering them, or by other wicked Means, hastening their End, *that is to say*, murthering of them: And Watchmen being set to guard Houses that were shut up, when there has been but one person left, and perhaps, that one lying sick, that they have broke in and murthered that Body, and immediately thrown them out into the Dead-Cart! and so they have gone scarce cold to the Grave.

I cannot say, but that some such Murthers were committed, and I think two were sent to Prison for it, but died before they could be try'd; and I have heard that three others, at several Times, were excused for Murthers of that kind; but I must say I believe nothing of its being so common a Crime, as some have since been pleas'd to say, nor did it seem to be so rational, where the People were brought so low as not to be able to help themselves, for such seldom recovered, and there was no Temptation to commit a Murder, at least, none equal to the Fact where they were sure Persons would die in so short a Time; and could not live.

That there were a great many Robberies and wicked Practises committed even in this dreadful Time I do not deny; the Power of Avarice was so strong in some, that they would run any Hazard to steal and to plunder, and particularly in Houses where all the Families, or Inhabitants have been dead, and carried out, they would break in at all Hazards, and without Regard to the Danger of Infection, take even the Cloths off, of the dead Bodies, and the Bed-cloaths from others where they lay dead.

This, *I suppose,* must be the Case of a Family in *Houndsditch,* where a Man and his Daughter, *the rest of the Family being, as I suppose, carried away before by the Dead-Cart,* were found stark naked, one in one Chamber, and one in another, lying Dead on the Floor; and the Cloths of the Beds, from whence, tis supposed they were roll'd off by Thieves, stoln, and carried quite away.

It is indeed to be observ'd, that the Women were in all this Calamity, the most rash, fearless, and desperate Creatures; and as there were vast Numbers that went about as Nurses, to tend those that were sick, they committed a great many petty Thieveries in the Houses where they were employed; and some of them were publickly whipt for it, when perhaps, they ought rather to have been hanged for Examples; for Numbers of Houses were robbed on these Occasions, till at length, the Parish Officers were sent to recommend Nurses to the Sick, and always took an Account who it was they sent, so as that they might call them to account,[9] if the House had been abused where they were placed.

But these Robberies extended chiefly to Wearing-Cloths, Linen, and what Rings, or Money they could come at, when the Person dyed who was under their Care, but not to a general Plunder of the Houses; and I could give an Account of one of these Nurses, who several Years after, being on her Death-bed, confest with the utmost Horror, the Robberries she had committed at the Time of her being a Nurse, and by which she had enriched herself to a great Degree: But as for murthers, I do not find that there was ever any Proof of the Facts, in the manner, as it has been reported, *except as above.*

They did tell me indeed of a Nurse in one place, that laid a wet Cloth upon the Face of a dying Patient, who she tended, and so put an End to his Life, who was just expiring before: And another that smother'd a young Woman she was looking to, when she was in a fainting fit, and would have come to her self: Some that kill'd them by giving them one Thing, some another, and some starved them by giving them nothing at all: But these Stories had two Marks of Suspicion that always attended them, which caused me always to slight them, and to look on them as meer Stories, that People continually frighted one another with. (1.) That wherever it was that we heard it, they always placed the Scene at the farther End of the Town, opposite, or most remote from where you were to hear it: If you heard it in *White-Chapel,* it had happened at *St. Giles's,* or at *Westminster,* or *Holborn,* or that End of the Town; if you heard of it at that End of the Town, then it was done in *White-Chapel,*

9. This practice is fictional. Part of Defoe's purpose in writing this book was to recommend better public administration during plagues.

or the *Minories*, or about *Cripplegate Parish*: If you heard of it in the City, why, then it had happened in *Southwark*; and if you heard of it in *Southwark*, then it was done in the City, and the like.

In the next Place, of what Part soever you heard the Story, the Particulars were always the same, especially that of laying a wet double Clout on a dying Man's Face, and that of smothering a young Gentlewoman; so that it was apparent, at least to my Judgment, that there was more of Tale than of Truth in those Things.

However, I cannot say, but it had some Effect upon the People, and particularly that, *as I said before,* they grew more cautious who they took into their Houses, and who they trusted their Lives with; and had them always recommended, if they could; and where they could not find such, for they were not very plenty, they applied to the Parish Officers.

But here again, the Misery of that Time lay upon the Poor, who being infected, had neither Food or Physick; neither Physician or Appothecary to assist them, or Nurse to attend them: Many of those died calling for help, and even for Sustenance out at their Windows, in a most miserable and deplorable manner; but it must be added, that when ever the Cases of such Persons or Families, were represented to my Lord-Mayor, they always were reliev'd.

It is true, in some Houses where the People were not very poor; yet, where they had sent perhaps their Wives and Children away; and if they had any Servants, they had been dismist; *I say it is true, that* to save the Expences, many such as these shut themselves in, and not having Help, dy'd alone.

A Neighbour and Acquaintance of mine, having some Money owing to him from a Shopkeeper in *White-Cross Street,*[1] or there abouts, sent his Apprentice, a youth about 18 Years of Age, to endeavour to get the Money: He came to the Door, and finding it shut, knockt pretty hard, and as he thought, heard some Body answer within, but was not sure, So he waited, and after some stay knockt again, and then a third Time, when he heard some Body coming down Stairs.

At length the Man of the House came to the Door; he had on his Breeches or Drawers, and a yellow Flannel Wastcoat; no Stockings, a pair of Slipt-Shoes,[2] a white Cap on his head; and as the young Man said, Death in his Face.

When he open'd the Door, says he, *what do you disturb me thus for?* the Boy, tho' a little surpriz'd, reply'd, *I come from such a one, and my Master sent me for the Money, which he says you know of: Very well Child,* returns the living Ghost, *call as you go by at* Cripplegate *Church, and bid them ring the Bell,* and with those Words, shut the Door again,

---

1. At the time of her death in 1732, Defoe's widow owned three houses in White Cross Alley, Cripplegate, which she probably inherited from her brother.

2. Waistcoats were short, soft garments worn next to the skin for additional warmth. Although some were beautiful and intended to show beneath an outergarment, the phrase would have signaled to Defoe's readers, as do the cap, the light slippers, and lack of stockings, that the man was not dressed for company or going out.

and went up again and Dy'd, The same Day; nay, perhaps the same Hour. This, the young Man told me himself, and I have Reason to believe it. This was while the Plague was not come to a Height: I think it was in *June*; Towards the latter End of the Month, it must be before the Dead Carts came about, and while they used the Ceremony of Ringing the Bell for the Dead, which was over for certain, in that Parish at least, before the Month of *July*; for by the *25th* of *July*, there died 550 and upward in a Week, and then they cou'd no more bury in Form, Rich or Poor.

I have mention'd above, that notwithstanding this dreadful Calamity; yet the Numbers of Thieves were abroad upon all Occasions, where they had found any Prey; and that these were generally Women. It was one Morning about 11 a Clock, I had walk'd out to my Brothers House in *Coleman's-street* Parish, as I often did, to see that all was Safe.

My Brother's House had a little Court before it, and a Brick-Wall with a Gate in it; and within that, several Ware-houses, where his Goods of several Sorts lay: It happen'd, that in one of these Ware-houses, were several Packs of Womens high-Crown'd Hats, which came out of the Country; and were, as I suppose, for Exportation; whither I know not.

I was surpriz'd that when I came near my Brother's Door, which was in a Place they call'd *Swan-Alley*, I met three or four Women with High-crown'd Hats on their Heads; and as I remembred afterwards, one, if not more, had some Hats likewise in their Hands: but as I did not see them come out at my Brother's Door, and not knowing that my Brother had any such Goods in his Ware-house, I did not offer to say any Thing to them, but went cross the Way to shun meeting them, as was usual to do at that Time, for fear of the Plague. But when I came nearer to the Gate, I met another Woman with more Hats come out of the Gate. *What Business Mistress*, said I, *have you had there?* There are more People there, said she, I have had no more Business there than they. I was hasty to get to the Gate then, and said no more to her; by which means she got away. But just as I came to the Gate, I saw two more coming cross the Yard to come out with Hats also on their Heads, and under their Arms; at which I threw the Gate to behind me, which having a Spring Lock fastened it self; and turning to the Women, forsooth said I, what are ye *doing here?* and seiz'd upon the Hats, and took them from them. One of them, who I confess, did not look like a Thief. Indeed says she, we are wrong; but we were told, they were Goods that had no Owner; be pleas'd to take them again, and look yonder, there are more such Customers as we: She cry'd and look'd pitifully; so I took the Hats from her, and opened the Gate, and bad them be gone, for I pity'd the Women indeed; But when I look'd towards the Ware-house, as she directed, there were six or seven more all, Women, fitting themselves with Hats, as unconcerned and quiet, as if they had been at a Hatters Shop, buying for their Money.

I was surpriz'd, not at the Sight of so many Thieves only, but at the

Circumstances I was in; being now to thrust my self in among so many People, who for some Weeks, had been so shye of my self, that if I met any Body in the Street, I would cross the Way from them.

They were equally surpriz'd, tho' on another Account: They all told me, they were Neighbours, that they had heard any one might take them, that they were no Bodies Goods, and the like. I talk't big to them at first; went back to the Gate, and took out the Key; so that they were all my Prisoners; threaten'd to Lock them all into the Ware-house, and go and fetch my Lord Mayor's Officers for them,

They beg'd heartily, protested they found the Gate open, and the Ware-house Door open; and that it had no doubt been broken open by some, who expected to find Goods of greater Value; which indeed, was reasonable to believe, because the Lock was broke, and a Padlock that hung to the Door on the out-side also loose; and not abundance of the Hats carry'd away.

At length I consider'd, that this was not a Time to be Cruel and Rigorous; and besides that, it would necessarily oblige me to go much about, to have several People come to me, and I go to several, whose Circumstances of Health, I knew nothing of; and that even, at this Time the Plague was so high, as that there dy'd 4000 a Week; so that in showing my Resentment, or even in seeking Justice for my Brother's Goods, I might lose my own Life; so I contented my self, with taking the Names and Places where some of them lived, who were really Inhabitants in the Neighbourhood; and threatning that my Brother should call them to an Account for it, when he return'd to his Habitation.

Then I talk'd a little upon another Foot with them; and ask'd them how they could do such Things as these, in a Time of such general Calamity; and as it were, in the Face of Gods most dreadful Judgments, when the Plague was at their very Doors; and it may be in their very Houses; and they did not know, but that the Dead-Cart might stop at their Doors in a few Hours, to carry them to their Graves.

I cou'd not perceive that my Discourse made much Impression upon them all that while; till it happened, that there came two Men of the Neighbourhood, hearing of the Disturbance, and knowing my Brother, for they had been both dependants upon his Family, and they came to my Assistance: These being as I said Neighbours, presently knew three of the Women, and told me who they were, and where they liv'd; and it seems, they had given me a true Account of themselves before.

This brings these two Men to a farther Remembrance: The Name of one was *John Hayward*,[3] who was at that Time under-Sexton, of the Parish of St. *Stephen Coleman-street*; by under Sexton, was understood at that Time Grave-digger and Bearer of the Dead. This Man carry'd or

---

3. Again, an actual historical person. Hayward was a Merchant Taylor and had been sexton in the ward where Defoe's father lived (Frank Bastian, *Defoe's Early Life* [Totowa: Barnes & Noble, 1981] 27). Defoe probably remembered him and enjoyed making him one of the stars of this story.

assisted to carry all the Dead to their Graves, which were bury'd in that
large Parish, and who were carried in Form; and after that Form of
Burying was stopt, went with the Dead Cart and the Bell, to fetch the
dead Bodies from the Houses where they lay, and fetch'd many of them
out of the Chambers and Houses; for the Parish was, and is still remarkable, particularly above all the Parishes in *London*, for a great Number
of Alleys, and Thorough fares very long, into which no Carts cou'd
come, and where they were oblig'd to go and fetch the Bodies a very
long Way; which Alleys now remain to Witness it; such as *Whites-Alley,
Cross-Key-Court, Swan-Alley, Bell-Alley, White-Horse-Alley*, and many
more: Here they went with a kind of Hand-Barrow, and lay'd the Dead
Bodies on it, and carry'd them out to the Carts; which work he performed, and never had the Distemper at all, but liv'd above 20 Year
after it, and was Sexton of the Parish to the Time of his Death. His Wife
at the same, time was Nurse to infected People, and tended many that
died in the Parish, being for her honesty recommended by the Parish
Officers, yet she never was infected neither.

He never used any Preservative against the Infection, other than holding *Garlick* and *Rue* in his Mouth, and smoaking Tobacco; this I also
had from his own Mouth; and his Wife's Remedy was washing her Head
in Vinegar, and sprinkling her Head-Cloths so with Vinegar, as to keep
them always Moist; and if the smell of any of those she waitd on was
more than ordinary Offensive, she snuft Vinegar up her Nose, and
sprinkled Vinegar upon her Head-Cloths, and held a Handkerchief wet-
ted with Vinegar to her Mouth.

It must be confest, that tho' the Plague was chiefly among the Poor;
yet, were the Poor the most Venturous and Fearless of it, and went about
their Employment, with a Sort of brutal Courage; I must call it so, for
it was founded neither on Religion or Prudence; scarse did they use any
Caution, but run into any Business, which they could get Employment
in, tho' it was the most hazardous; such was that of tending the Sick,
watching Houses shut up, carrying infected Persons to the Pest-House;
and which was still worse, carrying the Dead away to their Graves.

It was under this *John Hayward's* Care, and within his Bounds, that
the Story of the Piper,[4] with which People have made themselves so
merry, happen'd, and he assur'd me that it was true. It is said, that it
was a blind Piper; but as *John* told me, the Fellow was not blind, but an
ignorant weak poor Man, and usually walked his Rounds about 10 a
Clock at Night, and went piping along from Door to Door, and the
People usually took him in at Public Houses where they knew him, and

4. Many versions of the story of drunken men
presumed dead and carted away exist; see, for
instance, "Of One that Fell Drunke off from
his Horse taken for a Londoner Dead" in *The
Meeting of Gallants at an Ordinary* (London,
1604). As commemoration of the miraculous
survival of the "plague piper," a statue of him
by Caius Gabriel Cibber was erected in a garden on the Terrace in Tottenhamcourt Road,
near where the piper was allegedly picked up.
Cibber also carved reliefs for the base of The
Monument, the obelisk memorializing the
Great Fire, and "Melancholy" and "Raving
Madness" for the gates of Bethlehem Hospital.
He became Sculptor to King William III.

would give him Drink and Victuals, and sometimes Farthings; and he in Return, would Pipe and Sing, and talk simply, which diverted the People, and thus he liv'd: It was but a very bad Time for this Diversion, while Things were as I have told; yet the poor Fellow went about as usual, but was almost starv'd; and when any Body ask'd how he did, he would answer, the Dead Cart had not taken him yet, but that they had promised to call for him next Week.

It happen'd one Night, that this poor Fellow, whether some body had given him too much Drink or no, *John Hayward* said, he had not Drink in his House; but that they had given him a little more Victuals than ordinary at a Public House in *Coleman-Street*; and the poor Fellow having not usually had a Bellyfull, or perhaps not a good while, was laid all along upon the Top of a Bulk or Stall, and fast a sleep at a Door, in the Street near *London-Wall*, towards *Cripplegate*, and that upon the same Bulk or Stall, the People of some House, in the Alley of which the House was a Corner, hearing a Bell, which they always rung before the Cart came, had laid a Body really dead of the Plague just by him, thinking too, that this poor Fellow had been a dead Body as the other was, and laid there by some of the Neighbours.

Accordingly when *John Hayward* with his Bell and the Cart came along, finding two dead Bodies lie upon the Stall they took them up with the Instrument they used, and threw them into the Cart; and all this while the Piper slept soundly.

From hence they passed along, and took in other dead Bodies, till, as honest *John Hayward* told me, they almost burried him alive, in the Cart, yet all this While he slept soundly; at length the Cart came to the Place where the Bodies were to be thrown into the Ground, which, as I do remember, was at *Mount-mill*;[5] and as the Cart usually stopt some Time before they were ready to shoot out the melancholly Load they had in it, as soon as the Cart stop'd, the Fellow awaked, and struggled a little to get his Head out from among the dead Bodies, when raising himself up in the Cart, he called out, *Hey! where am I?* This frighted the Fellow that attended about the Work, but after some Pause *John Hayward* recovering himself said, *Lord bless us. There's some Body in the Cart not quite dead!* So another call'd to him and said, *Who are you?* the Fellow answered, *I am the poor Piper. Where am I? Where are you!* says *Hayward*; *why, you are in the Dead-Cart, and we are a-going to bury you. But I an't dead tho', am I?* says the Piper; which made them laugh a little, tho' as *John* said, they were heartily frighted at first; so they help'd the poor Fellow down, and he went about his Business.

I know the Story goes, he set up his Pipes in the Cart, and frighted the Bearers, and others, so that they ran away; but *John Hayward* did not tell the Story so, nor say any Thing of his Piping at all; but that he was a poor Piper, and that he was carried away as above I am fully satisfied of the Truth of.

5. This fort was built in 1642 to protect the City from the royalists; it was in Goswell Street, Aldersgate, near Moorfields.

It is to be noted here, that the Dead Carts in the City were not confin'd to particular Parishes, but one Cart went thro' several Parishes, according as the Numbers of Dead presented; nor were they ty'd to carry the Dead to their respective Parishes, but many of the Dead, taken up in the City, were carried to the Burying Ground in the Out-parts, for want of Room.

I have already mentioned the Surprize, that this Judgment was at first among the People, I must be allowed to give some of my Observations on the more serious and religious Part. Surely never City, at least, of this Bulk and Magnitude, was taken in a Condition so perfectly unprepar'd for such a dreadful Visitation, whether I am to speak of the Civil Preparations, or Religious; they were indeed, as if they had had no Warning, no Expectation, no Apprehensions, and consequently the least Provision imaginable, was made for it in a publick Way; for Example.

The Lord Mayor and Sheriffs had made no Provision as Magistrates, for [the enforcement of] the Regulations which were to be observed; they had gone into no Measures for Relief of the Poor.

The Citizens had no publick Magazines, or Store-Houses for Corn, or Meal, for the Subsistence of the Poor; which, if they had provided themselves, as in such Cases is done abroad, many miserable Families, who were now reduc'd to the utmost Distress, would have been reliev'd, and that in a better Manner, than now could be done.[6]

The Stock of the City's Money, I can say but little to; the Chamber of *London*[7] was said to be exceeding rich; and it may be concluded, that they were so, by the vast Sums of Money issued from thence, in the rebuilding the publick Edifices after the Fire of *London*, and in Building new Works, such as, for the first Part, the *Guild-Hall*, *Blackwell-Hall*, Part of *Leaden Hall*, Half the *Exchange*, the *Session-House*, the *Compter*; the Prisons of *Ludgate*, *Newgate*, &c. several of the Wharfs, and Stairs, and Landing-places on the River; all which were either burnt down or damaged by the great Fire of *London*, the next Year after the Plague; and of the second Sort, the Monument, *Fleet-ditch* with its Bridges, and the Hospital of *Bethlem*, or *Bedlam*, &c.[8] But possibly the Managers of the City's Credit, at that Time, made more Conscience of

6. Here Defoe is making suggestions to his own contemporaries as they face a possible plague.
7. The Chamber held the collected customs fees and the rents from City property.
8. These major buildings were rebuilt, but the City and the nation struggled to finance the work. Signs of the fire were still evident thirty years later; by 1670 none of the churches had been rebuilt, and special taxes such as the Coal Dues were repeatedly imposed. Guildhall and the Exchange were the heart of commercial London; most of the City's business transactions and administrative courts and meetings were in Guildhall. Blackwell Hall was the major cloth market; of all the London markets only part of Leadenhall survived. The Session House was what the people called Old Bailey Hall of Justice, London's main criminal court, because four "sessions" of the court were held there each year. The Compters were the prisons under the supervision of the City Sheriffs; they still required prisoners to "account for the cause of their commitment." The Monument was commissioned in 1667 as part of the Act for the Rebuilding of the City of London (18–19 Charles II. c.8). After the Fire, the Fleet River, which flows through Farringdon Ward Without through the City to the Thames, was dredged to improve navigation, and four bridges were built over it. Bethlehem Hospital was commonly called "Bedlam," and by 1377 was the hospital for the "distracted" and mentally ill. It did not burn in the Great Fire, but in 1674 it moved to a new building in Moorfields.

breaking in upon the Orphan's Money;[9] to shew Charity to the distress'd Citizens, than the Managers in the following Years did, to beautify the City, and re-edify the Buildings, tho' in the first Case, the Losers would have thought their Fortunes better bestow'd, and the Publick Faith of the City have been less subjected to Scandal and Reproach.

It must be acknowledg'd that the absent Citizens, who, tho' they were fled for Safety into the Country, were yet greatly interested in the Welfare of those who they left behind, forgot not to contribute liberally to the Relief of the Poor, and large Sums were also collected among Trading-Towns in the remotest Parts of *England*; and as I have heard also, the Nobility and the Gentry, in all Parts of *England*, took the deplorable Condition of the City into their Consideration, and sent up large Sums of Money in Charity, to the Lord Mayor and Magistrates, for the Relief of the Poor; the King also, as I was told, ordered a thousand Pounds a Week to be distributed in four Parts; one Quarter to the City and Liberties of *Westminster*: one Quarter, or Part, among the Inhabitants of the *Southwark* Side of the Water; one Quarter to the Liberty and Parts within, of the City, exclusive of the City, within the Walls; and, one fourth Part to the Suburbs in the County of *Middlesex*, and the East and North Parts of the City:[1] But this latter I only speak of as a Report.

Certain it is, the greatest Part of the Poor, or Families, who formerly liv'd by their Labour, or by Retail-Trade, liv'd now on Charity; and had there not been prodigious Sums of Money given by charitable, well-minded Christians, for the Support of such, the City could never have subsisted. There were, no Question, Accounts kept of their Charity, and of the just Distribution of it by the Magistrates: But as such Multitudes of those very Officers died, thro' whose Hands it was distributed; and also that, as I have been told, most of the Accounts of those Things were lost in the great Fire which happened in the very next Year, and which burnt even the Chamberlain's Office, and many of their Papers; so I could never come at the particular Account, which I used great Endeavours to have seen.

It may, however, be a Direction in Case of the Approach of a like Visitation, which God keep the City from; I say, it may be of use to observe that by the Care of the Lord Mayor and Aldermen, at that Time, in distributing Weekly, great Sums of Money, for Relief of the Poor, a Multitude of People, who would otherwise have perished, were relieved, and their Lives preservd. And here let me enter into a brief State of the Case of the Poor at that Time, and what Way apprehended from them, from whence may be judg'd hereafter, what may be expected, if the like Distress should come upon the City.

9. Defoe is making a true but risky accusation. The Orphan's Money was orphans' inheritances, which the City held in their behalf and used to pay for their upkeep. If there was any money left when an orphan came of age, he or she was entitled to it. They could not, however, collect the interest that their money earned, and it was an important source of income for the City. The City did use the Orphan's Money to rebuild after the fire, and by 1680 the Fund was bankrupt.

1. Defoe again offers a model of conduct, one not historically exact, to his contemporaries.

At the Beginning of the Plague, when there was now no more Hope, but that the whole City would be visited, when, as I have said, all that had Friends or Estates in the Country, retired with their Families, and when, indeed, one would have thought the very City it self was running out of the Gates, and that there would be no Body left behind. You may be sure, from that Hour, all Trade, except such as related to immediate Subsistence, was, *as it were*, at a full Stop.

This is so lively a Case, and contains in it so much of the real Condition of the People; that I think I cannot be too particular in it; and therefore I descend to the several Arrangements or Classes of People, who fell into immediate Distress upon this Occasion: For Example,

1. *All Master Work-men in Manufactures; especially such as belong'd to Ornament, and the less necessary Parts of the People dress Cloths and Furniture for Houses; such as Riband Weavers, and other Weavers; Gold and Silverlace-makers, and Gold and Silverwyer-drawers,* [2] *Seemstresses, Milleners, Shoe-makers, Hat-makers and Glove-makers: Also Upholdsterers, Joyners, Cabinet-makers, Looking-glass-makers; and innumerable Trades which depend upon such as these; I say the Master Workmen in such, stopt their Work, dismist their Journeymen, and Workmen, and all their Dependants.*

2. *As Merchandizing was at a full stop, for very few Ships ventur'd to come up the River, and none at all went out; so all the extraordinary Officers of the Customes, likewise the Watermen, Carmen,* [3] *Porters, and all the Poor, whose Labour depended upon the Merchants, were at once dismist, and put out of Business.*

3. *All the Tradesmen usually employ'd in building or repareing of Houses, were at a full Stop, for the People were far from wanting to build Houses, when so many thousand Houses were at once stript of their Inhabitants; so that this one Article turn'd all the ordinary Work-men of that Kind out of Business; such as Bricklayers, Masons, Carpenters, Joyners, Plasterers, Painters, Glaziers, Smiths, Plumbers; and all the Labourers depending on such.*

4. *As Navigation was at a Stop; our Ships neither coming in, or going out as before; so the Seamen were all out of Employment, and many of them in the last and lowest Degree of Distress, and with the Seamen, were all the several Tradesmen, and Workmen belonging to and depending upon the building, and fitting out of Ships; such as Ship Carpenters, Caulkers, Rope-makers, Dry-Coopers, Sail-makers, Anchor-Smiths, and other Smiths; Block-makers, Carvers, Gun Smiths, Ship-Chandlers, Ship-Carvers and the like; The Masters of those perhaps might live upon their Substance; but the Traders were Universally at a Stop, and conse-*

---

2. Drawers made wire by drawing metal through a series of increasingly small holes; the wire was used to make jewelry.

3. Licensed watermen's boats were for hire and taxied people and light cargo along the Thames. Carmen were carters who transported and delivered packages and heavy goods.

>   *quently all their Workmen discharged: Add to these, that the
>   River was in a manner without Boats, and all or most part of
>   the Watermen, Lightermen, Boat-builders, and Lighter-builders
>   in like manner idle, and laid by.*
>
> 5. *All Families retrench'd their living as much as possible, as well
>   those that fled, as those that stay'd; so that an innumerable Mul-
>   titude of Footmen, serving Men, Shop-keepers, Journey-men,
>   Merchants-Book-keepers, and such Sort of People, and especially
>   poor Maid Servants were turn'd off, and left Friendless and
>   Helpless without Employment, and without Habitation; and this
>   was really a dismal Article.*

I might be more particular as to this Part: But it may suffice to mention in general; all Trades being stopt, Employment ceased; the Labour,
and by that, the Bread of the Poor were cut off; and at first indeed, the
Cries of the poor were most lamentable to hear; tho' by the Distribution
of Charity, their Misery that way was greatly abated: Many indeed fled
into the Countries; but thousands of them having stay'd in *London*, till
nothing but Desperation sent them away; Death overtook them on the
Road, and they serv'd for no better than the Messengers of Death, indeed,
others carrying the Infection along with them; spreading it very unhappily into the remotest Parts of the Kingdom.

Many of these were the miserable Objects of Dispair which I have
mention'd before, and were remov'd by the Destruction which followed;
these might be said to perish, not by the Infection it self, but by the
Consequence of it; indeed, namely, by Hunger and Distress, and the
Want of all Things; being without Lodging, without Money, without
Friends, without Means to get their Bread, or without any one to give it
them, for many of them were without what we call legal Settlements,
and so could not claim of the Parishes,[4] and all the Support they had,
was by Application to the Magistrates for Relief, which Relief was, (to
give the Magistrates their Due) carefully and chearfully administred, as
they found it necessary; and those that stay'd behind never felt the Want
and Distress of that Kind, which they felt, who went away in the manner
above-noted.

Let any one who is acquainted with what Multitudes of People, get
their daily Bread in this City by their Labour, whether Artificers or meer
Workmen; I say, let any Man consider, what must be the miserable
Condition of this Town, if on a sudden, they should be all turned out
of Employment, that Labour should cease, and Wages for Work be no
more.

---

4. Residents of parishes and babies born within parishes were entitled to charity through the poor funds and other collected public funds. Forty days' residency as servant, apprentice, or householder was required for "legal settle-ment," but since many servants lived with the families for whom they worked, if fired or dis-placed by the deaths or departures of the mas-ter, they had trouble proving they were legal residents. In other novels Defoe writes of the plight of people without settled addresses and even of the homeless. Parish vestries could vote to include some of these people in the chari-table lists.

This was the Case with us at that Time, and had not the Sums of Money, contributed in Charity by well disposed People, of every Kind, as well abroad as at home, been prodigiously great, it had not been in the Power of the Lord Mayor and Sheriffs, to have kept the Publick Peace; nor were they without Apprehensions as it was, that Desparation should push the People upon Tumults, and cause them to rifle the Houses of rich Men, and plunder the Markets of Provisions; in which Case the Country People, who brought Provisions very freely and boldly to Town, would ha' been terrified from coming any more, and the Town would ha' sunk under an unavoidable Famine.[5]

But the Prudence of my Lord Mayor, and the Court of Aldermen within the City, and of the Justices of Peace in the Out-parts was such, and they were supported with Money from all Parts so well, that the poor People were kept quiet, and their Wants every where reliev'd, as far as was possible to be done.

Two Things, besides this, contributed to prevent the Mob doing any Mischief: One was, that really the Rich themselves had not laid up Stores of Provisions in their Houses, as indeed, they ought to have done, and which if they had been wise enough to have done, and lock'd themselves entirely up, as some few did, they had perhaps escaped the Disease better: But as it appear'd they had not, so the Mob had no Notion of finding Stores of Provisions there, if they had broken in, as it is plain they were sometimes very near doing, and which, if they had, they had finish'd the Ruin of the whole City, for there were no regular Troops to ha' withstood them, nor could the Traind-Bands have been brought together to defend the City, no Men being to be found to bear Arms.

But the Vigilance of the Lord Mayor, and such Magistrates as could be had, for some, even of the Aldermen were Dead, and some absent, prevented this; and they did it by the most kind and gentle Methods they could think of, as particularly by relieving the most desperate with Money, and putting others into Business and particularly that Employment of watching Houses that were infected and shut up; and as the Number of these were very great, for it was said, there was at one Time, ten thousand Houses shut up, and every House had two Watchmen to guard it, *viz* one by Night, and the other by Day; this gave Opportunity to employ a very great Number of poor Men at a Time.

The Women, and Servants, that were turned off from their Places, were likewise employed as Nurses to tend the Sick in all Places; and this took off a very great Number of them.

And, which tho' a melancholy Article in it self, yet was a Deliverance in its Kind, namely, the Plague which raged in a dreadful Manner from the Middle of *August* to the Middle of *October*, carried off in that Time thirty or forty Thousand of these very People, which had they been left,

5. Defoe surely has in mind the riots in Marseilles, France, and his account is intended to be more instructive than historically exact. See pp. 218–20 in this volume for reports on French desperation.

would certainly have been an unsufferable Burden, by their Poverty, *that is to say*, the whole City could not have supported the Expence of them, or have provided Food for them; and they would in Time have been even driven to the Necessity of plundering either the City it self, or the Country adjacent, to have subsisted themselves, which would first or last, have put the whole Nation, as well as the City, into the utmost Terror and Confusion.

It was observable then, that this Calamity of the People made them very humble; for now, for about nine Weeks together, there died near a thousand a-Day, one Day with another, even by the Account of the weekly Bills, which yet I have Reason to be assur'd never gave a full Account, by many thousands; the Confusion being such, and the Carts working in the Dark, when they carried the Dead, that in some Places no Account at all was kept, but they work'd on; the Clerks and Sextons not attending for Weeks together, and not knowing what Number they carried. This Account is verified by the following Bills of Mortality.

		Of all Diseases.	Of the Plague.
Aug. 8 to Aug. 15	— 5319	—— 3880
to 22	— 5568	—— 4237
to 29	— 7496	—— 6102
Aug. 29 to Sept. 5	— 8252	—— 6988
to 12	— 7690	—— 6544
to 19	— 8297	—— 7165
to 26	— 6460	—— 5533
Sept. 26 to Oct. 3	— 5720	—— 4929
to 10	— 5068	—— 4227
	———	———
	59870	49705

So that the Gross of the People were carried off in these two Months; for as the whole Number which was brought in, to die of the Plague, was but 68590 here, is fifty thousand of them, within a Trifle, in two Months; I say 50000, because, as there wants 295 in the Number above, so there wants two Days of two Months, in the Account of Time.

Now when, I say, that the Parish Officers did not give in a full Account, or were not to be depended upon for their Account, let any one but consider how Men could be exact in such a Time of dreadful Distress, and when many of them were taken sick themselves, and perhaps died in the very Time when their Accounts were to be given in, I mean the Parish Clerks; besides inferior Officers; for tho' these poor Men ventured at all Hazards, yet they were far from being exempt from the common Calamity, especially, if it be true, that the Parish of *Stepney* had within the Year, one hundred and sixteen Sextons, Grave-diggers, and their Assistants, that is to say, Bearers, Bell-men, and Drivers of Carts, for carrying off the dead Bodies.

Indeed the Work was not of a Nature to allow them Leisure, to take an exact Tale of the dead Bodies, which were all huddled together in the Dark into a Pit; which Pit, or Trench, no Man could come nigh, but at the utmost Peril. I observ'd often, that in the Parishes of *Algate*, and *Cripplegate*, *White-Chappel* and *Stepney*, there was five, six, seven, and eight hundred in a Week, in the Bills, whereas if we may believe the Opinion of those that liv'd in the City, all the Time, as well as I, there died sometimes 2000 a-Week in those Parishes; and I saw it under the Hand of one, that made as strict an examination into that Part as he could, that there really died an hundred thousand People of the Plague, in it that one Year, whereas the Bills, the Articles of the Plague, was but 68590.[6]

If I may be allowed to give my Opinion, by what I saw with my Eyes, and heard from other People that were Eye Witnesses, I do verily believe the same, *viz.* that there died, at least, 100000 of the Plague only, besides other Distempers, and besides those which died in the Fields, and High-ways, and secret Places, out of the Compass of the Communication, as it was called; and who were not put down in the Bills, tho' they really belonged to the Body of the Inhabitants. It was known to us all, that abundance of poor dispairing Creatures, who had the Distemper upon them, and were grown stupid, or melancholly[7] by their Misery, as many were, wandred away into the Fields, and Woods, and into secret uncouth Places, almost any where to creep into a Bush, or Hedge, and DIE.

The Inhabitants of the Villages adjacent would in Pity, carry them Food, and set it at a Distance, that they might fetch it, if they were able, and sometimes they were not able; and the next Time they went, they should find the poor Wretches lie dead, and the Food untouch'd. The Number of these miserable Objects were many, and I know so many that perish'd thus, and so exactly where, that I believe I could go to the very Place and dig their Bones up still; for the Country People would go and dig a Hole at a Distance from them, and then with long Poles, and Hooks at the End of them, drag the Bodies into these Pits, and then thro' the Earth in Form as far as they cou'd cast it to cover them; taking notice how the Wind blew, and so coming on that Side which the Sea-men call *to-Wind-ward*, that the Scent of the Bodies might blow from them; and thus great Numbers went out of the World, who were never known or any Account of them taken, as well within the Bills of Mor-tality as without.

This indeed I had, in the main, only from the Relation of others; for I seldom walk'd into the Fields, except towards *Bednal-green* and *Hackney*[8]; or as hereafter: But when I did walk I always saw a great many

6. Defoe's figures come from the printed Bills of Mortality.
7. The eighteenth-century reader would have recognized these terms as describing emotional breakdown. The stupid were stunned, stupe-fied, insensible, often so inattentive as to be suspected of deafness. Melancholy was a form of depression and a feared mental illness.
8. Bethnal Green and Hackney, hamlets in Middlesex, were near Defoe's home in Stoke Newington and the silk-weaving district of Spittlefields. "Bednal-greene" is the Elizabe-than spelling; in 1665 the Green was still a full seven acres.

poor Wanderers at a Distance, but I could know little of their Cases; for whether it were in the Street, or in the Fields, if we had seen any Body coming, it was a general Method to walk away; yet I believe the Account is exactly true.

As this puts me upon mentioning my walking the Streets and Fields, I cannot omit taking notice what a desolate Place the City was at that Time: The great Street I liv'd in, which is known to be one of the broadest of all the Streets of *London*. I mean of the Suburbs as well as the Liberties; all the Side where the Butchers lived, especially without the Bars was more like a green Field than a paved Street, and the People generally went in the middle with the Horses and Carts: It is true, that the farthest End towards *White-Chappel* Church, was not all pav'd, but even the Part that was pav'd was full of Grass also; but this need not seem strange since the great Streets within the City, such as *Leadenhall-Street*, *Bishopgate-Street*, *Cornhill*, and even the *Exchange* it self, had Grass growing in them, in several Places; neither Cart or Coach were seen in the Streets from Morning to Evening, except some Country Carts to bring Roots and Beans, or Pease, Hay and Straw, to the Market, and those but very few, compared to what was usual: As for Coaches they were scarce used, but to carry sick People to the Pest-House, and to other Hospitals; and some few to carry Physicians to such Places as they thought fit to venture to visit; for really Coaches were dangerous things, and People did not Care to venture into them, because they did not know who might have been carried in them last; and sick infected People were, *as I have said*, ordinarily carried in them to the Pest-Houses, and sometimes People expired in them as they went along.

It is true, when the Infection came to such a Height as I have now mentioned, there were very few Physicians, which car'd to stir abroad to sick Houses, and very many of the most eminent of the Faculty were dead as well as the Surgeons also, for now it was indeed a dismal time, and for about a Month together, not taking any Notice of the Bills of Mortality, I believe there did not die less than 1500 or 1700 a-Day, one Day with another.

One of the worst Days we had in the whole Time, as I thought, was in the Beginning of *September*, when indeed good People began to think, that God was resolved to make a full End of the People in this miserable City. This was at that Time when the Plague was fully come into the Eastern Parishes: The Parish of *Algate*, if I may give my Opinion buried above a thousand a Week for two Weeks, tho' the Bills did not say so many; but it surrounded me at so dismal a rate, that there was not a House in twenty uninfected; in the Minories, in *Houndsditch*, and in those Parts of *Algate* Parish about the *Butcher-Row*, and the Alleys over against me, I say in those places Death reigned in every Corner. *White Chapel* Parish was in the same Condition, and tho' much less than the Parish I liv'd in; yet bury'd near 600 a Week by the Bills; and in my Opinion, near twice as many; whole Families, and indeed, whole Streets

of Families were swept away together; insomuch, that it was frequent for
Neighbours to call to the Bellman, to go to such and such Houses, and
fetch out the People, for that they were all Dead.

And indeed, the Work of removing the dead Bodies by Carts, was
now grown so very odious and dangerous, that it was complain'd of, that
the Bearers did not take Care to clear such Houses, where all the Inhabitants were dead; but that sometimes the Bodies lay several Days unburied, till the neighbouring Families were offended with the Stench, and
consequently infect'd; and this neglect of the Officers was such, that the
Church Wardens and Constables were summon'd to look after it; and
even the Justices of the *Hamlets*, were oblig'd to venture their Lives
among them, to quicken and encourage them; for innumerable of the
Bearers dy'd of the Distemper, infected by the Bodies they were oblig'd
to come so near; and had it not been, that the Number of poor People
who wanted Employment, and wanted Bread, (as I have said before,)
was so great, that Necessity drove them to undertake any Thing, and
venture any thing, they would never have found People to be employ'd;
and then the Bodies of the dead would have lain above Ground, and
have perished and rotted in a dreadful Manner.

But the Magistrates cannot be enough commended in this, that they
kept such good Order for the burying of the Dead, that as fast as any of
those they employ'd to carry off, and bury the dead, fell sick or dy'd, as
was many Times the Case, they immediately supply'd the places with
others; which by reason of the great Number of Poor that was left out of
Business, *as above*, was not hard to do: This occasion'd, that notwithstanding the infinite Number of People which dy'd, and were sick almost
all together, yet, they were always clear'd away, and carry'd off every
Night; so that it was never to be said of *London*, that the living were not
able to bury the Dead.

As the Desolation was greater, during those terrible Times, so the
Amazement of the People encreas'd; and a thousand unaccountable
Things they would do in the violence of their Fright, as others did the
same in the Agonies of their Distemper, and this part was very affecting;
some went roaring, and crying, and wringing their Hands along the
Street; some would go praying, and lifting up their Hands to Heaven,
calling upon God for Mercy. I cannot say indeed, whether this was not
in their Distraction; *but be it so*, it was still an indication of a more
serious Mind, when they had the use of their Senses, and was much
better, *even as it was*, than the frightful yellings and cryings that every
Day, and especially in the Evenings, were heard in some Streets. I suppose the World has heard of the famous *Soloman Eagle* an Enthusiast:[9]
He tho' not infected at all, but in his Head; went about denouncing of

9. Solomon Eagle, whose real name was
Eccles, was a Quaker musician and shoe-
maker. He began these appearances in 1662
"crying repentance . . , and bad [people]
remember *Sodom*" after he "suffered some per-
secution in and near *Smithfield* in the Fair-
time" (A *Brief Relation of the Persecutions and
Cruelties that have been acted upon the People
called Quakers* [1662]).

Judgment upon the City in a frightful manner; sometimes quite naked, and with a Pan of burning Charcoal on his Head: What he said or pretended, indeed I could not learn.

I will not say, whether that Clergyman was distracted or not: Or whether he did it in pure Zeal for the poor People who went every Evening thro' the Streets of *White-Chapel*; and with his Hands lifted up, repeated that Part of the *Liturgy* of the Church continually; *Spare us good Lord, spare thy People whom thou hast redeemed with thy most precious Blood,*[1] I say, I cannot speak positively of these Things; because these were only the dismal Objects which represented themselves to me as I look't thro' my Chamber Windows, (for I seldom opened the Casements) while I confin'd my self within Doors, during that most violent rageing of the Pestilence; when indeed, as I have said, many began to think, and even to say, that there would none escape; and indeed, I began to think so too; and therefore kept within Doors, for about a Fortnight, and never stirr'd out: But I cou'd not hold it: Besides, there were some People, who notwithstanding the Danger, did not omit publickly to attend the Worship of God, even in the most dangerous Times; and tho' it is true, that a great many Clergymen did shut up their Churches, and fled as other People did, for the safety of their Lives; yet, all did not do so, some ventur'd to officiate, and to keep up the Assemblies of the People by constant Prayers; and sometimes Sermons, or Brief Exhortations to Repentance and Reformation, and this as long as any would come to hear them; and Dissenters did the like also, and even in the very Churches,[2] where the Parish Ministers were either Dead or fled, nor was there any Room for making Difference, at such a Time as this was.

It was indeed a lamentable Thing to hear the miserable Lamentations of poor dying Creatures, calling out for Ministers to Comfort them, and pray with them, to Counsel them, and to direct them, calling out to God for Pardon and Mercy, and confessing aloud their past Sins. It would make the stoutest Heart bleed to hear how many Warnings were then given by dying Penitents, to others not to put off and delay their Repentance to the Day of Distress, that such a Time of Calamity as this, was no Time for Repentance; was no Time to call upon God. I wish I could repeat the very Sound of those Groans, and of those Exclamations that I heard from some poor dying Creatures, when in the Height of their Agonies and Distress; and that I could make him that read this hear; as I imagine I now hear them, for the Sound seems still to Ring in my Ears.

If I could but tell this Part, in such moving Accents as should alarm

---

1. The line is from the Church of England's *Book of Common Prayer*, "The Order for the Visitation of the Sick."
2. Nonconformists had been removed from all the church pulpits after St. Bartholomew's Day 1662 (August 24). As Defoe says, many preached in the vacated pulpits during the plague and were promptly ousted when it ended.

the very Soul of the Reader, I should rejoice that I recorded those Things, however short and imperfect.

It pleased God that I was still spar'd, and very hearty and sound in Health, but very impatient of being pent up within Doors without Air, as I had been for 14 Days or thereabouts; and I could not restrain my self, but I would go to carry a Letter for my Brother to the Post-House;[3] then it was indeed, that I observ'd a profound Silence in the Streets; when I came to the Post-House, as I went to put in my Letter, I saw a Man stand in one Corner of the Yard, and talking to another at a Window; and a third had open'd a Door belonging to the Office; In the middle of the Yard lay a small Leather Purse, with two Keys hanging at it, and Money in it, but no Body would meddle with it: I ask'd how long it had lain there; the Man at the Window said, it had lain almost an Hour; but that they had not meddled with it, because they did not know, but the Person who dropt it, might come back to look for it. I had no such need of Money, nor was the Sum so big, that I had any Inclination to meddle with it, or to get the Money at the hazard it might be attended with; so I seem'd to go away, when the Man who had open'd the Door, said, he would take it up; but so, that if the right Owner came for it, he should be sure to have it: So he went in, and fetched a pail of Water, and set it down hard by the Purse; then went again, and fetch'd some Gun-powder, and cast a good deal of Powder upon the Purse, and then made a Train from that which he had thrown loose upon the Purse; the train reached about two Yards; after this he goes in a third Time, and fetches out a pair of Tongues[4] red hot, and which he had prepar'd, I suppose on purpose; and first setting Fire to the Train of Powder, that sing'd the Purse and also smoak'd the Air sufficiently: But he was not content with that; but he then takes up the Purse with the Tongs, holding it so long till the Tongs burnt thro' the Purse, and then he shook the Money out into the Pail of Water,[5] so he carried it in. The Money, as I remember, was about thirteen Shillings, and some smooth Groats, and Brass Farthings.

There might perhaps, have been several poor People, *as I have observ'd above*, that would have been hardy enough to have ventured for the sake of the Money; but you may easily see by what I have observ'd, that the few People, who were spar'd, were very careful of themselves, at that Time when the Distress was so exceeding great.

Much about the same Time I walk'd out into the Fields towards *Bow*; for I had a great mind to see how things were managed in the River, and among the Ships; and as I had some Concern in Shipping, I had a Notion that it had been one of the best Ways of securing ones self from

3. One of the many post offices in London.
4. Tongs.
5. England had no paper money, although people exchanged written notes, which could be transferred to pay debts or cashed at, for instance, goldsmiths' shops where the note writer was known.

the Infection to have retir'd into a Ship, and musing how to satisfy my Curiosity, in that Point, I turned away over the Fields, from *Bow* to *Bromley*, and down to *Blackwall*, to the Stairs,[6] which are there for landing, or taking Water.

Here I saw a poor Man walking on the Bank, or Sea-wall, as they call it, by himself, I walked a while also about, seeing the Houses all shut up; as last I fell into some Talk, at a Distance, with this poor Man; first I asked him, how People did thereabouts? *Alas, Sir! says he, almost all desolate; all dead or sick: Here are very few Families in this Part, or in that Village,* pointing at *Poplar; where half of them are not dead already, and the rest sick.* Then he pointed to one House, *There they are all dead,* said he, *and the House stands open; no Body dares go into it. A poor Thief,* says he, *ventured in to steal something, but he paid dear for his Theft; for he was carried to the ChurchYard too, last Night.* Then he pointed to several other Houses. *There,* says he, *they are all dead; the Man and his Wife, and five Children. There,* says he, *they are shut up, you see a Watchman at the Door;* and so of other Houses. *Why,* says I, *What do you here all alone? Why,* says he, *I am a poor desolate Man; it has pleased God I am not yet visited, tho' my Family is, and one of my Children dead. How do you mean then,* said I, *that you are not visited. Why,* says he, *that's my House,* pointing to a very little low boarded House, *and there my poor Wife and two Children live,* said he, *if they may be said to live,; for my Wife and one of the Children are visited, but I do not come at them.* And with that Word I saw the Tears run very plentifully down his Face; and so they did down mine too, I assure you.

But said I, *Why do you not come at them? How can you abandon your own Flesh, and Blood? Oh, Sir! says he, the Lord forbid; I do not abandon them; I work for them as much as I am able; and blessed be the Lord, I keep them from Want;* and with that I observ'd, he lifted up his Eyes to Heaven, with a Countenance that presently told me, I had happened on a Man that was no Hypocrite, but a serious, religious good Man, and his Ejaculation was an Expression of Thankfulness, that in such a Condition as he was in, he should be able to say his Family did not want. *Well,* says I, *honest Man, that is a great Mercy as things go now with the Poor: But how do you live then, and how are you kept from the dreadful Calamity that is now upon us all? Why Sir,* says he, *I am a Waterman, and there's my Boat,* says he, *and the Boat serves me for a House; I work in it in the Day, and I sleep in it in the Night; and what I get, I lay down upon that Stone,* says he, shewing me a broad Stone on the other Side of the Street, a good way from his House, *and then,* says he, *I halloo, and call to them till I make them hear; and they come and fetch it.*

6. Bow was the eastern suburb on the river Lea, Bromley was another market town familiar to Defoe, and Blackwall Stairs were slightly west of the mouth of the Lea. There was a myth that the plague spreading eastward would be stopped by the lime kilns at Bow.

Well Friend, says I, *but how can you get any Money as a Waterman? does any Body go by Water these Times? Yes Sir*, says he, *in the Way I am employ'd there does. Do you see there*, says he, *five Ships lie at Anchor*, pointing down the River, *a good way below the Town, and do you see*, says he, *eight or ten Ships lie at the Chain, there, and at Anchor yonder*, pointing above the Town. *All those Ships have Families on board, of their Merchants and Owners, and such like, who have lock'd themselves up, and live on board, close shut in, for fear of the Infection; and I tend on them to fetch Things for them, carry Letters, and do what is absolutely necessary, that they may not be obliged to come on Shore; and every Night I fasten my Boat on board one of the Ship's Boats, and there I sleep by my self, and blessed be God, I am preserv'd hitherto.*

Well, said I, *Friend, but will they let you come on board, after you have been on Shore here, when this is such a terrible Place, and so infected as it is?*

Why, as to that, said he, *I very seldom go up the Ship Side, but deliver what I bring to their Boat, or lie by the Side, and they hoist it on board; if I did, I think they are in no Danger from me, for I never go into any House on Shore, or touch any Body, no, not of my own Family; But I fetch Provisions for them.*

Nay, says I, *but that may be worse, for you must have those Provisions of some Body or other; and since all this Part of the Town is so infected, it is dangerous so much as to speak with any Body; for this Village*, said I, *is as it were, the Beginning of* London, *tho' it be at some Distance from it.*

That is true, added *he, but you do not understand me Right, I do not buy Provisions for them here; I row up to* Greenwich *and buy fresh Meat there, and sometimes I row down the River to* Woolwich[7] *and buy there; then I go to single Farm Houses on the Kentish Side, where I am known, and buy Fowls and Eggs, and Butter, and bring to the Ships, as they direct me, sometimes one, sometimes the other; I seldom come on Shore here; and I come now only to call to my Wife, and hear how my little Family do, and give them a little Money, which I receiv'd last Night.*

Poor Man! said I, *and how much hast thou gotten for them?*

I have gotten four Shillings, said he, *which is a great Sum, as things go now with poor Men; but they have given me a Bag of Bread too, and a Salt Fish and some Flesh; so all helps out.*

Well, said I, *and have you given it them yet?*

No, said he, *but I have called, and my Wife has answered, that she cannot come out yet, but in Half an Hour she hopes to come, and I am waiting for her: Poor Woman!* says he, *she is brought sadly down; she has*

---

7. Greenwich, a few miles east of London, is the site of Queen Henrietta Maria's "House of Delight," the palace designed by Inigo Jones for James I's queen, but completed for Charles I's. The National Maritime Museum is now there. Woolwich (pronounced "Wool-idge") is east of London and Greenwich, the only borough on both sides of the Thames.

a Swelling, and it is broke, and I hope she will recover;[8] *but I fear the Child will die; but it is the Lord!* ——Here he stopt, and wept very much.

Well, honest Friend, said I, *thou hast a sure Comforter, if thou hast brought thy self to be resign'd to the will of God, he is dealing with us all in Judgment.*

Oh, Sir, says he, *it is infinite Mercy, if any of us are spar'd; and who am I to repine!*

Sayest thou so, said I, *and how much less is my Faith than thine?* And here my Heart smote me, suggesting how much better this Poor Man's Foundation was, on which he staid in the Danger, than mine; that he had no where to fly; that he had a Family to bind him to Attendance, which I had not; and mine was meer Presumption, his a true Dependance, and a Courage resting on God: and yet, that he used all possible Caution for his Safety.

I turn'd a little way from the Man, while these Thoughts engaged me, for indeed, I could no more refrain from Tears than he.

At length, after some farther Talk, the poor Woman opened the Door, and call'd, *Robert, Robert*; he answered and bid her stay a few Moments, and he would come; so he ran down the common Stairs to his Boat, and fetch'd up a Sack in which was the Provisions he had brought from the Ships; and when he returned, he hallooed again; then he went to the great Stone which he shewed me, and emptied the Sack, and laid all out, every Thing by themselves, and then retired; and his Wife came with a little Boy to fetch them away; and he called, and said, such a Captain had sent such a Thing, and such a Captain such a Thing, and at the End adds, *God has sent it all, give Thanks to him.* When the Poor Woman had taken up all, she was so weak, she could not carry it at once in, *tho' the Weight was not much neither;* so she left the Biscuit which was in a little Bag, and left a little Boy to watch it till she came again.

Well, but says I to him, *did you leave her the four Shillings too, which you said was your Week's Pay?*

YES, YES, says he, *you shall hear her own it.* So he calls again, *Rachel, Rachel,*[9] which it seems was her Name, *did you take up the Money? YES,* said she. *How much was it,* said he? *Four Shillings and a Groat,* said she. *Well, well,* says he, *the Lord keep you all*; and so he turned to go away.

As I could not refrain contributing Tears to this Man's Story, so neither could I refrain my Charity for his Assistance; so I call'd him, *Hark thee Friend,* said I, *come hither; for I believe thou art in Health, that I may venture thee*; so I pull'd out my Hand, which was in my Pocket before, *here,* says I, *go and call thy* Rachel *once more, and give her a*

---

8. The breaking of swellings was considered a hopeful sign. See Hodges, "An Account of the First Rise, Progress, Symptoms, and Cure of the Plague Being the Substance of a Letter from Dr. Hodges to a Person of Quality," in *A Collection of very Valuable . . . Pieces* (25).

9. "Thus saith the Lord; A voice was heard in Ramah . . . Rachel weeping for her children refused to be comforted . . ." Jeremiah 31.15. Defoe, always a close reader of the Old Testament prophets, thought often of the book of Jeremiah as he wrote about the plague.

little more Comfort from me. God will never forsake a Family that trust in him as thou dost; so I gave him four other Shillings, and bade him go lay them on the Stone and call his Wife.

I have not Words to express the poor Man's thankfulness, neither could he express it himself; but by Tears running down his Face; he call'd his Wife, and told her God had mov'd the Heart of a Stranger upon hearing their Condition, to give them all that Money; and a great deal more such as that, he said to her. The Woman too, made Signs of the like Thankfulness, as well to Heaven, as to me, and joyfully pick'd it up; and I parted with no Money all that Year, that I thought better bestow'd.

I then ask'd the poor Man if the Distemper had not reach'd to *Greenwich*: He said it had not, till about a Fortnight before; but that then he feared it had; but that it was only at that End of the Town, which lay South towards *Deptford*-Bridge;[1] that he went only to a Butchers-Shop, and a Grocers, where he generally bought such Things as they sent him for; but was very careful.

I ask'd him then, how it came to pass, that those People who had so shut themselves up in the Ships, had not laid in sufficient Stores of all things necessary? He said some of them had, but on the other Hand, some did not come on board till they were frighted into it, and till it was too dangerous for them to go to the proper People, to lay in Quantities of Things, and that he waited on two Ships which he shewed me, that had lay'd in little or nothing but Biscuit Bread, and Ship Beer;[2] and that he had bought every Thing else almost for them. I ask'd him, if there was any more Ships that had separated themselves, as those had done. He told me yes, all the way up from the Point, right against *Greenwich*, to within the Shore of *Lime house* and *Redriff*,[3] all the Ships that could have Room, rid two and two in the middle of the Stream; and that some of them had several Families on Board, I ask'd him, if the Distemper had not reached them? He said he believ'd it had not, except two or three Ships, whose People had not been so watchful, to keep the Seamen from going on Shore as others had been; and he said it was a very fine Sight to see how the Ships lay up the Pool.[4]

When he said he was going over to *Greenwich*, as soon as the Tide began to come in. I ask'd if he would let me go with him, and bring me back, for that, I had a great mind to see how the Ships were ranged as he had told me? He told me if I would assure him on the Word of a Christian, and of an honest Man, that I had not the Distemper, he would: I assur'd him, that I had not, that it had pleased God to preserve me, That I liv'd in *White-Chapel*, but was too Impatient of being so

1. A pleasant town near Greenwich, its dock-yard was founded in 1513 by Henry VIII, and Francis Drake harbored his ship there.
2. Bread and beer made to be consumed on ships and thought to resist spoiling longer.
3. Settlements known for their shipyards, docks, and mariners. In 1689, Roger Cooper, a Redriff (Rothhithe) mariner, said he had known Defoe since childhood.
4. Slang name for Thames Harbor between Limehouse and Custom House Key where most of the ships unloaded.

long within Doors, and that I had ventured out so far for the Refreshment of a little Air; but that none in my House had so much as been touch't with it.

Well, Sir, says he, as your Charity has been mov'd to pity me and my poor Family; sure you cannot have so little pity left, as to put yourself into my Boat if you were not Sound in Health, which would be nothing less than killing me, and ruining my whole Family. The poor Man troubled me so much, when he spoke of his Family with such a sensible Concern, and in such an affectionate Manner, that I cou'd not satisfy my self at first to go at all. I told him, I would lay aside my Curiosity, rather than make him uneasy; tho' I was sure, and very thankful for it, that I had no more Distemper upon me, than the freshest Man in the World: Well, he would not have me put it off neither, but to let me see how confident he was, that I was just to him, he now importuned me to go; so when the Tide came up to his Boat, I went in, and he carry'd me to Greenwich: While he bought the Things which he had in his Charge to buy, I walk'd up to the Top of the Hill, under which the Town stands, and on the East-Side of the Town, to get a Prospect of the River: But it was a surprising Sight to see the Number of Ships which lay in Rows, two and two, and some Places, two or three such Lines in the Breadth of the River, and this not only up quite to the Town, between the Houses which we call Ratclif and Redriff, which they name the Pool, but even down the whole River, as far as the Head of Long-Reach,[5] which is as far as the Hills give us Leave to see it.

I cannot guess at the Number of Ships, but I think there must be several Hundreds of Sail; and I could not but applaud the Contrivance, for ten thousand People, and more, who attended Ship Affairs, were certainly sheltered here from the Violence of the Contagion, and liv'd very safe and very easy.

I returned to my own Dwelling very well satisfied with my Days Journey, and particularly with the poor Man; also I rejoyced to see that such little Sanctuaries were provided for so many Families, in a Time of such Desolation. I observ'd also, that as the Violence of the Plague had encreased, so the Ships which had Families on Board, remov'd and went farther off, till, as I was told, some went quite away to Sea, and put into such Harbours, and safe Roads on the North Coast, as they could best come at.

But it was also true, that all the People, who thus left the Land, and liv'd on Board the Ships, were not entirely safe from the Infection, for many died, and were thrown over board into the River, some in Coffins, and some, as I heard, without Coffins, whose Bodies were seen sometimes to drive up and down, with the Tide in the River.

But I believe, I may venture to say, that in those Ships which were thus infected, it either happened where the People had recourse to them

5. The Gravesend curve of the river. Ships departing the Thames and England stopped at Gravesend for customs clearance.

too late, and did not fly to the Ship till they had stayed too long on Shore, and had the Distemper upon them, tho' perhaps, they might not perceive it, and so the Distemper did not come to them, on Board the Ships, but they really carried it with them; OR it was in these Ships, where the poor Waterman said they had not had Time to furnish themselves with Provisions, but were obliged to send often on Shore to buy what they had Occasion for, or suffered Boats to come to them from the Shore; and so the Distemper was brought insensibly among them.

And here I cannot but take notice that the strange Temper of the People of *London* at that Time contributed extremely to their own Destruction. The Plague began, as I have observed, at the other End of the Town, namely, in *Long-Acre, Drury-Lane,* &c. and came on towards the City very gradually and slowly. It was felt at first in *December*, then again in *February*, then again in *April*, and always but a very little at a Time; then it stopt till *May*, and even the last Week in *May*, there was but 17, and all at that End of the Town; and all this while, even so long, as till there died above 3000 a-Week; yet had the People in *Redriff*, and in *Wapping*, and *Ratcliff* on both Sides the River, and almost all *Southwark Side*, a mighty Fancy, that they should not be visited, or at least that it would not be so violent among them. Some People fancied, the smell of the Pitch and Tar, and such other things, as Oil and Rosin, and Brimstone,[6] which is so much used by all Trades relating to Shipping, would preserve them. Others argued it, because it was in its extreamest Violence in *Westminster*, and the Parishes of St. *Giles's* and St. *Andrew's*, &c. and began to abate again, before it came among them, which was true indeed, in Part: *For Example*.

From the 8th to the 15th of *August*.

				Total this Week.
St. *Giles's in the Fields*	242	*Stepney* ——	197	
		St. *Mag. Bermondsey*	24	4030
Cripplegate	886	*Rotherhith* — —	3	

From the 15th to the 22d of *August*.

				Total this Week.
St. *Giles's in the Fields*	175	*Stepney* — —	273	
		St. *Mag. Bermondsey*	36	5319
Cripplegate	847	*Rotherhith* ——	2	

N.B. That it was observ'd the Numbers mention'd in *Stepney* Parish, at that time, were generally all on that Side where *Stepney* Parish joined to *Shoreditch*, which we now call *Spittle-fields*, where the Parish of *Stepney*, comes up to the very Wall of *Shoreditch* Church-Yard, and the Plague at this Time was abated at St. *Giles's in the Fields*, and raged most violently in *Cripplegate, Bishopsgate* and *Shoreditch* Parishes, but

6. Sulfur.

there was not 10 People a-Week that died of it in all that Part of *Stepney* Parish, which takes in *Lime-House*, *Ratcliff-high-way*, and which are now the Parishes of *Shadwell* and *Wapping*, even to St. *Katherines* by the Tower, till after the whole Month of *August* was expired; but they paid for it afterwards, as I shall observe by and by.

This, I say, made the People of *Redriff* and *Wapping*, *Ratcliff* and *Lime-House* so secure, and flatter themselves so much with the Plague's going off, without reaching them, that they took no Care, either to fly into the Country, or shut themselves up; nay, so far were they from stirring, that they rather receiv'd their Friends and Relations from the City into their Houses; and several from other Places really took Sanctuary in that Part of the Town, as a Place of Safety, and as a Place which they thought God would pass over and not visit as the rest was visited.

And this was the Reason, that when it came upon them they were more surprized, more unprovided and more at a Loss what to do than they were in other Places, for when it came among them really, and with Violence, as it did indeed, in *September* and *October*, there was then no stirring out into the Country, no Body would suffer a Stranger to come near them, no nor near the Towns where they dwelt; and as I have been told, several that wandred into the Country on *Surry* Side were found starv'd to Death in the Woods and Commons, that Country being more open and more woody, than any other Part so near *London*; especially about *Norwood*, and the Parishes of *Camberwell*, *Dullege*, and *Lusum*,[7] where it seems no Body durst relieve the poor distress'd People for fear of the Infection.

This Notion having, as I said, prevailed with the People in that Part of the Town, was in Part the Occasion, *as I said before*, that they had Recourse to Ships for their Retreat; and where they did this early, and with Prudence, furnishing themselves so with Provisions, that they had no need to go on Shore for Supplies, or suffer Boats to come on Board to bring them; I say where they did so they had certainly the safest Retreat of any People whatsoever: But the Distress was such, that People ran on Board in their Fright without Bread to eat, and some into Ships, that had no Men on Board to remove them farther off, or to take the Boat and go down the River to buy Provisions where it might be done safely; and these often suffered, and were infected on board as much as on Shore.

As the richer Sort got into Ships, so the lower Rank got into Hoys, Smacks, Lighters,[8] and Fishing boats; and many, especially Watermen,

7. Defoe knew Surrey well; his brother-in-law Samuel Tuffley owned property in Croyden, south of London. Norwood was at the edge of the Great North Wood, property of the Archbishop of Canterbury and reputed to be a dangerous place. The woods stretched from Camberwell to Croyden. Dullege is a phonetic spelling of Dulwich, a village south of Camberwell that, according to Defoe's *Tour*, was a holiday spot for "the common people."

8. Hoys were small ships rigged as sloops and used to carry passengers and freight short distance. Smacks were single-masted ships rigged like sloops and principally used for fishing. Lighters were flat-bottomed barges used to lighten or unload ships too large or heavy for parts of rivers or harbors.

lay in their Boats; but those made sad Work of it, especially the latter, for going about for Provision, and perhaps to get their Subsistence, the Infection got in among them and made a fearful Havock; many of the Watermen died alone in their Wherries, as they rid at their Roads,[9] as well above-Bridge as below, and were not found sometimes till they were not in Condition for any Body to touch or come near them.

Indeed the Distress of the People at this Sea-faring End of the Town was very deplorable, and deserved the greatest Commiseration: But alas! this was a Time when every one's private Safety lay so near them, that they had no Room to pity the Distresses of others; for every one had Death, as it were, at his Door, and many even in their Families, and knew not what to do, or whither to fly.

This, I say, took away all Compassion; self Preservation indeed appear'd here to be the first Law. For the Children ran away from their Parents, as they languished in the utmost Distress: And in some Places, tho' not so frequent as the other, Parents did the like to their Children; nay, some dreadful Examples there were, and particularly two in one Week of distressed Mothers, raveing and distracted, killing their own Children; one whereof was not far off from where I dwelt; the poor lunatick Creature not living herself long enough to be sensible of the Sin of what she had done, much less to be punish'd for it.

It is not indeed to be wondred at, for the Danger of immediate Death to ourselves, took away all Bowels of Love, all Concern for one another: I speak in general, for there were many Instances of immovable Affection, Pity, and Duty in many, and some that came to my Knowledg; that is to say, by here-say:

For I shall not take upon me to vouch the Truth of the Particulars.

To introduce one, let me first mention, that one of the most deplorable Cases, in all the present Calamity, was, that of Women with Child; who when they came to the Hour of their Sorrows, and their Pains came upon them, cou'd neither have help of one Kind or another; neither Midwife or Neighbouring Women to come near them; most of the Midwives were dead; especially, of such as serv'd the poor; and many, if not all the Midwives of Note were fled into the Country: So that it was next to impossible for a poor Woman that cou'd not pay an immoderate Price to get any Midwife to come to her, and if they did, those they cou'd get were generally unskilful and ignorant Creatures; and the Consequence of this was, that a most unusual and incredible Number of Women were reduc'd to the utmost distress. Some were deliver'd and spoil'd by the rashness and ignorance of those who pretended to lay them. Children without Number, were, I might say murthered by the same, but a more justifiable ignorance, pretending they would save the Mother, whatever became of the Child; and many Times, both Mother and Child were

9. Wherries were light rowboats or even barges so-called because of their rapid speed. Here Defoe shows his familiarity with boatmen's slang. "Roads" were sheltered places near the shore where boats could be anchored safely; they used "at road" to mean "riding at anchor."

lost in the same Manner; and especially, where the Mother had the Distemper, there no Body would come near them, and both sometimes perish'd: Sometimes the Mother has died of the Plague; and the Infant, it may be half born, or born but not parted from the Mother. Some died in the very Pains of their Travel,[1] and not deliver'd at all; and so many were the Cases of this Kind, that it is hard to Judge of them.

Something of it will appear in the unusual Numbers which are put into the Weekly Bills (tho' I am far from allowing them to be able to give any Thing of a full Account) under the Articles of

> *Child-Bed.*
> *Abortive* and *Stilborn.*
> *Chrisoms* and *Infants.*

Take the Weeks in which the Plague was most violent, and compare them with the Weeks before the Distemper began, even in the same Year: *For Example:*

		Child bed.	Abort.	Stil-born.
	Jan. 3 to *Jan.* 10	— 7	— 1	— 13
	to 17	— 8	— 6	— 11
	to 24	— 9	— 5	— 15
	to 31	— 3	— 2	— 9
From	*Jan.* 31 to *Feb.* 7	— 3	— 3	— 8
	to 14	— 6	— 2	— 11
	to 21	— 5	— 2	— 13
	to 28	— 2	— 2	— 10
	Feb. 7 to *March* 7	— 5	— 1	— 10
		48	— 24	— 100
	Aug. 1 to *Aug.* 8	— 25	— 5	— 11
	to 15	— 23	— 6	— 8
	to 22	— 28	— 4	— 4
	to 29	— 40	— 6	— 10
From	*Aug.* 1 to *Sept.* 5	— 38	— 2	— 11
	to 12	— 39	— 23	— 00
	to 19	— 42	— 5	— 17
	to 26	— 42	— 6	— 10
	Aug. 1 to *Octob.* 3	— 14	— 4	— 9
		291	— 61	— 80

To the Disparity of these Numbers, is to be considered and allow'd for, that according to our usual Opinion, who were then upon the Spot, there were not one third of the People in the Town, during the Months of *August* and *September*, as were in the Months of *January* and *Feb-*

1. Travail.

ruary: In a Word, the usual Number that used to die of these three Articles; and as I hear, did die of them the Year before, was thus:

$$1664 \begin{cases} \textit{Child-bed.} \ — \quad — \ 189 \\ \textit{Abortive} \text{ and } \textit{Stil-born.} \ \underline{458} \end{cases} \quad 1665 \begin{cases} \textit{Child-bed.} \ — \ — \ 625 \\ \textit{Abort. \& Stil-born.} \ \underline{617}^2 \end{cases}$$

$$\qquad\qquad\qquad 647 \qquad\qquad\qquad\qquad\qquad\qquad 1242$$

This inequallity, I say, is exceedingly augmented, when the Numbers of People are considered: I pretend not to make any exact Calculation of the Numbers of People, which were at this Time in the City; but I shall make a probable Conjecture at that part by and by: What I have said now, is to explain the misery of those poor Creatures above; so that it might well be said as in the Scripture. *Wo! be to those who are with Child; and to those which give suck in that Day.* [3] For indeed, it was a Woe to them in particular.

I was not conversant in many particular Families where these things happen'd; but the Out-cries of the miserable were heard afar off. As to those who were with Child, we have seen some Calculation made: 291 Women dead in Child bed in nine Weeks; out of one third Part of the Number, of whom there usually dy'd in that Time, but 48 of the same Disaster. Let the Reader calculate the Proportion.

There is no Room to doubt, but the Misery of those that gave Suck, was in Proportion as great. Our Bills of Mortality cou'd give but little Light in this; yet, some it did, there were several more than usual starv'd at Nurse, But this was nothing: The Misery was, where they were (*1st*) starved for want of a Nurse, the Mother dying, and all the Family and the Infants found dead by them, meerly for want; and if I may speak my Opinion, I do believe, that many hundreds of Poor helpless Infants perish'd in this manner. (*2dly*) Not starved (but poison'd) by the Nurse, Nay even where the Mother has been Nurse, and having receiv'd the Infection, has poison'd, that is, infected the Infant with her Milk, even before they knew they were infected themselves; nay, and the Infant has dy'd in such a Case before the Mother. I cannot but remember to leave this Admonition upon Record, if ever such another dreadful Visitation should happen in this City; that all Women that are with Child or that give Suck should be gone, if they have any possible Means out of the Place; because their Misery if infected, will so much exceed all other Peoples.

I could tell here dismal Stories of living Infants being found sucking the Breasts of their Mothers, or Nurses, after they have been dead of the Plague. Of a Mother, in the Parish where I liv'd, who having a Child that was not well, sent for an Apothecary to View the Child, and when he came, as the Relation goes, was giving the Child suck at her Breast,

---

2. Defoe has inadvertently erred in the figures for 1664. They were: childbed 250; abortive and stillborn 503; therefore, the increases were not quite as great as he says. In the year of the plague 48,737 women and 48,569 men died (Edward Brayley, *A Journal of the Plague Year* [London, 1839] 154–55).

3. Matthew 24.19.

and to all Appearance, was her self very well: But when the Apothecary came close to her, he saw the Tokens upon that Breast, with which she was suckling the Child. He was surpriz'd enough to be sure; but not willing to fright the poor Woman too much, he desired she would give the Child into his Hand; so he takes the Child, and going to a Cradle in the Room lays it in, and opening its Cloths, found the Tokens upon the Child too, and both dy'd before he cou'd get Home, to send a preventative Medicine to the Father of the Child, to whom he had told their Condition; whether the Child infected the Nurse-Mother, or the Mother the Child was not certain, but the last the most likely.

Likewise of a Child brought Home to the Parents from a Nurse[4] that had dy'd of the Plague; yet, the tender Mother would not refuse to take in her Child, and lay'd it in her Bosom, by which she was infected, and dy'd with the Child in her Arms dead also.

It would make the hardest Heart move at the Instances that were frequently found of tender Mothers, tending and watching with their dear Children, and even dying before them, and sometimes taking the Distemper from them, and dying when the Child, for whom the affectionate Heart had been sacrificed, has got over it and escap'd.

The like of a Tradesman in *East-Smith-field*, whose Wife was big with Child of her first Child; and fell in Labour, having the Plague upon her: He cou'd neither get Midwife to assist her, or Nurse to tend her; and two Servants which he kept fled both from her. He ran from House to House like one distracted, but cou'd get no help; the utmost he could get was, that a Watchman who attended at an infected House shut up, promis'd to send a Nurse in the Morning: The poor Man with his Heart broke, went back, assisted his Wife what he cou'd, acted the part of the Midwife; brought the Child dead into the World; and his Wife in about an Hour dy'd in his Arms, where he held her dead Body fast till the Morning, when the Watchman came and brought the Nurse as he had promised; and coming up the Stairs, for he had left the Door open, or only latched: They found the Man sitting with his dead Wife in his Arms; and so overwhelmed with Grief, that he dy'd in a few Hours after, without any Sign of the Infection upon him, but meerly sunk under the Weight of his Grief.

I have heard also of some, who on the Death of their Relations, have grown stupid with the insupportable Sorrow, and of one in particular, who was so absolutely overcome with the Pressure upon his Spirits, that by Degrees, his Head sunk into his Body, so between his Shoulders, that the Crown of his Head was very little seen above the Bones of his Shoulders; and by Degrees, loseing both Voice and Sense, his Face looking forward, lay against his Collar-Bone, and cou'd not be kept up any otherwise, unless held up by the Hands of other People; and the poor Man

4. Many seventeenth- and eighteenth-century women hired wet nurses for their babies. In *Conjugal Lewdness* (1727), Defoe condemned the practice as dangerous and motivated by vanity.

never came to himself again, but languished near a Year in that Condition and died: Nor was he ever once seen to lift up his Eyes, or to look upon any particular Object.

I cannot undertake to give any other than a Summary of such Passages as these, because it was not possible to come at the Particulars, where sometimes the whole Families, where such Things happen'd, were carry'd off by the Distemper: But there were innumerable Cases of this Kind, which presented to the Eye, and the Ear; even in passing along the Streets, as I have hinted above, nor is it easy to give any Story of this, or that Family, which there was not divers parallel Stories to meet with of the same Kind.

But as I am now talking of the Time, when the Plague rag'd at the Eastern-most Part of the Town; how for a long Time the People of those Parts had flattered themselves that they should escape; and how they were surprized, when it came upon them as it did; for indeed, it came upon them like an armed Man, when it did come. I say, this brings me back to the three poor Men, who wandered from *Wapping*, not knowing whether to go, or what to do, and who I mention'd before; one a Biscuit-Baker, one a Sail-Maker, and the other a Joiner; all of *Wapping*, or thereabouts.

The Sleepiness and Security of that Part as I have observ'd, was such; that they not only did not shift for themselves as others did; but they boasted of being safe, and of Safety being with them; and many People fled out of the City, and out of the infected Suburbs, to *Wapping*, *Ratcliff*, *Lime-house*, *Poplar*, and such Places, as to Places of Security; and it is not at all unlikely, that their doing this, help'd to bring the Plague that way faster, than it might otherwise have come. For tho' I am much for Peoples flying away and emptying such a Town as this, upon the first Appearance of a like Visitation, and that all People that have any possible Retreat, should make use of it in Time, and begone; yet, I must say, when all that will fly are gone, those that are left and must stand it, should stand stock still where they are, and not shift from one End of the Town, or one Part of the Town to the other; for that is the Bane and Mischief of the whole, and they carry the Plague from House to House in their very Clothes.

Wherefore, were we ordered to kill all the Dogs and Cats: But because as they were domestick Animals, and are apt to run from House to House, and from Street to Street; so they are capable of carrying the Effluvia or Infectious Steams of Bodies infected, even in their Furrs and Hair; and therefore, it was that in the beginning of the Infection, an Order was published by the Lord Mayor, and by the Magistrates, according to the Advice of the Physicians; that all the Dogs and Cats should be imediately killed, and an Officer was appointed for the Execution.

It is incredible, if their Account is to be depended upon, what a prodigious Number of those Creatures were destroy'd: I think they talk'd of forty thousand Dogs, and five times as many Cats, few Houses being without a Cat, and some having several, and sometimes five or six in a House. All possible Endeavours were us'd also to destroy the Mice and Rats, especially the latter; by laying Rats Bane, and other Poisons for them, and a prodigious multitude of them were also destroy'd.

I often reflected upon the unprovided Condition, that the whole Body of the People were in at the first coming of this Calamity upon them, and how it was for Want of timely entring into Measures, and Managements, as well publick as private, that all the Confusions that followed were brought upon us;[5] and that such a prodigious Number of People sunk in that Disaster, which if proper Steps had been taken, might, Providence concurring, have been avoided, and which, if Posterity think fit, they may take a Caution, and Warning from: But I shall come to this Part again.

I come back to my three Men: Their Story has a Moral in every Part of it, and their whole Conduct, and that of some who they join'd with, is a Pattern for all poor men to follow, or Women either, if ever such a Time comes again; and if there was no other End in recording it, I thing this a very just one, whether my Account be exactly according to Fact or no.

Two of them are said to be Brothers, the one an old Soldier, but now a Biscuit Baker; the other a lame Sailor, but now a Sail-Maker; the Third a Joiner. Says John the Biscuit Baker, one Day to Thomas his Brother, the Sail-maker, *Brother* Tom, *what will become of us? The Plague grows hot in the City, and encreases this way: What shall we do?*

Truly, says *Thomas, I am at a great Loss what to do, for I find, if it comes down into* Wapping, *I shall be turn'd out of my Lodging:* And thus they began to talk of it beforehand.

John, *Turn'd out of your Lodging,* Tom! *if you are, I don't know who will take you in; for People are so afraid of one another now, there's no getting a Lodging anywhere.*

Tho. *Why? The People where I lodge are good civil People, and have Kindness enough for me too; but they say I go abroad every Day to my Work, and it will be dangerous; and they talk of locking themselves up, and letting no Body come near them.*

John, *Why, they are in the right to be sure, if they resolve to venture staying in Town.*

Tho. *Nay, I might e'en resolve to stay within Doors too, for, except a Suit of Sails that my Master has in Hand, and which I am just a finishing, I am like to get no more Work a great while; there's no Trade stirs now; Workmen and Servants are turned off every where, so that I might be glad to be lock'd up too: But I do not see they will be willing to consent to that, any more than to the other.*

John, *Why, what will you do then Brother? and what shall I do? for I am almost as bad as you; the People where I lodge are all gone into the*

---

5. Defoe urged prompt, strong action in his journalistic writings on the plague as well as in his fiction.

Country but a Maid, and she is to go next Week, and to shut the House quite up, so that I shall be turn'd a drift to the wide World before you, and I am resolved to go away too, if I knew but where to go.

Tho. We were both distracted we did not go away at first, then we might ha' travelled any where; there's no stirring now; we shall be starv'd if we pretend to go out of Town; they won't let us have Victuals, no, not for our Money, nor let us come into the Towns, much less into their Houses.

John, And that which is almost as bad, I have but little Money to help my self with neither.

Tho. As to that we might make shift; I have a little, tho' not much; but I tell you there's no stirring on the Road. I know a Couple of poor honest Men in our Street have attempted to travel, and at Barnet, or Whetson,[6] or there about, the People offered to fire at them if they pretended to go forward; so they are come back again quite discourag'd.

John, I would have ventured their Fire, if I had been there; If I had been denied Food for my Money they should ha' seen me take it before their Faces; and if I had tendred Money for it, they could not have taken any Course with me by Law.

Tho. You talk your old Soldier's Language, as if you were in the Low-Countries now, but this is a serious thing. The People have good Reason to keep any Body off, that they are not satisfied are sound, at such a Time as this; and we must not plunder them.

John, No Brother, you mistake the Case, and mistake me too, I would plunder no Body; but for any Town upon the Road to deny me Leave to pass thro' the Town in the open High-Way, and deny me Provisions for my Money, is to say the Town has a Right to starve me to Death, which cannot be true.

Tho. But they do not deny you Liberty to go back again from whence you came, and therefore they do not starve you.

John, But the next Town behind me will by the same Rule deny me leave to go back, and so they do starve me between them; besides there is no Law to prohibit my travelling wherever I will on the Road.

Tho. But there will be so much Difficulty in disputing with them at every Town on the Road, that it is not for poor Men to do it, or to undertake it at such a Time as this is especially.

John, Why Brother? Our Condition at this Rate is worse than any Bodies else; for we can neither go away nor stay here; I am of the same Mind with the Lepers of Samaria,[7] If we stay here we are sure to die; I mean especially, as you and I are stated, without a Dwelling-House of our own, and without Lodging in any Bodies else; there is no lying in the Street at such a Time as this; we had as good go into the Dead-Cart at

6. On the Great North Road.

7. The four lepers came to the gates of Samaria and weighed starving there, entering the besieged and starving city, or surrendering to the enemy Syrians. They chose the last and found the Syrians fled but abundant supplies left behind (2 Kings 7.3–9).

once: *Therefore I say*, if we stay here we are sure to die, *and if we go away* we can but die: *I am resolv'd to be gone.*

Tho. *You will go away: Whither will you go? and what can you do? I would as willingly go away as you, if I knew whither: But we have no Acquaintance, no Friends. Here we were born, and here we must die.*

John, *Look you* Tom, *the whole Kingdom is my Native Country as well as this Town. You may as well say, I must not go out of my House if it is on Fire, as that I must not go out of the Town I was born in, when it is infected with the Plague. I was born in* England, *and have a Right to live in it if I can.*

Tho. *But you know every vagrant Person*[8] *may by the Laws of* England, *be taken up, and pass'd back to their last legal Settlement.*

John, *But how shall they make me vagrant; I desire only to travel on, upon my lawful Occasions.*

Tho. *What lawful Occasions can we pretend to travel, or rather wander upon, they will not be put off with Words.*

John, *Is not flying to save our Lives, a Lawful Occasion! and do they not all know that the Fact is true: We cannot be said to dissemble.*

Tho. *But suppose they let us pass, Whither shall we go?*

John, *Any where to save our Lives: It is Time enough to consider that when we are got out of this Town. If I am once out of this dreadful Place I care not where I go.*

Tho. *We shall be driven to great Extremities. I know not what to think of it.*

John, *Well* Tom, *consider of it a little.*

This was about the Beginning of *July*, and tho' the Plague was come forward in the West and North Parts of the Town, yet all *Wapping*, as I have observed before, and *Redriff*, and *Ratcliff*, and *Lime-House*, and *Poplar*, in short, *Deptford* and *Greenwich*, all both Sides of the River from the *Hermitage*,[9] and from over against it, quite down to *Blackwall*, was intirely free, there had not one Person died of the Plague in all *Stepney* Parish, and not one on the South Side of *White Chappel* Road, no, not in any Parish; and yet the Weekly Bill was that very Week risen up to 1006.

It was a Fortnight after this, before the two Brothers met again, and then the Case was a little altered, and the Plague was exceedingly advanced, and the Number greatly encreased, the Bill was up at 2785, and prodigiously encreasing, tho' still both Sides of the River, as below, kept pretty well: But some began to die in *Redriff*, and about five or six in *Ratclif-High-Way*, when the Sail Maker came to his Brother *John*, express, and in some Fright, for he was absolutely warn'd out of his

---

8. Vagrancy laws were harsh and rather arbitrarily applied. Occasionally they were extended to include such legitimate occupations as traveling theater companies. Vagrants could be whipped, imprisoned, and forcibly carted to another parish.

9. The southwestern entrance to the London Docks, formerly a brewhouse called the Hermitage because "an Hermit sometime being there" (Stowe, A *Survey of London* [1603]).

Lodging, and had only a Week to provide himself. His Brother *John* was in as bad a Case, for he was quite out, and had only beg'd Leave of his Master the Biscuit Baker to lodge in an Out-House[1] belonging to his Work-house, where he only lay upon Straw, with some Biscuit Sacks, or Bread-Sacks, as they call'd them, laid upon it, and some of the same Sacks to cover him.

Here they resolved, seeing all Employment being at an End, and no Work, or Wages to be had, they would make the best of their Way to get out of the Reach of the dreadful Infection; and being as good Husbands as they could, would endeavour to live upon what they had as long as it would last, and then work for more, if they could get Work any where, of any Kind, let it be what it would.

While they were considering to put this Resolution in Practice, in the best Manner they could, the third Man, who was acquainted very well with the Sail Maker, came to know of the Design, and got Leave to be one of the Number, and thus they prepared to set out.

It happened that they had not an equal share of Money, but as the Sail-maker, who had the best Stock, was besides his being Lame, the most unfit to expect to get any thing by Working in the Country, so he was content that what Money they had should all go into one publick Stock, on Condition, that whatever any one of them could gain more than another, it should, without any grudging, be all added to the same publick Stock.

They resolv'd to load themselves with as little Baggage as possible, because they resolv'd at first to travel on Foot; and to go a great way, that they might, if possible, be effectually Safe; and a great many Consultations they had with themselves, before they could agree about what Way they should travel, which they were so far from adjusting, that even to the Morning they set out, they were not resolv'd on it.

At last the Seaman put in a Hint that determin'd it; First, says he, the Weather is very hot, and therefore I am for travelling North, that we may not have the Sun upon our Faces and beating on our Breasts, which will heat and suffocate us; and I have been told, says he, that it is not good to over-heat our Blood at a Time when, for ought we know, the Infection may be in the very Air. In the next Place, says he, I am for going the Way that may be contrary to the Wind as it may blow when we set out, that we may not have the Wind blow the Air of the City on our Backs as we go. These two Cautions were approv'd of; if it could be brought so to hit, that the Wind might not be in the South when they set out to go North.

John the Baker, who had been a Soldier, then put in his Opinion; First, says he, we none of us expect to get any Lodging on the Road, and it will be a little too hard to lie just in the open Air; tho' it be warm Weather, yet it may be wet, and damp, and we have a double Reason

---

1. A small building adjoining the main house or building and used as a toolhouse, stable, or for some other similar purpose.

to take care of our Healths at such a time as this; and therefore, says he, you, Brother *Tom*, that are a Sail-maker, might easily make us a little Tent, and I will undertake to set it up every Night, and take it down, and a Fig for all the Inns in *England*; if we have a good Tent over our Heads; we shall do well enough.

The Joyner oppos'd this, and told them, let them leave that to him, he would undertake to build them a House every Night with his Hatchet and Mallet, tho' he had no other Tools, which should be fully to their satisfaction, and as good as a Tent.

The Soldier and the Joyner disputed that Point some time, but at last the Soldier carry'd it for a Tent; the only Objection against it was, that it must be carry'd with them, and that would encrease their Baggage too much, the Weather being hot; but the Sail-maker had a piece of good Hap fall in [2] which made that easie, for, his Master who he work'd for having a Rope-Walk [3] as well as his Sail-making Trade, had a little poor Horse that he made no use of then, and being willing to assist the three honest Men, he gave them the Horse for the carrying their Baggage; also for a small Matter of three Days Work that his Man did for him before he went, he let him have an old Top-gallant Sail that was worn out, but was sufficient and more than enough to make a very good Tent: The Soldier shew'd how to shape it, and they soon by his Direction made their Tent, and fitted it with Poles or Staves for the purpose, and thus they were furnish'd for their Journey; *viz*. three Men, one Tent, one Horse, one Gun, for the Soldier would not go without Arms, for now he said he was no more a Biscuit-Baker, but a Trooper.

The Joyner had a small Bag of Tools, such as might be useful if he should get any Work abroad, as well for their Subsistence as his own: What Money they had, they brought all into one publick Stock, and thus they began their Journey. It seems that in the Morning when they set out, the Wind blew as the Saylor said by his Pocket Compass, at N.W. by W. So they directed, or rather resolv'd to direct their Course N.W.

But then a Difficulty came in their Way, that as they set out from the hither end of *Wapping* near the *Hermitage*, and that the Plague was now very Violent, especially on the North side of the City, as in *Shoreditch* and *Cripplegate* Parish, they did not think it safe for them to go near those Parts; so they went away East through *Radcliff* High-way, as far as *Radcliff-Cross*, and leaving *Stepney* Church still on their Left-hand, being afraid to come up from *Radcliff-Cross* to *Mile-end*, because they must come just by the Church-yard, and because the Wind that seemed to blow more from the West, blow'd directly from the side of the City where the Plague was hottest. So I say, leaving *Stepney*, they fetched a long Compass, and going to *Poplar* and *Bromley*, came into the great Road just at *Bow*.

---

2. Luck came about.   3. Place where ropes are made.

Here the Watch plac'd upon *Bow* Bridge would have question'd them; but they crossing the Road into a narrow Way that turns out at the hither End of the Town of *Bow* to *Old-Ford*, avoided any Enquiry there, and travelled to *Old-Ford*.[4] The Constables every where were upon their Guard, not so much it seems to stop People passing by, as to stop them from taking up their Abode in their Towns, and withal because of a Report that was newly rais'd at that time, and that indeed was not very improbable, *viz*. That the poor People in *London* being distress'd and starv'd for want of Work, and by that means for want of Bread, were up in Arms, and had raised a Tumult, and that they would come out to all the Towns round to plunder for Bread. This, I say, was only a Rumour, and it was very well it was no more; but it was not so far off from being a Reality, as it has been thought, for in a few Weeks more the poor People became so Desperate by the Calamity they suffer'd, that they were with great difficulty kept from running out into the Fields and Towns, and tearing all in pieces where-ever they came; and, as I have observed before, nothing hinder'd them but that the Plague rag'd so violently, and fell in upon them so furiously, that they rather went to the Grave by Thousands than into the Fields in Mobs by Thousands: For in the Parts about the Parishes of St. *Sepulchres, Clerkenwell, Cripplegate, Bishopsgate* and *Shoreditch*, which were the Places where the Mob began to threaten, the Distemper came on so furiously, that there died in those few Parishes, even then, before the Plague was come to its height, no less than 5361 People in the first three Weeks in *August*, when at the same time, the Parts about *Wapping, Radcliffe*, and *Rotherhith*, were, as before describ'd, hardly touch'd, or but very lightly; so that in a Word, tho', as I said before, the good Management of the Lord Mayor and Justices did much to prevent the Rage and Desperation of the People from breaking out in Rabbles and Tumults, and in short, from the Poor plundering the Rich; I say, tho' they did much, the Dead Carts did more, for as I have said, that in five Parishes only there died above 5000 in 20 Days, so there might be probably three times that Number Sick all that time; for some recovered, and great Numbers fell sick every Day and died afterwards. Besides, I must still be allowed to say, that if the Bills of Mortality said five Thousand, I always believ'd it was near twice as many in reality; there being no room to believe that the Account they gave was right, or that indeed, they were, among such Confusions as I saw them in, in any Condition to keep an exact Account.

But to return to my Travellers; Here they were only examined, and as they seemed rather coming from the Country than from the City, they found the People the easier with them; that they talk'd to them, let them come into a publick House where the Constable and his Warders were, and gave them Drink and some Victuals, which greatly refreshed and encourag'd them; and here it came into their Heads to say, when they

---

4. A small town built at a popular ford of the river Lea. Here the main road from Essex, called Old Ford Road, entered London.

should be enquir'd of afterwards, not that they came from *London*, but that they came out of *Essex*.

To forward this little Fraud, they obtain'd so much Favour of the Constable at *Old-Ford*, as to give them a Certificate of their passing from Essex thro' that Village, and that they had not been at *London*; which tho' false in the common acceptation of *London* in the Country, yet was literally true; *Wapping* or *Radcliff* being no part either of the City or Liberty.

This Certificate directed to the next Constable that was at *Hummerton*, one of the Hamlets of the Parish of *Hackney*, was so serviceable to them, that it procured them not a free Passage there only, but a full Certificate of Health from a Justice of the Peace; who, upon the Constable's Application, granted it without much Difficulty; and thus they pass'd through the long divided Town of *Hackney*, (for it lay then in several separated Hamlets) and travelled on till they came into the great North Road on the top of *Stamford-Hill*.[5]

By this time they began to be weary, and so in the back Road from *Hackney* a little before it opened into the said great Road, they resolv'd to set up their Tent and encamp for the first Night; which they did accordingly, with this addition, that finding a Barn, or a Building like a Barn, and first searching as well as they could to be sure there was no Body in it, they set up their Tent, with the Head of it against the Barn; this they did also because the Wind blew that Night very high, and they were but young at such a way of Lodging, as well as at the managing their Tent.

Here they went to Sleep, but the Joyner, a grave and sober Man, and not pleased with their lying at this loose rate the first Night, could not sleep, and resolv'd, after trying to Sleep to no purpose, that he would get out, and taking the Gun in his Hand stand Centinel and Guard his Companions: So with the Gun in his Hand he walk'd to and again before the Barn, for that stood in the Field near the Road, but within the Hedge. He had not been long upon the Scout, but he heard a Noise of People coming on as if it had been a great Number, and they came on, as he thought, directly towards the Barn. He did not presently awake his Companions, but in a few Minutes more their Noise growing louder and louder, the Biscuit-Baker call'd to him and ask'd him what was the Matter, and quickly started out too: The other being the Lame Sailmaker and most weary, lay still in the Tent.

As they expected, so the People who they had heard, came on directly to the Barn, when one of our Travellers challenged, like Soldiers upon the Guard, with *Who comes there?* The People did not Answer immediately, but one of them speaking to another that was behind him, *Alas!*

5. A Middlesex landmark on the Great North Road. Burleigh House, the palace of the earl of Exeter built by William Cecil, Queen Elizabeth I's High Treasurer, stood there and gave visitors a fine view of the fens and a plain where horse races were held. Stamford, a prosperous town dating back to the Middle Ages, had been the home of architects Inigo Jones and the Adam brothers.

Alas! we are all disappointed, says *he, here are some People before us, the Barn is taken up.*

They all stopp'd upon that as under some Surprize, and it seems there was about Thirteen of them in all, and some Women among them: They consulted together what they should do, and by their Discourse our Travellers soon found they were poor distress'd People too like themselves, seeking Shelter and Safety; and besides, our Travellers had no need to be afraid of their coming up to disturb them; for as soon as they heard the Words, *Who comes there*, these could hear the Women say, *as if frighted, Do not go near them, how do you know but they may have the Plague?* And when one of the Men said, *Let us but speak to them*; the Women said, *No, don't by any means, we have escap'd thus far* by the Goodness of God, *do not let us run into Danger now, we beseech you.*

Our Travellers found by this that they were a good sober sort of People and flying for their Lives as they were; and, as they were encourag'd by it, so *John* said to the Joyner his Comrade, *Let us Encourage them too as much as we can*: So he called to them, *Hark ye good People* says the Joyner, we find by your Talk, that you are fleeing from the same dreadful Enemy as we are, do not be afraid of us, we are only three poor Men of us, if you are free from the Distemper you shall not be hurt by us; we are not in the Barn, but in a little Tent here in the outside, and we will remove for you, we can set up our Tent again immediately any where else; and upon this a Parly began between the Joyner, whose Name was *Richard*, and one of their Men, who said his Name was *Ford*.

Ford. And do you assure us that you are all Sound Men.

Rich. Nay, we are concern'd to tell you of it, that you may not be uneasy, or think your selves in Danger; but you see we do not desire you should put your selves into any Danger; and therefore I tell you, that as we have not made use of the Barn, so we will remove from it, that you may be Safe and we also.

Ford. That is very kind and charitable; But, if we have Reason to be satisfied that you are Sound and free from the Visitation, why should we make you remove now you are settled in your Lodging, and it may be are laid down to Rest? we will go into the Barn if you please, to rest our selves a while, and we need not disturb you.

Rich. Well, but you are more than we are, I hope you will assure us that you are all of you Sound too, for the Danger is as great from you to us, as from us to you.

Ford. Blessed be God that some do escape tho' it is but few; what may be our Portion still we know not, but hitherto we are preserved.

Rich. What part of the Town do you come from? Was the Plague come to the Places where you liv'd?

Ford. Ay ay, in a most frightful and terrible manner, or else we had not fled away as we do; but we believe there will be very few left alive behind us.

Rich. What Part do you come from?

Ford. We are most of us of *Cripplegate* Parish, only two or three of *Clerkenwell* Parish, but on the hither side.

Rich. How then was it that you came away no sooner?

Ford. We have been away some time, and kept together as well as we could at the hither End of *Islington,* where we got leave to lie in an old uninhabited House, and had some Bedding and Conveniencies of our own that we brought with us, but the Plague is come up into *Islington* too, and a House next Door to our poor Dwelling was Infected and shut up, and we are come away in a Fright.

Rich. And what Way are you going?

Ford. As our Lott shall cast us, we know not whither, but God will Guide those that look up to him.

They parlied no further at that time, but came all up to the Barn, and with some Difficulty got into it: There was nothing but Hay in the Barn, but it was almost full of that, and they accommodated themselves as well as they cou'd, and went to Rest; but our Travellers observ'd, that before they went to Sleep, an antient Man, who it seems was Father of one of the Women, went to Prayer with all the Company, recommending themselves to the Blessing and Direction of Providence, before they went to Sleep.

It was soon Day at that time of the Year; and as *Richard* the Joyner had kept Guard the first part of the Night, so *John* the Soldier Reliev'd him, and he had the Post in the Morning, and they began to be acquainted with one another. It seems, when they left *Islington,* they intended to have gone North away to *Highgate,* but were stop'd at *Holloway,*[6] and there they would not let them pass; so they cross'd over the Fields and Hills to the Eastward, and came out at the *Boarded-River,*[7] and so avoiding the Towns, they left *Hornsey* on the left Hand, and *Newington* on the right Hand, and came into the great Road about *Stamford-Hill* on that side, as the three Travellers had done on the other side: And now they had Thoughts of going over the River in the Marshes, and make forwards to *Epping* Forest,[8] where they hoped they should get leave to Rest. It seems they were not Poor, at least not so Poor as to be in Want; at least they had enough to subsist them moderately for two or three Months, when, as they said, they were in Hopes the cold Weather would check the Infection, or at least the Violence of it would have spent itself, and would abate, if it were only for want of People left alive to be Infected.

---

6. Three boroughs, Hornsey, St. Pancreas, and Islington, meet in the town of Highgate, which is four hundred feet above sea level. London is only eighty-six feet above sea level. Hollowell, (the modern spelling) is in the northern part of Islington, still on the Great North Road. Edward IV built a pesthouse there.

7. An artificial river that brought water to London. Wooden troughs made from broad boards carried the water.

8. Epping Forest, Essex, is still a vacation spot. In *A Tour* Defoe says that where it has not been "broken in upon" by enclosures or farming it shows "what the face of this island was before Roman time."

This was much the Fate of our three Travellers; only that they seemed to be the better furnish'd for Travelling, and had it in their View to go further off; for as to the first, they did not propose to go farther than one Day's Journey, that so they might have Intelligence every two or three Days how Things were at *London*.

But here our Travellers found themselves under an unexpected Inconvenience namely, that of their Horse, for by means of the Horse to carry their Baggage, they were obliged to keep in the Road, whereas the People of this other Band went over the Fields or Roads, Path or no Path, Way, or no Way, as they pleased; neither had they any Occasion to pass thro' any Town, or come near any Town, other than to buy such Things as they wanted for their necessary Subsistence, and in that indeed they were put to much Difficulty: Of which in its Place.

But our three Travellers were oblig'd to keep the Road, or else they must commit Spoil and do the Country a great deal of Damage in breaking down Fences and Gates, to go over enclosed Fields, which they were loth to do if they could help it.

Our three Travellers however had a great Mind to join themselves to this Company, and take their Lot with them; and after some Discourse, they laid aside their first Design which look'd Northward, and resolv'd to follow the other into *Essex*; so in the Morning they took up their Tent and loaded their Horse, and away they travelled all together.

They had some Difficulty in passing the Ferry at the River side, the Ferry-Man being afraid of them; but after some Parly at a Distance, the Ferry-Man was content to bring his Boat to a Place distant from the usual Ferry, and leave it there for them to take it; so putting themselves over, he directed them to leave the Boat, and he having another Boat, said he would fetch it again, which it seems however he did not do for above Eight Days.

Here giving the Ferry-Man Money before-hand, they had a supply of Victuals and Drink, which he brought and left in the Boat for them, but not without, as I said, having receiv'd the Mony before-hand. But now our Travellers were at a great Loss and Difficulty how to get the Horse over, the Boat being small and not fit for it, and at last cou'd not do it without unloading the Baggage, and making him swim over.

From the River they travelled towards the Forest, but when they came to *Walthamstow*[9] the People of that Town denied to admit them, as was the Case every where: The Constables and their Watchmen kept them off at a Distance, and Parly'd with them; they gave the same Account of themselves as before, but these gave no Credit to what they said, giving it for a Reason that two or three Companies had already come that Way and made the like Pretences, but that they had given several People the Distemper in the Towns where they had pass'd, and had been afterwards

9. The group continues to move north through Essex; Walthamstow is north of Chelmsford.

so hardly us'd by the Country, tho' with Justice too, as they had deserv'd; that about *Brent-Wood*[1] or that Way, several of them Perish'd in the Fields, whether of the Plague, or of mere Want and Distress, they could not tell.

This was a good Reason indeed why the People of *Walthamstow* shou'd be very cautious, and why they shou'd resolve not to entertain any Body that they were not well satisfied of. But as *Richard* the Joyner, and one of the other Men who parly'd with them told them, it was no Reason why they should block up the Roads, and refuse to let People pass thro' the Town, and who ask'd nothing of them, but to go through the Street: That if their People were afraid of them, they might go into their Houses and shut their Doors, they would neither show them Civility nor Incivility, but go on about their Business.

The Constables and Attendants, not to be perswaded by Reason, continued Obstinate, and wou'd hearken to nothing; so the two Men that talk'd with them went back to their Fellows, to consult what was to be done: It was very discouraging in the whole, and they knew not what to do for a good while: But at last *John* the Soldier and Biscuit-Baker considering a-while, Come, says he, leave the rest of the Parly to me; he had not appear'd yet, so he sets the Joyner *Richard* to Work to cut some Poles out of the Trees, and shape them as like Guns as he could, and in a little time he had five or six fair Muskets, which at a Distance would not be known; and about the Part where the Lock of a Gun is he caused them to wrap Cloths and Rags, such as they had, as Soldiers do in wet Weather, to preserve the Locks of their Pieces from Rust,[2] the rest was discolour'd with Clay or Mud, such as they could get; and all this while the rest of them sat under the Trees by his Direction, in two or three Bodies, where they made Fires at a good Distance from one another.

While this was doing, he advanc'd himself and two or three with him, and set up their Tent in the Lane within sight of the Barrier which the Town's Men had made, and set a Centinel just by it with the real Gun, the only one they had, and who walked to and fro with the Gun on his Shoulder, so as that the People of the Town might see them; also he ty'd the Horse to a Gate in the Hedge just by, and got some dry Sticks together and kindled a Fire on the other side of the Tent, so that the People of the Town cou'd see the Fire and the Smoak, but cou'd not see what they were doing at it.

After the Country People had look'd upon them very earnestly a great while, and by all that they could see, cou'd not but suppose that they were a great many in Company, they began to be uneasie, not for their

1. In *A Tour* Defoe says that there is little to be said for Brentwood, a small town northeast of London on the road to Chelmsford, except that it is a "large thorough-fair town, full of good inns, and chiefly maintained by the excessive multitude of carriers and passengers" on their way to London.

2. Defoe had fought with the duke of Monmouth's forces in 1685 in the rebellion against King James II. Throughout his life he was fascinated by the military and often wrote about it, as he did in his novel *Memoirs of a Cavalier* (1720).

going away, but for staying where they were; and above all perceiving they had Horses and Arms, for they had seen one Horse and one Gun at the Tent, and they had seen others of them walk about the Field on the inside of the Hedge, by the side of the Lane with their Muskets, as they took them to be, Shoulder'd: I say, upon such a Sight as this, you may be assured they were Alarm'd and terribly Frighted; and it seems they went to a Justice of the Peace to know what they should do; what the Justice advis'd them to I know not, but towards Evening they call'd from the Barrier, as above, to the Centinel at the Tent.

What do ye want? says John[3]

Why, what do ye intend to do? says the Constable.

To do, says John, *What wou'd you have us to do?*

Const. Why don't you be gone? what do you stay there for?

John. Why do you stop us on the King's Highway, and pretend to refuse us Leave to go on our Way?

Const. We are not bound to tell you our Reason, though we did let you know, it was because of the Plague.

John. We told you we were all sound, and free from the Plague, which we were not bound to have satisfied you of, and yet you pretend to stop us on the Highway.

Const. We have a Right to stop it up, and our own Safety obliges us to it; besides this is not the King's Highway, 'tis a Way upon Sufferance; you see here is a Gate, and if we do let People pass here, we make them pay Toll?[4]

John. We have a Right to seek our own Safety as well as you,[5] and you may see we are flying for our Lives, and 'tis very unchristian and unjust to stop us.

Const. You may go back from whence you came; we do not hinder you from that.

John. No, it is a stronger Enemy than you that keeps us from doing that; or else we should not ha' come hither.

Const. Well, you may go any other way then.

John. No, no: I suppose you see we are able to send you going, and all the People of your Parish, and come thro' your Town, when we will; but since you have stopt us here, we are content; you see, we have encamp'd here, and here we will live: we hope you will furnish us with Victuals.

---

3. It seems John was in the Tent, but hearing them call he steps out, and taking the Gun upon his Shoulder, talk'd to them as if he had been the Centinel plac'd there upon the Guard by some Officer that was his Superior [Defoe's note].

4. By the eighteenth century, the King's Highway was an abstract concept rather than the original four Great Roads. English people assumed a right of free passage, guaranteed to the monarch and all his subjects. The consta-

ble is insisting that the travelers were on one of the many lanes worn by local travel rather than on a recognized road.

5. The travelers shift ground and claim another "right." Defoe, John Locke, and many people of his time believed that certain rights were "natural," born in humankind. Among them were life, property, and the pursuit of happiness. Defoe went to prison for some of his defenses of these rights.

Const. We furnish you! What mean you by that?

John. Why you would not have us Starve, would you? If you stop us here, you must keep us.

Const. You will be ill kept at our Maintenance.

John. If you stint us, we shall make ourselves the better Allowance.

Const. Why you will not pretend to quarter upon us by Force, will you?

John. We have offer'd no Violence to you yet, why do you seem to oblige us to it? I am an old Soldier, and cannot starve, and if you think that we shall be obliged to go back for want of Provisions, you are mistaken.

Const. Since you threaten us, we shall take Care to be strong enough for you: I have Orders to raise the County upon you.

John. It is you that threaten, not we: And since you are for Mischief, you cannot blame us, if we do not give you time for it; we shall begin our March in a few Minutes.[6]

Const. What is it you demand of us?

John. At first we desir'd nothing of you, but Leave to go thro' the Town; we should have offer'd no Injury to any of you, neither would you have had any Injury or Loss by us. We are not Thieves, but poor People in distress, and flying from the dreadful Plague in *London*, which devours thousands every Week: We wonder how you could be so unmerciful!

Const. Self-preservation obliges us.

John. What! to shut up your Compassion in a Case of such Distress as this?

Const. Well, if you will pass over the Fields on your Left-hand, and behind that part of the Town, I will endeavour to have Gates open'd for you.

John. Our Horsemen cannot[7] pass with our Baggage that Way; it does not lead into the Road that we want to go; and why should you force us out of the Road? besides, you have kept us here all Day without any Provisions, but such as we brought with us; I think you ought to send us some Provisions for our Relief.

Const. If you will go another Way, we will send you some Provisions.

John. That is the way to have all the Towns in the County stop up the Ways against us.

Const. If they all furnish you with Food, what will you be the worse, I see you have Tents, you want no Lodging.

John. Well, what quantity of Provisions will you send us?

Const. How many are you?

John. Nay, we do not ask enough for all our Company, we are in three Companies; if you will send us Bread for twenty Men, and about

6. This frighted the Constable and the People that were with him, that they immediately chang'd their Note *[Defoe's note]*.

7. They had but one Horse among them *[Defoe's note]*.

six or seven Women for three Days, and shew us the Way over the Field you speak of, we desire not to put your People into any fear for us, we will go out of our Way to oblige you, tho' we are as free from Infection as you are.

Const. And will you assure us that your other People shall offer us no new Disturbance.

John. No, no, you may depend on it.

Const. You must oblige your self too that none of your People shall come a step nearer than where the Provisions we send you shall be set down.

John. I answer for it we will not.[8]

Accordingly they sent to the Place twenty Loaves of Bread, and three or four large pieces of good Beef, and opened some Gates thro' which they pass'd, but none of them had Courage so much as to look out to see them go, and, as it was Evening, if they had looked they cou'd not have seen them so as to know how few they were.

This was *John* the Soldier's Management. But this gave such an Alarm to the County, that had they really been two or three Hundred, the whole County would have been rais'd upon them, and they wou'd ha' been sent to Prison, or perhaps knock'd on the Head.

They were soon made sensible of this, for two Days afterwards they found several Parties of Horsemen and Footmen also about, in pursuit of three Companies of Men arm'd, *as they said,* with Muskets, who were broke out from *London,* and had the Plague upon them and that were not only spreading the Distemper among the People, but plundering the Country.[9]

As they saw now the Consequence of their Case, they soon see the Danger they were in, so they resolv'd by the Advice also of the old Soldier, to divide themselves again. *John* and his two Comrades with the Horse, went away as if towards *Waltham;* the other in two Companies, but all a little asunder, and went towards *Epping.*

The first Night they Encamp'd all in the Forest, and not far off of one another, but not setting up the Tent, lest that should discover them: On the other hand *Richard* went to work with his Axe and his Hatchet, and cutting down Branches of Trees, he built three Tents or Hovels, in which they all Encamp'd with as much Convenience as they could expect.

The Provisions they had had at *Walthamstow* serv'd them very plentifully this Night, and as for the next they left it to Providence; they had far'd so well with the old Soldier's Conduct, that they now willingly made him their leader; and the first of his Conduct appear'd to be very good: He told them that they were now at a proper Distance enough

8. Here he call'd to one of his Men, and bade him order Capt. *Richard* and his People to March the Lower Way on the Side of the Marshes, and meet them in the Forest; which was all a Sham, for they had no Captain *Richard,* or any such Company *[Defoe's note].*

[Defoe's text, prepared hastily to take advantage of concern over plague, has many printing lapses. There is no matching asterisk in the text for this note—*Editor.*]

9. Here again Defoe illustrates the power of rumor in times of crisis.

from *London*; that as they need not be immediately beholden to the County for Relief, so they ought to be as careful the Country did not infect them, as that they did not infect the Country; that what little Money they had they must be as frugal of as they could, that as he would not have them think of offering the Country any Violence, so they must endeavour to make the Sense of their Condition go as far with the Country as it could: They all referr'd themselves to his Direction; so they left their 3 Houses standing, and the next Day went away towards *Epping*; the Captain also, for so they now called him, and his two Fellow Travellers laid aside their Design of going to *Waltham*, and all went together.

When they came near *Epping* they halted, choosing out a proper Place in the open Forest, not very near the High-way, but not far out of it on the North-side, under a little cluster of low Pollard-Trees: [1] Here they pitched their little Camp, which consisted of three large Tents or Hutts made of Poles, which their Carpenter, and such as were his Assistants, cut down and fix'd in the Ground in a Circle, binding all the small Ends together at the Top, and thickning the sides with Boughs of Trees and Bushes, so that they were compleatly close and warm. They had besides this, a little Tent where the Women lay by themselves, and a Hutt to put the Horse in.

It happened that the next day, or next but one was Market-day at *Epping*; when Capt. *John*, and one of the other Men, went to Market, and bought some Provisions, that is to say Bread, and some Mutton and Beef; and two of the Women went separately, as if they had not belong'd to the rest, and bought more. *John* took the Horse to bring it Home, and the Sack (which the Carpenter carry'd his Tools in) to put it in: The Carpenter went to Work and made them Benches and Stools to sit on, such as the Wood he cou'd get wou'd afford, and a kind of a Table to dine on.

They were taken no Notice of for two or three Days, but after that, abundance of People ran out of the Town to look at them, and all the Country was alarmed about them. The People at first seem'd afraid to come near them, and on the other Hand they desir'd the People to keep off, for there was a Rumour that the Plague was at *Waltham*, and that it had been in *Epping* two or three Days So *John* called out to them not to come to them, *For*, says he, *we are all whole and sound People here, and we would not have you bring the Plague among us, nor pretend we brought it among you.*

After this the Parish Officers came up to them and parly'd with them at a Distance, and desir'd to know who they were, and by what Authority they pretended to fix their Stand at that Place? *John* answered very frankly, they were poor distressed People from *London*, who foreseeing the Misery they should be reduc'd to, if the Plague spread into the City, had fled out in time for their Lives, and having no Acquaintance or Rela-

1. Trees that have been polled or cut back so as to produce a thick growth of new branches at the cut.

tions to fly to, had first taken up at *Islington*, but the Plague being come into that Town, were fled further, and as they suppos'd that the People of *Epping* might have refus'd them coming into their Town, they had pitch'd their Tents thus in the open Field, and in the Forest, being willing to bear all the Hardships of such a disconsolate Lodging, rather than have any one think or be afraid that they should receive Injury by them.

At first the *Epping* People talk'd roughly to them, and told them they must remove; that this was no Place for them; and that they pretended to be Sound and Well, but that they might be infected with the Plague for ought they knew, and might infect the whole Country, and they cou'd not suffer them there.

John argu'd very calmly with them a great while, and told them, That *London* was the Place by which they, that is, the Townsmen of *Epping* and all the Country round them, subsisted, to whom they sold the produce of their Lands, and out of whom they made the Rent of their Farms; and to be so cruel to the Inhabitants of *London* or to any of those by whom they gain'd so much was very hard, and they would be loth to have it remembered hereafter, and have it told how barbarous, how unhospitable and how unkind they were to the People of *London*, when they fled from the Face of the most terrible Enemy in the World, that it would be enough to make the Name of an *Epping*-Man hateful thro' all the City, and to have the Rabble [2] Stone them in the very Streets, whenever they came so much as to Market; that they were not yet secure from being Visited themselves, and that as he heard, *Waltham* was already; that they would think it very hard that when any of them fled for Fear before they were touch'd, they should be deny'd the Liberty of lying so much as in the open Fields.

The *Epping* Men told them again, That they, indeed, said they were sound and free from the Infection, but that they had no assurance of it; and that it was reported, that there had been a great Rabble of People at *Walthamstow*, who made such Pretences of being sound, as they did, but that they threaten'd to plunder the Town, and force their Way whether the Parish Officers would or no; That they were near 200 of them, and had Arms and Tents like Low-Country Soldiers; that they extorted Provisions from the Town by threatening them with living upon them at free Quarter, shewing their Arms, and talking in the Language of Soldiers; and that several of them being gone away towards *Rumford* and *Brent-Wood*, the Country had been infected by them, and the Plague spread into both those large Towns, so that the People durst not go to Market there as usual; that it was very likely they were some of that Party, and if so, they deserv'd to be sent to the County Jail, and be secur'd till they had made Satisfaction for the Damage they had done, and for the Terror and Fright they had put the Country into.

2. Nonpropertied citizens; although the term is sometimes a synonym for lawless mob, such citizens were often considered a well of common sense and fair play.

John answered, That what other People had done was nothing to them; that he assured them they were all of one Company; that they had never been more in Number than they saw them at that time; (which by the way was very true) that they came out in two separate Companies, but joyn'd by the Way, their Cases being the same; that they were ready to give what Account of themselves any Body cou'd desire of them, and to give in their Names and Places of Abode, that so they might be call'd to an Account for any Disorder that they might be guilty of; that the Townsmen might see they were content to live hardly, and only desir'd a little Room to breath in on the Forest where it was wholesome, for where it was not they cou'd not stay, and wou'd decamp if they found it otherwise there.

But, said the Townsmen, we have a great charge of Poor upon our Hands already, and we must take care not to encrease it; we suppose you can give us no Security against your being chargeable to our Parish and to the Inhabitants, any more than you can of being dangerous to us as to the Infection.

Why look you, *says John*, as to being chargeable to you, we hope we shall not, if you will relieve us with Provisions for our present Necessity, we will be very thankful; as we all liv'd without Charity when we were at Home, so we will oblige ourselves fully to repay you, if God please to bring us back to our own Families and Houses in Safety, and to restore Health to the People of *London*.

As to our dying here, we assure you, if any of us die, we that survive, will bury them, and put you to no Expence, except it should be that we should all die, and then indeed the last Man not being able to bury himself, would put you to that single Expence which I am perswaded, says *John*, he would leave enough behind him to pay you for the Expence of.

On the other Hand, says *John*, if you will shut up all Bowels of Compassion and not relieve us at all, we shall not extort any thing by Violence, or steal from any one; but when what little we have is spent, if we perish for want, God's Will be done.

John wrought so upon the Townsmen by talking thus rationally and smoothly to them that they went away; and tho' they did not give any consent to their staying there, yet they did not molest them; and the poor People continued there three or four Days longer without any Disturbance. In this time they had got some remote Acquaintance with a Victualling-House[3] at the out-skirts of the Town, to whom they called at a Distance to bring some little Things that they wanted, and which they caus'd to to be set down at a Distance, and always paid for very honestly.

During this Time, the younger People of the Town came frequently pretty near them, and wou'd stand and look at them, and sometimes talk with them at some Space between; and particularly it was observed, that

---

3. A place that sold food, sometimes an inn or tavern.

the first Sabbath Day the poor People kept retir'd, worship'd God together, and were heard to sing Psalms.

These Things and a quiet inoffensive Behaviour, began to get them the good Opinion of the Country, and People began to pity them and speak very well of them; the Consequence of which was, that upon the occasion of a very wet rainy Night, a certain Gentleman who liv'd in the Neighbourhood, sent them a little Cart with twelve Trusses or Bundles of Straw, as well for them to lodge upon, as to cover and thatch their Huts, and to keep them dry: The Minister of a Parish not far off, not knowing of the other, sent them also about two Bushels of Wheat, and half a Bushel of white Peas.

They were very thankful to-be-sure for this Relief, and particularly the Straw was a very great Comfort to them; for tho' the ingenious Carpenter had made Frames for them to lie in like Troughs, and fill'd them with Leaves of Trees, and such Things as they could get, and had cut all their Tent-cloth out to make them Coverlids,[4] yet they lay damp, and hard, and unwholesome till this Straw came, which was to them like Feather-beds, and, as *John* said, more welcome than Feather-beds wou'd ha' been at another time.

This Gentleman and the Minister having thus begun and given an Example of Charity to these Wanderers, others quickly followed, and they receiv'd every Day some Benevolence or other from the People, but chiefly from the Gentlemen who dwelt in the Country round about; some sent them Chairs, Stools, Tables, and Such Houshold Things as they gave Notice they wanted; some sent them Blankets, Rugs and Coverlids; some Earthen-ware; and some Kitchin-ware for ordering[5] their Food.

Encourag'd by this good Usage, their Carpenter in a few Days, built them a large Shed or House with Rafters, and a Roof in Form, and an upper Floor in which they lodged warm, for the Weather began to be damp and cold in the beginning of *September*; But this House being very well Thatch'd, and the Sides and Roof made very thick, kept out the Cold well enough: He made also an earthen Wall at one End, with a Chimney in it; and another of the Company, with a vast deal of Trouble and Pains, made a Funnel to the Chimney to carry out the Smoak.

Here they liv'd very comfortably, tho' coarsely, till the beginning of *September*, when they had the bad News to hear, whether true or not, that the Plague, which was very hot at *Waltham-Abby* on one side, and at *Rumford* and *Brent-Wood* on the other side; was also come to *Epping*, to *Woodford*, and to most of the Towns upon the Forest, and which, as they said, was brought down among them chiefly by the Higlers[6] and such People as went to and from *London* with Provisions.

If this was true, it was an evident Contradiction to that Report which

4. Coverlets.
5. Literally "arranging," preparing, and managing.
6. People who buy or barter produce, poultry, and other commodities in the country and sell or barter them for supplies in the City. The name comes from "higgle," to haggle or bargain.

was afterwards spread all over *England*, but which, *as I have said*, I cannot confirm of my own Knowledge, namely, That the Market People carrying Provisions to the City, never got the Infection or carry'd it back into the Country; both which I have been assured, has been false.

It might be that they were preserv'd even beyond Expectation, though not to a Miracle, that abundance went and come, and were not touch'd, and that was much for the Encouragement of the poor People of *London*, who had been compleatly miserable, if the People that brought Provisions to the Markets had not been many times wonderfully preserv'd, or at least more preserv'd than cou'd be reasonably expected.

But now these new Inmates began to be disturb'd more effectually, for the Towns about them were really infected, and they began to be afraid to trust one another so much as to go abroad for such things as they wanted, and this pinch'd them very hard; for now they had little or nothing but what the charitable Gentlemen of the Country supply'd them with: But for their Encouragement it happen'd, that other Gentlemen in the Country who had not sent 'em any thing before, began to hear of them and supply them, and one sent them a large Pig, that is to say a Porker; another two Sheep; and another sent them a Calf: In short, they had Meat enough, and, sometimes had Cheese and Milk, and all such things; They were Chiefly put to it for Bread, for when the Gentlemen sent them Corn they had no where to bake it, or to grind it: This made them eat the first two Bushel of Wheat that was sent them in parched Corn, as the *Israelites* of old did without grinding or making Bread of it.[7]

At last they found means to carry their Corn to a Windmill near *Woodford*, where they had it ground; and afterwards the Biscuit Baker made a Hearth so hollow and dry that he cou'd bake Biscuit Cakes tolerably well; and thus they came into a Condition to live without any assistance or supplies from the Towns; and it was well they did, for the Country was soon after fully Infected, and about 120 were said to have died of the Distemper in the Villages near them, which was a terrible thing to them.

On this they call'd a new Council, and now the Towns had no need to be afraid they should settle near them, but on the contrary several Families of the poorer sort of the Inhabitants quitted their Houses, and built Hutts in the Forest after the same manner as they had done: But it was observ'd, that several of these poor People that had so remov'd, had the Sickness even in their Hutts or Booths; the Reason of which was plain, namely, not because they removed into the Air, but because they did not remove time enough, that is to say, not till by openly conversing with the other People their Neighbours, they had the Distemper upon

7. The Israelites' journey from Egypt is compared to the group's pilgrimage. Defoe may have in mind the way the Israelites renewed the thanksgiving festival of Passover before the assault on Jericho. They ate unleavened cakes and parched corn, which were from then on associated with the flight from Egypt and with sincerity and truth (*Interpreter's Bible*, Joshua 5.9–11).

them, or, (as may be said) among them, and so carry'd it about them whither they went: Or, (2.) Because they were not careful enough after they were safely removed out of the Towns, not to come in again and mingle with the diseased People.

But be it which of these it will, when our Travellers began to perceive that the Plague was not only in the Towns, but even in the Tents and Huts on the Forest near them, they began then not only to be afraid, but to think of decamping and removing; for had they stay'd, they wou'd ha' been in manifest Danger of their Lives.

It is not to be wondered that they were greatly afflicted, as being obliged to quit the Place where they had been so kindly receiv'd, and where they had been treated with so much Humanity and Charity; but Necessity, and the hazard of Life, which they came out so far to preserve, prevail'd with them, and they saw no Remedy. *John* however thought of a Remedy for their present Misfortune, namely, that he would first acquaint that Gentleman who was their principal Benefactor, with the Distress they were in, and to crave his Assistance and Advice.

The good charitable Gentleman encourag'd them to quit the Place, for fear they should be cut off from any Retreat at all, by the Violence of the Distemper; but whither they should go, that he found very hard to direct them to. At last *John* ask'd of him, whether he (being a Justice of the Peace) would give them Certificates of Health to other Justices who they might come before, that so whatever might be their Lot they might not be repulsed now they had been also so long from *London*. This his Worship immediately granted, and gave them proper Letters of Health, and from thence they were at Liberty to travel whither they pleased.

Accordingly they had a full Certificate of Health, intimating, That they had resided in a Village in the County of *Essex* so long, that being examined and scrutiniz'd sufficiently, and having been retir'd from all Conversation for above 40 Days, without any appearance of Sickness, they were therefore certainly concluded to be Sound Men, and might be safely entertain'd any where, having at last remov'd rather for fear of the Plague, which was come into *such a Town*, rather than for having any signal of Infection upon them, or upon any belonging to them.

With this Certificate they remov'd, tho' with great Reluctance; and *John* inclining not to go far from Home, they mov'd towards the Marshes on the side of *Waltham:* But here they found a Man, who it seems kept a Weer[8] or Stop upon the River, made to raise the Water for the Barges which go up and down the River, and he terrified them with dismal Stories of the Sickness having been spread into all the Towns on the River, and near the River, on the side of *Middlesex* and *Hertfordshire*; that is to say, into *Waltham, Waltham-Cross, Enfeld* and *Ware*,[9] and all the Towns on the Road, that they were afraid to go that way; tho' it

8. Properly spelled "weir," a barrier or dam to divert or change the water level in a stream.

9. Towns on the Great North Road to Hertford.

seems the Man impos'd upon them, for that the thing was not really true.

However it terrified them, and they resolved to move cross the Forest towards *Rumford* and *Brent-Wood*; but they heard that there were numbers of People fled out of *London* that way, who lay up and down in the Forest call'd *Henalt* Forest, reaching near *Rumford*,[1] and who having no Subsistence or Habitation, not only liv'd oddly, and suffered great Extremities in the Woods and Fields for want of Relief, but were said to be made so desperate by those Extremities, as that they offer'd many Violences to the County, robb'd and plunder'd, and kill'd Cattle, and the like; that others building Hutts and Hovels by the Road-side Begg'd, and that with an Importunity next Door to demanding Relief; so that the County was very uneasy, and had been oblig'd to take some of them up.

This, in the first Place intimated to them, that they would be sure to find the Charity and Kindness of the County, which they had found here where they were before, hardned and shut up against them; and that on the other Hand, they would be question'd where-ever they came, and would be in Danger of Violence from others in like Cases as themselves.

Upon all these Considerations, *John*, their Captain, in all their Names, went back to their good Friend and Benefactor, who had reliev'd them before, and laying their Case truly before him, humbly ask'd his Advice; and he as kindly advised them to take up their old Quarters again, or if not, to remove but a little further out of the Road, and directed them to a proper Place for them; and as they really wanted some House rather than Huts to shelter them at that time of the Year, it growing on towards *Michaelmas*, they found an old decay'd House, which had been formerly some Cottage or little Habitation, but was so out of repair as scarce habitable, and by the consent of a Farmer to whose Farm it belong'd, they got leave to make what use of it they could.

The ingenious Joyner and all the rest by his Directions, went to work with it, and in a very few Days made it capable to shelter them all in case of bad Weather, and in which there was an old Chimney, and an old Oven, tho' both lying in Ruins, yet they made them both fit for Use, and raising Additions, Sheds, and Leantoo's on every side, they soon made the House capable to hold them all.

They chiefly wanted Boards to make Window-Shutters, Floors, Doors, and several other Things; but as the Gentlemen above favour'd them, and the Country was by that Means made easy with them, and above all, that they were known to be all sound and in good health, every Body help'd them with what they could spare.

1. Rumford (Romford) is another village on the road to Colchester; it had two markets, one for calves and hogs and another for corn and other produce. Defoe invested in forest land in the area.

Here they encamp'd for good and all, and resolv'd to remove no more; they saw plainly how terribly alarm'd that County was every where, at any Body that came from *London*; and that they should have no admittance any where but with the utmost Difficulty, at least no friendly Reception and Assistance as they had receiv'd here.

Now altho' they receiv'd great Assistance and Encouragement from the Country Gentlemen and from the People round about them, yet they were put to great Straits, for the Weather grew cold and wet in *October* and *November*, and they had not been us'd to so much hardship; so that they got Colds in their Limbs, and Distempers, but never had the Infection: And thus about *December* they came home to the City again.

I give this Story thus at large, principally to give an Account [of] what became of the great Numbers of People which immediately appear'd in the City as soon as the Sickness abated: For, as I have said, great Numbers of those that were able and had Retreats in the Country, fled to those Retreats; So when it was encreased to such a frightful Extremity as I have related, the midling People who had not Friends, fled to all Parts of the Country where they cou'd get shelter, as well those that had Mony to relieve themselves; as those that had not. Those that had Mony always fled farthest, because they were able to subsist themselves; but those who were empty, suffer'd, as I have said, great Hardships, and were often driven by Necessity to relieve their Wants at the Expence of the Country: By that Means the Country was made very uneasie at them, and sometimes took them up, tho' even then they scarce knew what to do with them, and were always very backward to punish them, but often too they forced them from Place to Place, till they were oblig'd to come back again to *London*.

I have, since my knowing this Story of *John* and his Brother, enquir'd and found, that there were a great many of the poor disconsolate People, as above, fled into the Country every way, and some of them got little Sheds, and Barns, and Out-houses to live in, where they cou'd obtain so much Kindness of the Country, and especially where they had any the least satisfactory Account to give of themselves, and particularly that they did not come out of *London* too late. But others, and that in great Numbers, built themselves little Hutts and Retreats in the Fields and Woods, and liv'd like Hermits in Holes and Caves, or any Place they cou'd find; and where, we may be sure, they suffer'd great Extremities, such that many of them were oblig'd to come back again whatever the Danger was; and so those little Huts were often found empty, and the Country People suppos'd the Inhabitants lay Dead in them of the Plague, and would not go near them for fear, no not in a great while; nor is it unlikely but that some of the unhappy Wanderers might die so all alone, even sometimes for want of Help, as particularly in one Tent or Hutt, was found a Man dead, and on the Gate of a Field just by, was cut with

his Knife in uneven Letters, the following Words, by which it may be
suppos'd the other Man escap'd, or that one dying first, the other bury'd
him as well as he could;

> O mIsErY!
> We BoTH ShaLL DyE,
> WoE, WoE.

I have given an Account already of what I found to ha' been the Case
down the River among the Sea-faring Men, how the Ships lay in the
Offing, as 'tis call'd, in Rows or Lines a-stern of one another, quite down
from the *Pool* as far as I could see, I have been told, that they lay in the
same manner quite down the River as low as *Gravesend*, and some far
beyond, even every where, or in every Place where they cou'd ride with
Safety as to Wind and Weather; Nor did I ever hear that the Plague
reach'd to any of the People on board those Ships, except such as lay up
in the *Pool*, or as high as *Deptford* Reach, altho' the People went frequently on Shoar to the Country Towns and Villages, and Farmers
Houses, to buy fresh Provisions, Fowls, Pigs, Calves, and the like for
their Supply.

Likewise I found that the Watermen on the River above the Bridge,
found means to convey themselves away up the River as far as they cou'd
go; and that they had, many of them, their whole Families in their
Boats, cover'd with Tilts and Bales,[2] as they call them, and furnish'd
with Straw within for their Lodging; and that they lay thus all along by
the Shoar in the Marshes, some of them setting up little Tents with their
Sails, and so lying under them on Shoar in the Day, and going into
their Boats at Night; and in this manner, as I have heard, the River-sides
were lin'd with Boats and People as long as they had any thing to subsist
on, or cou'd get any thing of the Country; and indeed the Country People, as well Gentlemen as others, on these and all other Occasions, were
very forward to relieve them, but they were by no means willing to receive
them into their Towns and Houses, and for that we cannot blame them.

There was one unhappy Citizen within my Knowledge who had been
Visited in a dreadful manner, so that his Wife and all his Children were
Dead, and himself and two Servants only left, with an elderly Woman
a near Relation, who had nurs'd those that were dead as well as she
could: This disconsolate Man goes to a Village near the Town, tho' not
within the Bills of Mortality, and finding an empty House there, enquires
out the Owner, and took the House: After a few Days he got a Cart and
loaded it with Goods, and carries them down to the House; the People
of the Village oppos'd his driving the Cart along, but with some Argu-
ings, and some Force, the Men that drove the Cart along, got through
the Street up to the Door of the House, there the Constable resisted him
again, and would not let them be brought in. The Man caus'd the Goods

---

2. Awnings and bundles.

to be unloaden and lay'd at the Door, and sent the Cart away; upon which they carry'd the Man before a Justice of Peace; that is to say, they commanded him to go, which he did. The Justice order'd him to cause the Cart to fetch away the Goods again, which he refused to do; upon which the Justice order'd the Constable to pursue the Carters and fetch them back, and make them re-load the Goods and carry them away, or to set them in the Stocks till they came for farther Orders; and if they could not find them, nor the Man would not consent to take them away, they should cause them to be drawn with Hooks from the House-Door and burnt in the Street. The poor distress'd Man upon this fetch'd the Goods again, but with grievous Cries and Lamentations at the hardship of his Case. But there was no Remedy; Self-preservation oblig'd the People to those Severities, which they wou'd not otherwise have been concern'd in: Whether this poor Man liv'd or dy'd I cannot tell, but it was reported that he had the Plague upon him at that time; and perhaps the People might report that to justify their Usage of him; but it was not unlikely, that either he or his Goods, or both, were dangerous, when his whole Family had been dead of the Distemper so little a while before.

I kno' that the Inhabitants of the Towns adjacent to *London*, were much blamed for Cruelty to the poor People that ran from the Contagion in their Distress; and many very severe things were done, as may be seen from what has been said; but I cannot but say also that where there was room for Charity and Assistance to the People, without apparent Danger to themselves, they were willing enough to help and relieve them. But as every Town were indeed Judges in their own Case, so the poor People who ran a-broad in their Extremities, were often ill-used and driven back again into the Town; and this caused infinite Exclamations and Out-cries against the Country Towns, and made the Clamour very popular.[3]

And yet more or less, maugre[4] all their Caution, there was not a Town of any Note within ten (or I believe twenty) Miles of the City, but what was more or less Infected, and had some died among them. I have heard the Accounts of several; such as they were reckon'd up as follows.

In *Enfeld*	32	*Hertford*	90	*Brent-Wood*	70
In *Hornsey*	58	*Ware*	160	*Rumford*	109
In *Newington*	17	*Hodsdon*	30	*Barking* abt.	200
In *Tottenham*	42	*Waltham* Ab.	23	*Branford*	432
In *Edmonton*	19	*Epping*	26	*Kingston*	122
In *Barnet* and		*Deptford*	623	*Stanes*	82
Hadly	43	*Greenwich*	231	*Chertsey*	18
In *St. Albans*	121	*Eltham* and		*Windsor*	103
In *Watford*	45	*Lusum*	85		
In *Uxbridge*	117	*Croydon*	61	*cum aliis.*[5]	

3. "Made the Clamour very popular": ordinary people repeated and deplored this conduct until it was a public, common chorus.
4. In spite of.
5. With others.

Another thing might render the Country more strict with respect to the Citizens, and especially with respect to the Poor; and this was what I hinted at before, namely, that there was a seeming propensity, or a wicked Inclination in those that were Infected to infect others.

There have been great Debates among our Physicians, as to the Reason of this; some will have it to be in the Nature of the Disease, and that it impresses every one that is seized upon by it, with a kind of a Rage, and a hatred against their own Kind, as if there was a malignity, not only in the Distemper to communicate it self, but in the very Nature of Man, prompting him with evil Will, or an evil Eye, that *as they say* in the Case of a mad Dog, who tho' the gentlest Creature before of any of his Kind, yet then will fly upon and bite any one that comes next him and those as soon as any, who had been most observ'd by him before.

Others plac'd it to the Account of the Coruption of humane Nature, which cannot bear to see itself more miserable than others of its own Specie, and has a kind of involuntary Wish, that all Men were as unhappy, or in as bad a Condition as itself.

Others say, it was only a kind of Desperation, not knowing or regarding what they did, and consequently unconcern'd at the Danger or Safety, not only of any Body near them, but even of themselves also: And indeed when Men are once come to a Condition to abandon themselves, and be unconcern'd for the Safety, or at the Danger of themselves, it cannot be so much wondered that they should be careless of the Safety of other People.

But I choose to give this grave Debate a quite different turn, and answer it or resolve it all by saying, *That I do not grant the Fact.* On the contrary, I say, that the Thing is not really so, but that it was a general Complaint rais'd by the People inhabiting the out-lying Villages against the Citizens, to justify, or at least excuse those Hardships and Severities so much talk'd of, and in which Complaints, both Sides may be said to have injur'd one another; that is to say, the Citizens pressing to be received and harbour'd in time of Distress, and with the Plague upon them, complain of the Cruelty and Injustice of the Country People, in being refused Entrance, and forc'd back again with their Goods and Families; and the Inhabitants finding themselves so imposed upon, and the Citizens breaking in as it were upon them whether they would or no, complain, that when they were infected, they were not only regardless of others, but even willing to infect them; neither of which were really true, that is to say, in the Colours they were describ'd in.

It is true, there is something to be said for the frequent Alarms which were given to the Country, of the resolution of the People in *London* to come out by Force, not only for Relief, but to Plunder and Rob, that they ran about the Streets with the Distemper upon them without any control; and that no Care was taken to shut up Houses, and confine the sick People from infecting others; whereas, to do the *Londoners* Justice, they never practised such things, except in such particular Cases as I have mention'd above, and such-like. On the other Hand every thing was managed with so much Care, and such excellent Order was observ'd in the whole City and Suburbs, by the Care of the Lord Mayor and Aldermen; and by the Justices of the Peace, Churchwardens, &c. in the out-Parts; that *London* may be a Pattern to all the Cities in the World for the good Government and the excellent Order that was every where kept, even in the time of the most violent Infection; and when the People were in the utmost Consternation and Distress. But of this I shall speak by itself.

One thing, it is to be observ'd, was owing principally to the Prudence of the Magistrates, and ought to be mention'd to their Honour, *(viz.)* The Moderation which they used in the great and difficult Work of shutting up of Houses: It is true, as I have mentioned, that the shutting up of Houses was a great Subject of Discontent, and I may say indeed the only Subject of Discontent among the People at that time; for the confining the Sound in the same House with the Sick, was counted very terrible, and the Complaints of People so confin'd were very grievous; they were heard into the very Streets, and they were sometimes such that called for Resentment, tho' oftner for Compassion; they had no way to converse with any of their Friends but out at their Windows, where they wou'd make such piteous Lamentations, as often mov'd the Hearts of those they talk'd with, and of others who passing by heard their Story; and as those Complaints oftentimes reproach'd the Severity, and sometimes the Insolence of the Watchmen plac'd at their Doors, those Watchmen wou'd answer saucily enough; and perhaps be apt to affront the People who were in the Street talking to the said Families; for which, or for their ill Treatment of the Families, I think seven or eight of them in several Places were kill'd; I know not whether I shou'd say murthered [6] or not, because I cannot enter into the particular Cases. It is true, the Watchmen were on their Duty, and acting in the Post where they were plac'd by a lawful Authority; and killing any publick legal Officer in the Execution of his Office, is always in the Language of the Law call'd Murther. But as they were not authoriz'd by the Magistrate's Instructions, or by the Power they acted under, to be injurious or abusive, either to the People who were under their Observation, or to any that concern'd themselves for them; so when they did so, they might be said to act themselves, not their Office; to act as private Persons, not as Persons employ'd; and consequently if they brought Mischief upon themselves by such an undue Behaviour, that Mischief was upon their own Heads; and indeed they had so much the hearty Curses of the People, whether they deserv'd it or not, that whatever befel them no body pitied them, and every Body was apt to say, they deserv'd it, whatever it was;

6. A common spelling for "murdered."

nor do I remember that any Body was ever punish'd, at least to any considerable Degree, for whatever was done to the Watchmen that guarded their Houses.

What variety of Stratagems were used to escape and get out of Houses thus shut up, by which the Watchmen were deceived or overpower'd, and that the People got away, I have taken notice of already, and shall say no more to that: But I say the Magistrates did moderate and ease Families upon many Occasions in this Case, and particulary in that of taking away, or suffering to be remov'd the sick Persons out of such Houses, when they were willing to be remov'd either to a Pest-House, or other Places, and sometimes giving the well Persons in the Family so shut up, leave to remove upon Information given that they were well, and that they would confine themselves in such Houses where they went, so long as should be requir'd of them. The Concern also of the Magistrates for the supplying such poor Families as were infected; I say, supplying them with Necessaries, as well Physick as Food, was very great, and in which they did not content themselves with giving the necessary Orders to the Officers appointed, but the Aldermen in Person, and on Horseback frequently rid to such Houses, and caus'd the People to be ask'd at their Windows, whether they were duly attended, or not?[7] Also, whether they wanted anything that was necessary, and if the Officers had constantly carry'd their Messages, and fetch'd them such things as they wanted, or not? And if they answered in the Affirmative, all was well; but if they complain'd, that they were ill supply'd, and that the Officer did not do his Duty, or did not treat them civilly, they (the Officers) were generally remov'd, and others plac'd in their stead.

It is true, such Complaint might be unjust, and if the Officer had such Arguments to use as would convince the Magistrate, that he was right, and that the People had injur'd him, he was continued, and they reproved. But this part could not well bear a particular Inquiry, for the Parties could very ill be brought face to face, and a Complaint could not be well heard and answer'd in the Street, from the Windows, as was the Case then; the Magistrates therefore generally chose to favour the People, and remove the Man, as what seem'd to be the least Wrong, and of the Least ill Consequence; seeing, if the Watchman was injur'd yet they could readily make him amends by giving him another Post of the like Nature; but if the Family was injur'd, there was no Satisfaction could be made to them, the Damage perhaps being irreparable, as it concern'd their Lives.

A great variety of these Cases frequently happen'd between the Watchmen and the poor People shut up, besides those I formerly mention'd about escaping; sometimes the Watchmen were absent, sometimes drunk, sometimes asleep when the People wanted them, and such never fail'd to be punish'd severely, as indeed they deserv'd.

7. This is an idealistic fiction intended as instructive example for good city administration.

But after all that was or could be done in these Cases, the shutting up of Houses, so as to confine those that were well, with those that were sick, had very great Inconveniences in it, and some that were very tragical, and which merited to have been consider'd if there had been room for it; but it was authoriz'd by a Law, it had the publick Good in view, as the End chiefly aim'd at, and all the private Injuries that were done by the putting it in Execution, must be put to the account of the publick Benefit.

It is doubtful to this day, whether in the whole it contributed any thing to the stop of the Infection, and indeed, I cannot say it did; for nothing could run with greater Fury and Rage than the Infection did when it was in its chief Violence; tho' the Houses infected were shut up as exactly, and as effectually as it was possible. Certain it is, that if all the infected Persons were effectually shut in, no sound Person could have been infected by them, because they could not have come near them. But the Case was this, and I shall only touch it here, namely, that the Infection was propagated insensibly, and by such Persons as were not visibly infected, who neither knew who they infected, or who they were infected by.

A House in *White-Chapel* was shut up for the sake of one Infected Maid, who had only Spots, not the Tokens come out upon her, and recover'd; yet these People obtain'd no Liberty to stir, neither for Air or Exercise forty Days; want of Breath, Fear, Anger, Vexation, and all the other Griefs attending such an injurious Treatment, cast the Mistress of the Family into a Fever, and Visitors came into the House, and said it was the Plague, tho' the Physicians declar'd it was not; however the Family were oblig'd to begin their Quarantine anew, on the Report of the Visitor or Examiner, tho' their former Quarantine wanted but a few Days of being finish'd. This oppress'd them so with Anger and Grief, and, *as before*, straiten'd them also so much as to Room, and for want of Breathing and free Air, that most of the Family fell sick, one of one Distemper, one of another, chiefly Scorbutick Ailments;[8] *only one a violent Cholick,*[9] 'till after several prolongings of their Confinement, some or other of those that came in with the Visitors to inspect the Persons that were ill, in hopes of releasing them, brought the Distemper with them, and infected the whole House, and all or most of them died, not of the Plague, as really upon them before, but of the Plague that those People brought them, who should ha' been careful to have protected them from it; and this was a thing which frequently happen'd, and was indeed one of the worst Consequences of shutting Houses up.

I had about this time a little Hardship put upon me, which I was at first greatly afflicted at, and very much disturb'd about; tho' as it prov'd, it did not expose me to any Disaster; and this was being appointed by the

8. Scurvy.
9. Colic, severe cramping pains of the stomach and abdomen.

Alderman of *Portsoken* Ward,[1] one of the Examiners of the Houses in the Precinct where I liv'd; we had a large Parish, and had no less than eighteen Examiners, as the Order call'd us, the People call'd us Visitors. I endeavour'd with all my might to be excus'd from such an Employment, and used many Arguments with the Alderman's Deputy to be excus'd; particularly I alledged, that I was against shutting up Houses at all, and that it would be very hard to oblige me, to be an Instrument in that which was against my Judgment, and which I did verily believe would not answer the End it was intended for, but all the Abatement I could get was only, that whereas the Officer was appointed by my Lord Mayor to continue two Months, I should be obliged to hold it but three Weeks, on Condition, nevertheless that I could then get some other sufficient House-keeper to serve the rest of the Time for me, which was, in short, but a very small Favour, it being very difficult to get any Man to accept of such an Employment, that was fit to be intrusted with it.

It is true that shutting up of Houses had one Effect, which I am sensible was of Moment, namely, it confin'd the distemper'd People, who would otherwise have been both very troublesome and very dangerous in their running about Streets with the Distemper upon them, which when they were dilirious, they would have done in a most frightful manner; and as indeed they began to do at first very much, 'till they were thus restrain'd; nay, so very open they were, that the Poor would go about and beg at peoples Doors, and say they had the Plague upon them, and beg Rags for their Sores, or both, or any thing that dilirious Nature happen'd to think of.

A poor unhappy Gentlewoman, a substantial Citizen's Wife was (if the Story be true) murther'd by one of these Creatures in *Aldersgate-street*, or that Way: He was going along the Street, raving mad to be sure, and singing, the People only said, he was drunk; but he himself said, he had the Plague upon him, which, it seems, was true; and meeting this Gentlewoman, he would kiss her;[2] she was terribly frighted as he was only a rude Fellow, and she run from him, but the Street being very thin of People, there was no body near enough to help her: When she see he would overtake her, she turn'd, and gave him a Thrust so forcibly, he being but weak, and push'd him down backward: But very unhappily, she being so near, he caught hold of her, and pull'd her down also; and getting up first, master'd her, and kiss'd her; and which was worst of all, when he had done, told her he had the Plague, and why should not she have it as well as he. She was frighted enough before, being also young with Child; but when she heard him say, he had the Plague, she scream'd out and fell down in a Swoon, or in a Fit, which tho' she recover'd a little, yet kill'd her in a very few Days, and I never heard whether she had the Plague or no.

1. On the east side of the City, the large ward that included H. F.'s parish of St. Botolph Aldgate.
2. Was determined to kiss her.

Another infected Person came, and knock'd at the Door of a Citizen's House, where they knew him very well; the Servant let him in, and being told the Master of the House was above, he ran up, and came into the Room to them as the whole Family was at Supper: They began to rise up a little surpriz'd, not knowing what the Matter was, but he bid them sit still, he only came to take his leave of them. They ask'd him. Why Mr. —— where are you going? Going, says he, I have got the Sickness, and shall die to morrow Night. 'Tis easie to believe, though not to describe the Consternation they were all in, the Women and the Man's Daughters which were but little Girls, were frighted almost to Death, and got up, one running out at one Door, and one at another, some down-Stairs and some up-Stairs, and getting together as well as they could, lock'd themselves into their Chambers, and screamed out at the Window for Help, as if they had been frighted out of their Wits: the Master more compos'd than they, tho' both frighted and provok'd, was going to lay Hands on him, and thro'[3] him down Stairs, being in a Passion, but then considering a little the Condition of the Man and the Danger of touching him, Horror seiz'd his Mind, and he stood still like one astonished. The poor distemper'd Man all this while, being as well diseas'd in his Brain as in his Body, stood still like one amaz'd; at length he turns round, *Ay! says he,* with all the seeming calmness imaginable, *Is it so with you all! Are you all disturb'd at me? why then I'll e'en go home and die there.* And so he goes immediately down Stairs: The Servant that had let him in goes down after him with a Candle, but was afraid to go past him and open the Door, so he stood on the Stairs to see what he wou'd do; the Man went and open'd the Door, and went out and flung the Door after him: It was some while before the Family recover'd the Fright, but as no ill Consequence attended, they have had occasion since to speak of it (you may be sure) with great Satisfaction. Tho' the Man was gone it was some time, nay as I heard, some Days before they recover'd themselves of the Hurry they were in, nor did they go up and down the House with any assurance, till they had burnt a great variety of Fumes and Perfumes in all the Rooms, and made a great many Smoaks of Pitch, of Gunpowder, and of Sulphur, all separately shifted;[4] and washed their Clothes, and the like: As to the poor Man whether he liv'd or dy'd I don't remember.

It is most certain, that if by the Shutting up of Houses the sick had not been confin'd, multitudes who in the height of their Fever were Dilirious and Distracted, wou'd ha' been continually running up and down the Streets, and even as it was, a very great number did so, and offer'd all sorts of Violence to those they met, even just as a mad Dog runs on and bites at every one he meets; nor can I doubt but that shou'd one of those infected diseased Creatures have bitten any Man or Woman,

3. Throw.   4. Changed.

while the Frenzy of the Distemper was upon them, they, I mean the Person so wounded, wou'd as certainly ha' been incurably infected, as one that was sick before and had the Tokens upon him.

I heard of one infected Creature, who running out of his Bed in his Shirt, in the anguish and agony of his Swellings, of which he had three upon him, got his Shoes on and went to put on his Coat, but the Nurse resisting and snatching the Coat from him, he threw her down, run over her, run down Stairs and into the Street directly to the *Thames* in his Shirt, the Nurse running after him, and calling to the Watch to stop him; but the Watchmen frighted at the Man, and afraid to touch him, let him go on; upon which he ran down to the Still-yard Stairs,[5] threw away his Shirt, and plung'd into the *Thames*, and, being a good swimmer, swam quite over the River; and the Tide being coming in, as they call it, that is running West-ward, he reached the Land not till he came about the Falcon Stairs,[6] where landing, and finding no People there, it being in the Night, he ran about the Streets there, Naked as he was, for a good while, when it being by that time High-water, he takes the River again, and swam back to the Still-yard, landed, ran up the Streets again to his own House, knocking at the Door, went up the Stairs, and into his Bed again; and that this terrible Experiment cur'd him of the Plague, that is to say, that the violent Motion of his Arms and Legs stretch'd the Parts where the Swellings he had upon him were, that is to say under his Arms and his Groin, and caused them to ripen and break; and that the cold of the Water abated the Fever in his Blood.

I have only to add, that I do not relate this any more than some of the other, as a Fact within my own Knowledge, so as that I can vouch the Truth of them, and especially that of the Man being cur'd by the extravagant Adventure, which I confess I do not think very possible, but it may serve to confirm the many desperate Things which the distress'd People falling into, Diliriums, and what we call Lightheadedness, were frequently run upon at that time, and how infinitely more such there wou'd ha' been, if such People had not been confin'd by the shutting up of Houses; and this I take to be the best, *if not the only good thing* which was perform'd by that severe Method.

On the other Hand, the Complaints and the Murmurings were very bitter against the thing itself.

It would pierce the Hearts of all that came by to hear the piteous Cries of those infected People, who being thus out of their Understandings by the Violence of their Pain, or the heat of their Blood, were either shut in, or perhaps ty'd in their Beds and Chairs, to prevent their doing themselves Hurt, and who wou'd make a dreadful outcry at their being con-

5. Stairs from the bank to the docks or water's edge were common along the Thames, for it was a major transportation route. The Still-yard Stairs were at the Steelyard, the location of the hall of the German merchants of the Hanse in England, at Dowgate Dock. In 1598 this hall was taken by the Queen and made the Navy Office.
6. In Southwark near the Falcon Tavern.

fin'd, and at their being not permitted to die at large, as they call'd it, and as they wou'd ha' done before.

This running of distemper'd People about the Streets was very dismal, and the Magistrates did their utmost to prevent it, but as it was generally in the Night and always sudden, when such attempts were made, the Officers cou'd not be at hand to prevent it, and even when any got out in the Day, the Officers appointed did not care to meddle with them, because, as they were all grievously infected to *be sure* when they were come to that Height, so they were more than ordinarily infectious, and it was one of the most dangerous things that cou'd be to touch them; on the other Hand, they generally ran on, not knowing what they did, till they dropp'd down stark Dead, or till they had exhausted their Spirits so, as that they wou'd fall and then die in perhaps half an Hour or an Hour, and which was most piteous to hear, they were sure to come to themselves intirely in that half Hour or Hour, and then to make most grievous and piercing Cries and Lamentations in the deep afflicting Sense of the Condition they were in. This was much of it before the Order for shutting up of Houses was strictly put in Execution, for at first the Watchmen were not so vigorous and severe, as they were afterward in the keeping the people in; that is to say, before they were, I mean some of them, severely punish'd for their Neglect, failing in their Duty, and letting People who were under their Care slip away, or conniving at their going abroad whether sick or well. But after they saw the Officers appointed to examine into their Conduct, were resolv'd to have them do their Duty, or be punish'd for the omission, they were more exact, and the People were strictly restrain'd; which was a thing they took so ill, and bore so impatiently, that their Discontents can hardly be describ'd: But there was an absolute Necessity for it, that must be confess'd, unless some other Measures had been timely enter'd upon, and it was too late for that.

Had not this particular of the Sicks been restrain'd as above, been our Case at that time, *London* wou'd ha' been the most dreadful Place that ever was in the World, there wou'd for ought I kno' have as many People dy'd in the Streets as dy'd in their Houses; for when the Distemper was at its height, it generally made them Raving and Dilirious, and when they were so, they wou'd never be perswaded to keep in their Beds but by Force; and many who were not ty'd, threw themselves out of Windows, when they found they cou'd not get leave to go out of their Doors.

It was for want of People conversing one with another, in this time of Calamity, that it was impossible any particular Person cou'd come at the Knowledge of all the extraordinary Cases that occurr'd in different Families; and particularly I believe it was never known to this Day how many People in their Diliriums drowned themselves in the *Thames*, and in the River which runs from the Marshes by *Hackney*, which we generally call'd *Ware* River, or *Hackney* River; as to those which were set down in the Weekly Bill, they were indeed few; nor cou'd it be known of any of those, whether they drowned themselves by Accident or not: But I believe, I might reckon up more, who, within the compass of my Knowledge or Observation, really drowned themselves in that Year, than are put down in the Bill of all put together, for many of the Bodies were never found, who, yet were known to be so lost; and the like in other Methods of Self-Destruction. There was also One Man in or about *Whitecross-Street*, burnt himself to Death in his Bed; some said it was done by himself, others that it was by the Treachery of the Nurse that attended him; but that he had the Plague upon him was agreed by all.

It was a merciful Disposition of Providence also, and which I have many times thought of at that time, that no Fires, or no considerable ones at least, happen'd in the City, during that Year, which, if it had been otherwise, would have been very dreadful; and either the People must have let them alone unquenched, or have come together in great Crowds and Throngs, unconcern'd at the Danger of the Infection, not concerned at the Houses they went into, at the Goods they handled, or at the Persons or the People they came among: But so it was that excepting that in *Cripplegate* Parish, and two or three little Eruptions of Fires, which were presently extinguish'd, there was no Disaster of that kind happen'd in the whole Year. They told us a Story of a House in a Place call'd *Swan-Alley*,[7] passing from *Goswell-street* near the End of *Olaf-street* into *St. Johnstreet*, that a Family was infected there, in so terrible a Manner that every one of the House died; the last person lay dead on the Floor, and as it is supposed, had laid her self all along to die just before the Fire; the Fire, it seems had fallen from its Place, being of Wood, and had taken hold of the Boards and the Joists they lay on, and burnt as far as just to the Body, but had not taken hold of the dead Body, tho' she had little more than her Shift on, and had gone out of itself, not hurting the Rest of the House, tho' it was a slight Timber House. How true this might be, I do not determine, but the City being to suffer severely the next Year by Fire, this Year it felt very little of that Calamity.

Indeed considering the Deliriums, which the Agony threw People into, and how I have mention'd in their Madness, when they were alone, they did many desperate Things; it was very strange there were no more Disasters of that kind.

It has been frequently ask'd me, and I cannot say, that I ever knew how to give a direct Answer to it, How it came to pass that so many infected People appear'd abroad in the Streets, at the same time that the Houses which were infected were so vigilantly searched, and all of them shut up and guarded as they were.

I confess, I know not what Answer to give to this, unless it be this, that in so great and populous a City as this is, it was impossible to discover every House that was infected as soon as it was so, or to shut up

---

7. Olave Street; this is the neighborhood of Defoe's earliest childhood.

all the Houses that were infected: so that People had the Liberty of going about the Streets, even where they pleased, unless they were known to belong to such and such infected Houses.

It is true, that as several Physicians told my Lord Mayor, the Fury of the Contagion was such at some particular Times, and People sicken'd so fast, and died so soon, that it was impossible and indeed to no purpose to go about to enquire who was sick and who was well, or to shut them up with such Exactness, as the thing required; almost every House in a whole Street being infected, and in many Places every Person in some of the Houses; and that which was still worse, by the time that the Houses were known to be infected, most of the Persons infected would be stone dead, and the rest run away for Fear of being shut up; so that it was to very small Purpose, to call them infected Houses and shut them up; the Infection having ravaged, and taken its Leave of the House, before it was really known, that the Family was any way touch'd.

This might be sufficient to convince any reasonable Person, that as it was not in the Power of the Magistrates, or of any humane [8] Methods or Policy, to prevent the spreading the Infection; so that this way of shutting up of Houses was perfectly insufficient for that End. Indeed it seemed to have no manner of publick Good in it, equal or proportionable to the grievous Burthen that it was to the particular Families, that were so shut up; and as far as I was employed by the publick in directing that Severity, I frequently found occasion to see, that it was incapable of answering the End. For Example as I was desired as a Visitor or Examiner to enquire into the Particulars of several Families which were infected, we scarce came to any House where the Plague had visibly appear'd in the Family, but that some of the Family were Fled and gone; the Magistrates would resent this, and charge the Examiners with being remiss in their Examination or Inspection: But by that means Houses were long infected before it was known. Now, as I was in this dangerous Office but half the appointed time, which was two Months, it was long enough to inform myself, that we were no way capable of coming at the Knowledge of the true state of any Family, but by enquiring at the Door, or of the Neighbours; as for going into every House to search, that was a part, no Authority wou'd offer to impose on the Inhabitants, or any Citizen wou'd undertake, for it wou'd ha' been exposing us to certain Infection and Death, and to the Ruine of our own Families as well as of ourselves, nor wou'd any Citizen of Probity, and that cou'd be depended upon, have staid in the Town, if they had been made liable to such a Severity.

Seeing then that we cou'd come at the certainty of Things by no Method but that of Enquiry of the Neighbours, or of the Family, and on that we cou'd not justly depend, it was not possible, but that the incertainty of this Matter wou'd remain as above.

It is true, Masters of Families were bound by the Order, to give Notice

8. Human; eighteenth-century writers frequently added an "e" but did not mean "humane."

to the Examiner of the Place wherein he liv'd, within two Hours after
he shou'd discover it, of any Person being sick in his House, that is to
say, having Signs of the Infection, but they found so many ways to evade
this, and excuse their Negligence, that they seldom gave that Notice, till
they had taken Measures to have every one Escape out of the House,
who had a mind to Escape, whether they were Sick or Sound; and while
this was so, it is easie to see, that the shutting up of Houses was no way
to be depended upon, as a sufficient Method for putting a stop to the
Infection, because, as I have said elsewhere, many of those that so went
out of those infected Houses, had the Plague really upon them, tho'
they might really think themselves Sound: And some of these were the
People that walk'd the Streets till they fell down Dead, not that they
were suddenly struck with the Distemper, as with a Bullet that kill'd with
the Stroke, but that they really had the Infection in their Blood long
before, only, that, as it prey'd secretly on the Vitals, it appear'd not till
it seiz'd the heart with a mortal Power, and the Patient died in a Moment,
as with a sudden Fainting, or an Apoplectick Fit.

I know that some, even of our Physicians, thought, for a time, that
those People that so died in the Streets, were seiz'd but that Moment
they fell, as if they had been touch'd by a Stroke from Heaven, as Men
are kill'd by a flash of Lightning; but they found Reason to alter their
Opinion afterward; for upon examining the Bodies of such after they
were Dead, they always either had Tokens upon them, or other evident
Proofs of the Distemper having been longer upon them, than they had
otherwise expected.

This often was the Reason that, as I have said, we, that were Examiners, were not able to come at the Knowledge of the Infection being
enter'd into a House, till it was too late to shut it up; and sometimes not
till the People that were left, were all Dead. In *Petticoat-Lane*[9] two
Houses together were infected, and several People sick; but the Distemper was so well conceal'd, the Examiner, who was my Neighbour, got
no Knowledge of it, till Notice was sent him that the People were all
Dead, and that the Carts should call there to fetch them away. The two
Heads of the Families concerted their Measures, and so order'd their
Matters, as that when the Examiner was in the Neighbourhood, they
appeared generally one at a time, and answered, that is, lied for one
another, or got some of the Neighbourhood to say they were all in Health,
and perhaps knew no better, till Death making it impossible to keep it
any longer as a Secret, the dead-Carts were call'd in the Night, to
both the Houses, and so it became publick: But when the Examiner order'd
the Constable to shut up the houses, there was no Body left in them but
three People, two in one House, and one in the other just dying, and a
Nurse in each House, who acknowledg'd that they had buried five before,
that the Houses had been infected nine or ten Days, and that for all the

9. The western side is in Portsoken Ward, where H. F. was an Examiner. The French weavers
settled there, and it terminated in Spittlefields.

rest of the two Families, which were many, they were gone, some sick, some well, or whether sick or well could not be known.

In like manner, at another House in the same Lane, a Man having his Family infected, but very unwilling to be shut up, when he could conceal it no longer, shut up himself; that is to say, he set the great red Cross upon his Door with the words LORD HAVE MERCY UPON US; and so deluded the Examiner, who suppos'd it had been done by the Constable, by Order of the other Examiner, for there were two Examiners to every District or Precinct; by this means he had free egress and regress into his House again, and out of it, as he pleas'd notwithstanding it was infected; till at length his Strategem was found out, and then he, with the sound part of his Servants and Family, made off and escaped; so they were not shut up at all.

These things made it very hard, if not impossible, *as I have said*, to prevent the spreading of an Infection by the shutting up of Houses, unless the People would think the shutting up of their Houses no Grievance, and be so willing to have it done, as that they wou'd give Notice duly and faithfully to the Magistrates of their being infected, as soon as it was known by themselves: But as that can not be expected from them, and the Examiners can not be supposed, as above, to go into their Houses to visit and search, all the good of shutting up Houses, will be defeated, and few Houses will be shut up in time, except those of the Poor, who can not conceal it, and of some People who will be discover'd by the Terror and Consternation which the Thing put them into.

I got myself discharg'd of the dangerous Office I was in, as soon as I cou'd get another admitted, who I had obtain'd for a little Mony to accept of it; and so, instead of serving the two Months, which was directed, I was not above three Weeks in it; and a great while too, considering it was in the Month of *August*, at which time the Distemper began to rage with great Violence at our end of the Town.

In the execution of this Office, I cou'd not refrain speaking my Opinion among my Neighbours, as to this shutting up the People in their Houses; in which we saw most evidently the Severities that were used *tho' grievous in themselves*, had also this particular Objection against them, namely, that they did not answer the End, *as I have said*, but that the distemper'd People went Day by Day about the Streets; and it was our united Opinion, that a Method to have removed the Sound from the Sick in Case of a particular House being visited, wou'd ha' been much more reasonable on many Accounts, leaving no Body with the sick Persons, but such as shou'd on such Occasion request to stay and declare themselves content to be shut up with them.

Our Scheme for removing those that were Sound from those that were Sick, was only in such Houses as were infected, and confining the sick was no Confinement; those that cou'd not stir, wou'd not complain, while they were in their Senses, and while they had the Power of judging: Indeed, when they came to be Delirious and Light-headed, then they wou'd cry out of the Cruelty of being confin'd; but for the removal of those that were well, we thought it highly reasonable and just, for their own sakes, they shou'd be remov'd from the Sick, and that, for other People's Safety, they shou'd keep retir'd for a while, to see that they were sound, and might not infect others; and we thought twenty or thirty Days enough for this.

Now certainly, if houses had been provided on purpose for those that were found to perform this demy[1] Quarantine in, they wou'd have much less Reason to think themselves injur'd in such a restraint, than in being confin'd with infected People, in the Houses where they liv'd.

It is here, however, to be observ'd, that after the Funerals became so many, that People could not Toll the Bell, Mourn, or Weep, or wear Black for one another, as they did before; no, nor so much as make Coffins for those that died; so after a while the fury of the Infection appeared to be so encreased, that in short, they shut up no Houses at all, it seem'd enough that all the Remedies of that Kind had been used till they were found fruitless, and that the Plague spread itself with an irresistible Fury, so that, as the Fire the succeeding Year, spread itself and burnt with such Violence, that the Citizens in Despair, gave over their Endeavours to extinguish it, so in the Plague, it came at last to such Violence that the People sat still looking at one another, and seem'd quite abandon'd to Despair; whole Streets seem'd to be desolated, and not to be shut up only, but to be emptied of their Inhabitants; Doors were left open, Windows stood shattering with the Wind in empty Houses, for want of People to shut them: In a Word, People began to give up themselves to their Fears, and to think that all regulations and Methods were in vain, and that there was nothing to be hoped for, but an universal Desolation; and it was even in the height of this general Despair, that it pleased God to stay his Hand, and to slacken the Fury of the Contagion, in such a manner as was even surprizing like its beginning, and demonstrated it to be his own particular Hand, and that above, if not without the Agency of Means, as I shall take Notice of in its proper Place.

But I must still speak of the Plague as in its height, raging even to Desolation, and the People under the most dreadful Consternation, even, as I have said, to Despair. It is hardly credible to what Excesses the Passions of Men carry'd them in this Extremity of the Distemper; and this Part, I think, was as moving as the rest; What cou'd affect a Man in his full Power of Reflection; and what could make deeper Impressions on the Soul, than to see a Man almost Naked and got out of his House, or perhaps out of his Bed into the Street, come out of *Harrow-Alley*, a populous Conjunction or Collection of Alleys, Courts, and Passages, in the Butcher-row in *Whitechappel?* I say, What could be more Affecting, than to see this poor Man come out into the open Street, run Dancing

1. Demi, half.

and Singing, and making a thousand antick Gestures, with five or six Women and Children running after him, crying, and calling upon him, for the Lord's sake to come back, and entreating the help of others to bring him back, but all in vain, no Body daring to lay a Hand upon him, or to come near him.

This was a most grievous and afflicting thing to me, who see it all from my own Windows; for all this while, the poor afflicted Man, was, as I observ'd it, even then in the utmost Agony of Pain, having, as they said, two Swellings upon him, which cou'd not be brought to break, or to suppurate; but by laying strong Causticks on them, the Surgeons had, it seems, hopes to break them, which Causticks were then upon him, burning his Flesh as with a hot Iron: I cannot say what became of this poor Man, but I think he continu'd roving about in that manner till he fell down and Died.

No wonder the Aspect of the City itself was frightful, the usual concourse of People in the Streets, and which used to be supplied from our end of the Town, was abated; the Exchange [2] was not kept shut indeed, but it was no more frequented; the Fires were lost; they had been almost extinguished for some Days by a very smart and hasty Rain: But that was not all, some of the Physicians insisted that they were not only no Benefit, but injurious to the Health of People: This they made a loud Clamour about, and complain'd to the Lord Mayor about it: On the other Hand, others of the same Faculty, and Eminent too, oppos'd them, and gave their Reasons why the Fires were and must be useful to asswage the Violence of the Distemper. I cannot give a full Account of their Arguments on both Sides, only this I remember, that they cavil'd very much with one another; some were for Fires, but that they must be made of Wood and not Coal, and of particular sorts of Wood too, such as Fir in particular, or Cedar, because of the strong effluvia of Turpentine; Others were for Coal and not Wood, because of the Sulphur and Bitumen; and others were for neither one or other. Upon the whole, the Lord Mayor ordered no more Fires, and especially on this Account, namely, that the Plague was so fierce that they saw evidently it defied all Means and rather seemed to encrease than decrease upon any application to check and abate it; and yet this Amazement of the Magistrates, proceeded rather from want of being able to apply any Means successfully, than from any unwillingness either to expose themselves, or undertake the Care and Weight of Business; for, to do them Justice, they neither spared their Pains or their Persons; but nothing answer'd, the Infection rag'd, and the People were now frighted and terrified to the last Degree, so that, as I may say, they gave themselves up, and, as I mention'd above, abandon'd themselves to their Despair.

But let me observe here, that when I say the People abandon'd themselves to Despair, I do not mean to what Men call a religious Despair,

2. The Exchange was finally closed on August 2 for lack of business; it reopened around September 27. The *Newes* for that date reported that "repairs" were completed.

or a Despair of their eternal State, but I mean a Despair of their being able to escape the Infection, or to out-live the Plague, which they saw was so raging and so irresistible in its Force, that indeed few People that were touch'd with it in its height about *August*, and *September*, escap'd: And, which is very particular, contrary to its ordinary Operation in *June* and *July*, and the beginning of *August*, when, as I have observ'd many were infected, and continued so many Days, and then went off, after having had the Poison in their Blood a long time; but now on the contrary, most of the People who were taken during the two last Weeks in *August*, and in the three first Weeks in *September*, generally died in two or three days at farthest, and many the very same Day they were taken; Whether the Dog-days,[3] or as our Astrologers pretended to express themselves, the Influence of the Dog-Star had that malignant Effect; or all those who had the seeds of Infection before in them, brought it up to a maturity at that time altogether I know not; but this was the time when it was reported, that above 3000 People died in one Night; and they that wou'd have us believe they more critically observ'd it, pretend to say, that they all died within the space of two Hours, *(viz.)* Between the Hours of One and three in the Morning.

As to the Suddenness of People's dying at this time more than before, there were innumerable Instances of it, and I could name several in my Neighbourhood; one Family without the Barrs, and not far from me, were all seemingly well on the Monday, being Ten in Family, that Evening one Maid and one Apprentice were taken ill, and dy'd the next Morning, when the other Apprentice and two Children were touch'd, whereof one dy'd the same Evening, and the other two on Wednesday: In a Word, by Saturday at Noon, the Master, Mistress, four Children and four Servants were all gone, and the House left entirely empty, except an ancient Woman, who came in to take Charge of the Goods for the Master of the Family's Brother, who liv'd not far off, and who had not been sick.

Many Houses were then left desolate, all the People being carry'd away dead, and especially in an Alley farther, on the same Side beyond the Barrs, going in at the Sign of *Moses* and *Aaron*;[4] there were several Houses together, which (they said) had not one Person left alive in them, and some that dy'd last in several of those Houses, were left a little too long before they were fetch'd out to be bury'd; the Reason of which was not as some have written very untruly, that the living were not sufficient to bury the dead; but that the Mortality was so great in the yard or Alley, that there was no Body left to give Notice to the Buriers or Sextons, that there were any dead Bodies there to be bury'd. It was said; how true I

3. The most sultry period of summer, from about July 3 to August 11. So-named in ancient Mediterranean cultures, it extended twenty days before and twenty days after the conjunction of Sirius (the dog star) with the sun and was considered likely to bring disease and plague. Defoe traces to the Middle and Near East many of the superstitions to which he refers.
4. This sign was on a coffeehouse at the corner of Moses and Aaron Alley and White Chapel.

know not, that some of those Bodies were so much corrupted, and so rotten, that it was with Difficulty they were carry'd; and as the Carts could not come any nearer than to the Alley-Gate in the high Street, it was so much the more difficult to bring them along; but I am not certain how many Bodies were then left, I am sure that ordinarily it was not so.

As I have mention'd how the People were brought into a Condition to despair of Life and abandon themselves, so this very Thing had a strange Effect among us for three or four Weeks, that is, it made them bold and venturous, they were no more shy of one another, or restrained within Doors, but went any where and every where, and began to converse; one would say to another, I do not ask you how you are, or say how I am, it is certain we shall all go, so 'tis no Matter who is sick or who is sound, and so they run desperately into any Place or any Company.

As it brought the People into publick Company, so it was surprizing how it brought them to crowd into the Churches, they inquir'd no more into who they sat near to, or far from, what offensive Smells they met with, or what condition the People seemed to be in, but looking upon themselves all as so many dead Corpses, they came to the Churches without the least Caution, and crowded together, as if their Lives were of no Consequence, compar'd to the Work which they came about there: Indeed, the Zeal which they shew'd in Coming, and the Earnestness and Affection they Shew'd in their Attention to what they heard, made it manifest what a Value People would all put upon the Worship of God, if they thought every Day they attended at the Church that it would be their Last.

Nor was it without other strange Effects, for it took away all Manner of Prejudice at, or Scruple about the Person who they found in the Pulpit when they came to the Churches. It cannot be doubted, but that many of the Ministers of the Parish-Churches were cut off among others in so common and so dreadful a Calamity; and others had not Courage enough to stand it, but removed into the Country as they found Means for Escape, as then some Parish-Churches were quite vacant and forsaken, the People made no Scruple of desiring such dissenters as had been a few Years before depriv'd of their Livings, by Virtue of the Act of Parliament call'd, *The Act of Uniformity* to preach in the Churches, nor did the Church Ministers in that Case make any Difficulty of accepting their Assistance, so that many of those who they called silenced Ministers,[5] had their Mouths open'd on this Occasion, and preach'd publickly to the People.

Here we may observe, and I hope it will not be amiss to take notice

---

5. See p. 26 in this volume. Those forbidden to preach because they would not accept the *Book of Common Prayer* and all thirty-nine Articles of the Church of England called themselves "silenced," and they used the term eloquently. As the Rev. John Whitlock said, "God now calls us and many others to preach to you by silence. And the very silence of so many ministers . . . may prove the most powerful . . . sermon to people that they have ever had" (Backscheider, *Defoe* 131).

of it, that a near View of Death would soon reconcile Men of good
Principles one to another, and that it is chiefly owing to our easy Scitua-
tion in Life, and our putting these Things far from us, that our Breaches
are fomented, ill Blood continued, Prejudices, Breach of Charity and of
Christian Union so much kept and so far carry'd on among us, as it is:
Another Plague Year would reconcile all these Differences, a close conversing with Death, or with Diseases that threaten Death, would scum
off the Gall from our Tempers, remove the Animosities among us, and
bring us to see with differing Eyes, than those which we look'd on Things
with before; as the People who had been used to join with the Church,
were reconcil'd at this Time, with the admitting the Dissenters to preach
to them: So the Dissenters, who with an uncommon Prejudice, had
broken off from the Communion of the Church of England, were now
content to come to their Parish-Churches, and to conform to the Worship which they did not approve of before; but as the Terror of the Infection abated, those Things all returned again to their less desirable Channel,
and to the Course they were in before.

I mention this but historically, I have no mind to enter into Arguments to move either, or both Sides to a more charitable Compliance
one with another; I do not see that it is probable such a Discourse would
be either suitable or successful; the Breaches seem rather to widen, and
tend to a widening farther, than to closing, and who am I that I should
think myself able to influence either one Side or other? But this I may
repeat again, that 'tis evident Death will reconcile us all; on the other
Side the Grave we shall be all Brethren again: In Heaven, whether, I
hope we may come from all Parties and Perswasions, we shall find neither Prejudice or Scruple; there we shall be of one Principle and of one
Opinion, why we cannot be content to go Hand in Hand to the Place
where we shall join Heart and Hand without the least Hesitation, and
with the most compleat Harmony and Affection; I say, why we cannot
do so here I can say nothing to, neither shall I say any thing more of it,
but that it remains to be lamented.

I could dwell a great while upon the Calamities of this dreadful time,
and go on to describe the Objects that appear'd among us every Day,
the dreadful Extravagancies which the Distraction of sick People drove
them into; how the Streets began now to be fuller of frightful Objects,
and Families to be made even a Terror to themselves: But after I have
told you, as I have above, that One Man being tyed in his Bed, and
finding no other Way to deliver himself, set the Bed on fire with his
Candle, which unhappily stood within his reach, and Burnt himself in
his Bed. And how another, by the insufferable Torment he bore, daunced
and sung naked in the Streets, not knowing one Extasie from another, I
say, after I have mention'd these Things, What can be added more?
What can be said to represent the Misery of these Times, more lively to
the Reader, or to give him a more perfect Idea of a complicated Distress?

I must acknowledge that this time was Terrible, that I was sometimes at the End of all my Resolutions, and that I had not the Courage that I had at the Beginning. As the Extremity brought other People abroad, it drove me Home, and except, having made my Voyage down to *Blackwall* and *Greenwich*, as I have related, which was an Excursion, I kept afterwards very much within Doors, as I had for about a Fortnight before; I have said already, that I repented several times that I had ventur'd to stay in Town, and had not gone away with my Brother, and his Family, but it was too late for that now; and after I had retreated and stay'd within Doors a good while, before my Impatience led me Abroad, than they call'd me, as I have said, to an ugly and dangerous Office, which brought me out again; but as that was expir'd, while the hight of the Distemper lasted, I retir'd again, and continued close ten or twelve Days more. During which many dismal Spectacles represented themselves in my View, out of my own Windows, and in our own Street, as that particularly from *Harrow-Alley*, of the poor outrageous Creature which danced and sung in his Agony, and many others there were: Scarce a Day or Night Pass'd over, but some dismal Thing or other happened at the End of that *Harrow-Alley*, which was a Place full of poor People, most of them belonging to the Butchers, or to Employments depending upon the Butchery.

Sometimes Heaps and Throngs of People would burst out of that Alley, most of them Women, making a dreadful Clamour, mixt or Compounded of Skreetches, Cryings and Calling one another, that we could not conceive what to make of it; almost all the dead Part of the Night the dead Cart stood at the End of that Alley, for it went in it could not well turn again, and could go in but a little Way. There, I say, it stood to receive dead Bodys, and as the Church-Yard was but a little Way off, if it went away full it would soon be back again: It is impossible to describe the most horrible Cries and Noise the poor People would make at their bringing the dead Bodies of their Children and Friends out to the Cart, and by the Number one would have thought, there had been none left behind, or that there were People enough for a small City liveing in those Places: Several times they cryed Murther, sometimes Fire; but it was easie to perceive it was all Distraction, and the Complaints of Distress'd and distemper'd People.

I believe it was every where thus at that time, for the Plague rag'd for six or seven Weeks beyond all that I have express'd; and came even to such a height, that in the Extremity, they began to break into that excellent Order, of which I have spoken so much, in behalf of the Magistrates, namely, that no dead Bodies were seen in the Streets or Burials in the Day-time, for there was a Necessity, in this Extremety, to bear with its being otherwise, for a little while.

One thing I cannot omit here, and indeed I thought it was extraordinary, at least, it seemed a remarkable Hand of Divine Justice, *(viz)* That all the Predictors, Astrologers, Fortune-tellers, and what they call'd cunning-Men, Conjurers, and the like; calculators of Nativities, and dreamers of Dreams, and such People, were gone and vanish'd, not one of them was to be found: I am, verily, perswaded that a great Number of them fell in the heat of the Calamity, having ventured to stay upon the Prospect of getting great Estates; and indeed their Gain was but too great for a time through the Madness and Folly of the People; but now they were silent, many of them went to their long Home, not able to foretel their own Fate, or to calculate their own Nativities; some have been critical enough to say, that every one of them dy'd; I dare not affirm that, but this I must own, that I never heard of one of them that ever appear'd after the Calamity was over.

But to return to my particular Observations, during this dreadful part of the Visitation: I am now come, as I have said, to the Month of *September*, which was the most dreadful of its kind, I believe, that ever *London* saw; for by all the Accounts which I have seen of the preceding Visitations which have been in *London*, nothing has been like it; the Number in the Weekly Bill amounting to almost 40,000 from the 22d of *August*, to the 26th of *September*, being but five Weeks, the particulars of the Bills are as follows, *(viz.)*

From *August* the 22d to the 29th	7496
To the 7th of *September*	8252
To the 12th	7690
To the 19th	8297
To the 26th	6460
	38195[6]

This was a prodigious Number of itself, but if I should add the Reasons which I have to believe that this Account was deficient, and how deficient it was, you would with me, make no Scruple to believe that there died above ten Thousand a Week for all those Weeks, one Week with another, and a proportion of several Weeks both before and after: The Confusion among the People, especially within the City at that time, was inexpressible; the Terror was so great at last, that the Courage of the People appointed to carry away the Dead, began to fail them; nay, several of them died altho' they had the Distemper before, and were recover'd; and some of them drop'd down when they have been carrying the Bodies even at the Pitside, and just ready to throw them in; and this Confusion was greater in the City, because they had flatter'd themselves with Hopes of escaping: And thought the bitterness of Death was past: One Cart they told us, going up *Shoreditch*,[7] was forsaken of the Drivers, or being left to one Man to drive, he died in the Street, and the Horses going on, overthrew the Cart, and left the Bodies, some thrown out

6. This figure includes all deaths; the Bills of Mortality list 32,332 plague deaths for this period.
7. This borough is north of London and between Hackney and Bethnal Green on the east and Islington on the west. St. Leonard was the major parish and had a church of Saxon origin.

here, some there, in a dismal manner; Another Cart was it seems found in the great Pit in *Finsbury* Fields, the Driver being Dead, or having been gone and abandon'd it, and the Horses running too near it, the Cart fell in and drew the Horses in also: It was suggested that the Driver was thrown in with it, and that the Cart fell upon him, by Reason his Whip was seen to be in the Pit among the Bodies; but that, I suppose, cou'd not be certain.

In our Parish of *Aldgate*, the dead-Carts were several times, as I have heard, found standing at the Church-Yard Gate, full of dead bodies, but neither Bell man or Driver, or any one else with it; neither in these, or many other Cases, did they know what Bodies they had in their Cart, for sometimes they were let down with Ropes out of Balconies and out of Windows; and sometimes the Bearers brought them to the Cart, sometimes other People; nor, *as the Men themselves said*, did they trouble themselves to keep any Account of the Numbers.

The Vigilance of the Magistrate was now put to the utmost Trial, and it must be confess'd, can never be enough acknowledg'd on this Occasion also, whatever Expence or Trouble they were at, two Things were never neglected in the City or Suburbs either.

1. Provisions were always to be had in full Plenty, and the Price not much rais'd neither, hardly worth speaking.

2. No dead Bodies lay unburied or uncovered; and if one walk'd from one end of the City to another, no Funeral or sign of it was to be seen in the Day-time, except a little, as I have said above, in the three first Weeks in *September*.

This last Article perhaps will hardly be believ'd, when some Accounts which others have published since that shall be seen, wherein they say, that the Dead lay unburied, which I am assured was utterly false; at least, if it had been any where so, it must ha' been in Houses where the Living were gone from the Dead, having found means, as I have observed, to Escape, and where no Notice was given to the Officers: All which amounts to nothing at all in the Case in Hand; for this I am positive in, having myself been employ'd a little in the Direction of that part in the Parish in which I liv'd, and where as great a Desolation was made in proportion to the Number of Inhabitants as was any where. I say, I am sure that there were no dead Bodies remain'd unburied; that is to say, none that the proper Officers knew of; none for want of People to carry them off, and Buriers to put them into the Ground and cover them; and this is sufficient to the Argument; for what might lie in Houses and Holes as in *Moses* and *Aaron* Ally is nothing; for it is most certain, they were buried as soon as they were found. As to the first Article, namely, of Provisions, the scarcity or dearness, tho' I have mention'd it before, and shall speak of it again; yet I must observe here,

(1.) The Price of Bread in particular was not much raised; for in the beginning of the Year *(viz.)* In the first Week in *March*, the Penny Wheaten Loaf was ten Ounces and a half; and in the height of the

Contagion, it was to be had at nine Ounces and an half, and never dearer, no not all that Season: And about the beginning of *November* it was sold ten Ounces and a half again; the like of which, I believe, was never heard of in any City, under so dreadful a Visitation before.

(2.) Neither was there (which I wondred much at) any want of Bakers or Ovens kept open to supply the People with Bread; but this was indeed alledg'd by some Families, *viz.* That their Maid-Servants going to the Bake-houses with their Dough to be baked,[8] which was then the Custom, sometimes came Home with the Sickness, that is to say, the Plague upon them.

In all this dreadful Visitation, there were, as I have said before, but two Pest-houses made use of, *viz.* One in the Fields beyond *Old-Street*, and one in *Westminster;*[9] neither was there any Compulsion us'd in carrying People thither: Indeed there was no need of Compulsion in the Case, for there were Thousands of poor distressed People, who having no Help, or Conveniences, or Supplies but of Charity, would have been very glad to have been carryed thither, and been taken Care of, which indeed was the only thing that, I think, was wanting in the whole publick Management of the City; seeing no Body was here allow'd to be brought to the Pest-house, but where Money was given, or Security for Money, either at their introducing, or upon their being cur'd and sent out; for very many were sent out again whole, and very good Physicians were appointed to those Places, so that many People did very well there, of which I shall make Mention again. The principal Sort of People sent thither were, as I have said, Servants, who got the Distemper by going of Errands to fetch Necessaries to the Families where they liv'd; and who in that Case, if they came Home sick, were remov'd to preserve the rest of the House, and they were so well look'd after there in all the time of the Visitation, that there was but 156 buried in all at the *London* Pest-house, and 159 at that of *Westminster.*

By having more Pest-houses, I am far from meaning a forcing all People into such Places. Had the shutting up of Houses been omitted, and the Sick hurried out of their Dwellings to Pest-houses, as some proposed it seems, at that time as well as since, it would certainly have been much worse than it was; the very removing the Sick would have been a spreading of the Infection, and [that] rather because that removing could not effectually clear the house, where the sick Person was, of the Distemper, and the rest of the Family being then left at Liberty would certainly spread it among others.

The Methods also in private Families, which would have been universally used to have concealed the Distemper, and to have conceal'd the Persons being sick, would have been such, that the Distemper would

---

8. Not all homes had ovens; bread baked from customers' own dough was called "wives bread."
9. There were five pesthouses, but Defoe insists that only two functioned adequately: that beyond Bunhill Fields and one at Tothill Fields, Westminster. It is unlikely that all five together held as many as six hundred patients.

sometimes have seiz'd a whole Family before any Visitors or Examiners could have known of it: On the other hand, the prodigious Numbers which would have been sick at a time, would have exceeded all the Capacity of publick Pest-houses to receive them, or of publick Officers to discover and remove them.

This was well considered in those Days, and I have heard them talk of it often: The Magistrates had enough to do to bring People to submit to having their Houses shut up, and many Ways they deceived the Watchmen, and got out, as I have observed: But that Difficulty made it apparent, that they would have found it impracticable to have gone the other way to Work; for they could never have forced the sick People out of their Beds and out of their Dwellings; it must not have been my Lord Mayor's Officers, but an Army of Officers that must have attempted it; and the People, on the other hand, would have been enrag'd and desperate, and would have kill'd those that should have offered to have meddled with them or with their Children and Relations, whatever had befallen them for it; so that they would have made the People, who, *as it was*, were in the most terrible Distraction imaginable; I say, they would have made them stark mad; whereas the Magistrates found it proper on several Accounts to treat them with Lenity and Compassion, and not with Violence and Terror, such as dragging the Sick out of their Houses, or obliging them to remove themselves would have been.

This leads me again to mention the Time, when the Plague first began, that is to say, when it became certain that it would spread over the whole Town, when, as I have said, the better sort of People first took the Alarm, and began to hurry themselves out of Town: It was true, as I observ'd in its Place, that the Throng was so great, and the Coaches, Horses, Waggons and Carts were so many, driving and dragging the People away, that it look'd as if all the City was running away; and had any Regulations been publish'd that had been terrifying at that time, especially such as would pretend to dispose of the People, otherwise than they would dispose of themselves, it would have put both the City and Suburbs into the utmost Confusion.

But the Magistrates wisely caus'd the People to be encourag'd, made very good By-Laws for the regulating the Citizens, keeping good Order in the Streets, and making every thing as eligible as possible to all Sorts of People.

In the first Place, the Lord Mayor and the Sheriffs, the Court of Aldermen and a certain Number of the Common Council-Men, or their Deputies came to a Resolution and published it, *viz.* That *they* would not quit the City themselves, but that they would be always at hand for the preserving good Order in every Place, and for the doing Justice on all Occasions; as also for the distributing the publick Charity to the Poor; and in a Word, for the doing the Duty, and discharging the Trust repos'd in them by the Citizens to the utmost of their Power.

In Pursuance of these Orders, the Lord Mayor, Sheriffs, &c. held

Councils every Day more or less, for making such Dispositions as they found needful for preserving the Civil Peace; and tho' they used the People with all possible Gentleness and Clemency, yet all manner of presumptuous Rogues, such as Thieves, House-breakers, Plunderers of the Dead, or of the Sick, were duly punish'd, and several Declarations were continually publish'd by the Lord Mayor and Court of Aldermen against such.

Also all Constables and Church-wardens were enjoin'd to stay in the City upon severe Penalties, or to depute such able and sufficient House-keepers, as the Deputy Aldermen, or Common Council-men of the Precinct should approve, and for whom they should give Security; and also Security in case of Mortality, that they would forthwith constitute other Constables in their stead.

These things re-establish'd the Minds of the People very much, especially in the first of their Fright, when they talk'd of making so universal a Flight, that the City would have been in Danger of being entirely deserted of its Inhabitants, except the Poor; and the Country of being plunder'd and laid waste by the Multitude. Nor were the Magistrates deficient in performing their Part as boldly as they promised it; for my Lord Mayor and the Sheriffs were continually in the Streets, and at places of the greatest Danger; and tho' they did not care for having too great a Resort of People crouding about them, yet, in emergent Cases, they never denyed the People Access to them, and heard with Patience all their Grievances and Complaints; my Lord Mayor had a low Gallery built on purpose in his Hall, where he stood a little remov'd from the Croud when any Complaint came to be heard, that he might appear with as much Safety as possible.

Likewise the proper Officers, call'd *my Lord Mayor's Officers*, constantly attended in their Turns, as they were *in waiting*; and if any of them were sick or infected, as some of them were, others were instantly employed to fill up and officiate in their Places, till it was known whether the other should live or die.

In like manner the Sheriffs and Aldermen did in their several Stations and Wards, where they were placed by Office; and the Sheriff's Officers or Sergeants were appointed to receive Orders from the respective Aldermen in their Turn; so that Justice was executed in all Cases without Interruption. In the next Place, it was one of their particular Cares, to see the Orders for the Freedom of the Markets observ'd; and in this part either the Lord Mayor, or one or both of the Sheriffs, were every Market-day on Horseback to see their Orders executed, and to see that the Country People had all possible Encouragement and Freedom in their coming to the Markets, and going back again; and that no Nuisances or frightful Objects should be seen in the Streets to terrify them, or make them unwilling to come. Also the Bakers were taken under particular Order, and the Master of the Bakers Company was, with his Court of Assistance, directed to see the Order of my Lord Mayor for their Regulation put in Execution, and the due Assize of Bread, which was weekly appointed by my Lord Mayor, observ'd, and all the Bakers were oblig'd to keep their Ovens going constantly, on pain of losing the Privileges of a Freeman of the City of *London*.

By this means, Bread was always to be had in Plenty, and as cheap as usual, as I said above; and Provisions were never wanting in the Markets, even to such a Degree, that I often wonder'd at it, and reproach'd my self with being so timorous and cautious in stirring abroad, when the Country People came freely and boldly to Market, as if there had been no manner of Infection in the City, or Danger of catching it.

It was indeed one admirable piece of Conduct in the said Magistrates, that the Streets were kept constantly clear, and free from all manner of frightful Objects, dead Bodies, or any such things as were indecent or unpleasant, unless where any Body fell down suddenly or died in the Streets, *as I have said above*, and these were generally covered with some Cloth or Blanket, or remov'd into the next Church-yard, till Night: All the needful Works, that carried Terror with them, that were both dismal and dangerous, were done in the Night; if any diseas'd Bodies were remov'd, or dead Bodies buried, or infected Cloths burnt, it was done in the Night; and all the Bodies, which were thrown into the great Pits in the several Church-yards, or burying Grounds, *as has been observ'd*, were so remov'd in the Night; and every thing was covered and closed before Day: So that in the Day-time there was not the least Signal of the Calamity to be seen or heard of, except what was to be observ'd from the Emptiness of the Streets, and sometimes from the passionate Outcries and Lamentations of the People, out at their Windows, and from the Numbers of Houses and Shops shut up.

Nor was the Silence and Emptiness of the Streets so much in the City as in the Out-parts, except just at one particular time, when, as I have mention'd, the Plague came East, and spread over all the City: It was indeed a merciful Disposition of God, that as the Plague began at one End of the Town first, *as has been observ'd at large*, so it proceeded progressively to other Parts, and did not come on this way or Eastward, till it had spent its Fury in the West part of the Town; and so as it came on one way, it abated another. *For Example.*

It began at St. *Giles's* and the *Westminster* End of the Town, and it was in its Height in all that part by about the Middle of *July*, *viz.* in St. *Giles* in the *Fields*, St. *Andrew's Holborn*, St. *Clement-Danes*, St. *Martins* in the *Fields*, and in *Westminster:* The latter End of *July* it decreased in those Parishes, and coming East, it encreased prodigiously in *Cripplegate*, St. *Sepulchers*, St. *Ja. Clarkenwell*, and St. *Brides*, and *Aldersgate*; while it was in all these Parishes, the City and all the Parishes of the *Southwark* Side of the Water, and all *Stepney*, *White-Chapel*, *Aldgate*, *Wapping*, and *Ratcliff* were very little touch'd; so that People went about their Business unconcern'd, carryed on their Trades, kept open their Shops, and conversed freely with one another in all the City, the

East and North-East Suburbs, and in *Southwark*, almost as if the Plague had not been among us.

Even when the North and North-west Suburbs were fully infected, *viz. Cripplegate, Clarkenwell, Bishopsgate,* and *Shoreditch,* yet still all the rest were tolerably well. For Example,

From 25th *July* to 1st *August* the Bill stood thus of all Diseases:

St. *Giles Cripplegate* _____	554
St. *Sepulchers* _____	250
Clarkenwell _____	103
Bishopsgate _____	116
Shoreditch _____	110
Stepney Parish _____	127
Aldgate _____	92
White-Chappel _____	104
All the 97 Parishes within the Walls __	228
All the Parishes in *Southwark* _____	205
	1889

So that in short there died more that Week in the two Parishes of *Cripplegate* and St. *Sepulchers* by 48 than in all the City, and all the East Suburbs, and all the *Southwark* Parishes put together: This caused the Reputation of the City's Health to continue all over *England,* and especially in the Counties and Markets adjacent, from whence our Supply of Provisions chiefly came, even much longer than that Health it self continued; for when the People came into the Streets from the Country, by *Shoreditch* and *Bishopsgate,* or by *Oldstreet* and *Smithfield,* they would see the out Streets empty, and the Houses and Shops shut, and the few People that were stirring there walk in the Middle of the Streets; but when they came within the City, *there things look'd better,* and the Markets and Shops were open, and the People walking about the Streets as usual, tho' not quite so many; and this continued till the latter End of *August,* and the Beginning of *September.*

But then the Case alter'd quite, the Distemper abated in the West and North-West Parishes, and the Weight of the Infection lay on the City and the Eastern Suburbs and the *Southwark* Side, and this in a frightful manner.

Then indeed the City began to look dismal, Shops to be shut, and the Streets desolate; in the High-Street indeed Necessity made People stir abroad on many Occasions; and there would be in the middle of the Day a pretty many People, but in the Mornings and Evenings scarce any to be seen, even there, no not in *Cornhill* and *Cheapside.*

These Observations of mine were abundantly confirm'd by the Weekly Bills of Mortality for those Weeks, an Abstract of which, as they respect the Parishes which I have mention'd, and as they make the Calculations I speak of very evident, take as follows.

The Weekly Bill, which makes out this Decrease of the Burials in the West and North side of the City, stand thus.

From the 12th of *September* to the 19th.

St. *Giles's Cripplegate*	456
St. *Giles* in the Fields	140
Clarkenwell	77
St. *Sepulchers*	214
St. *Leonard Shoreditch*	183
Stepney Parish	716
Aldgate	623
White-Chapel	532
In the 97 Parishes within the Walls	1493
In the 8 Parishes on *Southwark* Side	1636
	‾‾‾
	6060

Here is strange change of Things indeed, and a sad Change it was, and had it held for two Months more than it did, very few People would have been left alive: But then such, I say, was the merciful Disposition of God, that when it was thus the West and North part which had been so dreadfully visited at first, grew *as you see*, much better; and as the People disappear'd here, they began to look abroad again there; and the next Week or two altered it still more, that is, more to the Encouragement of the other Part of the Town. *For Example*:

From the 19th of *September* to the 26th;

St. *Giles's Cripplegate*	277
St. *Giles* in the Fields	119
Clarkenwell	76
St. *Sepulchers*	193
St. *Leonard Shoreditch*	146
Stepney Parish	616
Aldgate	496
White-Chapel	346
In the 97 Parishes within the Walls	1268
In the 8 Parishes on *Southwark* Side	1390
	‾‾‾
	4900

From the 26th of *Septemb.* to the 3d of *October*.

St. *Giles's Cripplegate*	196
St. *Giles* in the Fields	95
Clarkenwell	48
St. *Sepulchers*	137
St. *Leonard Shoreditch*	128

Stepney Parish _____	674
Aldgate _____	372
White-Chapel _____	328
In the 97 Parishes within the Walls __	1149
In the 8 Parishes on *Southwark* Side _	1201
	4328

And now the Misery of the City, and of the said East and South Parts was complete indeed; for as you see the Weight of the Distemper lay upon those Parts, that is to say, the City, the eight Parishes over the River, with the Parishes of *Aldgate*, *White-Chapel*, and *Stepney*, and this was the Time that the Bills came up to Such a monstrous Height, as that I mention'd before; and that Eight or Nine, and, as I believe, Ten or Twelve Thousand a Week died; for 'tis my settled Opinion, that they never could come at any just Account of Numbers, for the Reasons which I have given already.

Nay one of the most eminent Physicians,[1] who has since publish'd in Latin an Account of those Times, and of his Observations, says, that in one Week there died twelve Thousand People, and that particularly there died four Thousand in one Night; tho' I do not remember that there ever was any such particular Night, so remarkably fatal, as that such a Number died in it: However all this confirms what I have said above of the Uncertainty of the Bills of Mortality, &c. of which I shall say more hereafter.

And here let me take leave to enter again, tho' it may seem a Repetition of Circumstances, into a Description of the miserable Condition of the City it self, and of those Parts where I liv'd at this particular Time: The City, and those other Parts, not withstanding the great Numbers of People that were gone into the Country, was vastly full of People, and perhaps the fuller, because People had for a long time a strong Belief, that the Plague would not come into the City, nor into *Southwark*, no nor into *Wapping*, or *Ratcliff* at all; nay such was the Assurance of the People on that Head, that many remov'd from the Suburbs on the West and North Sides, into those Eastern and South Sides as for Safety, and as I verily believe, carry'd, the Plague amongst them there, perhaps sooner than they would otherwise have had it.

Here also I ought to leave a farther Remark for the use of Posterity, concerning the Manner of Peoples infecting one another, namely, that it was not the sick People only, from whom the Plague was immediately receiv'd by others that were sound, but THE WELL. *To explain myself*; by *the sick* People I mean those who were known to be sick, had ·taken their Beds, had been under Cure, or had Swellings and Tumours upon them, and the like; these every Body could beware of, they were either in their Beds, or in such Condition as cou'd not be conceal'd.

1. Dr. Nathaniel Hodges; his *Loimologia* was first published in 1671 in Latin and had recently appeared in English translation (1720); see p. 214 in this volume.

By *the Well*, I mean such as had received the Contagion, and had it really upon them, and in their Blood, yet did not shew the Consequences of it in their Countenances, nay even were not sensible of it themselves, *as many were not* for several Days: These breathed Death in every Place, and upon every Body who came near them; nay their very Cloaths retained the Infection, their Hands would infect the Things they touch'd, especially if they were warm and sweaty, and they were generally apt to sweat too.

Now it was impossible to know these People, nor did they sometimes, as I have said, know themselves to be infected: These were the People that so often dropt down and fainted in the Streets; for oftentimes they would go about the Streets to the last, till on a sudden they would sweat, grow faint, sit down at a Door and die: It is true, finding themselves thus, they would struggle hard to get Home to their own Doors, or at other Times would be just able to go in to their Houses and die instantly; other Times they would go about till they had the very Tokens come out upon them, and yet not know it, and would die in an Hour or two after they came Home, but be well as long as they were Abroad: These were the dangerous People, these were the People of whom the well People ought to have been afraid; but then *on the other side* it was impossible to know them.

And this is the Reason why it is impossible in a Visitation to prevent the spreading of the Plague by the utmost human Vigilance, *(viz.)* that it is impossible to know the infected People from the sound; or that the infected People should perfectly know themselves: I knew a Man who conversed freely in *London* all the Season of the Plague in 1665, and kept about him an Antidote or Cordial, on purpose to take when he thought himself in any Danger, and he had such a Rule to know, or have warning of the Danger by, as indeed I never met with before or since, how far it may be depended on I know not: He had a Wound in his Leg, and whenever he came among any People that were not sound, and the Infection began to affect him, he said he could know it by that Signal, *(viz.)* That his Wound in his Leg would smart, and look pale and white; so as soon as ever he felt it smart, it was time for him to withdraw, or to take care of himself, taking his Drink, which he always carried about him for that Purpose. Now it seems he found his Wound would smart many Times when he was in Company with such, who thought themselves to be sound, and who appear'd so to one another; but he would presently rise up, and say publickly, Friends, here is some Body in the Room that has the Plague, and so would immediately break up the Company. This was indeed a faithful Monitor to all People, that the Plague is not to be avoided by those that converse promiscuously in a Town infected, and People have it when they know it not, and that they likewise give it to others when they know not that they have it themselves; and in this Case, shutting up the WELL or removing the SICK will not do it, unless they can go back and shut up all those that the Sick had Convers'd with, even before they knew themselves to be sick, and none knows how far to carry that back, or where to stop; for none knows when, or where, or how they may have received the Infection, or from whom.

This I take to be the Reason, which makes so many People talk of the Air being corrupted and infected, and that they need not be cautious of whom they converse with, for that the Contagion was in the Air. I have seen them in strange Agitations and Surprises on this Account, I have never come near any infected Body! *says the disturbed Person*, I have Convers'd with none, but sound healthy People, and yet I have gotten the Distemper! I am sure I am struck from Heaven, *says another*, and he falls to the serious Part; again the first goes on exclaiming, I have come near no Infection, or any infected Person, *I am sure it is in the Air*; We draw in Death when we breath, and therefore 'tis the Hand of God, there is no withstanding it; and this at last made many People, being hardened to the Danger, grow less concern'd at it, and less cautious towards the latter End of the Time, and when it was come to its height, than they were at first; then with a kind of a *Turkish* Predestinarianism, they would say, if it pleas'd God to strike them, it was all one whether they went Abroad or staid at Home, they cou'd not escape it, and therefore they went boldly about even into infected Houses, and infected Company; visited sick People, and in short, lay in the Beds with their Wives or Relations when they were infected; and what was the Consequence? But the same that is the Consequence in *Turkey*, and in those Countries where they do those Things; namely, that they were infected too, and died by Hundreds and Thousands.

I would be far from lessening the Awe of the Judgments of God, and the Reverence to his Providence, which ought always to be on our Minds on such Occasions as these; doubtless the Visitation it self is a Stroke from Heaven upon a City, or Country, or Nation where it falls; a Messenger of his Vengeance, and a loud Call to that Nation, or Country, or City, to Humiliation and Repentance, according to that of the Prophet *Jeremiah* xviii. 7, 8. *At what instant I shall speak concerning a Nation, and concerning a Kingdom to pluck up, and to pull down, and destroy it: If that Nation against whom I have pronounced, turn form their evil, I will repent of the evil that I thought to do unto them.* [2] Now to prompt due Impressions of the Awe of God on the Minds of Men on such Occasions, and not to lessen them it is that I have left those Minutes upon Record.

I say, therefore I reflect upon no Man for putting the Reason of those Things upon the immediate Hand of God, and the Appointment and

---

2. Again Defoe turns to the book of Jeremiah for a parallel to London's situation. The parable of the potter and his clay from which these verses come was one of Defoe's favorites; he retold it in his first surviving manuscript, the *Meditations*. The potter spoils the vessel he was making on his wheel but reworks it into another vessel. At that point God speaks, "O house of Israel, cannot I do with you as this potter?" (Jeremiah 18.1–12). Defoe is beginning to move his novel to its conclusion, the rebirth and refashioning of London.

Direction of his Providence; nay, on the contrary, there were many wonderful Deliverances of Persons from Infection, and Deliverances of Persons when Infected, which intimate singular and remarkable Providence,[3] in the particular Instances to which they refer, and I esteem my own Deliverance to be one next to miraculous, and do record it with Thankfulness.

But when I am speaking of the Plague, as a Distemper arising from natural Causes, we must consider it as it was really propagated by natural Means, nor is it at all the less a Judgment for its being under the Conduct of humane Causes and Effects;[4] for as the divine Power has form'd the whole Scheme of Nature, and maintains Nature in its Course; so the same Power thinks fit to let his own Actings with Men, whether of Mercy or Judgment, go on in the ordinary Course of natural Causes, and he is pleased to act by those natural Causes as the ordinary Means; excepting and reserving to himself nevertheless a Power to act in a Supernatural Way when he sees occasion: Now 'tis evident, that in the Case of an Infection, there is no apparent extraordinary occasion for supernatural Operation, but the ordinary Course of Things appears sufficiently arm'd, and made capable of all the Effects that Heaven usually directs by a Contagion. Among these Causes and Effects this of the secret Conveyance of Infection imperceptible, and unavoidable, is more than sufficient to execute the Fierceness of divine Vengeance, without putting it upon Supernaturals and Miracle.

The acute penetrating Nature of the Disease itself was such, and the Infection was receiv'd so imperceptibly, that the most exact Caution could not secure us while in the Place: But I must be allowed to believe, and I have so many Examples fresh in my Memory, to convince me of it, that I think none can resist their Evidence; I say, I must be allowed to believe, that no one in this whole Nation ever receiv'd the Sickness or Infection, but who receiv'd it in the ordinary Way of Infection from some Body, or the Cloaths, or touch, or stench of some Body that was infected before.

The Manner of its coming first to *London*, proves this also, *(viz.)* by Goods brought over from *Holland*, and brought thither from the *Levant*; the first breaking of it out in a House in *Long-Acre*, where those Goods were carried, and first opened; its spreading from that House to other Houses, by the visible unwary conversing with those who were sick, and the infecting the Parish Officers who were employed about the Persons dead, *and the like*; these are known Authorities for this great Foundation Point, that it went on, and proceeded from Person to Person, and from

3. Some writers collected "particular Providences," instances that seemed to indicate the direct hand of God in human affairs. Defoe had contributed to such a collection, William Turner's A *Compleat History of the Most Remarkable Providences, Both of Judgment and Mercy* (1697), and his own books from *The Storm* in 1704 to A *Political History of the Devil* in 1726 to show his interest in the subject.

4. Defoe takes this position in all his writings. Although he does not deny the possibility of miracles, he carefully reveals natural causes, causes firmly based on the laws of physics, biology, or psychology.

House to House, and no otherwise: In the first House that was infected there died four Persons, a Neighbour hearing the Mistress of the first House was sick, went to visit her, and went Home and gave the Distemper to her Family, and died, and all her Houshold. A Minister call'd to pray with the first sick Person in the second House, was said to sicken immediately, and die with several more in his House: Then the Physicians began to consider, for they did not at first dream of a general Contagion. But the Physicians being sent to inspect the Bodies, they assur'd the People that it was neither more or less than *the Plague* with all its terrifying Particulars, and that it threatened an universal Infection, so many People having already convers'd with the Sick or Distemper'd, and having, as might be suppos'd, received Infection from them, that it would be impossible to put a stop to it.

Here the Opinion of the Physicians agreed with my Observation afterwards, namely, that the Danger was spreading insensibly; for the Sick cou'd infect none but those that came within reach of the sick Person; but that one Man, who may have really receiv'd the Infection, and knows it not, but goes Abroad, and about as a sound Person, may give the Plague to a thousand People, and they to greater Numbers in Proportion, and neither the Person giving the Infection, or the Persons receiving it, know any thing of it, and perhaps not feel the Effects of it for several Days after.

For Example, Many Persons in the Time of this Visitation never perceiv'd that they were infected, till they found to their unspeakable Surprize, the Tokens come out upon them, after which they seldom liv'd six Hours; for those Spots they call'd the Tokens were really gangreen Spots, or mortified Flesh in small Knobs as broad as a little silver Peny, and hard as a piece of Callous or Horn; so that when the Disease was come up to that length, there was nothing could follow but certain Death, and yet *as I said* they knew nothing of their being Infected, nor found themselves so much as out of Order, till those mortal Marks were upon them: But every Body must allow, that they were infected in a high Degree before, and must have been so some time; and consequently their Breath, their Sweat, their very Cloaths were contagious for many Days before.

This occasion'd a vast Variety of Cases, which Physicians would have much more opportunity to remember than I; but some came within the Compass of my Observation, or hearing, of which I shall name a few.

A certain Citizen who had liv'd safe, and untouch'd, till the Month of *September*, when the Weight of the Distemper lay more in the City than it had done before, was mighty chearful, and something too bold, as I think it was, in his Talk of how secure he was, how cautious he had been, and how he had never come near any sick Body: Says another Citizen, a Neighbour of his to him, one Day, *Do not be too confident* Mr. —— *It is hard to say who is sick and who is well; for we see Men alive, and well to outward Appearance one Hour, and dead the next.*

That is true, says the first Man, for he was not a Man presumptuously secure, but had escap'd a long while, and Men, as I said above, especially in the City, began to be over-easie upon that Score. *That is true*, says he, I do not think my self secure, *but I hope I have not been in Company with any Person that there has been any Danger in*. No! Says his Neighbour, *was not you at the* Bullhead *Tavern in* Gracechurch Street[5] *with* Mr. —— *the Night before last:* YES, says the first, *I was*, but *there was no Body there, that we had any Reason to think dangerous:* Upon which his Neighbour said no more, being unwilling to surprize him; but this made him more inquisitive, and as his Neighbour appear'd backward, he was the more impatient, and in a kind of Warmth, says he aloud, *why he is not dead, is he!* upon which his Neighbour still was silent, but cast up his Eyes, and said something to himself; at which the first Citizen turned pale, and said no more but this, *then I am a dead Man too*, and went Home immediately, and sent for a neighbouring Apothecary to give him something preventive, for he had not yet found himself ill; but the Apothecary opening his Breast, fetch'd a Sigh, and said no more, but this, *look up to God*; and the Man died in a few Hours.

Now let any Man judge from a Case like this, if it is possible for the Regulations of Magistrates, either by shutting up the Sick, or removing them, to stop an Infection, which spreads it self from Man to Man, even while they are perfectly well, and insensible of its Approach, and may be so for many Days.

It may be proper to ask here, how long it may be supposed, Men might have the Seeds of the Contagion in them, before it discover'd it self in this fatal Manner; and how long they might go about seemingly whole, and yet be contagious to all those that came near them? I believe the most experienc'd Physicians cannot answer this Question directly, any more than I can; and something an ordinary Observer may take notice of, which may pass their Observation. The opinion of Physicians Abroad seems to be, that it may lye Dormant in the Spirits, or in the Blood Vessels, a very considerable Time; why else do they exact a Quarantine of those who come into their Harbours, and Ports, from suspected Places? Forty Days is, one would think, too long for Nature to struggle with such an Enemy as this, and not conquer it, or yield to it: But I could not think by my own Observation that they can be infected so, as to be contagious to others, above fifteen or sixteen Days at farthest; and on that score it was, that when a House was shut up in the City, and any one had died of the Plague, but no Body appear'd to be ill in the Family for sixteen or eighteen Days after, they were not so strict, but that they would connive at their going privately Abroad; nor would People be much afraid of them afterward, but rather think they were fortified

---

5. London had a number of Bulls Head taverns. This one, however, is an anachronism; in 1722 there was a Bulls Head Tavern that Defoe knew well on Gracechurch Street; in 1665, however, the nearest Bulls Head was probably on Cheapside.

the better, having not been vulnerable when the Enemy was in their own House; but we sometimes found it had lyen much longer conceal'd.

Upon the foot of all these Observations, I must say, that tho' Providence seem'd to direct my Conduct to be otherwise; yet it is my opinion, and I must leave it as a Prescription, *(viz.) that the best Physick against the Plague is to run away from it.* I know People encourage themselves, by saying, God is able to keep us in the midst of Danger, and able to overtake us when we think our selves out of Danger; and this kept Thousands in the Town, whole Carcasses went into the great Pits by Cart Loads; and who, if they had fled from the Danger, had, I believe, been safe from the Disaster; at least 'tis probable they had been safe.

And were this very Fundamental only duly consider'd by the People, on any future occasion of this, or the like Nature, I am persuaded it would put them upon quite different Measures for managing the People, from those that they took in 1665, or than any that have been taken Abroad that I have heard of; in a Word, they would consider of seperating the People into smaller Bodies, and removing them in Time farther from one another, and not let such a Contagion as this, which is indeed chiefly dangerous, to collected Bodies of People, find a Million of People in a Body together, as was very near the Case before, and would certainly be the Case, if it should ever appear again.

The Plague like a great Fire, if a few Houses only are contiguous where it happens, can only burn a few Houses; or if it begins in a single, or as we call it a loan House,[6] can only burn that loan House where it begins: But if it begins in a close built Town, or City, and gets a Head, there its Fury encreases, it rages over the whole Place, and consumes all it can reach.

I could propose many Schemes, on the foot of which, the Government of this City, if ever they should be under the Apprehensions of such another Enemy, (God forbid they should) might ease themselves of the greatest Part of the dangerous People that belong to them; I mean such as the begging, starving, labouring Poor, and among them chiefly those who in Case of a Siege, are call'd the useless Mouths; who being then prudently, and to their own Advantage dispos'd of, and the wealthy Inhabitants disposing of themselves, and of their Servants, and Children, the City, and its adjacent Parts would be so effectually evacuated, that there would not be above a tenth Part of its People left together, for the Disease to take hold upon: But suppose them to be a fifth Part, and that two Hundred and fifty Thousand People were left, and if it did seize upon them, they would by their living so much at large, be much better prepar'd to defend themselves against the Infection, and be less liable to the Effects of it, than if the same Number of People lived close together in one smaller City, such as *Dublin*, or *Amsterdam*, or the like.

It is true, Hundreds, yea Thousands of Families fled away at this last

6. Lane house, house at the end of a lane and, therefore, not contiguous to others.

Plague, but then of them, many fled too late, and not only died in their Flight, but carried the Distemper with them into the Countries where they went, and infected those whom they went among for Safety; which confounded the Thing, and made that be a Propagation of the Distemper, which was the best means to prevent it; and this too is an Evidence of it, and brings me back to what I only hinted at before, but must speak more fully to here; namely, that Men went about apparently well, many Days after they had the taint of the Disease in their Vitals, and after their Spirits were so seiz'd, as that they could never escape it; and that all the while they did so, they were dangerous to others. *I say*, this proves, *that so it was*; for such People infected the very Towns they went thro', as well as the Families they went among, and it was by that means, that almost all the great Towns in *England* had the Distemper among them, more or less; and always they would tell you such a *Londoner* or such a *Londoner* brought it down.

It must not be omitted, that when I speak of those People who were really thus dangerous, I suppose them to be utterly ignorant of their own Condition; for if they really knew their Circumstances to be such as indeed they were, they must have been a kind of *willful Murtherers*, if they would have gone Abroad among healthy People, and it would have verified indeed the Suggestion *which I mention'd above, and which I thought seem'd untrue, (viz.)* That the infected People were utterly careless as to giving the Infection to others, and rather forward to do it than not; and I believe it was partly from this very Thing that they raised that Suggestion, which I hope was not really true in Fact.

I confess no particular Case is sufficient to prove a general, but I cou'd name several People within the Knowledge of some of their Neighbours and Families yet living, who shew'd the contrary to an extream. One Man, a Master of a Family in my Neighbourhood, having had the Distemper, he thought he had it given him by a poor Workman whom he employ'd, and whom he went to his House to see, or went for some Work that he wanted to have finished, and he had some Apprehensions even while he was at the poor Workman's Door, but did not discover it fully, but the next day it discovered it self, and he was taken very ill; upon which he immediately caused himself to be carried into an out Building which he had in his Yard, and where there was a Chamber over a Work-house, the Man being a Brazier; here he lay, and here he died, and would be tended by none of his Neighbours, but by a Nurse from Abroad, and would not suffer his Wife, or Children, or Servants, to come up into the Room lest they should be infected, but sent them his Blessing and Prayers for them by the Nurse, who spoke it to them at a Distance, and all this for fear of giving them the Distemper, and without which, he knew as they were kept up, they could not have it.

And here I must observe also, that the Plague, as I suppose all Distempers do, operated in a different Manner, on differing Constitutions; some were immediately overwhelm'd with it, and it came to violent Fevers,

Vomitings, unsufferable Head-achs, Pains in the Back, and so up to Ravings and Ragings with those Pains: Others with Swellings and Tumours in the Neck or Groyn, or Arm-pits, which till they could be broke, put them into insufferable Agonies and Torment; while others, as I have observ'd, were silently infected, the Fever preying upon their Spirits insensibly, and they seeing little of it, till they fell into swooning, and faintings, and Death without pain.

I am not Physician enough to enter into the particular Reasons and Manner of these differing Effects of one and the same Distemper, and of its differing Operation in several Bodies; nor is it my Business here to record the Observations, which I really made, because the Doctors themselves, have done that part much more effectually than I can do, and because my opinion may in some things differ from theirs: I am only relating what I know, or have heard, or believe of the particular Cases, and what fell within the Compass of my View, and the different Nature of the Infection, as it appeared in the particular Cases which I have related; but this may be added too, that tho' the former Sort of those Cases, namely those openly visited, were the worst for themselves as to Pain, I mean those that had such Fevers, Vomitings, Head-achs, Pains and Swellings, because they died in such a dreadful Manner, yet the latter had the worst State of the Disease; for in the former they frequently recover'd, especially if the Swellings broke, but the latter was inevitable Death; no cure, no help cou'd be possible, nothing could follow but Death; and it was worse also to others, because as, above, it secretly, and unperceiv'd by others, or by themselves, communicated Death to those they convers'd with, the penetrating Poison insinuating it self into their Blood in a Manner, which it is impossible to describe, or indeed conceive.

This infecting and being infected; without so much as its being known to either Person, is evident from two Sorts of Cases, which frequently happened at that Time; and there is hardly any Body living who was in *London* during the Infection, but must have known several of the Cases of both Sorts.

1. Fathers and Mothers have gone about as if they had been well, and have believ'd themselves to be so, till they have insensibly infected, and been the Destruction of their whole Families: Which they would have been far from doing, if they had the least Apprehensions of their being unsound and dangerous themselves. A Family, whose Story I have heard, was thus infected by the Father, and the Distemper began to appear upon some of them, even before he found it upon himself; but searching more narrowly, it appear'd he had been infected some Time, and as soon as he found that his Family had been poison'd by himself, he went distracted, and would have laid violent Hands upon himself, but was kept from that by those who look'd to him, and in a few Days died.

2. The other Particular is, that many People having been well to the best of their own Judgment, or by the best Observation which they could make of themselves for several Days, and only finding a Decay of Appe-

tite, or a light Sickness upon their Stomachs; nay, some whose Appetite has been strong, and even craving, and only a light Pain in their Heads; have sent for Physicians to know what ail'd them, and have been found to their great Surprize, at the brink of Death, the Tokens upon them, or the Plague grown up to an incurable Height.

It was very sad to reflect, how such a Person *as this last mentioned above*, had been a walking Destroyer, perhaps for a Week or Fortnight before that; how he had ruin'd those, that he would have hazarded his Life to save, and had been breathing Death upon them, even perhaps in his tender Kissing and Embracings of his own Children: Yet thus certainly it was, and often has been, and I cou'd give many particular Cases where it has been so; if then the Blow is thus insensibly stricken; if the Arrow flies thus unseen, and cannot be discovered; to what purpose are all the Schemes for shutting up or removing the sick People? those Schemes cannot take place, but upon those that appear to be sick, or to be infected; whereas there are among them, at the same time, Thousands of People, who seem to be well, but are all that while carrying Death with them into all Companies which they come into.

This frequently puzzled our Physicians, and especially the Apothecaries and Surgeons, who knew not how to discover the Sick from the Sound; they all allow'd *that it was really so*, that many People had the Plague in their very Blood, and preying upon their Spirits, and were in themselves but walking putrified Carcasses, whose Breath was infectious, and their Sweat Poison; and yet were as well to look on as other People, and even knew it not themselves: I say, they all allowed that it was really true in Fact, but they knew not how to propose a Discovery.

My Friend Doctor *Heath* was of Opinion, that it might be known by the smell of their Breath; but then, *as he said*, who durst Smell to that Breath for his Information? Since to know it, he must draw the Stench of the Plague up into his own Brain, in order to distinguish the Smell! I have heard, it was the opinion of others, that it might be distinguish'd by the Party's breathing upon a piece of Glass, where the Breath condensing, there might living Creatures be seen by a microscope[7] of strange monstrous and frightful Shapes, such as Dragons, Snakes, Serpents, and Devils, horrible to behold: But this I very much question the Truth of, and we had no Microscopes at that Time, as I remember, to make the Experiment with.

It was the opinion also of another learned Man, that the Breath of such a Person would poison, and instantly kill a Bird; not only a small Bird, but even a Cock or Hen, and that if it did not immediately kill the latter, it would cause them to be roupy[8] *as they call it*; particularly that if they had laid any Eggs at that Time, they would be all rotten: But those are Opinions which I never found supported by any Experiments,

---

7. Microscopes and magnifying glasses were something of a rage in Defoe's time. Available since the early 1600s, microscopes were greatly popularized by Robert Hooke's *Micrographia; or Some Physiological Descriptions of Minute* *Bodies* (1665). Charles Morton's academy in Stoke Newington, where Defoe was educated, had one.

8. Infected with a poultry disease causing a swollen rump.

or heard of others that had seen it; so I leave them as I find them, only with this Remark; namely, that I think the Probabilities are very strong for them.

Some have proposed that such Persons should breath hard upon warm Water, and that they would leave an unusual Scum upon it, or upon several other things, especially such as are of a glutinous Substance and are apt to receive a Scum and support it.

But from the whole I found, that the Nature of this Contagion was such, that it was impossible to discover it at all, or to prevent its spreading from one to another by any human Skill.

Here was indeed one Difficulty, which I could never throughly get over to this time, and which there is but one way of answering that I know of, and it is this, *viz.* The first Person that died of the Plague was in *Decemb.* 20th, or thereabouts 1664, and in, or about *Long-acre*, whence the first Person had the Infection, was generally said to be, from a Parcel of Silks imported from *Holland*, and first opened in that House.

But after this we heard no more of any Person dying of the Plague, or of the Distemper being in that Place, till the 9th of *February*; which was about 7 Weeks after, and then one more was buried out of the same House: Then it was hush'd, and we were perfectly easy as to the publick, for a great while; for there were no more entered in the Weekly Bill to be dead of the Plague, till the 22[d] of *April*, when there was 2 more buried not out of the same House, but out of the same Street; and as near as I can remember, it was out of the next House to the first: this was nine Weeks asunder, and after this we had No more till a Fortnight, and then it broke out in several Streets and spread every way. Now the Question seems to lye thus, *where lay the Seeds of the Infection all this while? How came it to stop so long, and not stop any longer?* Either the Distemper did not come immediately by Contagion from Body to Body, or if it did, then a Body may be capable to continue infected, without the Disease discovering itself, many Days, nay Weeks together, even not a Quarentine of Days only, but Soixantine,[9] not only 40 Days but 60 Days or longer.

It's true, there was, as I observed at first, and is well known to many yet living, a very cold Winter, and a long Frost, which continued three Months, and this, the Doctors say, might check the Infection; but then the learned must allow me to say, that if according to their Notion, the Disease was, as I may say, only frozen up, it would like a frozen River, have returned to its usual Force and Current when it thaw'd, whereas the principal Recess of this Infection, which was from *February* to *April*, was after the Frost was broken, and the Weather mild and warm.

But there is another way of solving all this Difficulty, which I think my own Remembrance of the thing will supply; and that is, the Fact is not granted, namely, that there died none in those long Intervals, *viz.* from the 20th of *December* to the 9th of *February*, and from thence to the

9. A period of sixty days.

22^d of *April*. The Weekly Bills are the only Evidence on the other side, and those Bills were not of Credit enough, at least with me, to support an *Hypothesis*, or determine a Question of such Importance as this: For it was our receiv'd Opinion at that time, and I believe upon very good Grounds, that the Fraud lay in the Parish Officers, Searchers, and Persons appointed to give Account of the Dead, and what Diseases they died of: And as People were very loth at first to have the Neighbours believe their Houses were infected, so they gave Money to procure, or otherwise procur'd the dead Persons to be return'd as dying of other Distempers; and this I know was practis'd afterwards in many Places, I believe I might say in all Places, where the Distemper came, as will be seen by the vast Encrease of the Numbers plac'd in the Weekly Bills under other Articles of Diseases, during the time of the Infection: *For Example*, in the Month of *July* and *August*, when the Plague was coming on to its highest Pitch; it was very ordinary to have from a thousand to twelve hundred, nay to almost fifteen Hundred a Week of other Distempers; not that the Numbers of those Distempers were really encreased to such a Degree: But the great Number of Families and Houses where really the Infection was, obtain'd the Favour to have their dead be return'd of other Distempers to prevent the shutting up their Houses. *For Example*,

Dead of other Diseases besides the *Plague*.

From the 18th	to the 25th *July*	942
	to the 1st *August*	1004
	to the 8th	1213
	to the 15th	1439
	to the 22d	1331
	to the 29th	1394
	to the 5th *September*	1264
	to the 12th	1056
	to the 19th	1132
	to the 26th	927

Now it was not doubted, but the greatest part of these, or a great part of them, were dead of the Plague, but the Officers were prevail'd with to return them as above, and the Numbers of some particular Articles of Distempers discover'd is, as follows;

From the 1st to the 8th of *Aug.* to the 15th. to the 22. to the 29.

Fever	314	353	348	383
Spotted Fever[1]	174	190	166	165
Surfeit	85	87	74	99
Teeth	90	113	111	133
	663	743	699	780

1. Any of a group of infectious diseases, including typhus, that are spread by ticks and mites and characterized by skin eruptions.

From *August* 29th to the 5th *Sept.* to the 12. to the 19. to the 26.

Fever	364	332	309	268
Spotted Fever	157	97	101	65
Surfeit	68	45	49	36
Teeth	138	128	121	112
	728	602	580	481

There were several other Articles which bare a Proportion to these, and which it is easy to perceive, were increased on the same Account, as *Aged, Consumptions, Vomitings, Imposthumes,*[2] *Gripes,* and the like, many of which were not doubted to be infected People; but as it was of the utmost Consequence to Families not to be known to be infected, if it was possible to avoid it, so they took all the measures they could to have it not believ'd; and if any died in their Houses to get them return'd to the Examiners, and by the Searchers, as having died of other Distempers.

This, I say, will account for the long Interval, which, *as I have said,* was between the dying of the first Persons that were returned in the Bill to be dead of the Plague, and the time when the Distemper spread openly, and could not be conceal'd.

Besides, the Weekly Bills themselves at that time evidently discover this Truth; for while there was no Mention of the Plague, and no Increase, after it had been mentioned, yet it was apparent, that there was an Encrease of those Distempers which bordered nearest upon it, for Example there were Eight, Twelve, Seventeen of the Spotted Fever in a Week, when there were none, or but very few of the Plague; whereas before *One, Three,* or *Four,* were the ordinary Weekly Numbers of that Distemper; likewise, as I observed before, the Burials increased Weekly in that particular Parish, and the Parishes adjacent, more than in any other Parish, altho' there were none set down of the Plague; all which tells us, that the Infection was handed on, and the Succession of the Distemper really preserv'd, tho' it seem'd to us at that time to be ceased, and to come again in a manner surprising.

It might be also, that the Infection might remain in other parts of the same Parcel of Goods which at first it came in, and which might not be perhaps opened, or at least not fully, or in the Cloths of the first infected Person; for I cannot think, that any Body could be seiz'd with the Contagion in a fatal and mortal Degree for nine Weeks together, and support his State of Health so well, as even not to discover it to themselves; yet if it were so, the Argument is the stronger in Favour of what I am saying; namely, that the Infection is retain'd in Bodies apparently well, and convey'd from them to those they converse with, while it is known to neither the one nor the other.

---

2. Abscesses, cysts.

Great were the Confusions at that time upon this very Account; and when People began to be convinc'd that the Infection was receiv'd in this surprising manner from Persons apparently well, they began to be exceeding shie and jealous of every one that came near them. Once in a publick Day, whether a Sabbath Day or not I do not remember, in *Aldgate* Church in a Pew full of People, on a sudden, one fancy'd she smelt an ill Smell, immediately she fancies the Plague was in the Pew, whispers her Notion or Suspicion to the next, then rises and goes out of the Pew, it immediately took with the next, and so to them all; and every one of them, and of the two or three adjoining Pews, got up and went out of the Church, no Body knowing what it was offended them or from whom.

This immediately filled every Bodies Mouths with one Preparation or other, such as the old Women directed, and some perhaps as Physicians directed, in order to prevent Infection by the Breath of others; insomuch that if we came to go into a Church, when it was any thing full of People, there would be such a Mixture of Smells at the Entrance, that it was much more strong, tho' perhaps not so wholesome, than if you were going into an Apothecary's or Druggist's Shop; in a Word, the whole Church was like a smelling Bottle, in one Corner it was all Perfumes, in another Aromaticks, Balsamicks, and Variety of Drugs, and Herbs; in another Salts and Spirits, as every one was furnish'd for their own Preservation; yet I observ'd, that after People were possess'd, *as I have said*, with the Belief or rather Assurance, of the Infection being thus carryed on by Persons apparently in Health, the Churches and Meeting-Houses were much thinner of People than at other times before that they us'd to be; for this is to be said of the People of *London*, that during the whole time of the Pestilence, the Churches or Meetings were never wholly shut up, nor did the People decline coming out to the public Worship of God, except only in some Parishes when the Violence of the Distemper was more particularly in that Parish at that time; and even then no longer, than it continued to be so.

Indeed nothing was more strange, than to see with what Courage the People went to the public Service of God, even at that time when they were afraid to stir out of their own Houses upon any other Occasion; this I mean before the time of Desperation, which I have mention'd already; this was a Proof of the exceeding Populousness of the City at the time of the Infection, notwithstanding the great Numbers that were gone into the Country at the first Alarm, and that fled out into the Forests and Woods when they were farther terrifyed with the extraordinary Increase of it. For when we came to see the Crouds and Throngs of People, which appear'd on the Sabbath Days at the Churches, and especially in those parts of the Town where the Plague was abated, or where it was not yet come to its Height, it was amazing. But of this I shall speak again presently; I return in the mean time to the Article of infecting one another at first; before People came to right Notions of the Infection, and of infecting one another, People were only shye of those that were really sick, a Man with a Cap upon his Head, or with Cloths round his Neck, *which was the Case of those that had Swellings there*; such was indeed frightful: But when we saw a Gentleman dress'd with his Band on and his Gloves in his Hand, his Hat upon his Head, and his Hair comb'd, of such we had not the least Apprehensions; and People converse a great while freely, *especially with their Neighbours and such as they knew.* But when the Physicians assured us, that the Danger was as well from the Sound, that is *the seemingly sound*, as the Sick; and that those People, who thought themselves entirely free, were oftentimes the most fatal; and that it came to be generally understood, that People were sensible of it, and of the reason of it: Then I say they began to be jealous of every Body, and a vast Number of People lock'd themselves up, so as not to come abroad into any Company at all, nor suffer any, that had been abroad in promiscuous Company, to come into their Houses, or near them; at least not so near them, as to be within the Reach of their Breath, or of any Smell from them; and when they were oblig'd to converse at a Distance with Strangers, they would always have Preservatives in their Mouths, and about their Cloths to repell and keep off the Infection.

It must be acknowledg'd, that when People began to use these Cautions, they were less exposed to Danger, and the Infection did not break into such Houses so furiously as it did into others before, and thousands of Families were preserved, *speaking with due Reserve to the Direction of Divine Providence*, by that Means.

But it was impossible to beat any thing into the Heads of the Poor, they went on with the usual Impetuosity of their Tempers full of Outcries and Lamentations when taken, but madly careless of themselves, Fool-hardy and obstinate, while they were well: Where they could get Employment they push'd into any kind of Business, the most dangerous and the most liable to Infection; and if they were spoken to, their Answer would be, *I must trust to God for that; if I am taken, then I am provided for, and there is an End of me*, and the like: OR THUS, *Why, What must I do? I can't starve, I had as good have the Plague as perish for want. I have no Work, what could I do? I must do this or beg:* Suppose it was burying the dead, or attending the Sick, or watching infected Houses, which were all terrible Hazards, but their Tale was generally the same. It is true Necessity was a very justifiable warrantable Plea, and nothing could be better; but their way of Talk was much the same, where the Necessities were not the same: This adventurous Conduct of the Poor was that which brought the Plague among them in a most furious manner, and this join'd to the Distress of their Circumstances, when taken, was the reason why they died so by Heaps; for I cannot say, I could observe one jot of better Husbandry among them, I mean the labouring Poor, while they were well and getting Money, than there was before, but as lavish, as extravagant, and as thoughtless for to Morrow as ever; so that when they came to be taken sick, they were immediately in the utmost Distress as well for want, as for Sickness, as well for lack of Food, as lack of Health.

This Misery of the Poor I had many Occasions to be an Eye-witness of, and sometimes also of the charitable Assistance that some pious People daily gave to such, sending them Relief and Supplies both of Food, Physick and other Help, as they found they wanted; and indeed it is a Debt of Justice due to the Temper of the People of that Day to take Notice here, that not only great Sums, *very great* Sums of Money were charitably sent to the Lord Mayor and Aldermen for the Assistance and Support of the poor distemper'd People; but abundance of private People daily distributed large Sums of Money for their Relief, and sent People about to enquire into the Condition of particular distressed and visited Families, and relieved them; nay some pious Ladies were so transported with Zeal in so good a Work; and so confident in the Protection of Providence in Discharge of the great Duty of Charity, that they went about in person distributing Alms to the Poor, and even visiting poor Families, tho' sick and infected in their very Houses, appointing Nurses to attend those that wanted attending, and ordering Apothecaries and Surgeons, the first to supply them with Drugs or Plaisters, and such things as they wanted; and the last to lance and dress the Swellings and Tumours, where such were wanting; giving their Blessing to the Poor in substantial Relief to them, as well as hearty Prayers for them.

I will not undertake to say, as some do, that none of these charitable People were suffered to fall under the Calamity itself; but this I may say, that I never knew any one of them that miscarried, which I mention for the Encouragement of others in case of the like Distress; and doubtless, *if they that give*[3] *to the Poor, lend to the Lord, and he will repay them*; those that hazard their Lives to give to the Poor, and to comfort and assist the Poor in such a Misery as this, may hope to be protected in the Work.

Nor was this Charity so extraordinary eminent only in a few; but, *(for I cannot lightly quit this Point)* the Charity of the rich as well in the City and Suburbs as from the Country, was so great, that in a Word, a prodigious Number of People, who must otherwise inevitably have perished for want as well as Sickness, were supported and subsisted by it; and tho' I could never, nor I believe any one else come to a full Knowledge of what was so contributed, yet I do believe, that as I heard one say, that was a critical Observer of that Part, there was not only many Thousand Pounds contributed, but many hundred thousand Pounds, to the Relief of the Poor of this distressed afflicted City; nay one Man affirm'd to me that he could reckon up above one hundred thousand Pounds a Week, which was distributed by the Church Wardens at the several Parish Vestries, by the Lord Mayor and the Aldermen in the several Wards and Precincts, and by the particular Direction of the Court and of the

3. Proverbs 19.17.

Justices respectively in the parts where they resided; over and above the private Charity distributed by pious Hands in the manner I speak of, and this continued for many Weeks together.

I confess this is a very great Sum; but if it be true, that there was distributed in the Parish of *Cripplegate* only 17800 Pounds in one Week[4] to the Relief of the Poor, as I heard reported, and which I really believe was true, the other may not be improbable.

It was doubtless to be reckon'd among the many signal good Providences which attended this great City, *and of which there were many other worth recording*; I say, this was a very remarkable one, that it pleased God thus to move the Hearts of the People in all parts of the Kingdom, so chearfully to contribute to the Relief and Support of the poor at *London*; the good Consequences of which were felt many ways, and particularly in preserving the Lives and recovering the Health of so many thousands, and keeping so many Thousands of Families from perishing and starving.

And now I am talking of the merciful Disposition of Providence in this time of Calamity, I cannot but mention again, tho' I have spoken several times of it already on other Account, I mean that of the Progression of the Distemper; how it began at one end of the Town, and proceeded gradually and slowly from one Part to another, and like a dark Cloud that passes over our Heads, which as it thickens and overcasts the Air at one End, clears up at the other end: So while the Plague went on raging from West to East, as it went forwards East, it abated in the West, by which means those parts of the Town, which were not seiz'd, or who were left, and where it had spent its Fury, were (as it were) spar'd to help and assist the other; whereas had the Distemper spread it self over the whole City and Suburbs at once, raging in all Places alike, as it has done since in some Places abroad, the whole Body of the People must have been overwhelmed, and there would have died twenty thousand a Day, as they say there did at *Naples*,[5] nor would the People have been able to have help'd or assisted one another.

For it must be observ'd that where the Plague was in its full Force, there indeed the People were very miserable, and the Consternation was inexpressible. But a little before it reach'd even to that place, or presently after it was gone, they were quite another Sort of People, and I cannot but acknowledge, that there was too much of that common Temper of Mankind to be found among us all at that time; namely to forget the Deliverance, when the Danger is past: But I shall come to speak of that part again.

It must not be forgot here to take some Notice of the State of Trade, during the time of this common Calamity, and this with respect to Foreign Trade, as also to our Home-trade.

As to Foreign Trade, there needs little to be said; the trading Nations

4. This is the parish in which Defoe's sisters were baptized, and he may have heard this improbably large figure from his family.
5. See p. 169, in this volume.

of Europe were all afraid of us, no Port of *France*, or *Holland*, or *Spain*, or *Italy* would admit our Ships or correspond with us; indeed we stood on ill Terms with the *Dutch*, and were in a furious War with them,[6] but tho' in a bad Condition to fight abroad, who had such dreadful Enemies to struggle with at Home.

Our Merchants accordingly were at a full Stop, their Ships could go no where, that is to say to no place abroad; their Manufactures and Merchandise, that is to say, of our Growth, would not be touch'd abroad; they were as much afraid of our Goods, as they were of our People; and indeed they had reason, for our woolen Manufactures are as retentive of Infection as human Bodies, and if pack'd up by Persons infected would receive the Infection, and be as dangerous to touch, as a Man would be that was infected; and therefore when any *English* Vessel arriv'd in Foreign Countries, if they did take the Goods on Shore, they always caused the Bales to be opened and air'd in Places appointed for that Purpose: But from *London* they would not suffer them to come into Port, much less to unlade their Goods upon any Terms whatever; and this Strictness was especially us'd with them in *Spain* and *Italy*, in *Turkey* and the Islands of the *Arches*[7] indeed as they are call'd, as well those belonging to the *Turks* as to the *Venetians*, they were not so very rigid; in the first there was no Obstruction at all; and four Ships, which were then in the River loading for *Italy*, that is for *Leghorn*[8] and *Naples*, being denyed Product, *as they call it*, went on to *Turkey*, and were freely admitted to unlade their Cargo without any Difficulty, only that when they arriv'd there, some of their Cargo was not fit for Sale in that Country, and other Parts of it being consign'd to Merchants at *Leghorn*, the Captains of the Ships had no Right nor any Orders to dispose of the Goods; so that great Inconveniences followed to the Merchants. But this was nothing but what the Necessity of Affairs requir'd, and the Merchants at *Leghorn* and at *Naples* having Notice given them, sent again from thence to take Care of the Effects, which were particularly consign'd to those Ports, and to bring back in other Ships such as were improper for the Markets at *Smyrna* and *Scanderoon*.[9]

The Inconveniences in *Spain* and *Portugal* were still greater; for they would, by no means, suffer our Ships, especially those from *London*, to come into any of their Ports, much less to unlade; there was a Report, that one of our Ships having by Stealth delivered her Cargo, among which, was some Bales of *English* Cloth, Cotton, Kersyes,[1] and such like Goods, and *Spaniards* caused all the Goods to be burnt, and punished the Men with Death who werre concern'd in carrying them on Shore. This I believe was in Part true, tho' I do not affirm it: But it is

6. England had declared war on the Dutch on February 22, and the Second Anglo-Dutch War lasted until 1667.

7. Sailors' slang for "archipelago."

8. City in northwestern Italy on the Ligurian Sea.

9. Smyrna is one of the best ports in Turkey; its modern name is Izmir. Scanderoon is a seaport in Syria.

1. Coarse, ribbed wool cloth.

not at all unlikely, seeing the Danger was really very great, the Infection being so violent in *London*.

I heard likewise that the Plague was carryed into those Countries by some of our Ships, and particularly to the Port of *Faro* in the Kingdom of *Algarve*,[2] belonging to the King of *Portugal*; and that several Persons died of it there, but it was not confirm'd.

On the other Hand, tho' the *Spaniards* and *Portuguese* were so shie of us, it is most certain, that the Plague, *as has been said*, keeping at first much at that end of the Town next *Westminster*, the merchandising part of the Town, such as the City and the Water-side, was perfectly sound, till at least the Beginning of *July*; and the Ships in the River till the Beginning of *August*; for to the 1st of *July*, there had died but seven within the whole City, and but 60 within the Liberties; but one in all the Parishes of *Stepney*, *Aldgate*, and *White-Chapel*; and but two in all the eight Parishes of *Southwark*. But it was the same thing abroad, for the bad News was gone over the whole World, that the City of *London* was infected with the Plague; and there was no inquiring there, how the Infection proceeded, or at which part of the Town it was begun, or was reach'd to.

Besides, after it began to spread, it increased so fast, and the Bills grew so high, all on a sudden, that it was to no purpose to lessen the Report of it, or endeavour to make the People abroad think it better than it was, the Account which the Weekly Bills gave in was sufficient; and that there died two thousand to three or four thousand a Week, was sufficient to alarm the whole trading part of the World, and the following time being so dreadful also in the very City it self, put the whole World, *I say*, upon their Guard against it.

You may be sure also, that the Report of these things lost nothing in the Carriage, the Plague was it self very terrible, and the Distress of the People very great, as you may observe by what I have said: But the Rumor was infinitely greater, and it must not be wonder'd, that our Friends abroad, as my Brother's Correspondents in particular were told there, namely in *Portugal* and *Italy* where he chiefly traded, that in *London* there died twenty thousand in a Week; that the dead Bodies lay unburied by Heaps; that the living were not sufficient to bury the dead, or the Sound to look after the Sick; that all the Kingdom was infected likewise, so that it was an universal Malady, such as was never heard of in those parts of the World; and they could hardly believe us, when we gave them an Account how things really were, and how there was not above one Tenth part of the People dead; that there was 500000 left that lived all the time in the Town; that now the People began to walk the Streets again, and those, who were fled, to return, there was no Miss of the usual Throng of people in the Streets, except as every Family might miss their Relations and Neighbours, and the like; I say they could not believe

2. Faro was an important seventeenth-century trading center on the southern coast of Portugal; Algarve is the coastal strip of southern Portugal.

these things; and if Enquiry were now to be made in *Naples*, or in other Cities on the Coast of *Italy*, they would tell you that there was a dreadful Infection in *London* so many Years ago; in which, *as above*, there died Twenty Thousand in a Week, &c. Just as we have had it reported in *London*, that there was a Plague in the City of *Naples*, in the Year 1656, in which there died 20000 People in a Day, of which I have had very good Satisfaction, that it was utterly false.

But these extravagant Reports were very prejudicial to our Trade as well as unjust and injurious in themselves; for it was a long Time after the Plague was quite over, before our Trade could recover it self in those parts of the World; and the *Flemings* and *Dutch*, but especially the last, made very great Advantages of it, having all the Market to themselves, and even buying our Manufactures in the several Parts of *England* where the Plague was not, and carrying them to *Holland*, and *Flanders*, and from thence transporting them to *Spain*, and to *Italy*, as if they had been of their own making.

But they were detected sometimes and punish'd, that is to say, their Goods confiscated, and Ships also; for if it was true, that our Manufactures, as well as our People, were infected, and that it was dangerous to touch or to open, and receive the Smell of them; then those People ran the hazard by that clandestine Trade,[3] not only of carrying the Contagion into their own Country, but also of infecting the Nations to whom they traded with those Goods; which, considering how many Lives might be lost in Consequence of such an Action, must be a Trade that no Men of Conscience could suffer themselves to be concern'd in.

I do not take upon me to say, that any harm was done, I mean of that Kind, by those People: But I doubt, I need not make any such Proviso in the Case of our own Country; for either by our People of *London*, or by the Commerce, which made their conversing with all Sorts of People in every Country, and of every considerable Town, necessary, I say, by this means the Plague was first or last spread all over the Kingdom, as well in *London* as in all the Cities and great Towns, especially in the trading Manufacturing Towns, and Sea-Ports; so that first or last, all the considerable Places in *England* were visited more or less, and the Kingdom of *Ireland* in some Places, but not so universally; how it far'd with the People in *Scotland*, I had no opportunity to enquire.

It is to be observ'd, that while the Plague continued so violent in *London*, the *out Ports*, as they are call'd, enjoy'd a very great Trade, especially to the adjacent Countries, and to our own Plantations; for Example, the Towns of *Colchester*, *Yarmouth*, and *Hull*,[4] on that side of *England*, exported to *Holland* and *Hamburgh*, the Manufactures of the adjacent Counties for several Months after the Trade with *London* was as it were entirely shut up; likewise the Cities of *Bristol* and *Exeter*

3. Smuggling. All nations, including England, increased the severity of punishments for smuggling during times of plague. On March 7, 1722, George I gave his royal assent to such an act of Parliament.

4. "Out ports" on the east coast of England.

with the Port of *Plymouth*,[5] had the like Advantage to *Spain*, to the
Canaries, to *Guinea*, and to the *West Indies*; and particularly to *Ireland*;
but as the Plague spread it self every way after it had been in *London*, to
such a Degree as it was in *August* and *September*; so all, or most of those
Cities and Towns were infected first or last, and then Trade was as it
were under a general Embargo, or at a full stop, as I shall observe farther, when I speak of our home Trade.

One thing however must be observed, that as to Ships coming in from
Abroad, as many you may be sure did, some, who were out in all Parts
of the World a considerable while before, and some who when they
went out knew nothing of an Infection, or at least of one so terrible;
these came up the River boldly, and delivered their Cargoes as they were
oblig'd to do, except just in the two Months of *August* and *September*,
when the Weight of the Infection lying, as I may say, all below Bridge,
no Body durst appear in Business for a while: But as this continued but
for a few Weeks, the Homeward bound Ships, especially such whose
Cargoes were not liable to spoil, came to an Anchor for a Time, short
of THE POOL,[6] or fresh Water part of the River, even as low as the
River *Medway*, where several of them ran in, and others lay at the *Nore*,
and in the *Hope* below *Gravesend*: So that by the latter end of *October*,
there was a great Fleet of Homeward bound Ships to come up, such as
the like had not been known for many Years.

Two particular Trades were carried on by Water Carriage all the while
of the Infection, and that with little or no Interruption, very much to
the Advantage and Comfort of the poor distressed People of the City,
and those were the coasting Trade for Corn, and the *Newcastle* Trade
for Coals.

The first of these was particularly carried on by small Vessels, from
Port of *Hull*, and other Places in the *Humber*, by which great Quantities
of Corn were brought in from *Yorkshire* and *Lincolnshire*: The other part
of this Corn-Trade was from *Lynn* in *Norfolk*, from *Wells*, and *Burn-
ham*, and from *Yarmouth*, all in the same County; and the third Branch
was from the River *Medway*, and from *Milton*, *Feversham*, *Margate*,
and *Sandwich*, and all the other little Places and Ports round the Coast
of *Kent* and *Essex*.[7]

There was also a very good Trade from the Coast of *Suffolk* with
Corn, Butter and Cheese; these Vessels kept a constant Course of Trade,
and without Interruption came up to that Market known still by the
Name of *Bear-Key*,[8] where they supply'd the City plentifully with Corn,

5. Bristol is in the west of England on the Bristol Channel; Exeter and Plymouth are south
coast ports.
6. That Part of the River where the Ships lye
up when they come Home, is call'd the *Pool*,
and takes in all the River on both Sides of the
Water, from the *Tower* to *Cuckold's* Point, and
Limehouse [*Defoe's note*].

7. Defoe described all of these places and their
trade in *A Tour* (1724–7), which he had probably already begun writing.
8. One of the two major corn markets in London. Defoe says in *A Tour* that, except for Holland, "the whole world cannot equal the
quantity . . . bought and sold there." It was a
few blocks from the Custom House.

when Land Carriage began to fail, and when the People began to be sick of coming from many Places in the Country.

This also was much of it owning to the Prudence and Conduct of the Lord Mayor, who took such care to keep the Masters and Seamen from Danger, when they came up, causing their Corn to be bought off at any time they wanted a Market, (which however was very seldom) and causing the Corn-Factors immediately to unlade and deliver the Vessels loaden with Corn, that they had very little occasion to come out of their Ships or Vessels, the Money being always carried on Board to them, and put into a Pail of Vinegar before it was carried.

The Second Trade was, that of Coals from *Newcastle* upon *Tyne;* without which the City could have been greatly distressed; for not in the Streets only, but in private Houses and Families, great Quantities of Coals were then burnt, even all the Summer long, and when the Weather was hottest, which was done by the Advice of the Physicians; some indeed oppos'd it, and insisted that to keep the Houses and Rooms hot, was a means to propagate the Distemper, which was a Fermentation and Heat already in the Blood, that it was known to spread, and increase in hot Weather, and abate in cold, and therefore they alledg'd that all contagious Distempers are the worse for Heat, because the Contagion was nourished, and gain'd Strength in hot Weather, and was as it were propagated in Heat.

Others said, they granted, that Heat in the Climate might propagate Infection, as sultry hot Weather fills the Air with Vermine, and nourishes innumerable Numbers, and Kinds of venomous Creatures, which breed in our Food, in the Plants, and even in our Bodies, by the very stench of which, Infection may be propagated; also, that heat in the Air, or heat of Weather, *as we ordinarly call it,* makes Bodies relax and faint, exhausts the Spirits, opens the Pores, and makes us more apt to receive Infection, or any evil Influence, be it from noxious pestilential Vapors, or any other Thing in the Air: But that the heat of Fire, and especially of Coal Fires kept in our Houses, or near us, had a quite different Operation, the Heat being not of the same Kind, but quick and fierce, tending not to nourish but to consume, and dissipate all those noxious Fumes, which the other kind of Heat rather exhaled, and stagnated, than separated, and burnt up; besides it was alledg'd, that the sulphurous and nitrous Particles, that are often found to be in the Coal, with that bituminous Substance which burns, are all assisting to clear and purge the Air, and render it wholsom and safe to breath in, after the noctious Particles as above are dispers'd and burnt up.

The latter Opinion prevail'd at that Time, and as I must confess I think with good Reason, and the Experience of the Citizens confirm'd it, many Houses which had constant Fires kept in the Rooms, having never been infected at all; and I must join my Experience to it, for I found the keeping good Fires kept our Rooms sweet and wholsom, and

I do verily believe made our whole Family so, more than would other-wise have been.

But I return to the Coals as a Trade, it was with no little difficulty that this Trade was kept open, and particularly because as we were in an open War with the *Dutch*, at that Time, the *Dutch* Capers[9] at first took a great many of our Collier Ships, which made the rest cautious, and made them to stay to come in Fleets together: But after some time, the Capers were either afraid to take them, or their Masters, the States, were afraid they should, and forbad them, lest the Plague should be among them, which made them fare the better.

For the Security of those *Northern* Traders, the Coal Ships were order'd by my Lord Mayor, not to come up into the *Pool* above a certain Num-ber at a Time, and order'd Lighters, and other Vessels, such as the Wood-mongers,[1] that is the *Wharf* Keepers, or Coal-Sellers furnished, to go down, and take out the Coals as low as *Deptford* and *Greenwich*, and some farther down.

Others deliver'd great Quantities of Coals in particular Places, where the Ships cou'd come to the Shoar, as at *Greenwich*, *Blackwal*, and other Places, in vast Heaps, as if to be kept for Sale; but were then fetch'd away, after the Ships which brought them were gone; so that the Seamen had no Communication with the River-Men, nor so much as came near one another.

Yet all this Caution, could not effectually prevent the Distemper get-ting among the Colliery, that is to say, among the Ships, by which a great many Seamen died of it; and that which was still worse, was, that they carried it down to *Ipswich*, and *Yarmouth*, to *Newcastle* upon *Tyne*, and other Places on the Coast; where, especially at *Newcastle* and at *Sunderland*, it carried off a great Number of People.

The making so many Fires as above, did indeed consume an unusual Quantity of Coals; and that upon one or two stops of the Ships coming up, whether by contrary Weather, or by the Interruption of Enemies, I do not remember, but the Price of Coals was exceeding dear, even as high as 4 l. a Chalder,[2] but it soon abated when the Ships came in, and as afterwards they had a freer Passage, the Price was very reasonable all the rest of that Year.

The publick Fires which were made on these Occasions, as I have calculated it, must necessarily have cost the City about 200 Chalder of Coals a Week, if they had continued, which was indeed a very great Quantity; but as it was, thought necessary, nothing was spar'd; however as some of the Physicians cry'd them down, they were not kept a-light above four or five Days; the Fires were order'd thus.

One at the *Custom-house*, one at *Billingsgate*, one at *Queen-hith*, and one at the *Three Cranes*, one in *Black Friers*, and one at the Gate of

---

9. Privateers; pirates licensed by a government to prey on the ships of hostile nations.
1. Sellers of wood.

2. A regulated amount or measure; Defoe says thirty-six bushels.

Bridewel,[3] one at the Corner of *Leadenhal* Street, and *Grace-church*, one at the *North*, and one at the *South* Gate of the *Royal Exchange*, one at *Guild Hall*, and one at *Blackwell-hall* Gate,[4] one at the Lord *Mayor's* Door, in St. *Helens*, and one at the West Entrance into St. *Paul's*, and one at the Entrance into *Bow* Church:[5] I do not remember whether there was any at the City Gates, but one at the *Bridge* foot there was, just by St. *Magnus* Church.[6]

I know, some have quarrell'd since that at the Experiment, and said, that there died the more People, because of those Fires; but I am persuaded thoses that say so, offer no Evidence to prove it, neither can I believe it on any Account whatever.

It remains to give some Account of the State of Trade at home in *England* during this dreadful Time, and particularly as it relates to the Manufactures, and the Trade in the City: At the first breaking out of the Infection, there was, as it is easie to suppose, a very great fright among the People, and consequently a general stop of Trade; except in Provisions and Necessaries of Life, and even in those Things, as there was a vast Number of People fled, and a very great Number always sick, besides the Number which died, so there could not be above two Thirds, if above one Half of the Consumption of Provisions in the City as used to be.

It pleas'd God, to send a very plentiful Year of Corn and Fruit, but not of Hay or Grass; by which means, Bread was cheap, by Reason of the Plenty of Corn: Flesh was cheap, by Reason of the Scarcity of Grass; but Butter and Cheese were dear for the same Reason, and Hay in the Market just beyond *White-Chapel* Bars, was sold at 4 l. *per* Load. But that affected not the Poor; there was a most excessive Plenty of all Sorts of Fruit, such as Apples, Pears, Plumbs, Cherries, Grapes; and they were the cheaper, because of the want of People; but this made the Poor eat them to excess, and this brought them into Fluxes, griping of the Guts, Surfeits, and the like, which often precipitated them into the Plague.

But to come to Matters of Trade; first, Foreign Exportation being stopt, or at least very much interrupted, and rendred difficult; a general Stop of all those Manufactories followed of Course, which were usually bought for Exportation; and tho' sometimes Merchants Abroad were

---

3. Defoe is tracing the fires from east to west along the major docks on the Thames. The Custom House was at Wool Wharf, south out of Lower Thames Street; official weights were kept there, and ship arrivals and departures were registered. Billingsgate is the most famous fish-market and became synonymous with coarse language and verbal abuse, because of that used by the sellers and hawkers. Queen Hith was the second large corn market and, according to Defoe, specialized in malt. The Three Cranes was another wharf south of Thames Street; its name came from the cranes used to lift casks of wines from ships to dock. Blackfriars was a wharf west of Three Cranes at the east end of Fleet Ditch. Bridewell Gate, west of Black-friars, led into the workhouse and prison from a dock on Fleet Ditch.

4. These fires were at heavily traveled points in the heart of the City. Leadenhall and Grace Church Street, both broad streets, intersected near the Hide and Green Markets and Merchants' Hall. Blackwell Hall Gate led to Guild-hall from a major wool cloth market.

5. St. Mary Le Bow Church was commonly called Bow Church and dated from the time of William the Conqueror. It was on Cheapside, a wide thoroughfare.

6. St. Magnus the Martyr was at the north end of London Bridge.

importunate for Goods, yet little was sent, the Passages being so generally stop'd, that the *English* Ships would not be admitted, as is said
already, into their Port.

This put a stop to the Manufactures, that were for Exportation in most
Parts of *England*, except in some out Ports; and even that was soon
stop'd, for they all had the Plague in their Turn: But tho' this was felt all
over *England*, yet what was still worse, all Intercourse of Trade for Home
Consumption of Manufactures, especially those which usually circulated thro' the *Londoners* Hands,[7] was stop'd at once, the Trade of the
City being stop'd.

All Kinds of Handicrafts in the City, &c. Tradesmen and Mechan-
icks, were, as I have said before, out of Employ, and this occasion'd the
putting off, and dismissing an innumerable Number of Journey-men,
and Work-men of all Sorts, seeing nothing was done relating to such
Trades, but what might be said to be absolutely necessary.

This caused the Multitude of single People in *London* to be unprovided for; as also of Families, whose living depended upon the Labour
of the Heads of those Families; I say, this reduced them to extream
Misery; and I must confess it is for the Honour of the City of *London*,
and will be for many Ages, as long as this is to be spoken of, that they
were able to supply with charitable Provision, the Wants of so many
Thousands of those as afterwards fell sick, and were distressed; so that it
may be safely aver'd that no Body perished for Want, at lest that the
Magistrates had any notice given them of.

This Stagnation of our Manufacturing Trade in the Country, would
have put the People there to much greater Difficulties, but that the Mas-
ter-Workmen, Clothiers and others, to the uttermost of their Stocks and
Strength, kept on making their Goods to keep the Poor at Work, believing that as soon as the Sickness should abate, they would have a quick
Demand in Proportion to the Decay of their Trade at That Time: But as
none but those Masters that were rich could do thus, and that many
were poor and not able, the Manufacturing Trade in *England* suffer'd
greatly, and the Poor were pinch'd all over *England* by the Calamity of
the City of *London* only.

It is true, that the next Year made them full amends by another terrible Calamity upon the City; so that the City by one Calamity impov-
erished and weaken'd the Country, and by another Calamity even terrible
too of its Kind, enrich'd the Country and made them again amends: For
an infinite Quantity of Houshold Stuff, wearing Apparel, and other
Things, besides whole Ware-houses fill'd with Merchandize and Man-
ufacturies, such as come from all Parts of *England*, were consum'd in
the Fire of *London*, the next Year after this terrible Visitation: It is
incredible what a Trade this made all over the whole Kingdom, to make

7. London functioned as the hub of domestic as well as foreign trade. Almost all commodities
were transported to London and then redistributed.

good the Want, and to supply that Loss: so that, in short, all the manu-facturing Hands in the Nation were set on Work, and were little enough, for several Years, to supply the Market and answer the Demands; all Foreign Markets, also were empty of our Goods, by the stop which had been occasioned by the Plague, and before an open Trade was allow'd again; and the prodigious Demand at Home falling in join'd to make a quick Vent for all Sorts of Goods; so that there never was known such a Trade all over *England* for the Time, as was in the first seven Years after the Plague, and after the Fire of *London*.

It remains now, that I should say something of the merciful Part of this terrible Judgment: The last Week in *September* the Plague being come to its Crisis, its Fury began to asswage. I remember my Friend Doctor *Heath* coming to see me the Week before, told me, he was sure that the Violence of it would asswage in a few Days; but when I saw the weekly Bill of that Week, which was the highest of the whole Year, being 8297 of all Diseases, I upbraided him with it, and ask'd him, what he had made his Judgment from? His Answer, however, was not so much to seek, as I thought it would have been; look you, *says he*, by the Number which are at this Time sick and infected, there should have been twenty Thousand dead the last Week, instead of eight Thousand, if the inveterate mortal Contagion had been, as it was two Weeks ago; for then it ordinarily kill'd in two or three Days, now not under Eight or Ten; and then not above One in Five recovered; whereas I have observ'd, that now not above Two in Five miscarry; and observe it from me, the next Bill will decrease, and you will see many more People recover than used to do; for tho' a vast Multitude are now every where infected, and as many every Day fall sick; yet there will not so many die as there did, for the Malignity of the Distemper is abated; adding, that he began now to hope, nay more than hope, that the Infection had pass'd its Crisis, and was going off; and accordingly so it was, for the next Week being, as I said, the last in *September*, the Bill decreased almost two Thousand.

It is true, the Plague was still at a frightful Height, and the next Bill was no less than 6460, and the next to that 5720; but still my Friend's Observation was just, and it did appear the People did recover faster, and more in Number, than they used to do; and indeed if it had not been so, what had been the Condition of the City of *London?* for according to my Friend there were not fewer than sixty Thousand People at that Time infected, whereof, as above, 20477 died, and near 40000 recovered; whereas had it been as it was before, Fifty thousand of that Number would very probably have died, if not more, and 50000 more would have sickned; for in a Word, the whole Mass of People began to sicken, and it look'd as if none would escape.

But this Remark of my Friend's appear'd more evident in a few Weeks more; for the Decrease went on, and another Week in *October* it decreas'd 1849. So that the Number dead of the Plague was but 2665, and the next Week it decreased 1413 more, and yet it was seen plainly, that there was abundance of People sick, nay abundance more than ordinary, and abundance fell sick every Day, but (as above) the Malignity of the Disease abated.

Such is the precipitant Disposition of our People, whether it is so or not all over the World, that's none of my particular Business to enquire; but I saw it apparently here, that as upon the first Fright of the Infection, they shun'd one another, and fled from one another's Houses, and from the City with an unaccountable, and, as I thought, unnecessary Fright; so now upon this Notion spreading, (*viz.*) that the Distemper was not so catching as formerly, and that if it was catch'd, it was not so mortal, and seeing abundance of People who really fell sick, recover again daily; they took to such a precipitant Courage, and grew so entirely regardless of themselves, and of the Infection, that they made no more of the Plague than of an ordinary Fever, nor indeed so much; they not only went boldly into Company, with those who had Tumours and Carbuncles upon them, that were running, and consequently contagious, but eat and drank with them, nay into their Houses to visit them, and even, as I was told, into their very Chambers where they lay sick.

This I cou'd not see rational; my Friend Doctor *Heath* allow'd, and it was plain to Experience, that the Distemper was as catching as ever, and as many fell sick, but only he alledg'd, that so many of those that fell sick did not die; but I think that while many did die, and that, at best, the Distemper it self was very terrible, the Sores and Swellings very tormenting, and the Danger of Death not left out of the Circumstance of Sickness, tho' not so frequent as before; all those things, together with the exceeding Tediousness of the Cure, the Loathsomeness of the Disease, and many other Articles, were enough to deter any Man living from a dangerous Mixture with the sick People, and make them as anxious almost to avoid the Infection as before.

Nay there was another Thing which made the meer catching of the Distemper frightful, and that was the terrible burning of the Causticks, which the Surgeons laid on the Swellings to bring them to break, and to run; without which the Danger of Death was very great, even to the last; also the unsufferable Torment of the Swellings, which tho' it might not make People raving and distracted, as they were before, and as I have given several Instances of already, yet they put the Patient to inexpressible Torture; and those that fell into it, tho' they did escape with Life, yet they made bitter Complaints of those, that had told them there was no Danger, and sadly repented their Rashness and Folly in venturing to run into the reach of it.

Nor did this unwary Conduct of the People end here, for a great many that thus cast off their Cautions suffered more deeply still; and tho' many escap'd, yet many died; and at least it had this publick Mischief attending it, that it made the Decrease of Burials flower than it would otherwise have been; for as this notion run like Lightning thro' the City, and People Heads were possess'd with it, even as soon as the first great Decrease in the Bills appear'd, we found, that the two next Bills did not decrease in Proportion; the Reason I take to be the Peoples running so rashly into Danger, giving up all their former Cautions, and Care, and all the Shyness which they used to practice; depending that the Sickness would not reach them, or that if it did, they should not die.

The Physicians oppos'd this thoughtless Humour of the People with all their Might, and gave out printed Directions, spreading them all over the City and Suburbs, advising the People to continue reserv'd, and to use still the utmost Caution in their ordinary Conduct, notwithstanding the Decrease of the Distemper, terrifying them with the Danger of bringing a Relapse upon the whole City, and telling them how such a Relapse might be more fatal and dangerous than the whole Visitation that had been already; with many Arguments and Reasons to explain and prove that part to them, and which are too long to repeat here.

But it was all to no Purpose, the audacious Creatures were so possess'd with the first Joy, and so surpriz'd with the Satisfaction of seeing a vast Decrease in the weekly Bills, that they were impenetrable by any new Terrors, and would not be persuaded, but that the Bitterness of Death was pass'd; and it was to no more purpose to talk to them, than to an East-wind; but they open'd Shops, went about Streets, did Business, and conversed with any Body that came in their Way to converse with, whether with Business, or without, neither inquiring of their Health, or so much as being Apprehensive of any Danger from them, tho' they knew them not to be sound.

This imprudent rash Conduct cost a great many their Lives, who had with great Care and Caution shut themselves up, and kept retir'd as it were from all Mankind, and had by that means, under God's Providence, been preserv'd thro' all the heat of that Infection.

This rash and foolish Conduct, *I say*, of the People went so far, that the Ministers took notice to them of it at last, and laid before them both the Folly and Danger of it; and this check'd it a little, so that they grew more cautious, but it had another Effect, which they cou'd not check; for as the first Rumour had spread not over the City only, but into the Country, it had the like Effect, and the People were so tir'd with being so long from *London*, and so eager to come back, that they flock'd to Town without Fear or Forecast,[8] and began to shew themselves in the Streets, as if all the Danger was over: It was indeed surprising to see it, for tho' there died still from a Thousand to eighteen Hundred a Week, yet the People flock'd to Town, as if all had been well.

The Consequence of this was, that the Bills encreas'd again Four Hundred the very first Week in *November*; and if I might believe the Physicians, there was above three Thousand fell sick that Week, most of them new Comers too.

---

8. "Fear or forecast" was a cliché, suggesting that neither remembering past experience nor imagining future consequences deterred present behavior.

One JOHN COCK, a Barber in St. *Martins le Grand*,[9] was an eminent Example of this; I mean of the hasty Return of the People, when
the Plague was abated: This *John Cock* had left the Town with his whole
Family, and lock'd up his House, and was gone in the Country, as many
others did, and finding the Plague so decreas'd in *November*, that there
died but 905 *per* Week of all Diseases, he ventur'd home again; he had
in his Family Ten Persons, that is to say, himself and Wife, five Children, two Apprentices, and a Maid Servant; he had not been return'd to
his House above a Week, and began to open his Shop, and carry on his
Trade, but the Distemper broke out in his Family, and within about five
Days they all died, except one, that is to say, himself, his Wife, all his
five Children, and his two Apprentices, and only the Maid remain'd
alive.

But the Mercy of God was greater to the rest than [we] had Reason to
expect; for the Malignity, as I have said, of the Distemper was spent, the
Contagion was exhausted, and also the Winter Weather came on apace,
and the Air was clear and cold, with some sharp Frosts; and this encreasing still, most of those that had fallen sick recover'd, and the Health of the
City began to return: There were indeed some Returns of the Distemper,
even in the Month of *December*, and the Bills encreased near a Hundred,
but it went off again and so in a short while, Things began to return to
their own Channel. And wonderful it was to see how populous the City
was again all on a sudden; so that a Stranger could not miss the Numbers
that were lost, neither was there any miss of the Inhabitants as to their
Dwellings: Few or no empty Houses were to be seen,[1] or if there were
some, there was no want of Tenants for them.

I wish I cou'd say, that as the City had a new Face, so the Manners
of the People had a new Appearance: I doubt not but there were many
that retain'd a sincere Sense of their Deliverance, and that were heartily
thankful to that sovereign Hand, that had protected them in so dangerous a Time; it would be very uncharitable to judge otherwise in a City
so populous, and where the People were so devout, as they were here in
the Time of the Visitation it self; but except what of this was to be found
in particular Families, and Faces, it must be acknowledg'd that the general Practice of the People was just as it was before, and very little Difference was to be seen.

Some indeed said Things were worse, that the Morals of the People
declin'd from this very time; that the People harden'd by the Danger
they had been in, like Sea-men after a Storm is over, were more wicked
and more stupid, more bold and hardened in their Vices and Immoral-
ities than they were before; but I will not carry it so far neither: It would
take up a History of no small Length, to give a Particular of all the

9. Aldersgate Street narrowed after the Aldersgate into St. Martin's Le Grand and intersected
Newgate Street in the City.

1. London had been severely overcrowded.
Living nine to a room was not uncommon.

Gradations, by which the Course of Things in this City came to be restor'd again, and to run in their own Channel as they did before.

Some Parts of *England* were now infected as violently as *London* had been; the Cities of *Norwich, Peterborough, Lincoln, Colchester*, and other Places[2] were now visited; and the Magistrates of *London* began to set Rules for our Conduct, as to corresponding with those Cities: It is true, we could not pretend to forbid their People coming to *London*, because it was impossible to know them asunder, so after many Consultations, the Lord Mayor, and Court of Aldermen were oblig'd to drop it: All they cou'd do, was to warn and caution the People, not to entertain in their Houses, or converse with any People who they knew came from such infected Places.

But they might as well have talk'd to the Air, for the People of *London* thought themselves so Plague-free now, that they were past all Admonitions; they seem'd to depend upon it, that the Air was restor'd, and that the Air was like a Man that had had the Small Pox, not capable of being infected again; this reviv'd that Notion, that the Infection was all in the Air, that there was no such thing as Contagion from the sick People to the Sound; and so strongly did this Whimsy prevail among People, that they run all together promiscuously, sick and well; not the *Mahometans*, who, prepossess'd with the Principle of Predestination value nothing of Contagion, let it be in what it will, could be more obstinate than the People of *London*; they that were perfectly sound, and came out of the wholesome Air, as we call it, into the City, made nothing of going into the same Houses and Chambers nay even into the same Beds, with those that had the Distemper upon them, and were not recovered.

Some indeed paid for their audacious Boldness with the Price of their Lives; an infinite Number fell sick, and the Physicians had more Work than ever, only with this Difference, that more of their Patients recovered; that is to say, they generally recovered, but certainly there were more People infected, and fell sick now, when there did not die above a Thousand, or Twelve Hundred in a Week, than there was when there died Five or Six Thousand a Week; so entirely negligent were the People at that Time, in the great and dangerous Case of Health and Infection; and so ill were they able to take or accept of the Advice of those who cautioned them for their Good.

The People being thus return'd, as it were in general, it was very strange to find, that in their inquiring after their Friends, some whole Families were so entirely swept away, that there was no Remembrance of them left; neither was any Body to be found to possess or shew any Title to that little they had left; for in such Cases, what was to be found was generally embezzled, and purloyn'd some gone one way, some another.

2. These are inland towns north-northeast of London. At various times in his life, Defoe had trading ventures with all of them.

It was said such abandon'd Effects, came to the King as the universal
Heir, upon which we were told, and I suppose it was in part true, that
the King granted all such as Deodands[3] to the Lord Mayor and Court of
Aldermen of *London*, to be applied to the use of the Poor, of whom
there were very many: For it is to be observ'd, that tho' the Occasions of
Relief, and the Objects of Distress were very many more in the Time of
the Violence of the Plague, than now after all was over; yet the Distress
of the Poor was more now, a great deal than it was then, because all the
Sluices of general Charity were now shut; People suppos'd the main
Occasion to be over, and so stop'd their Hands; whereas particular Objects
were still very moving, and the Distress of those that were Poor, was very
great indeed.

Tho' the Health of the City was now very much restor'd, yet Foreign
Trade did not begin to stir, neither would Foreigners admit our Ships
into their Ports for a great while; as for the *Dutch*, the Misunderstand-
ings between our Court and them had broken out into a War the Year
before; so that our Trade that way was wholly interrupted; but *Spain* and
Portugal, *Italy* and *Barbary*, as also *Hamburgh*, and all the Ports in the
Baltick, these were all shy of us a great while, and would not restore
Trade with us for many Months.

The Distemper sweeping away such Multitudes, as I have observ'd,
many, if not all the out Parishes were oblig'd to make new burying
Grounds, besides that I have mention'd in *Bunhil-Fields*, some of which
were continued, and remain in Use to this Day; but others were left off,
and which, I confess, I mention with some Reflection, being converted
into other Uses, or built upon afterwards, the dead Bodies were disturb'd, abus'd, dug up again, some even before the Flesh of them was
perished from the Bones, and remov'd like Dung or Rubbish to other
Places; some of those which came within the Reach of my Observation,
are as follow.

1. A piece of Ground beyond *Goswel* Street, near *Mount-Mill*, being
some of the Remains of the old Lines or Fortifications of the City, where
Abundance were buried promiscuously from the Parishes of *Aldergate*,
Clerkenwell, and even out of the City. This Ground, as I take it, was
since made a Physick Garden, and after that has been built upon.

2. A piece of Ground just over the *Black Ditch*, as it was then call'd,
at the end of *Holloway Lane*,[4] in *Shoreditch* Parish; it has been since
made a Yard for keeping Hogs, and for other ordinary Uses, but is quite
out of Use as a burying Ground.

3. The upper End of *Hand-Alley* in *Bishopsgate* Street, which was
then a green Field, and was taken in particularly for *Bishopsgate* Parish,

---

3. Strictly speaking, a forfeit upon the death of
a person as a propitiatory offering to God and
to be converted to pious uses. Although the
forfeitures were probably carried out as convenient administrative actions, Defoe links them

to the theme of the possibility of God's judgment on the city.
4. Holywell Lane in Shoreditch, Middlesex,
ran between the Curtain and Shoreditch, the
main road to Hackney.

tho' many of the Carts out of the City brought their dead thither also, particularly out of the Parish of St. *All-hallows* on the *Wall*;[5] this Place I cannot mention without much Regret, it was, as I remember, about two or three Year after the Plague was ceas'd that Sir *Robert Clayton* came to be possest of the Ground; it was reported, how true I know not, that it fell to the King for want of Heirs, all those who had any Right to it being carried off by the Pestilence, and that Sir *Robert Clayton* obtain'd a Grant of it from King *Charles* II. But however he came by it, certain it is, the Ground was let out to build on, or built upon by his Order: The first House built upon it was a large fair House still standing, which faces the Street, or Way, now call'd *Hand-Alley*, which, tho' call'd an *Alley*, is as wide as a Street:[6] The Houses in the same Row with that House Northward, are built on the very same Ground where the poor People were buried, and the Bodies on opening the Ground for the Foundations, were dug up, some of them remaining so plain to be seen, that the Womens Sculls were distinguish'd by their long Hair, and of others, the Flesh was not quite perished; so that the People began to exclaim loudly against it, and some suggested that it might endanger a Return of the Contagion: After which the Bones and Bodies, as fast as they came at them, were carried to another part of the same Ground, and thrown all together into a deep Pit, dug on purpose, which now is to be known, in that it is not built on, but is a Passage to another House, at the upper end of *Rose Alley*, just against the Door of a Meeting-house,[7] which has been built there many Years since; and the Ground is palisadoed off from the rest of the Passage, in a little square, there lye the Bones and Remains of near Two thousand Bodies, carried by the Dead-Carts to their Grave in that one Year.

4. Besides this, there was a piece of Ground in *Moorfields*, by the going into the Street which is now call'd *Old Bethlem*,[8] which was enlarg'd much, tho' not wholly taken in on the same occasion.

N. B. The Author of this Journal, lyes buried in that very Ground, being at his own Desire, his Sister having been buried there a few Years before.

5. *Stepney* Parish, extending it self from the East part of *London* to the *North*, even to the very Edge of *Shoreditch* Church-yard, had a piece of Ground taken in to bury their Dead, close to the said Church-yard; and which for that very Reason was left open, and is since, I suppose, taken into the same Church-yard; and they had also two other burying

---

5. Defoe recounts accurately which parishes used that burial ground. Hand Alley was an L-shaped street not far from Spittlefields.

6. Clayton made a fortune in investments and pioneered mortgage banking. He became both Lord Mayor and a member of Parliament. Defoe knew this street well, for the famous Presbyterian clergyman Daniel Williams had his meeting house there.

7. Rose Alley was also off Bishopsgate Street.

As a Nonconformist, Defoe often used the meeting houses as landmarks.

8. Moorfields had the reputation for being unhealthy, for it was a marsh and had been used as a dumping ground. In the early 1600s rubbish was used to raise the ground, and Moorfields became the first designated public park in London. Old Bethlem Street ran along Bethlem Burying Ground between Moorfields and New Broad Street.

Places in *Spittlefields*, one where since a Chapel or Tabernacle has been
built for ease to this great Parish, and another in *Petticoat-lane*.

There were no less than Five other Grounds made use of for the
Parish of *Stepney* at that time; one where now stands the Parish Church
of St. *Paul's Shadwel*, and the other, where now stands the Parish Church
of St. *John* at *Wapping*, both which had not the Names of Parishes at
that time, but were belonging to *Stepney* Parish.

I cou'd name many more, but these coming within my particular
Knowledge, the Circumstance I thought made it of Use to record them;
from the whole, it may be observ'd, that they were oblig'd in this Time
of Distress, to take in new burying Grounds in most of the out Parishes,
for laying the prodigious Numbers of People which died in so short a
Space of Time; but why Care was not taken to keep those Places separate
from ordinary Uses, that so the Bodies might rest undisturb'd, that I
cannot answer for, and must confess, I think it was wrong; who were
to blame, I know not.

I should have mention'd, that the Quakers had at that time also a
burying Ground,[9] set a-part to their Use, and which they still make use
of, and they had also a particular *dead Cart* to fetch their Dead from
their Houses; and the famous *Solomon Eagle*, who, as I mentioned before,
had predicted the Plague as a Judgment, and run naked thro' the Streets,
telling the People, that it was come upon them, to punish them for their
Sins, had his own Wife died the very next Day of the Plague, and was
carried one of the first in the Quakers *dead Cart*, to their new burying
Ground.

I might have throng'd this Account with many more remarkable Things,
which occur'd in the Time of the Infection, and particularly what pass'd
between the Lord Mayor and the Court, which was then at *Oxford*, and
what Directions were from time to time receiv'd from the Government
for their Conduct on this critical Occasion. But really the Court concern'd themselves so little, and that little they did was of so small Import,
that I do not see it of much Moment to mention any Part of it here,
except that of appointing a Monthly Fast in the City, and the sending
the Royal Charity to the Relief of the Poor, both which I have mention'd
before.

Great was the Reproach thrown on those Physicians who left their
Patients during the Sickness, and now they came to Town again, no
Body car'd to employ them; they were call'd Deserters, and frequently
Bills were set up upon their Doors, and written, *Here is a Doctor to be
let!* So that several of those Physicians were fain for a while to sit still
and look about them, or at least remove their Dwellings, and set up in
new Places, and among new Acquaintance; the like was the Case with
the Clergy, who the People were indeed very abusive to, writing Verses

---

9. Bunhill Fields. It was never consecrated, and, therefore, people could be buried there without
the use of the *Book of Common Prayer*.

and scandalous Reflections upon them, setting upon the Church Door, *here is a Pulpit to be let*, or sometimes *to be sold*, which was worse.

It was not the least of our Misfortunes, that with our Infection, when it ceased, there did not cease the Spirit of Strife and Contention, Slander and Reproach, which was really the great Troubler of the Nation's Peace before: It was said to be the Remains of the old Animosities, which had so lately involv'd us all in Blood and Disorder. But as the late Act of Indemnity had laid asleep the Quarrel it self, so the Government had recommended Family and Personal Peace upon all Occasions, to the whole Nation.

But it cou'd not be obtain'd, and particularly after the ceasing of the Plague in *London*, when any one that had seen the Condition which the People had been in, and how they caress'd one another at that time, promis'd to have more Charity for the future, and to raise no more Reproaches: I say, any one that had seen them then, would have thought they would have come together with another Spirit at last. But, I say, it cou'd not be obtain'd; the Quarrel remain'd, the Church and the Presbyterians were incompatible; as soon as the Plague was remov'd, the dissenting outed Ministers who had supplied the Pulpits, which were deserted by the Incumbents, retir'd, they cou'd expect no other; but that they should immediately fall upon them, and harrass them, with their penal Laws, accept their preaching while they were sick, and persecute them as soon as they were recover'd again, this even we that were of the Church thought was very hard, and cou'd by no means approve of it.

But it was the Government, and we cou'd say nothing to hinder it; we cou'd only say, it was not our doing, and we could not answer for it.

On the other Hand, the Dissenters reproaching those Ministers of the Church with going away, and deserting their Charge, abandoning the People in their Danger, and when they had most need of Comfort and the like, this we cou'd by no means approve; for all Men have not the same Faith, and the same Courage, and the Scripture commands us to judge the most favourably, and according to Charity.

A Plague is a formidable Enemy, and is arm'd with Terrors, that every Man is not sufficiently fortified to resist, or prepar'd to stand the Shock against: It is very certain, that a great many of the Clergy, who were in Circumstances to do it, withdrew, and fled for the Safety of their Lives; but 'tis true also, that a great many of them staid, and many of them fell in the Calamity, and in the Discharge of their Duty.

It is true, some of the Dissenting turn'd out Ministers staid, and their Courage is to be commended, and highly valued, but these were not abundance; it cannot be said that they all staid, and that none retir'd into the Country, any more than it can be said of the Church Clergy, that they all went away; neither did all those that went away, go without substituting Curates, and others in their Places, to do the Offices needful, and to visit the Sick, as far as it was practicable; so that upon the whole, an Allowance of Charity might have been made on both Sides,

and we should have consider'd, that such a time as this of 1665, is not
to be parallel'd in History, and that it is not the stoutest Courage that
will always support Men in such Cases; I had not said this, but had
rather chosen to record the Courage and religious Zeal of those of both
Sides, who did hazard themselves for the Service of the poor People in
their Distress, without remembring that any fail'd in their Duty on either
side. But the want of Temper among us, has made the contrary to this
necessary; some that staid, not only boasting too much of themselves,
but reviling those that fled, branding them with Cowardice, deserting
their Flocks, and acting the Part of the Hireling, and the like: I recommend it to the Charity of all good People to look back, and reflect duly
upon the Terrors of the Time; and whoever does so will see, that it is
not an ordinary Strength that cou'd support it, it was not like appearing
in the Head of an Army, or charging a Body of Horse in the Field; but
it was charging Death it self on his pale Horse; to stay was indeed to die,
and it could be esteemed nothing less, especially as things appear'd at
the latter End of *August*, and the Beginning of *September*, and as there
was reason to expect them at that time; for no Man expected, and I dare
say, believed, that the Distemper would take so sudden a Turn as it did,
and fall immediately 2000 in a Week, when there was such a prodigious
Number of People sick at that Time, as it was known there was; and
then it was that many shifted away, that had stay'd most of the time
before.

Besides, if God gave Strength to some more than to others, was it to
boast of their Ability to abide the Stroak, and upbraid those that had not
the same Gift and Support, or ought not they rather to have been humble and thankful, if they were render'd more useful than their Brethren?

I think it ought to be recorded to the Honour of such Men, as well
Clergy as Physicians, Surgeons, Apothecaries, Magistrates and Officers
of every kind, as also all useful People, who ventur'd their Lives in Dis-
charge of their Duty, as most certainly all such as stay'd did to the last
Degree, and several of all these Kinds did not only venture but lose their
Lives on that sad Occasion.

I was once making a List of all such, I mean of all those Professions
and Employments, who thus died, as I call it, in the way of their Duty,
but it was impossible for a private Man to come at a Certainty in the
Particulars; I only remember, that there died sixteen Clergy-men, two
Aldermen, five Physicians, thirteen Surgeons, within the City and Liberties before the beginning of *September*: But this being, as I said before,
the great Crisis and Extremity of the Infection, it can be no compleat
List: As to inferior People, I think there died six and forty Constables
and Headboroughs in the two Parishes of *Stepney* and *White-Chapel*;
but I could not carry my List on, for when the violent Rage of the
Distemper in *September* came upon us, it drove us out of all Measures:
Men did then no more die by Tale[1] and by Number, they might put

1. By tally, by lists.

out a Weekly Bill, and call them seven or eight Thousand, or what they pleas'd; 'tis certain they died by Heaps, and were buried by Heaps, that is to say without Account; and if I might believe some People, who were more abroad and more conversant with those things than I, tho' I was public enough for one that had no more Business to do than I had, I say, if I may believe them, there was not many less buried those first three Weeks in *September* than 20000 *per* Week; however the others aver the Truth of it, yet I rather chuse to keep to the public Account; seven and eight thousand *per* Week is enough to make good all that I have said of the Terror of those Times; and it is much to the Satisfaction of me that write, as well as those that read, to be able to say, that every thing is set down with Moderation, and rather within Compass than beyond it.

Upon all these Accounts I say I could wish, when we were recover'd, our Conduct had been more distinguish'd for Charity and Kindness in Remembrance of the past Calamity, and not so much a valuing our selves upon our Boldness in staying, as if all Men were Cowards that fly from the Hand of God, or that those, who stay, do not sometimes owe their Courage to their Ignorance, and despising the Hand of their Maker, which is a criminal kind of Desperation, and not a true Courage.

I cannot but leave it upon Record, that the Civil Officers, such as Constables, Headboroughs, Lord Mayor's, and Sheriff's-men, as also Parish-Officers, whose Business it was to take Charge of the Poor, did their Duties in general with as much Courage as any, and perhaps with more, because their Work was attended with more Hazards, and lay more among the Poor, who were more subject to be infected and in the most pitiful Plight when they were taken with the Infection: But then it must be added too, that a great Number of them died, indeed it was scarce possible it should be otherwise.

I have not said one Word here about the Physick or Preparations that we ordinarily made use of on this terrible Occasion, I mean we that went frequently abroad up and down Street, as I did; much of this was talk'd of in the Books and Bills of our Quack Doctors, of whom I have said enough already. It may however be added, that the College of Physicians were daily publishing several Preparations, which they had consider'd of in the Process of their Practice, and which being to be had in Print, I avoid repeating them for that reason.

One thing I could not help observing, what befell one of the Quacks, who publish'd that he had a most excellent Preservative against the Plague, which whoever kept about them, should never be infected, or liable to Infection; this Man, who we may reasonably suppose, did not go abroad without some of this *excellent Preservative* in his Pocket, yet was taken by the Distemper, and carry'd off in two or three Days.

I am not of the Number of the Physic-Haters, or Physic-Despisers; on the contrary, I have often mentioned the regard I had to the Dictates of my particular Friend Dr. *Heath*; but yet I must acknowledge, I made use of little or nothing, except as I have observ'd, to keep a Preparation of strong Scent to have ready, in case I met with any thing of offensive Smells, or went too near any burying place, or dead Body.

Neither did I do, what I know some did, keep the Spirits always high and hot with Cordials, and Wine, and such things, and which, as I observ'd, one learned Physician used himself so much to, as that he could not leave them off when the Infection was quite gone, and so became a Sot for all his Life after.[2]

I remember, my Friend the Doctor us'd to say, that there was a certain Set of Drugs and Preparations, which were all certainly good and useful in the case of an Infection; out of which, or with which, Physicians might make an infinite Variety of Medicines, as the Ringers of Bells make several Hundred different Rounds of Musick by the changing and Order of Sound but in six Bells; and that all these Preparations shall be really very good; therefore, said he, I do not wonder that so vast a Throng of Medicines is offer'd in the present Calamity; and almost every Physician prescribes or prepares a different thing, as his Judgment or Experience guides him: but, says my Friend, let all the Prescriptions of all the Physicians in *London* be examined; and it will be found, that they are all compounded of the same things, with such Variations only, as the particular Fancy of the Doctor leads him to; so that, says he, every Man judging a little of his own Constitution and manner of his living, and Circumstances of his being infected, may direct his own Medicines out of the ordinary Drugs and Preparations: Only that, says he, some recommend one thing as most sovereign, and some another; some, says he, think that *Pill. Ruff.*[3] which is call'd itself the Antipestilential Pill, is the best Preparation that can be made; others think, that V*enice* Treacle[4] is sufficient of it self to resist the Contagion, and I, says he, think as both these think, *viz.* that the last is good to take beforehand to prevent it, and the last, if touch'd, to expel it. According to this Opinion. I several times took V*enice Treacle* and a sound Sweat upon it, and thought my self as well fortified against the Infection as any one could be fortifyed by the Power of Physic.

As for Quackery and Mountebank, of which the Town was so full, I listened to none of them, and have observ'd often since with some Wonder, that for two Years after the Plague, I scarcely saw or heard of one of them about Town. Some fancied they were all swept away in the Infection to a Man, and were for calling it a particular Mark of God's Vengeance upon them, for leading the poor People into the Pit of Destruction, merely for the Lucre of a little Money they got by them; but I cannot go

2. Cordials, believed to stimulate the heart and arouse the spirit, often included as much alcohol as wine. Many contained wine; a typical recipe for a cordial called for a pint of Malmsey wine, a spoonful of cardamom seeds, and a spoonful of treacle (a mild syrup made from molasses and corn syrup) beaten together. Wine had long had the reputation of aiding digestion and helping maintain good health. Landa says that Defoe may have had Dr. Hodges in mind as the physician who became a "sot." Hodges had written that wine was "deservedly" considered an antidote to the plague (285n.).
3. *Pilulae Rufi*, a mixture of myrrh and aloe.
4. A cordial water or confection containing over fifty ingredients, including opium.

that Length neither; that Abundance of them died is certain, many of them came within the Reach of my own Knowledge; but that all of them were swept off I much question; I believe rather, they fled into the Country, and tryed their Practices upon the People there, who were in Apprehension of the Infection, before it came among them.

This however is certain, not a Man of them appear'd for a great while in or about *London;* there were indeed several Doctors, who published Bills, recommending their several physical Preparations for cleansing the Body, as they call it, after the Plague, and needful, as they said, for such People to take, who had been visited and had been cur'd; whereas I must own, I believe that it was the Opinion of the most eminent Physicians at that time, that the Plague was itself a sufficient Purge; and that those who escaped the Infection needed no Physic to cleanse their Bodies of any other things; the running Sores, the Tumors, &c. which were broke and kept open by the Directions of the Physicians, having sufficiently cleansed them; and that all other Distempers and Causes of Distempers were effectually carried off that Way; and as the Physicians gave this as their Opinions, wherever they came, the Quacks got little Business.

There were indeed several little Hurries, which happen'd after the Decrease of the Plague, and which whether they were contriv'd to fright and disorder the People, as some imagin'd, I cannot say, but sometimes we were told the Plague would return by such a Time; and the famous *Solomon Eagle* the naked Quaker, I have mention'd, prophesy'd evil Tidings every Day; and several others telling us that *London* had not been sufficiently scourg'd, and the sorer and severer Strokes were yet behind; had they stop'd there, or had they descended to Particulars, and told us that the City should the next Year be destroyed by Fire; then indeed, when we had seen it come to pass, we should not have been to blame to have paid more than a common Respect to their Prophetick Spirits, at least we should have wonder'd at them, and have been more serious in our Enquiries after the meaning of it, and whence they had the Fore-knowledge: But as they generally told us of a Relapse into the Plague, we have had no Concern since that about them; yet by these frequent Clamours, we were all kept with some kind of Apprehensions constantly upon us, and if any died suddenly, or if the spotted Fevers at any time increased, we were presently alarm'd; much more if the Number of the Plague encreased, for to the End of the Year, there were always between 2 and 300 of the Plague; on any of these Occasions, I say, we were alarm'd anew.

Those, who remember the City of *London* before the Fire, must remember, that there was then no such Place as that we now call *Newgate-*Market. But that in the Middle of the Street, which is now call'd *Blow-bladder Street*,[5] and which had its Name from the Butchers, who us'd to

5. In 1665, Newgate Market was an important meat market with row after row of sheds for butchers. Blow Bladder Street was at the east end of Newgate Street. Processed sheep blad-

kill and dress their Sheep there; (and who it seems had a Custom to blow up their Meat with Pipes to make it look thicker and fatter than it was, and were punish'd there for it by the Lord Mayor) I say, from the End of the Street towards *Newgate*, there stood two long Rows of Shambles for the selling Meat.

It was in those Shambles, that two Persons falling down dead, as they were buying Meat, gave Rise to a Rumor that the Meat was all infected, which tho' it might affright the People, and spoil'd the Market for two or three Days; yet it appear'd plainly afterwards, that there was nothing of Truth in the Suggestion: [6] But no Body can account for the Possession of Fear when it takes hold of the Mind.

However it pleas'd God by the continuing of the Winter Weather to restore the Health of the City, that by *February* following, we reckon'd the Distemper quite ceas'd, and then we were not so easily frighted again.

There was still a Question among the Learned, and at first it perplex'd the People a little, and that was, in what manner to purge the Houses and Goods, where the Plague had been; and how to render them habitable again, which had been left empty during the time of the Plague; Abundance of Perfumes and Preparations were prescrib'd by Physicians, some of one kind and some of another, in which the People, who listened to them, put themselves to a great, and indeed in my Opinion, to an unnecessary Expence; and the poorer People, who only set open their Windows Night and Day, burnt Brimstone, Pitch, and Gun-powder and such things in their Rooms, did as well as the best; nay, the eager People, who as I said above, came Home in haste and at all Hazards, found little or no Inconvenience in their Houses nor in the Goods, and did little or nothing to them.

However, in general, prudent cautious People did enter into some Measures for airing and sweetning their Houses, and burnt Perfumes, Incense, Benjamin, Rozin, and Sulphur in the Rooms close shut up, and then the Air carry it all out with a Blast of Gun-powder; others caused large Fires to be made all Day and all Night, for several Days and Nights; by the same Token, that two or three were pleas'd to set their Houses on Fire, and so effectually sweetned them by burning them down to the Ground; as particularly one at *Ratcliff*, one in *Holbourn*, and one at *Westminster*; besides two or three that were set on Fire, but the Fire was happily got out again, before it went far enough to burn down the Houses; and one Citizen's Servant, I think it was in *Thames* Street, carried so much Gunpowder into his Master's House for clearing

---

ders were in demand for, among other things, making balls used in children's games and even the equivalent of adult soccer matches played between rival parishes or sections of town. It has been speculated that the games between St. Michael's and St. Paul's were played at the intersection of Newgate and Paternoster Row— Blow Bladder Street (Ronald Baker and Rich-

ard Frushell, "Defoe's Blow-bladder Street," *Journal of American Folklore* 87 (1974): 160–62).

6. This story, like the one featuring Hayward, may have been one told by Defoe's father, a member and officer in the Butchers' Company.

it of the Infection, and managed it so foolishly, that he blew up part of the Roof of the House. But the Time was not fully come, that the City was to be purg'd by Fire, nor was it far off; for within Nine Months more I saw it all lying in Ashes; when, as some of our Quacking Philosophers pretend, the Seeds of the Plague were entirely destroy'd and not before; a Notion too ridiculous to speak of here, since, had the Seeds of the Plague remain'd in the Houses, not to be destroyed but by Fire, how has it been, that they have not since broken out? Seeing all those Buildings in the Suburbs and Liberties, and in the great Parishes of *Stepney, White-Chapel, Aldgate, Bishopsgate, Shoreditch, Cripplegate* and St. *Giles's,* where the Fire never came, and where the Plague rag'd with the greatest Violence, remain still in the same Condition they were in before.

But to leave these things just as I found them, it was certain, that those People, who were more than ordinarily cautious of their Health, did take particular Directions for what they called Seasoning of their Houses, and Abundance of costly Things were consum'd on that Account, which, I cannot but say, not only seasoned those Houses, as they desir'd, but fill'd the Air with very grateful and wholesome Smells, which others had the Share of the Benefit of, as well as those who were at the Expences of them.

And yet after all, tho' the Poor came to Town very precipitantly, as I have said, yet I must say, the rich made no such Haste; the Men of Business indeed came up, but many of them did not bring their Families to Town, till the Spring came on, and that they saw Reason to depend upon it, that the Plague would not return.

The Court indeed came up soon after Christmas, but the Nobility and Gentry, except such as depended upon, and had Employment under the Administration, did not come so soon.

I should have taken Notice here, that notwithstanding the Violence of the Plague in *London* and in other Places, yet it was very observable, that it was never on Board the Fleet;[7] and yet for some time there was a strange Press[8] in the River, and even in the Streets for Sea-Men to man the Fleet. But it was in the Beginning of the Year, when the Plague was scarce begun, and not at all come down to that part of the City, where they usually press for Seamen; and tho' a War with the *Dutch* was not at all grateful to the People at that time, and the Seamen went with a kind of Reluctancy into the Service, and many complain'd of being drag'd into it by Force, yet it prov'd in the Event a happy Violence to several of them, who had probably perish'd in the general Calamity, and who after the Summer Service was over, tho' they had Cause to lament the Desolation of their Families, who, when they came back, were many of

7. Some ships in the fleet were infected in spite of the fact that sailors were not allowed ashore and the Navy issued orders forbidding impressing colliers returning from London. Defoe often wrote propaganda to help recruit seamen.
8. "Press" is slang for "impress"; recruiting officers had warrants with quotas giving them the right to impress men into the British military, usually the navy. This compulsory conscription was usually enforced with warrants but kidnapping occurred.

them in their Graves; yet they had room to be thankful, that they were carried out of the Reach of it, tho' so much against their Wills; we indeed had a hot War with the *Dutch* that Year, and one very great Engagement at Sea, in which the *Dutch* were worsted; but we lost a great many Men and some Ships. But, as I observ'd, the Plague was not in the Fleet, and when they came to lay up the Ships in the River, the violent part of it began to abate.

I would be glad, if I could close the Account of this melancholy Year with some particular Examples historically; I mean of the Thankfulness to God our Preserver for our being delivered from this dreadful Calamity; certainly the Circumstances of the Deliverance, as well as the terrible Enemy we were delivered from, call'd upon the whole Nation for it; the Circumstances of the Deliverance were indeed very remarkable, as I have in part mention'd already, and particularly the dreadful Condition, which we were all in, when we were, to the Surprize of the whole Town, made joyful with the Hope of a Stop of the Infection.

Nothing, but the immediate Finger of God, nothing, but omnipotent Power could have done it; the Contagion despised all Medicine, Death rag'd in every Corner; and had it gone on as it did then, a few Weeks more would have clear'd the Town of all, and every thing that had a Soul: Men every where began to despair, every Heart fail'd them for Fear, People were made desperate thro' the Anguish of their Souls, and the Terrors of Death sat in the very Faces and Countenances of the People.

In that very Moment, when we might very well say, Vain was the Help of Man;[9] I say in that very Moment it pleased God, with a most agreeable Surprize, to cause the Fury of it to abate, even of it self, and the Malignity declining, as I have said, tho' infinite Numbers were sick, yet fewer died; and the very first Week's Bill decreased 1843; a vast Number indeed!

It is impossible to express the Change that appear'd in the very Countenances of the People, that *Thursday* Morning, when the Weekly Bill came out; it might have been perceived in their Countenances, that a secret Surprize and Smile of Joy sat on every Bodies Face; they shook one another by the Hands in the Streets, who would hardly go on the same Side of the way with one another before; where the Streets were not too broad, they would open their Windows and call from one House to another, and ask'd how they did, and if they had heard the good News, that the Plague was abated; Some would return when they said good News, and ask, *what good News?* and when they answered, that the Plague was abated, and the Bills decreased almost 2000, they would cry out, *God be praised*; and would weep aloud for Joy, telling them

9. Psalms 60.11. This psalm was a lamentation and appeal for God's help in a time of national calamity. The verse reads, "Give us help from trouble: for vain *is* the help of man."

they had heard nothing of it; and such was the Joy of the People that it was as it were Life to them from the Grave. I could almost set down as many extravagant things done in the Excess of their Joy, as of their Grief; but that would be to lessen the Value of it.

I must confess my self to have been very much dejected just before this happen'd; for the prodigious Number that were taken sick the Week or two before, besides those that died, was such, and the Lamentations were so great every where, that a Man must have seemed to have acted even against his Reason, if he had so much as expected to escape; and as there was hardly a House, but mine, in all my Neighbourhood, but what was infected; so had it gone on, it would not have been long, that there would have been any more Neighbours to be infected; indeed it is hardly credible, what dreadful Havock the last three Weeks had made, for if I might believe the Person, whose Calculations I always found very well grounded, there were not less than 30000 People dead, and near 100 thousand fallen sick in the three Weeks I speak of; for the Number that sickened was surprising, indeed it was astonishing, and those whose Courage upheld them all the time before, sunk under it now.

In the Middle of their Distress, when the Condition of the City of *London* was so truly calamitous, just then it pleased God, as it were, by his immediate Hand to disarm this Enemy; the Poyson was taken out of the Sting, it was wonderful, even the Physicians themselves were sur-prized at it; wherever they visited, they found their Patients better, either they had sweated kindly, or the Tumours were broke, or the Carbuncles went down, and the Inflammations round them chang'd Colour, or the Fever was gone, or the violent Headach was asswag'd, or some good Symptom was in the Case; so that in a few Days, every Body was recover-ing, whole Families that were infected and down, that had Ministers praying with them, and expected Death every Hour, were revived and healed, and none died at all out of them.

Nor was this by any new Medicine found out, or new Method of Cure discovered, or by any Experience in the Operation, which the Physi-cians or Surgeons had attain'd to; but it was evidently from the secret invisible Hand of him, that had at first sent this Disease as a Judgment upon us; and let the Atheistic part of Mankind call my Saying this what they please, it is no Enthusiasm; it was acknowledg'd at that time by all Mankind; the Disease was enervated, and its Malignity spent, and let it proceed from whencesoever it will, let the Philosophers search for Rea-sons in Nature to account for it by, and labour as much as they will to lessen the Debt they owe to their Maker; those Physicians, who had the least Share of Religion in them, were oblig'd to acknowledge that it was all supernatural, that it was extraordinary, and that no Account could be given of it.

If I should say, that this is a visible Summons to us all to Thankful-ness, especially we that were under the Terror of its Increase, perhaps it

may be thought by some, after the Sense of the thing was over, an offi-
cious canting of religious things, preaching a Sermon instead of writing
a History, making my self a Teacher instead of giving my Observations
of things; and this restrains me very much from going on here, as I might
otherwise do: But if ten Leapers were healed, and but one return'd to
give Thanks, I desire to be as that one,[1] and to be thankful for my self.

Nor will I deny, but there were Abundance of People who to all
Appearance were very thankful at that time; for their Mouths were stop'd
even the Mouths of those, whose Hearts were not extraordinary long
affected with it: But the Impression was so strong at that time, that it
could not be resisted, no not by the worst of the People.

It was a common thing to meet People in the Street, that were Strangers,
and that we knew nothing at all of, expressing their Surprize. Going one
Day thro' *Aldgate*, and a pretty many People being passing and repass-
ing, there comes a Man out of the End of the *Minories*, and looking a
little up the Street and down, he throws his Hands abroad, *Lord, what
an Alteration is here!* Why, last Week I came along here, and hardly
any Body was to be seen; another Man, I heard him, adds to his Words,
'tis all wonderful, 'tis all a Dream: Blessed be God, says a third Man,
and let us give Thanks to him, for 'tis all his own doing: Human Help
and human Skill was at an End. These were all Strangers to one another:
But such Salutations as these were frequent in the Street every Day; and
in Spight of a loose Behaviour, the very common People went along the
Streets, giving God Thanks for their Deliverance.

It was now, as I said before, the People had cast off all Apprehensions,
and that too fast; indeed we were no more afraid now to pass by a Man
with a white Cap upon his Head, or with a Cloth wrapt round his Neck,
or with his Leg limping, occasion'd by the Sores in his Groyn, all which
were frightful to the last Degree, but the Week before; but now the Street
was full of them, and these poor recovering Creatures, give them their
Due, appear'd very sensible of their unexpected Deliverance; and I should
wrong them very much, if I should not acknowledge, that I believe many
of them were really thankful; but I must own, that for the Generality of
the People it might too justly be said of them, as was said of the Children
of *Israel*, after their being delivered from the Host of *Pharaoh*, when
they passed the *Red-Sea*, and look'd back, and saw the *Egyptians* overwhelmed in the Water, *viz.* That *they sang his Praise, but they soon
forgot his Works.*[2]

I can go no farther here, I should be counted censorious, and perhaps
unjust, if I should enter into the unpleasant Work of reflecting, whatever

1. Luke 17.12–17; this passage is one of Defoe's
favorites, and he compared himself to that one
leper several times in his nonfiction prose and
in his letters to benefactors.
2. Psalms 106.12–13. Defoe is probably quoting from memory. This psalm would have

seemed appropriate to him because it includes
a review of Israel's history, deliverance, and
repeated lapses into sin and forgetfulness, and
it concludes with thanks for God's repeated
mercy and forgiveness.

Cause there was for it, upon the Unthankfulness and Return of all manner of Wickedness among us, which I was so much an Eye-Witness of my self; I shall conclude the Account of this calamitous Year therefore with a coarse but sincere Stanza of my own, which I plac'd at the End of my ordinary Memorandums, the same Year they were written:

> *A dreadful Plague in* London *was,*
> *In the Year Sixty Five,*
> *Which swept an Hundred Thousand Souls*
> *Away; yet I alive!*

H. F.

FINIS[3]

---

3. The visual emblem of the phoenix printed at the end of the text symbolizes the city's rebirth and return to life, health, and prosperity.

BACKGROUNDS: THE PLAGUE OF 1665 AND THE THREAT OF 1720–21

Orders
Conceived and Published by the Lord MAIOR and Aldermen of the City of *London*, concerning the Infection of the Plague. 1665.

Whereas in the reign of our late sovereign King James,[1] of happy memory, an act was made for the charitable relief and ordering of persons infected with the plague; whereby authority was given to justices of peace, mayors, bailiffs, and other head officers, to appoint within their several limits, examiners, searchers, watchmen, keepers, and buriers for the persons and places infected, and to minister unto them oaths for the performance of their offices. And the same statute did also authorize the giving of other directions, as unto them for the present necessity should seem good in their discretions. It is now upon special consideration, thought very expedient for preventing and avoiding of infection of sickness (if it shall so please Almighty God) that these officers following be appointed, and these orders hereafter duly observed.

Examiners to Be Appointed in Every Parish

First, it is thought requisite, and so ordered, that in every parish there be one, two, or more persons of good sort and credit, chosen and appointed by the alderman, his deputy, and common council of every ward, by the name of examiners, to continue in that office the space of two months at least: and if any fit person so appointed, shall refuse to undertake the same, the said parties so refusing, to be committed to prison until they shall conform themselves accordingly.

The Examiner's Office

That these examiners be sworn by the aldermen, to enquire and learn from time to time what houses in every parish be visited, and what persons be sick, and of what diseases, as near as they can inform themselves; and upon doubt in that case, to command restraint of access, until it appear what the disease shall prove: and if they find any person sick of the infection, to give order to the constable that the house be shut up; and if the constable shall be found remiss or negligent, to give present notice thereof to the alderman of the ward.

Watchmen

That to every infected house there be appointed two watchmen, one, for every day, and the other for the night: and that these watchmen have

1. James I.

a special care that no person go in or out of such infected houses, whereof they have the charge, upon pain of severe punishment. And the said watchman to do such further offices as the sick house shall need and require: and if the watchman be sent upon any business, to lock up the house, and take the key with him: and the watchman by day to attend until ten of the clock at night: and the watchman by night until six in the morning.

Searchers

That there be a special care to appoint women searchers in every parish, such as are of honest reputation, and of the best sort as can be got in this kind: and these to be sworn to make due search, and true report to the utmost of their knowledge, whether the persons whose bodies they are appointed to search, do die of the infection, or of what other diseases, as near as they can. And that the physicians who shall be appointed to cure and prevention of the infection, do call before them the said searchers, who are or shall be appointed for the several parishes under their respective cares, to the end they may consider whether they are fitly qualified for that employment; and charge them from time to time as they shall see cause, if they appear defective in their duties.

That no searcher during this time of visitation be permitted to use any publick work or employment, or keep any shop or stall, or be employed as laundress, or in any other common employment whatsoever.

Chirurgeons

For better assistance of the searchers, for as much as there hath been heretofore great abuse in misreporting the disease, to the further spreading of the infection: it is therefore ordered, that there be chosen and appointed able and discreet chirurgeons, besides those that do already belong to the pesthouse: amongst whom the city and the liberties to be quartered as the places lie most apt and convenient; and every of these to have one quarter for his limit: and the said chirurgeons in every of their limits to join with the searchers for the view of the body, to the end there may be a true report made of the disease.

And further, that the said chirurgeons shall visit and search such like persons as shall either send for them, or be named and directed unto them, by the examiners of every parish, and inform themselves of the disease of the said parties.

And forasmuch as the said chirurgeons are to be sequestered from all other cures, and kept only to this disease of the infection; it is ordered that every of the said chirurgeons shall have twelve pence a body searched by them, to be paid out of the goods of the party searched, if he be able, or otherwise by the parish.

※   ※   ※

JOHN GRAUNT

From *Reflections on the Weekly Bills of Mortality* and *Natural and Political Observations upon the Bills of Mortality* †

So Far as They Relate to All the Plagues That Have Happen'd in London *From the Year 1592, to the Great Plague in 1665, and Some Other Particular Diseases.*

There have been in *London*, within about 130 Years, four great Mortalities.

The first in 1592. when there died between *March* and *December*, 25886.

Whereof of the Plague, 11503.

The second in 1603. when there died from *March* to *December*, 37294.

Whereof of the Plague, 30561.

The fourth in 1636. from *April* to *December*, 23357.

Whereof of the Plague, 10400.

In the first and last of these Years, *viz.* 1592. and 1636. the Proportion of those that died of the *Plague*, to those that died of all other Diseases or Casualties, was about two to five.

In the second, *viz.* 1603. it was four to five.

In the third, it was seven to ten.

And so the greatest Plague Year was 1603.

And yet the greatest Year of Mortality was 1625.

When the Burials were 54265. $\Big\}$ Or as $\begin{cases} 8 \\ 1 \end{cases}$
The Christenings were 6983.

This Business lying here, that there lieth an Error in the Accounts or Distinctions of Casualties, that is, more died of the *Plague* than were accounted for under that Name, as many as one to four, there being a fourth Part more dead of other Casualties that Year, than the Years preceding or subsequent. Whence we may collect a good Rule, *viz.* That whereas it is doubted we have not a true Account of the Number that died in 1665. of the *Plague*, the poor Searchers, out of Ignorance, Respect, Love of Money, or Malice, returning, it's suspected, more or less, as they were inclined; we may discern the Truth, by comparing the Number that died of other Diseases, and the Casualties the Weeks immediately before the *Plague* begun, and the Number reported to have been dead every Week of those Diseases and Casualties after, and observing that the Surplusage that died at one Time, above what did then of those

† John Graunt, the first important English demographer, published *Reflections* in 1665 and *Observations* in 1662. This excerpt includes material from both. He is sometimes called the father of modern statistics.

Diseases, are indeed dead of the *Plague*, tho' returned under the Notion of those other Diseases.

And here it will not be unseasonable to observe That the keeping of Bills of Mortality began A. D 1592. being a Year of great Sickness, and after some Disuse, was established by Order, A.D. 1603. the next Year of Sickness: The first of the continued weekly Bills of Mortality commencing *October* 29. 1603. the first Year of King *James*.

❈   ❈   ❈

The Diseases, and Casualties this year being 1632.

ABortive, and Stilborn	445
Affrighted	1
Aged	628
Ague	43
Apoplex, and Meagrom	17
Bit with a mad dog	1
Bleeding	3
Bloody flux, scowring, and flux	348
Brused, Issues, sores, and ulcers,	28
Burnt, and Scalded	5
Burst, and Rupture	9
Cancer, and Wolf	10
Canker	1
Childbed	171
Chrisomes, and Infants	2268
Cold, and Cough	55
Colick, Stone, and Strangury	56
Consumption	1797
Convulsion	241
Cut of the Stone	5
Dead in the street, and starved	6
Dropsie, and Swelling	267
Drowned	34
Executed, and prest to death	18
Falling Sickness	7
Fever	1108
Fistula	13
Flocks, and small Pox	531
French Pox	12
Gangrene	5
Gout	4
Grief	11
Jaundies	43
Jawfaln	8
Impostume	74
Kil'd by several accidents	46
King's Evil	38
Lethargie	2
Livergrown	87
Lunatique	5
Made away themselves	15
Measles	80
Murthered	7
Over-laid, and starved at nurse	7
Palsie	25
Piles	1
Plague	8
Planet	13
Pleurisie, and Spleen	36
Purples, and spotted Feaver	38
Quinsie	7
Rising of the Lights	98
Sciatica	1
Scurvey, and Itch	9
Suddenly	62
Surfet	86
Swine Pox	6
Teeth	470
Thrush, and Sore mouth	40
Tympany	13
Tissick	34
Vomiting	1
Worms	27

Christened { Males . . . . 4994 Females . . . . . 4590 In all . . . . 9584 }   Buried { Males . . . . 4932 Females . . . . . 4603 In all . . . . 9535 } Whereof, of the Plague. 8

Increased in the Burials in the 122 Parishes, and at the Pesthouse this year 993

Decreased of the Plague in the 122 Parishes, and at the pesthouse this year 266

These Bills are made and composed in this manner: When any one dies, then, either by tolling, or ringing of a Bell, or by bespeaking of a Grave of the *Sexton*, the same is known to the *Searchers*, corresponding with the said *Sexton*.

The *Searchers* hereupon (who are antient Matrons, sworn to their Office) repair to the place, where the dead Corps lies, and by view of the same, and by other enquiries, they examine by what *Disease*, or *Casualty* the Corps died. Hereupon they make their Report to the *Parish-Clerk*, and he, every *Tuesday* night, carries in an Accompt of all the *Burials*, and *Christnings*, hapning that Week, to the *Clerk* of the *Hall*. On *Wednesday* the general Accompt is made up, and Printed, and on *Thursdays* published, and dispersed to the several Families, who will pay four shillings *per* Annum for them.

Now altho the Searchers are ignorant and careless, yet in such Diseases and Casualties as are obvious to Sense, as Age, Consumptions, or inward Decayings, signified by the outward Leanness, Coughs, Wind, Teeth, Convulsions, Thrush, Scowring, Abortions, Head-ach, or Sudden Deaths, or by Apoplexy, &c. Drowning, Vomiting, &c. Small-Pox, Stone, Gout, they may be relied on, as they may also in such Cases as those wherein they have the Opinion of the Physicians.

Memorandum, That although the general yearly *Bills* have been set out in the several varieties aforementioned, yet the Original Entries in the *Hall-books* were as exact in the very first Year as to all particulars, as now; and the specifying of *Casualties* and *Diseases*, was probably more.

In the year 1636, the Accompt of the *Burials*, and *Christnings* in the Parishes of *Islington, Lambeth, Stepney, Newington, Hackney*, and *Redriff*, were added in the manner following, making a seventh Canton, *viz.*

Covent Garden being made a Parish, the nine out-Parishes were called the ten out-Parishes, the which in former years were but eight.

In Margaret Westminster	Christned	440		Christned	99
	Buried	890	Newington	Buried	181
	Plague	0		Plague	0
Islington	Christned	36			
	Buried	113			
	Plague	0	Hackney	Christned	30
Lambeth	Christned	132		Buried	91
	Buried	220		Plague	0
	Plague	0			
Stepney	Christned	892		Christned	16
	Buried 1486		Redriff	Buried	48
	Plague	0		Plague	0

The total of all the Burials in the seven last Parishes this Year 2958
Whereof of the Plague 0
The total of all the Christnings 1645

Parish	Bur.	Plag.
Alban Woodstreet	23	19
Alhallows Barking	41	32
Alhallows Breadstreet	4	3
Alhallows Great	59	53
Alhallows Honylane	1	
Alhallows Lesse	29	26
Alhallows Lumbardstreet	8	7
Alhallows Staining	16	10
Alhallows the Wall	41	30
St Alphage	25	13
St Andrew Hubbard	6	5
St Andrew Undershaft	25	22
St Andrew Wardrobe	63	54
St Ann Aldersgate	33	28
St Ann Blackfryers	79	65
St Antholins Parish	6	5
St Austins Parish	2	2
St Barholomew Exchange	3	3
St Bennet Fynck	1	
St Bennet Gracechurch	5	4
St Bennet Paulswharf	35	15
St Bennet Sherehog	1	
St Botolph Billingsgate	4	4
Christs Church	55	48
St Christophers	6	5
St Clement Eastcheap	3	3
St George Botolphlane	5	3
St Gregory by St Pauls	32	23
St Hellen	8	8
St James Dukes place	29	26
St James Garlickhithe	13	11
St John Baptist	7	6
St John Evangelist		
St John Zachary	3	2
St Katharine Coleman	44	36
St Katharine Crechurch	35	31
St Lawrence Jewry	8	6
St Lawrence Pountney	22	17
St Leonard Eastcheap	5	4
St Leonard Fosterlane	34	32
St Magnus Parish	7	6
St Margaret Lothbury	8	8
St Margaret Moses	5	5
St Margaret Newfishstreet	17	13
St Margaret Pattons	5	3
St Mary Abchurch	13	9
St Mary Aldermanbury	20	16
St Mary Aldermary	11	10
St Mary le Bow	4	2
St Mary Bothaw	9	8
St Mary Colechurch	2	1
St Mary Hill	12	8
St Martin Ludgate	21	11
St Martin Orgars	9	7
St Martin Outwitch	8	3
St Martin Vintrey	64	61
St Matthew Fridaystreet	1	1
St Maudlin Milkstreet	5	3
St Maudlin Oldfishstreet	16	11
St Michael Bassishaw	17	12
St Michael Cornhil	14	11
St Michael Crookedlane	10	10
St Michael Queenhithe	11	6
St Michael Quern	4	3
St Michael Royal	20	17
St Michael Woodstreet	6	2
St Mildred Breadstreet	6	3
St Mildred Poultrey	4	2
St Nicholas Acons	8	7
St Nicholas Coleabby	14	13
St Nicholas Olaves	12	9
St Olave Hartstreet	20	18
St Olave Jewry	7	5
St Olave Silverstreet	23	17
St Pancras Soperlane	2	2
St Peter Cheap	4	3
St Peter Cornhil	10	6
St Peter Paulswharf	12	12

Parish	Buried	Plague
St Dionis Backchurch	10	3
St Dunstan East	20	10
St Edmund Lumbardstr.	4	4
St Ethelborough	16	6
St Faith	7	6
St Foster	10	9
St Gabriel Fenchurch	6	3
St Mary Mounthaw	9	9
St Mary Sommerset	36	34
St Mary Stayning	2	1
St Mary Woolchurch	2	2
St Mary Woolnoth	9	6
St Martin Iremongerlane	1	1
St Peter Poor	6	6
St Steven Colemanstreet	47	40
St Steven Walbrook	5	5
St Swithin	11	9
St Thomas Apostle	19	17
Trinity Parish	13	13

Christned in the 97 Parishes within the Walls . . 40   Buried . . 1493   Plague . . 1189

Parish	Buried	Plague
St Andrew Holborn	271	247
St Bartholomew Great	21	17
St Bartholomew Lesse	14	12
St Bridget	236	180
Bridewel Precinct	32	31
St Botolph Aldersgate	68	62
St Botolph Aldgate	623	589
St Botolph Bishopsgate	294	256
St Dunstan West	88	79
St George Southwark	195	176
St Giles Cripplegate	456	373
St Olave Southwark	530	363
Saviours Southwark	427	403
S. Sepulchres Parish	301	214
St Thomas Southwark	57	52
Trinity Minories	12	10
At the Pesthouse	6	6

Christned in the 16 Parishes without the Walls . 65   Buried, and at the Pesthouse . 3631   Plague . 3070

Parish	Buried	Plague
St Giles in the fields	140	125
Hackney Parish	22	18
St James Clerkenwel	77	67
St Kath. near the Tower	93	66
Lambeth Parish	48	43
St Leonard Shoreditch	183	173
St Magdalen Bermondsey	207	180
St Mary Newington	155	152
St Mary Islington	68	66
St Mary Whitechappel	532	502
Rothorith Parish	17	13
Stepney Parish	716	686

Christned in the 12 out Parishes in Middlesex and Surry . . 42   Buried . . 2258   Plague . . 2091

Parish	Buried	Plague
St Clement Danes	168	140
St Paul Covent Garden	30	29
St Martin in the fields	286	228
St Mary Savoy	20	19
St Margaret Westminster	411	399
Whereof at the Pesthouse	—	7

Christned in the 5 Parishes in the City and Liberties of Westminster . 29   Buried . 915   Plague . 815

The Diseases and Casualties This Week.
[12–19 September 1665]

ABORTIVE	5	Kingsevil	2
Aged	43	Lethargy	1
Ague	2	Palsie	1
Apoplexie	1	Plague	7165
Bleeding	2	Rickets	17
Burnt in his Bed by a Candle at		Rising of the Lights	11
St. Giles Cripplegate	1	Scowring	5
Canker	1	Scurvy	2
Childbed	42	Spleen	1
Chrisomes	18	Spotted Fever	101
Consumption	134	Stilborn	17
Convulsion	64	Stone	2
Cough	2	Stopping of the Stomach	9
Dropsie	33	Strangury	1
Feaver	309	Suddenly	1
Flox and Small-pox	5	Surfeit	49
Frighted	3	Teeth	121
Gowt	1	Thrush	5
Grief	3	Timpany	1
Griping in the Guts	51	Tissick	11
Jaundies	5	Vomiting	3
Imposthume	11	Winde	3
Infants	16	Wormes	15
Killed by a fall from the Belfrey at			
Alhallows the Great	1		

Christned { Males...... 95 / Females.... 81 / In all ......176 }   Buried { Males.....4095 / Females...4202 / In all .....8297 } Plague 7165

Increased in the Burials this Week 607
Parishes clear of the Plague 4   Parishes Infected 126

The Assize of Bread set forth by Order of the Lord Maior and Court of Aldermen,
A penny Wheaten Loaf to contain Nine Ounces and a half, and three
half-penny White Loaves the like weight.

In the year 1660. the last-mentioned ten Parishes, with *Westminster, Islington, Lambeth, Stepney, Newington, Hackney,* and *Redriff,* are entered under two Divisions, *viz.* the one containing the twelve Parishes lying in *Middlesex,* and *Surrey,* and the other the five Parishes within the City, and Liberties of *Westminster,* viz. St. *Clement-Danes,* St. *Paul's-Covent-Garden,* St. *Martin's* in the *Fields,* St. *Mary-Savoy,* and St. *Margaret's Westminster.*

The Diseases and Casualties This Year.
[1665]

ABORTIVE and Stilborne	617	Jaundies	110
Aged	1545	Impostume	227
Ague and Feaver	5257	Kild by severall accidents	46
Appoplex and Suddenly	116	Kings Evill	86
Bedrid	10	Leprosie	2
Blasted	5	Lethargy	14
Bleeding	16	Livergrown	20
Bloody Flux, Scowring & Flux	185	Meagrom and Headach	12
Burnt and Scalded	8	Meazles	7
Calenture	3	Murthered and Shot	9
Cancer, Gangrene, and Fistula	56	Overlaid & Starved	45
Canker, and Thrush	111	Palsie	30
Childbed	625	Plague	68596
Chrisomes and Infants	1258	Plannet	6
Cold and Cough	68	Plurisie	15
Collick and Winde	134	Poysoned	1
Consumption and Tissick	4808	Quinsie	35
Convulsion and Mother	2036	Rickets	557
Distracted	5	Rising of the Lights	397
Dropsie and Timpany	1478	Rupture	34
Drowned	50	Scurvy	105
Executed	21	Shingles and Swine pox	2
Flox and Small-pox	655	Sores, Ulcers, broken and bruised	
Found dead in streets, fields, &c	20	Limbs	82
French Pox	86	Spleen	14
Frighted	23	Spotted Fever and Purples	1929
Gout and Sciatica	27	Stopping of the Stomack	332
Grief	46	Stone and Strangury	98
Griping in the Guts	1288	Surfet	1251
Hangd & made away them-		Teeth and Worms	2614
selves	7	Vomiting	51
Headmouldshot & Mouldfallen	14	Wenn	1

Christned	Males.....5114 Females...4853 In all 9967	Buried	Males....48569 Females..48737 In all 97306	Of the Plague	...68596

Increased in the Burials in the 130 Parishes and at the Pest-house this year . . . 79009
Increased of the Plague in the 130 Parishes and at the Pest-house this year 68590

A General Bill for This Present Year.
[from 27 Dec. 1664–19 Dec. 1665]

Parish	Bur.	Plag.	Parish	Bur.	Plag.	Parish	Bur.	Plag.
St Albans Woodstreet	200	121	St George Botolphlane	41	27	St Martins Ludgate	196	128
St Alhallowes Barking	514	330	St Gregories by Pauls	376	232	St Martins Orgars	110	71
St Alhallowes Breadst	35	16	St Hellens	108	75	St Martins Outwitch	60	34
St Alhallowes Great	455	426	St James Dukes place	262	190	St Martins Vintrey	417	349
St Alhallowes Honila	10	5	St James Garlickhithe	189	118	St Matthew Fridaystreet	24	6
St Alhallowes Lesse	239	175	St John Baptist	138	83	St Maudlins Milkstreet	44	22
St Alhall. Lumbardstr.	90	62	St John Evangelist	9		St Maudlins Oldfishstr.	176	121
St Alhallowes Staining	185	112	St John Zacharie	85	54	St Michael Bassishaw	253	164
St Alhallowes the Wall	500	356	St Katherine Coleman	299	213	St Michael Cornhill	104	52
St Alphage	271	115	St Katherine Creechu	335	231	St Michael Crookedla	179	133
St Andrew Hubbard	71	25	St Lawrence Jewry	94	48	St Michael Queenhit	203	122
St Andrew Undershaft	274	189	St Lawrence Pountney	214	140	St Michael Querne	44	18
St Andrew Wardrobe	476	308	St Leonard Eastcheap	42	27	St Michael Royall	152	116
St Anne Aldersgate	282	197	St Leonard Fosterlane	335	255	St Michael Woodstreet	122	62
St Anne Blacke Friers	652	467	St Magnus Parish	103	60	St Mildred Breadstreet	59	26
St Antholins Parish	58	33	St Margaret Lothbury	100	66	St Mildred Poultrey	68	46
St Austins Parish	43	20	St Margaret Moses	38	25	St Nicholas Acons	46	28
St Barthol. Exchange	73	51	St Margaret Newfishst.	114	66	St Nicholas Coleabby	125	91
St Bennet Fynch	47	22	St Margaret Pattons	49	24	St Nicholas Olaves	90	62
St Benn. Grace-church.	57	41	St Mary Abchurch	99	54	St Olaves Hartstreet	237	160
St Bennet Pauls Wharf	355	172	St Mary Aldermanbury	181	109	St Olaves Jewry	54	32
St Bennet Sherehog	11	1	St Mary Aldermary	105	75	St Olaves Silverstreet	250	132
St Botolph Billingsgate	83	50	St Mary le Bow	64	36	St Pancras Soperlane	30	15
Christs Church	653	467	St Mary Bothaw	55	30	St Peters Cheape	61	35
St Christophers	60	47	St Mary Colechurch	17	6	St Peters Cornehill	136	76
St Clements Eastcheap	38	20	St Mary Hill	94	64	St Peters Pauls Wharfe	114	86

Buried in the 97 Parishes within the Walls

Parish			Parish			Parish		
St Dionis Back-church	78	27	St Mary Mounthaw	56	37	St Peters Poore	79	47
St Dunstans East	265	150	St Mary Summerset	342	262	St Stevens Colemanstr.	560	391
St Edmunds Lumbard	70	36	St Mary Staynings	47	27	St Stevens Walbrooke	34	17
St Ethelborough	195	106	St Mary Woolchurch	65	33	St Swithins	93	56
St Faiths	104	70	St Mary Woolnoth	75	38	St Thomas Apostle	163	110
St Fosters	144	105	St Martins Iremonger	21	11	Trinitie Parish	115	79
St Gabriel Fen-church	69	39						

Buried in the 97 Parishes within the Walls . . 15207   Whereof, of the Plague . . 9887

Buried in the 16 Parishes without the Walls

Parish			Parish			Parish		
St Andrew Holborne	3958	3103	St Botolph Aldgate	4926	4051	St Saviours Southwark	4235	3446
St Bartholomew Great	493	344	St Botolph Bishopsg	3464	2500	St Sepulchres Parish	4509	2746
Bartholomew Lesse	193	139	St Dunstans West	958	665	St Thomas Southwark	475	371
St Bridget	2111	1427	St George Southwark	1613	1260	Trinity Minories	168	123
Bridewell Precinct	230	179	St Giles Cripplegate	8069	4838	At the Pesthouse	159	156
St Botolph Aldersga.	997	755	St Olaves Southwark	4793	2785			

Buried in the 16 Parishes without the Walls . . 41351   Whereof, of the Plague . . 28888

Buried in the 12 out Parishes in Middlesex and Surrey

Parish			Parish			Parish		
St Giles in the fields	4457	3216	Lambeth Parish	798	537	St Mary Islington	696	593
Hackney Parish	232	132	St Leonard Shorditch	2669	1949	St Mary Whitechappel	4766	3855
St James Clerkenwel	1863	1377	St Magdalen Bermon	1943	1363	Redriffe Parish	304	210
St Katherines Tower	956	601	St Mary Newington	1272	1004	Stepney Parish	8598	6583

Buried in the 12 out Parishes in Middlesex and Surrey . . 28554   Whereof, of the Plague . . 21420

Buried in the 5 Parishes in the City and Liberties of Westminster

Parish			Parish			Parish		
St Clement Danes	1969	1319	St Martins in the fields	4804	2883	St Margaret Westminst.	4710	3742
St Paul Covent Garden	408	261	St Mary Savoy	303	198	Whereof at the Pesthouse	—	156

Buried in the 5 Parishes in the City and Liberties of Westminster . . 12194   Whereof, of the Plague . . 8403

COLLEGE OF PHYSICIANS

Necessary Directions for the *Prevention* and *Cure* of the PLAGUE in 1665 †

With divers Remedies of Small Charge, by the College of Physicians.

I. DOCTORS, CHIRURGEONS AND APOTHECARIES

The church orders for prayers being first observed, as in former times, it might be desired, that by the government of the city there be appointed six or four doctors at least, who may apply themselves to the cure of the infected; and that these doctors be stipendiaries to the city for their lives; and that to each doctor there be assigned two apothecaries, and three chirurgeons, who are also to be stipended by the city; that so due and true care may be taken in all things, that the people perish not without help, and that the infection spread not, while none take particular care to resist it, as in Paris, Venice and Padua, and many other cities.

And if any doctor, chirurgeon or apothecary stipended by the city, shall happen to die in the service of the attendance of the plague, then their widows surviving shall have their pensions during their lives.

II. PREVENTION OF PROPAGATING THE INFECTION FROM PLACE TO PLACE

As the provision already made by authority, upon occasion of prohibiting persons and goods coming from foreign countries and places infected, to be landed for forty days, is most rational, for preventing the bringing in of the contagion from any such places; so it is advisable, that some suitable provision be made in relation to persons within the kingdom, who may remove or travel from places much infected, to sound: as, that none might travel without certificate of health; that persons justly suspected might not be suffered to enter such places free from infection, but speedily sent away, or kept in some house or houses set apart to receive such persons (with accommodation of necessaries) for forty or thirty days at least, till their soundness might appear; and that any goods coming from the like places might be opened and aired, before received into houses free and clear.

*   *   *

† This publication was issued by the College of Physicians; it, the *Orders*, and Graunt's *Reflections* were available to Defoe in an opportunistically published book, A *Collection of very* *Valuable and Scarce Pieces Relating to the Last Plague in the Year 1665* (London, 1721). These excerpts are from pp. 36–41 and 43–47.

IV. TO BE CAUTELOUS UPON ANY SUSPICION

It is to be presumed, because every one desireth his own liberty, that none will give notice of any suspicion of the plague against themselves; wherefore that must be the overseer's care, upon any notice or suspicion of infection, by the help of the doctors, chirurgeons, keepers or searchers, to find out the truth thereof, and so to proceed accordingly, but not to depend upon the testimony of women searchers alone.

* * *

VI. THE CARE TO BE TAKEN WHEN A HOUSE IS VISITED

That upon the discovery of the infection in any house, there be presently means used to preserve the whole, as well as to cure the infected: and that no sick persons be removed out of any house, though to another of his own, without notice thereof to be given to the overseers, and to be by them approved: or if the whole be to be removed, that notice be given to the overseers of their remove; and that caution be given that they shall not wander about till they be sound.

The house that is known to be infected though none be dead therein, to be shut up, and carefully kept watched by more trusty men than ordinary wardens, till a time after the party be well recovered, and that time to be forty days at the least, or rather remove them all immediately to the pest houses.

VII. CAUTION ABOUT APPAREL AND HOUSEHOLD STUFF

That no apparel or household stuff be removed, or sold out of the infected house, for six months after the infection is ceased in the house; and that all the brokers and inferior criers for apparel be restrained in that behalf, and such apparel or household stuff to be aired and fumed.

VIII. CORRECTION OF THE AIR

Fires made in the streets, and often with stinkpots, and good fires kept in and about the houses of such as are visited, and their neighbours may correct the infectious air; as also frequent discharging of guns.

Also fumes of these following materials; rosin, pitch, tar, turpentine, frankincense, myrrhe, amber; the woods of juniper, cypress, cedars; the leaves of bays, rosemary; to which, especially to the less grateful scented, may be added somewhat of labdanum, storax, benzoin, lignum aloes: one or more of these, as they are at hand, or may be procured, are to be put upon coals, and consumed with the least flame that may be, in rooms, houses, churches, or other places.

Brimstone burnt plentifully in any room or place, though ill to be endured for the present, may effectually correct the air for the future.

Vapours from vinegar exhaled in any room, may have the like efficacy; especially after it hath been impregnated, by infusing or steeping in it any one or more of these ingredients; wormwood, angelica, master-wort, bay leaves, rosemary, rue, sage, scordium, or water germander, valerium, or setwall root, zedoary, camphire. To which vinegar also, to render it less ungrateful, may be added rosewater, to a fourth or third part: these are cooler, and so more proper for hot seasons.

The vapour of vinegar raised by slaking of lime in it, may effectually correct the air near about it.

Take saltpeter, amber, brimstone, of each two parts, of juniper one part, mix them in a powder, put thereof upon a red hot iron, or coals, a little at once.

*   *   *

XIII. BY INWARD MEDICINES

Let none go fasting forth; every one according as they can procure, let them take some such thing as may resist putrefaction.

Some may take garlick with butter, a clove, two or three, according as it shall agree with their bodies, some may take fasting, some of the electuary with figs and rue hereafter expressed: some may use London treacle, the weight of eight pence in the morning, taking more or less, according to the age of the party; after one hour let them eat some other breakfast, as bread and butter with some leaves of rue, or sage moistened with vinegar, and in the heat of summer, of sorrel or wood sorrel.

Pure water with so much salt as may be but tasted, or well born; or with flour of brimstone, or common brimstone boiled in it, an ounce in three pints, to a quart; a draught being taken every morning, hath proved effectual and successful.

To steep rue, wormwood or sage all night in their drink, and to drink a good draught in the morning fasting, is very wholesome, or to drink a draught of such drink, after the taking of any of the preservatives, will be very good.

Take of sage bruised well, two handfuls, of wormwood one handful, of rue half a handful; put them into a jug of four quarts, put to them of mild beer ready to drink four quarts; in the morning, let every one of the family drink a draught of it fasting together, eating after it bread and butter.

*   *   *

XVI. FOR WOMEN WITH CHILD, CHILDREN, AND SUCH AS CANNOT TAKE BITTER THINGS, USE THIS

Take conserve of red roses, conserve of wood sorrel, of each two ounces, conserves of borage, of sage flowers, of each six drams, bole armoniack, shavings of harts horn, sorrel seeds, of each two drams, yellow or white saunders half a dram, saffron one scruple, syrup of wood sorrel, enough to make it a moist electuary; mix them well, take so much as a chesnut at a time, once or twice a day, as you shall find cause.

XVII. FOR THE RICHER SORT

Take the shavings of harts horn, of pearl, of coral, of tormentil roots, zedoary, true terra sigillata, of each one dram, citron pills, yellow, white and red saunders, of each half a dram, white amber, hyacinth stone prepared, of each two scruples, bezoar stone of the east, unicorns horn, of each four and twenty grains, citron and orange peels candied, of each three drams, lignum aloes one scruple, white sugar candy twice the weight of all the rest; mix them well, being made into a dredge powder. Take the weight of twelve pence at a time every morning fasting, and also in the evening about five a clock, or an hour before supper.

With these powders and sugar there may be made lozenges, or Manus Christi's, and with convenient conserves they may be made into electuaries. All which, and many more for their health, they may have ben the advice and directions of their own physicians.* * *

THOMAS VINCENT

From *God's Terrible Voice in the City* †
     ✻   ✻   ✻

From Sect. II.

WHAT ARE THOSE TERRIBLE THINGS BY WHICH GOD DOTH SOMETIMES SPEAK?

The word in the Original is נוֹרָאוֹת from יָרֵא which signifieth, he feared: Terrible things are such great Judgements of God, as do usually make a general impression of *fear* upon the hearts of people.

Take some instances.

1. *The Plague is a Terrible Judgement by which God speaks unto men.* The Hebrew word is דֶּבֶר from דָּבַר he spake. It is a *speaking* Judgement; where God sends the Plague, he speaks, and he speaks terribly; the Plague is very terrible, as it effecteth terrour; the *Pestilence which walketh in darkness*, is called *the Terrour by night*, Psal. 91.5,6.

The Plague is very *terrible*, in that

1. It is so *poysonous* a disease; it poysons the blood and spirits, breeds

---

†Thomas Vincent received an M.A. from Christ Church College, Oxford, became a Nonconformist minister, was ejected from his pulpit, and eventually opened a school near Bunhill Fields and a meeting house at Hoxton. During the plague he remained in London and preached almost daily, sometimes twice daily. *God's Terrible Voice* was published in 1667.

a strange kind of venom in the body, which breaketh forth sometimes in Boils, and Blains, and great Carbuncles, or else works more dangerously, when it preyeth upon the vitals more inwardly.

2. It is so *noysome* a disease; it turns the good humors into putrefaction, which putting forth it self in the issues of running sores, doth give a most noysome smell: Such a disease for loathsomeness we read of, *Psa.* 38.5,7,11. *My wounds stink and are corrupt, my loins are filled with a loathsome disease, and there is no soundness in my flesh; my lovers and my friends stand aloof from my sore, and my Kinsmen stand afar off.*

3. It is so *infectious* a disease; it spreadeth it self worse than the Leprosie amongst the *Jews*; it infecteth not only those of which are weak, and infirm in body, and full of ill humors, but also those which are young, strong, healthful, and of the best temperature; and that sometimes sooner than others. The Plague is infectious, and greatly infectious, whole Cities have been depopulated through its spreading, many whole families have received infection, and death one from another thereby, which is the third thing that rendreth the Plague so terrible.

4. It is so *deadly*; it kills where it comes without mercy; it kills (I had almost said *certainly*) very few do escape, especially upon its first entrance, and before its malignity be spent; few are touched by it, but they are killed by it: and it kills *suddenly*; as it gives no warning before it comes, suddenly the arrow is shot which woundeth unto the heart; so it gives little time of preparation before it brings to the Grave: Under other diseases men may linger out many weeks and moneths; under some divers years; but the Plague usually killeth within a few daies; sometimes within a few hours after its first approach, though the body were never so strong and free from disease before.

The Plague is very terrible; it is terrible to them that have it; insomuch as it usually comes with Grim Death, the *King of Terrours*, in its hand: and it is terrible to them which have it not; because of their danger of being infected by it; the fear of which hath made such an impression upon some, that it hath rased out of their hearts, for the while, all affections of love and pitty to their nearest Relations and dearest Friends; so that when the Disease hath first seized upon them, and they have had the greatest need of succour, they have left their friends in distress, and flown away from them, as if they had been their Enemies.

*   *   *

From Sect. V

In *August* how dreadful is the increase? from 2010 the number amounts up to 2817 in one week; and thence to 3880 the next; thence to 4237 the next; thence to 6102 the next; and all these of the Plague, besides other diseases.

Now the cloud is very black, and the storm comes down upon us very sharp. Now death rides triumphantly on his pale horse through our streets, and breaks into every house almost where any inhabitants are to be found. Now people fall as thick as leaves from the trees in Autumn, when they are shaken by a mighty wind. Now there is a dismal solitude in *London* streets, every day looks with the face of a Sabbath day, observed with greater solemnity than it used to be in the City. Now shops are shut in, people rare and very few that walk about, in so much that the grass begins to spring up in some places, and a deep silence almost in every place, especially within the walls; no ratling Coaches, no prancing Horses, no calling in Customers, nor offering Wares; no *London* cries sounding in the ears; if any voice be heard, it is the groans of dying persons, breathing forth their last, and the funeral knells of them that are ready to be carried to their graves. Now shutting up of visited houses (there being so many) is at an end, and most of the well are mingled among the sick which otherwise would have got no help. Now in some places where the people did generally stay; not one house in an hundred but is infected; and in many houses half the family is swept away; in some the whole, from the eldest to the youngest; few escape with the death of but one or two: never did so many husbands and wives die together; never did so many parents carry their children with them to the grave, and go together into the same house under earth, who had lived together in the same house upon it. Now the nights are too short to bury the dead, the whole day though at so great a length is hardly sufficient to light the dead that fall therein into their beds.

Now we could hardly go forth, but we should meet many coffins, and see many with sores, and limping in the streets; amongst other sad spectacles, methought two were very affecting: one of a woman comming alone, and weeping by the door where I lived (which was in the midst of the infection) with a little Coffin under her arm carrying it to the new Church yard; I did judge that it was the mother of the childe, and that all the family besides was dead, and she was forced to coffin up and bury with her own hands this her last dead childe. Another, was of a man at the corner of the Artillery wall, that as I judge through the diziness of his head with the disease, which seised upon him there, had dasht his face against the wall, and when I came by he lay hanging with his bloody face over the rails, and bleeding upon the ground; and as I came back he was removed under a tree in More-fields, and lay upon his back; I went and spake to him; he could make me no answer, but ratled in the throat, and as I was informed, within half an hour died in the place.

It would be endless to speak what we have seen and heard of some of their frensie, rising out of their beds, and leaping about their rooms; others crying and roaring at their windows; some comming forth almost naked, and running into the streets, strange things have others spoken and done when the disease was upon them: But it was very sad to hear of one who being sick alone, and it is like phrantick, burnt himself in his bed. Now the plague had broken in much amongst my acquaintance; and of about 16. or more whose faces I used to see every day in our house, within a little while I could finde but 4. or 6. of them alive; scarcely a day past over my head for I think a moneth or more together, but I should hear of the death of some one or more than I knew. The first day that they were smitten, the next day some hopes of recovery, and the third day that they were dead.

The *September*, when we hoped for a decrease, because of the season, because of the number gone, and the number already dead; yet it was not come to its height; but from 6102, which died by the Plague the last week of *August*, the number is augmented to 6988 the first week in *September*; and when we conceived some little hopes in the next weeks abatement to 6544; our hopes were quite dashed again, when the next week it did rise to 7165. which was the highest Bill; And a dreadful Bill it was! and of the 130. Parishes in and about the City, there were but 4 Parishes which were not infected: and in those, few people remaining that were not gone into the Country.

Now the grave doth open its mouth without measure. Multitudes! multitudes! in the valley of the shadow of death, thronging daily into eternity; the Church-yards now are stufft so full with dead corpses, that they are in many places swell'd two or three foot higher than they were before; and new ground is broken up to bury the dead.

*   *   *

NATHANIEL HODGES

From *Loimologia: Or, an Historical Account of the Plague in London in 1665* †

*   *   *

After then all endeavours to restrain the contagion proved of no effect, we applied ourselves to the care of the diseased; and in the prosecution of which, it may be affirmed without boasting, no hazards to ourselves were avoided. But it is incredible to think how the plague raged amongst the common people, insomuch that it came by some to be called "the poor's plague." Yet, although the more opulent had left the town, and that it was almost left uninhabited, the commonality that were left felt little of want; for their necessities were relieved with a profusion of good things from the wealthy, and their poverty was supported with plenty. A more manifest cause therefore for such a devastation amongst them I shall assign in another place.

In the months of August and September, the contagion changed its

† Nathaniel Hodges was a member of the College of Physicians. During the plague, he remained in London and saw all who sought his advice. Published in Latin in 1671 by Joseph Nevill and in another edition in 1672, *Loimologia* was published in an English translation by J. Quincy in 1720 and was in a third edition by 1721.

former slow and languid pace, and having as it were got master of all, made a most terrible slaughter, so that three, four, or five thousand died in a week, and once eight thousand. Who can express the calamities of such times? The whole British nation wept for the miseries of her metropolis. In some houses carcasses lay waiting for burial, and in others persons in their last agonies; in one room might be heard dying groans, in another the raving of delirium, and not far off relations and friends bewailing both their loss and the dismal prospect of their own sudden departure. Death was the sure midwife to all children, and infants passed immediately from the womb to the grave. Who would not burst with grief to see the stock for a future generation hanging upon the breasts of a dead mother? Or the marriage-bed changed the first night into a sepulchre, and the unhappy pair meet with death in their first embraces? Some of the infected ran about staggering like drunken men, and fell and expired in the streets; while others lie half-dead and comatose, but never to be waked but by the last trumpet; some lie vomiting as if they had drunk poison; and others fell dead in the market, while they were buying necessaries for the support of life. Not much unlike was it in the following conflagration,[1] where altars themselves became so many victims, and the finest churches in the whole world carried up to heaven supplications in flames, while their marble pillars wet with tears melted like wax; nor were monuments secure from the inexorable flames, where many of their venerable remains passed a second martyrdom; the most august palaces were soon laid waste, and the flames seemed to be in a fatal engagement to destroy the great ornament to commerce; and the burning of all the commodities of the world together seemed a proper epitome of this conflagration; neither confederate crowns nor the drawn swords of kings could restrain its phanatic and rebellious rage; large halls, stately houses, and the sheds of the poor were together reduces to ashes; the sun blushed to see himself set, and envied those flames the government of the night, which had rivalled him so many days. As the city, I say, was afterwards burnt without any distinction, in like manner did this plague spare no order, age, or sex. The divine was taken in the very exercise of his priestly office to be enrolled amongst the saints above; and some physicians, as before intimated, could not find assistance in their own antidotes, but died in the administration of them to others; and although the soldiery retreated from the field of death, and encamped out of the city, the contagion followed and vanquished them. Many in their old age, others in their prime, sunk under its cruelties. Of the female sex most died; and hardly any children escaped; and it was not uncommon to see an inheritance pass successively to three or four heirs in as many days. The number of sextons was not sufficient to bury the dead; the bells seemed hoarse with continual tolling, until at last they quite ceased; the burying places would not hold the dead, but they were

1. The Great Fire of London in 1666.

thrown into large pits dug in waste grounds, in heaps, thirty or forty
together; and it often happened that those who tended the funerals of
their friends one evening were carried the next to their long home.

> . . . *Quis talia fundo*
> *Temperet a lachrymis?* [2]

Even the relation of this calamity melts me into tears. And yet the worst
was not certain, although the city was near drained by her funerals, for
the disease as yet had no relaxation.

About the beginning of September, the disease was at its height; in
the course of which month more than twelve thousand died in a week.
But at length, that nothing might go untried to divert the contagion, it
was ordered by the governors who were left to superintend those calamitous affairs (for the Court was then removed to Oxford), to burn fires in
the streets for three days together; yet while this was in debate, the physicians concerned were diffident of the success, as the air in itself was
uninfected, and therefore rendered such a showy and expensive a project
superfluous and of no effect; and these conjectures we supported by the
authority of antiquity, and Hippocrates himself; notwithstanding which,
the fires were kindled in all the streets. But alas! the controversy was
soon decided, for before the three days were quite expired the heavens
both mourned so many funerals, and wept for the fatal mistake, so as to
extinguish even the fires with their showers. I shall not determine any
other person's conjecture in this case, whether these fires may more
properly be deemed the ominous forerunners of the ensuing conflagra-
tions, or the ensuing funerals; but whether it was from the suffocating
qualities of the fuel, or the wet constitution of the air that immediately
followed, the most fatal night ensued wherein more than four thousand
perished. May posterity by this mistake be warned, and not, like empir-
ics, apply a remedy where they are ignorant of the cause.

The reader is by the way to be advertised that the year was luxuriant
in most fruits, especially cherries and grapes which were at so low a price
that the common people surfeited with them; for this might very much
contribute to the disposition of the body, as made this pestilential taint
more easily take place.

Nor ought we here to pass by the beneficent assistance of the rich,
and the care of the magistrates; for the markets being open as usual, and
a great plenty of all provisions was a great help to support the sick, so
that there was the reverse of a famine which hath been observed to be so
fatal to pestilential contagions; and in this the goodness of heaven is
always to be remembered, in alleviating a common misery by such a
provision of good things from the stores of nature.

But as it were to balance this immediate help of Providence, nothing

---

2. "Who in telling such [stories] might hold back from tears?" Virgil, *Aeneid* 2.6–8 [trans. Thomas
Hahn].

was otherwise wanting to aggravate the common destruction, and to which nothing more contributed than the practice of chymists and quacks, and of whose audacity and ignorance it is impossible to be altogether silent. They were indefatigable in spreading their antidotes; and although equal strangers to all learning as well as physic, they thrust into every hand some trash or other under the disguise of a pompous title. No country, surely, ever abounded with such wicked imposters; for all events contradicted their pretensions, and hardly a person escaped that trusted to their delusions. Their medicines were more fatal than the plague, and added to the numbers of the dead. But these blowers of the pestilential flame were caught in the common ruin, and by their death in some measure excused the neglect of the magistrates in suffering their practice.

Nor in this account are we to neglect, that the contagion spread its cruelties into the neighbouring countries; for the citizens, which crowded in multitudes into the adjacent towns, carried the infection along with them, where it raged with equal fury; so that the plague, which at first crept from one street to another, now reigned over whole counties, leaving hardly any place free from its insults; and the towns upon the Thames were more severely handled, not perhaps from a great moisture in the air from thence, but from the tainted goods rather that were carried up it. Moreover, some cities and towns of the most advantageous situation for a wholesome air, did notwithstanding feel the common ruin. Such was the rise and such the progress of this cruel destroyer which first began at London.

But the worst part of the year being now over, and the height of the disease, the plague by leisurely degrees declined, as it had gradually made its first advances; and before the number infected decreased, its malignity began to relax, insomuch that few died, and those chiefly such as were ill managed. Hereupon that dread which had been upon the minds of the people wore off; and the sick cheerfully used all the means directed for their recovery; and even the nurses grew either more cautious or more faithful; insomuch that after some time a dawn of health appeared as sudden and as unexpected as the cessation of the following conflagration, wherein after blowing up of houses, and using all means for its extinction to little purpose, the flames stopped as it were of themselves, for want of fuel or out of shame for having devoured so much.

The pestilence however did not stop for want of subjects to act upon (as then commonly rumoured), but from the nature of the distemper its decrease was like its beginning, moderate.

*　　*　　*

About the close of the year, that is, on the beginning of November, people grew more healthful, and such a different face was put upon the public, that although the funerals were yet frequent, yet many who had made most haste in retiring, made the most to return, and came into the city without fear; insomuch that in December they crowded back as thick as they fled. The houses which before were so full of the dead, were inhabited now by the living, and the shops which had been most part of the year shut up were again opened, and the people again cheerfully went about their wonted affairs of trade and employ; and even, what is almost beyond belief, those citizens who before were afraid of their friends and relations, would without fear enter the houses and rooms where infected persons had but a little while before breathed their last. Nay, such comforts did inspire the languishing people, and confidence, that many went into the beds where persons had died, before they were even cold or cleansed from the stench of the diseased. They had the courage now to marry again, and betake to the means of repairing the past mortality; and even women before deemed barren were said to prove prolific, so that although the contagion had carried off, as some computed, about one hundred thousand, after a few months their loss was hardly discernible, and thus ended this fatal year.

But the next Spring, indeed, appeared some remains of the contagion, which was easily conquered by the physicians, and, like the termination of a common intermittent, ended in a healthful recovery; whereupon the whole malignity ceasing, the city returned to a perfect health; not unlike what happened also after the last conflagration, when a new city suddenly arose out of the ashes of the old, much better able to stand the like flames another time.

[DANIEL DEFOE]

From *Applebee's Original Weekly Journal* †

October 1, 1720

Our letters from Marseilles continue to bring very bad news; the dismal Accounts of the Plague in that City are such, that they are scarce credible; three most dreadful Evils attend the People of the City, besides the contagion. (1). The dead Bodies lying in Heaps unbury'd, the Stench of which is unsufferable; and tho' the Slaves of the Gallies, and Carts appointed by the Magistrates, have carry'd away thousands, yet the Numbers are very great, where they are so putrify'd and perish'd, that no Body dare come near them. (2). The second Disaster is the Want of Provisions, which is such, and the condition of the Inhabitants has been thereby render'd so desperate, that the Country People not daring to bring Provisions to them, the several Bodies of the People,—furious and raging for mere Hunger,—have cut the Guards in Pieces at the Gates,

---

† A loophole in the Stamp Tax Act made magazine-length weekly papers more economical than short newspapers. John Applebee's weekly journal was but one that carried Defoe's lively columns.

have broken out, Sword in Hand, and made their Way into the Country to seek Bread. (3). The Third is the Troops of Thieves and Murderers, that range the infected Streets, there being no Guards or Officers who dare come into those Places; and these break into the Houses where the Plague is most raging, murder the Sick and Sound, and rob and rifle them of all that comes to Hand. 'Tis incredible what Mischief these last have done, and how many they have destroy'd, the Particulars it is impossible to know; but they say that one of these Wretches, who was executed for his Thefts and Murders, confess'd that he had been concern'd in the Murder of above a thousand, many of whom he had destroy'd with his own Hands. Several of these have been kill'd, several taken and hang'd; and they tell us one Passage, which, if true, is remarkably just, tho' a very terrible Execution; namely that the Troops having fir'd upon some of these Bloody Creatures, besides the slain, five were wounded, and lay in the Streets disabled, but alive, whom the Magistrates order'd to be thrown upon a Heap of dead Bodies who had died of the Plague, and there suffer'd them to lye and languish till they died, whether of their Wounds, or of the Infection, they do not write: It is true, the Thing is shocking and terrible even in the Relation; but if it be true, that they were such a cruel harden'd Sort of Villains, as is related, nothing can be esteem'd severe to such. N.B. *We do not assert this Part of the Story at all, but relate it as we find it.*[1]

May 20, 1720

PLAGUE AT THOULON.[2]

We have very dismal Accounts from France of the Ravages which the Plague makes in Provence, and particularly at the City of Thoulon. But they tell one Story which indeed strikes every Body with Horror that reads it; and this relates to the terrible Famine which rages in Thoulon, where the want of Bread, and indeed of all Provisions, is such, that the People are made desperate and distracted. 'Tis said that they have devoured entirely all the Corn, or Flesh, that was in the City, and have eaten the most loathsome and nauseous Things,—such as Dogs, Cats, Rats, Mice, Leather, Starch, Soap,—and, in a Word, that they are ready to Prey even upon one another. They add, that in Troops they break into the Houses which are shut up, and rob the richer Inhabitants of what they had laid up for their Provisions. But that which is most horrible of all is, that on the 9th, a Rabble of the People, Men, Women, and Children, to the number of 1700,—made desperate by their Diseases, and quite raging by their Hunger,—Sally'd out into the Fields by force, and wandering about to seek Food, came up to the Lines, which are guarded by several Regiments of regular Troops. They demanded Bread; the Sol-

1. Note that Defoe uses this same disclaimer   2. Seaport in southeast France.
frequently in A *Journal of the Plague Year.*

diers told them they had none but the Ammunition-Bread, that was allow'd them for their daily Subsistence, but seeing their Distress, they threw them what they had, which the poor Creatures devoured like ravenous Beasts. They then desir'd they might pass into the plain Country, to get Bread, that they might not be starved; when the Soldiers told them they could not let them do so, it being contrary to their Orders. But the poor desperate Wretches told them they must, and would go, for they could but dye; and accordingly attempted the Lines in sixteen or seventeen Places. At the same Time the Soldiers kept them back as long as they could with Blows, and with the Muzzles of their Pieces; but were at length obliged to fire at them, by which about 178 were killed, and, as they say, 137 wounded. Among the first were three and thirty Women and Children, and four and fifty among the latter; so that most of them were driven back into the City, where they must inevitably perish. They add, that notwithstanding this, several hundreds of them got over the Lines, and spread themselves every way over the Fields; but 'tis thought that most of those that are got over will fall into the Soldiers' Hands, and be killed in cold Blood, or will be starv'd in the Mountains. The same Letters say, that the Government, having had an Account of this dreadful Story, has order'd that the Guards shall be doubled in the said Lines, but that a sufficient Quantity of Corn and Cattle, and Salt should be furnish'd by the Intendants of Dauphine, and be deliver'd weekly to the Officers commanding in the Lines, to be deliver'd by them to the Magistrates of Thoulon, for the supply of the City; and, that the City shall be liable to be tax'd for the Value of the said Provisions, after they are restor'd to their former State of Health. The Numbers that Dye every Day in the City, are Diversly reported; some say about two hundred,—others, that there die above three hundred a Day, but that as many perish for Want of Food,—that is, are starved to Death,—as dye of the Plague; so that the Misery of that Place is not to be express'd, and is infinitely worse than it was at Marseilles.

July 29, 1721

CITIZENS OPPOSE PRECAUTIONS AGAINST PLAGUE.

Sir, Before I begin what I am going to write, give me leave to let your Reader into the true Design of the Story, which is thus: The House of Commons, upon mature Consideration, and at the Motion of those who very well understand the Interest of their Country, had brought in a Bill for the more effectual preventing the running on Shore of Infected Goods; a Caution which they found very necessary, without question, for preserving us from the Dangers which surround us;—several Countries around us, and perhaps more than we are yet aware of, being infected with the Plague,—and that such a Plague, as has not been known in these Parts of the World, perhaps in the Memory of the oldest Man living.

In the middle of this, we find some of our worthy Citizens setting up against it,—worthy Gentlemen! I must confess,—and whose Concern for the Trade of their Fellow Citizens, more than for their Lives, is very well worth your Notice.

That the House of Commons are careful and Concern'd for the Pub-lick Safety in such a Time of Danger, is our Happiness, and what I think we ought to be very thankful for. Certainly then, tho' some Inconve-niences had happen'd to our immediate Imports, such as are now peti-tion'd against, 'tis hard any Discouragement should be given to whatever Measures should be taken for our Security.

If these Gentlemen, who are so Tenacious of their Trading Liberty, should, for want of due Care being taken, import the Plague upon us, as was really the Case in the poor unhappy City of Toulon, who had the Distemper brought among them in a Bale of Silk from Marseilles; I say, if it should be so here, I think those Merchants, that would have Room left for it, ought to be remember'd.

If I were to propose an equal and just Treatment of such Men, it should be, that if such a dreadful Thing should ever happen among us, (as God forbid,) they who had concern'd themselves to obstruct the mak-ing needful Laws to prevent, or who had endeavour'd to leave out proper Clauses in such Laws, to make them more effectual; should be oblig'd, by the same Law, to stay in the City, and take their Risk with the Poor, who are not able to fly, and have not wherewith to shift from one Coun-try to another, as the Rich have.

This is but equal; for those Men who are made Instrumental to bring the Distemper in, it is but just that they and their Families should bear their Share, at least, of the Hazard.

It is a just Observation, which I might enlarge on here, how Avarice hardens Men against all Dangers of every kind; and how Men will risk their Lives, and the Lives of a whole City, nay, a whole Nation, for their present Profit; by not putting any Dangers, any Disasters which they may fall into, in the Scale with their present Advantages. Give them the Gain they have in View, and the present Advances of their Fortunes and Estates; and as for the Consequences, leave it to them, and leave them to their Fate. What else but this could be the Language of the Furrier who was shot to Death at Lyons, for presuming to bring Goods into that City from Infected Countries? Or of the Merchant at Toulon, who ventur'd to receive five Bales of Silk, and other Goods from Marseilles, at the Time of the Infection? He ventur'd for himself, 'tis true; but he ventur'd for his Fellow-Citizens too, whose Lives were all at his Mercy, as I may say, the whole City being since desolated by that one Action.

What we venture for ourselves is one Thing, but when we venture for other People, and that without their Consent too, we so far injure them;

and if the Danger be of Life, we are so far Guilty of their Death, (if that should be the Consequence,) and ought to be punish'd in proportion. Such Men would do well to tell us who they are; that if they should be the unhappy Instruments of bringing their Country into such a Calamity, the World may be able to do themselves Justice upon them.

Another Thing to be complain'd of in this Affair is the eager running of Goods from Ships, which are oblig'd to perform Quarantine; a Practice which, if continu'd, destroys the very End and Reason of the Thing itself, and not only makes the Quarantine itself be of no effect, but indeed may make that very means, which is intended to preserve us from the Plague, be the Occasion of bringing it among us.

Recommend it, Sir, in the most pressing Terms possible to our Representatives and Governors, to put a speedy stop to this pernicious Practice. In vain the Merchants are oblig'd to lay their Ships up in little Holes, and remote Creeks, to the Hazard of spoiling their Goods, and to the delay of their Returns, and to their great Detriment many Ways; if some effectual Means be not used to prevent avaricious Minds, for private Gain, conveying Goods on Shore at the Hazard of bringing a Contagion upon their Country.

No Mercy is due to a Crime so merciless in its own Nature; nothing can in itself be more cruél. No Thought can be more barbarous, than to venture the Welfare of the whole Kingdom, and the Lives of Men, Women, and Children, for the wretched Gain of a private Man, and perhaps that Gain a Trifle. Such a Man should dye without Mercy, and would dye unpity'd, if ever Man did so.

The Damage of obliging Ships to Quarantine, is, as I have said above, very considerable to the Merchants; it spoils their Goods, and many sorts of Goods are perishable, and subject to decay in others. The Profit of the whole Voyage depends upon the Season of coming into the Market; as new Fruit, for Example, from Alicant and Malaga, Currants from Zant and Cephalonia, Lemons from Malaga, and the like; also new Wines, Oyl, Pickles &c. Raw and Thrown Silk must come to its Time, for the Demands of the Manufacturers for their Spring Trade; and all these are very much interrupted, and, as the Case may happen, may be some Times quite disappointed, the Profits of the Voyage lost, and the Merchants perhaps ruin'd, by the Ships lying for six Weeks for PRODUCT, as 'tis called.

Besides this, it stagnates Trade, makes Returns home, heavy and tedious, raises the Freight, and brings Goods to the Market dear, encreases the Risk, and every way harrasses the Merchant in his Business.

Yet all this we chearfully submit to for the Reason of it; 'tis allow'd to be just, to be necessary, and what really ought to be done. But if one Villain can pass the Barriers set,—if one Man can escape out of these Ships, with but one Bundle of Silk, or a Parcel of any sort of Goods, dangerous to Health,—he may lodge the Plague among us, the Merchants suffer all the Inconveniences for nothing, the Distemper spreads, and we are all undone.

Your Friend,   QUARANTINE.

From *The Daily Journal* †

Monday January 1. 172½.

Yesterday arrived a Mail from Holland, and last Night one from France, with the following Advices.
From the Amsterdam Gazette.
Avignon, Dec. 4.

The Contagion still rages very violently here, and they reckon that since the 19th of September there have died 4000 Persons; they say that there now are 1500 actually Sick. The Quarantine which is just finish'd, has not been well observ'd, by which the Sickness has been increas'd, and we are now beginning another. Some few Days ago two Women were Whip'd for coming out of their Houses contrary to the general Order. The Beds on which our Sick lay are so full of Insects, that they perfectly devour them, for which reason those who are visited chuse rather to lay on the Ground out of Town, than in the Hospitals. The only Physitian that was left amongst them is dead. The Infection has reach'd a Monastery, the Vice-Legate's Palace, and several Farm Houses in the Territory. They are erecting a 4th Hospital big enough to hold about a thousand sick Persons.

Orange, Dec. 6. There is no Infection but in one quarter of the Town, and they take all the care they can to prevent its being communicated to any Houses out of that quarter; but it gets ground in the Farm Houses which are in the Road to Avignon, and especially in them nearest the Town. Caumont, Sorgues, and Monteux, are still in a very bad Condition; Serrians has been visited within these few Days; things mend at Bedarides and Chateauneuf.

Marseilles, Dec. 11. We are still in perfect Health here, and the Village of Alauch, where the Plague has again broke out, is so closely block'd up, that 'tis impossible for any of the Inhabitants to come out; in all the other Villages of our Territory they are in perfect Health. At Besse and Roquebrousane it continues, and has again broke out at Pemes; Carpentras is also suspected. The Marquiss of Brancas is perfecting the Lines which separate us from the Comtat.

---

† *The Daily Journal* was the third London daily paper and at the height of its popularity in 1722. It was, according to James Sutherland, an authority on early British newspapers, "the one with the best news service, domestic and for-

eign," and clearly superior to the others in style and substance (*The Restoration Newspaper and Its Development* [Cambridge: Cambridge UP, 1986] 32, 37–38). The dates here are Old Style; England did not begin 1722 until 25 March.

There are some other Accounts from the Gevaudan which shall be inserted to Morrow.

Tuesday January 2. 172$\frac{1}{2}$.

* * * At Mendes the Plague decreas'd with the Moon; they reckon there 756 dead to the 26th of November, besides 4 Physitians and 8 Surgeons. At Marvejols the Infection seems to be just at an end; but it has again broke out in 3 neighbouring Hamlets. * * * It has also broke out again at Bournons, where they had been free for 50 days, there having now died a Girl with Buboes upon her, and another fallen sick. There have died two lately at Laurac, and several more have fallen sick; 2 more have also died at St. Paul la Cote, and the blockade is continu'd. At St. Genaix the Sickness is violent. Genouillac, Concoul, the Banassac, are still in the same condition. The 4 Hamlets of St. George's Parish, are now free from Infection, but of 60 Inhabitants there are but 13 left, and most of those have been visited. Of 87 Inhabitants of Font-Jullian, there remain but 39, and 7 or 8 of these are not quite well. Chambonet, and another Village near Moulins, are visited; and there is this remarkable in the former not one recovers, in the latter, where there is neither Physitian nor Surgeon, no one dies. * * * Five Soldiers of the Regiment of Piemont having pass'd a Line, the Duke of Roquelaure has made them cast Lots in order to have one shot, and the other 4 are sent into Quarentine till farther orders, the Duke having chose to be merciful because the Sickness is at a great distance from the Line. M. de Cassade, Lieutenant Colonel of the Regiment of Beaujolois, has had the Skull of a Peasant of Prades split, who was convicted of having traded with some of the Gevaudan; and to make the greater Example of him, he order'd that two Peasants of every Village in the Line of low Auvergne shou'd be present at the Execution. There is no infection in the Velai. The Sickness does not spread towards Auvergne, but towards Languedoc it does. The Plague every where increases with the increase of the Moon.

Tuesday January 9. 172$\frac{1}{2}$.

TO THE AUTHOR OF THE DAILY JOURNAL.

SIR,

I Cannot think that a Dissertation upon the Plague (when all Europe seems apprehensive of it, and most of our Papers are stuff'd with dismal accounts) can be very foreign to the Province of a News-monger. The Curious, who have not time enough of their own to enquire into the Nature and Cause of this dreadful Distemper, will doubtless be pleas'd with a short view of it, and the ignorant, according to custom, will admire what they cannot understand.

Dissertations of this Nature are generally of Service, the more Man-

kind is let into Secrets of this Nature, the less reason they see to apprehend it; and 'tis very evident, that in some Countries the fear of the
Plague might be worse than the *Plague* it self, and might prove so to *us*,
cou'd People of all degrees be so terrify'd as to fly out of Town, how
must our *Commerce* then suffer! What wretched *Poverty* must this *once
flourishing City*, and all its Inhabitants labour under.

But this is foreign to my present purpose, what I intend to examine,
is, whether this *Epidemical* Distemper proceeds from the *Steams* issuing
from *Minerals*, or from *Insects* which we suck in with our Breath; and if
we allow it to be the latter, we ought to inquire how those *Insects* are
bred and *nourish'd*, and how *destroy'd*. Nor shall I on this Head pretend
to offer new Reasons of my own, but give you such as I have met with
in an excellent little Treatise sent by a Friend to *Mr. Bradley* and by
him printed in his *New Improvements of Planting and Gardening*.

"It is the common receiv'd Opinion (says this ingenious Author) that
the *Plague* proceeds from an Infection in the Air, and so undoubtedly it
does; but then it will be ask'd, why the Air is not at all times thus infected?

"Some will have it from *Steams* or *Vapours* arising from some *poisonous Minerals* at certain bad Seasons. * * *"

THE LONDON GAZETTE

[Quarantine Act of 1721] †

Published by Authority.

FROM SATURDAY FEBRUARY 4, TO TUESDAY FEBRUARY 7, 1721.

*An Act for repealing an Act made in the ninth Year of the Reign of
Her late Majesty Queen Anne, Initialed, An Act to oblige Ships coming
from Places infected, more effectually to perform their Quarentine; and
for the better preventing the Plague being brought from foreign Parts into
Great Britain or Ireland, or the Isles of Guernsey, Jersey, Alderney, Sark
or Man; and to hinder the Spreading of Infection.*

Whereas in the Parliament begun and holden at Westminster in the
ninth Year of the Reign of her late Majesty Queen Anne, an Act passed,
intituled, *An Act to oblige Ships coming from Places infected, more effectually to perform their Quarentine*; and whereas Marseilles, and other
Places in the Southern Parts of France, have, for some time past, been
visited with the Plague, which occasioned just Apprehensions lest the
Infection might be brought into this Kingdom from the Places so infected,
or other Places trading or corresponding therewith, unless timely Care

† The *London Gazette* was the official government newspaper. Its editor worked for the Undersec-
retary of one of the Secretaries of State. The 1721 dates here are Old Style. England did not begin
1722 until 25 March.

were taken to prevent the same; and whereas it has been found by Experience, that the said Act is defective and insufficient for the Purposes
intended; and the Penalties inflicted by the same not adequate to the
Offences thereby prohibited; and some further Provisions are necessary
to be made, in case it should please Almighty God to permit these King-
doms to be afflicted with the Plague: For Remedy thereof, be it enacted
by the King's most excellent Majesty, by and with the Advice and Consent of the Lords Spiritual and Temporal, and Commons in Parliament
assembled, and by the Authority of the same, that during the present
Infection, and in all future Times, when any Country or Place shall be
infected with the Plague, all Ships, Vessels, Persons, Goods and Merchandizes whatsoever, coming or imported in such Ships or Vessels,
into any Port or Place within Great Britain or Ireland, or the Isles of
Guernsey, Jersey, Alderney, Sark or Man, from any Places so infected,
or from any Place the Inhabitants whereof are known to trade or correspond with any Country or Place actually infected, or from any Place
from whence his Majesty, his Heirs or Successors, by and with the Advice
of his or their Privy-Council, shall judge it probable that the Infection
may be brought, shall be obliged to make their Quarentine in such Place
and Places, for such Time and in such Manner as hath been or shall,
from time to time, be directed by His Majesty, his Heirs or Successors,
by his or their Order or, Orders made in his or their Privy Council, and
notified by Proclamation; and that until such Ships, Vessels, Persons,
Goods, and Merchandizes, shall have respectively performed, and be
discharged from such Quarentine, no such Persons, Goods, or Merchandizes, or any of them, shall come or be brought on Shore, or go or
be put on board any other Ship or Vessel in any Place within His Majesty's Dominions, unless in such Cases, and by such proper License, as
shall be directed or permitted by such Order or Orders made by His
Majesty, his Heirs or Successors, in Council, and notified, as aforesaid;
and that all such Ships and Vessels, and the Persons and Goods coming
or imported in, or going or being put on board the same, and all Ships,
Vessels, Boats, and Persons receiving any Goods or Persons out of the
same, shall be subject to such Orders, Rules, and Directions concerning
Quarentine. and the prevention of Infection, as have been or shall be
made by His Majesty, his Heirs and Successors, in Council, and notified
by Proclamations, as aforesaid.

And to the End it may be the better known, whether any Ship or
Vessel be actually infected with the Plague, or whether such Ship or
Vessel, or the Mariners or Cargo coming and imported in the same, are
liable to any Orders touching Quarentine; be it enacted by the Authority
aforesaid, That during the present Infection * * * the principal Officer
of His Majesty's Customs in such Port or Place, or such Person as shall
be authorized to see Quarentine duly performed, shall go off, or cause
some other Person to be by him appointed for that Purpose, to go off to
such Ship or Vessel; and such Officer or other Person authorized to see

Quarentine performed, as aforesaid, or the Person so by him appointed for that Purpose, shall, at a convenient Distance from such Ship or Vessel, demand of the Commander, Master, or other Person having Charge of such Ship or Vessel, and such Commander, Master, or other Person having Charge of such Ship or Vessel, shall, upon such Demand, give a true Account of the following Particulars; (that is to say) the Name of such Ship or Vessel; the Name of the Commander or the Person having Charge thereof; at what Place the Cargo was taken on board; what Place or Places the Ship or Vessel touched at in her Voyage; Whether such Places, or any, and which of them, were infected with the Plague; how long such Ship or Vessel had been in her Passage; how many Persons were on board when the said Ship or Vessel set Sail; whether any, and what Persons, during that Voyage, on board such Ship or Vessel, had been or shall be then infected with the Plague; how many died in the Voyage, and of what Distemper; what Ships or Vessels he or any of his Ships Company with his Privity went on board, or had any of their Company come on board his Ship or Vessel in the Voyage; and to what Place such Ships or Vessels belonged; and also the true Contents of his Lading to the best of his Knowledge. And in case it shall appear upon such Examination or otherwise, that any Person then on board such Ship or Vessel, shall at the time of such Examination be actually infected with the Plague, in such case it shall and may be lawful to and for the Officers of any of His Majesty's Ships of War, or any of His Majesty's Ports or Garrisons, and all other His Majesty's Officers, whom it may concern * * * are hereby required to resist and oppose the Entrance of such Ship or Vessel into any such Port or Place, or to oblige such Ship or Vessel to depart out of the same, and to use all necessary Means for the Purposes aforesaid, or either of them, be it by firing of Guns upon such Ship or Vessel, or any other kind of Force and Violence whatsoever; and in case any such Ship or Vessel shall come from any Place visited with the Plague, or have any Person on board actually infected, and the Commander, Master, or other Person having Charge of such Ship or Vessel, shall not discover the same, such Commander, Master, or other Person having Charge of such Ship or Vessel, shall be adjudged guilty of Felony, and suffer Death, as in case of Felony, without Benefit of Clergy; and in case such Commander, Master, or other Person having Charge of such Ship or Vessel, shall, upon such Demand made, as aforesaid, not make a true Discovery in any other of the Particulars beforementioned, such Commander, Master or other Person having Charge of such Ship or Vessel, for every such Offence shall forfeit the Sum of two hundred Pounds; one Moiety thereof to the King, his Heirs and Successors, and the other Moiety to him or them who will sue for the same, by Action, Bill, Plaint, or Information, in any of His Majesty's Courts of Record at Westminster, Edinburgh, Dublin, or in the proper Courts of the Isles of Guernsey, Jersey, Alderney, Sark or Man, respectively.

*   *   *

And be it further enacted by the Authority aforesaid, That during the present Infection, and in all future Times, when any Country or Place shall be infected with the Plague, it shall and may be lawful to and for His Majesty, his Heirs and Successors, to order Ships to be provided, or to cause Houses or Lazarets for the receiving and entertaining of Persons infected with the Plague, or obliged to perform Quarentine, during such Time as they shall continue infected, or until they shall have performed Quarentine. . . .

*   *   *

And be it further enacted, That if any Person infected with the Plague, or obliged to perform Quarentine, shall wilfully refuse or neglect to repair within convenient time, after due Notice for that Purpose given to him, her, or them, by the proper Officer, to the Ship, House, Lazaret, or other Place duly appointed for him, her, or them; or having been placed in such Ship, House, Lazaret, or other Place, shall escape, or attempt to escape out of the same, whilst he, she, or they shall continue infected, or before Quarentine fully performed respectively; it shall and may be lawful to and for the Watchmen and other Persons, appointed to see Quarentine performed, by any kind of Violence that the Case shall require to compel every such Person.

And be it further enacted by the Authority aforesaid, That if at any time or times hereafter, any City, Town, or Place within Great Britain, or Ireland, shall be infected with the Plague, it shall and may be lawful to and for His Majesty, his Heirs and Successors, to cause one or more Line or Lines, Trench or Trenches, to be cast up or made about such infected City, Town, or Place, at a convenient Distance from the same, in order to cut off the Communication between such infected City, Town, or Place, and the rest of the Country; and to prohibit all Persons, Goods, and Merchandizes whatsoever, to enter, pass, or be carried over such Lines or Trenches and in case any Person or Persons, being within such Lines or Trenches or any of them, shall, during the time of such Infection, presume or attempt to come out of the same, unless in such Cases, and by such proper Licence, and subject to such Regulations and Restrictions for Performance of Quarentine, as shall be directed or permitted by such Order or Orders, made or to be made and notified, as aforesaid; it shall and may be lawful to and for the Watchmen, or Persons appointed to guard or secure such Lines or Trenches, or any of them, by any kind of Violence that the Case shall require, to compel all and every such Person and Persons to return back within such Lines or Trenches; and in case any Person shall actually come out of such Lines or Trenches, or any of them (unless in such Cases, and by such proper License, and subject to such Regulations and Restrictions as aforesaid) every such Person shall be adjudged guilty of Felony, and suffer Death as a Felon without Benefit of Clergy.

*   *   *

RICHARD MEAD

A Short Discourse concerning Pestilential Contagion, and the Methods to be Used to Prevent It †

To the Right Honourable James Craggs, Esq; One of His Majesty's Principal Secretaries of State

SIR,

I Most humbly offer to You my Thoughts concerning the Prevention of the Plague, which I have put together by your Command. As soon as you was pleased to signify to me, in his Majesty's Absence; that their Excellencies the Lords Justices thought it necessary for the Publick Safety, upon the Account of the Sickness now in France, that proper Directions should be drawn up to defend our selves from such a Calamity; I most readily undertook the Task, though upon short Warning, and with little Leisure: I have therefore rather put down the principal Heads of Caution, than a Set of Directions Form.

The first, which relate to the performing Quarentines, &c. You, who are perfectly versed in the History of Europe, will see are agreable to what is practised in other Countries, with some new Regulations. The next, concerning the suppressing Infection here, are very different from the Methods taken in former Times among Us, and from what they commonly Do Abroad: But, I persuade myself, will be found agreable to Reason.

I most heartily wish, that the wise Measures, the Government has already taken, and will continue to take, with Regard to the former of these, may make the Rules about the latter unnecessary. However it is fit, we should be always provided with proper Means of Defence against so terrible an Enemy.

May this short Essay be received as one Instance, among many others, of the Care, you always shew for Your Country; and as a Testimony of the great Esteem and Respect, with which I have the Honour to be,
SIR,

Your most obedient,
Most humble Servant,
Novemb. 25.
1720

R. Mead.

† Dr. Richard Mead was a Nonconformist like Defoe and, therefore, barred from English schools and universities. He was educated at Utrecht, Leyden, and Padua, where he received his M.D. in 1695. He could not be licensed either but was allowed to practice in Stepney, perhaps because it was on the edge of the College of Physicians' jurisdiction. He was elected to the Royal Society in 1703 and finally became a member of the College of Physicians in 1708. The king, Robert Walpole, and Isaac Newton were his patients, and the Lords Justices, through Secretary of State Craggs, asked him to write this treatise on preventing an outbreak of plague.

*   *   *

There is no *Evil* in which the great Rule of *Resisting the Beginning*, more properly takes place, than in the present Case; and yet it has unfortunately happened, that the common Steps formerly taken have had a direct Tendency to hinder the putting *this Maxim* in Practice.

As the *Plague* always breaks out in some particular Place, it is certain, that the Directions of the *Civil Magistrate* ought to be such, as to make it as much for the Interest of Families to discover their Misfortune, as it is, when a House is on *Fire*, to call in the Assistance of the Neighbourhood: Whereas on the contrary, the Methods taken by the Publick, on such Occasions, have always had the Appearance of a severe *Discipline*, and even *Punishment*, rather than of a *Compassionate Care:* Which must naturally make the *Infected* conceal the Disease as long as was possible.

The main Import of the *Orders* issued out at these Times was, As soon as it was found that any House was infected, to keep it shut up, with a *large red Cross*, and *Lord have Mercy upon us* on the Door; and Watchmen attending Day and Night to prevent any one's going in or out, except *Physicians, Surgeons, Apothecaries, Nurses, Searchers,* &c. allowed by Authority: And this to continue at least a Month after all the Family was *dead* or *recovered.*[1]

It is not easy to conceive a more dismal Scene of Misery, than this; Families seized with a Distemper, which the most of any in the World requires Help and Comfort, lockt up from all their Acquaintance; left it may be to the Treatment of an inhumane Nurse (for such are often found at these Times about the Sick;) and Strangers to every thing but the Melancholy sight of the Progress, Death makes among themselves; with small Hopes of Life, and those mixed with Anxiety and Doubt, whether it be not better to Dye, than to survive the Loss of their best Friends, and nearest Relations.

*   *   *

1. Vid. *Directions for the Cure of the* Plague, *by the* College *of* Physicians; *and Orders by the* Lord Mayor *and* Aldermen *of* London, *published* 1665 [*Mead's note*].

CONTEXTS:
REFLECTIONS ON
PLAGUES AND THEIR
EFFECTS

THUCYDIDES

[The Plague at Athens] †

* * *

The plague began for the first time to show itself among the Athenians. It is said, indeed, to have broken out before in many places, both in Lemnos and elsewhere, though no pestilence of such extent nor any scourge so destructive of human lives is on record anywhere. For neither were physicians able to cope with the disease, since they at first had to treat it without knowing its nature, the mortality among them being greatest because they were most exposed to it, nor did any other human art avail. And the supplications made at sanctuaries, or appeals to oracles and the like, were all futile, and at last men desisted from them, overcome by the calamity.

XLVIII. The disease began, it is said, in Ethiopia beyond Egypt, and then descended into Egypt and Libya and spread over the greater part of the King's territory. Then it suddenly fell upon the city of Athens, and attacked first the inhabitants of the Peiraeus, so that the people there even said that the Peloponnesians had put poison in their cisterns; for there were as yet no public fountains there. But afterwards it reached the upper city also, and from that time the mortality became much greater.

* * *

While the plague lasted there were none of the usual complaints, though if any did occur it ended in this. Sometimes death was due to neglect, but sometimes it occurred in spite of careful nursing. And no one remedy was found, I may say, which was sure to bring relief to those applying it—for what helped one man hurt another—and no constitution, as it proved, was of itself sufficient against it, whether as regards physical strength or weakness, but it carried off all without distinction, even those tended with all medical care. And the most dreadful thing about the whole malady was not only the despondency of the victims, when they once became aware that they were sick, for their minds straightway yielded to despair and they gave themselves up for lost instead of resisting, but also the fact that they became infected by nursing one another and died like sheep. And this caused the heaviest mortality; for if, on the one hand, they were restrained by fear from visiting one another, the sick perished uncared for, so that many houses were left empty through lack of anyone to do the nursing; or if, on the other hand, they visited

---

† Thucydides had the plague sometime between 430 and 427 B.C. It is not known when various parts of his *The History of the Peloponnesian War* were composed; he intended to carry it to 404, but it concludes before the winter of 411. The excerpt is from book 2. Rather than bubonic plague, this epidemic may have been typhus or cholera.

the sick, they perished, especially those who made any pretensions to goodness. For these made it a point of honour to visit their friends without sparing themselves at a time when the very relatives of the dying, overwhelmed by the magnitude of the calamity, were growing weary even of making their lamentations. But still it was more often those who had recovered who had pity for the dying and the sick, because they had learnt what it meant and were themselves by this time confident of immunity; for the disease never attacked the same man a second time, at least not with fatal results. And they were not only congratulated by everybody else, but themselves, in the excess of their joy at the moment, cherished also a fond fancy with regard to the rest of their lives that they would never be carried off by any other disease.

LII. But in addition to the trouble under which they already laboured, the Athenians suffered further hardship owing to the crowding into the city of the people from the country districts; and this affected the new arrivals especially. For since no houses were available for them and they had to live in huts that were stifling in the hot season, they perished in wild disorder. Bodies of dying men lay one upon another, and half-dead people rolled about in the streets and, in their longing for water, near all the fountains. The temples, too, in which they had quartered themselves were full of the corpses of those who had died in them; for the calamity which weighed upon them was so overpowering that men, not knowing what was to become of them, became careless of all law, sacred as well as profane. And the customs which they had hitherto observed regarding burial were all thrown into confusion, and they buried their dead each one as he could. And many resorted to shameless modes of burial because so many members of their households had already died that they lacked the proper funeral materials. Resorting to other people's pyres, some, anticipating those who had raised them, would put on their own dead and kindle the fire; others would throw the body they were carrying upon one which was already burning and go away.

LIII. In other respects also the plague first introduced into the city a greater lawlessness. For where men hitherto practised concealment, that they were not acting purely after their pleasure, they now showed a more careless daring. They saw how sudden was the change of fortune in the case both of those who were prosperous and suddenly died, and of those who before had nothing but in a moment were in possession of the property of the others. And so they resolved to get out of life the pleasures which could be had speedily and would satisfy their lusts, regarding their bodies and their wealth alike as transitory. And no one was eager to practise self-denial in prospect of what was esteemed honour, because everyone thought that it was doubtful whether he would live to attain it, but the pleasure of the moment and whatever was in any way conducive to it came to be regarded as at once honourable and expedient. No fear of gods or law of men restrained; for, on the one hand, seeing that all men were perishing alike, they judged that piety and impiety came to the same thing, and, on the other, no one expected that he would live to be called to account and pay the penalty of his misdeeds. On the contrary, they believed that the penalty already decreed against them, and now hanging over their heads, was a far heavier one, and that before this fell it was only reasonable to get some enjoyment out of life.

*   *   *

GIOVANNI BOCCACCIO

The First Day †

*   *   *

To the cure of these maladies nor counsel of physician nor virtue of any medicine appeared to avail or profit aught; on the contrary,—whether it was that the nature of the infection suffered it not or that the ignorance of the physicians (of whom, over and above the men of art, the number, both men and women, who had never had any teaching of medicine, was become exceeding great,) availed not to know whence it arose and consequently took not due measures thereagainst,—not only did few recover thereof, but well nigh all died within the third day from the appearance of the aforesaid signs, this sooner and that later, and for the most part without fever or other accident. And this pestilence was the more virulent for that, by communication with those who were sick thereof, it gat hold upon the sound, no otherwise than fire upon things dry or greasy, whenas they are brought very near thereunto. Nay, the mischief was yet greater; for that not only did converse and consortion with the sick give to the sound infection or cause of common death, but the mere touching of the clothes or of whatsoever other thing had been touched or used of the sick appeared of itself to communicate the malady to the toucher.

*   *   *

From these things and many others like unto them or yet stranger divers fears and conceits were begotten in those who abode alive, which well nigh all tended to a very barbarous conclusion, namely, to shun and flee from the sick and all that pertained to them, and thus doing, each thought to secure immunity for himself. Some there were who conceived that to live moderately and keep oneself from all excess was the best defence against such a danger; wherefore, making up their company, they lived removed from every other and shut themselves up in those houses where none had been sick and where living was best; and there, using very temperately of the most delicate viands and the finest

---

† In *The Decameron* Boccaccio constructs the fiction of seven women and three men telling each other one hundred tales in order to pass the time during the great plague of Florence in 1348. This excerpt is from the introduction to the first day, in which Boccaccio tells how the people "who are hereinafter presented assembled for the purpose of telling stories."

wines and eschewing all incontinence, they abode with music and such other diversions as they might have, never suffering themselves to speak with any nor choosing to hear any news from without of death or sick folk. Others, inclining to the contrary opinion, maintained that to carouse and make merry and go about singing and frolicking and satisfy the appetite in everything possible and laugh and scoff at whatsoever befell was a very certain remedy for such an ill. That which they said they put in practice as best they might, going about day and night, now to this tavern, now to that, drinking without stint or measure; and on this wise they did yet more freely in other folk's houses, so but they scented there aught that liked or tempted them, as they might lightly do, for that every one—as he were to live no longer—had abandoned all care of his possessions, as of himself, wherefore the most part of the houses were become common good and strangers used them, whenas they happened upon them, like as the very owner might have done; and with all this bestial preoccupation, they still shunned the sick to the best of their power.

In this sore affliction and misery of our city, the reverend authority of the laws, both human and divine, was all in a manner dissolved and fallen into decay, for [lack of] the ministers and executors thereof, who, like other men, were all either dead or sick or else left so destitute of followers that they were unable to exercise any office, wherefore every one had license to do whatsoever pleased him. Many others held a middle course between the two aforesaid, not straitening themselves so exactly in the matter of diet as the first neither allowing themselves such license in drinking and other debauchery as the second, but using things in sufficiency, according to their appetites; nor did they seclude themselves, but went about, carrying in their hands, some flowers, some odoriferous herbs and other some divers kinds of spiceries, which they set often to their noses, accounting it an excellent thing to fortify the brain with such odours, more by token that the air seemed all heavy and attainted with the stench of the dead bodies and that of the sick and of the remedies used.

Some were of a more barbarous, though, peradventure, a surer way of thinking, avouching that there was no remedy against pestilences better than—no, nor any so good as—to flee before them; wherefore, moved by this reasoning and recking of nought but themselves, very many, both men and women, abandoned their own city, their own houses and homes, their kinsfolk and possessions, and sought the country seats of others, or, at the least, their own, as if the wrath of God, being moved to punish the iniquity of mankind, would not proceed to do so wheresoever they might be, but would content itself with afflicting those only who were found within the walls of their city, or as if they were persuaded that no person was to remain therein and that its last hour was come. And albeit these, who opined thus variously, died not all, yet neither did they all escape; nay, many of each way of thinking and in every place sickened of the plague and languished on all sides, well nigh abandoned, having themselves, what while they were whole, set the example to those who abode in health.

Indeed, leaving be that townsman avoided townsman and that well nigh no neighbour took thought unto other and that kinsfolk seldom or never visited one another and held no converse together save from afar, this tribulation had stricken such terror to the hearts of all, men and women alike, that brother forsook brother, uncle nephew and sister brother and oftentimes wife husband; nay (what is yet more extraordinary and well nigh incredible) fathers and mothers refused to visit or tend their very children, as they had not been theirs. By reason whereof there remained unto those (and the number of them, both males and females, was incalculable) who fell sick, none other succour than that which they owed either to the charity of friends (and of these there were few) or the greed of servants, who tended them, allured by high and extravagant wage; albeit, for all this, these latter were not grown many, and those men and women of mean understanding and for the most part unused to such offices, who served for well nigh nought but to reach things called for by the sick or to note when they died; and in the doing of these services many of them perished with their gain.

THOMAS DEKKER

From *The Wonderful Year* †

*　*　*

What an unmatchable torment were it for a man to be barred up every night in a vast, silent charnel-house hung, to make it more hideous, with lamps dimly and slowly burning in hollow and glimmering corners; where all the pavement should instead of green rushes be strewed with blasted rosemary, withered hyacinths, fatal cypress and yew, thickly mingled with heaps of dead men's bones—the bare ribs of a father that begat him lying there, here the chapless hollow skull of a mother that bore him; round about him a thousand corpses, some standing bolt upright in their knotted winding-sheets, others half mouldered in rotten coffins that should suddenly yawn wide open filling his nostrils with noisome stench and his eyes with the sight of nothing but crawling worms. And to keep such a poor wretch waking, he should hear no noise but of toads croaking, screech-owls howling, mandrakes shrieking. Were not this an infernal prison? Would not the strongest-hearted man beset with such a ghastly horror look wild? And run mad? And die?

† Dekker is best known as a dramatist, contemporary of Ben Jonson and William Shakespeare. Like Defoe, he was repeatedly imprisoned for debt, and his short *The Won-* *derful Year* (1603) is a mixture of poignant observations and "wonderful" (that is, amazing) tales.

And even such a formidable shape did the diseased City appear in. For he that durst in the dead hour of gloomy midnight have been so valiant as to have walked through the still and melancholy streets—what think you should have been his music? Surely the loud groans of raving sick men, the struggling pangs of souls departing; in every house grief striking up an alarum—servants crying out for masters, wives for husbands, parents for children, children for their mothers. Here, he should have met some franticly running to knock up sextons; there, others fearfully sweating with coffins to steal forth dead bodies lest the fatal handwriting of Death should seal up their doors. And to make this dismal concert more full, round about him bells heavily tolling in one place and ringing out in another. The dreadfulness of such an hour is inutterable. Let us go further.

If some poor man, suddenly starting out of a sweet and golden slumber, should behold his house flaming about his ears, all his family destroyed in their sleeps by the merciless fire, himself in the very midst of it woefully and like a madman calling for help—would not the misery of such a distressed soul appear the greater if the rich usurer dwelling next door to him should not stir, though he felt part of the danger, but suffer him to perish when the thrusting out of an arm might have saved him? Oh, how many thousands of wretched people have acted this poor man's part! How often hath the amazed husband, waking, found the comfort of his bed lying breathless by his side, his children at the same instant gasping for life, and his servants mortally wounded at the heart by sickness! The distracted creature beats at death's doors, exclaims at windows; his cries are sharp enough to pierce Heaven but on earth no ear is opened to receive them.

And in this manner do the tedious minutes of the night stretch out the sorrows of ten thousand. It is now day. Let us look forth and try what consolation rises with the sun. Not any, not any. For before the jewel of the morning be fully set in silver, a hundred hungry graves stand gaping and every one of them, as at a breakfast, hath swallowed down ten or eleven lifeless carcases. Before dinner in the same gulf are twice so many more devoured. And before the sun takes his rest those numbers are doubled.

* * *

But, wretched man! when thou shalt see and be assured by tokens sent thee from Heaven that tomorrow thou must be fumbled into a muckpit and suffer thy body to be bruised and pressed with threescore dead men lying slovenly upon thee, and thou to be undermost of all— yea, and perhaps half of that number were thine enemies, and see how they may be revenged, for the worms that breed out of their putrefying carcases shall crawl in huge swarms from them and quite devour thee—

what agonies will this strange news drive thee into? If thou art in love
with thyself this cannot choose but possess thee with frenzy.

*   *   *

Never let any man ask me what became of our physicians in this
massacre. They hid their synodical heads as well as the proudest. And I
cannot blame them. For their phlebotomies, lozenges and electuaries,
with their diacatholicons, diacodions, amulets and antidotes had not so
much strength to hold life and soul together as a pot of Pinder's ale and
a nutmeg. Their drugs turned to dirt; their simples were simple things.
Galen could do no more good than Sir Giles Goosecap, Hippocrates,
Avicenna, Paracelsus, Rhazes, Fernelius, with all their succeeding rabble of doctors and water-casters, were at their wits' end—or I think rather
at the world's end, for not one of them durst peep abroad or, if any one
did take upon him to play the venturous knight, the plague put him to
his *nonplus*. In such strange and such changeable shapes did this cha-
meleon-like sickness appear that they could not, with all the cunning in
their budgets, make purse-nets to take him napping.

Only a band of desperviews, some few empirical madcaps (for they
could never be worth velvet caps) turned themselves into bees—or, more
properly, into drones—and went humming up and down with honey-
brags in their mouths sucking the sweetness of silver and now and then
of *aurum potabile* out of the poison of blains and carbuncles. And these
jolly mountebanks clapped up their bills upon every post like a fencer's
challenge, threatening to canvas the plague and to fight with him at all
his own several weapons. I know not how they sped but some they sped,
I am sure, for I have heard them banned for the Heavens because they
sent those thither that were wished to tarry longer upon earth.

*   *   *

I will let the churchwarden in Thames St sleep (for he's now past
waking) who, being requested by one of his neighbours to suffer his wife
or child that was then dead to lie in the churchyard, answered in a
mocking sort, he kept that lodging for himself and his household; and
within three days after was driven to hide his head in a hole himself.
Neither will I speak a word of a poor boy, servant to a chandler dwelling
thereabouts, who being struck to the heart by sickness was first carried
away by water to be left anywhere but, landing being denied by an army
of brown bill men that kept the shore, back again was he brought and
left in an out-cellar where, lying grovelling and groaning on his face
amongst faggots (but not one of them set on fire to comfort him), there
continued all night and died miserably for want of succour. Nor of another
poor wretch in the Parish of St Mary Overy's who, being in the morning
thrown, as the fashion is, into a grave upon a heap of carcases that stayed
for their complement, was found in the afternoon gasping and gaping

for life. But by these tricks imagining that many a thousand have been turned wrongfully off the ladder of life, and praying that Derrick or his executors may live to do those a good turn that have done so to others, *hic finis Priami*, here's an end of an old song;[1] *et iam tempus equum fumantia solvere colla.*[2]

*   *   *

A tinker came sounding through the town, mine host's house being the ancient watering-place where he did use to cast anchor. You must understand he was none of those base rascally tinkers that, with a bandog and a drag at their tails and a pikestaff on their necks, will take a purse sooner than stop a kettle: no, this was a devout tinker—he did honour God Pan; a musical tinker that upon his kettledrum could play any country-dance you called for, and upon holidays had earned money by it when no fiddler could be heard of. He was only feared when he stalked through some towns where bees were, for he struck so sweetly on the bottom of his copper instrument that he would empty whole hives and lead the swarms after him only by the sound.

This excellent egregious tinker calls for his draught, being a double jug. It was filled for him but, before it came to his nose, the lamentable tale of the Londoner was told, the chamber-door where he lay being thrust open with a long pole because none durst touch it with their hands, and the tinker bidden if he had the heart to go in and see if he knew him. The tinker, being not to learn what virtue the medicine had which he held at his lips, poured it down his throat merrily and crying 'Trillil!' he feared no plagues. In he stepped, tossing the dead body to and fro, and was sorry—he knew him not.

Mine host, that with grief began to fall away villainously, looking very ruefully on the tinker and thinking him a fit instrument to be played upon, offered a crown out of his own purse if he would bury the party. A crown was a shrewd temptation to a tinker: many a hole might he stop before he could pick a crown off it. Yet being a subtle tinker (and to make all sextons pray for him, because he would raise their fees) an angel he wanted to be his guide: and under ten shillings, by his ten bones, he would not put his finger in the fire. The whole parish had warning of this presently. Thirty shillings was saved by the bargain, and the town likely to be saved, too: therefore ten shillings was levied out of hand, put into a rag which was tied to the end of a long pole and delivered in sight of all the parish, who stood aloof stopping their noses, by the headborough's own self in proper person to the tinker, who with one hand received the money and with the other struck the board, crying

---

1. "Here's the end of Priam," Virgil, *Aeneid* 2.554. An allusion to the speech that Hamlet asks the players to perform on the death of Priam may also be intended, Shakespeare, *Hamlet* (1603), 2.2.441ff [note and trans. Thomas Hahn].

2. "And now it's time to release the smoking [i.e., steaming, hot] necks of our horses," Virgil, *Georgics* 2.542. In other words, it's the end of the race, and the horses are to be given their heads.

'Hey! a fresh double pot!' Which armour of proof being fitted to his body, up he hoists the Londoner on his back like a schoolboy, a shovel and pickaxe standing ready for him.

And thus furnished, into a field some good distance from the town he bears his deadly load and there throws it down, falling roundly to his tools—upon which the strong beer having set an edge, they quickly cut out a lodging in the earth for the citizen. But the tinker, knowing that worms needed no apparel saving only sheets, stripped him stark naked; but first dived nimbly into his pockets to see what linings they had, assuring himself that a Londoner would not wander so far without silver. His hopes were of the right stamp, for from one of his pockets he drew a leathern bag with £7 in it. This music made the tinker's heart dance. He quickly tumbled his man into the grave, hid him over head and ears in dust, bound up his clothes in a bundle and, carrying that at the end of his staff on his shoulder, with the purse of £7 in his hand, back again comes he through the town, crying aloud 'Have ye any more Londoners to bury? Hey down a down derry! Have ye any more Londoners to bury?'—the Hobbinolls running away from him as if he had been the dead citizen's ghost, and he marching away from them in all the haste he could with that song still in his mouth.

ALBERT CAMUS

From *The Plague* †

*   *   *

Michel's death marked, one might say, the end of the first period, that of bewildering portents, and the beginning of another, relatively more trying, in which the perplexity of the early days gradually gave place to panic. Reviewing that first phase in the light of subsequent events, our townsfolk realized that they had never dreamed it possible that our little town should be chosen out for the scene of such grotesque happenings as the wholesale death of rats in broad daylight or the decease of concierges through exotic maladies. In this respect they were wrong, and their views obviously called for revision. Still, if things had gone thus far and no farther, force of habit would doubtless have gained the day, as usual. But other members of our community, not all menials or poor people, were to follow the path down which M. Michel had led the way. And it was then that fear, and with fear serious reflection, began.

*   *   *

† Camus, the French author and playwright, was born in Algiers. His *The Plague* (1947) shows Defoe's influence clearly, but in Camus's novel the plague is often self consciously used as a metaphor. Reprinted from Camus, *The Plague* with permission of Random House and Hamish Hamilton, Ltd.

The word "plague" had just been uttered for the first time. At this stage of the narrative, with Dr. Bernard Rieux standing at his window, the narrator may, perhaps, be allowed to justify the doctor's uncertainty and surprise—since, with very slight differences, his reaction was the same as that of the great majority of our townsfolk. Everybody knows that pestilences have a way of recurring in the world; yet somehow we find it hard to believe in ones that crash down on our heads from a blue sky. There have been as many plagues as wars in history; yet always plagues and wars take people equally by surprise.

In fact, like our fellow citizens, Rieux was caught off his guard, and we should understand his hesitations in the light of this fact; and similarly understand how he was torn between conflicting fears and confidence. When a war breaks out, people say: "It's too stupid; it can't last long." But though a war may well be "too stupid," that doesn't prevent its lasting. Stupidity has a knack of getting its way; as we should see if we were not always so much wrapped up in ourselves.

In this respect our townsfolk were like everybody else, wrapped up in themselves; in other words they were humanists: they disbelieved in pestilences. A pestilence isn't a thing made to man's measure; therefore we tell ourselves that pestilence is a mere bogy of the mind, a bad dream that will pass away. But it doesn't always pass away and, from one bad dream to another, it is men who pass away, and the humanists first of all, because they haven't taken their precautions. Our townsfolk were not more to blame than others; they forgot to be modest, that was all, and thought that everything still was possible for them; which presupposed that pestilences were impossible. They went on doing business, arranged for journeys, and formed views. How should they have given a thought to anything like plague, which rules out any future, cancels journeys, silences the exchange of views. They fancied themselves free, and no one will ever be free so long as there are pestilences.

Indeed, even after Dr. Rieux had admitted in his friend's company that a handful of persons, scattered about the town, had without warning died of plague, the danger still remained fantastically unreal. For the simple reason that, when a man is a doctor, he comes to have his own ideas of physical suffering, and to acquire somewhat more imagination than the average. Looking from his window at the town, outwardly quite unchanged, the doctor felt little more than a faint qualm for the future, a vague unease.

He tried to recall what he had read about the disease. Figures floated across his memory, and he recalled that some thirty or so great plagues known to history had accounted for nearly a hundred million deaths. But what are a hundred million deaths? When one has served in a war, one hardly knows what a dead man is, after a while. And since a dead man has no substance unless one has actually seen him dead, a hundred million corpses broadcast through history are no more than a puff of smoke in the imagination. The doctor remembered the plague at Constantinople that, according to Procopius, caused ten thousand deaths in a single day. Ten thousand dead made about five times the audience in a biggish cinema. Yes, that was how it should be done. You should collect the people at the exits of five picture-houses, you should lead them to a city square and make them die in heaps if you wanted to get a clear notion of what it means. Then at least you could add some familiar faces to the anonymous mass. But naturally that was impossible to put into practice; moreover, what man knows ten thousand faces? In any case the figures of those old historians, like Procopius, weren't to be relied on; that was common knowledge. Seventy years ago, at Canton, forty thousand rats died of plague before the disease spread to the inhabitants. But, again, in the Canton epidemic there was no reliable way of counting up the rats. A very rough estimate was all that could be made, with, obviously, a wide margin for error. "Let's see," the doctor murmured to himself, "supposing the length of a rat to be ten inches, forty thousand rats placed end to end would make a line of . . ."

He pulled himself up sharply. He was letting his imagination play pranks—the last thing wanted just now. A few cases, he told himself, don't make an epidemic; they merely call for serious precautions. He must fix his mind, first of all, on the observed facts: stupor and extreme prostration, buboes, intense thirst, delirium, dark blotches on the body, internal dilatation, and, in conclusion . . . In conclusion, some words came back to the doctor's mind; aptly enough, the concluding sentence of the description of the symptoms given in his medical handbook: "The pulse becomes fluttering, dicrotic, and intermittent, and death ensues as the result of the slightest movement." Yes, in conclusion, the patient's life hung on a thread, and three people out of four (he remembered the exact figures) were too impatient not to make the very slight movement that snapped the thread.

The doctor was still looking out of the window. Beyond it lay the tranquil radiance of a cool spring sky; inside the room a word was echoing still, the word "plague." A word that conjured up in the doctor's mind not only what science chose to put into it, but a whole series of fantastic possibilities utterly out of keeping with that gray and yellow town under his eyes, from which were rising the sounds of mild activity characteristic of the hour; a drone rather than a bustling, the noises of a happy town, in short, if it's possible to be at once so dull and happy. A tranquillity so casual and thoughtless seemed almost effortlessly to give the lie to those old pictures of the plague: Athens, a charnel-house reeking to heaven and deserted even by the birds; Chinese towns cluttered up with victims silent in their agony; the convicts at Marseille piling rotting corpses into pits; the building of the Great Wall in Provence to fend off the furious plague-wind; the damp, putrefying pallets stuck to the mud floor at the Constantinople lazar-house, where the patients were hauled up from their beds with hooks; the carnival of masked doctors at the Black Death; men and women copulating in the cemeteries of Milan; cartloads of dead bodies rumbling through London's ghoul-haunted darkness—nights and days filled always, everywhere, with the

eternal cry of human pain. No, all those horrors were not near enough
as yet even to ruffle the equanimity of that spring afternoon. The clang
of an unseen streetcar came through the window, briskly refuting cruelty
and pain. Only the sea, murmurous behind the dingy checkerboard of
houses, told of the unrest, the precariousness, of all things in this world.
And, gazing in the direction of the bay, Dr. Rieux called to mind the
plague-fires of which Lucretius tells, which the Athenians kindled on
the seashore. The dead were brought there after nightfall, but there was
not room enough, and the living fought one another with torches for a
space where to lay those who had been dear to them; for they had rather
engage in bloody conflicts than abandon their dead to the waves. A
picture rose before him of the red glow of the pyres mirrored on a wine-
dark, slumbrous sea, battling torches whirling sparks across the darkness,
and thick, fetid smoke rising toward the watchful sky. Yes, it was not
beyond the bounds of possibility. . . .

But these extravagant forebodings dwindled in the light of reason.
True, the word "plague" had been uttered; true, at this very moment
one or two victims were being seized and laid low by the disease. Still,
that could stop, or be stopped. It was only a matter of lucidly recognizing
what had to be recognized; of dispelling extraneous shadows and doing
what needed to be done. Then the plague would come to an end, because
it was unthinkable, or, rather, because one thought of it on misleading
lines. If, as was most likely, it died out, all would be well. If not, one
would know it anyhow for what it was and what steps should be taken
for coping with and finally overcoming it.

The doctor opened the window, and at once the noises of the town
grew louder. The brief, intermittent sibilance of a machine-saw came
from a near-by workshop. Rieux pulled himself together. There lay cer-
titude; there, in the daily round. All the rest hung on mere threads and
trivial contingencies; you couldn't waste your time on it. The thing was
to do your job as it should be done.

*   *   *

MICHEL FOUCAULT

Panopticism †

The following, according to an order published at the end of the seventeenth century, were the measures to be taken when the plague appeared
in a town. [1]

† The historical investigations of the French philosopher Michel Foucault (1926–84) examine the enabling conditions and relations of areas of knowledge, institutions, and forms of social practice. His methods of studying culture through the analysis of power have been among the most influential in the late twentieth century. This excerpt is reprinted by permission of Georges Borchardt, Inc. and Penguin Books Ltd. from the final chapter of Foucault's *Discipline and Punish* (translated by Alan Sheridan, 1977). *Discipline and Punish* exposes the increasingly carceral nature of our society.

1. Archives militaires de Vincennes, A 1,516

First, a strict spatial partitioning: the closing of the town and its out-lying districts, a prohibition to leave the town on pain of death, the killing of all stray animals; the division of the town into distinct quarters, each governed by an intendant. Each street is placed under the authority of a syndic, who keeps it under surveillance; if he leaves the street, he will be condemned to death. On the appointed day, everyone is ordered to stay indoors: it is forbidden to leave on pain of death. The syndic himself comes to lock the door of each house from the outside; he takes the key with him and hands it over to the intendant of the quarter; the intendant keeps it until the end of the quarantine. Each family will have made its own provisions; but, for bread and wine, small wooden canals are set up between the street and the interior of the houses, thus allowing each person to receive his ration without communicating with the sup-pliers and other residents; meat, fish and herbs will be hoisted up into the houses with pulleys and baskets. If it is absolutely necessary to leave the house, it will be done in turn, avoiding any meeting. Only the inten-dants, syndics and guards will move about the streets and also, between the infected houses, from one corpse to another, the 'crows', who can be left to die: these are 'people of little substance who carry the sick, bury the dead, clean and do many vile and abject offices'. It is a segmented, immobile, frozen space. Each individual is fixed in his place. And, if he moves, he does so at the risk of his life, contagion or punishment.

Inspection functions ceaselessly. The gaze is alert everywhere: 'A con-siderable body of militia, commanded by good officers and men of sub-stance', guards at the gates, at the town hall and in every quarter to ensure the prompt obedience of the people and the most absolute authority of the magistrates, 'as also to observe all disorder, theft and extortion'. At each of the town gates there will be an observation post; at the end of each street sentinels. Every day, the intendant visits the quarter in his charge, inquires whether the syndics have carried out their tasks, whether the inhabitants have anything to complain of; they 'observe their actions'. Every day, too, the syndic goes into the street for which he is responsible; stops before each house: gets all the inhabitants to appear at the windows (those who live overlooking the courtyard will be allocated a window looking onto the street at which no one but they may show themselves); he calls each of them by name; informs himself as to the state of each and every one of them—'in which respect the inhabitants will be com-pelled to speak the truth under pain of death'; if someone does not appear at the window, the syndic must ask why: 'In this way he will find out easily enough whether dead or sick are being concealed.' Everyone locked up in his cage, everyone at his window, answering to his name and showing himself when asked—it is the great review of the living and the dead.

This surveillance is based on a system of permanent registration: reports

---

91 sc. Pièce. This regulation is broadly similar to a whole series of others that date from the same period and earlier.

from the syndics to the intendants, from the intendants to the magistrates or mayor. At the beginning of the 'lock up', the role of each of the inhabitants present in the town is laid down, one by one; this document bears 'the name, age, sex of everyone, notwithstanding his condition': a copy is sent to the intendant of the quarter, another to the office of the town hall, another to enable the syndic to make his daily roll call. Everything that may be observed during the course of the visits—deaths, illnesses, complaints, irregularities—is noted down and transmitted to the intendants and magistrates. The magistrates have complete control over medical treatment; they have appointed a physician in charge; no other practitioner may treat, no apothecary prepare medicine, no confessor visit a sick person without having received from him a written note 'to prevent anyone from concealing and dealing with those sick of the contagion, unknown to the magistrates'. The registration of the pathological must be constantly centralized. The relation of each individual to his disease and to his death passes through the representatives of power, the registration they make of it, the decisions they take on it.

Five or six days after the beginning of the quarantine, the process of purifying the houses one by one is begun. All the inhabitants are made to leave; in each room 'the furniture and goods' are raised from the ground or suspended from the air; perfume is poured around the room; after carefully sealing the windows, doors and even the keyholes with wax, the perfume is consumed; those who have carried out the work are searched, as they were on entry, 'in the presence of the residents of the house, to see that they did not have something on their persons as they left that they did not have on entering'. Four hours later, the residents are allowed to re-enter their homes.

This enclosed, segmented space, observed at every point, in which the individuals are inserted in a fixed place, in which the slightest movements are supervised, in which all events are recorded, in which an uninterrupted work of writing links the centre and periphery, in which power is exercised without division, according to a continuous hierarchical figure, in which each individual is constantly located, examined and distributed among the living beings, the sick and the dead—all this constitutes a compact model of the disciplinary mechanism. The plague is met by order; its function is to sort out every possible confusion: that of the disease, which is transmitted when bodies are mixed together; that of the evil, which is increased when fear and death overcome prohibitions. It lays down for each individual his place, his body, his disease and his death, his well-being, by means of an omnipresent and omniscient power that subdivides itself in a regular, uninterrupted way even to the ultimate determination of the individual, of what characterizes him, of what belongs to him, of what happens to him. Against the plague, which is a mixture, discipline brings into play its power, which is one of analysis. A whole literary fiction of the festival grew up around the plague: suspended laws, lifted prohibitions, the frenzy of passing time, bodies mingling together without respect, individuals unmasked, abandoning their statutory identity and the figure under which they had been recognized, allowing a quite different truth to appear. But there was also a political dream of the plague, which was exactly its reverse: not the collective festival, but strict divisions; not laws transgressed, but the penetration of regulation into even the smallest details of everyday life through the mediation of the complete hierarchy that assured the capillary functioning of power; not masks that were put on and taken off, but the assignment to each individual of his 'true' name, his 'true' place, his 'true' body, his 'true' disease. The plague as a form, at once real and imaginary, of disorder had as its medical and political correlative discipline. Behind the disciplinary mechanisms can be read the haunting memory of 'contagions', of the plague, of rebellions, crimes, vagabondage, desertions, people who appear and disappear, live and die in disorder.

If it is true that the leper gave rise to rituals of exclusion, which to a certain extent provided the model for and general form of the great Confinement, then the plague gave rise to disciplinary projects. Rather than the massive, binary division between one set of people and another, it called for multiple separations, individualizing distributions, an organization in depth of surveillance and control, an intensification and a ramification of power. The leper was caught up in a practice of rejection, of exile-enclosure; he was left to his doom in a mass among which it was useless to differentiate; those sick of the plague were caught up in a meticulous tactical partitioning in which individual differentiations were the constricting effects of a power that multiplied, articulated and subdivided itself; the great confinement on the one hand; the correct training on the other. The leper and his separation; the plague and its segmentations. The first is marked; the second analysed and distributed. The exile of the leper and the arrest of the plague do not bring with them the same political dream. The first is that of a pure community, the second that of a disciplined society. Two ways of exercising power over men, of controlling their relations, of separating out their dangerous mixtures. The plague-stricken town, traversed throughout with hierarchy, surveillance, observation, writing; the town immobilized by the functioning of an extensive power that bears in a distinct way over all individual bodies—this is the utopia of the perfectly governed city. The plague (envisaged as a possibility at least) is the trial in the course of which one may define ideally the exercise of disciplinary power. In order to make rights and laws function according to pure theory, the jurists place themselves in imagination in the state of nature; in order to see perfect disciplines functioning, rulers dreamt of the state of plague. Underlying disciplinary projects the image of the plague stands for all forms of confusion and disorder; just as the image of the leper, cut off from all human contact, underlies projects of exclusion.

They are different projects, then, but not incompatible ones. We see them coming slowly together, and it is the peculiarity of the nineteenth century that it applied to the space of exclusion of which the leper was the symbolic inhabitant (beggars, vagabonds, madmen and the disorderly formed the real population) the technique of power proper to disciplinary partitioning. Treat 'lepers' as 'plague victims', project the subtle segmentations of discipline onto the confused space of internment, combine it with the methods of analytical distribution proper to power, individualize the excluded, but use procedures of individualization to mark exclusion—this is what was operated regularly by disciplinary power from the beginning of the nineteenth century in the psychiatric asylum, the penitentiary, the reformatory, the approved school and, to some extent, the hospital. Generally speaking, all the authorities exercising individual control function according to a double mode; that of binary division and branding (mad/sane; dangerous/harmless; normal/abnormal); and that of coercive assignment, of differential distribution (who he is; where he must be; how he is to be characterized; how he is to be recognized; how a constant surveillance is to be exercised over him in an individual way, etc.). On the one hand, the lepers are treated as plague victims; the tactics of individualizing disciplines are imposed on the excluded; and, on the other hand, the universality of disciplinary controls makes it possible to brand the 'leper' and to bring into play against him the dualistic mechanisms of exclusion. The constant division between the normal and the abnormal, to which every individual is subjected, brings us back to our own time, by applying the binary branding and exile of the leper to quite different objects; the existence of a whole set of techniques and institutions for measuring, supervising and correcting the abnormal brings into play the disciplinary mechanisms to which the fear of the plague gave rise. All the mechanisms of power which, even today, are disposed around the abnormal individual, to brand him and to alter him, are composed of those two forms from which they distantly derive.

Bentham's *Panopticon*[2] is the architectural figure of this composition. We know the principle on which it was based: at the periphery, an annular building; at the centre, a tower; this tower is pierced with wide windows that open onto the inner side of the ring; the peripheric building is divided into cells, each of which extends the whole width of the building; they have two windows, one on the inside, corresponding to the windows of the tower; the other, on the outside, allows the light to cross the cell from one end to the other. All that is needed, then, is to place

---

2. The Panopticon was the plan of Jeremy Bentham (lawyer and philosopher, 1748–1832) for an efficient prison. As its name suggests, the Panopticon was designed to provide for the isolation and continued surveillance of its inmates, while simultaneously preventing them from observing their warder. Reading the Panopticon as a metonymy of the technique of coercion in contemporary society, Foucault notes that it fashions subjects who are continually self-policing and who monitor their conduct under an internalized, unlocalized gaze. Segregation and self-consciousness are the means by which subjects are disciplined [John Roberts].

a supervisor in a central tower and to shut up in each cell a madman, a patient, a condemned man, a worker or a schoolboy. By the effect of backlighting, one can observe from the tower, standing out precisely against the light, the small captive shadows in the cells of the periphery. They are like so many cages, so many small theatres, in which each actor is alone, perfectly individualized and constantly visible. The panoptic mechanism arranges spatial unities that make it possible to see constantly and to recognize immediately. In short, it reverses the principle of the dungeon; or rather of its three functions—to enclose, to deprive of light and to hide—it preserves only the first and eliminates the other two. Full lighting and the eye of a supervisor capture better than darkness, which ultimately protected. Visibility is a trap.

To begin with, this made it possible—as a negative effect—to avoid those compact, swarming, howling masses that were to be found in places of confinement, those painted by Goya or described by Howard. Each individual, in his place, is securely confined to a cell from which he is seen from the front by the supervisor; but the side walls prevent him from coming into contact with his companions. He is seen, but he does not see; he is the object of information, never a subject in communication. The arrangement of his room, opposite the central tower, imposes on him an axial visibility; but the divisions of the ring, those separated cells, imply a lateral invisibility. And this invisibility is a guarantee of order. If the inmates are convicts, there is no danger of a plot, an attempt at collective escape, the planning of new crimes for the future, bad reciprocal influences; if they are patients, there is no danger of contagion; if they are madmen there is no risk of their committing violence upon one another; if they are schoolchildren, there is no copying, no noise, no chatter, no waste of time; if they are workers, there are no disorders, no theft, no coalitions, none of those distractions that slow down the rate of work, make it less perfect or cause accidents. The crowd, a compact mass, a locus of multiple exchanges, individualities merging together, a collective effect, is abolished and replaced by a collection of separated individualities. From the point of view of the guardian, it is replaced by a multiplicity that can be numbered and supervised; from the point of view of the inmates, by a sequestered and observed solitude (Bentham, 60–64).

Hence the major effect of the Panopticon: to induce in the inmate a state of conscious and permanent visibility that assures the automatic functioning of power. So to arrange things that the surveillance is permanent in its effects, even if it is discontinuous in its action; that the perfection of power should tend to render its actual exercise unnecessary; that this architectural apparatus should be a machine for creating and sustaining a power relation independent of the person who exercises it; in short, that the inmates should be caught up in a power situation of which they are themselves the bearers. To achieve this, it is at once too much and too little that the prisoner should be constantly observed by

an inspector: too little, for what matters is that he knows himself to be
observed; too much, because he has no need in fact of being so. In view
of this, Bentham laid down the principle that power should be visible
and unverifiable. Visible: the inmate will constantly have before his eyes
the tall outline of the central tower from which he is spied upon. Unverifiable: the inmate must never know whether he is being looked at at any
one moment; but he must be sure that he may always be so. In order to
make the presence or absence of the inspector unverifiable, so that the
prisoners, in their cells, cannot even see a shadow, Bentham envisaged
not only venetian blinds on the windows of the central observation hall,
but, on the inside, partitions that intersected the hall at right angles and,
in order to pass from one quarter to the other, not doors but zig-zag
openings; for the slightest noise, a gleam of light, a brightness in a half-
opened door would betray the presence of the guardian.[3] The Panopticon is a machine for dissociating the see/being seen dyad: in the peripheric ring, one is totally seen, without ever seeing; in the central tower,
one sees everything without ever being seen.[4]

*   *   *

SUSAN SONTAG

From *AIDS and Its Metaphors* †

"Plague" is the principal metaphor by which the AIDS epidemic is
understood. And because of AIDS, the popular misidentification of cancer as an epidemic, even a plague, seems to be receding: AIDS has
banalized cancer.

Plague, from the Latin *plaga* (stroke, wound), has long been used
metaphorically as the highest standard of collective calamity, evil
scourge—Procopius, in his masterpiece of calumny, *The Secret History*,
called the Emperor Justinian worse than the plague ("fewer escaped")—
as well as being a general name for many frightening diseases. Although
the disease to which the word is permanently affixed produced the most
lethal of recorded epidemics, being experienced as a pitiless slayer is not
necessary for a disease to be regarded as plague-like. Leprosy, very rarely
fatal now, was not much more so when at its greatest epidemic strength,

3. In the *Postscript to the Panopticon*, London, 1791, Bentham adds dark inspection gal-
leries painted in black around the inspector's
lodge, each making it possible to observe two
storeys of cells.
4. In his first version of the *Panopticon*, Bentham had also imagined an acoustic surveillance, operated by means of pipes leading from
the cells to the central tower. In the *Postscript*
he abandoned the idea, perhaps because he
could not introduce into it the principle of dis-
symmetry and prevent the prisoners from hearing the inspector as well as the inspector hearing
them. Julius tried to develop a system of dis-
symmetrical listening (N. H. Julius, *Leçons sur
les prisons* vol. 1 [Paris, 1831] 18).
† Susan Sontag, author and film director, counts
among her many books the groundbreaking *On
Photography* (1977) and *Illness as Metaphor*
(1978). This excerpt is chapter 5 of her 1988
book, *AIDS and Its Metaphors*, and is reprinted
with the permission of Farrar, Straus & Giroux
and Penguin Books Ltd.

between about 1050 and 1350. And syphilis has been regarded as a plague—Blake speaks of "the youthful Harlot's curse" that "blights with plagues the Marriage hearse"—not because it killed often, but because it was disgracing, disempowering, disgusting.

It is usually epidemics that are thought of as plagues. And these mass incidences of illness are understood as inflicted, not just endured. Considering illness as a punishment is the oldest idea of what causes illness, and an idea opposed by all attention to the ill that deserves the noble name of medicine. Hippocrates, who wrote several treatises on epidemics, specifically ruled out "the wrath of God" as a cause of bubonic plague. But the illnesses interpreted in antiquity as punishments, like the plague in *Oedipus*, were not thought to be shameful, as leprosy and subsequently syphilis were to be. Diseases, insofar as they acquired meaning, were collective calamities, and judgments on a community. Only injuries and disabilities, not diseases, were thought of as individually merited. For an analogy in the literature of antiquity to the modern sense of a shaming, isolating disease, one would have to turn to Philoctetes and his stinking wound.

The most feared diseases, those that are not simply fatal but transform the body into something alienating, like leprosy and syphilis and cholera and (in the imagination of many) cancer, are the ones that seem particularly susceptible to promotion to "plague." Leprosy and syphilis were the first illnesses to be consistently described as repulsive. It was syphilis that, in the earliest descriptions by doctors at the end of the fifteenth century, generated a version of the metaphors that flourish around AIDS: of a disease that was not only repulsive and retributive but collectively invasive. Although Erasmus, the most influential European pedagogue of the early sixteenth century, described syphilis as "nothing but a kind of leprosy" (by 1592 he called it "something worse than leprosy"), it had already been understood as something different, because sexually transmitted. Paracelsus speaks (in Donne's paraphrase) of "that foule contagious disease which then had invaded mankind in a few places, and since overflowes in all, that for punishment of general licentiousness God first inflicted that disease." Thinking of syphilis as a punishment for an individual's transgression was for a long time, virtually until the disease became easily curable, not really distinct from regarding it as retribution for the licentiousness of a community—as with AIDS now, in the rich industrial countries. In contrast to cancer, understood in a modern way as a disease incurred by (and revealing of) individuals, AIDS is understood in a premodern way, as a disease incurred by people both as individuals and as members of a "risk group"—that neutral-sounding, bureaucratic category which also revives the archaic idea of a tainted community that illness has judged.

Not every account of plague or plague-like diseases, of course, is a vehicle for lurid stereotypes about illness and the ill. The effort to think critically, historically, about illness (about disaster generally) was attempted throughout the eighteenth century: say, from Defoe's *A Journal of the Plague Year* (1722) to Alessandro Manzoni's *The Betrothed* (1827). Defoe's historical fiction, purporting to be an eyewitness account of bubonic plague in London in 1665, does not further any understanding of the plague as punishment or, a later part of the script, as a transforming experience. And Manzoni, in his lengthy account of the passage of plague through the duchy of Milan in 1630, is avowedly committed to presenting a more accurate, less reductive view than his historical sources. But even these two complex narratives reinforce some of the perennial, simplifying ideas about plague.

One feature of the usual script for plague: the disease invariably comes from somewhere else. The names for syphilis, when it began its epidemic sweep through Europe in the last decade of the fifteenth century, are an exemplary illustration of the need to make a dreaded disease foreign.[1] It was the "French pox" to the English, *morbus Germanicus* to the Parisians, the Naples sickness to the Florentines, the Chinese disease to the Japanese. But what may seem like a joke about the inevitability of chauvinism reveals a more important truth: that there is a link between imagining disease and imagining foreignness. It lies perhaps in the very concept of wrong, which is archaically identical with the non-us, the alien. A polluting person is always wrong, as Mary Douglas has observed. The inverse is also true: a person judged to be wrong is regarded as, at least potentially, a source of pollution.

The foreign place of origin of important illnesses, as of drastic changes in the weather, may be no more remote than a neighboring country. Illness is a species of invasion, and indeed is often carried by soldiers. Manzoni's account of the plague of 1630 (chapters 31 to 37) begins:

> The plague which the Tribunal of Health had feared might enter the Milanese provinces with the German troops had in fact entered, as is well known; and it is also well known that it did not stop there, but went on to invade and depopulate a large part of Italy.

Defoe's chronicle of the plague of 1665 begins similarly, with a flurry of ostentatiously scrupulous speculation about its foreign origin:

1. As noted in the first accounts of the disease: "This malady received from different peoples whom it affected different names," writes Giovanni di Vigo in 1514. Like earlier treatises on syphilis, written in Latin—by Nicolo Leoniceno (1497) and by Juan Almenar (1502)—the one by di Vigo calls it *morbus Gallicus*, the French disease. (Excerpts from this and other accounts of the period, including *Syphilis: Or a Poetical History of the French Disease* [1530] by Girolamo Fracastoro, who coined the name that prevailed, are in *Classic Descriptions of Disease*, edited by Ralph H. Major [1932].) Moralistic explanations abounded from the beginning. In 1495, a year after the epidemic started, the Emperor Maximilian issued an edict declaring syphilis to be an affliction from God for the sins of men.

The theory that syphilis came from even farther than a neighboring country, that it was an entirely new disease in Europe, a disease of the New World brought back to the Old by sailors of Columbus who had contracted it in America, became the accepted explanation of the origin of syphilis in the sixteenth century and is still widely credited. It is worth noting that the earliest medical writers on syphilis did not accept the dubious theory. Leoniceno's *Libellus de Epidemia, quam vulgo morbum Gallicum vocant* starts by taking up the question of whether "the French disease under another name was common to the ancients," and says he believes firmly that it was.

It was about the beginning of September, 1664, that I, among the rest of my neighbours, heard in ordinary discourse that the plague was returned again in Holland; for it had been very violent there, and particularly at Amsterdam and Rotterdam, in the year 1663, whither, they say, it was brought, some said from Italy, others from the Levant, among some goods which were brought home by their Turkey fleet; others said it was brought from Candia; others from Cyprus. It mattered not from whence it came; but all agreed it was come into Holland again.

The bubonic plague that reappeared in London in the 1720s had arrived from Marseilles, which was where plague in the eighteenth century was usually thought to enter Western Europe: brought by seamen, then transported by soldiers and merchants. By the nineteenth century the foreign origin was usually more exotic, the means of transport less specifically imagined, and the illness itself had become phantasmagorical, symbolic.

At the end of *Crime and Punishment* Raskolnikov dreams of plague: "He dreamt that the whole world was condemned to a terrible new strange plague that had come to Europe from the depths of Asia." At the beginning of the sentence it is "the whole world," which turns out by the end of the sentence to be "Europe," afflicted by a lethal visitation from Asia. Dostoevsky's model is undoubtedly cholera, called Asiatic cholera, long endemic in Bengal, which had rapidly become and remained through most of the nineteenth century a worldwide epidemic disease. Part of the centuries-old conception of Europe as a privileged cultural entity is that it is a place which is colonized by lethal diseases coming from elsewhere. Europe is assumed to be by rights free of disease. (And Europeans have been astoundingly callous about the far more devastating extent to which they—as invaders, as colonists—have introduced *their* diseases to the exotic "primitive" world: think of the ravages of smallpox, influenza, and cholera on the aboriginal populations of the Americas and Australia.) The tenacity of the connection of exotic origin with dreaded disease is one reason why cholera, of which there were four great outbreaks in Europe in the nineteenth century, each with a lower death toll than the preceding one, has continued to be more memorable than smallpox, whose ravages increased as the century went on (half a million died in the European smallpox pandemic of the early 1870s) but which could not be construed as, plague-like, a disease with a non-European origin.

Plagues are no longer "sent," as in Biblical and Greek antiquity, for the question of agency has blurred. Instead, peoples are "visited" by plagues. And the visitations recur, as is taken for granted in the subtitle of Defoe's narrative, which explains that it is about that "which happened in London during the Last Great Visitation in 1665." Even for non-Europeans, lethal disease may be called a visitation. But a visitation on "them" is invariably described as different from one on "us." "I believe that about one half of the whole people was carried off by this visitation," wrote the English traveler Alexander Kinglake, reaching Cairo at a time of the bubonic plague (sometimes called "oriental plague"). "The Orientals, however, have more quiet fortitude than Europeans under afflictions of this sort." Kinglake's influential book *Eothen* (1844)—suggestively subtitled "Traces of Travel Brought Home from the East"—illustrates many of the enduring Eurocentric presumptions about others, starting from the fantasy that peoples with little reason to expect exemption from misfortune have a lessened capacity to *feel* misfortune. Thus it is believed that Asians (or the poor, or blacks, or Africans, or Muslims) don't suffer or don't grieve as Europeans (or whites) do. The fact that illness is associated with the poor—who are, from the perspective of the privileged, aliens in one's midst—reinforces the association of illness with the foreign: with an exotic, often primitive place.

Thus, illustrating the classic script for plague, AIDS is thought to have started in the "dark continent," then spread to Haiti, then to the United States and to Europe, then . . . It is understood as a tropical disease: another infestation from the so-called Third World, which is after all where most people in the world live, as well as a scourge of the *tristes tropiques*. Africans who detect racist stereotypes in much of the speculation about the geographical origin of AIDS are not wrong. (Nor are they wrong in thinking that depictions of Africa as the cradle of AIDS must feed anti-African prejudices in Europe and Asia.) The subliminal connection made to notions about a primitive past and the many hypotheses that have been fielded about possible transmission from animals (a disease of green monkeys? African swine fever?) cannot help but activate a familiar set of stereotypes about animality, sexual license, and blacks. In Zaire and other countries in Central Africa where AIDS is killing tens of thousands, the counterreaction has begun. Many doctors, academics, journalists, government officials, and other educated people believe that the virus was sent to Africa from the United States, an act of bacteriological warfare (whose aim was to decrease the African birth rate) which got out of hand and has returned to afflict its perpetrators. A common African version of this belief about the disease's provenance has the virus fabricated in a CIA-Army laboratory in Maryland, sent from there to Africa, and brought back to its country of origin by American homosexual missionaries returning from Africa to Maryland.[2]

2. The rumor may not have originated as a KGB-sponsored "disinformation" campaign, but it received a crucial push from Soviet propaganda specialists. In October 1985 the Soviet weekly *Literaturnaya Gazeta* published an article alleging that the AIDS virus had been engineered by the U.S. government during biological warfare research at Fort Detrick, Maryland, and was being spread abroad by U.S. servicemen who had been used as guinea pigs. The source cited was an article in the Indian newspaper *Patriot*. Repeated on Moscow's "Radio Peace and Progress" in English, the story was taken up by newspapers and magazines throughout the world. A year later it was featured on the front page of London's conservative, mass-circulation *Sunday Express*. ("The killer AIDS virus was artificially created by American scientists during laboratory experiments which went disastrously wrong—and a massive cover-up has kept the secret from the world until today.") Though ignored by most American newspapers, the *Sunday Express* story was recycled in virtually every other country.

At first it was assumed that AIDS must become widespread elsewhere in the same catastrophic form in which it has emerged in Africa, and those who still think this will eventually happen invariably invoke the Black Death. The plague metaphor is an essential vehicle of the most pessimistic reading of the epidemiological prospects. From classic fiction to the latest journalism, the standard plague story is of inexorability, inescapability. The unprepared are taken by surprise; those observing the recommended precautions are struck down as well. *All* succumb when the story is told by an omniscient narrator, as in Poe's parable "The Masque of the Red Death" (1842), inspired by an account of a ball held in Paris during the cholera epidemic of 1832. Almost all—if the story is told from the point of view of a traumatized witness, who will be a benumbed survivor, as in Jean Giono's Stendhalian novel *Horseman on the Roof* (1951), in which a young Italian nobleman in exile wanders through cholera-stricken southern France in the 1830s.

Plagues are invariably regarded as judgments on society, and the metaphoric inflation of AIDS into such a judgment also accustoms people to the inevitability of global spread. This is a traditional use of sexually transmitted diseases: to be described as punishments not just of individuals but of a group ("generally licentiousnes"). Not only venereal diseases have been used in this way, to identify transgressing or vicious populations. Interpreting any catastrophic epidemic as a sign of moral laxity or political decline was as common until the later part of the last century as associating dreaded diseases with foreignness. (Or with despised and feared minorities.) And the assignment of fault is not contradicted by cases that do not fit. The Methodist preachers in England who connected the cholera epidemic of 1832 with drunkenness (the temperance movement was just starting) were not understood to be claiming that *everybody* who got cholera was a drunkard: there is always room for "innocent victims" (children, young women). Tuberculosis, in its identity as a disease of the poor (rather than of the "sensitive"), was also linked by late-nineteenth-century reformers to alcoholism. Responses to illnesses associated with sinners and the poor invariably recommended the adoption of middle-class values: the regular habits, productivity, and emotional self-control to which drunkenness was thought the chief impediment.[3] Health itself was eventually identified with these values, which were religious as well as mercantile, health being evidence of

As recently as the summer of 1987, it appeared in newspapers in Kenya, Peru, Sudan, Nigeria, Senegal, and Mexico. Gorbachev-era policies have since produced an official denial of the allegations by two eminent members of the Soviet Academy of Sciences, which was published in *Izvestia* in late October 1987. But the story is still being repeated—from Mexico to Zaire, from Australia to Greece.

3. According to the more comprehensive diagnosis favored by secular reformers, cholera was the result of poor diet and "indulgence in irregular habits." Officials of the Central Board of Health in London warned that there were no specific treatments for the disease, and advised paying attention to fresh air and cleanliness, though "the true preventatives are a healthy body and a cheerful, unruffled mind." Quoted in R. J. Morris, *Cholera 1832* (1976).

virtue as disease was of depravity. The dictum that cleanliness is next to godliness is to be taken quite literally. The succession of cholera epidemics in the nineteenth century shows a steady waning of religious interpretations of the disease; more precisely, these increasingly coexisted with other explanations. Although, by the time of the epidemic of 1866, cholera was commonly understood not simply as a divine punishment but as the consequence of remediable defects of sanitation, it was still regarded as the scourge of the sinful. A writer in *The New York Times* declared (April 22, 1866): "Cholera is especially the punishment of neglect of sanitary laws; it is the curse of the dirty, the intemperate, and the degraded."[4]

That it now seems unimaginable for cholera or a similar disease to be regarded in this way signifies not a lessened capacity to moralize about diseases but only a change in the kind of illnesses that are used didactically. Cholera was perhaps the last major epidemic disease fully qualifying for plague status for almost a century. (I mean cholera as a European and American, therefore a nineteenth-century, disease; until 1817 there had never been a cholera epidemic outside the Far East.) Influenza, which would seem more plague-like than any other epidemic in this century if loss of life were the main criterion, and which struck as suddenly as cholera and killed as quickly, usually in a few days, was never viewed metaphorically as a plague. Nor was a more recent epidemic, polio. One reason why plague notions were not invoked is that these epidemics did not have enough of the attributes perennially ascribed to plagues. (For instance, polio was construed as typically a disease of children—of the innocent.) The more important reason is that there has been a shift in the focus of the moralistic exploitation of illness. This shift, to diseases that can be interpreted as judgments on the individual, makes it harder to use epidemic disease as such. For a long time cancer was the illness that best fitted this secular culture's need to blame and punish and censor through the imagery of disease. Cancer was a disease of an individual, and understood as the result not of an action but rather of a failure to act (to be prudent, to exert proper self-control, or to be properly expressive). In the twentieth century it has become almost impossible to moralize about epidemics—except those which are transmitted sexually.

The persistence of the belief that illness reveals, and is a punishment for, moral laxity or turpitude can be seen in another way, by noting the persistence of descriptions of disorder or corruption as a disease. So indispensable has been the plague metaphor in bringing summary judgments about social crisis that its use hardly abated during the era when collective diseases were no longer treated so moralistically—the time between the influenza and encephalitis pandemics of the early and mid-1920s and the acknowledgment of a new, mysterious epidemic illness in the early 1980s—and when great infectious epidemics were so often and

4. Quoted in Charles E. Rosenberg, *The Cholera Years: The United States in 1832, 1849, and 1866* (1962).

confidently proclaimed a thing of the past.[5] The plague metaphor was common in the 1930s as a synonym for social and psychic catastrophe. Evocations of plague of this type usually go with rant, with antiliberal attitudes: think of Artaud on theatre and plague, of Wilhelm Reich on "emotional plague." And such a generic "diagnosis" necessarily promotes antihistorical thinking. A theodicy as well as a demonology, it not only stipulates something emblematic of evil but makes this the bearer of a rough, terrible justice. In Karel Čapek's *The White Plague* (1937), the loathsome pestilence that has appeared in a state where fascism has come to power afflicts only those over the age of forty, those who could be held morally responsible.

Written on the eve of the Nazi takeover of Czechoslovakia, Čapek's allegorical play is something of an anomaly—the use of the plague metaphor to convey the menace of what is defined as barbaric by a mainstream European liberal. The play's mysterious, grisly malady is something like leprosy, a rapid, invariably fatal leprosy that is supposed to have come, of course, from Asia. But Čapek is not interested in identifying political evil with the incursion of the foreign. He scores his didactic points by focusing not on the disease itself but on the management of information about it by scientists, journalists, and politicians. The most famous specialist in the disease harangues a reporter ("The disease of the hour, you might say. A good five million have died of it to date, twenty million have it and at least three times as many are going about their business, blithely unaware of the marble-like, marble-sized spots on their bodies"); chides a fellow doctor for using the popular terms, "the white plague" and "Peking leprosy," instead of the scientific name, "the Cheng Syndrome"; fantasizes about how his clinic's work on identifying the new virus and finding a cure ("every clinic in the world has an intensive research program") will add to the prestige of science and win a Nobel Prize for its discoverer; revels in hyperbole when it is thought a cure has been found ("it was the most dangerous disease in all history, worse than the bubonic plague"); and outlines plans for sending those with symptoms to well-guarded detention camps ("Given that every carrier of the disease is a potential spreader of the disease, we *must* protect the uncontaminated from the contaminated. All sentimentality in this regard is fatal and therefore criminal"). However cartoonish Čapek's ironies may seem, they are a not improbable sketch of catastrophe (medical, ecological) as a managed public event in modern mass society. And however conventionally he deploys the plague metaphor, as an agency of retribution (in the end the plague strikes down the dictator himself), Čapek's feel for public relations leads him to make explicit in the play the under-

5. As recently as 1983, the historian William H. McNeill, author of *Plagues and Peoples*, started his review of a new history of the Black Death by asserting: "One of the things that separate us from our ancestors and make contemporary experience profoundly different from that of other ages is the disappearance of epidemic disease as a serious factor in human life" (*The New York Review of Books*, July 21, 1983). The Eurocentric presumption of this and many similar statements hardly needs pointing out.

standing of disease as a metaphor. The eminent doctor declares the accomplishments of science to be as nothing compared with the merits of the dictator, about to launch a war, "who has averted a far worse scourge: the scourge of anarchy, the leprosy of corruption, the epidemic of barbaric liberty, the plague of social disintegration fatally sapping the organism of our nation."

Camus's *The Plague*, which appeared a decade later, is a far less literal use of plague by another great European liberal, as subtle as Čapek's *The White Plague* is schematic. Camus's novel is not, as is sometimes said, a political allegory in which the outbreak of bubonic plague in a Mediterranean port city represents the Nazi occupation. This plague is not retributive. Camus is not protesting anything, not corruption or tyranny, not even mortality. The plague is no more or less than an exemplary event, the irruption of death that gives life its seriousness. His use of plague, more epitome than metaphor, is detached, stoic, aware—it is not about bringing judgment. But, as in Čapek's play, characters in Camus's novel declare how unthinkable it is to have a plague in the twentieth century . . . as if the belief that such a calamity could not happen, could not happen *anymore*, means that it must.

GEORGE WHITMORE

Epilogue to *Someone Was Here* †

Early in 1985, when I suggested an article to the editors of *The New York Times Magazine* on "the human cost of AIDS," most reporting on the epidemic was scientific in nature and people with AIDS were often portrayed as faceless victims. I wanted to show the devastating impact AIDS was having on individual lives. It had certainly had an impact on mine. I was pretty sure I was carrying the virus and I was terrified.

Plainly, some of my reasons for wanting to write about AIDS were altruistic, others selfish. AIDS was decimating the community around me; there was a need to bear witness. AIDS had turned me and others like me into walking time-bombs; there was a need to strike back, not just sit and wait to die. What I didn't fully appreciate then, however, was the extent to which I was trying to bargain with AIDS: if I wrote about it, maybe I wouldn't get it.

My article on Jim Sharp and Edward Dunn ran in the *Times Magazine* in May 1985. But AIDS didn't keep its part of the bargain. Less

---

† George Whitmore's *Someone Was Here: Profiles in the AIDS Epidemic* is composed of three extended profiles of different communities coming to terms with AIDS. The author was a novelist, playwright, and journalist who died in 1989. Copyright © 1988 by George Whitmore. Used by permission of New American Library, a division of Penguin Books USA Inc.

than a year later, after discovering a small strawberry-colored spot on my calf, I was diagnosed with Kaposi's sarcoma.

Ironically, I'd just agreed to write this book. The prospect suddenly seemed absurd and out of the question, but "Write it," my doctor urged without hesitation. And on reflection, I had to agree. I don't believe in anything like fate. And yet clearly, along with what looked like a losing hand, I'd just been dealt the assignment of a lifetime.

Needless to say, reporting on the epidemic from my particular point of view has had its advantages and handicaps, but they're perhaps not the obvious ones. If I felt a special affinity for Manuella Rocha, it wasn't in small part due to the fact that I recognized in her eyes the same thing I saw in my own mother's eyes the day I gave her the news about myself. If I was scared sitting for hours in an airless room with a bunch of addicts with AIDS, it wasn't because I was scared of *them*. It was because their confusion and rage were precisely what I was feeling myself. The journalist's vaunted shield of objectivity was of little use at times like those. On the contrary, what counted most in the long run—on this story at least—was not my ability to function as a disinterested observer, but my ability to identify with my so-called subjects.

Nevertheless, long after I began writing, I worried about the morality, and even the feasibility, of producing a documentary-style piece of reportage like the one I'd contracted for—that is, without literally putting myself into it, in the first person, so to speak. It wasn't until I returned to the transcripts of my original interviews with Jim Sharp that I realized Jim was now speaking for me, too. Jim's grief, his despair, his terror—they were mine, too. But Jim's special gift was for anger. Life-affirming anger was the lesson Jim taught me, and anger has enabled me to write about the ocean of pain that engulfs us without drowning in it.

When I met Jim, I have to confess, I could only see a dying man. A chasm separated me from him and all the other men with AIDS I interviewed. Even though they were gay, as I am, even though most of them were my own age, even though after I left those interviews I had to stop on the street to cry, each one of them remained safely "on the other side of the fence" for me. But now, for good or ill, there is no "other side of the fence" and no safety.

When I first met Jim, I could only see a dying man. Last summer in Houston, when Jim came to his front door to greet me, I met myself.

A few months after my article on him ran in the *Times*, Jim announced without fanfare that he was moving back to Houston, accepting an old friend's longstanding offer of a room and sanctuary. Since I'd first interviewed them, there had been plenty of indications that Jim and Dennis weren't going to be able to make a go of it, so I wasn't surprised. Jim needed, he said, to be with people who loved and understood him best.

On the morning of his departure, Jim called and asked if I'd do him a favor. He had some parcels he needed to ship to Houston. Could I take care of them for him? A car service was going to drive him to the airport that afternoon and he'd drop the boxes by my place on his way out of town.

I met Jim at his apartment to say good-bye. The little studio had taken on a distinctly Gothic flavor since I first saw it. Dennis had brought some of his furniture out of storage—dark, carved Germanic pieces that included straight-backed chairs suitable for a rectory. A pewlike bench with carved finials stood at the foot of the bed. The funeral atmosphere was augmented by black walls.

The place was tidy. Jim was packed and ready to go. We sat and talked a while, waiting for the car, both avoiding saying what was really on our minds. I felt sad for Jim.

"You know if you ever need anything whatsoever, I'm as close as the phone."

"Sure, sure."

He didn't seem to believe it.

Jim watched through the shutters. At the appointed hour, the car pulled up across the street. The driver came in and picked up some bags. Jim insisted on carrying one himself.

We got everything into the car and, while the driver and I waited, Jim locked up. Crossing the street, he looked defeated and frail. He got into the back of the car. His cane, the one Dennis had given him for Valentine's Day, was at his side. I sat up front with the driver and gave him directions to my apartment.

We drove down Carmine Street, past the corner grocery where Jim bought his cigarettes—by the pack, as if that made them somehow less lethal—past the coffeehouse where Jim and I had once spent a pleasant hour without mentioning AIDS once, past our Lady of Pompeii, past the pasta shop, the luncheonette, the bagel store. This was my neighborhood, too.

As the car turned up Sixth Avenue, I felt a need to memorize the scene before my eyes—pedestrians crossing the intersection against the light, the sun falling on the brick facades of the apartment houses, the olive-drab leaves on the trees. I turned in my seat to look back at Jim. He was staring out the window, in his own trance. I was sure I'd never see him alive again.

Soon after the *Times* article on him and Jim was published, Edward Dunn brought me a gift. It was a little teddy bear—a nice ginger-colored teddy bear with a gingham ribbon tied around its neck. Since I didn't collect toys, I didn't know quite what to make of it. But Edward explained to me that he often gave teddy bears to friends because they represented warmth and gentleness to him. Later, he asked me what I was going to name mine.

"I hadn't thought of naming it."

"Oh, you have to name him," Edward said.

"I don't know, what do you think?"

"I thought you might call him Robert."

Since Robert was the pseudonym we'd chosen for his late lover, I saw Edward's gift in a new light. I realized that after the grueling interviews I'd put him through, Edward was paying me an enormous compliment. He was, in a way, placing a share of Robert's memory in my hands.

That fall, after over 20 years in New York, Edward moved to Los Angeles, saying it was time to begin a new life. Perhaps grandiosely, I wondered if our interviews didn't play a part in Edward's decision to leave the city—that they'd served as something of a catharsis or a watershed.

Over the next year and a half, "Robert" sat on the bookshelf in the hall and only came down when the cat knocked him down. Every once in a while I'd find "Robert" on the floor, dust him off and put him back on the shelf. I felt vaguely guilty about "Robert." I was no longer in touch with Edward.

One gloomy Saturday afternoon, a month after I began visiting Lincoln Hospital, I interviewed Sr. Fran Whelan at her home in East Harlem. That day she told me about the child I've called Frederico and I asked if I could meet him.

"If you go up with me. Then the nurses on the floor won't get upset."

"Why would they get upset?"

"They would wonder who you are. And then, too, I had a seminary student working with me and she wanted to do something in pediatrics. She told me that when she didn't wear gloves and that kind of thing, when she'd just play with him, they'd get upset."

That next week, I went up to the fourth floor with Sr. Fran. Frederico was asleep. The room was dim.

I peered into Frederico's crib. He was wearing mitts that day because he hadn't been eating well and they'd had to insert a feeding tube into one nostril.

There was a din from the hall—children crying, conversation, slamming doors.

"Kids develop a high tolerance for noise," Sr. Fran commented. "If you're tired, you sleep."

I peered into the crib. I heard a ringing in my ears. I almost bolted out of the room. Somehow, I kept my two feet planted where they were on the floor.

I'd seen eyes unblinking from lesions. I'd spoken to deaf ears. I'd held the hand of the dying man. But nothing had prepared me for this.

I wanted to snatch Frederico out of his crib, snatch him up and run away, run away with him. It was horribly, cruelly clear that I wanted for him what I wanted for myself, and I was powerless.

Later, as I walked down the hall beside Sr. Fran, I struggled to retain my composure. I hadn't, of course, told anyone at the hospital that I had AIDS.

"It's good the nurse saw you with us," Sr. Fran was saying. "Now you can come visit him lots, whenever you like, and there'll be no questions." In her quiet way, Sr. Fran is a real snakecharmer. She knew I'd go back.

And I did, more than once. I held Frederico in my arms. He smelled like piss and baby powder and he was quite a handful. He squirmed in my arms. I was a stranger. He didn't know me. He wanted to be put down.

The day I first saw Frederico, when Sr. Fran was distracted for a moment, I took "Robert" out of the plastic bag I was carrying and set him down among the other stuffed animals in the crib. I knew Edward would approve. What I didn't know was that Edward had AIDS and would die before the year was out.

It's taken me months to write this. I'm afraid to finish this book. I'm afraid of what will happen next.

When I met Jim, all I could see was a dying man. The day he left New York, I was sure I'd never see him alive again. But I did see him again, in Houston last time. He lives in a modest bungalow house on a tree-lined street. He's something of a celebrity. Until recently, he served on the board of the local AIDS foundation and he spends lots of time every day on the phone, dispensing comfort and advice to other people with AIDS. Among his other distinctions, Jim is probably the only man with AIDS in Texas who's lived long enough to collect Medicaid there.

A week after I got back from Texas, Mr. Schult called to tell me Frederico was dead.

Things had finally been looking up for Frederico. Sr. Barletta had finally gotten him into day care. The agency had finally placed him in a foster home. But on his second night outside the hospital, inexplicably, Frederico turned blue. By the time the ambulance arrived, he was dead. For some reason, the emergency medical service didn't even try to revive him.

I went to the funeral home. Frederico lay in a little coffin lined with swagged white satin. He was dressed in a blue playsuit with speedboats on it.

"You dressed him in a playsuit," I said to Mr. Schult.

"And now he's at play," Mr. Schult sobbed, at my side. "He's romping in heaven now with Jesus like he never was able to down here."

I held Mr. Schult's arm tightly until the sobbing passed. The coffin was too small for the top of catafalaque. You could see gouges and scrapes and scars in the wood in the parts the coffin didn't cover. I looked down at the body in the coffin, beyond help. I agreed aloud with Mr. Schult that Frederico was in heaven now because it seemed to make him feel a little better.

I don't know why, but I always thought Frederico would live.

New York City
December 1987

Public Informational Material about AIDS †

Our society is using the same methods of distributing information on AIDS that Defoe's did in 1665 and 1720. Posters, brochures, and handbills are aimed at educating the public, helping them prevent infection, and urging them to get proper treatment. Just as they were in Defoe's time, they are often in simple lists or eye-catching question-answer form.

AIDS

AIDS is a disease caused by a virus which enters the body. When this happens, the body's defenses can have trouble fighting off other diseases. The virus is most often spread through semen and blood, mainly through sexual activity and sharing needles. It is not spread by casual contact.

You are in greatest danger of getting AIDS . . .

• If you have had sex with someone who is already infected.
• If you have shared I.V. drug "works" (needles, syringes, etc.).
Babies can be infected during pregnancy

Is there a test for AIDS?

There is no blood test for AIDS. There is a blood test to detect the presence of the antibody to HIV, the virus which causes AIDS. Blood banks are now using the test to screen donated blood to detect if donors have been exposed to the virus. You can be tested to find out if at some time you were exposed to the virus and now have the antibody. You can get the test from your own doctor or clinic, or at a testing site set up by the New York City Department of Health.

How Don't You Get AIDS?

• You don't get AIDS from sharing meals, shaking hands or touching doorknobs.

† Reprinted from an information card and from the New York State Department of Health brochure "What Parents Need to Tell Children about AIDS." I am grateful for permission to publish.

- You don't get AIDS from swimming pools, showers, drinking fountains or toilet seats.
- You don't get AIDS from being in school or at work with someone who has AIDS.
- You don't get AIDS from hugging, petting or cuddling.
- You don't get AIDS by donating blood.
- You don't get AIDS from being near or even from living with a person who has AIDS.
- The AIDS virus is *not* in the air. It's in blood, semen and other body fluids.

CRITICISM

SIR WALTER SCOTT

Daniel De Foe †

*   *   *

That De Foe was a man of powerful intellect and lively imagination is obvious from his works; that he was possessed of an ardent temper, a resolute courage, and an unwearied spirit of enterprise, is ascertained by the events of his changeful career; and whatever may be thought of that rashness and improvidence, by which his progress in life was so frequently impeded, there seems no reason to withhold from him the praise of as much, nay more, integrity, sincerity, and consistency, than could have been expected in a political author writing for bread, and whose chief protector, Harley, was latterly of a different party from his own. As the author of *Robinson Crusoe*, his fame promises to endure as long as the language in which he wrote.

*   *   *

We must, in the first place, remark that the fertility of De Foe was astonishing. He wrote on all occasions, and on all subjects, and seemingly had little time for preparation upon the subject in hand, but treated it from the stores which his memory retained of early reading, and such hints as he had caught up in society, not one of which seems to have been lost upon him. A complete list of De Foe's works, notwithstanding the exertions of the late George Chalmers, has not yet been procured, and a perfect collection even of such books as he is well known to have written can scarce be procured, even by the most active bibliomaniac. The preceding memoir[1] does not notice one half of his compositions, all, even the meanest of which, have something in them to distinguish them as the works of an extraordinary man. It cannot, therefore, be doubted that he possessed a powerful memory to furnish him with materials, and a no less copious vein of imagination to weave them up into a web of his own, and supply the rich embroidery which in reality constitutes their chief value. De Foe does not display much acquaintance with classic learning, neither does it appear that his attendance on the Newington seminary had led him deep into the study of ancient languages. His own language is genuine English, often simple even to vulgarity, but always so distinctly impressive that its very vulgarity had, as we shall presently show, an efficacy in giving an air of truth or probability to the

---

† Sir Walter Scott, the Scottish poet, novelist, and critic, was one of the first collectors of Defoe's work (exactly what Defoe wrote is still a matter of dispute). The excerpt is from Scott's *Lives of the Novelists*. Notes are by the editor.

1. The biographical part of the original essay on Defoe was by John Ballantyne, who published one of the first collections of Defoe's novels and best-known works (1810).

facts and sentiments it conveys. Exclusive of politics, De Foe's studies led chiefly to those popular narratives, which are the amusement of children and of the lower classes; those accounts of travellers who have visited remote countries; of voyagers who have made discoveries of new lands and strange nations; of pirates and buccaneers who have acquired wealth by their desperate adventures on the ocean.

*   *   *

Shylock[2] observes, there are land thieves and water thieves; and as De Foe was familiar with the latter, so he was not without some knowledge of the practices and devices of the former. We are afraid we must impute to his long and repeated imprisonments the opportunity of becoming acquainted with the secrets of thieves and mendicants, their acts of plunder, concealment, and escape. But whatever way he acquired his knowledge of low life, De Foe certainly possessed it in the most extensive sense, and applied it in the composition of several works of fiction, in the style termed by the Spaniards *Gusto Picaresco*, of which no man was ever a greater master. This class of the fictitious narrative may be termed the Romance of Roguery, the subjects being the adventures of thieves, rogues, vagabonds, and swindlers, including viragoes and courtesans. The improved taste of the present age has justly rejected this coarse species of amusement, which is, besides, calculated to do an infinite deal of mischief among the lower classes, as it presents in a comic, or even heroic shape, the very crimes and vices to which they are otherwise most likely to be tempted. Nevertheless, the strange and blackguard scenes which De Foe describes are fit to be compared to the gipsy-boys of the Spanish painter Murillo,[3] which are so justly admired, as being, in truth of conception, and spirit of execution, the very *chef d'oeuvres* of art, however low and loathsome the originals from which they are taken. Of this character is the *History of Colonel Jack*, for example, which had an immense popularity among the lower classes; that of *Moll Flanders*, a shoplifter and prostitute; that of *Mrs. Christian Davis*, called *Mother Ross*;[4] and that of *Roxana*, as she is termed, a courtesan in higher life. All of these contain strong marks of genius; in the last they are particularly predominant. But from the coarseness of the narrative, and the vice and vulgarity of the actors, the reader feels as a well-principled young man may do, when seduced by some entertaining and dissolute libertine into scenes of debauchery, that, though he may be amused, he must be

---

2. Shakespeare's character, *The Merchant of Venice*.

3. Bartolomé Esteban Murillo (1617–82). This comparison is not entirely complimentary. Murillo was largely self-taught and for many years sold his small paintings in marketplaces. Lord Treasurer Godolphin once paid eight guineas (a little more than £8) for "some boxes" of Murillo's paintings, and John Evelyn declared that "deare enough." Murillo's fame is now based on the paintings he did for the Convent of San Francisco in Seville.

4. Defoe did not write *The Life and Adventures of Mrs. Christian Davies, commonly call'd Mother Ross; who, in Several Campaigns under King William and the late Duke of Marlborough, In the Quality of a Foot-Soldier and Dragoon, Gave many signal Proofs of an unparallel'd Courage and Personal Bravery* (1739).

not a little ashamed of that which furnishes the entertainment. So that, though we could select from these *picaresque* romances a good deal that is not a little amusing, we let them pass by, as we would persons, howsoever otherwise interesting, who may not be in character and manners entirely fit for good society.

A second species of composition, to which the author's active and vigorous genius was peculiarly adapted, was the account of great national convulsions, whether by war, or by the pestilence, or the tempest. These were tales which are sure, when even moderately well told, to arrest the attention, and which, narrated with that impression of reality which De Foe knew so well how to convey, make the hair bristle and the skin creep. In this manner he has written the *Memoirs of a Cavalier*, which have been often read and quoted as a real production of a real personage.

* * *

The *History of the Great Plague in London* is one of that particular class of compositions which hovers between romance and history. Undoubtedly De Foe embodied a number of traditions upon this subject with what he might actually have read, or of which he might otherwise have received direct evidence. The subject is hideous almost to disgust, yet, even had he not been the author of *Robinson Crusoe*, De Foe would have deserved immortality for the genius which he has displayed in this work, as well as in the *Memoirs of a Cavalier*. This dreadful disease, which, in the language of Scripture, might be described as "the pestilence which walketh in darkness, and the destruction that wasteth at noonday," was indeed a fit subject for a pencil so veracious as that of De Foe; and, accordingly, he drew pictures almost too horrible to look upon.

* * *

LOUIS A. LANDA

[Religion, Science, and Medicine in A *Journal of the Plague Year*] †

A *Journal of the Plague Year*, professedly an authentic account of the Great London Plague in 1665, was published in the spring of 1722,[1] a year in which its indefatigable author also published, among other works, two of his novels, *Moll Flanders* and *Colonel Jack*. Defoe's name was not on the title-page of the *Journal*. Instead it is ascribed to 'a Citizen who continued all the while in London'; and on the final page the citizen is identified by the initials H.F. Tradition has it that the initials

† From the Introduction to A *Journal of the Plague Year* (Oxford: Oxford English Novels, 1969). Reprinted by permission of Oxford University Press.

1. It was advertised in *The Post-Boy* 15–17 Mar., and in *The Daily Courant*, 19 Mar. 1722.

stand for Defoe's uncle, Henry Foe, a saddler who lived in Aldgate. Although we have no firm evidence, it is not unlikely that Henry Foe remained in London during the Plague and certainly not improbable that the youthful Daniel Defoe, aged fourteen when his uncle died, heard of his relative's experiences at first hand. That Defoe should adopt Henry Foe's initials and occupation for the putative narrator of the *Journal* must strike one as more than mere coincidence. Nevertheless, it is fruitless to speculate on the identity of H.F., or to presume that the uncle (or some unknown person) prepared a journal of the Plague which was later available to Defoe. The most easily acceptable hypothesis is that the *Journal* presents one more instance of a device characteristic of Defoe's narratives, the fictional *persona* relating his experiences; and the book itself may be accepted without cavil as the fruit of that remarkable surge of energy and imagination which characterized Defoe in 1722, his *annus mirabilis*.

The immediate stimulus to the writing of the *Journal* was the epidemic raging in the south of France in 1720, in the city and region of Marseilles, an event which generated dire apprehension in England and prompted the publication of a formidable number of tracts about plague, some reprinted from 1665 and some new ones, setting forth cures and preventive measures in the event that England was visited again. Defoe is thus one of a chorus; but it is misleading to view his *Journal* merely as the product of the moment, the result of a single event written on impulse or, as has been suggested, composed in support of austere measures, as a quarantine of ships, to prevent bringing infected goods into England.[2] However plausible this view may be, we do better to consider the *Journal* not as an isolated work: it is, in fact, the culmination of a persistent interest in plague expressed in Defoe's writing for at least a decade before he wrote the *Journal*. The very idea of plague seems to have been an abiding fact in his consciousness, perhaps implanted by his childhood memories or by his reading, perhaps by the concern he shared with his contemporaries that England lay constantly under the threat of another epidemic such as the awesome one of 1665. Even in the so-called plague-free years of the seventeenth century, sporadic cases of plague occurred; and many Englishmen accepted the inevitability of epidemics. Witness the ominous words of one of Defoe's most distinguished contemporaries, Sir William Petty: 'It is to be remembered that one time with another, a *Plague* happeneth in *London* once in 20 Years, or thereabouts; for in the last hundred Years, between the Years 1582

---

2. See John Robert Moore, *Daniel Defoe: Citizen of the Modern World* (1958), p. 320; and particularly Alfred James Henderson, *London and the National Government, 1721–1742* (1945), pp. 33 ff. Henderson gives a full account of the struggle over the Quarantine Act, in which Defoe played a part. Defoe's various works on the Plague may have helped to create an atmosphere which made the public and the mercantile interest more willing to accept the unpopular Quarantine Act of 1721. At the same time these works, especially *Due Preparations for the Plague* and certain articles in *Applebee's Weekly Journal*, by calling attention to the despotic French measure against plague, reinforced the opposition to Walpole's proposals.

and 1682, there have been five great *Plagues, viz. Anno* 1592, 1603, 1625, 1636 and 1665. And it is to be remembered that the *Plagues* of *London* do commonly kill one fifth part of the *Inhabitants.*'[3]

               ✳   ✳   ✳

[As early as 1709 Defoe began to write extensively about plague and especially about the danger to England of another epidemic.[4]] Then in the autumn of 1720, his fears aroused by the epidemic in Marseilles, he began to write once again of England's danger. In the pages of several periodicals, *The Daily Post, Applebee's Journal*, and *Mist's Journal*, he took occasion no fewer than ten times within the year to describe the horrors and ravages of the plague in France. These journalistic accounts are of special interest because they reflect the frame of mind which prompted Defoe to write his longer works on the plague; and have an additional interest because they put him in the centre of a conflict between the government, then seeking a stringent quarantine act, and mercantile interests opposed to rigorous control of commerce. Despite his lifelong convictions about the importance of trade, Defoe defended the need for a strict quarantine act designed to prevent importations which, it was believed, harboured pestilential particles. Although he was concerned about other emergency measures sought by the government—such despotic regulations as prevailed in France—he approved the Quarantine Act which received royal assent on 12 February 1722.[5] Four days earlier the first of Defoe's plague tracts was published.

Some bent in his temperament turned Defoe easily into a man prophetic and admonitory; and it is apparent that he was in a receptive frame of mind in the autumn of 1720, when plague raged in the south of France, to write a book on the subject in which prophecy, admonition, and practical advice were mingled in proper proportions. This work Defoe titled *Due Preparations for the Plague, as well for Soul as Body.* It appeared on 8 February 1722, little more than a month before the *Journal.*[6] The sub-title of the book is revealing: *Being some seasonable Thoughts upon the visible Approach of the present dreadful Contagion in France, the properest Measures to prevent it, and the great Work of Submitting to it.* In a tone persistently monitory Defoe shows how a family may save both body and soul, the body by 'due preparations' in shutting out the world after diligent, far-sighted arrangements, the soul by understanding that plague is a divine visitation and that one should submit to it by penitence, reformation, and dependence upon infinite mercy. As

---

3. Ibid.
4. Landa, *A Journal of the Plague Year* (Oxford, 1969) xi–xiii *[Editor].*
5. See *Applebee's Journal,* 29 July 1721. This and the other issues of the journals mentioned are reprinted in William Lee, *Daniel Defoe: His Life and Recently Discovered Writings* (1869), ii. 265, 277, 281, 284, 291, 294, 296,

378, 399, 407. For the controversy over the Quarantine Act see Alfred James Henderson, *London and the National Government, 1721–1742: A Study of City Politics and the Walpole Administration* (1945), pp. 33 ff.
6. Advertised in *The Post-Boy* on this date as 'This Day is publish'd, (very proper to be given away)'.

so often in Defoe, the practical and the religious join hands amiably. *Due Preparations* has some resemblances to the *Journal*, a number of parallels in fact and situation; but it suffers greatly by any comparison. The proximity of their publication suggests that Defoe was writing both at the same time. Certainly they were composed within the brief compass of a few weeks, thus raising the question as to why Defoe wished to write two books on the same subject simultaneously or nearly so. Any answer must be surmise. It is possible that he was so possessed by the subject that a single book left him dissatisfied. It is more likely that he thought of the two as different, though complementary. Although *Due Preparations* is narrative in form, it is intended as a manual of instruction, a guide to behaviour both practical and religious. It is utilitarian, an anticipation in spirit of such other works by Defoe as *The Complete English Tradesman* and *A New Family Instructor*. Defoe clearly wanted something more, a tale which would reflect the profound agony, the dark and mysterious tragedy which enveloped London in 1665. The *Journal* was to achieve that.

No other historical event so captivated the mind and imagination of Defoe as did the awesome Plague of London. If it had not occurred, Defoe (one is tempted to say) would have invented it. The problems it posed, the questions it raised—social, religious, economic, philosophic—are similar to the ones found in his works generally, even in the reflective passages of his various novels. Not least in significance is that the tragedy of 1665 was a tragedy of London, a city of perennial fascination to Defoe. There was something voracious in his relation to the metropolis, a zest for every aspect of it, inns, streets, markets, buildings, its beauty *and* its ugliness, that often generates a lyrical energy in his prose when London is the subject. Defoe was the laureate of eighteenth-century London as Dickens was of Victorian London; and what appealed to him most of all was the spectacle of a teeming, bustling, dynamic city, infinitely complex, a pageant of movement and colour, splendid despite its tawdry aspects, impressive and intricate by virtue of the intertwining of the lives and fates of its massive population. What the Great Plague of 1665 presented to Defoe's imagination was London in a wholly different guise, diametrical and yet fascinating in the very magnitude of the change, its vitality withered, its streets deserted, a city desolate, stricken, dying. Although Defoe's *Journal* is many things, it is perhaps first and foremost a story of London. People die by the thousands, families and parishes are decimated, physicians, clergymen, tradesmen, the rich and the poor, are carted off to graves; but these are nameless dead and the tragedies, with a few exceptions, are not individual. Where deaths are so abundant, poignancy is diffused. The real tragedy is corporate. It applies less to this or that person or family, more to the greater organism, the stricken city ravished by plague, its people either fled or dying, its marts closed, its vast energies replaced by silence and inaction. Defoe, I suggest, wished this to be a paramount impression of his narrative; and he has ordered his material to gain that end. He was so intent on depicting a city lying desolate and inert that he may have gone beyond the historical facts. Although large numbers fled and certain activities ceased, we know from Pepys, Evelyn, and others that many of the customary routines of daily life continued; and even Defoe has not wholly obscured this fact, however much he has minimized it.

If the *Journal* is then a historical narrative of London in a year of agony—a variety, so to speak, of local history as limited temporally as it is geographically—it has also an affinity with another kind of 'history' congenial to the age: histories or accounts of natural calamities, of extraordinary manifestations in nature, as storms, floods, earthquakes, fires, blazing stars (i.e. comets), and plagues. Such great and catastrophic events, with their awesome power of destruction, raised questions about the cosmic plan generally and their meaning for man particularly. They generated a perennial strain of philosophic reflection in homiletic literature and elsewhere, whether they dated from biblical times or belonged to the living present. Defoe did not escape their fascination. Almost two decades before he wrote about the Great Plague of London, he had published a work entitled *The Storm* (1704), an account of one of the most dramatic natural calamities of his own day, the 'Dreadful Tempest' which struck England in November 1703, leaving vast destruction in its wake. Like his contemporaries, Defoe had a strong conviction that these convulsions in the microcosm had significance beyond the event itself. 'The treasury of immediate cause', he wrote, 'is generally committed to nature itself' and 'the philosopher's business [i.e. the scientist's] is not to look through nature; but the Christian begins just where the philosopher ends.' The Christian, if he is to understand the true meaning of these striking natural calamities, looks 'to the vast open field of infinite power'. This is a distinction Defoe elaborates in the opening chapters of *The Storm*, and it serves usefully as a comment on the pervasive religious strain in the *Journal*. The *Journal*, as any reader will quickly observe, is not merely the narrative of a great natural calamity; for its narrator, H. F., it becomes a religious experience as well, something to be explained in terms of God's government of 'all his creatures and all their actions'. One of Defoe's deepest convictions was that the life of man is providentially ordered down to the most trivial detail, a view persistently found in his writings, sometimes implicit, at other times explicit, as at the end of *Robinson Crusoe*, where Crusoe explains the ultimate meaning of his strange, surprising adventures: 'And thus I have given the first part of a life of fortune and adventure, a life of Providence's chequer-work.'

Defoe's narrator in the *Journal* is similarly aware that his experiences in the Plague reflect a providential pattern. H. F., like Robinson Crusoe, received signs or intimations from heaven, and is no less the object of 'particular providence'. A man of faith from the beginning, he resolves by his faith the agonizing problem of whether to flee the plague or remain.

He interprets properly certain intimations as the will of heaven that he should remain in London; and he reinforces the divine promptings by the old practice of *Sortes Biblicae* (as did Robinson Crusoe) to discover that he has opened the Bible at the 91st Psalm, which promises him safety from the noisome pestilence 'that walketh in darkness', even though thousands shall die. Thus fortified in his faith, H. F. remains and is untouched by the plague, his deliverance being in his view 'next to miraculous'; and like the 'wonderful Deliverances' of some others, an intimation of 'singular and remarkable Providence in the particular Instances'. Nevertheless, H. F. qualifies this attitude by observing 'that tho' Providence seem'd to direct my Conduct to be otherwise; yet it is my opinion . . . *that the best Physick against the Plague is to run away from it*'.

If the religious attitudes expressed by H. F. appear to be ambivalent, the reason is that Defoe reflects both traditional and contemporary views of plague, as on the one hand a divine visitation and on the other a natural calamity—a viewpoint which invited inconsistencies. As I have implied, Defoe might well have given to his *Journal* the revealing title used by an anonymous pamphleteer of the eighteenth century, *Providence Displayed*. H. F. pauses from time to time to remark on the plague as a 'terrible Judgment upon the whole Nation'. He recognizes that it is from 'the Hand of God': 'I look'd upon this dismal Time to be a particular Season of Divine Vengeance.' It is a moment, he reflects, when God has 'his Sword drawn in his Hand, on purpose to take Vengeance . . . on the whole Nation'. The narrative moves to the accompaniment of such remarks, to a final affirmation near the end as H. F. comments on the utter failure of physicians to discover a cure, understandably since the plague is 'evidently from the secret invisible Hand of him, that had at first sent this Disease as a Judgment upon us'. Even 'those Physicians, who had the least Share of Religion in them, were oblig'd to acknowledge that it was all supernatural, that it was extraordinary, and that no Account [i.e. no scientific or medical explanation] could be given of it'.

As Defoe's narrator meditates philosophically on this great natural calamity, he falls into the phraseology of those who sought the meaning of plagues in the relationship of man to the cosmic order. A plague was ultimately explicable only in a theological or Christian context. To the extent that Defoe relies on this historiography, he is reflecting strong convictions and feelings which possessed people of all degrees in 1665 and 1721, though in passing we may note that this is the kind of history Gibbon was to reject in the second half of the century, history in terms of divine rather than in terms of human or natural causes. The wrath of God theory was a commonplace, its strength derived from both classical and biblical sources and from constant repetition throughout the ages in scores of plague tracts, both medical and lay. Its stress on a punitive deity, on the concept of 'afflictive providence', was congenial to Defoe's way of thinking. Ovid had ascribed the plague at Aegina to 'angry Juno's wrath' (*Metamorphoses*, vii. 532 ff.). The 'divinity' of plagues was affirmed often in the Old Testament (Numbers, Deuteronomy, 2 Samuel, 2 Kings, Psalms), and even in a special sense in Hippocrates and Galen. Procopius of Caesarea took the same view of the Plague of Justinian (*History of the Wars*, bk. ii, chs. xxii–xxiii). In the Introduction to the *Decameron* Boccaccio asserted that the visitation in Florence, 1348, resulted from the just wrath of God. Thus the tradition is rich and extended; and it came down to the seventeenth and eighteenth centuries with its strength little diminished. It is not surprising that clergymen adopted it with zeal. As the plague at Marseilles posed its threat to England, the clergy of all persuasions told their auditors that pestilence is a scourge from God, that 'National Calamities are the Sure Consequence of Publick Iniquities', and that national punishments, such as plagues, are part of 'God's Gracious Design'.[7] Sermons embodying this message were preached and printed by the score. They help to define the atmosphere in which Defoe wrote his *Journal*; and in fact many of them have something in common with the *Journal* and *Due Preparations* other than the conviction that plagues are instruments of a wrathful God: they too are often monitory, and they reinforce the admonitions by horrendous pictures of the pestilence of 1665.

The vitality of the wrath of God theory is attested to all the more forcibly by its wide prevalence in the medical tracts on plague. Typical is Dr. Nathaniel Hodges, one of the few physicians who is mentioned by name in the *Journal* and whose work influenced Defoe. He declared that a plague might properly be viewed as 'the Rod of the Almighty to punish men's Impieties': 'The sacred Pages clearly and demonstratively prove, that the Almighty . . . may draw the Sword, bend the Bow, or shoot the Arrows of Death'; and he particularly mentions that the London epidemic of 1665 revealed 'the Footsteps of an over-ruling Power'.[8] Hodges is the voice of the seventeenth century, but it is sounded again and again by eighteenth-century medical practitioners contemporary with Defoe. Consider, for example, Sir Richard Blackmore, perhaps more successful as physician than as poet (he was physician to Queen Anne), who published *A Discourse upon the Plague* in 1721:

> This dreadful Calamity is inflicted immediately by the Hand of God, or at his Command by the Ministry of his invisible Angels. . . . When He intends to manifest his being, Providence and just Government over Mankind, to chastise extraordinary Provocations, He pours down from Heaven Divine Vengeance upon a Nation harden'd in Impiety and obstinate in Wickedness. . . . And when Physicians and Naturalists have puzzled their Reason in searching after the Origine of any particular Plague . . . it will be

7. The quoted words are from two sermons, one preached before the House of Commons, 8 Dec. 1721, by Erasmus Saunders, the other before the University of Oxford a week later by Thomas Newlin.
8. *Vindiciae Medicinae & Medicorum* (1666), p. 34; *Loimologia* (1720), pp. 30–1.

an Argument of their Wisdom, Penetration and Piety to ascribe it
to the Finger of God (pp. 28–9).

Similarly Richard Boulton, author of several medical works, including
An Essay on the Plague in 1721, assented to the view that a plague may
happen 'by the extraordinary Interposition of God Almighty, provoked
by Men's Sins'. In such a case, he adds, 'Repentance, with a lively Faith
in God's Mercies, is the only Remedy' (p. 36). This is much the view
Defoe has put into the mouth of his narrator (though it is not the whole
view, as we shall see); and it was the entrenched view. As final evidence
of its remarkable persistence, we may note that it had been succinctly
uttered in 1544 by Thomas Phaer—'The first roote superiour and cause
of the pestilence is the wil of God rightfullye punishinge wicked men'—
whose treatise on plague still seemed of sufficient value to be republished
in 1722, endorsed by a physician.[9]

Nevertheless, the theory of divine wrath in its full implications ran
counter to the rationalistic spirit of the Enlightenment. The horrors of a
plague and its magnitude, along with the human failure to cope with it,
gave cogency to the idea that a divine agency is involved; but only an
occasional writer on plague in Defoe's day was willing to defend the
extreme position that the plague is an extraordinary, direct, and immediate interposition of the deity, an intervention in or suspension of the
laws of nature. In 1721 William Hendley, a clergyman who wrote a
plague tract, argued that the plague 'never proceeds from any first natural Cause, but is sent immediately from God'. To assert otherwise, he
says, is 'bad Philosophy and worse divinity'.[1] But Hendley was one of a
small minority. The more widely accepted view, at least in intellectual
circles or among those with any pretensions to authority, was that the
deity did not intervene in the natural order, that miraculous intervention
was a thing of the past (though possible if the deity wished), and that
plagues, like other diseases, were explicable in terms of natural or secondary causes. Physicians, such as Nathaniel Hodges and Sir Richard
Blackmore, might admit that plague came from God, but they moved
from this position to a realistic one for the medical scientist: Hodges,
once he has paid his respects to the theological view, says that 'it is
sufficient to the Purpose of a Physician, to assign natural and obvious
Causes'.[2] Support for this view came from one of Europe's most respected
authorities on plague, the Dutch physician Isbrand de Diemerbroeck,
whose famous work, *Tractatus de Peste*, Defoe apparently possessed. It
was translated into English by the surgeon Thomas Stanton in 1722.
Diemerbroeck granted, so Stanton remarks, that 'this deplorable Disease

9. A *Treatise of the Plague, written in English
about Two Hundred Years ago, by Thomas
Phaer. Publish'd, with a Preface, by a Physician* (1722), p. 6.
1. See *Loimologia Sacra: Or, A Discourse
shewing that the Plague never proceeds from any*

first *Natural Cause, but is sent immediately
from God, and that as a Punishment to a People for their Sins* (1721), title-page, and pp. 6,
41.
2. *Loimologia* (1720), p. 31.

comes by a divine and special Appointment. . . . But though he supposes the severe Anger of God to be the principal Cause, he nevertheless asserts it may secondarily proceed from some secret, malignant, and virulent Seeds. . . .'[3] One of the more emphatic rejections of the theory of divine interposition came from the learned apothecary William Boghurst, who remained in London during the visitation of 1665 and set down extensive observations on the nature of plague. 'Now,' he wrote, 'as God brings warr and Famine not by any new-created Agents, but by the ministry of known and second Causes, making them the Executioners of his Decree upon Mankind, soe wee cannot without reason suppose hee doth otherwise in the Pestilence.'[4] Both the logic and the argument, it hardly needs to be said, are venerable. The problem of first and second causes reached far back in time; and philosophers and clergymen revived it, or gave it new vitality and expression, in times of natural calamity. It had a special appeal to writers on the plague. As for Defoe, it was a question he pondered often, even as early as 1709 when he wrote in the *Review*: God 'generally speaking always works by, tho' he is not prescrib'd to Human Means'.[5] Not surprisingly it is this conviction which informs his *Due Preparations*, in which he commits himself to a view of plague in terms of second or natural causes but is cautious enough to assert that this is not a denial of 'the agency of providence'.

Now it is perfectly clear that Defoe wished the *Journal* to reflect the theory of divine wrath. Yet it is also clear, despite H. F.'s description of the plague as 'a Stroke from Heaven', 'a Messenger of [God's] Vengeance', 'the immediate Finger of God', that Defoe did not wish this phraseology to signify that the order of nature had been broken by divine intervention. He is, on the contrary, firmly aligned with those writers on plague who affirmed that the deity 'undoubtedly operates by natural Causes'. For the orthodox rationalism of the period it was sufficient to maintain that God is 'the undoubted original Source and prime Cause of all Natural Causes' and Himself the 'true original Cause' of the plague. It 'doth altogether proceed from his divine Command'.[6] But, as Defoe had remarked, God 'generally speaking always works by . . . Human Means'; and it is this view we find set forth in the *Journal*. In a significant passage H. F. comments on the plague as by 'the Appointment and Direction of [God's] Providence', and he judges his own 'Deliverance to be one next to miraculous'. Then, as though he has gone too far, he declares: 'But when I am speaking of the Plague, as a Distemper arising from natural Causes, we must consider it as it was really propagated by natural Means':

3. *A Treatise concerning the Pestilence . . . written Originally in Latin . . . and abridg'd and translated into English, by Thomas Stanton, Surgeon* (1722), p. 3.
4. *Loimographia: An Account of the Great Plague of London in the Year 1665*, ed. by Joseph Frank Payne, for the Epidemiological Society of London (1894), p. 16.
5. *Review*, no. 89, 29 Oct. 1709.
6. This is the phraseology of P. Kennedy, *A Discourse on Pestilence* (1721), p. 2.

> nor is it at all the less a Judgment for its being under the Conduct
> of humane Causes and Effects; for as the divine Power has form'd
> the whole Scheme of Nature, and maintains Nature in its Course;
> so the same Power thinks fit to let his own Actings with Men . . .
> go on in the ordinary Course of natural Causes, and he is pleased
> to act by those natural Causes as the ordinary Means. . . .

H. F. adds, as a qualification, that God reserves to himself 'a Power to act in a supernatural Way when he sees occasion'. But the spread of the plague calls for 'no apparent extraordinary occasion'. The ordinary course of things is sufficient 'without putting it upon Supernaturals and Miracle'. This is the voice of Defoe, adapting himself easily to the climate of contemporary opinion and affirming that providence displayed itself in the natural order. Thus it is that Defoe has H. F. look with contempt upon the 'Ignorance and Enthusiasm' of those who 'talk of its being an immediate Stroke from Heaven, without the Agency of Means, having Commission to strike this or that particular Person, and none other'.

How, then, does Defoe view the plague, its nature, causes, and transmission? H. F. expresses his opinions from time to time, rather positively in some instances. He rejects at the outset (with one passing moment of credulity) the views of the astrologers that the plague is the result of the malign influence of planets or that comets are omens of approaching evils. The tradition of planetary influence lingered in the eighteenth century and occasionally found utterance even in medical works, particularly in those reprinted from earlier periods, as in the sixteenth-century work already referred to, Thomas Phaer's A *Treatise of the Plague*, where we are told that 'there be two bodies called evil and malicious, that is *Saturne* and *Mars*, which oftentimes by their unwholesome influence are causes of manifold infirmities, specially of the Pestilence' (p. 8). Defoe makes vivid use of astrological lore and its impact on the credulous in depicting the terror and confusion which seized Londoners as rumours of the plague spread; but H. F.'s refusal to credit the astrologers is at once a reflection of the scepticism found in many contemporary plague tracts and an anticipation of Defoe's own views as they appeared in *Applebee's Journal* later (2 February, 7 December 1723, 10 July 1725).

Defoe likewise rejects a more serious opinion concerning the cause of plague: the view, in H. F.'s words, that the infection is 'carried on by the Air only, by carrying with it vast Numbers of Insects, and invisible Creatures, who enter into the Body with the Breath, or even at the Pores, and there generate or emit most acute Poisons, or poisonous Ovae, or Eggs, which mingle with the Blood, and so infect the Body'. This is Defoe's simplified version of the theory advanced by the German-born Jesuit priest, Athanasius Kircher (1602–80), whose epidemiological views were supported in England by Defoe's contemporary, Richard Bradley. Bradley's contention that 'all Pestilential Distempers . . . are occasion'd by poisonous Insects convey'd from Place to Place by the Air' was known to Defoe—and to many other writers on the plague in the 1720s—and he was criticized sharply by such physicians as Hodges, Mead, and Blackmore, among others. The anonymous author of *Medicina Flagellata* (1721), who devoted himself to exposing the 'Remarkable Errors in the late Writings on the Plague', refers to Dr. Bradley, 'who hatches this Distemper by the smaller Kind of Insects floating in the Air', as being 'jealous of his favourite Egg, from which that fatal Cockatrice breaks forth and disperses Death in Every Quarter' (p. 200). It may be observed that Kircher and Bradley have a place in the development of the modern doctrine of *contagium vivum*, but Defoe follows some of his respected contemporaries in brushing aside the view which, as later developed and formulated, holds that living microscopic organisms are the agents of communicable disease.

Defoe had no special knowledge of medical theory, and we cannot easily gauge the extent to which he read beyond the readily available plague literature. He was obliged, if he thought about the matter at all, to maintain the authenticity of the temporal setting of the *Journal*, the year 1665, by restricting himself to the medical knowledge then current. He may have been saved from anachronisms by the failure of epidemiology to make advances from 1665 to 1720. The plague literature of 1665 and that of 1720 show marked similarities and only inconsequential differences. Defoe knew some of the tracts published shortly before he wrote the *Journal*, though he made more extensive use of those which had appeared in 1665, particularly the group of tracts from that year reprinted under the title, *A Collection of Very Valuable and Scarce Pieces relating to the Last Plague in the Year 1665*, 1721. Here he found the theories of Dr. Nathaniel Hodges; and from Hodges and Dr. Richard Mead, whose *Short Discourse concerning Pestilential Contagion* (1720) was authorized by the government, Defoe seems to have formed his general conception of the plague. He repeats their view, which was widely though not universally accepted, that plagues were not of English origin and that the Plague of 1665 came to London by means of imported goods from the Levant transhipped from Holland. It was believed that certain kinds of goods with high porosity, as cottons and woollens, might for long periods retain pestilential particles or effluvia. H. F. mentions that 'the infection was generally said to be, from a Parcel of Silks imported from Holland'; and he remarks that 'our woollen Manufactures are as retentive of Infection as human bodies'. The 'seeds of the infection' as conceived by Defoe, following Mead and others, were chemical and inanimate, not the living effluvia of Kircher and Bradley.

A related matter touching the medical science of the period is concerned with the way in which the plague was transmitted from person to person. Obviously this was predicated on the nature of the disease and, ultimately, on its cause or causes. In the hotly debated controversy over miasma and contagion, inherited by the seventeenth and eighteenth centuries from earlier ages, Defoe aligns himself with the contagionists.

The miasmatic view held that plagues resulted from corrupted or putrid air, chiefly the poisonous exhalations of the earth, with these intensified by foul emanations from rotten vegetable matter, human corpses, mines, pools, streams, dunghills, and filth of various kinds. The air thus becomes laden with pestilential particles. Philip Rose, a Fellow of the Royal College of Physicians, writing in 1721, stated the theory briefly: one 'domestic cause' of plague is

> a Pestilential Air, occasioned by Poisonous, Mineral, Arsenical Exhalations, which sometimes Ascend out of the Bowels of that part of the Globe of the Earth, where we do Inhabit, and do impregnate our Atmosphere, with deleterious volatile Salts and Sulphurs, wherewith our Bodies are not encompassed, but even are admitted into the Lungs by Inspiration, and thence communicated and dispersed through the whole Machine of the Body.[7]

In the same year Sir Richard Blackmore, like Rose, stimulated to write by the threat from Marseilles, asserted that 'Plagues are often bred in the Bowels of the Earth' where 'Reeks and Fumes of various Kinds' are generated and then 'burst their Prisons by furious Earthquakes, and break thro' the Chasms and Disruptions of the Ground in violent and contagious Tempests [filling] the Regions of the Air with crude pestilential Seeds'. These 'hurtful particles', Blackmore wrote, are 'drawn into the Lungs by the Breath, infect the Vitals, and execute their terrible Tragedy'. Blackmore, who took exception to Kircher's 'worms', that is, to living effluvia, argued strongly that the 'fatal Vapours can be nothing else but the Crude Streams of Nitre, Vitriol and Sulphur blended together, with which the Caverns of the Earth so much abound, and the Exhalations of other Minerals and Metals of the like noxious Quality . . . combin'd with them'.[8] Rose and Blackmore, physicians Defoe could have known, are representative of the traditional miasmatic view, a view argued as forcibly in 1665 as it was in 1721: 'the earth [is] the seminary and seed-plot of these venemous vapours and pestiferous effluvia, which vitiate and corrupt the Aire, and consequently induce the pestilence.'[9]

But Defoe's *Journal* rejects the telluric theory: it is pervasively contagionist and even explicitly anti-miasmatic. He did not, of course, have our modern view that a biological agency occasions the spread of plague. The notion that fleas from infected rodents transmit bubonic plague was still generations in the future; but Defoe did not subscribe to the contemporary theory of a corrupted atmosphere saturated with pestilential particles, a pestilential miasma. H. F. is at pains to reject this view at some length, both by direct statement and by examples of how infections actually occur. 'I must be allowed to believe', he says, 'that no one in this whole Nation ever receiv'd the Sickness or Infection, but who receiv'd it in the

7. A *Theorico-Practical, Miscellaneous and Succinct Treatise of the Plague* (1721), p. 9.
8. A *Discourse upon the Plague* (1721), pp.

34–5.
9. Boghurst, *Loimographia*, p. 13.

ordinary Way of Infection from some Body, or the Cloaths, or touch, or stench of some Body that was infected before.' The threat of 'an universal Infection' was real enough, but not from an infective principle in the air: it came from the highly contagious nature of the disease whereby a single man 'may give the Plague to a thousand People, and they to greater Numbers in Proportion'. H. F. observes that his opinion and the opinions of physicians coincided, that 'the Sick cou'd infect none but those that came within reach of the sick Person'. He was particularly struck by instances in which the victims were not aware that they were infected, no cutaneous signs having appeared, such instances as might today be labelled *pestis minor* or *pestis ambulans*. These he thought most dangerous of all as they went unwittingly among people: 'These breathed Death in every Place, and upon every Body who ever came near them; nay their very Cloaths retained the Infection, their Hands would infect the Things they touch'd, especially if they were warm and sweaty.'

*　　*　　*

No reader can miss Defoe's preoccupation with the flight of the clergy and the physicians, or the tone of satisfaction in his remarks on the courage and fidelity of the dissenting clergy who remained to minister to the spiritual needs of the people, in sharp contrast to the shameful flight of Anglican clerics. He also has ample praise for the magistrates who filled their responsibilities. Clergy, physicians, magistrates, these three professions are the instruments Defoe uses for insinuating into his narrative the vexed problem of flight with its theological and social implications.[1] It would not have been lost on Defoe's contemporary readers that H. F., without wife or children, faced a dilemma less agonizing than a man with family. With few or no responsibilities, he might flee without anguish. Nevertheless he had servants and a flourishing business to consider, as well as his own safety, by no means minor considerations, so that Defoe depicts him vividly in the throes of indecision. But there is more to it: even the single man without any special responsibilities stands in a certain relationship to God; and Defoe, as we see, gives substance to H. F.'s indecision by putting the matter in a theological context. To the elder brother's arguments that he should flee, H. F. replied that 'fleeing from my habitation [would be] a kind of flying from God, and that he could cause Justice to overtake me when and where he thought fit'. This is precisely the logic Bèze had examined in his treatise in the sixteenth century, that flight in effect means men 'thinke themselves stronger than God, and that they can escape his hande'; and we

1. Landa points out that, shortly before the publication of Defoe's novel, William Hendley's *Loimologia Sacra* (1721) explored "what Circumstances persons may with good Conscience fly from the *Plague*" and concluded that clergymen, magistrates, physicians, apothecaries, surgeons, and midwives were obliged to stay. This work, along with many others published in 1665 and the early 1720s, suggests that the interest that Defoe's contemporaries had in the question (xxx–xxxi) [Editor].

find it an equally momentous matter to Defoe's contemporaries. Witness the words of William Hendley in 1721. If the plague comes from God as 'his just Anger for the Sins of men, there seems to be no Security in flying from it, and it doth betray a want of that Trust and Confidence which every good Christian ought to have in the Mercies and Providence of God'.[2]

'Is it a fruit of faithlessness to shun the Plague?' This is the traditional theological question which Defoe lets H. F. and his brother debate; and in effect H. F.'s answer is affirmative. Thus he resolutely announces that he will not flee. 'I resolved that I would stay in Town, and casting myself entirely upon the Goodness and Protection of the Almighty, would not seek any other Shelter whatever.' It is the proper decision for a man of austere faith, exhibiting an exemplary Christianity. On the other hand, the brother represented the 'Rule of the *Physicians*, that in time of a *Pestilence, to make haste away, to get at a great Distance off*, and *to be slow in returning back*, is the only . . . *sure Remedy.*'[3] But often in the theological discussions of plague the austerity of the rule of faith was modified and reconciled with the rule of the physicians. If faith that the deity would provide a protective shield was felt to be an exemplary Christian attitude, God also demanded, so others maintained, that each person should take all available means to preserve himself. The deity sends pestilence, but he also sends life. When Richard Kephale, to whom we have already referred, examined the question, may a Christian in good conscience fly from the plague, he emphasized this more pragmatic and less austere view, which Defoe puts into the mouth of H. F.'s brother. Kephale, seeking to support his opinion by authority, relied on Joseph Hall, the highly respected Anglican bishop who had lived through several great plagues in the first half of the seventeenth century:

> The Angel of God follows you [Hall wrote], and you doubt, whether you shall fly; if a Lyon out of the Forrest should pursue you, you would make no question, yet could hee do it unsent; what is the difference? Both instruments of Divine Revenge; both threaten death, one by spilling the blood, the other by Infecting it . . . you say it is Gods visitation; What evil is not? If war have wasted the confines of your Countrey, you save your throats by flight, why are you more favourable to Gods immediate Sword of Pestilence. . . . If you honor his Rod . . . if you mislike not the affliction, because hee sends it, then love the life, which you have of his sending. . . . Because death will overtake us, shall we run and meet him . . .?[4]

The ambivalence in the theological discussions is mirrored in Defoe's *Journal*. H. F.'s elder brother, as we are told by H. F. himself, was 'a very religious man'; and it is clear that he does not have 'a wrong notion

2. Theodore de Bèze, A *Short Learned and Pithie Treatise* (1580), sig. B[8]; Hendley, *Loimologia Sacra* (1721), pp. 76–7.

3. William Hendley, op. cit., p. 76.

4. *Medela Pestilentiae*, pp. 28–9.

of divinity' any more than H. F. has *the* right notion. Each brother represents a prevailing view, reflecting the conflicting opinions about Christian duty in time of plague as these opinions were warmly debated in plague tracts and homiletic literature from the Reformation to Defoe's time. For a summation of the controversy from the vantage of one who lived through the epidemic of 1665, we may turn to Boghurst, the apothecary already mentioned:

> Beza and some other Divines treating of this point [i.e. flight] and commending and advising it, doe not like well to have it called flying away, perhaps thinking it a scandalous term, but would have it called only going aside, a more moderate word. All physicians terme it Flight, and many of them scruple much the advising it, soe that some will . . . neither persuade or dissuade, but leave every man to his choice, but the Divines have been more bold and advise it more eagerly and condemn those that betake not themselves to their heels. Nay, they say people are wicked and provoke God in not doing it.[5]

From the foregoing discussion we may infer that Defoe wished his narrator to be something more than merely the recorder of objective events. H. F. is not simply a utilitarian *persona*. A few touches give him humanity: his religious reflections, his scepticism, his respect for the authorities, his curiosity, his indecision.

* * *

It is singularly inappropriate to call the *Journal* a novel, but there remains the vexed question of whether it is history or fiction. Here we are confronted with the difficult, possibly insoluble, problem of Defoe's sources. Little can be said with confidence on this subject. It is profitless to speculate about his childhood memories of 1665, or about what he heard later from older people who lived to report their experiences. He may have recalled something; he is likely to have heard more; yet there is no way to discover that any part of the *Journal* has levied on memory and report. In his Introduction to *Due Preparations*, the companion piece to the *Journal*, Defoe wrote: 'I very particularly remember the last visitation of this kind which afflicted this nation in 1665, and have had occasion to converse with many other persons who lived in this city all the while'; and he is at pains to insist on the essential accuracy of his facts, many of which parallel the factual material of the *Journal*. Yet we must remember that he referred to *Robinson Crusoe* as 'a just history of *fact*' and to *Moll Flanders* as a 'genuine' private history. These assertions may be little more than the customary desire to gain verisimilitude by claiming that one's fiction is fact. But there may also be semantic confusion in the remarks, a result of his apparent conviction that fiction in

5. *Loimographia*, pp. 58–9.

the service of man, intended for ethical and religious improvement, is somehow not only legitimate but a kind of truth.

We must tread as warily in seeking Defoe's printed sources. The sale catalogue of his library (in which, unfortunately, his books are listed with those of another) lists the plague tracts of Richard Kephale, William Kemp, and Isbrand de Diemerbroeck. It is a reasonable, if not a wholly safe, assumption that he drew details and general information from them. The single printed source possibly most useful, along with the Bills of Mortality, was A *Collection of Very Valuable and Scarce Pieces relating to the Last Plague*, 1721. As mentioned earlier, this compilation contained a 'Letter' by the physician, Dr. Nathanial Hodges, in which an account is given of the 'first Rise, Progress, Symptoms and Cure of the *Plague*'. A *Collection* included two other pieces which seem to have served Defoe well. One of these, 'Orders conceived and published by the Lord Mayor and Aldermen of the City of London concerning the Infection of the Plague, 1665', Defoe reprinted verbatim in the *Journal*, adding only the names of the lord mayor and the sheriffs who were in office at the time of the Plague.[6] The other piece is almost as important: 'Necessary Directions for the Prevention and Cure of the Plague in 1665. With divers Remedies of small Charge, by the College of Physicians', a separate copy of which is listed in the sale catalogue of Defoe's library. The 'Letter' of Dr. Hodges and the 'Necessary Directions' of the College of Physicians, if added to the tracts of Mead,[7] Kephale, and Kemp, could have supplied him with most of his factual information about the origin, nature, and treatment of the plague, as well as with current theories and religious attitudes. There remains to be mentioned one printed source of surpassing importance, the Bills of Mortality, those weekly compilations by the Company of Parish Clerks in which deaths from all causes were listed for the individual parishes. These weekly Bills supplied Defoe with the chronological progression of the Plague as it spread inexorably from parish to parish, from its beginning in the western parts of London to north, south, and east. The structure of the *Journal* is determined, temporally and geographically, by the weekly Bills. Defoe may have possessed the separate weekly Bills, or the annual compilation entitled *London's Dreadful Visitation: Or, A Collection of all the Bills of Mortality for this Present Year . . . 1665*. I have no doubt that he read additional plague literature and some of the numberless sermons on the subject, all of which became a staple of publishers in 1665 and later. It is likely too that he knew commentaries on the classi-

6. Walter George Bell, who indicts Defoe's accuracy in a number of instances, points out that the 'Orders' reprinted by Defoe are in fact those issued in 1646. The differences between those of 1646 and 1665 were not great. Bell attacks Defoe for the unwarranted assumption that 'these authorized and printed Orders were necessarily carried out'; and he concludes that Defoe was 'not an historical writer' (see *The Great Plague in London in 1665* (rev. edn., 1951, pp. 72 ff.).

7. In his *Due Preparations for the Plague* (1722) Defoe quotes from Richard Mead's *Short Discourse concerning Pestilential Contagion* (1720) and takes issue with some of Mead's assertions. See *Due Preparations* (1895 edn.), pp. 11, 32, 39–40.

cal plagues and the Black Death by Thucydides, Lucretius, Procopius, Boccaccio, and others. The resemblances between these earlier epidemics and the epidemics in England in 1592, 1603, 1625, 1636, and 1665, were frequently the subject of comment. Indeed, it is hardly an exaggeration to say that the plague tractates of the seventeenth and eighteenth centuries constitute a sub-literary genre. In view of his sustained interest in plagues, Defoe may have read them extensively, repeating and adapting material which writers had passed on from plague to plague. One who has read the plague tracts of such authors as Thomas Dekker and George Wither will read Defoe's *Journal* with the shock of recognition.

But the *Journal* is not a thing 'suckt out of other bookes', however much Defoe has absorbed from others. It has the aura of history just as it has, as a memoir, the aura of autobiography. The story of an actual occurrence, it is at best history ordered and infused with an interpretation. Though history is used to authenticate the narrative, the *Journal* is essentially a work of the imagination, a reshaping of a voluminous body of fact, embellished and ascribed to a single individual who, even if he has a historical prototype, is still fictional as presented in a pattern of actions, motives, and thoughts, the whole selected and arranged to achieve certain effects and to suggest certain truths about helpless man as he rolls 'darkling down the torrent of his fate'.

EVERETT ZIMMERMAN

H.F.'s Meditations: A *Journal of the Plague Year* †

A *Journal of the Plague Year* follows historical sources rather scrupulously: in a recent analysis, F. Bastian concludes that "the invented detail . . . is small and inessential."[1] This historical material is narrated by H.F., who experiences and survives the plague year. He does more, however, than merely communicate details about the plague. In the Puritan religious tradition that informs both H.F.'s view of reality and Defoe's fiction generally, historical events have a spiritual meaning: the world is providentially ordered and the ultimate reality is metaphysical. For H.F., then, the plague is a spiritually significant experience, not just a physical phenomenon.[2]

In the Puritan tradition, the isolation of man in his relationship to God is emphasized, and the significance of ordinary physical reality (apart from the spiritual meanings that it may reveal) is limited. For these

† Reprinted by permission of the Modern Language Association of America from *PMLA* 87 (1972): 417–23.

1. "Defoe's *Journal of the Plague Year* Reconsidered," *RES*, 16 (1965), 172.

2. For a discussion of the Puritan view of reality and history, see J. Paul Hunter, *The Reluctant Pilgrim: Defoe's Emblematic Method and Quest for Form in* Robinson Crusoe (Baltimore, Md.: Johns Hopkins Press, 1966), esp. Ch. v, "Metaphor, Type, Emblem, and the Pilgrim 'Allegory.' "

reasons, Puritan writings tend to turn inward. For example, Bunyan in *Grace Abounding* writes a great deal of what the modern reader thinks of as psychological analysis. But, to the Puritan, this analysis reveals not primarily a mind, but rather the process by which God brings a man to an understanding of spiritual realities. Bunyan is writing to direct other men to the same truths that he has discovered. Defoe's *Journal*, while it contains elements of several traditions of pious writings, has a different emphasis.[3] When H.F. attempts to find a coherent spiritual purpose governing the physical world, material reality presents itself to him so powerfully that he cannot fully reconcile it with his religious assumptions. The disorienting forces of the plague expose the tensions within him, and we see his conflicts and mounting anxiety. The focus in Defoe is on the narrator: we are left with a character, not a lesson.

The multitude of details about the plague (the "verisimilitude") are brought into relationship with H.F.'s spiritual and psychological development by several means: (1) H.F. structures his account around his repentance of the decision to remain in London; (2) he frequently comments on his not entirely successful attempts to comprehend the nature of morality in a time of plague; (3) he uses many biblical references to suggest spiritual interpretations of physical reality.

H.F. obliquely invites the reader's attention to what is always implicit in the writing—the personal spiritual concern that informs and shapes it: "Such Intervals as I had, I employed in reading Books, and in writing down my Memorandums of what occurred to me every Day. . . . What I wrote of my private Meditations I reserve for private Use, and desire it may not be made publick on any Account whatever."[4] [65–66] Among the "private meditations" that do in fact appear in the public account are those concerning his choosing to stay in London during the plague. He reconsiders the implications of his choice and finally repents of it, seeing it as sinful presumption, not trust in God. His changing attitudes reflect his deepening understanding of the human condition in a time of plague.

Self-consciously and defensively H.F. asserts that he writes of his decision only to give advice to those who may find themselves in a similar situation (p. 9) [11] Yet, his initial account is ambiguous, leading to questions rather than solutions. He advises the reader, ". . . if he be one that makes Conscience of his Duty, and would be directed what to do in it, namely, that he should keep his Eye upon the particular Providences which occur at that Time, and look upon them complexly, as they regard one another, and as altogether regard the Question before him" (p. 12) [13]. But he goes on to accept as "providences" events that

3. Hunter suggests that the *Journal* should be read "in relation to the providence and diary traditions" (p. 204). It also contains elements of the "Guide" tradition. G. A. Starr, *Defoe and Spiritual Autobiography* (Princeton, N.J.: Princeton Univ. Press, 1965), also deals with

background relevant to this work.
4. P.94. All references are to the Shakespeare Head Edition (Oxford: Basil Blackwell, 1928). Page numbers in brackets are to this Norton Critical Edition.

his brother, "tho' a very Religious Man himself, laught at . . . that I should take it as an Intimation from Heaven, that I should not go out of Town, only because I could not hire a Horse to go, or my Fellow was run away that was to attend me, was ridiculous" (p. 13) [13–14].

H.F. is left "greatly oppress'd . . . irresolute, and not knowing what to do" (p. 14) [14]. At this point he resorts to bibliomancy—choosing at random a passage from the Bible for advice about the future (p. 15) [15]. The passage he reads is in the 91st Psalm—one that was traditionally thought to be written by David in time of plague—and its promises of deliverance convince him to remain in town. Bibliomancy was a subject of controversy in Defoe's time. It was commonly accepted that one might be divinely prompted through the Bible. However, arbitrarily selecting a passage from the Bible might also be a usurpation of a divine preroga-tive; the practice could result in a man's choosing or accepting only that which is in accord with his own will. Whatever Defoe thought of bib-liomancy generally, he calls attention here to a dubiety in H.F.'s method.[5] H.F. refers only to several verses from the psalm—the second through the seventh and also the tenth. This emphasized selectivity invites a rereading of the psalm to see what has been omitted. The first verse places a qualification on the assurances that follow: "He that dwelleth in the secret place of the most High shall abide under the shadow of the Almighty" (Psalm xci.1). More important, he has omitted verses 11–12: "For he shall give his angels charge over thee, to keep thee in all thy ways. They shall bear thee up in their hands, lest thou dash thy foot against a stone." These are, of course, the words that Satan quotes when tempting Christ to cast himself down from a pinnacle of the temple, a temptation to presume on God's mercy. Is H.F. to be commended for his trust in God or is he wrongfully presuming on God's mercy? The narrator's confidence in his decision cannot be the reader's.

H.F. recognizes his sin and repents. During the initial stage of repen-tance, he is terror stricken: "Terrified by those frightful Objects," he spends much time in the "Confession of my Sins, giving my self up to God every Day, and applying to him with Fasting, Humiliation, and Meditation" (pp. 93–94) [65]. His later response to a waterman, who has genuinely been obliged to remain, reveals his increased understand-ing: "And here my Heart smote me, suggesting how much better this Poor Man's Foundation was, on which he stayed in Danger, than mine; that he had no where to fly; that he had a Family to bind him to Atten-dance, which I had not; and mine was mere Presumption, his a true Dependence, and a Courage resting on God; and yet, that he used all possible Caution for his Safety" (p. 132) [90].

These are not only temporary emotional outbursts, for he later sets up

5. See Rodney M. Baine, *Daniel Defoe and the Supernatural* (Athens: Univ. of Georgia Press, 1968), pp. 6–7, 9–11, for a discussion of Defoe, bibliomancy, and *A Journal of the Plague Year*. Baine gives an interpretation of the *Journal* differing from the one in this paper. He believes that Defoe generally accepted bib-liomancy, and sees no irony in Defoe's treat-ment of H.F.'s decision.

a "prescription" that condemns his own conduct: "Upon the foot of all these Observations, I must say, that tho' Providence seemed to direct my Conduct to be otherwise; yet it is my Opinion, and I must leave it as a Prescription, (viz) *that the best Physick against the Plague is to run away from it*" (pp. 240–41) [156]. And in case his survival should be regarded as a validation of his choice, he states near the end of the *Journal* that those who remained may owe their "Courage to their Ignorance, and despising the Hand of their Maker, which is a criminal kind of Desperation, and not a true Courage" (p. 290) [185]. The *Journal* makes clear that H.F.'s decision to remain was wrong. The advice he finally gives is not to imitate his choice but to recognize his folly.

The focus that is established in the opening account of the approaching plague supports the internal emphasis that is predominant in the narrator's account of himself. The plague is dealt with secondarily; in the foreground are the confusions of the people: "It was about the Beginning of *September* 1664, that I, among the Rest of my Neighbours, heard in ordinary Discourse, that the Plague was return'd again in *Holland*; for it had been very violent there, and particularly at *Amsterdam* and *Roterdam*, in the year 1663, whither *they say*, it was brought, some said from *Italy*, others from the *Levant* among some Goods, which were brought home by their Turkey Fleet; others said it was brought from *Candia*; others from Cyprus." What they hear subsequently is also unverifiable, and their apprehensiveness mounts. The plague bills seem to be something they can trust, but it is soon obvious that the seeming veracity of numbers and dates is as confused and confusing as the rumors. After several fluctuations of hope and fear, "All our Extenuations abated" and the reports of low death rates are known to be "all Knavery and Collusion" (p. 6) [9]. This pattern of diminishing trust in external authority, and the consequent abandoning of the individual to his own possibly false perceptions, continues after the focus narrows to the problems of H.F. He includes himself among the confused populace in the opening pages, and then tells us of his own morally ambiguous decision to remain in London.

As H.F. presents the multitude of details about the plague year, we can see his confusion and anxiety reflected in his manner of narration. The numbers, the lists, the incidents are somehow expected to fix the truth, but the truth is evasive. He always sees the alternatives, other possibilities that might be relevant, and seems almost temperamentally incapable of reaching a conclusion. His very style frequently reflects his turmoil: "I cou'd give a great many such Stories as these, diverting enough, which in the long Course of that dismal Year, I met with, *that is* heard of, and which are very certain to be true, or very near the Truth; that is to say, true in the General, for no Man could at such a Time learn all the Particulars" (p. 63) [47]. The interrupting qualifications and the many dependent clauses characteristically undermine his assertions. He deals with the murder of watchmen in a similar equivocal fashion:

It is true, the Watchmen were on their Duty, and acting in the Post where they were plac'd by a lawful Authority; and killing any pub-lick legal Officer in the Execution of his Office, is always in the Language of the Law called Murther. But as they were not author-iz'd by the Magistrate's Instructions, or by the Power they acted under, to be injurious or abusive, either to the People who were under their Observation, or to any that concern'd themselves for them; so when they did so, they might be said to act themselves, not their Office; to act as private Persons, not as Persons employ'd; and consequently if they brought Mischief upon themselves by such an undue Behaviour, that Mischief was upon their own Heads; and indeed they had so much the hearty Curses of the People, whether they deserv'd it or not, that whatever befel them no body pitied them, and every Body was apt to say, they deserv'd it, whatever it was. (pp. 189–90) [125].

As the clauses pile up, the repeated qualifications finally obscure mur-der.

In his evaluations of people and policies, he is usually ambiguous and sometimes contradictory. Perhaps the most obvious example is his com-mentary on the shutting up of houses: "This is one of the Reasons why I believ'd then, and do believe still, that the shutting up Houses thus by Force, and restraining, or rather imprisoning People in their own Houses, as is said above, was of little or no Service in the Whole; nay, I am of Opinion, it was rather hurtful . . ." (p. 87) [61]. But he later writes: "It is most certain, that if by the Shutting up of Houses the sick had not been confin'd, multitudes who in the height of their Fever were Dili-rious and Distracted, wou'd ha' been continually running up and down the Streets, and even as it was, a very great number did so, and offer'd all sorts of Violence to those they met, even just as a mad Dog runs on and bites at every one he meets" (pp. 196–97) [129]. He refers to the shutting up of houses obsessively, and, although generally against it, is unable to rest on any conclusion.

In making other judgments, he has similar difficulties. Although he distinguishes between physicians and quacks, the "Plague defied all Medicines." The physicians go about "prescribing to others and telling them what to do, till the Tokens were upon them, and they dropt down dead, destroyed by that very Enemy, they directed others to oppose" (p. 43) [34]. With apparently unintentional irony he then comments, "Abundance of Quacks too died, who had the folly to trust to their own Medicines . . ." (p. 43) [34]. He is unwilling or unable to reach a clear judgment about the clergymen. He is contemptuous of the rabble-rous-ing predictions of doom by the soothsayers, but must condemn the min-isters for similar behavior (pp. 30–31) [25–26]. Those ministers who flee from their charges seem to be blameworthy, but at the end he finds too many complications to be able either to blame or to exculpate them (pp. 286–87) [183–84]. This evasiveness is so persistent that even if one concedes individual cases in which Defoe was merely careless, the overall design cannot easily be explained as fortuitous.

The narrator believes unequivocally that the first cause of the plague is God, although the plague operates in general through natural means (pp. 235–36, e.g) [152–53][6] But this belief raises other questions. To what end is the city plagued? What should be the effect of the plague on the individual moral life? Although the narrator feels that the plague should bring men to repentance, he notices that while fear causes some to repent, it leads many others to "extremes of folly" (p. 36) [29]. And afterward "it must be acknowledg'd that the general Practice of the People was just as it was before, and very little Difference was to be seen" (p. 279) [178].

What has the most vivid effect upon H.F. is not the repentance of the people but the almost total moral collapse brought by the plague: "But, alas! this was a Time when every one's private Safety lay so near them, that they had no Room to pity the Distresses of others; for every one had Death, as it were, at his Door . . . and knew not what to do, or whither to fly. This, I say, took away all Compassion; self Preservation indeed appear'd here to be the first Law" (p. 140) [95]. Even parents and children abandon each other (pp. 140–41) [95–96], and Death is a "deliverance" (p. 119) [81]. His grim account of how the deaths of the poor are fortunate for others suggests a new perspective on conventional human feelings and values: ". . . they would in Time have been even driven to the Necessity of plundering either the City it self, or the Country adjacent, to have subsisted themselves, which would first or last, have put the whole Nation, as well as the City, into the utmost Terror and Confusion" (p. 120) [82].

The symbolic and psychological meanings in the account of the "great Pit," a mass grave in the churchyard in Aldgate, are relevant to the narrator's attempts to find a moral meaning in the human condition (pp. 72–77) [52–55]. This "terrible Pit" suggests some of the many biblical uses of the image, both literal and figurative. Korah's rebellion against Moses was ended when he and his followers "went down alive into the pit, and the earth closed upon them: and they perished from among the congregation" (Numbers xvi.33). The Psalmist prays, "Hear me speedily, O Lord: my spirit faileth: hide not thy face from me, lest I be like unto them that go down into the pit" (cxlii.7). The symbolic suggestions of the pit, a fearsome death, and alienation from God, are underlined by the narrator's calling it a "dreadful Gulph . . . for such it was rather than a Pit" (p. 73) [53]—a suggestion of the "great gulf fixed" between

6. In considering the causes of the plague, H.F. adopts the usual Puritan view of God's interventions in His providentially ordered universe: God uses natural means to accomplish something beyond the ordinary course of nature. This is a "special providence" and differs from a "miracle" because it does not set aside the laws of nature. Some Puritans thought that miracles ceased after biblical times. For a full discussion, see Perry Miller, *The New England Mind: The Seventeenth Century* (Cambridge, Mass.: Harvard Univ. Press, 1939), esp. pp. 226–28.

the rich man in hell and Lazarus, who is with Abraham (St. Luke xvi. 26).

Because of the danger of infection, it is forbidden to go near the pit. But the narrator "resolv'd to go in the Night and see some of them thrown in" (p. 74) [53], an example of the seemingly brutal curiosity that sometimes inspires him. With the argument that "it might be an Instructing Sight" he gains admittance, the sexton responding, " 'Tis a speaking Sight . . . and has a Voice with it, and a loud one, to call us all to Repentance . . ." (p. 75) [54]. The narrator's curiosity about the appalling sight is not idle: he desires, in the fullest metaphoric sense, to see into the pit, to comprehend the plague and the human condition that it reveals. This same compulsive desire appears at other times. For example, after the plague intensifies, H. F. admits that he need not leave his house; nevertheless, "tho' I confin'd my Family, I could not prevail upon my unsatisfy'd Curiosity to stay within entirely my self; and tho' I generally came frighted and terrified Home, yet I cou'd not restrain; only that indeed, I did not do it so frequently as at first" (p. 98) [68].

The same night in which he visits the pit, H. F. has an altercation with the "dreadful Set of Fellows" at the Pye-Tavern (p. 78) [56]. The tavern is "within View of the Church Door" (p. 82) [58], and the men mock those who attend public worship and laugh at the narrator's "calling the Plague the Hand of God" (p. 81) [57]. H. F. is presented with two possible responses to the plague—that of the tavern or that of the church. The episode is related to the story of Korah. Several accounts of people going alive into the pit had previously been mentioned, and the roisterers taunt the "poor Gentleman," about whom the narrator is concerned, "with want of Courage to leap into the great Pit and go to Heaven" (p. 79) [57]. The narrator leaves their company "lest the Hand of that Judgment which had visited the whole City should glorify his Vengeance upon them, and all that were near them" (p. 81) [58]. He follows the advice of Moses to those near Korah and his followers: "Depart, I pray you, from the tents of these wicked men, and touch nothing of their's, lest ye be consumed in all their sins" (Numbers xvi. 26). The men of the tavern *do* meet the end of Korah, thus vindicating the narrator's faith in a controlling moral order: ". . . they were every one of them carried into the great Pit, which I have mentioned above, before it was quite filled up, which was not above a Fortnight or thereabout" (p. 82) [58].

But this episode is not a resolution of the questions that have preoccupied H. F. Although his faith in a moral scheme is confirmed, he continues to be baffled in his attempts to understand the complexities of divine justice. Also at this time his concern turns more profoundly inward: he seriously wonders whether he rebuked the men at the Pye-Tavern for pious or for egotistical reasons (pp. 84–85) [59–60]. Although he finally vindicates himself, his self-assurance is shaken. Shortly thereafter, he endures the first terror-filled stage of his repentance (pp. 93–94) [65–66].

Biblical allusions and parallels give even the seemingly circumstantial accounts a spiritual dimension. Many traditional typological interpretations were accepted by the dissenters, and in the seventeenth century typology was frequently extended to postbiblical history. Biblical types could be prefigurations not only of later biblical events but also of later history. In J. Paul Hunter's words, ". . . the broadened typology offered contemporary history an extended mythic dimension based upon past history frozen into static form."[7] The plague and the great fire almost demanded typological treatment. The word "plague" is itself the term persistently used in the English Bible for God's judgments, especially those on the Egyptians before the exodus and on the Israelites afterward. Fire is another common image of God's judgments, especially of those that are final, and the narrator refers frequently to the fire which will destroy London after the plague. His prophetic tone suggests the apocalyptic: "But the Time was not fully come, that the City was to be purg'd by Fire, nor was it far off; for within Nine Months more I saw it all lying in Ashes" (pp. 295–96 [189]; cf. II Peter iii. 11–12).

The narrator specifically suggests a relationship between the conduct of the Israelites and the Londoners: ". . . it might too justly be said of them, as was said of the children of *Israel*, after their being delivered from the host of *Pharaoh*, when they passed the *Red Sea*, and look'd back, and saw the *Egyptians* overwhelmed in the water, *viz.* That *they sang his Praise, but they soon forgot his Works*" (p. 302) [192]. The wanderings of Israel were usually interpreted typologically as the spiritual journey of Everyman. For example, Matthew Henry comments or the Red Sea: "Israel's passage through it was typical of the conversion of souls (Isa. xi. 15), and the Egyptian's perdition in it was typical of the final ruin of all impenitent sinners (Rev. xx. 14)."[8] The allusion suggests, then, multiple levels of significance: it refers to both the historical situation after the plague and man's personal salvation.

Some of the allusions relate London to the cities of Nineveh and, more important, Jerusalem. Nineveh suggests the possibility of repentance (pp. 35–36) [29]. Jerusalem is related, however, to repeated and increasing punishments: the dispersions of the Jews; the occupation of Jerusalem and the profanation of the temple by Antiochus Epiphanes; and the conquest by Titus. The narrator refers specifically to Jeremiah's comments to Jerusalem's impending doom (pp. 84, 235) [59, 152], and to the later destruction by the Romans (pp. 22, 25) [19–20, 22]. In addition, he alludes to biblical passages traditionally interpreted as prophetic of the destruction of Jerusalem. The reference to Josephus' account of a man crying "woe to *Jerusalem*" (p. 25) [22] suggests Christ's mourning for Jerusalem (St. Matthew xxiii. 37–39; St. Mark xiii. 1–2). Christ's prophetic warnings are also mentioned as applicable to Londoners in

7. *The Reluctant Pilgrim*, pp. 100–01. See the entire discussion, pp. 99–102.
8. *An Exposition of the Old and New Testa-ment* ("Author's Preface," 1706; 1st American ed., Philadelphia: Barrington and Haswell, 1828), I, 281.

plague: "Wo! be to those who are with Child, and to those which give suck in that Day" (p. 144 [000]; St. Matthew xxiv. 19). A related allusion occurs in H.F.'s meeting with the waterman, who was obliged to remain in London with his wife and family. His wife's name is Rachel and their child has plague (pp. 132–33) [89–90], details that are reminiscent of Jeremiah's prophecy: "A voice was heard in Ramah, lamentation and bitter weeping; Ra[c]hel weeping for her children refused to be comforted for her children, because they were not" (Jeremiah xxxi. 15; see also St. Matthew ii. 16–18).

These references are connected with the narrator's specific situation as well as generally with the city. In each of the gospels in which Christ prophesies the destruction of Jerusalem, he also warns his listeners to flee (St. Matthew xxiv. 16; St. Mark xiii. 14; St. Luke xxi. 21); woes are predicted for those who cannot flee—for example, those who are with child. The story of the three men from Stepney parish—the soldier, sailor, and carpenter—reinforces the warning implied by these allusions. As Bastian notes, "No effort is made to fit the story convincingly into the rest, by pretending, for instance, that H.F. was connected with any of the participants."[9] However, the story is thematically relevant; the decision of these men to leave is the appropriate one and provides an indirect comment on H.F.

In his introduction to the story of the three men, H.F. implies that he thinks the account has a moral significance beyond its literal one. His first abortive introduction states that even if the plague does not return "still the Story may have its Uses so many ways as that it will, I hope, never be said, that the relating has been unprofitable" (p. 72) [52]. Later, just before he actually begins the story, he not only recommends the conduct of these men as a pattern to follow in time of plague, but also states that the "Story has a Moral in every Part of it" (p. 149) [100]. The broad outlines are obviously parallel to the biblical account of the Israelites leaving Egypt to find the Promised Land, typologically mankind seeking salvation. The men flee a plague-stricken city and live nomadically in a hostile environment. Eventually they and their company establish themselves in an abandoned house, where they remain until the plague has abated. What the story seems to inculcate is the personal effort that, in addition to reliance on God, is necessary for salvation. H.F.'s passive trust in God is presumptuous.

There are other more explicit biblical references in this story. After the wanderers are given wheat, they must eat it "in parched Corn, as the *Israelites* of old did without grinding or making Bread of it" (p. 178) [118], an allusion to the Israelites before the city of Jericho (Joshua v. 11). The major difficulties that the wanderers from Stepney parish face are those of finding food and gaining permission to pass through towns (p. 150) [101–2]. Finding food was a recurrent difficulty for the Israelites,

9. Defoe's *Journal of the Plague Year* Reconsidered," p. 170.

and both the Edomites and Amorites refused to allow passage, even though the Israelites offered to "go by the high way: and if I and my cattle drink of thy water, then I will pay for it: I will only, without doing any thing else, go through on my feet" (Numbers xx.19; see also xxi.22–23; see *Journal*, p. 164 [109–10]).

The care with which Defoe's allusions are selected is attested to by the pertinence of even the seemingly casual reference to the lepers of Samaria. The old soldier John says, "I am of the same Mind with the Lepers of Samaria: 'If we stay here we are sure to die' " (p. 151) [101]. The complete story of these lepers is found in II Kings vii. The Israelites, besieged by the Syrians, had no food. In desperation the lepers among them went to the Syrian camp, where they discovered that the Syrians had fled, leaving plenty of food: "For the Lord had made the host of the Syrians to hear a noise of chariots, and a noise of horses, even the noise of a great host . . ." (II Kings vii.6). This same John who mentions the lepers subsequently devises the stratagem by which the wanderers, pretending to be a large armed band, get food from the people of Walthamstow (pp. 165–69) [110–13]. This is certainly an example of the combination of personal effort and divine prompting.

H.F.'s advice—"*the best Physick against the Plague is to run away from it*" (p. 241) [156]—reflects not only his increased understanding but also the limits of his understanding. He sees the plague as a terrifying evil that frustrates his attempts at moral discriminations. The prophecies of Christ that H.F. alludes to cannot increase his understanding greatly. Christ's injunction is to flee: although there is an overall moral order, no promises are made to those unable to flee: woes are pronounced upon them, no matter how morally worthy they may be. This sense of a judgment that evades man's usual moral discriminations pervades *A Journal of the Plague Year* and produces the anxiety in the narrator that is so common among Defoe's characters. One of the frequently repeated words in Defoe's writings is "hardened," and the ultimate evil is the hardened heart that cannot respond to God's judgments.[1] The narrator of the *Journal* seeks calm, but he cannot confidently distinguish this state from hardening. He continuously alternates between trust and fear, seeking to escape his terrors but also believing them to be evidence of his responsiveness to God.[2]

It is the intensity of the focus on the narrator that makes *A Journal of the Plague Year* something more like a novel than like either history or the seventeenth-century pious writings that lie in the background. *The Pilgrim's Progress* continues to be interesting because of its Christian, but he is contained within the boundaries of the work's didacticism. In

1. See Starr's chapter on *Moll Flanders* in *Defoe and Spiritual Autobiography* for a discussion of "the classic process of hardening" (p. 134).
2. It seems clear that at times Defoe had a detached and even ironic attitude toward his narrator; at other times H.F.'s uncertainties may reflect Defoe's own anxieties. Although the question of Defoe's relationship to his narrator cannot be given a definitive answer, the coherence of the book can, nevertheless, be seen.

contrast, H.F.'s attempts to instruct the reader frequently become only further evidence of his psychological turmoil; the lesson is sometimes poorly taught, but the character's emotional difficulties are powerfully communicated. A *Journal of the Plague Year* contains signs of the hasty writing that flaws so much of Defoe, but the aptness of the allusions and the clear development of H.F. imply a coherent design. Defoe organized his factual material to suggest the spiritual reality that lies beyond the physical one. But instead of directing the spiritual meanings primarily outward toward the reader for a didactic purpose, Defoe used these meanings to create a psychologically complex and interesting character.[3]

JOHN J. RICHETTI

Epilogue: A *Journal of the Plague Year* as Epitome †

> . . . for the face of things so often alters, and the situation of affairs in this great British Empire gives such new turns, even to nature it self, that there is matter of new observation every day presented to the traveller's eye.
>
> Defoe, *A Tour Through the Whole Island of Great Britain*, I.

Among Defoe's longer narratives, A *Journal of the Plague Year* is *sui generis*. His other narrators are autobiographers who place themselves at once in the middle of events, shaping and altering their surroundings from act to act. Their task is to present themselves at the expense, finally, of the world, to extract freedom from various kinds of necessity. In place of these expansive conquests, the *Journal* offers a detailed and carefully compelling picture of necessity in the ultimate human forms of disease and death. The semi-anonymous H. F. lives at the contemplative edge of that necessity, mysteriously immune to the plague so that he can record the inscrutability of natural process. Defoe's other narrators appropriate their environments, converting them from historical and geographical entities into emanations of the infinitely resourceful self.[1]

3. Two important works that deal with the *Journal* have appeared subsequent to my writing of this paper: A *Journal of the Plague Year*, ed. Louis Landa (London: Oxford Univ. Press, 1969); George Starr, *Defoe and Casuistry* (Princeton, N.J.: Princeton Univ. Press, 1971).
† Reprinted with some revisions from *Defoe's Narratives: Situations and Structures* (Oxford: Clarendon, 1975) by permission of Oxford University Press.
1. Robinson Crusoe, for example, domesticates his deserted island by introducing agriculture and animal husbandry and even, at the end of the narrative, by establishing a colony that he leaves behind when he returns to England. Moll Flanders survives in London's urban labyrinth by her mastery of larcenous techniques as shoplifter and pickpocket, so that in time the city's intricacy and immensity become essential aspects of her art of thievery. In both novels, an oppressive and dangerous environment is transformed by the protagonist's distinctive energy into an arena for the expression of personality. *Roxana* and *Colonel Jack* have much more varied settings, and the relationships between their protagonists and the environments through which they travel are never simply or clearly self-expressive.

The saddler's account is rooted in and limited by the historical moment of the plague, and it is surrounded as well by the verifiable documents and maps of an actual London.[2]

These differences are hardly surprising. The *Journal* is pseudo-history in the service of expert political propaganda,[3] and the saddler is necessarily an adjunct to these purposes, a witness to events whose reactions support rather than convert their reality. But as Louis Landa has remarked and as every reader of the book can affirm, H. F. 'achieves a measure of individuality, enough at least to insinuate concern for his fate into a reader's mind'.[4] It seems to me, moreover, that our concern for the saddler's fate is never a matter of crude anxiety over his survival. That, after all, is given from the start. The source of our concern and what we participate in as readers is the process of ordering an unprecedented intrusion of natural chaos called the plague, and what the saddler leads us to fear is the dominance of disorder. In short, the saddler is not a lesser Crusoe; he is an intensified and almost abstract version of the ordering self that we have seen in Defoe's other narratives.[5]

The plague is an extended moment of total uncertainty, an exaggerated, nearly metaphysical version provided by history of the random destructiveness of an environment. Perfectly, one can add, that environment is both natural and social. The plague is a natural disaster attendant upon commerce and urban crowding, perpetuated and complicated by the conditions of social life. What we are delighted witnesses to as readers is the simultaneous resolute stillness and efficient movement of the saddler in the plague. The special trick he manages is what all Defoe's narrators aspire to achieve in the larger spaces and more extensive rhythms

2. F. Bastian has asserted that Defoe's major source was his own experience and 'a considerable mass of first-hand information, critically sifted by an acute mind'. (See 'Defoe's *Journal of the Plague Year* Reconsidered', *RES*, 16 (1965), 166) The traditional praise of the book has involved marvelling over Defoe's powers of literary reconstruction and research, so Bastian's affirmations mark an important if exaggerated critical shift. Freed as it is from the conventions of popular narrative format, the *Journal* is free to make use of Defoe's own experience of walking the streets of London as a private citizen. Manuel Schonhorn has reinforced that common-sense view of the matter by pointing out that although Defoe reconstructed in his narrative the topography of an older London, he concentrated on those locations and structures still a part of the London scene in 1720. (See 'Defoe's *Journal of the Plague Year*: Topography and Intention', *RES*, 19 [1968], 387.)

3. J. R. Moore says that the *Journal* and *Due Preparations for the Plague* were published in 1722 to create support for Walpole's unpopular Quarantine Act. (See *Daniel Defoe: Citizen of the Modern World* [Chicago, 1958], p. 320.)

4. *The Journal of the Plague Year* (Oxford English Novels, 1969), Introduction, p. xxxiv. All further references in the text are to this edition.

5. *Defoe's Narratives* argues that his novels, in different ways, are concerned with the dilemma built into individualist consciousness during what historians call the early modern period, when identity is still for most people intertwined with traditional communal institutions but when the possibilities for a specifically individual sense of selfhood begin to be imagined by increasing numbers. Defoe's protagonists balance their extraordinary individual presence (or at least their narrative attempt to communicate it) against their narration of the social circumstances that forced them to be what they are. The novels, I argue, "communicate by their arrangements and strategies an implicit grasp of the tangled relationships between the free self and the social and ideological realities which that self seems to require. What they show us as we read is character carefully separating itself from that unsatisfactory tangle of private and public, personal and social, and establishing an unimpeachable selfhood, at least in the privileged space of the narrative" (*Defoe's Narratives*, p. 17).

of their lives: to balance the claims of action and submission and to extend that pattern to their environments. The saddler stays because he has a hunch. His inactivity is a form of action which reconciles movement and stillness in a perfect manner. Moreover, his solution to the problem set by the plague is entirely personal, private. Others did well to fly.

> Upon the foot of all these Observations, I must say, that tho' Providence seem'd to direct my Conduct to be otherwise; yet it is my opinion, and I must leave it as a Prescription, *(viz.) that the best Physick against the Plague is to run away from it.* I know People encourage themselves, by saying, God is able to keep us in the midst of Danger, and able to overtake us when we think our selves out of Danger; and this kept Thousands in the Town, whose Carcasses went into the great Pits by Cart Loads; and who, if they had fled from the Danger, had, I believe, been safe from the Disaster; at least 'tis probable they had been safe. (197–8)[156]

Note the last qualifying phrase. The saddler is nothing if not reasonable. He rejects 'Turkish Predestinarism' (193)[152] and its extremes of trust and careless fatalism in favour of Christian moderating action; he refines the plague from the direct visitation of an angry God to the result of natural causes. And yet he sympathizes with those who are distracted nearly to belief in the consoling clarity of such simplicities. All this reasonableness and more serve to obscure that initial irrationality, the decision to stay. Like Crusoe, H. F. presents a detailed brief for the existence of personal providential signals. He surrounds his decision to stay with circumstances which confirm his initial inclination to stay. He thought of going away but could get no horse, resolved to walk and sleep in a tent but his servant left him. He opens his Bible at random and the 91st Psalm advises him to trust in God, advice we might add maliciously to be found almost everywhere in that book.[6] All these details add up to 'Intimations from Heaven of what is his unquestion'd Duty to do' (10)[13], even though the saddler's brother tells him that Providence does not work through such trivial and particular means. The theological question of particular Providences remained in doubt in the early eighteenth century,[7] but the needs of narrative are always clear. The central self must in some way assert itself at the expense of the other, and H. F. must stay if we are to have a book to read. That fact is both cause and effect of the narrator's power over what he sees and experiences. The sheer necessity of wanting and having this kind of first-person observer (in events and yet outside them) involves not just journalistic efficiency but a fundamentally superior self that can participate in the world with

6. See p. 6 in this volume.
7. R. M. Baine notes that in Defoe's day the doctrine of particular Providence 'was beginning to weaken', and sees its defence as a pervasive theme in Defoe's works, especially in the *Journal,* where 'the pattern of Providence is most frequently felt and most variously apprehended'. (See *Daniel Defoe and the Supernatural* [Athens, Georgia, 1968], pp. 3, 6.)

involvement but without loss. We have forgotten how important such truisms are and how coherently and intensely Defoe's narratives work them out. In so far as we are readers, the theological arguments are thereby after the fact, a handy ideological justification of what is given by the functional and structural requirements of the narrative. The special privilege of the narrator in the novel is given, to return to Lukács's phrase, in the 'affirmation of a dissonance' between the immanence of being and empirical life.[8] In other forms, says Lukács, that situation is a prelude to form; in the novel it is the form itself. The *Journal* is an almost pure articulation of that form implicit in the situation which may be said to create the novel as a genre.[9]

The saddler's search for justification is the first indicator in the narrative of his essentially gratuitous resistance to the demands of empirical life raised to the nth power by the plague. Gratuitous at least at first, for the narrator's function is to protect himself from the formlessness of that horrendous physical reality. It is only paradoxical at first glance that he has to stay in the middle of death and disorder in order to live and establish the order of his narrative. More overtly and clearly than Defoe's other narratives, the *Journal* allows us to see that the self does not so much resist disorder as exploit it to create its own order.

H. F.'s narrative is the unfolding of a mystery and its reduction to facts—statistics, measurements, causes, and effects. He explains at the very beginning that there were no newspapers to give false reports, so he thought that official documents like the weekly Bills of Mortality could be used and trusted. But even they are unreliable, invaded by 'Knavery and Collusion' (6)[9], and H. F. depends upon his own observations for the truth of the spreading infection. Those observations are impelled by what he repeatedly calls his 'curiosity'. In turn, the plague in all its exact details compels the saddler: 'I mention'd above shutting of Houses up; and it is needful to say something particularly to that; for this Part of the History of the Plague is very melancholy; *but the most grievous Story must be told*' (36)[35]. H. F.'s horror is consistently coupled with an exactness which is obviously a means of controlling and intensifying that horror at a measured pace. The narrating self is a measuring intelligence whose strength is expanded by that exactness. Thus the description of

8. *The Theory of the Novel*, p. 72. See also, Chapter 1, *Defoe's Narratives*.

9. The most influential Marxist critic of the early twentieth century, the Hungarian Georg Lukács began his critical career with a Hegelian treatise on the distinctiveness of the novel and its philosophical implications as a new literary form (*The Theory of the Novel* [London: Merlin Press, 1971, trans. Anna Bostock; first published in German, 1920]) Lukács argued there that the novel does not, like older literary genres, dramatize pre-existing ethical systems and exploit the "dissonance" between life and artistic representation to constitute itself as a form. Rather, the novel, says Lukács, enacts in the biographical patterns of individuals the process of a peculiarly modern ethical dissonance in which there is a gap between the empirical self and the transcendental subject, that is, between the historical individual (the "I") produced by material and social circumstances and the free self glimpsed in the liberating act of narration whereby those circumstances are understood and to that extent mastered. To put it another way, Lukács sees the novel in general as mimetic (representing the world as we experience it) and form-giving (understanding that world and coming to self-consciousness of our place in it by the act of narration).

the great pit at Aldgate begins with measurements, an engineer's survey: 'it was about 40 Foot in Length, and about 15 or 16 Foot broad; and at the Time I first looked at it, about nine Foot deep; but it was said, they dug it near 20 Foot deep afterwards, in one Part of it, till they could go no deeper for the Water' (59)[52]. But that order is less than the truth, and he goes to see it at night to count the bodies it conceals. What he sees is a sort of authentic disorder:

> It was about the 10th of *September*, that my Curiosity led, or rather drove me to go and see this Pit again, when there had been near 400 People buried in it; and I was not content to see it in the Day-time, as I had done before; for then there would have been nothing to have seen but the loose Earth; for all the Bodies that were thrown in, were immediately covered with Earth, by those they call'd the Buryers, which at other Times were call'd Bearers; but I resolv'd to go in the Night and see some of them thrown in. (60)[53]

The saddler's 'curious' enumeration of these things precludes, of course, the inarticulate horror which is the natural reaction to them. He admits as much: 'This may serve a little to describe the dreadful Condition of that Day, tho' it is impossible to say any Thing that is able to give a true Idea of it to those who did not see it, other than this; that it was indeed *very, very, very* dreadful, and such as no Tongue can express' (60)[00]. Such clumsy underlinings mark the end of his attempts to render his feelings about the plague and to concentrate solely on his relationship to it. After the great pit at Aldgate, the saddler tells us he is 'almost over-whelm'd', and his narrative shifts noticeably about this point towards description of what others did about the plague. His 'curiosity' contin-ues, but leading now in more positive directions to the discovery no longer of pure horror but of resourceful ordering by others in the face of the plague. In Defoe's other stories, the narrators are the only ones per-mitted to function that way; they observe themselves. Here the saddler becomes a pure and disinterested intelligence who has earned the right by staying in the middle of disorder to claim the rewards of order around him. He claims those rewards in the sense that the novelistic narrator tends to appropriate for himself and for us what he sees, claims them in the novelistic sense that to narrate is to supply the perception which supplies being. Having stayed by himself and for his own inscrutable reasons, he presides over the order he discovers in the absolute middle of the plague. The narrative sequence is such that a powerful apartness such as we have seen at times achieved by Defoe's other characters with great labour is the saddler's privilege, the result of his actively staying still in the centre of the whirlwind. Having endured disorder, having looked steadily into it, and having done that for no reason except a sense of secret and special destiny, the saddler discovers that the plague is the source of an order greater than that which prevailed before the plague struck. That pattern stands from our perspective on Defoe's narratives as a remarkable epitome of their imaginative strategies.

The saddler finds virtue, courage, and ingenuity: in the Waterman whose family is stricken and then provided for by means of a large flat stone, in those who have taken refuge aboard ships in the harbour, in the biscuit-baker, sail-maker, and joiner who establish with their skills a community of survival for themselves in the middle of it all. London itself is a source of joyful satisfaction as a model of order, 'a Pattern to all the Cities in the World for the good Government and the excellent Order that was every where kept, even in the time of the most violent Infection; and when the People were in the utmost Consternation and Distress' (155)[125]. Order and decency, he records, are preserved to such an extent that nothing extraordinary is seen during the day, 'not the least Signal of the Calamity to be seen or heard of, except what was to be observ'd from the Emptiness of the Streets, and sometimes from the passionate Outcries and Lamentations of the People, out at their Windows, and from the Number of Houses and Shops shut up' (186)[147]. As Manuel Schonhorn has observed, the book is a tribute to the city itself,[1] but that tribute must be read as a means of enlarging and solidifying the observing self which has remained in the city. H. F. combines personal experience, anecdote, and socio-political observation in such a way that they co-operate to place him beyond confusion or ideological simplification. He examines questions of origins and effects with informed nicety. He establishes physical contagion over miasma and natural causes (tempered by awareness of ultimate providence) over supernatural intervention. The individual depravity of the sick in spreading the infection is proved to be the understandable defence of the hard-pressed provincial towns. The validity of his observations and opinions as well as their consonance with Defoe's opinions are interesting but irrelevant questions for the purpose of grasping the imaginative base of the book. Those observations function as an endorsement of the narrative self. The act of discovery that we read about is what matters, the transition from the natural chaos of the plague and the brief uncertainty of the self that it engenders to the serene contemplation of an extended human order.

The ultimate step in that contemplation, in logic if not quite in sequence, is the overt realization that the plague is a fruitful crisis, a set of circumstances which made men forget their sectarian alliances.[2] And finally, the economic disaster wrought by the plague produced, like the Great Fire before it, tremendous prosperity afterwards. Though offered pages apart from each other, those two consolidations explain the special sort of transforming privilege the narrator now has. He is able to see on the one hand how the plague restores natural conditions, encourages the survival of the resourceful, and destroys artificial distinctions in the

---

1. 'Defoe's *Journal of the Plague Year*: Topography and Intention', *RES*, 19 (1968), 398.
2. See H. F.'s observations on "a near View of Death would soon reconcile Men of good Principles . . . ," pp. 139–40 in this volume.

brotherhood of survival. On the other, he can see that the plague coop-
erates with what we might call the normal business cycle and is as much
a metaphor for social-economic conditions as a hyperbolic version of
natural conditions. The natural and the social interact in the *Journal*
with a quiet perfection nowhere else achieved in Defoe's narratives; the
'truth' of human nature resides in the natural environment, and in the
privileged moment elaborated by the narrator's intelligence that environment and the social-economic setting where that truth is normally
obscured coalesce. The narrator possesses that unique resolution of the
antithesis between the natural and the social by virtue of his obstinate or
perhaps singular and privileged refusal to run.

The saddler concludes by spending a good number of his last pages in
sorrow at the return of careless disorder. The plague subsides and people
forget the danger of contagion and return to normal religious strife. The
plague, then, is a brief moment of clarity when nature and society coin-
cide and allow the self to observe and to order, to act without moving.
History presented Defoe with the materials to solve the problem that his
other narratives confront in overtly personal and therefore quite impossible ways. *A Journal of the Plague Year* remains a thickly factual, even
grossly truthful, book. But the imagination which flares up occasionally
and dominates those facts is the secret and smiling and still quite impossible self for which we read Defoe.

MAXIMILLIAN E. NOVAK

Defoe and the Disordered City †

Few readers of *A Journal of the Plague Year* (1722) would argue with the
notion that the most compelling aspect of the book involves the terrible
scenes of pain and death, the cries of the victims, or such vivid triumphs
of style as that involving the apprentice who attempts to collect money
for his master from one of the plague victims: "At length the Man of the
House came to the Door; he had on his Breeches or Drawers, and a
yellow Flannel Wastcoat; no Stockings, a pair of Slipt-Shoes, a white
Cap on his head; and as the young Man said, Death in his Face."[1] But
with many theologians and even more physicians insisting that there was
no more a cure for the plague than for an earthquake, that it was a direct
visitation from God, many writers on the pestilence concerned themselves less with nostrums than with the problem of disorder; for if there
appeared to be no way to prevent the plague from extinguishing a major

† Reprinted by permission of the Modern
Language Association of America from *PMLA*
92 (1977): 241–52.
1. Daniel Defoe, *A Journal of the Plague Year*,
ed. Louis Landa (London: Oxford Univ. Press,
1969), p. 86 [72]. All quotations from this work
refer to this edition. Page numbers in brackets
are to this Norton Critical Edition.

part of the population, there might at least be some way of preventing a complete breakdown of communal and political organization.[2] In his influential *Short Discourse concerning Pestilential Contagion*, which appeared in an eighth edition in 1722, Richard Mead wrote:

> It is no small Part of the Misery, that attends this terrible Enemy of Mankind, that whereas moderate Calamities open the Hearts of Men to *Compassion* and *Tenderness*, this greatest of Evils is found to have the contrary effect. Whether Men of wicked Minds, through Hopes of Impunity, at these Times of Disorder and Confusion, give their evil Disposition full Scope, which ordinarily is restrained by the Fear of Punishment; or whether it be, that a constant View of Calamaties and Distress, does so pervert the Minds of Men as to blot out all Sentiments of Humanity: or whatever else be the Cause, certain it is, that at such Times, when it should be expected to see all Men unite in one common Endeavour, to moderate the publick Misery; quite otherwise, they grow regardless of each other, and Barbarities are often practised, unknown at other times.[3]

Defoe was to report on one man, captured by the French authorities when the plague was raging around Marseilles in 1721, who confessed to murdering more than a thousand victims.[4] Richard Bradley warned that when plague struck, "The Father abandon'd the Child, and the Son the Father; the Husband the Wife, and the Wife the Husband." And another pamphlet remarked that "The most intimate Friends are afraid of and abandon each other."[5] *A Journal of the Plague Year* offers a different view of human life under the stress of the plague, and in this paper I want to examine some of the reasons for Defoe's perspective and its implications for fiction.

Recent discussions of *A Journal of the Plague Year* have centered on questions of historical accuracy and on the character of H. F., the Saddler narrator.[6] But historians have long assured readers that it must be read as a "historical novel."[7] And though the thoughts of Defoe's narrator are unquestionably important as our way into the work of fiction,

2. See, e.g., Sir John Colbatch, *A Scheme for Proper Methods to Be Taken Should It Please God to Visit Us with the Plague* (London: J. Roberts, 1721), pp. vii–viii.
3. *Short Discourse concerning Pestilential Contagion*, 8th ed. (London: Sam Buckley, 1722), pp. xvii–xviii.
4. *Applebee's Journal*, 1 Oct. 1720, rpt. in William Lee, *Daniel Defoe: His Life and Recently Discovered Writings* (London: John Hotten, 1869), ii, 285. All references to *Applebee's Journal* are to this edition.
5. Bradley, *The Plague at Marseilles Consider'd* (Dublin: Patrick Dugan, 1721), sig. a4; and *The Late Dreadful Plague at Marseilles Considered* (Dublin: Patrick Dugan, 1721), pp. 3, 13. This pamphlet has been ascribed to Dr. Joseph Browne.
6. See, e.g., Everett Zimmerman, "H. F.'s

Meditations: A *Journal of the Plague Year*," PMLA, 87 (1972), 417–22; and Frank Bastian, "Defoe's *Journal of the Plague Year* Reconsidered," *Review of English Studies*, 16 (1965), 151–73.
7. Walter G. Bell, *The Great Plague in London in 1665* (London: John Lane, 1924), p. v. Bell insists that Defoe's method was unhistorical, that the narrative, based on the Orders of London's Lord Mayor, a set of regulations never actually carried out, was essentially fictional. Thus what Watson Nicholson showed as long ago as 1919 in his study of Defoe's use of history, *The Historical Sources of Defoe's Journal of the Plague Year*, that Defoe drew heavily on contemporary reports of the plague, is not really important for Bell's argument. As a narrative, *A Journal of the Plague Year* is a work of fiction.

what we apprehend of his life and inner state merely satisfies Lengelet du Fresnoy's contemporary characterization of the ideal historical narrator—a man whom we trust for his judgment and impartiality.[8] Our focus is seldom on his personal problems except as he shares those problems with the victims of the plague; and those victims were, for the most part, not businessmen. "It came by some to be called the *Poors Plague,*" Dr. Nathaniel Hodges remarked in his firsthand account of the holocaust of 1665, and what distinguishes Defoe's narrative is its remarkable concern for the ordinary man and his anguish as the city struggled to survive.[9] As Landa has remarked in his excellent introduction to the *Journal,* the book is "first and foremost a story of London. . . . Where deaths are so abundant, poignancy is diffused. The real tragedy is corporate" (p. xvi). But it was a London from which the rich had fled, and H. F. must be the first fictional narrator whose sympathies embrace even the swarming poor of the city.[1]

Landa is, of course, not wrong to remind us that in Defoe's vision of the plague everyone is a victim, "the rich and the poor" (p. xvi). H. F. remarks that the burials in the plague pits were

> full of Terror, the Cart had in it sixteen or seventeen Bodies, some were wrapt up in Linen Sheets, some in Rugs, some little other than naked, or so loose, that what Covering they had, fell from them, in the shooting out of the Cart, and they fell quite naked among the rest; but the Matter was not much to them, or the Indecency much to any one else, seeing they were all dead, and were to be huddled together into the common Grave of Mankind, as we may call it, for here was no Difference made, but Poor and Rich went together. (p. 62)[55]

But what is surprising is not the presence of this theme, which appears in all of Dekker's plague pamphlets, but its comparative absence.[2] Unlike the heavy metaphors and moralizing we find in Dekker, Defoe continues, "there was no other way of Burials, neither was it possible there

8. *A New Method of Studying History,* trans. Richard Rawlinson (London: W. Burton, 1728), I, 281.
9. See Hodges, *Loimologia,* 3rd ed. (London: E. Bell, 1721), p. 15. The connection between the conditions under which the poor lived and the plague was commonplace. Reports of the plague in Marseilles noted that "the Distemper having seized only the poorest sort of People" might pass as soon as the government sent in supplies of better food than the poor usually ate. *The Present State of Europe,* trans. John Philipps et al. (London: Henry Rhodes, 1720), XXI, 306.
1, The flight of the rich from the city at the onset of the plague was part of the ordinary pattern of life during the 17th century. In his *A Rod for Run-awaies* written in 1625, Thomas Dekker wrote, "I send this newes to you, the great Masters of Riches, who haue forsaken your

Habitations, left your disconsolate Mother (the City) in the midst of her sorrowes, in the height of her distresse, in the heauinesse of her lamentations." In *The Plague Pamphlets,* ed. Frank P. Wilson (Oxford: Clarendon, 1925), p. 145.
2. Typical of Dekker's style is the following: "The World is our common Inne, in which wee haue no certaine abyding: It stands in the Road-way for all passengers. . . . A sicke-mans bed is the gate or first yard to this Inne, where death at our first arriuall stands like the Chamberlaine to bid you welcome, and is so bold, as to aske if you will alight, and he will shew you a Lodging" (*Plague Pamphlets,* pp. 182–83). Defoe's rejection of images like the dance of death is reminiscent of Dickens' refusal to get emotional mileage from such easy ironies; see Alexander Welsh, *The City of Dickens* (Oxford: Clarendon, 1971), p. 13.

should, for Coffins were not to be had for the prodigious Numbers that fell in such a Calamity as this" (pp. 62–63)[55]. The reason, then, for the observation has more to do with the scarcity of goods than with a moral reflection.

Technically, the most obvious device for displaying general human sympathy is the use of the words "poor" and "people" in an ambiguous sense; sometimes "poor" is used in the manner of George Eliot in expressing pity for an individual, sometimes as a description of those who were too indigent to escape from the city.[3] But is is clear that when he speaks of "People made desperate" (p. 55)[49], he is not merely speaking of those with property as was customary at the time, but of all Londoners. H. F. and some wealthier citizens manage to shut themselves away, living a kind of Robinson Crusoe existence for a time, completely self-sufficient, but he knows that those without money cannot do that:

> However, the poor People cou'd not lay up Provisions, and there was a necessity, that they must go to Market to buy, and others to send Servants of their Children; and as this was a Necessity which renew'd it self daily; it brought abundance of unsound People to the Markets, and a great many that went thither Sound, brought Death Home with them. (p. 78)[67]

And comments on these poor blend into accounts of a "poor unhappy Gentlewoman" (p. 160)[128], "the Passions of the Poor People" (p. 80)[69], "poor People, terrified, and even frighted to Death" (p. 55)[50], and, toward the end, "these poor recovering Creatures" (p. 248[192].

What is more remarkable is that H. F. writes with considerable sympathy for the people of London when they are in a state of complete confusion:

> It is impossible to describe the most horrible Cries and Noise the poor People would make at their bringing the dead Bodies of their Children and Friends out to the Cart, and by the Number one would have thought, there had been none left behind, or that there were People enough for a small City liveing in those Places: Several times they cryed Murther, sometimes Fire; but it was easie to perceive it was all Distraction, and the Complaints of Distress'd and distemper'd People. (p. 178)[141]

Instead of the usual contempt heaped on any action of the mob, he describes the rumor of an insurrection in the city with compassion, arguing that the poor were "starv'd for want of Work, and by that means for want of Bread" (p. 128)[105]. He denies, however, that there was ever any real plunge into chaos:

> This, I say, was only a Rumour, and it was very well it was no more; but it was not so far off from being a Reality, as it had been

3. For a discussion of the use of sympathy in George Eliot's fiction, see Barbara Hardy, *The Novels of George Eliot* (New York: Oxford Univ. Press, 1967), pp. 14–31.

thought, for in a few Weeks more the poor People became so Desperate by the Calamity they suffer'd, that they were with great difficulty kept from running out into the Fields and Towns, and tearing all in pieces where ever they came; and, as I observed before, nothing hinder'd them but that the Plague rag'd so violently and fell in upon them so furiously, that they rather went to the Grave by Thousands than into the Fields in Mobs by Thousands: For . . . where the Mob began to threaten, the Distemper came on so furiously, that there died in those few Parishes, even then, before the Plague was come to its height, no less than 5361 People in the first three Weeks in August. (pp. 128–29)[105]

But the compassionate treatment of individuals is even more striking. Robert the Waterman, whom H. F. meets walking on the bank of the Thames, is described as a "poor Man"; yet in the midst of his sufferings for the loss of one of his children and probable death of another, Robert is capable of pitying a "*poor Thief*" who has died of the plague while robbing a nearby house (p. 106)[88]. Robert weeps as he tells of how he continues working to support his remaining family, and H. F. is moved:

> And here my Heart smote me, suggesting how much better this Poor Man's Foundation was, on which he staid in the Danger, than mine; that he had no where to fly; that he had a Family to bind him to Attendance, which I had not; and mine was meer Presumption, his a true Dependance, and a Courage resting on God: and yet, that he used all possible Caution for his Safety.
>
> I turn'd a little way from the Man, while these Thoughts engaged me, for indeed, I could no more refrain from Tears than he. (pp. 108–09)[90]

Now, as Walter Bell remarks in his book on the plague, if some doctors died, no magistrate succumbed (*The Great Plague*, p. 9). Though Pepys shows distress throughout the plague, after remarking that "the likelihood of the increase of the plague this week makes us a little sad," he immediately adds, "But then again, the thoughts of the late prizes [in the war] make us glad." And in his last entry for 1665, he summarizes his sense of the year's events in a burst of good feeling: "I have never lived so merrily (besides that I never got so much) as I have done this plague-time, by my Lord Brouncker's and Captain Cocke's good company, and the acquaintance of Mrs. Knipp, Coleman and her husband, and Mr. Laneare; and great store of dancings we have had at my cost (which I was willing to indulge myself and wife) at my lodgings."[4] Pepys is a little inconvenienced and sometimes a little frightened. Like H. F., he is fascinated by the spectacle of death, but, for the most part, his concerns focus on the war with the Dutch, on his efforts at bringing together the shy couple, Philip Carteret and Jemima Montagu, and on

4. Samuel Pepys, *The Diary*, ed. Robert Latham and William Matthews (Berkeley: Univ. of California Press, 1971), vi, 226, 342.

his pursuit of various ladies, recorded in a mixture of Spanish, French, and Latin.

Pepys' *Diary* indicates just how odd *A Journal of the Plague Year* is. It represents a concentration on the life of the poor such as never had been attempted before. Unlike Defoe's experimental *The Storm*, an account of the violent tempest of 1703, with its focus on a few days spread over a wide geographical area, the *Journal* focuses exclusively on London and its surroundings and is, in spite of considerable historical accuracy, fictional in its narrative viewpoint and overall structure.[5] Neither the life of the time nor even the life of the plague went on in quite the way Defoe presented it. It is a novel with a collective hero—the London poor—and though it ends with the triumphant voice of the Saddler proclaiming his survival, it is the survival of London that matters.

The trouble with the plague of 1665 from a teleological standpoint was that the wrong people were punished. Defoe argued that the vices of the upper classes gradually drifted down to corrupt the manners of the poor.[6] The plague of 1665 should have been visited on the "Lewd, Lascivious" court of Charles II. But as he knew from William Kemp's *A Brief Treatise of . . . the Pestilence*, which appears in Defoe's library, the plague flourished in the poorer parts of cities "and more in narrow Streets and Lanes of those Cities, . . . because usually there are narrow and little rooms, which are soonest fill'd with infectious vapours, and longer keep them in."[7] And so in one of his mock-prophetic pieces, which invariably included predictions of an imminent plague, he envisioned a pestilence that would harm the rich more than the poor.

> Shall Britain be free! flatter not your selves with Expectations of it, many Plagues visit this Nation and whole Parties of Men suffer the Infection; all sorts of Men shall die, some politickly, some really, the Grave makes no Distinction of *Whigg* or *Tory*, High or Low *Church*. Three Bishops go off the Stage first, Dukes, Earls, Barons and Privy-Counsellors follow; a great Rot fall among the Court-Sheep, and the Murrain upon the Stallions of this *Sodomitish* City. The Infection spares none: But alas, for the Sheepherds of our Flocks! they fly and leave their Flocks to be scattered . . . the Number,

5. Although Thucydides' account of the plague in Athens was justly admired as a distinguished piece of writing, the study of a single natural phenomenon, such as a storm, earthquake, or plague, was not regarded as a historical genre. The preface to *The Storm* (London: J. Nutt, 1704) clearly indicates that Defoe considered his work as entirely original. He remarked in his preface, "I have not undertaken this Work without the serious Consideration of what I owe to Truth, and to Posterity; nor without a Sence of the extraordinary Variety and Novelty of the Relation" (sig. A4). See also Thomas Sprat, *The Plague of Athens* (London: H. Hills, 1709), p. 2.

6. See particularly *The Poor Man's Plea*, in *A True Collection of the Writings of the Author of the True Born English-man* (London, 1703–05), I, 286–87.

7. *A Brief Treatise of the Nature, Causes, Signes, Preservation from, and Cure of the Pestilence* (London: D. Kemp, 1665), p. 35. See also *The Libraries of Daniel Defoe and Phillips Farewell*, ed. Helmut Heidenreich (Berlin, 1970). A general discussion of contemporary theories regarding the plague may be found in Charles F. Mullett, *The Bubonic Plague and England* (Lexington: Univ. of Kentucky Press, 1956).

whose Carkasses shall fall in the Wilderness, is not to be Numbered. . . . Yet for the Encouragement and Support of the Poor,
Heaven promises Plenty in the Fields, and there shall be no want
of Bread.[8]

Defoe was not uncritical in his admiration of the common people, but
he believed in a class mobility which would allow the common soldier,
"poor Wretches, that are (too many of them) the refuse and off-scow-
rings of the worst parts of our Nation," to become "Orderly, and Sensible, and Clean, and have an Ayre and a Spirit."[9] And he could sympathize
with "that black Throng" of London street children who "perish young,
and dye miserable, before they may be said to look into Life."[1] Defoe's
attitudes appear oddly humane even next to those two other depicters of
the sublime and miserable in human life—James Thomson and Edward
Young.[2]

And behind H. F.'s willingness to sympathize with the distractions of
the mob under the fear of the plague and starvation lies Defoe's refusal
to condemn completely the mobs of his day. When we think of Dryden's
ignorant rout or Thomas Southerne's venial rabble, it is hardly surprising that Pope should have made the mob the symbol of universal chaos.
But in his recent study of radical movements, Christopher Hill rightly
detects behind Defoe's Harringtonian respect for property more radical
elements of thought.[3] For if Defoe believed that only those with a share
in the wealth of the nation should participate in elections, the fact is
that he recognized that in times of national crisis the crowd always became
involved. Thus, though he thought mobs to be the very antithesis of
government, his theory of the chaos from which government emerged
and into which it could fall involved mob action.[4] As a result, while
depreciating all mobs, he found himself distinguishing between good
mobs and bad mobs and arguing that, unless deceived by false propaganda, they were usually a manifestation of some wrong that needed to
be redressed.

When he called upon the House of Commons to pay attention to the

8. *The British Visions: Or, Isaac Bickerstaff,
Sen.* (London: J. Baker, 1711), p. 10. For other
predictions of a coming plague, see *The Second-Sighted Highlander* (London: J. Baker,
1713), p. 13; and *The Second-Sighted Highlander. Being Four Visions of the Eclypse* (London: J. Baker, 1715), p. 17.
9. A *Short Narrative of the Life and Actions of
His Grace John, D. of Marlborough* (London:
J. Baker, 1711), pp. 42–43.
1. *Some Considerations on the Reasonableness
and Necessity of Encreasing and Encouraging
the Seamen* (London: J. Roberts, 1728), p. 44.
2. George Eliot rightly suggests some of Young's
failures of sympathy in her essay "Worldliness
and Other-Worldliness: The Poet Young."
Thomson's depiction of the plague, like his other
descriptions of human distress, tends to dimin-

ish human suffering in relation to the power of
nature and its God.
3. *The World Turned Upside Down* (London:
Temple Smith, 1972), p. 308.
4. Defoe's contemporaries always stressed the
radical elements implied by works like *The
Original Power of the Collective Body of the
People of England* (London, 1702 [1701]). His
stress on the importance of property as the basis
of government was neither new nor excessive,
but the suggestion of a chaotic brew at the bottom of all political action was suspect. See, e.g.,
Charles Leslie, *The Rehearsal*, 28 Sept. 1706,
where Defoe's theories are attacked for laying
"a Foundation for Perpetual Changes and Revolutions, without any Possible Rest or Settle-
ment."

Kentish Petitioners, he signed himself "Legion," with all its Satanic reference to Mark v.9, *"our Name is Legion, and we are Many."*[5] Thus, all his treatment of the people acting as a political force has an edge to it, and when he wrote to his patron, Harley, about the mob he encountered in Edinburgh, there is more than that; indeed, there is something close to exhilaration: "[I] Saw a Terrible Multitude Come up the High street with A Drum at the head of Them shouting and swearing and Cryeing Out all scotland would stand together, No Union, No Union, English Dogs, and the like."[6] One would think that this fear of being torn apart by the mob ("Nor was Monsr *De Witt* quite Out of my Thoughts"—*Letters*, p. 135) would bring out an attack on mob violence, but in his *History of the Union of Great Britain*, in which the mobs are brilliantly described, we have a sympathetic picture of a nation completely "divided . . . and as the Event began to be feared on every side, People stood strangely doubtful of one another."[7] The plight of these people resembles that of the people of London during the plague, and yet the blame is placed entirely on those in power:

> It was not for the poor People, to distinguish the Original of Causes and Things. . . . it was not for them to distinguish the hand of *Joab* in all this; whether *Jacobite* or Papist was the Original of this Matter was not for them to examine; They saw their Superiors joyning in the same Complaint, and every Party saw some of their respective Chiefs embark'd.
>
> The common People could look no further; the Episcopal Poor saw their Curates Tooth and Nail against it; the Ignorant and Indifferent Poor, saw their *Jacobite* Land-Lords and Masters Railing at it; and which was worse still, the Honest Presbyterian poor People saw some of their Gentlemen, and such as they had remarked and noticed *to be Hearty Presbyterians*, yet appearing against it;—Who then can censure the poor depending, uninformed and abused People?
>
> (*History of the Union*, Pt. II, p. 56)

In this picture of a nation in a state of division and panic, there are major parallels with the central situation of *A Journal of the Plague Year*, and if it may be argued that the *Journal* was hardly about 1706, it may be answered that neither was it about 1665. The chaos Defoe really had in mind was that of 1721. And the cause of that chaos was not merely the fear of the plague in Provence but also the awareness of the "plague of avarice" that had ruled England and much of Europe for a number of years. Though writing long after the event, Tobias Smollett gives an effective and accurate picture of the consternation created by the collapse of the South Sea Bubble:

5. *Legion's Memorial* (1701), in *The Shortest Way with the Dissenters and Other Pamphlets* (Oxford: Basil Blackwell, 1927), p. 112.
6. *The Letters*, ed. George H. Healey (Oxford: Clarendon, 1955), p. 135.
7. *History of the Union of Great Britain* (Edinburgh: Andrew Anderson, 1709), Pt. II, p. 34.

During the infatuation produced by this infamous scheme, luxury, vice, and profligacy, increased to a shocking degree of extravagance. The adventurers, intoxicated by their imaginary wealth, pampered themselves with the rarest dainties, and the most expensive wines that could be imported: They purchased the most sumptuous furniture, equipage, and apparel, though without taste or discernment: they indulged their criminal passions to the most scandalous excess: their discourse was the language of pride, insolence, and the most ridiculous ostentation. They affected to scoff at religion and morality, and even to set heaven at defiance.[8]

Amid a general feeling of chagrin in 1721, there seemed to be unanimous agreement that a good dose of bubonic plague would be a proper punishment for the sins of the nation. A bill against atheism and profaneness aimed at reminding the nation of its errors raised bitter debate and recrimination in the House of Lords. A mass hanging of everyone associated with the South Sea Company might have had a calming effect, but the great Skreen-Master General, Walpole, deprived everyone of that pleasure.[9]

In such an atmosphere, the plague at Marseilles, which was to spread to Arles, Toulon, and other cities of Provence, was regarded with apprehension. This apprehension was reinforced by the connection between the plague and commercial adventurers. An infected ship had arrived at Marseilles on 20 May 1720 carrying goods from Syria, and the plague spread rapidly from the docks. Captain Chataud's vessel and its disastrous cargo became a familiar object lesson. Fairly typical of the connection made between trade and the plague is Thomas Newlin's sermon *God's Gracious Design in Inflicting National Judgments*, preached on 16 December 1720, a day set aside by George I "for a General Fast and Humiliation . . . particularly for beseeching God to preserve Us from the Plague." After quoting from Isaiah xxv.8, *"Her Merchants were Princes, her Traffickers the Honourable of the Earth,"* he remarked that "the channels by which our Riches are convey'd, may convey the Plague to our Houses," and made a direct causal connection between England's avarice and the seemingly inexorable approach of the plague.[1]

Incidentally, Newlin's sermon was hardly intended to quiet the fears of his audience. He sounded the familiar theme from Lamentations, *"How doth the City sit solitary that was full of People! How is she become a Widow!"* And he reminded his audience that "not only the Offices of Friendship were Destroy'd, but all Relations were frequently Taken away" during a plague. He pretended to spare the feelings of his listeners ("I fear I have trespass'd upon your Humanity, and may be charg'd with violating the Tenderness of Nature, unless I draw a Veil over this melan-

8. A *Complete History of England*, 3rd ed. (London: James Rivington, 1759), x, 273.
9. See John Carswell, *The South Sea Bubble* (London: Cresset, 1961), pp. 223–24; and Smollett, *A Complete History of England*,

pp. 273–74.
1. *God's Gracious Design in Inflicting National Judgments* (Oxford: Stephen Fletcher, 1721), title page, pp. 11, 21.

cholly Scene"), but included some horrendous descriptions of the dead and dying (*God's Gracious Design*, pp. 11, 14, 15). Equally vivid in its implications was a Jacobite tract, *The Best Preservative against the Plague*, which warned that a more likely cause for the approaching pestilence was the sin of rebellion and that the best means of keeping it away was a speedy return of the Stuarts to the throne.[2]

Adding somewhat to the feeling of terror was the passage of the new Quarantine Act on 25 January 1721, containing three clauses which ordered immediate death for anyone sick who attempted to leave a house that was quarantined, or for anyone well who attempted to leave after coming in contact with anyone in such a house. The third clause gave the King the right "*to cause* one or more Line, or Lines, Trench, or Trenches, *to be cast up, or made, about such infected City, Town or Place, at a convenient Distance.*" Anyone attempting to cross these lines could be shot as a person "*Guilty of* Felony." The arguments against these clauses, presented in a petition of the Lord Mayor of London, Aldermen, and Commons of the City, were that such measures could not be put into effect without military force, "And the *violent* and *inhuman* Methods which on these Occasions may, as we apprehend, be practised, will we fear, rather draw down the Infliction of a new Judgment from Heaven, than contribute any way to remove that, which shall have befallen us." The petitioners further maintained that these measures were copied from France, a tyrannical nation, that nothing of the kind had been done in 1665, and that they would "keep the Minds of the People perpetually *alarm'd* with those Apprehensions under which they now labour."[3] To Londoners, with the lesson of Toulon before them, a city that lost two thirds of its population through similar measures, the thought of being ringed by soldiers must have been particularly terrifying. On 20 May 1721, Defoe wrote an account for *Applebee's Journal* describing the massacre of 178 people who attempted to flee Toulon:

> People, Men, Women, and Children, to the number of 1700,— made desperate by their Diseases, and quite raging by their Hunger,—Sally'd out into the Fields by force, and wandering about to seek Food, came up to the Lines, which are guarded by several Regiments of regular Troops. They demanded Bread; the Soldiers told them they had none but the Ammunition-Bread, that was allow'd them for their daily Subsistence, but seeing their Distress, they threw them what they had, which the poor Creatures devoured like ravenous Beasts. They then desir'd they might pass into the plain Country, to get Bread, that they might not be starved; when the Soldiers told them they could not let them do so, it being contrary to their Orders. But the poor desperate Wretches told them they

2. *The Best Preservative against the Plague* (London: J. Leminge, 1721), pp. IV–XI.
3. *A Compleat Collection of the Protests of the*

Lords (London: J. Jones, 1722), pp. 6–8. See also Abel Boyer, *The Political State* (London: A. Boyer, 1721), XXII, 640–44.

must, and would go, for they could but dye; and accordingly attempted the Lines in sixteen or seventeen Places. At the same Time the Soldiers kept them back as long as they could with Blows, and with the Muzzles of their Pieces; but were at length obliged to fire at them, by which about 178 were killed, and, as they say, 137 wounded. Among the first were three and thirty Women and Children, and four and fifty among the latter; so that most of them were driven back into the City, where they must inevitably perish.[4]

Defoe remarks that, in spite of this slaughter, some hundreds did get through the lines; so the effort to quarantine the city, for all its slaughter, was ineffectual.

Defoe's vivid account in *Applebee's* was fairly symptomatic of his attitudes. His sympathies are with the starving people of Toulon and, to some extent, with the soldiers who had to follow orders. His anger is directed against a nation that could treat its population with such cruelty. But Defoe's situation is not at all simple. John Robert Moore argued that *A Journal of the Plague Year* and other writings on the plague were intended to support Walpole's government. Indeed, the Quarantine Act had been introduced by Walpole,[5] and, in the House of Lords, the petition of the Lord Mayor had the support of only a few Jacobites and Tories.[6] Yet Defoe is clearly for the elimination of the three clauses.[7] When they were finally repealed in 1722, it was only after Walpole's supporters noticed that their leader "seemed to remain silent" (Boyer, *Political State*, XXIII, 118). As we shall see, while supporting Walpole's efforts at bringing order and stability out of the chaos of the time, Defoe followed his own theory that a certain amount of anarchy need not subvert the general order of society.

Defoe's unusual attitudes emerge in this period in his writings for *The Manufacturer*, a journal supporting the riots of the weavers against the import of calicoes. The weavers actually went so far as to tear calico clothing off women in London streets, and when Defoe's role in defending the weavers was discovered, he was taunted for espousing such a cause.[8] I have no intention of making Defoe into a proto-Marxist, defending proletarian class interests; Diana Spearman, in her *The Novel and Society*, has rightly cautioned us against anachronistic treatments of

4. Printed in William Lee, *Daniel Defoe: His Life and Recently Discovered Writings* (London: John Hotten, 1869), II, 378–79.

5. *Daniel Defoe: Citizen of the Modern World* (Chicago: Univ. of Chicago Press, 1958), p. 320. See also Mullett, *Bubonic Plague and England*, p. 271.

6. See *The History and Proceedings of the House of Lords from the Restoration in 1660 to the Present Time* (London: Ebenezer Timberland, 1742), III, 198–200. A large number of those voting for repeal participated in the Jacobite plot in 1722.

7. The government gave official approval to a

pamphlet by Edmund Gibson, *The Causes of the Discontents in Relation to the Plague* (London: J. Roberts, 1721), and had it distributed around the country. Gibson scoffed at the idea that the liberties of Englishmen were being undermined by the Quarantine Act and accused the enemies of the Act of Jacobite leanings. See Norman Sykes, *Edmund Gibson Bishop of London* (London: Oxford Univ. Press, 1926), p. 81.

8. See *The British Merchant*, 24 Nov. 1719, 1 Dec. 1719; and Defoe's reply in *The Manufacturer*, 2 Dec. 1719.

the concept of class in eighteenth-century fiction.[9] On the other hand, she is wholly wrong in thinking that no distinct idea of class existed, whether in literature or life, until the nineteenth century. In Richardson's *Clarissa*, both Lovelace and Anna Howe use the word "class" with clear socioeconomic implications, and so did Defoe and his contemporaries earlier in the century.[1] Actually, since Defoe had supported striking keelmen at Newcastle years before *The Manufacturer* and given his sympathy for what was called the "working poor" throughout his life, his championship of the poor in case of a possible plague should not be surprising. For all of his respect for property as the basis of government, he made an even more significant division between those who added to the wealth of the nation through their labor and those who did not, and in this division neither aristocrat nor beggar fared well.[2]

But if he was willing to excuse the violent acts of the weavers, the concurrence of the South Sea Bubble and the possibility of an approaching plague led him toward efforts at soothing the nerves of the nation. An early opponent of stock jobbing, he linked the two events together constantly. On 25 March 1720, in *The Commentator*, he remarked on the similarity of the two:

> The Fury of Gaming may perhaps go in Courses, like the Plague, from one Quarter of the World to another; and the Seat of it at present seems to be in *England*, where it begins to rage with more Violence, than has been ever known in these Parts. It is not indeed of that mortal Kind as the *Sickness* in the Year 1665. But tho' it does not sweep away whole Families without Distinction of Age or Sex, yet there have been lately some Houses lock'd up.

And on 1 October 1720, after the bursting of the South Sea Bubble, he made the same comparison through the eyes of a man visiting the Exchange from the Country:

> I concluded these were either some honest sorrowful Persons, come together to some great Burial, and so they had put on the most dismal Countenances they could frame for themselves; or, that some Sickness was broke out in the Place, and these walking Ghosts were all infected with the Plague; for never Men look'd so wretchedly.

9. *The Novel and Society* (London: Routledge & Kegan Paul, 1966), pp. 37–50.

1. See Samuel Richardson, *Clarissa* (London: Dent, 1959), II, 281, 442. Defoe attacked the "Impudence" of servants in *The Great Law of Subordination Consider'd* (1724), but a careful reading of that work next to Swift's *Directions to Servants* (1745) reveals how much Defoe places the blame for the misbehavior of servants and workers on their masters. In *The Generous Projector* (1731), he concluded that if the servants had the wit to get good wages, they probably deserved them and added, "However, if they are honest and diligent, I would have them encourag'd, and Handsome Wages allow'd 'em; because, by this Means, we provide for the Children of the inferior Class of People, who otherwise could not maintain themselves."

2. For a discussion of Defoe's attitude toward people according to their productivity, see my *Economics and the Fiction of Daniel Defoe* (Berkeley: Univ. of California Press, 1962), pp. 16–17, 74. For a typical qualification about the evil of mobs, see A *Review of the Affairs of France*, ed. Arthur W. Secord (New York: Facsimile Text Society, 1938), VIII, 17–18.

Someone takes the Countryman aside to explain that these are South Sea men by their "South Sea Face" which makes the victim appear "Pale, Frighted, Angry, and out of his Wits" (*Applebee's Journal*, in Lee, II, 283–84).[3]

A more straightforward effort at quieting the frenzy was a journal called *The Director*, which fought a losing battle against the hysteria of investors, attempting to defend the idea of a South Sea Company even after the dishonesty of the directors was apparent. He also warned that it would be inevitable that Jacobites would use the distracted state of the nation to plot against the government. Meanwhile, in a satire printed in *Applebee's Journal*, on 14 January 1721, he complained that too many deaths were being blamed on the fall of stocks. Noting that one madam had blamed the South Sea Company for the closing of her bordello, he composed a mock Bill of Mortality for deaths of this kind:

Drowned herself *(in the South Sea)* at St. *Paul's*, Shadwell, One.
Kill'd by a *(South Sea)* Sword, at St. *Margaret's*, *Westminster*, One.
Smother'd in a *(South Sea)* House of Office, at St. *Augustine's*, One.
Cut his Throat with a *(South Sea)* Razor, at St. *Anne*, *Blackfryers*, One.
Frighted *(by the Fall of South Sea Stock)* at St. *Mary-le-Bow*, Two.
Overlaid *(by South Sea)* at St. *Dunstan's*, *Stepney*, Three.
Grief *(at the Fall of South Sea)* at St. *Giles Cripplegate*, One.
Scalded to Death in a *(South Sea)* Caldron, at St. *Botolph* without, *Bishopgate*, One.
Shot himself with a *(South Sea)* Pistol, at St. *Mary*, *Whitechapel*, One.
Kill'd by Excessive Drinking of *(South Sea)* Geneva, Five, (viz.) Two at St. *Martin-Outwich*, and three at St. *Peter's Poor*.

(in Lee, II, 324–25)

Such satire was gentle enough. Much earlier, in an issue of *The Commentator* (4 July 1720), he applauded an act of Parliament that would regulate trade in such a way as to prevent it from going in the direction of "Tricking and Cheating . . . and made all Men afraid of one another as well as ready to devour one another."[4] And to cheer up those still blaming themselves for their ruinous avarice, he reminded them that it was almost impossible to tell when the quest after money turned from a virtue to a vice.

Though he used many of the same methods to relieve anxieties over the plague, as might be expected, he was usually more somber. In an article in *The Commentator* of 15 August 1720, he played down the likelihood of any plague coming to England:

3. There is a probable connection between the idea of a "South Sea Face" and a "plague face," a particular facial appearance which marked a person as a victim of the plague. See William Boghurst, *Loimographia* (1666), in *Transactions of the Epidemiological Society*, 13 (1894),

28; and *The Late Dreadful Plague at Marseilles*, p. 6.
4. This was the so-called Bubble Act, which the Directors of the South Sea Co. approved, since by eliminating smaller bubbles, it also removed competition.

> Now I am none of those that are for frighting People with Appre-
> hensions of the Judgment of Heaven; nor is it my Business, who
> am not of the Pulpit to tell them what they might expect, if they
> were to have what they merit from their Maker. Blessed be God,
> *Marseilles* is a great Way off; and the *French* are obliged, for their
> own Safety, to keep it from spreading this Way, if it be possible:
> Besides, the Plague has been much nearer to *England* than *Mar-
> seilles*, and yet we have escaped it; . . . And therefore we have no
> reason to be allarm'd yet, unless a Ship was to come in here directly
> from *Marseilles*. In which Case, no question, due Care will be
> taken by the Government to prevent any Mischief of that Kind, at
> least as far as possible: And which is better than all, I am informed
> the Case is not so bad as is reported, but that even at Marseilles
> they have been more afraid than hurt.

Defoe himself tells of a number of deaths through sheer terror in *A
Journal of the Plague Year*, and while he may have believed some of the
reports circulated by the French government to belittle the virulence of
the plague, it is clear that his chief concern is to prevent panic in England.

Along similar lines are his efforts to preach the uses of adversity, whether
associated with the stock market or the plague, and to argue that affliction brought men together:

> How easy were it for the Master-Governor of the World to correct
> Mankind for their Dissentions, and teach them Peace by the Pun-
> ishment of their Contentions? How easily would we be all recon-
> cil'd by our own Sufferings, and reduc'd by the Terrors of the Divine
> Hand, either in Pestilence, Earthquakes, Famine, or a long ruin-
> ous War; we should soon be better Friends with one another. . . .
> Men would lay aside their Strife, when they are oppress'd with pub-
> lick Mischief; and are easily inclin'd to go Hand in Hand to the
> Grave, tho' they never shook Hands before.[5]

And in a letter to *Applebee's Journal*, in an issue filled with news of the
plague, Defoe commented through a mask with the significant name,
T. Saddler, "why do you not walk about the Streets of this half-ruin'd
City, and make Observations upon such frequent and just Occasions, as
the present Circumstances of Things would present you? Certainly no
Age ever gave the like Instances of human Misery, or the like Variety
for Speculation" (in Lee, II, 292). The cause of this misery was not a
plague but the final bursting of the bubble, though both had one similar
effect—that of causing widespread unemployment.[6] "In a Word," he
remarked, "every Place is full of the Ruines of Exchange Alley, and the
Desolations of the Bubble-Adventurers." And he urged his audience to
a general sympathy. "If Pity was ever a Tribute from the Hearts of Men
unconcern'd to Men in Disaster," he wrote, "now is the Time to shew
it."[7]

5. *Commentator*, 13 June 1720.
6. See, e.g., Colbatch, p. 13.

7. *Applebee's Journal*, 22 Oct. 1720, in Lee,
II, 292–93.

What this suggests, then, is that the main impulse behind A *Journal of the Plague Year* was a demonstration of human pity and fellowship in the worst of disasters. What Robinson Crusoe felt for himself and asked his readers to feel for his isolation, the Saddler asks for an entire community. And Defoe achieves his effect by showing a London in 1665 in which family love frequently triumphed over the drive for self-preservation. With such warnings in mind from contemporary tracts that "everyone is left to die ALONE,"[8] Defoe has his Saddler tell stories of family sacrifice such as that of the Tradesman who attends his wife during the birth of their child:

> The poor Man with his Heart broke, went back, assisted his Wife what he cou'd, acted the part of the Midwife; brought the Child dead into the World; and his Wife in about an Hour dy'd in his Arms, where he held her dead Body fast till the Morning, when the Watchman came and brought the Nurse as he had promised; and coming up the Stairs, for he had left the Door open, or only latched: They found the Man sitting with his dead Wife in his Arms; and so overwhelmed with Grief, that he dy'd in a few Hours after, without any Sign of the Infection upon him, but meerly sunk under the Weight of his Grief. (pp. 119–20)[98]

The Saddler offers to show examples of the plague taking away "all Bowels of Love, all concern for one another" (p. 115)[95], but the only example he gives is that of a pitiable woman who kills her children in a frenzy of delirium. "Self Preservation indeed appear'd here to be the first Law" (p. 115)[95], writes H. F., but the example of Robert the Waterman bringing food and money to keep his infected family alive contradicts such statements. James Sutherland is right to speak of a Wordsworthian effect to achieve sympathy, much as Barbara Hardy does with George Eliot.[9] The parallels are striking:

> *But how do you live then, and how are you kept from the dreadful Calamity that is now upon us all? Why Sir, says he, I am a Waterman, and there's my Boat, says he, and the Boat serve me for a House; I work in it in the Day, and I sleep in it in the Night; and what I get, I lay down upon that Stone, says he, shewing me a broad Stone on the other Side of the Street, a good way from his House, and then, says he, I halloo, and call to them till I make them hear; and they come and fetch it.* (p. 107)[88]

H. F. remarks how deeply he is moved "when he spoke of his Family with such a sensible Concern, and in such an affectionate Manner" (p. 111)[92]. A breakdown in human relationships is always presented as a possibility within the *Journal*, but instead we are given a picture of sacrifice. And as for the evidence that people who had the plague sometimes tried to communicate it to the healthy, H. F. flatly denies that it is so (p. 154)[124].

---

8. *The Late Dreadful Plague*, p. 13.
9. See Sutherland, *Daniel Defoe* (Cambridge, Mass.: Harvard Univ. Press, 1971), pp. 226–27; and Hardy, pp. 196–98.

If those who remain in the city are depicted with such compassion, so the more radical stance, the flight of the brothers, John and Thomas, and their friend Richard, the Joiner, is presented as a "Pattern for all poor Men to follow, or Women either, if ever such a Time comes again" (p. 122)[100]. Thus, the leader of the group, the former soldier John, asserts the liberty of Englishmen to spread through the countryside in fleeing from the plague. Doubtless the individual towns which attempted to prevent such exodus were less efficient than the lines of soldiers proposed in 1721, but, in any case, John will have none of it. "Look you Tom," he tells his brother, "*the whole Kingdom is my Native Country as well as this Town. You may as well say, I must not go out of my House if it is on Fire, as that I must not go out of the Town I was born in, when it is infected with the Plague*" (p. 124)[102]. This is a speech that Defoe seconded in his *Due Preparations for the Plague*, in which he argued, "I cannot but think men have a natural right to flee for the preservation of their lives, especially while they are sound and untainted with the infection."[1]

The flight is not presented as a mob raging through the countryside. Rather it resembles a highly organized communal retreat before an inexorable enemy (*Due Preparations*, xv, 21–27).[2] And though John argues for self-preservation at first, when he is stopped by a country Constable, he argues that self-preservation must come behind "Compassion" (p. 145)[116]. The three Londoners use considerable ingenuity, but their survival depends on the charity of the countryside.

In his *Tour through the Whole Island of Great Britain*, Defoe commented on the increased population of the city as being due in part to large numbers of people living on money invested in government annuities and in the great stock companies and speculates on whether paying off the public debt would depopulate the city. But however mixed were his feelings about the "luxuriant age which we live in, and . . . the overflowing riches of the citizens," he still views London as "the most glorious sight without exception, that the whole world at present can show, or perhaps ever cou'd show since the sacking of Rome in the European, and the burning of the Temple of Jerusalem in the Asian part of the World." And while he refers to London as "this great and monstrous thing," he also praises it as having "perhaps, the most regular and well-ordered government that any city, of above half its magnitude, can boast of."[3] But when Walter Bell accuses Defoe of naïveté in believing that the orders of the Lord Mayor were actually carried out in 1665, it is Bell who is naïve (*The Great Plague*, pp. 72–75). What Defoe was trying to show was the possibility of maintaining order in the midst of disaster and to show that what happened in France could not occur in

1. In *Romances and Narratives by Daniel Defoe*, ed. George A. Aitken (London: Dent, 1901), xv, 19.

2. The plan to evacuate the children of London is reminiscent of a similar effort in World War II.

3. *Tour through the Whole Island of Great Britain*, Everyman Library Ed., introd. George D. H. Cole (London: Dent, n.d.), I, 168, 322, 323.

England. Judging conditions in London in 1665 and Marseilles in 1720 "pretty much the same," one writer spoke of the bodies left to rot on the streets unburied and of famine everywhere (*The Late Dreadful Plague*, pp. 12–13).[4] But, however questionable his facts, Defoe's London has neither bodies left on the street nor actual starvation. If the death carts are objects of horror, they are relatively efficient, and charity is seen to supply vast amounts of food. The paradigm of history is not a Jerusalem destroyed from within before falling to Titus, but a city refusing to succumb to chaos and disaster however great its agony.[5] If, as Alexander Welsh has shown, the London of Victorian fiction was a symbol of death, Defoe's London functions as the victory of life over death (*The City of Dickens*, pp. 180–95).

What I have been suggesting is that some of Defoe's peculiar attitudes toward disorder and the events of the time led to the creation of a completely humane narrator whose all-pervading sympathy for human suffering, extended to characters from the laboring poor, like Robert and John, takes in even the *"poor Thief."* Even God's role in punishing the sins of the nation is played down.[6] Though the Saddler is reluctant to arrive at his conclusion, he admits, "I must be allowed to believe that no one in this whole Nation ever receiv'd the Sickness or Infection, but who receiv'd it in the ordinary Way of Infection." A *Journal of the Plague Year*, then, is about the despair of 1721 through the suffering and triumph of 1665, and the charity of the narrator embraces those who fled the city and those who stayed, Church of England man and Nonconformist, the living and the dead.

Twenty-seven years after the publication of A *Journal of the Plague Year*, Henry Fielding was to argue that, among the four qualities necessary in a good novelist, humanity or "a good Heart" had to be considered among the most important. "Nor will all the Qualities I have hitherto given my Historian avail him," he writes, "unless he have what is generally meant by a good Heart, and be capable of feeling. The Author who will make me weep, says *Horace*, must first weep himself. In reality, no Man can paint a Distress well, which he doth not feel while he is painting it; nor do I doubt but that the most pathetic and affecting Scenes have been writ with Tears."[7] Given the satiric basis of

4. See also A *Brief Journal of What Passed in the City of Marseilles While It Was Afflicted with the Plague* (London: J. Roberts, 1721), p. 36.

5. For the influence of Josephus' account on A *Journal of the Plague Year*, see Watson Nicholson, *The Historical Sources of Defoe's Journal of the Plague Year* (Boston: Stratford, 1919), p. 166. A better passage than that suggested by Nicholson is from Bk. v, Secs. 27 and 33, in which Josephus speaks of how "The city being now on all sides beset by these battling conspirators and their rabble, between them the people, like some huge carcase, was torn in pieces," *The Jewish War*, trans. H. St. J. Thackeray, Loeb Library (Cambridge, Mass.:

Harvard Univ. Press, 1966), pp. 209, 211. The comparison between London in plague and Jerusalem under seige was a typological commonplace. See Dekker, pp. 31, 72.

6. Cf. Defoe's tone to that of the Quaker, Richard Ashby, in A *Faithful Warning to the Inhabitants of Great-Britain* (London, 1721), or even to that of Sir Richard Blackmore's *Just Prejudices against the Arian Hypothesis* (London: J. Peele, 1721), which threatens some terrible punishment for the avarice and irreligion of the time.

7. *The History of Tom Jones A Foundling*, ed. Martin Battestin and Fredson Bowers (Middletown: Wesleyan Univ. Press, 1975), I, 495.

so much eighteenth-century fiction and Fielding's own ironic stance in *Jonathan Wild*, it was a portentous statement for the many English novels that followed with their humane view of the entire cast of characters. Such a perspective led to those novels in which saints and sinners tended to blend into a brew of erring mortals on whom the narrator could lavish his universal pity.

So far as I can tell, no narrator in realistic prose fiction before H. F. reveals this type of general sympathy for the human condition. I do not find it in those fictions of Defoe influenced by picaresque models. In *Moll Flanders* and *Colonel Jack* there is too much of a concern with self and individual experience to have the kind of combination of sympathy and detachment to be found in H. F. And the same may be said of "poor Robinson Crusoe," as the parrot calls Defoe's castaway. Crusoe obviously has to teach his parrot to repeat that self-pitying title. Like Fielding's humane historian, H. F. resists all temptation to blame and scold. He is the invention of a moment in English history when Defoe wanted to spread feelings of hope and charity. In the process, he set a pattern for fictional narrators that has been central to the development of the novel.

JOHN BENDER

The City and the Rise of the Penitentiary: A *Journal of the Plague Year* †

> *There are in* London, *and the far*
> *extended Bounds, which I now call so,*
> *notwithstanding we are a Nation of Liberty,*
> *more publick and private Prisons,*
> *and Houses of Confinement,*
> *than any City in* Europe, *perhaps as many*
> *as in all the Capital Cities of*
> Europe *put together.*
>
> DANIEL DEFOE
> *A Tour Thro' the Whole Island of Great Britain*

*   *   *

Defoe's narratives record the onset of an epoch-making revision in men's exercise of final authority over one another. This change occurred as

† Reprinted from chapter 3 of *Imagining the Penitentiary: Fiction and the Architecture of Mind in Eighteenth-Century England* (1987) with the permission of the University of Chicago Press. Mr. Bender has edited this chapter slightly, and he and I have added a few notes and identified people and places mentioned in the text but discussed in other chapters. For full understanding of Bender's use of the old-style liminal prison and the eighteenth-century invention of the modern penitentiary, the reader should refer to chapter 1 of *Imagining the Penitentiary*. Also of interest may be chapter 2, on Defoe's *Robinson Crusoe* as a history of civic settlement, and his book's tracing of the ideological underpinnings and formal similarities

London was assuming distinctive metropolitan features, including an unprecedented immensity of scale. Just as cities had originally implied walls and bounded, hierarchical social forms,[1] they also had dictated the transient use of prison—a threshold marking off ordinary life from death, banishment, or vindication. Thus both the decrees of imperial Rome and civil law, right through the seventeenth century, ruled against imprisonment as a punishment.[2] Liminal prisons, which temporarily detained those awaiting trial or sentencing, had meaning only within a network of social boundaries, and frequently were built at the civic threshold or gateway directly within city walls. Such liminal places are, etymologically, "seclusion sites"; their inmates are at once neither living nor dead and both living and dead. The randomness, the reign of chance, and the confusion of categories so abhorrent to reformers prevailed horrifyingly within the old style prisons Defoe overtly depicted in his novels. The new style penitentiaries his work implies would impose the ordered sequence of a narrative reformation of self through discipline. These new penitentiaries did not come physically into being until the late eighteenth century.[3]

City walls by their nature could shield and govern, or enforce exile. But the London of Defoe's youth already had outgrown its walls. The original enclosure of the old City increasingly merged into sprawling suburbs at once congenial to real estate speculation and necessary to accommodate the commerce and the luxurious display that supported early urban industry.[4] Defoe lived through the period when the proto-

---

between novelistic narrative and the development of the concept of the modern penitentiary as parallel expressions of structures of feeling in urban England.

1. Anthony Giddens, A Contemporary Critique of Historical Materialism (Berkeley: University of California Press, 1981), chap. 4; and Mason Hammond, The City in the Ancient World (Cambridge: Harvard University Press, 1972), pp. 43–46.

2. See Max Grünhut, Penal Reform: A Comparative Study (Oxford: Clarendon Press, 1948), pp. 11–14. Thus Justinian reaffirmed in A.D. 533 the principle articulated under Caracalla (A.D. 211–217) that "prison ought to be used for detention only, but not for punishment": and the medieval code of Ferrara, like that of many Italian states, decreed that "prison has been 'invented' for custody, not for punishment." Quotations cited from Grünhut. In England imprisonment was used chiefly for debt and in the Star Chamber, and, as on the Continent, became increasingly common during the seventeenth century.

3. See the discussion of the old-style liminal prisons in Imagining the Penitentiary (10–40).

4. Consolidated building had extended well outside the city walls when Wenceslaus Hollar's A Map or Ground-plot of the Citty of London . . . after the Fire of 1666 was published.

Hollar's map refers specifically to the "Suburbes," which reach out much farther than on earlier maps. See Philippa Glanville, London in Maps (London: Connoisseur, 1972), pp. 92–94 on Hollar and passim for earlier maps. Glanville stresses the concern about the extramural growth of London during this period: "The Stuarts recognised the problems created by an outer belt beyond the City's control, and the Council offered in 1633 'whether they woulde accept of parte of the suburbs into their jurisdiction and liberty for better government,' but the City rejected the offer and it was not repeated" (p. 86).

Ian Watt says of Defoe's attitude toward London, by way of contrast with Richardson's suspicious negativity:

Yet although the picture has its selfish and sordid aspects, it has one very significant difference from that presented by the modern city. Defoe's London is still a community, a community composed by now of an almost infinite variety of parts, but at least of parts which still recognise their kinship; it is large, but somehow remains local, and Defoe and his characters are part of it, understanding and understood.

There are probably many reasons for Defoe's buoyant and secure tone. He had

typical pattern of blocks and squares characteristic of the modern
metropolis unmistakably asserted itself in the speculative development
of the West End.[5] The economic and social implications of this development were considerable. London moved swiftly from a distribution of
real estate on the medieval pattern of irregular precincts, parishes, and
plots to modern gridiron development whereby land is parceled out and
standardized as a commodity subject to exchange. Roger North's
autobiography[6] indicates that speculative building on a large scale began
with Dr. Nicholas Barbone's ventures following the Great Fire: "He was
the inventor of the new method of building by casting of ground into
streets and small houses, and selling the ground to workmen by so much
per front foot, and what he could not sell, built himself. This had made
ground rents high for the sake of mortgaging, and others, following his
steps, have refined and improved upon it, and made a superfoetation of
houses around London."[7] Immediately after the fire, Wren[8] presented
a new plan for London to Charles II and a rebuilding committee was
established by royal proclamation. Wren and Evelyn[9] swiftly proposed
schemes in which largely regular gridirons of blocks were overlain by
axial radiants linking major monuments. These schemes adopted the
outlines of authoritarian baroque order even though they were somewhat hobbled by the absence of the court, traditionally resident upriver.
Wren's city would have focused on a gigantic circus centered by the
Royal Exchange and surrounded by the Mint, the Post Office, the Excise
Office, and the Insurance Office—a grand seat of commercial power to
which even Saint Paul's was subordinated. Under pressure of circumstance, London opted instead for renovations superficially following the
ancient street plan but conducted in the manner of modern parceled
development, with zoning and codes of construction specified by the
government. Thus Richard Newcourt's rebuilding scheme, extending
the ancient walls and realigning parishes on a strict grid with a church

some memory of the days before the Great
Fire, and the London he had grown up in
was still an entity, much of it enclosed by
the City Wall. But the major reason is surely
that although Defoe had since seen enormous changes, he himself had participated
in them actively and enthusiastically; he lived
in the hurly-burly where the foundations of
the new way of life were being laid: and he
was at one with it. (*The Rise of the Novel*
[Berkeley: University of California Press,
1959], p. 181)

Although I lay more stress than does Watt on
Defoe's registration of London's metropolitan
traits, my case depends upon the situation he
so aptly describes. Defoe lives at a turning point;
and his way of writing narrative works to preserve the minute particulars of the old life while
reshaping them according to new predicates.

5. See map, p. 2.
6. Roger North (1653–1734) was Attorney

General to James II's Queen Mary and the
biographer of his three older brothers. He lost
his position when William of Orange became
king of England. His autobiography, *Notes of
Mee*, was not published until 1887 [*Editor*].
7. On gridiron development, see Lewis Mumford, *The City in History* (New York: Harcourt, Brace and World, 1961), pp. 421–23;
he quotes North on p. 418.
8. Sir Christopher Wren (1631–1723) was a
founding member of the Royal Society. Rather
than overseeing the rebuilding of the City, he
was appointed surveyor of the City churches
and designed fifty-two of them, including St.
Paul's. The Sheldonian Theatre at Oxford is
also his [*Editor*].
9. John Evelyn (1620–1706), another founder
of the Royal Society, is remembered today primarily for his diary. He wrote, however, influential books on reforestation, horticulture,
navigation, and commerce, and held several
government positions [*Editor*].

at the center of each block, graphs the reorientation of London's growth during Defoe's lifetime more meaningfully than Wren's or Evelyn's.[1]

The novel represented "this great and monstrous Thing, called *London*" to itself, rendering its sprawling scope accessible, comprehensible, and controllable.[2] Coherence now lay not in the permanent shape of the city as a whole (its acropolis, its close, its bounding walls, its social hierarchy), but in the formal order, the internal governance, of partial representations of metropolitan life (its consumption of goods, its cultural and social foundations, its state institutions, its literature and art). The realistic novel is above all a means of perception and disposition that validates itself in the multifarious urban setting by means of an apparent reflective completeness. The novelistic refiguration of the liminal prison into the narrative penitentiary is part of the web of generation, representation, and regeneration that creates and maintains the identity of the modern city. As Lewis Mumford says, "The abstractions of money, spatial perspective, and mechanical time provided the enclosing frame of the new life. Experience was progressively reduced to just those elements that were capable of being split off from the whole and measured separately." Or again, in a passage citing Defoe's eulogies to the sheer size of London as a force in magnifying trade, "The expansion of the market . . . is involved in the whole scheme of substituting vicarious satisfactions for direct ones, and money goods for life experiences."[3]

1. Newcourt's plan is described in Glanville, *London in Maps*, p. 95. For discussion of plans by Wren, Evelyn, and others, see Michael Hanson, *Two Thousand Years of London* (London: Country Life, 1967), pp. 94–99. See also Thomas F. Reddaway, *The Rebuilding of London after the Great Fire* (London: Jonathan Cape, 1940).

Despite the occasion offered by the Great Fire, London traversed the seventeenth century with few marks of baroque city planning. Not even after the Great Fire did London adopt the axial symmetry that typified Continental urban renovations of the period. According to Mumford, the palatial forms, uniform street elevations, and repetitious patterning of these plans enforced the dominance of absolutist courts by repeating the ancient urban "implosion" in self-conscious, formally abstracted terms (*The City in History*, p. 367). The rebuilding of Saint Paul's and the City churches in Wren's vernacular adaptation of the baroque typifies the selective approach taken by a London that for the most part remained casual toward monumental architecture. The aristocratic attempt to perpetuate the illusion that the whole of urban life was identical to that of the court had its counterpart in a variety of English public buildings, ironically including Robert Hooke's palatial Bedlam Hospital (1675); but purely from the point of view of urban planning, London bypassed the elaborations of the authoritarian baroque in favor of a direct move to the prototypical grid. The reasons for this situation had

to do in some measure with insular politics; in the 1660s the imperious symbolism of ceremonial avenues cutting across the City surely would have gone against the grain of many Londoners. But the long-term significance of London's westward development is not so very different from that of systematic baroque planning, for both broke with the existing city forms in favor of ordered parcels arranged in reduplicating units, and both proposed idealized representations of the law, order, and uniformity necessary to mercantile trade. See Mumford (chaps. 12–14).

2. Daniel Defoe, *A Tour . . . of Great Britain*, 2 vols. (London: Peter Davies, 1927), 1: 325.

3. Mumford, *The City in History*, pp. 365–66 and 437–38. See also E. P. Thompson, "Time, Work-Discipline, and Industrial Capitalism," *Past and Present* 38 (1967): 56–97; and Niklas Luhmann, *The Differentiation of Society*, trans. Stephen Holmes and Charles Larmore (New York: Columbia University Press, 1982), pp. 239 and 248. Mumford's substitutional model, though suggestive in this context, oversimplifies: vicarious experience may indeed be diminished in emotional intensity and perceptual vividness but is also a symptom of the metropolitan organization and deployment of information, which allows both to individuals and to entities a vastly enlarged scope of comprehension and an unprecedented capacity to calculate plans and predict behavior. The emergence of organized philanthropy is a case

More specifically, we may add, the substitution of private novel reading for action in the public sphere.

One characteristic method of abstraction mentioned by Mumford is casuistry, an analytic procedure for correlating general principles and particular cases that provides the matrix within which Defoe weaves his fictional universe. Casuistry is "that part of Ethics which resolves cases of conscience, applying the general rules of religion and morality to particular instances in which 'circumstances alter cases,' or in which there appears to be a conflict of duties."[4] A recognition of the affinity of casuistry to the novel allows us to grasp the paradox that realism is a method of schematization that employs dense particularity of reference as its means. The novel appears as the veritable opposite of abstraction only if we look at its content rather than its methods. As Mikhail Bakhtin says of the distinctively modern moment in the vast history of the novel as he embracingly defines it: "When the novel becomes the dominant genre, epistemology becomes the dominant discipline."[5]

In the particular kind of material realism that Defoe initiated (the novel of "Things" as Maximillian E. Novak has called it, following Defoe's division of the "Subject of Trade" into "Things" and "Persons") what is abstracted is not the referents—the narrative content or subject matter per se—but the medium itself.[6] Modern novelistic realism in general is marked by its self-representation as a transparent medium, a mode of writing that one sees through rather than a form one looks at. The convention in Defoe's fiction that his novels are transparent or, as Ian Watt has suggested, "ethically neutral," requires prior acceptance of the abstract premise that formal realism itself is intrinsically fair and evenhanded—requires in short the unacknowledged acceptance of a certain kind of authority diffused throughout the text. Watt assumes this point in his basic definition of the realist novel:

> The narrative method whereby the novel embodies this circum-
> stantial view of life may be called its formal realism; formal, because
> the term realism does not here refer to any special literary doctrine
> or purpose, but only to a set of narrative procedures which are so
> commonly found together in the novel, and so rarely in other lit-
> erary genres, that they may be regarded as typical of the form itself.

study in the large-scaled effectuality of com-
modified, vicarious experience in modern
society. On this, see Thomas Haskell, "Capitalism and the Origins of the Humanitarian
Sensibility," *American Historical Review* 90
(1985): 339–61 and 547–66.

4. G. A. Starr, *Defoe and Casuistry* (Princeton University Press, 1971), especially chap. 1.
Starr begins his book with the *OED*'s crisp definition, which continues: "Often (and perhaps
originally) applied to a quibbling and evasive
way of dealing with difficult cases of duty."
Casuistry is, strictly, a device for dealing with
the conflict of laws or rules in specific cases.

Starr broadens the idea of casuistry (convincingly in my view) to include narration of the
cases themselves.

5. Mikhail Bakhtin, *The Dialogic Imagination*, ed. and trans. Michael Holquist and Caryl
Emerson (Austin: University of Texas Press,
1981), p. 15.

6. Maximillian E. Novak, "Crime and Punishment in Defoe's *Roxana*," *Journal of English
and Germanic Philology* 65 (1966): 445. This
essay appears in another form as chapter 5 of
Realism, Myth, and History in Defoe's Fiction
(Lincoln: University of Nebraska Press, 1983).

Formal realism, in fact, is the narrative embodiment of a premise that Defoe and Richardson accepted very literally, but which is implicit in the novel form in general: the premise, or primary convention, that the novel is a full and authentic report of human experience. . . . Formal realism is, of course, like the rules of evidence, only a convention; and there is no reason why the report on human life which is presented by it should be in fact any truer than those presented through the very different conventions of other literary genres. The novel's air of total authenticity, indeed, does tend to authorise confusion on this point.[7]

The authority latent in the convention of representational neutrality is explicitly manipulated in novels such as Fielding's. While pretending all the while to hew to the values of formal realism, his narrator shapes our judgment, leading us along and supplying or withholding information so as to order our perceptions.

*   *   *

I am arguing at the most general level, then, that novelistic conventions of transparency, completeness, and representational reliability (perhaps especially where the perceptions being represented are themselves unreliable) subsume an assent to regularized authority. This assent finds its cultural counterpart in the societal consent whereby, according to Weber,[8] our reliance on the consistency, orderliness, and rationality of bureaucratic institutions—our acceptance of them as transparent and ethically neutral—validates the power of the state and indeed enables us to conceive its existence.[9] The penitentiary idea represents this acceptance at an extreme of ideological concentration in which it is rarely formulated except in what Erving Goffman has described as "total institutions."[1] Because of that doubleness and paradox specific to art and

7. Watt, *The Rise of the Novel*, p. 32. As Watt says, "the novel in general, as much in Joyce as in Zola, employs the literary means [of] formal realism." The force of transparency as a primary convention is shown by the lengths to which novelists must go in order to call attention to their medium. The self-referential novel from *Tristram Shandy* to the present day defines itself in opposition to, and therefore depends upon, the convention of realism and the transparency it implies. These values implied by formal realism are borne by novelistic conventions in themselves, with no necessary reference to the specific subject matter.

8. Max Weber (1864–1920) is best known as author of *The Protestant Ethic and the Spirit of Capitalism* (1920), which argues that Calvinism fostered capitalism [*Editor*].

9. "Only with the bureaucratization of the state and of law in general can one see a definite possibility of separating sharply and conceptually an 'objective' legal order from the 'subjective rights' of the individual which it guarantees. . . . This conceptual separation presupposes the conceptual separation of the 'state,' as an abstract bearer of sovereign prerogatives and the creator of 'legal norms,' from all personal 'authorizations' of individuals. These conceptual forms are necessarily remote from the nature of pre-bureaucratic, and especially from patrimonial and feudal, structures of authority. This conceptual separation of private and public was first conceived and realized in urban communities" (from "Bureaucracy," pp. 196–244, in *From Max Weber*, trans. and ed. H. H. Gerth and C. Wright Mills [New York: Oxford University Press, 1958], p. 239). This section translates part 3, chap. 6, pp. 650–78, of Weber's *Wirtschaft und Gesellschaft*.

1. Erving Goffman, "On the Characteristics of Total Institutions," in *Asylums: Essays on the Social Situation of Mental Patients and Other Inmates* (Garden City, N.Y.: Anchor Books, 1961), pp. 1–124; reprinted from *The Prison*, ed. Donald R. Cressey (New York: Holt, Rinehart and Winston, 1961).

literature (what Louis Althusser calls "internal distantiation"), there probably is no such thing as the "total" novel, but a profound affinity exists between the penal law and the traditional canons of consistent representation, which the novel brings to their most detailed realization. As Roland Barthes maintains, "That particular psychology, in the name of which you can very well today have your head cut off, comes straight from our traditional literature, that which one calls in bourgeois style literature of the Human Document."[2]

Whereas Moll Flanders's Newgate[3] had held a topographically and emblematically distinct place within London's delineating walls, sites of imprisonment in A Journal of the Plague Year (1722) are diffused into every street marked by the disease. Defoe's feigned historical memoir, published only two months after Moll Flanders, tacitly abandons the old prisons by granting them no delimited location in a text otherwise obsessed with places. H. F., the narrator of the Journal, never describes a single one of the twenty-seven public gaols listed in Defoe's Tour nor says anything about their condition during the plague.[4] Instead, H. F. considers the whole of London as a place of confinement bounded by hostile villages whose citizens allow no passage by road. In London and its environs, where sick people are guarded under quarantine in their own houses, there "were just so many Prisons in the Town, as there were Houses shut up" (p. 52)[47].

When H. F. laments at the very end of his journal that most people who survived the scourge went back to their own routines without registering the transformational force of their experience, he chooses the overtly liminal metaphor of the Israelites' passage into the promised land:

> I must own, that for the Generality of the People it might too justly be said of them, as was said of the Children of Israel, after their being delivered from the Host of Pharaoh, when they passed the Red-Sea, and look'd back, and saw the Egyptians overwhelmed in the Water, viz. That they sang his Praise, but they soon forgot his Works. (p. 248)[192]

2. Roland Barthes, "Dominici, or the Triumph of Literature," in Mythologies, trans. Annette Lavers (New York: Hill and Wang, 1972), p. 45. Earlier in this essay, Barthes says, "It is in the name of a 'universal' psychology that old Dominici has been condemned: descending from the charming empyrean of bourgeois novels and essentialist psychology, Literature has just condemned a man to the guillotine" (p. 43). See too The Pleasure of the Text, trans. Richard Miller (New York: Hill and Wang, 1975), p. 3: "How much penal evidence is based on a psychology of consistency!" See also D. A. Miller, "The Novel and the Police," Glyph 8 (1981): 127–47, as well as my chapter 7 below. On "internal distantiation," see Louis Althusser, "A Letter on Art in Reply to André Daspre," in Lenin and Philosophy, trans. Ben

Brewster (New York: Monthly Review Press, 1971), pp. 221–27, especially p. 222.
3. The London prison in which Defoe was confined several times and to which he sends his character Moll Flanders. Chapter 1 of Imagining the Penitentiary gives a good description of Newgate [Editor].
4. For a listing of references, see Manuel Schonhorn, "Defoe's Journal of the Plague Year: Topography and Intention," Review of English Studies, n.s. 19 (1968): 399–402; and A Journal of the Plague Year, ed. Louis Landa (London: Oxford University Press, 1969), pp. 291–98). Citations appearing parenthetically in the text refer to this edition. The only mention of actual prisons occurs on p. 92, where H.F. lists several among the rebuilding projects undertaken after the Great Fire.

This amounts to a denial of the liminal magic to Londoners who lived out the plague confined in the city at large.

The whole *Journal* depicts the uncertainty, danger, and sense of finality characteristic of rites of passage, but liminality is shorn of its transformative effects. H.F. allows lasting alteration only to those few sick people who recovered against odds. And, as to them, "confining the sick was no Confinement; those that cou'd not stir, wou'd not complain, while they were in their Senses, and while they had the Power of judging: Indeed, when they came to be Delirous and Light-headed, then they wou'd cry out of the Cruelty of being confin'd" (p. 170)[135–36]. Alone among others, he as narrator receives a perfect score. His final test is the remembrance over time of the sentence of plague under which the city had suffered, measured against his awareness of how self-conscious discipline and reflection validated his own sense of being an individual with a place in the order of things:

> I wish I cou'd say, that as the City had a new Face, so the Manners of the People had a new Appearance: I doubt not but there were many that retain'd a sincere Sense of their Deliverance . . . but except what of this was to be found in particular Families, and Faces, it must be acknowledg'd that the general Practice of the People was just as it was before. . . . Some indeed said Things were worse, that the Morals of the People declin'd from this very time; that the People harden'd by the Danger they had been in, like Seamen after a Storm is over, were more wicked and more stupid, more bold and hardened in their Vices and Immoralities than they were before; but I will not carry it so far neither. (p. 229)[178]

Although H. F. here seems to retreat from opinions closely similar to those of later reformers who attacked the old prisons, his doubts arise in a context of generalizations about the whole populace of London. But the alleged moral decline, even the terminology in which H.F. characterizes it, is precisely that of Moll and her cohorts in the Old Newgate. In the *Journal*'s archaeology of urban crisis, we find Defoe's account of the social and mental states requisite to the reformation of confinement in *Robinson Crusoe* and *Moll Flanders*.[5] H.F. prefigures the absolute contradiction of the liminal prison later found in Gay; and, through his real if tentative or casuistic embrace of authority, he assumes traits of the judgmental narrators in Fielding's novels.[6]

---

5. See chapter 2, *Imagining the Penitentiary* (42–61).

6. Maximillian E. Novak, citing Fielding's assertion in *Tom Jones* that the true novelist must above all have "a good Heart, and be capable of feeling," argues that "no narrator in realistic prose fiction before H.F. reveals this type of general sympathy for the human condition. . . . Like Fielding's humane historian, H.F. resists all temptation to blame and scold. . . . He set a pattern for fictional narrators that has been central to the development of the novel" ("Defoe and the Disordered City," *PMLA* 92 [1977]: 249–50). While I accept Novak's general characterization of H.F.'s empathetic quality and agree that the *Journal* defines this type of narrator, my stress lies on the formulation of authority latent in the methods of realistic fiction. From the point of view maintained in the following pages, the humane qualities Novak describes in H.F., as well as in later narrators, are themselves part of

In the *Journal* Defoe looks back from the period when the novel was becoming a recognizable mode of writing to the time, following the Restoration and prior to the great depopulations of plague and fire, when London, already engulfed by suburban progeny, had assumed an early modern form and was on the verge of its endless sprawl into an industrial metropolis. Defoe formulates a multiplex account of urban values by adopting the fiction of a retrospective journal assembled at least thirty years afterwards from memoranda supposedly kept during the plague of 1665 by one H.F., a saddler now deceased and buried in Moorfields.[7] H.F. reflects as follows on the spread of the town after the Civil War:

> It must not be forgot here, that the City and Suburbs were pro-digiously full of People, at the time of this Visitation . . . for tho' I have liv'd to see a farther Encrease . . . the Numbers of People, which the Wars being over, the Armies disbanded, and the Royal Family and the Monarchy being restor'd . . . was such, that the Town was computed to have in it above a hundred thousand people more than ever it held before; nay, some took upon them to say, it had twice as many. . . .
>
> I often thought, that as *Jerusalem* was besieg'd by the *Romans*, when the *Jews* were assembled together, to celebrate the Passover . . . the Plague entred *London,* when an incredible Increase of People had happened occasionally, by the particular Circumstances above-nam'd: As this Conflux of the People, to a youthful and gay Court, made a great Trade in the City, especially in every thing that belong'd to Fashion and Finery; So it drew by Consequence, a great Number of Work-men, Manufacturers, and the like, being mostly poor Peo-ple, who depended upon their Labour. (pp. 18–19)[19–20][8]

Defoe's history, staged in multiple repetitions within the psychology of a single narrator, allows him to preserve the contradictory sense that H.F. lives simultaneously in modern, metropolitan London and in an old city that, following presentiments of future growth after the Civil War, died away at the height of the plague into a kind of archaeological site:

> The great Streets within the City, such as *Leaden-hall-Street, Bish-opgate-Street, Cornhill,* and even the *Exchange* it self, had Grass growing in them, in several Places; neither Cart or Coach were seen in the Streets from Morning to Evening, except some Country Carts to bring Roots and Beans, or Pease, Hay and Straw, to the Market, and those but very few, compared to what was usual. (p. 101)[84]

a representational alliance of self with author-ity that is characteristic of the realist novel. In these works effective magistrates and judges, like persuasive narrators, must be men of good heart. Similarly, this kind of speaker pervades refor-mist tracts and, in descriptions of the ideal keeper or warden, becomes central to the penitentiary idea.

7. On the (fictional) time of composition, see Schonhorn, "Defoe's *Journal,*" p. 388.
8. Even in H.F.'s neighborhood beyond Ald-gate on the far east, where growth was slower than on the west and north, development had extended to some depth beyond the walls and was spreading well down the river banks.

Defoe immerses the disease whereby "the Face of *London* was now indeed strangely alter'd" in the reflective consciousness of a narrator whose recollection, from a vantage point following the Glorious Revolution, encompasses the decimation of the old "Mass of Buildings, City, Liberties, Suburbs, *Westminster, Southwark* and altogether" by plague and fire, as well as their resurgence with the "mighty Throngs of People settling in *London*" during the rebuilding thereafter (pp. 16, 18)[17–18, 19]

The *Journal,* through its exacting literalism of reference, fuses the metropolitan grid into realist narrative. H.F.'s story unites inseparably with the history of a London that confines him under martial law. Such is the *Journal's* historical precision that, having for some while been taken as a real document, it has since inspired a commentary obsessed with grading the degree of its accuracy and with certifying its title to one generic description or another. At the same time, the London of 1665 depicted in the *Journal* is really composed of landmarks that survived, however altered, in Defoe's city of the 1720s.[9] The lifeblood of the work seems to lie in an obsessively overdetermined double representationality: it behaves as if any depiction short of the literal is somehow insufficient. In reducing realism to an essence, the *Journal* risks becoming another substance—the zero degree of novelism. Paradoxically, by this same token, the work approaches a standing as the impossible "total" novel alluded to above.

The literalism of the *Journal* constitutes a narrational move to protect authority by presenting the text as a real documentary account of London under sentence of plague. Since the factuality of the work therefore cannot be questioned within its own boundaries (indeed H.F. preempts doubt by incorporating continual disclaimers concerning what he can and cannot know precisely), questions about the authenticity of the text as regards London are displaced into issues of authority in the mind of H.F.[1] Given that Defoe wrote the *Journal* in part to justify the unpopular Quarantine Act, proposed by the government following the spread of plague from Marseilles in the early 1720s, the issue of the proper relationship between the force of the state and individual freedom presents itself directly in the work's history.[2] Thus I view the refiguration of the authority latent in cities, especially as its representation directs and inhabits mental life in the urban metropolis, as the *Journal's* elemental

9. Schonhorn, "Defoe's *Journal,*" p. 389.

1. See Barthes, *The Pleasure of the Text,* pp. 56–57: "Of course, it very often happens that representation takes desire itself as an object of imitation; but then, such desire never leaves the frame, the picture; it circulates among the characters; if it has a recipient, that recipient remains interior to the fiction (consequently, we can say that any semiotics that keeps desire within the configuration of those upon whom it acts, however new it may be, is a semiotics of representation). That is what representation is: when nothing emerges, when nothing leaps out of the frame: of the picture, the book, the screen." Barthes's actual word, translated as "those upon whom it acts," is *actants,* a technical term in the structuralist analysis of narrative morphology. *Actants* are narrative roles usually lodged in single characters, but sometimes spread across several characters or vested in things: villain, hero, guide, quest object, and so forth. For the original see *Le Plaisir du texte* (Paris: Seuil, 1973), p. 90.

2. See Landa edition, pp. ix–x; and John Robert Moore, *Daniel Defoe,* p. 320.

concern.[3] And therefore I join with other critics who have treated the passages on the shutting up of houses as tropes for the claustrophobic, solipsistic, isolating aspects of the modern city—qualities that attain "total" representation in the penitentiary. As W. B. Carnochan suggests, H.F.'s watching from windows "prefigures Bentham's[4] inspector".[5]

> I cannot speak positively of these Things; because these were only the dismal Objects which represented themselves to me as I look'd thro' my Chamber Windows (for I seldom opened the Casements) while I confin'd my self within Doors, during that most violent rageing of the Pestilence; when indeed, as I have said, many began to think, and even to say, that there would none escape; and indeed, I began to think so too; and therefore kept within Doors, for about a Fortnight, and never stirr'd out: But I cou'd not hold it. (p. 103)[86]

H.F.'s self-confinement, though for want of enforcement he cannot "hold it" at this comparatively early stage of the narrative, anticipates his later acceptance of the role of examiner despite strong disagreement with official policy. The good citizen is both watched and watcher.

Defoe adopts the conceit that fully deployed legal authority in the city turns its houses into prisons and its citizens into criminals. From the specific case the *Journal* proposes, a generalized version of the reformist penitentiary follows by converse inference: "total" authority represented through physically enforced mental solitude—through a narratively ordered, sequential control of the particulars of daily life—will make citizens of criminals. Of course the bluntness of these propositions is a function of their exposition here. Defoe naturalizes their shading in a thousand ways by embedding them in the historically specific and highly unusual events of his journal, and by personifying them psychologically through his casuistic narrator's exposition of the debate over the shutting up of houses. The viability of the narrative depends upon a certain density of factual and emotional texture, upon the ebb and flow of multiple reports and competing interpretations.[6]

A number of strands lace through Defoe's network of claim and counterclaim, fact and counterfact, case and countercase. First, H.F. discredits liminal confinement by depicting the policy of shutting up houses as unfair and cruel in terms that precisely describe rites of passage. Sec-

3. See the last section of chapter two for full discussion of these ideas as they pertain to *Robinson Crusoe, Imagining the Penitentiary*.
4. For Foucault's description of Jeremy Bentham's design, see pp. 248–50 in this volume [*Editor*].
5. W. B. Carnochan, *Confinement and Flight*. (Berkeley: University of California Press, 1977), p. 75. I allude especially to Max Byrd, *London Transformed: Images of the City in the Eighteenth Century* (New Haven: Yale University Press, 1978), pp. 30–43; and to W. Austin Flanders, "Defoe's *Journal of the Plague Year* and the Modern Urban Experience." *Centen-*

nial Review 16 (1972): 328–48, reprinted in *Daniel Defoe: A Collection of Critical Essays*, ed. Max Byrd (Englewood Cliffs, N.J.: Prentice-Hall, 1976), pp. 150–69. See also Jack Lindsay, *The Monster City: Defoe's London, 1688–1730* (New York: St. Martin's Press, 1978).
6. This density of texture extends outside the *Journal*'s formal boundaries in the sense that the work is one of several writings by Defoe which appear, simultaneously, to have increased public acceptance of the Quarantine Act and to have "reinforced the opposition to Walpole's proposals" (see Landa edition, p. x).

ond, permanent mental reformation, not mere change of status, is the standard against which H.F. judges the effect of confinement under siege of plague on the populace. Third, he traces the reach of authority into every aspect of urban life and illustrates the force of its psychic claims through his acceptance of the official role as examiner despite his deep reservations concerning the shutting up of houses. In the metropolis, as in prison, one is either watched or watcher, and those who refuse to be examiners are themselves "committed to Prison until they shall conform themselves accordingly" (p. 38)[36]. Finally, H.F.'s narrative certifies isolation, reflection, and solitude as means of survival and thus as final values. In H.F. we witness the private self being constituted narratively through isolated reflection on its relation to circumstance; individual personality appears as the internal restatement of external authority, as a principle of order in face of chaos, comprehension in face of the arbitrary, representation in face of endless disordered perception, a principle of life as opposed to death, reformation as opposed to execution.

H.F.'s all but obsessive recurrence to the issue of shutting up houses throws these ideological predicates into relief. The debate about the effectiveness of sequestering any household touched with plague symptoms dates back as far as the practice of shutting up houses itself, and Defoe's use of this controversy, along with his literal inscription of the entire legislation on which the decrees of 1665 were based, is part of his minute re-creation of social practices that accommodated rites of passage and used them expressively.[7] But the terms in which H.F. couches his rejection of this type of forced quarantine strongly condemn the liminality that he sees as characterizing the shut-up houses.

It is precisely the chaotic, uncontrolled mixture of categories—well and sick, master and servant—that H.F. deplores most strongly in the shut-up houses. He attends much to the numerous methods of escape from shut-up houses—to the lack of system and regularity in enforcement—though from the liminal perspective the possibility of escape is itself part of the symbolism. The myth of the penitentiary is, conversely, that one cannot get out except by a regulated course of life.

Although H.F. views the measure of shutting up houses as inhumane, his objections focus at least as much on its ineffectiveness as on its cruelty: "I believed then, and do believe still, that the shutting up of Houses . . . was of little or no Service in the Whole; nay I am of the Opinion it was rather hurtful, having forc'd those desperate People to wander abroad with the Plague upon them who would otherwise have died quietly in their Beds" (p. 71)[61]. He advocates a more discriminating quarantine in pesthouses, where only those stigmatized with signs of the disease would be confined in solitary rooms, and therefore effectively monitored:

7. See ibid., p. 267n, for an account of the debate. On the expressive function of punishment, see Joel Feinberg, *Doing and Deserving:* *Essays in the Theory of Responsibility* (Princeton: Princeton University Press, 1970), pp. 95–118.

> I say, had there instead of that one been several Pest-houses, every one able to contain a thousand People without lying two in a Bed, or two Beds in a Room . . . I am perswaded, and was all the While of that Opinion, that not so many, by several Thousands, had died. (p. 74)[63–64]

H.F. seems to envision a system of voluntary confinement in the pesthouses, for he denies the intention of "forcing all People into such Places" (p. 182)[144]. Yet his proposal is directed chiefly at servants, who spread the plague by coming and going to fetch necessaries for their households, and he vests the power to commit them in their masters, not in the servants themselves.[8] Similarly, for all that it contradicts his conviction that shutting up houses by force was ineffectual, H.F. never wavers in his belief that forcible confinement would prevent spread of the disease by crazed victims dashing frantically about the streets:

> Had not this particular of the Sick's been restrain'd . . . *London* wou'd ha' been the most dreadful Place that ever was in the World; there wou'd for ought I know have as many People dy'd in the Streets as dy'd in their Houses; for when the Distemper was at its height, it generally made them Raving and Delirious, and when they were so, they wou'd never be perswaded to keep in their Beds but by Force; and many who were not ty'd, threw themselves out of Windows, when they found they cou'd not get leave to go out of their Doors. (p. 164)[131]

Thus, while opposing the method of shutting up houses, H.F. endorses its most practical aim, advancing a scheme in which solitary confinement would protect society and increase the survival rate of the infected.[9]

More important than the specific content of H.F.'s objections, however, is his rejection of symbolic boundedness as a method for organizing and allocating authority. The shutting up of houses was an old practice by which authority placed itself in a distinct relation to material circumstance, drawing putative boundaries around arenas within which the arbitrary and the bizarre not only were tolerated but expected. Liminal symbolism forms part of a cultural system alien to H.F.'s way of conceiving reality, and thus to his proposals. He advocates a much more individual and focused discrimination, a much finer symptomatic classification for separating the diseased from the not-diseased. In the old

---

8. See *Journal*, pp. 73–75 [63–65]. Since, even under H.F.'s proposal, the master's only other choice would be the hated alternative of shutting up the house containing himself and his entire family along with the infected servant, avowals against force seem disingenuous. The assumption that disease, like crime, originates among the poor underlies the very legislation that Defoe transcribes into the *Journal*. The section on beggars closely resembles a number of criminal statutes. On Defoe's own, more sympathetic, attitude toward the poor, see Novak, "Defoe and the Disordered City."

9. See *Journal*, p. 182 [145]. In another passage, H.F. claims that greater ills would have resulted from carrying the sick to the pesthouses than would have followed from leaving them shut up at home (pp. 181–82) [144–45]. But here he refers to dangerous proposals that would have relied on the two grossly inadequate existing pest houses while abandoning the shutting up of houses.

system, one could talk of infected houses; H.F. would deal in infected persons. By contrast with the demonstrative power that liminal boundaries symbolize, his representation of authority is more penetrating, diffused, and internalized. A person is no longer one with a status (bachelor, widow, citizen, councillor, magistrate, etc.) but one who has a self that continually rehearses, situates, and internalizes the force of authority. This is why casuistry takes such a central place in the formal structure of Defoe's fictions, and why it serves as an element of structure as well as style. H.F.'s representational mode is consonant with Defoe's Hobbesian ideas on government as a construct devised by men to protect themselves against the savagery of human nature, and consonant as well with the Lockean presumption that the self remains in total subjection to perceptual experience. Reality lies within, and therefore to the degree any external authority is realized, it must be as a mental phenomenon represented in words or images.[1]

H.F.'s position on shutting up houses unfolds during a course of extended personal deliberation in which he comes to identify with the established order in the city and, while rejecting liminality, to endorse solitude as a final, life- and self-preserving value. This occurs despite H.F.'s specific disapproval of and distaste for the formal policies of quarantine. To the degree the book tells his inner story, these events outline its plot. But he is caught up during the historical time of the plague itself in the contradiction of living between old world and new: H.F. the compulsive walker and watcher; H.F. the man who believes himself providentially sheltered yet tries to shut himself up to gain safety; H.F. the reluctant examiner; H.F. the social projector and reformer. His supposed plague journal is fused with retrospection and reflection, and his narrative, as opposed to its historical object (the plague in 1665), formulates the self in a private, internally isolated manner. His final values consist of solitude and respect for the balanced, moderate, bureaucratic order of modern society:

> Every thing was managed with so much Care . . . that *London* may be a Pattern to all the Cities in the World for the good Government and the excellent Order that was everywhere kept, even in the time of the most violent Infection. . . . One thing, it is to be observ'd, was owing principally to the Prudence of the Magistrates, and ought to be mention'd to their Honour, *(viz.)* The Moderation which they used in the great and difficult work of shutting up of Houses. . . . But after all that was or could be done in these Cases, the shutting up of Houses, so as to confine those that were well with those that were sick, had very great Inconveniences in it, and some that were very tragical . . . but it was authoriz'd by a Law, it had the publick Good in view, as the End chiefly aim'd at, and all the private Inju-

1. See Maximillian E. Novak, *Defoe and the Nature of Man* (Oxford: Oxford University Press, 1963), pp. 14–21, passim, on Hobbes and pp. 157–58 on Locke. Novak cites *An Essay Concerning Human Understanding*, 3.11.24–25.

ries that were done by the putting it in Execution, must be put to
the account of the publick Benefit. (pp. 155, 158)[125, 127]

In context, the stress lies solidly on H.F.'s transaction with authority in
itself, for a flat denial of the value of shutting up houses follows at once.
Yet again, a few pages later:

> The Lord Mayor and the Sheriffs, the Court of Aldermen, and a
> certain Number of the Common Council-Men, or their Deputies
> came to a Resolution and published it, *viz.* 'That *they* would not
> quit the City themselves, but that they would be always at hand for
> the preserving good Order in every Place, and for the doing Justice
> on all Occasions. . . . These things re-establish'd the Minds of the
> People very much. . . . Nor were the Magistrates deficient in per-
> forming their Part as boldly as they promised it; for my Lord Mayor
> and the Sheriffs were continually in the Streets, and at places of the
> greatest Danger. (pp. 183–84)[145–46]

Significantly, these passages enclose the episode in which H.F., "greatly
afflicted" by the "Hardship" of being appointed an examiner for his parish, gains slight remission by pleading opposition to official policy.

But H.F. does serve, and the crisis of his personal history comes when,
as an appointed bureaucrat, he must himself maintain order and respect
for authority by enforcing the quarantine. The random fury of the plague
opposes the systematic conduct of the urban magistrates who encounter
it with written legislation, computation of casualties, printed plague bills,
routine sweeping away of bodies, control of food supplies, and, above
all, the shutting up of infected houses. To have a self is to take individual
narrative account of the regulating, discriminating forces that control
the chaos of human nature just as they display and order the abstract
grid of the metropolis. Otherwise, like many people at the height of the
plague, he would begin to give up himself to "Fears, and to think that
all regulations and Methods were in vain, and that there was nothing to
be hoped for, but an universal Desolation" (p. 171)[136]. Authority both
requires coherent personal identity and supplies the occasion for its production.

H.F. lives at a historical threshold, himself betwixt and between, a
personified contradiction. He simultaneously considers his "own Deliverance to be one next to miraculous," a special providence that saved
him personally, yet condemns "*Turkish* Predestinarianism" and insists
that the plague was "really propagated by natural Means, nor is it at all
the less a Judgment for its being under the Conduct of human Causes
and Effects" (pp. 193–94)[152–53]. Certainly his recommendations and
his relation to secular authority embrace human causes and effects—the
regulated, measured order of the metropolis, the private house, the individual consciousness, and the penitentiary cell. When H.F. once
approaches the despair he has earlier described, schemes of social engi-
neering allay his doubt:

> Now let any Man judge . . . if it is possible for the Regulations of
> Magistrates . . . to stop an Infection, which spreads it self from
> Man to Man, even while they are perfectly well and insensible of
> its Approach. . . . Tho' Providence seem'd to direct my Conduct
> to be otherwise; yet it is my opinion, and I must leave it as a Pre-
> scription, *(viz.) that the best Physick against the Plague is to run
> away from it.* I know People encourage themselves, by saying, God
> is able to keep us in the midst of Danger, and able to overtake us
> when we think our selves out of Danger; and this kept Thousands
> in the Town, whose Carcasses went into the great Pits by Cart Loads.
> [But] were this very Fundamental only duly consider'd . . . on any
> future occasion of this, or the like Nature, I am persuaded it would
> put them upon quite different Measures for managing the People,
> from those that they took in 1665 . . . in a Word, they would con-
> sider of separating the People into smaller Bodies, and removing
> them in Time farther from one another. (pp. 197–98)[155–56]

While noticing himself as a seeming exception, H.F. turns not to
worship but to a rationalistic authoritarian project for thinning out the
city by systematic evacuation to a density below that critical to the spread
of plague. His cure dissolves the city into its solitary citizens, a cure
applicable to the fire and, by extension of H.F.'s language about the
poor, to crime:

> I could propose many Schemes, on the foot of which the Govern-
> ment of this City . . . might ease themselves of the greatest Part of
> the dangerous People that belong to them; I mean such as the beg-
> ging, starving, labouring Poor, and among them chiefly those
> who in Case of a Siege, are call'd the useless Mouths; who be-
> ing then prudently, and to their own Advantage dispos'd of, and
> the wealthy Inhabitants disposing of themselves, and of their Ser-
> vants, and Children, the City and its adjacent Parts would be so
> effectually evacuated, that there would not be above a tenth Part of
> its People left together, for the Disease to take hold upon. (pp. 198–
> 99)[156][2]

For all this, as H.F. immediately points out, the fact remains that even
among those who fled, many had died, and even retreat implies confinement elsewhere. The only unimpeachable method of survival cited
in the entire *Journal* is in fact total self-imposed isolation based on fore-
sight, rational planning and storage of provision, and relentless vigilance:

> Many Families foreseeing the Approach of the Distemper, laid up
> Stores of Provisions, sufficient for their whole Families, and shut

2. This passage suggests a more negative attitude toward the poor than Novak argues for in
"Defoe and the Disordered City," but a sympathetic stance does not rule out accepting
necessary solutions. Defoe's understanding of
the social conditions that drove women to
prostitution did not prevent his advocacy of
shutting up their houses because they shelter
robbers. See *An Effectual Scheme for the
Immediate Preventing of Street Robberies* (1731).

themselves up, and that so entirely, that they were neither seen or heard of, till the Infection was quite ceased, and then came abroad Sound and Well: I might recollect several such as these, and give you the Particular of their Management; for doubtless, it was the most effectual secure Step that cou'd be taken for such, whose Circumstance would not admit them to remove, or who had not Retreats abroad proper for the Case. . . . Nor do I remember, that any one of those Families miscary'd; among these, several *Dutch* Merchants were particularly remarkable, who kept their Houses like little Garrisons besieged, suffering none to go in or out, or come near them. (p. 55)[49]

While H.F. advocates self-imposed physical isolation as the only sure method of survival, he cannot require it of himself both for want of provision and patience. Yet psychologically he remains more alone on the streets of plague-stricken London than the Dutch merchants barricaded in their houses. Their siege retreat invokes the proto-urban form of the garrisoned tribe. H.F.'s project for guarding the city by stripping it down to a molecular array of isolated citizens anticipates metropolitan civil defense and could be implemented only by a disciplined population in collaboration with bureaucratic authority.

The *Journal* hovers near an explicit denial of liminality as a principle of justice. Counteractively, the mental life of Defoe's narrator illustrates the sustaining power of reflective isolation, which is validated within the fiction by the narrator's acceptance of authority, and maintained within the larger novelistic construct as a principle of absolute representational order diffused throughout the whole text. The interior affirmation of consistently present authority registers psychologically as the persistence of self. As in *Robinson Crusoe*, the narrative acts this out in terms of a mental plot that hinges on a contract with God on the one hand and with societal order on the other. The *Journal*'s minute realism certifies the truth of its basic metaphor of London as prison and demonstrates total confinement as a mode of positive self-construction. The narrative is deeply contradictory, however, because the authority it validates enforces those old methods of confinement that it rejects. In this respect, Defoe has moved toward greater explicitness than in *Robinson Crusoe* and *Moll Flanders*, where the surface detail that refers to liminal practice is used to construct a mentality organized along quite different lines. Here the narrator questions liminal boundedness outright and proposes specific alternatives. But the casuistry of the narration tends to erode their concreteness in turn, and Defoe's narrative never breaks over into reformist discourse. Instead, what counts is the *Journal*'s demonstration of the salubrious, life-giving, self-creating effect—the formulative power—of the contract between authority and isolated self. The work lays bare the central paradox of the urban metropolis (so vividly and totally crystallized in its corollary, the penitentiary) that the more tightly people pack together the more isolated they become, and concomitantly, the more dependent for their conception of self and their communication with others upon the authority latent in fine-grained representational forms: rationalized bureaucratic government, realistic narration, geographic placement in the metropolitan grid. As Crusoe says in "Of Solitude," the first chapter of *Serious Reflections*.[3]

> I can affirm, that I enjoy much more solitude in the middle of the greatest collection of mankind in the world, I mean, at London, while I am writing this, than ever I could say I enjoyed in eight and twenty years' confinement to a desolate island. (p. 4)

Solitude is redefined not merely as a physical state, not merely as a state of mind, but as a condition of being.

My argument, then, is not that the *Journal* advocates the penitentiary but that Defoe articulates the conditions of its possibility by formulating the network of subjective circumstances—the structure of feeling—under which reformative confinement becomes part of the institutional texture of the city. Prison and the authority it assumes lie deep within the origins and structure of the city, but the city changes and so too do forms of confinement. The shift from the liminal to the penitentiary prison that I have been describing in terms of Defoe's rendering of consciousness can be viewed as a shift from the emblematic display of power within bounded walls, which also were literally prisons, to schematic forms of power that are increasingly removed, projected, and displaced into symbolically transparent, ideologically reified forms such as the novel and the penitentiary. This is not to assert that metropolitan life, the realist novel, and the penitentiary regime are identical. On the contrary, I view the penitentiary as the extreme case—the "total" instance, to use Goffman's term—of the narrative construction of self that the realistic novel portrays as normative. The novel bears these forms early and persuasively by virtue of its structural identity with urban life and its authoritative fusion of material specificity with detailed narrative causation. Finally, in attempting to anchor the rise of the penitentiary in novelistic form, one must observe the simple fact that the reformers of the modern penitentiary are not its occupants any more than the heroes and heroines of Newgate novels were readers. In other words, the penitentiary idea originally was a representation, a reformist construct, aimed at the literate public; only later, in the eighteenth century, once having attained architectural form, could it claim an audience of criminals, and even then its literary life continued through interminable debates over its refinements, controversies that preoccupied the nineteenth century and continue even to the present day.

---

3. Defoe elaborates on many of the subjects raised in *Robinson Crusoe* in a book of essays, *Serious Reflections during the Life and Surpris-* *ing Adventures of Robinson Crusoe, with his Vision of the Angelick World* (1720) [Editor].

MICHELLE BRANDWEIN

Formation, Process, and Transition in A *Journal of the Plague Year*†

Daniel Defoe's A *Journal of the Plague Year* is a "formative" work in a way that few novels are, in both its subject and the treatment of it. Its subject, the Great Plague in England in 1665, was in and of itself a cataclysmic event that had a powerful and unalterable effect on the minds and lives of all who lived through it. For his fictional treatment of the plague Defoe chose for his narrator one "H. F.," who undoubtedly bears a certain finite relationship to Defoe's actual uncle, Henry Foe, but for the purposes of an analysis of the novel might be considered a character "in process" in that his stature lies somewhere between that of an undeveloped character and that of a fully developed one. Any plague-stricken city constitutes, in addition, a severe and instant disruption of an existing society, which must bend to meet urgent new needs, and is consequently itself replaced, temporarily, if not permanently, by a new society. A *Journal of the Plague Year* is an ongoing account of the (imperfect) efforts of H. F., and others as seen through him, to come to terms with the causes, fact of, and effect of the Great Plague, and its skewing of their world.

A *Journal of the Plague Year* thus privileges shifting grounds, transformations (of society, institutions, laws), and incipience (of patterns of thinking and ideas). It constitutes in fact a fictional outline of certain of the theories, themes, and methods of approach of Michel Foucault that obviously predates his work, in that its text deals with the movement to the center of marginal sections of society (the poor and the ill), it makes highly visible what is ordinarily unseen, and it reverses the typical relationship of dominance of the mind over the body. Given the turbulent and uncertain nature of the material of A *Journal of the Plague Year*, and the fact that it deals fictionally with an actual plague while purporting (falsely) to be a true history of it, its particular novelistic "zone of contact," or the point, as described by Mikhail Bakhtin, at which it "comes into contact with the spontaneity of the inconclusive present," is especially problematic and complex.[1] It is therefore not surprising that critics have often been confused about how to "take" the *Journal*, and

† This essay is originally published here. Michelle Brandwein holds an M.Phil. from Oxford University and an M.A. in English from the University of Rochester.

1. M. M. Bakhtin, *The Dialogic Imagination*, ed. Michael Holquist, trans. Caryl Emerson and Michael Holquist (Austin and London: University of Texas Press, 1981), p. 27.

The "zone of contact" is further complicated by the fact that Defoe wrote the *Journal* (as well as his plague tract *Due Preparations for the Plague, As Well as for Soul and Body*, which appeared about a month before the *Journal*) in response to the threat of plague from Marseilles, and in support of Walpole's proposed Quarantine Act.

there lies behind it a long history of critical dispute about what "kind" of work it is. It has at various times been judged to be authentic history, completely—or predominantly—fictional, a hybrid form of history and fiction, a historical novel, and a nonfiction novel.[2] The immense impact of this "unclassifiable" piece of writing is nevertheless attested to by the descriptions given of it as a *"tour de force* of literary aeronautics,*"* as "Defoe's masterpiece," and as "an immortal work." Its style has been described by James Joyce as "masterly" and "orchestral," and it has inspired such comments as the following from Louis Landa: "If [the plague] had not occurred, Defoe (one is tempted to say) would have invented it."[3]

My focus will be on the illumination of A *Journal of the Plague Year* through the ideas of Foucault and other contemporary theorists. But there is also a way in which such an analysis of the novel might then be applied toward something of an elucidation of various aims of Foucault's, characterized by him as answering the questions: how conscious change is possible and how new ways of thinking take place;[4] "how, from the seventeenth and eighteenth centuries onward, there was a veritable technological take-off in the productivity of power";[5] and how "a human being turns him- or herself into a subject" and is made into an object.[6] I claim that this type of dual elucidation is viable on the basis of the Bakhtinian idea that

2. "Authentic history" by Watson Nicholson in *The Historical Sources of Defoe's Journal of the Plague Year* (Boston: The Stratford Co., 1919);

"fiction" by Walter G. Bell in *The Great Plague in London in 1665* (London: John Lane The Bodley Head, 1924), v–vi, 72–75; and Arthur Wellesley Secord in *Studies in the Narrative Method of Defoe* (New York: Russell & Russell, 1963), pp. 231–33;

"a hybrid form of history and fiction" attributed to Sir Walter Scott and then others by Robert Mayer in "The Reception of A *Journal of the Plague Year* and the Nexus of Fiction and History in the Novel," *ELH*, 57 (1990), pp. 533, 541–44. Mayer surveys the "biography" of the reception of the *Journal* starting from the premise that the *Journal's* history of problematic classification provides a key to the theoretical definition of the novel as genre, and argues that "the *Journal* constitutes the most forceful assertion in the whole discourse of the novel in English that the nexus of history and fiction is a constitutive feature of the form" (546).

"historical novel" by Paula R. Backscheider in *Daniel Defoe: Ambition and Innovation* (Lexington: The University Press of Kentucky, 1986), pp. 135–45, and John J. Burke, Jr. in "Observing the Observer in the Historical Fictions by Defoe," *Philological Quarterly*, 61 (1982), pp. 13–32;

"nonfiction novel" by Mas'ud Zavarzadeh in *The Mythopoeic Reality: The Postwar American Nonfiction Novel* (University of Illinois Press, 1976), pp. 102–12.

3. By, respectively:

F. Bastian, "Defoe's *Journal of the Plague Year* Reconsidered," *Review of English Studies*, n.s. 25, no. 62 (1965), p. 173.

Anthony Burgess, "Introduction" to A *Journal of the Plague Year* (Penguin, 1966, rpt. 1987), p. 19.

George A. Aitken, "Introduction" to A *Journal of the Plague Year* (London: J. M. Dent & Co., 1895), p. x.

James Joyce, "Daniel Defoe," ed. and trans. Joseph Prescott, *Buffalo Studies* 1 (1964), p. 17; quoted in Paula R. Backscheider, *Daniel Defoe: His Life* (Baltimore and London: The Johns Hopkins University Press, 1989), p. 532.

Louis Landa, "Introduction" to A *Journal of the Plague Year* (London: Oxford University Press, 1969), p. xv.

4. Michel Foucault, *Technologies of the Self* (Amherst: The University of Massachusetts Press, 1988), p. 14. Foucault states that all of *Discipline and Punish* is an attempt to answer this question.

5. Michel Foucault, *Power/Knowledge*, ed. Colin Gordon, trans. Colin Gordon et al. (New York: Pantheon, 1972), p. 119. Foucault gives this as one of his aims for *Discipline and Punish*.

6. Michel Foucault, "Afterword: The Subject and Power," in Hubert L. Dreyfus and Paul Rabinow, *Michel Foucault: Beyond Structuralism and Hermeneutics* (Chicago: The University of Chicago Press, 1982), p. 208.

> the novel is the only developing genre and therefore it reflects more
> deeply, more essentially, more sensitively and rapidly, reality itself
> in the process of its unfolding. Only that which is itself developing
> can comprehend development as a process. The novel has become
> the leading hero in the drama of literary development in our time
> precisely because it best of all reflects the tendencies of a new world
> still in the making; it is, after all, the only genre born of this new
> world and in total affinity with it.[7]

Because a plague results in the inevitable erasure of the society that
stands and the urgent formation of a new one, a novel virtually enclosed
by a plague, as A *Journal of the Plague Year* is, would in a dual sense be
"a new world still in the making." This relationship might be thought
to hold even more "firmly" for a novel based on an actual bubonic
plague, as a historical novel (which is the way I would classify A *Journal
of the Plague Year*) is, by Georg Lukács's definition, a novel whose "proper
hero . . . is life itself."[8] We should therefore, in A *Journal of the Plague
Year*, be able to watch the emergence of the new ways of thinking, production of power, and subjectivization/objectivization of human beings
with which Foucault is, in general, concerned. When examining a novel
that intersects with so much, there are many places to begin. But I will
begin where Foucault's *Discipline and Punish* begins: with "the body of
the condemned."

Discipline and Punish, intended to be "a correlative history of the
modern soul and of a new power to judge"[9] written "against the background of a history of bodies,"[1] opens, appropriately enough, with a
gruesome account of the 1757 torture and execution of the regicide
Damiens in front of an audience. Like this scene, Defoe's plague-stricken
London is dominated by bodies, and in it too the raging plague functions
as spectacle. Victims escape from their shut-up houses and run wildly
through the streets "with the Plague visibly upon them,"[2] throw themselves into plague pits and out of their windows, shoot themselves in the
violence of their pain, and drop down "stark dead" in the streets.[3]

H. F., the observer and recorder who remains healthy throughout,
partakes of the ghastly drama by visiting a giant plague pit in Aldgate

---

7. Bakhtin, *The Dialogic Imagination*, p. 7.

8. Georg Lukács, *The Historical Novel*, trans.
Hannah and Stanley Mitchell (London: Merlin Press, 1962), p. 149.

9. Michel Foucault, *Discipline and Punish: The
Birth of the Prison*, trans. Alan Sheridan (New
York: Vintage, 1979), p. 23.

1. Ibid., p. 25.

2. 48. Subsequent references will be to this
Norton Critical Edition and will be given in
the text.

3. It must be noted that in none of Defoe's
sources for the *Journal*—such as Nathaniel
Hodges's *Loimologia: Or, an Historical Account
of the Plague in London in 1665: With Precau-*

tionary Directions against the Like Contagion
(trans. John Quincy [London: E. Bell, 1720];
excerpt rpt. in *London in Plague and Fire 1665–
1666*, ed. Roland Bartel [Boston: Heath, 1957],
pp. 33–46) or Thomas Vincent's *God's Terrible Voice in the City* (1667, rpt. 1722)—is the
body so overwhelmingly present, its power and
pain so menacing, pervasive, and real. (Nor is
this the case in Defoe's own *Due Preparations
for the Plague* or in accounts unavailable to
Defoe, such as the *Diary* of Samuel Pepys,
Walter Bell's history of the plague, or even
Foucault's own section on a plague-stricken
town in *Discipline and Punish* [pp. 195–200].)

that eventually holds 1,114 bodies because he is "press'd in [his] Mind to go" and see it (54), watching from his windows the agonized sufferings of plague victims dashing through the streets, and accompanying the waterman, Robert, on his boat to Greenwich, where he can see the hundreds of ships in rows in which families have shut themselves away to remain safe from the plague. Indeed, H. F. refers to what he can see of the plague from his windows as "dismal Spectacles" (141). The stories H. F. designates as of uncertain authority have even more sensational characteristics than his actual experiences of the plague as spectacle, such as the tale of the infected man who jumped out of his bed and cured his swellings by swimming the Thames and the tale of the plague piper.

Foucault explains in *Discipline and Punish* that public spectacles of torture, such as those of the execution of Damiens, were political rituals. The condemned man's breach of the law was seen as an attack on the body of the king, who must himself retaliate in kind; the tortured body of the condemned man became "the place where the vengeance of the sovereign was applied, the anchoring point for a manifestation of power."[4] The punished man's "lack of power" is contrasted with the "surplus power" possessed by the person of the sovereign.[5] The manner of impact such an execution was intended to have on its audience was unmistakable:

> A body effaced, reduced to dust and thrown to the winds, a body destroyed piece by piece by the infinite power of the sovereign constituted not only the ideal, but the real limit of punishment.[6]

There is a battle between the criminal and the sovereign in which the sides are unequal, the length of attack is undetermined, and the outcome is decided in advance.

Whereas *Discipline and Punish* begins with the disappearance of this form of punishment itself, *A Journal of the Plague Year* begins with its (metaphoric) establishment. The London of the Great Plague, filled with pain, tortured bodies, and spectacles of suffering, is a society at its utmost limits—a society undergoing perpetual punishment. The specter of the punishing king appears in *A Journal of the Plague Year* with H. F.'s reference to the fact that the abandoned effects of whole families who had been swept away by the plague came after the plague's end "to the King as the universal Heir" (180). The significance of such an evocation of the figure of the king, would, as Foucault could tell us, be substantial. "The function of the king," Northrop Frye writes in *The Great Code*,

> is primarily to represent, for his subjects, the unity of their society in an individual form. Even yet Elizabeth II can draw crowds wherever she appears, not because there is anything remarkable about her appearance, but because she dramatizes the metaphor of society

4. Foucault, *Discipline and Punish*, p. 55.   6. Ibid., p. 50.
5. Ibid., p. 29.

as a single "body." Other societies have other figures, but there seems to be a special symbolic eloquence, even a pathos, about the *de jure* monarch, whose position has been acquired by the pure accident of birth, and who has no executive power.[7]

To supplement the actual reversion during the plague to the supremacy of body over mind, *A Journal of the Plague Year* abounds in metaphors of the body. H. F. describes the plague as coming upon the easternmost part of town "like an armed Man" (99) and depicts London during the crisis as having a "strangely alter'd" face (17). "*London*," he tells us, "might well be said to be all in Tears" (18). London, in metaphorical terms, becomes a human body with its limbs, or roads and ports, cut off from interaction with the outside world: the country people no longer come to London's markets but sell their provisions in outside fields or at the entrances into town, inhabitants of London who desire to escape it are barred from entry onto outer roads, and London's ships are refused entry into foreign ports while foreign ships do not dare to enter London's.

A society thus engulfed by bodies constitutes a return to the primitive: the ordinarily dominant partner in the mind/body dualism—the mind—has been overthrown. There are two ways in which the privileging of the body's power leads to a primitive, basic state, both of which I shall deal with in turn: (1) the plague results in a return to primitive society, as the collapse of the existent society necessitates the formation of new and embryonic societies to fill its void; (2) the plague results in the reconstitution and reflection of the primitive and precognitive individual mind.

The connection of a plague of society begins with the diseased individual himself. As Elizabeth Wright observes:

> The patient with his symptom is an example of inadequacy at the meeting-place of body and society. Where the inadequacy is to be lodged, in the body in question or the society of which it is a member, or both, cannot be simply decided.[8]

To elaborate on Wright's point, the body depends on society for its survival, yet by virtue of its foreignness from it must struggle against it. The body is society's precursor: the body with its needs and desires existed before language, intellectual activity, culture, and societal institutions and laws. The body was a whole before it was a part (of society).

Bodily illness is thus a potential lever for exposing a society's insecurity: the fact that the society exists and operates in incongruous juxtaposition with bodies will by this circumstance be revealed. A plague as such, which constitutes the (numerically) extended elaboration of this problem, is consequently an attack on the very foundations of a society.

---

7. Northrop Frye, *The Great Code: The Bible and Literature* (New York and London: Harcourt Brace Jovanovich, 1981), p. 87.
8. Elizabeth Wright, *Psychoanalytic Criticism: Theory in Practice* (London and New York:

Methuen, 1984), p. 175. Wright is here talking about bodies and symptoms as they relate to psychoanalytic treatment and practice, not strictly physical disease as such, but I extrapolate.

The epidemic and its victims make immediate dents in the structures on which the society rests; those who are ordinarily in power—such as politicians and the rich—are forced to adapt to the needs of the poor and the ill, who are usually invisible and unheard.[9] We see this adaptation taking place very clearly in the *Journal*.

A further severe attack on an existing society during a plague comes from something that is more intrinsic to a plague than any other form of illness: it effectively turns crime and disease into identical things. A plague, as a contagious illness, breaks down the distinction between ordinary, noncontagious illness (understood as harmful only to the self) and crime (understood as harmful to others); because a plague is harmful to both the sick person and others it forms a bridge between illness and crime, and all who suffer from it are both victims and criminals at the same time.[1] As Paul Slack tells us in *The Impact of Plague in Tudor and Stuart England*, if plague victims did not cooperate with being confined to their places of abode, "they could be accounted murderers."[2]

This conflation of illness and crime is as true in regard to the physical manifestations of plague—at least the bubonic kind—as in the conception of it in society's mind. Bubonic plague marks its victims with buboes, or "tokens," in the way that the tortured bodies of condemned criminals like Damiens were branded with stigmata. As Defoe describes the sufferings of the plague victims,

> The Pain of the Swelling was in particular very violent, and to some intollerable; the Physicians and Surgeons may be said to have tortured many poor Creatures, even to Death. The Swellings in some grew hard, and they apply'd violent drawing Plasters, or Pultices, to break them; and if these did not do, they cut and scarified them in a terrible Manner: In some, those Swellings were made hard, partly by the Force of the Distemper, and partly by their being too violently drawn, and were so hard, that no Instrument could cut them, and then they burnt them with Caustiks, so that many died raving mad with the Torment; and some in the very Operation. (69–70)

And so the parallel from *Discipline and Punish*:

> It was the task of the guilty man to bear openly his condemnation and the truth of the crime that he had committed. His body, displayed, exhibited in procession, tortured, served as the public sup-

9. London's Great Plague, like plagues in general, was overwhelmingly a disease of the poor, and Nathaniel Hodges in an excerpt from *Loimologia* said that it "came by some to be called the Poors Plague" (p. 36).

Paul Slack in *The Impact of Plague in Tudor and Stuart England* (London: Routledge & Kegan Paul, 1985), also asserts: "what was special about plague was the fact that it combined high mortality and unpredictable incidence with a particular, and increasingly obvious, association with poverty. The first two features caused shock, anxiety and insecurity. The third gave these emotions an outlet: it provided an external target against which they could be directed, and moreover a target which was already being attacked for other reasons" (p. 309).

1. Pointed out by Thomas S. Szasz in *The Manufacture of Madness: A Comparative Study of the Inquisition and the Mental Health Movement* (New York: Harper & Row, 1970), p. 20.

2. Slack, *The Impact of Plague*, p. 40.

port of a procedure that had hitherto remained in the shade; in him, on him, the sentence had to be legible for all.[3]

The crime/illness relationship becomes even more complex in regard to the *Journal* than it would otherwise be because of the historical period that the *Journal* covers. Sixteen years before the Great Plague, in 1649, King Charles I was executed by his own subjects, and the knowledge of this (shameful) execution would have hovered over Defoe and his readers in 1722, when the *Journal* was written, as it would have been even more vividly present to the minds of London's inhabitants in 1665. The executed king was betrayed by his subjects just as plague sufferers are betrayed by their bodies, for all sufferers of illness experience their bodies as sources of pain external to themselves (that is, to their minds)—as antagonistic things apart. W. H. Auden describes this experience in this way:

> At first the baby sees his limbs as belonging to the outside world. When he has learnt to control them, he accepts them as part of himself. What we call the 'I', in fact, is the area over which our will is immediately operative. Thus, if we have a toothache, we seem to be two people, the suffering 'I' and the hostile outer world of the tooth.[4]

The relationship of the human body to the whole "person" is at once the simplest and the most complex. People are and are not their bodies, as the centuries-old debate on the mind/body problem has made clear; the mind and the body are dependent on one another for survival, yet always in a strong sense remain distinct and, ultimately, alien entities. In the end the body betrays one—it sickens, and dies—providing unwanted evidence of one's own weakness and mortality. Like torture and execution, disease is experienced—emotionally, if not rationally—as punishment.

The *Journal* is permeated by associations to the contradictory figures of two kinds of kings: the first, the severely judging, punishing king; the second king—betrayed, executed, and robbed of power. What might be called the "power" of the punishing king is reinforced within the novel through H. F.'s quite snide references to the conduct of the Court during the plague:

> I should observe that the Court removed early, (*viz.*) in the Month of *June,* and went to *Oxford,* where it pleas'd God to preserve them; and the Distemper did not, *as I heard of,* so much as touch them; for which I cannot say, that I ever saw they shew'd any great Token of Thankfulness, and hardly any thing of Reformation, tho' they did not want being told that their crying Vices might, without Breach of Charity, be said to have gone far, in bringing that terrible Judgment upon the whole Nation. (17)

3. Foucault, *Discipline and Punish*, p. 43.
4. W. H. Auden, *The English Auden*, ed. Edward Mendelson (London: Faber and Faber, 1977), p. 394.

But really the Court concern'd themselves so little, and that little they did was of so small import, that I do not see it of much Moment to mention any Part of it here, except that of appointing a Monthly Fast in the City, and the sending the Royal Charity to the Relief of the Poor, both which I have mention'd before. (182)

The power behind the king would be of course the power of God, and the opinion that the plague was an expression of God's wrath upon the people of London as retribution for their sins was entertained not only by Defoe/H. F., but by the writers of Defoe's historical sources for the *Journal*, such as Thomas Vincent and Nathaniel Hodges, for whom it was a commonly held and longstanding viewpoint.[5] The actual execution of Charles I in 1649 constituted the ultimate reversal, the unthinkable case in which the people's power actually triumphed over the power of the monarch, and was accordingly blasphemous in that it was simultaneously an attack on "God." Yet when placed side by side the glaring events of the regicide and the Great Plague constitute what by Foucault's logic would be considered a clean fight in that they consist of bodies facing off against bodies. The body of the king confronts the bodies of the common people before the bodies of the people become the "docile bodies" that are at the mercy of the "micro-power" of modern (and hypocritical) disciplinary technology, the changeover that Foucault so graphically delineates in *Discipline and Punish*. The predictable result of the pitting of the power of an avenging king against the power of his guilty subjects—"bodies of the condemned" en masse—is an unadulterated explosion, not just a physical one but in all possible ways.

What is thus displayed for us in the *Journal* is an entire society turned upside down by the uncontrolled power of the body. In the *Journal* we see society under the sway of power distilled, power before the declaration took effect that "punishment . . . should strike the soul rather than the body."[6] Among Foucault's various definitions of "power" is the following:

> In reality power means relations, a more-or-less organised, hierarchal, co-ordinated cluster of relations.[7]

The Great Plague was, if nothing else, a manifestation of the "relations" among men, since the predominant concern of the people in London (and outside it), while the plague raged, was whether they were going to catch it from one another or not. In the *Journal* the citizens who do not flee London or lock themselves in their houses walk only in the middle of the street to avoid others, go to great lengths to keep from touching money or provisions that it is necessary for them to exchange with other people, and converse only at a distance and carry preservatives in their

---

5. Slack, *The Impact of Plague*, p. 39.
6. G. de Mably, *De la legislation, Oeuvres completes*, IX, 1789; quoted in Foucault, *Discipline and Punish*, p. 16.
7. Foucault, *Power/Knowledge*, p. 198.

clothes to repel infection. Likewise, the country people outside London refuse to take in wanderers on the road in case they are infected with the plague.

H. F. is continually obsessed with the problem of not being able to tell "the Sick from the Sound" (133–34, 150–51, 154, 156–57, 159), and again and again he refutes the public idea that plague sufferers purposely attempt to infect others (49, 60–61, 124, 157). The potential power of the body extends even beyond death: plague victims (the Londoners believe) can infect others after they have died. "Communication" among men has been relegated to the level of the body, and thus to a level beneath discourse; the mind's role has been supplanted.

Defoe's *Journal* makes apparent that it is the poor and the ill who wield—for the duration of a plague, at least—all the power: the power to infect as well as to kill others, and the power to bend their society's current laws. The Great Plague thus brings together two kinds of reversals: the societal reversal in which the ordinarily marginal poor and ill move to the center, and the individualized reversal in which the body completes a revolution over the mind (with both reversals, naturally, to an extent overlapping). In these respects Defoe's plague functions like plagues considered collectively, but the *Journal* also contains further reversals and contradictions that are peculiar to it and distinguish it sharply from its historical sources. While the plague is in full force, for instance, the living get mixed up with the dead, as in the cases of the sleeping piper who is thrown into the dead cart, the plague victims near their end who "bury themselves" (54) by jumping into plague pits, and the men who drop down dead while pulling dead carts and burying bodies. As H. F. uncomfortably relates to us on several occasions, rumors circulate abroad that "the living were not sufficient to bury the dead, or the Sound to look after the Sick" (138–39, 143, 168), rumors that H. F. is at pains to deny.

There is a confusion as well between the healthy and the sick (in addition to the fact that they cannot always be told apart) in that the healthy are forced to be shut up together with their sick family members in infected houses, and are thus transformed into victims and potential "criminals" in the same way that plague victims are: they are victims because they suffer (and in fact sometimes die) from being unfairly confined, and criminals because they can be punished if they escape from their infected houses, as indeed many of them do.

The "living versus dead" reversals and contradictions that run throughout the *Journal* come to include H. F. himself. Although H. F. ends the *Journal* with a short poem emphatically affirming his survival of the plague:

> A *dreadful plague in* London *was,*
> *In the Year Sixty Five,*
> *Which swept an Hundred Thousand Souls*
> *Away; yet I alive!* (193)

Defoe also inserts into the text the following information in regard to a burial ground at Moorfields:

> N.B. The Author of this Journal, lyes buried in that very Ground, being at his own Desire, his Sister having been buried there a few Years before. (181)

The uneasy identification within the world of the *Journal* of the categories of living and dead engulfs and contains the healthy observer H. F., even as it traps London and stops it from functioning normally for the duration of the plague. The life of London itself, as well as of its inhabitants, seems to hang in the balance as all its laws and normal ways of thinking and operating are suspended.

One might expect, once a society's controlling structures and systems of belief are substantially overthrown, that new societies would arise to replace the old, and this is precisely what happens in the *Journal*. Two kinds of new societies actually develop within the novel: societies that are merely altered versions of the original, pre-plague society, and societies that are completely oppositional to the society that spawned them. The former kind of society begins with the publishing and enforcement of the *Orders Conceived and Published by the Lord Mayor and Aldermen of the City of London Concerning the Infection of the Plague, 1665*, printed in full near the beginning of the *Journal* (36–43). The *Orders* determine the course to be taken by London, as a community, during the plague. The society that creates and follows the *Orders* is what the original pre-plague society of London has turned into.

The second type of society is one that never engages with the authority and consequences of the *Orders* at all; it remains unaffected by the *Orders* because it separates itself from the transformed society of London during the plague and begins anew. The members of this type of society include the Londoners who resort to living in their ships, those who completely seclude themselves in their own houses in London, and others who set up tents in the fields and live in them "as Hermits in a Cell" (51). Defoe gives us only one detailed description of a group of people who strike out for themselves and aggressively form a new society: the tale of the three men who wander from Wapping and set up camp on the outskirts of the town of Epping. They develop their own social, economic, and moral laws: they pool their money on the condition that any further money any one of them gains will be added to the public stock; they manage, with no compunction, to accomplish "the little Fraud" (106) of gaining a certificate of having come not from London, but Essex; and they fool the people of the town of Walthamstow into thinking that they, together with the small band of fellow escapees they have joined, are really a large group of men in three companies, furnished with horses and arms. Even the self-righteous H. F. (with Defoe behind him) applauds their trickery, as well as the rest of their behavior, during this extreme situation.

The salient characteristics of these two kinds of new societies—the alternative, competing kind of society that the story of the three men exemplifies, and the transformed, but still recognizable, "ordered" society of London under the plague—are the new ways of thinking and behaving that follow from them. The three men, out of necessity, resort to a primitive and marginalized way of living. They build their own shelter, kill their own food, and almost totally avoid interaction with anyone outside their group. The inhabitants of London as it exists under the direction of the *Orders* similarly become extremely isolated from the rest of England and from their usual trading nations. They too come to think and respond in entirely different ways from previously, as illustrated by the mind and actions of H. F.   H. F.'s very printing of the *Orders* is one indication of the (Foucaultian) endeavor that he is engaged in throughout the *Journal*, of imposing order on chaos. This kind of attempt, from any thinking inhabitant of a society as unhinged as Defoe's plague-stricken London, needs no explanation, and H. F.'s relentless recountings of facts and figures, such as the *Bills of Mortality*, can also be seen as efforts in this direction.[8] H. F. prints the *Bills of Mortality* over and over again even though he expresses his belief on at least five occasions that they are inaccurate (82, 105, 142, 148–50, 160–62).

Walter Bell, a historian of the plague who was intent in 1924 on proving how "fictional" *A Journal of the Plague Year* was, condemns Defoe both for his printing of the *Orders* (because this makes the *Journal* appear "authentic") and for his assuming, "wholly without warrant," that the *Orders* were actually carried out.[9] The greater or lesser extent, however, to which the *Orders* were carried out in 1665 seems to have little bearing on a judgment of their significance in regard to the fictional narrator H. F., who chooses to call attention to their existence and importance. It is obvious that both the *Orders* and the *Bills* affect the actions of Londoners—who exit and re-enter London and stay in or out of their houses in response to them—and thus affect the spreading of the plague; but the *Orders* and *Bills* also, independently of their effect on action, affect human thought. It is most fully possible to gauge this effect in terms of H. F., since his are the only thoughts Defoe gives us. H. F.'s obsessive meditations on the shutting up of infected houses stem from the *Orders*, as does his conflict about having to serve as an examiner—an office specified by the *Orders*—which he is at last forced to do. The sizes of the weekly bills cause constant fluctuations in his state of mind (as they do in the minds of all others); thus the *Bills* together with the *Orders* influence the course of "his" *Journal*, which is the (retrospective) product of his thought for the duration of the plague.

It is a measure of the incongruity engendered by a plague that in spite

8. Backscheider in *Daniel Defoe: His Life*, p. 504, points out Defoe's own preoccupation with order and disorder in his work, and the pervasiveness of his need (especially during the 1720s) for order and regulation.

9. Bell, *The Great Plague in London in 1665*, pp. v–vi, 72–75.

of the attempt made by the magistrates of London to impose rigid control upon the outbreak through the *Orders*, disorder, to a significant extent, reigns. Notwithstanding the intention of the Lord Mayor and other authorities that every resident of London take his place and behave as directed, often it is "self Preservation [that comes] to be the first Law" (95); all compassion for others and respect for authority are forced into abeyance among those threatened by the plague. The drive to maintain order manifested by the officials of London in the proclamations they make and actions they take is counteracted by the wild response of the masses, who are unable to control their emotional reactions to the menace of the plague.

The Great Plague in Defoe's *Journal* functions in fact as one of Foucault's central concepts: the "discursive formation" (previously called by Foucault an "episteme"), defined in *The Order of Things* as:

> the fundamental code . . . of a culture . . . [which] govern[s] its language, its schemas of perception, its exchanges, its techniques, its values, the hierarchy of its practices,[1]

and in *The Archaeology of Knowledge* as:

> being something like a world-view, a slice of history common to all branches of knowledge, which imposes on each one the same norms and postulates, a general stage of reason, a certain structure of thought that the men of a particular period cannot escape—a great body of legislation written once and for all by some anonymous hand. By *episteme*, we mean, in fact, the total set of relations that unite, at a given period, the discursive practices that give rise to epistemological figures, sciences, and possibly formalized systems.[2]

Like a discursive formation, the Great Plague—in the real London of 1665 as well as in the fictional world of the *Journal*—determined what it was possible to think, know, and say at that time. In the *Journal* we can see the plague's effects, although not its causes, just as the causes of Foucault's epistemes are hidden; epistemes, as depicted by Foucault, simply appear alongside one another, in ruptures. Society during the plague is reduced to basic life and death situations: people can think only in terms of their own survival, and everything else, such as compassion for others and adherence to law, is expendable.[3] Londoners frustrated at being shut up in their infected houses, for instance, at times kill the watchmen who are authorized to guard them and are not punished for it. H. F. tells us that nurses entrusted with the care of plague victims are reported to smother, starve, and by other means murder their charges,

---

1. Michel Foucault, *The Order of Things: An Archaeology of the Human Sciences*, trans. Alan Sheridan (New York: Pantheon, 1970), p. xx.
2. Michel Foucault, *The Archaeology of Knowledge*, trans. Alan Sheridan (New York: Pantheon, 1972), p. 191.

3. There are exceptions to this, which Defoe is happy to give, such as the ongoing conduct of the Lord Mayor, the story of the waterman (88–92), and the story of the three men (100–21).

behavior given even more credence in various factual histories of the plague than in Defoe's novel.[4] Crime is frequent, tolerated, relatively routine, in the shattered world of the plague.

The changes that occur in London's governing structures and economy are also signs of the new discursive formation. Even religious division during the plague is temporarily suspended: people put aside their religious quarrels and flock to worship, losing "all Manner of Prejudice at, or Scruple about the Person whom they found in the Pulpit when they came to the Churches" (139, 26, 86).

Overall, both Defoe's Great Plague and Foucault's discursive formation can be viewed as instruments of "imprisonment": just as human thoughts are imprisoned by discursive formations in that it is impossible to think by means of a different discursive formation while the current one is in operation, so the lives of Londoners cannot extend beyond the "prison" of what is currently determined by the plague. The plague forces the physical imprisonment of the sick and their relations in their houses as well; and even healthy Londoners without sick family members, such as H. F., resort to locking themselves up simply out of their justifiable fear of going outside.

The *Journal* thus provides a literary stage on which we can observe the accelerated development of what is effectively one of Foucault's discursive formations. By eradicating the prior discursive formation, the plague clears the way for the development of a new one: it returns humans to a basic state from which we can watch their evolution as if it is happening all over again. After the plague has ended, admittedly, the new societies collapse again into the previous society: citizens who have shut themselves up in their boats and houses re-emerge, the party of the three men returns to London as presumably other voluntary exiles do, and the streets and shops fill again. The course taken by religion immediately after the plague could serve as a concrete example of this kind of reversion:

> as soon as the Plague was remov'd, the dissenting ousted Ministers . . . cou'd expect no other; but that [Anglicans] should immediately fall upon them, and harrass them, with their penal Laws, accept their preaching while they were sick, and persecute them as soon as they were recover'd again. (183)

However this reversion back into the pre-plague society is not complete. To take the matter of religion, again, as an example, with the end of the plague, as Paula Backscheider points out,

> England becomes far more secular in its public utterances. Issues that had been discussed in theological terms become pragmatic and are not religious or even ethical, although in most cases civil and

4. Such as Bell, *The Great Plague in London in 1665*, pp. 108–10; and Hodges, *Loimologia*, p. 34.

religious virtues were synonymous. H.F.'s account has far more directions for the conduct of life than the practice of piety; he gives more instructions to magistrates than to clergymen. . . . Joining with the fading of the Puritan influence, the experience of the plague decreased the tendency to interpret every experience, no matter how trivial, as a message from God.[5]

Out of the tragedy of the plague, new societal beginnings are born.

All of the transformations in English society—temporary and permanent—in *A Journal of the Plague Year* have been achieved through the power of the body: its attainment during the plague of dominance over the mind. The path left in the wake of the plague in the *Journal* lends support to Foucault's contention that it is always really the body (not the soul) that is at issue; the object of power and knowledge and punishment alike is the body itself. It is, in the *Journal*, the privileging of the power of the body that results in the destruction of the standing discursive formation and the creation of a new one, and thus strips the screen from a civilization and exposes its workings and the inner lives and beliefs of its members to view.

It is also significant that Defoe's account of the plague was written at a time (1722) when affective individualism was "emergent," about a time (1665) when affective individualism was "pre-emergent."[6] In light of W. H. Auden's idea that infectious diseases are "a sign of the unconscious sense of unity between men,"[7] individualism as a concept stands in direct contradistinction to what was physically occurring among plague sufferers during the epidemic—that is, a manifestation of "relations," a merging together of bodies. The unique contribution to the story of the plague made by Defoe, retelling it fifty-seven years later, was to present it in the context of upcoming individualism as a split experience. Defoe manages this by incorporating equally into the story, on the one hand, the uniform experiences of the masses who were infected with the plague, and, on the other, the isolated experience of H. F., who observes the plague and transmits its tale.

Louis Landa has noted that H. F., like Robinson Crusoe, is a "lonely" character;[8] and John Bender, arguing in *Imagining the Penitentiary* that Defoe, in the *Journal*, "articulates the conditions of [the penitentiary's]

---

5. Backscheider, *Daniel Defoe: Ambition and Innovation*, pp. 141–42.

6. I am using "emergent" and "pre-emergent" as defined by Raymond Williams in *Marxism and Literature* (Oxford: Oxford University Press, 1977), pp. 123–26.

"Affective individualism," as defined by Lawrence Stone in *The Family, Sex and Marriage In England 1500–1800*, Abridged Edition (Harper & Row, 1977), is "firstly, a growing introspection and interest in the individual personality; and secondly, a demand for personal autonomy and a corresponding respect for the individual's right to privacy, to self-expression, and to the free exercise of his will within limits set by the need for social cohesion: a recognition that it is morally wrong to make exaggerated demands for obedience, or to manipulate or coerce the individual beyond a certain point in order to achieve social or political ends" (p. 151).

7. Auden, *The English Auden*, p. 299.

8. Landa, "Introduction," p. xxiv.

possibility," states that H. F. "comes to . . . endorse solitude as a final, life- and self-preserving value"; "his narrative, as opposed to its historical object (the plague in 1665), formulates the self in a private, internally isolated manner."[9] "What counts" in the *Journal*, Bender asserts, is its "demonstration of the salubrious, life-giving, self-creating effect—the formulative power—of the contract between authority and isolated self."[1] The strongest representation in the *Journal* of "the contract between authority and the self" is H. F.'s eventual acceptance of the role of examiner although he is personally opposed to the shutting up of houses. H. F. demonstrates elsewhere in his narrative that he is quite aware of the dichotomy between public and private roles, as his comments upon the killing of watchmen by the inhabitants of the infected houses they were appointed to guard (125–26) make clear.

In the case of this opposition, too, the body is fundamental. As Elaine Scarry points out in *The Body in Pain*,

> the degree to which body and state are interwoven with one another can be most quickly appreciated by noticing the most obvious and ongoing manifestation of that relation such as the fact that one's citizenship ordinarily entails physical *presence* within the boundaries of that country.[2]

She maintains, in addition, that "the felt experience of physical pain" results in "an almost obscene conflation of private and public":

> It brings with it all the solitude of absolute privacy with none of its safety, all the self-exposure of the utterly public with none of its possibility for camaraderie or shared experience.[3]

While the plague understandably results in the consolidation of all aspects of the society of London as well as the corollary separation into new and smaller societal islands that I have outlined above, it also paradoxically conduces to the formation of the solitary, unique individual. Considered from the perspective of Foucault's theories this latter consequence is not a paradox at all because the individual, in Foucault's terms, is produced at the crossroads of power and knowledge,[4] which are themselves discursively inscribed upon bodies. Through the medium of *A Journal of the Plague Year*, Defoe locates and illuminates for us the point at which individualism and the communality from which it developed stood juxtaposed.

H. F. is a character "in process" not only because he treads the fine line between an underdeveloped and more fully developed literary char-

9. John Bender, *Imagining the Penitentiary: Fiction and the Architecture of Mind in Eighteenth-Century England* (Chicago and London: The University of Chicago Press, 1987), pp. 83, 79.

1. Ibid., p. 83.

2. Elaine Scarry, *The Body in Pain: The Making and Unmaking of the World* (Oxford: Oxford University Press, 1985), p. 111.

3. Ibid., p. 53.

4. For example, Foucault, in *Discipline and Punish*: "the examination is at the centre of the procedures that constitute the individual as effect and object of power, as effect and object of knowledge" (192).

acter, but because his mind is continuously groping for information and answers; he is always at the point of being "constructed" by knowledge. He exemplifies the kind of "subject" that Foucault states it has been his task to study, the subject who is definitively *not* "either transcendental in relation to the field of events or run[ning] in its empty sameness throughout the course of history." Thus

> one has to dispense with the constituent subject, to get rid of the subject itself, that's to say, to arrive at an analysis which can account for the constitution of the subject within a historical framework.[5]

It is in this vein that Foucault rejects Marxism and other "analyses which prioritise ideology," because

> there is always presupposed a human subject on the lines of the model provided by classical philosophy, endowed with a consciousness which power is then thought to seize on.[6]

In contrast to this kind of subject to which Foucault denies validity, H. F. is a character whose consciousness and its creation, throughout *A Journal of the Plague Year*, is lucidly displayed. The state of H. F.'s consciousness consistently reflects the progress and eventual ending of the plague. While the plague reigns, for instance, H. F. together with his fellow Londoners find themselves unable to arrive at true knowledge of the plague—of either its causes, means of transmittal, or likely end, and therefore of the possible part they should play during it. Their failure to acquire necessary knowledge is evident in such excerpts as the following (as well as on pp. 131, 151, 159):

> I cou'd give a great many such Stories as these, diverting enough, which in the long Course of that dismal Year, I met with, *that* is, heard of, and which are very certain to be true, or very near the Truth; that is to say, true in the General: for no Man could at such a Time, learn all the Particulars. (47)

> Seeing then that we cou'd come at the certainty of Things by no Method but that of Enquiry of the Neighbours, or of the family, and on that we cou'd not justly depend, it was not possible, but that the incertainty of this Matter wou'd remain. (133)

Foucault sees knowledge as arising from power in the following ways:

> What makes power hold good, what makes it accepted, is simply the fact that it doesn't only weigh on us as a force that says no, but that it traverses and produces things, it induces pleasure, forms knowledge, produces discourse.[7]

> [power] produced effects at the level of desire—and also at the level of knowledge. Far from preventing knowledge, power produces it.[8]

5. Foucault, *Power/Knowledge*, p. 117.   7. Ibid., p. 119.
6. Ibid., p. 58.   8. Ibid., p. 59.

Because the form of power chiefly operating during the plague is the power of the body, with the body functioning in an uncharacteristic relationship of ascendancy over the mind, the kind of knowledge in which this power results is accordingly warped. "Knowledge" during, and at the very beginning of, the plague either does not exist or is extrasensory—as in the many cases of predictions made by fortune-tellers and astrologers, and the interpretations of signs and dreams.[9] H. F.'s very manner of writing throughout the *Journal* evinces the indeterminacy the plague has generated, as many of the exceedingly long sentences in the novel make apparent.[1] Several commentators have noted that the "effort" of a Defoean sentence is devoted to "postponing the decision as to how it shall end."[2] H. F.'s vacillating, repetitive, almost hysterical, endless sentences demonstrate that during the particular discursive formation of the plague, unequivocal thinking is impossible to maintain, and accurate knowledge is elusive.

As further evidence of such perpetual uncertainty, H. F. often (blatantly) defers both the facts and the opinions of his narrative. For example, citing the cruel practices of nurses who attended the sick, he tells us: "But I shall say more of this in its Place" (55), and then twenty pages later does so (70–72); he states that he "shall come to speak of that part again" which concerns the people's lack of thankfulness for their deliverance from the plague (166), and then subsequently on several occasions goes into detail about it (178, 190, 192); he mentions early on the efforts he made toward preventing infection by the plague (66), and then much later gives us the whole story of what he did and didn't do (185–86). There are numerous instances of deferrals like these; while the plague is in force, H. F. cannot even maintain the appearance of possessing knowledge.

At the height of the plague, the astrologers and fortune-tellers have vanished completely, together with their false knowledge. It is then H. F.'s turn to construct his own false knowledge, although he does not come to recognize it as false (and neither, for that matter, does Defoe).

9. Backscheider in *Daniel Defoe: His Life* points out that "most of Defoe's characters have extrasensory experiences and feel the presence of the devil" (523).
1. The following is a sample of a typical extremely long sentence (others can be found on pp. 105, 125–126, 133–34): "And now I am talking of the merciful Disposition of Providence in this time of Calamity, I cannot but mention again, tho' I have spoken several times of it already on other Account, I mean that of the Progression of the Distemper; how it began at one end of the Town, and proceeded gradually and slowly from one Part to another, and like a dark Cloud that passes over our Heads, which as it thickens and overcasts the Air at one End, clears up at the other end. So while the Plague went on raging from West to East, as it went forwards East, it abated in the West, by which means those parts of the Town, which were not seiz'd, or who were left, and where it had spent its Fury, were (as it were) spar'd to help and assist the other; whereas had the Distemper spread it self over the whole City and Suburbs at once, raging in all Places alike, as it has done since in some Places abroad, the whole Body of the People must have been overwhelmed, and there would have died twenty thousand a Day, as they say there did at *Naples*; nor would the People have been able to have help'd or assisted one another" (166).
2. P. N. Furbank and W. R. Owens, *The Canonisation of Daniel Defoe* (New Haven: Yale University Press, 1988), p. 130. Furbank and Owens call Defoe's style of writing "improvisatory." Compare Everett Zimmerman, *Defoe and the Novel* (Berkeley: University of California Press, 1975), p. 114.

H. F. constructs an answer to his question of why, at the time the plague first broke out, there elapsed months between the earliest sicknesses and deaths, in order to make the facts conform to his contagion theory as an explanation of the transmission of the plague. He decides, to his own satisfaction, that the weekly bills for those times were in error and were deliberately attributing deaths from the plague to other causes. However, as medicine now knows, bubonic plague was spread by rats and fleas. Fleas carried the infection from rat to human, and it was thus not necessary for humans to be ill in uninterrupted chains. In a way, therefore, lack of knowledge at the beginning of the plague is matched by lack of knowledge at the end of it; false knowledge is both destroyed and created.

The Great Plague in Defoe's *Journal*, like discourse in Foucault's view of things, is ultimately a way of knowing. H. F.'s entire journal is first and foremost a communication—his scattered attempt through language, in a world where discourse has fallen to bodies, to contain the upheaval of the plague. "In the Classical Age [i.e., the period of the seventeenth and eighteenth centuries]," Foucault tells us,

> discourse is that translucent necessity through which representations and beings must pass—as beings are represented to the mind's eye, and as representation renders beings visible in their truth. The possibility of knowing things and their order passes, in the Classical experience, through the sovereignty of words: words are, in fact, neither marks to be deciphered (as in the Renaissance period) nor more or less faithful and masterable instruments (as in the positivist period); they form rather a colourless network on the basis of which beings manifest themselves and representations are ordered.[3]

Words and events at the time of the plague and of Defoe's composition of the *Journal* were thus interdependent; reality, and the persons—or fictional characters—who experienced it took on the characteristics of the language in which they were represented. H. F. is, of course, unaware of the relationship of his own manner of reporting the plague to the plague itself (although he is aware of the great changes the plague has wrought in communities and individuals). The explanation for his lack of awareness can be found in Foucault's concept of the "archive," defined as "the general system of the formation and transformation of statements." "It is not possible," according to Foucault, "for us to describe our own archive, since it is from within these rules that we speak."[4] H. F. speaks out from an archive of indeterminacy about the unstable reality in which he lives.

During the time the Great Plague has stamped out the old discursive formation, and temporarily created a new one, H. F. defers his own knowledge and the reader's. Only at the end of the plague, when the field is cleared for the appearance of a new discursive formation, does

3. Foucault, *The Order of Things*, p. 311.
4. Foucault, *The Archeaology of Knowledge*, p. 130.

he construct (false) knowledge. He is exemplifying the construction of the human being by discourse—which is exactly the way in which Foucault believes the "human being" was constructed and then suddenly "appeared" at the end of the eighteenth century.[5] H. F., the creation of an author who was in numerous ways ahead of his time, is the precursor of this new kind of individual, described by Foucault as "a primary reality with his own density, . . . the difficult object and sovereign subject of all possible knowledge."[6] In Foucault's view, the rise of this modern individual (who comes to be "objectified" by the social sciences) and of the modern idea of society are complementary sides of the same process.[7]

Far from leaping onto the scene already formed and intact the way a character does in the novels of Richardson or Fielding, H. F. is hazy around the edges—as much a product of, and subject to being shaped by, the turbulence of the plague as the plague is subject to his manner of recounting it. H. F.'s searching, shifting, incipient consciousness is contiguous with the impact of his journal; A Journal of the Plague Year serves on the whole as an eloquent piece of evidence for one of Bakhtin's assertions about the novel:

> [the novel] is, by its very nature, not canonic. It is plasticity itself. It is a genre that is ever questing, ever examining itself and subjecting its established forms to review.[8]

Through H. F.'s developing consciousness and construction of knowledge, and through the triumph and defeat of the power of the body, the point at which one discursive formation changes into another is made visible to us at A Journal of the Plague Year's end.

More than any other writer Defoe arrests for us the sense of the plague being "visibly upon" (a phrase he employs over and over again) the sufferers in London, of the body—and civilization—entering chaos. Ian Watt, discussing how Defoe and Richardson were forced to break with traditional prose style in order to fulfill their realistic intentions and achieve "immediacy and closeness of the text to what is being described," comments that "with Defoe this closeness is mainly physical, with Richardson mainly emotional."[9] By Watt's description, therefore, Defoe was the ideal person to write about the plague.

5. Foucault, The Order of Things, pp. 310–12.
6. Ibid., p. 310.
7. Foucault states in Discipline and Punish: "there is the small historical problem of the emergence, towards the end of the eighteenth century, of what might generally be termed the 'clinical' sciences; the problem of the entry of the individual (and no longer the species) into the field of knowledge; the problem of the entry of the individual description, of the cross-examination, of anamnesis, of the 'file' into the general functioning of scientific discourse"

(191).
    Consider also Raymond Williams in Marxism and Literature: "The major emphasis on language as activity began in the eighteenth century, in close relation to the idea of men having made their own society," which follows from the fact that "a definition of language is always, implicitly or explicitly, a definition of human beings in the world" (21–22).
8. Bakhtin, The Dialogic Imagination, p. 39.
9. Ian Watt, The Rise of The Novel (Berkeley: University of California Press, 1962), p. 29.

The eighteenth century in England saw the rise of the middle class, the birth of a police force, the growth of affective individualism, the cementing of the concept of society, the rise of the novel, the development of disciplinary technology, the weakening of religious belief. All these things can be seen emerging in microcosm in A *Journal of the Plague Year.* "The *Journal*," writes Paula Backscheider, "is full of beautiful rhythms."[1] These are the rhythms of "a new world in the making"; the *Journal* captures the flux of a changing, developing world.

Like Foucaultian theory itself, the effect of the *Journal* is more accurately described as that of an unending evolution than a determinate point of view. The *Journal* is also like Foucault's writings in that it seems to come at us as if from two worlds at once. Although acknowledging that his work might be as much the product of discursive practices as the work of anyone else,[2] Foucault simultaneously asks that we treat his discourse as an exception to this rule. Foucault speaks to us from both our world and the one outside discourse—the one we cannot see. The *Journal* looks backward—to the regicide in 1649, the Restoration in 1660, the Puritan rise and fall, and the plague and Great Fire in 1665 and 1666; takes in the present—the threat of a new outbreak of plague from Marseilles, secularization, and the intensification of human self-consciousness; and looks ahead to the future. In it the residual and the emergent sensitively, hauntingly touch. This is undoubtedly the reason critics have noted its "bi-referentiality," "double representationality," and dual chronological perspective.[3] Charting social and individual chaos, the *Journal* is a discursive formation reflected and revealed, vulnerably displayed. It moves to a plane of transparency the forcible construction of society and thought and the individual subject.

1. Backscheider, *Daniel Defoe: His Life*, p. 504.
2. Foucault, *The Order of Things:* "It would hardly behoove me, of all people, to claim that my discourse is independent of conditions and rules of which I am largely unaware, and which determine other work that is being done today" (xiv).
3. Mas'ud Zavarzadeh in *The Mythopoeic Reality:* "[the *Journal*] is essentially a bi-referential narrative with two fields of meaning: the external and the internal" (pp. 103, 111). See also Bender, *Imagining the Penitentiary*, pp. 75–76.

Discussing George Starr's point of view that "the 'gaze' of Defoe's narrators 'is obsessively purposeful,' " Paula Backscheider in *Daniel Defoe: Ambition and Innovation* states: "And so it is in A *Journal of the Plague Year*, but it is also directed toward describing Defoe's own time" (136).

Daniel Defoe: A Chronology†

1660	Convention Parliament invites Charles II to return to England on April 25. Daniel Defoe probably born in the autumn, the son of James Foe, a London tallow chandler, and his wife, Alice.
1662	Nonconformist clergy ejected from their churches on August 24 by the Act of Uniformity; among other things, the act required clergymen to assent to everything in the *Book of Common Prayer*, which some had not had the opportunity to see.
1665	The Plague strikes London; more than 97,000 die.
1666	War between England and France breaks out. The Great Fire of London breaks out on September 2; 13,000 houses burned.
1674–78?	Studies at Charles Morton's Newington Green Academy, a school for Nonconformists that earned a great reputation.
1681	Decides not to go into the Nonconformist ministry.
1681–92	Is a hose factor and an investor in import/export trade and in such things as a diving bell and civet cats.
1684	On January 1 marries Mary Tuffley, daughter of a wealthy cooper, who brings him a large dowry, £3700.
1685	Charles II dies February 6 and is succeeded by James II. Monmouth rebels June 11 and Defoe joins his army. Monmouth is defeated at Sedgemoor July 6. Defoe manages to escape being captured.
1692	Bankrupt and imprisoned for debt in the Fleet Prison on October 29 and again on November 4.
1693	Imprisoned for debt in the King's Bench Prison on February 12; negotiates terms with his creditors; begins to work for Thomas Neale as a manager-trustee for Neale's private lotteries.
1695	Becomes an accountant to one of the commissioners of the Glass Duty and proprietor of a brick and tile works in Essex.

†Copyright © 1990 and excerpted from *Moll Flanders: The Making of a Criminal Mind* by Paula R. Backscheider with the permission of Twayne Publishers, a division of G.K. Hall & Co., Boston.

1697   Publishes *An Essay upon Projects*, his first long work.

1701   *The True-Born Englishman*, one of the most popular poems of the century; it ridicules those who resented King William because he was Dutch. After this time, sometimes signed his published works, "By the Author of *The True-Born Englishman.*"

1702   The Bill to Prevent Occasional Conformity—legislature intended to bar Nonconformists like Defoe from public office and to restrict other civil rights—is introduced into Parliament. *The Shortest Way with the Dissenters*, a satire of Anglican High Church severity toward the Nonconformists, is published.

1703   *The Shortest Way with the Dissenters* is declared a seditious libel, ordered burned by the Common Hangman, and a warrant for Defoe's arrest is sworn out. Defoe is captured May 21 at the home of a Spittlefields weaver and is imprisoned in Newgate. On June 5 he is released on bail.

1703   Convicted of seditious libel July 7 and sentenced to stand in the pillory three times, pay a fine of 200 marks, and find sureties for good behavior for seven years. Released from Newgate Prison November 8 through Robert Harley's intercessions; is bankrupt again.

1704   First issue of the *Review*, his essay periodical, published Feburary 19.

1704   Begins traveling through the south and east of England for Secretary of State Robert Harley in the summer; samples public opinion and identifies important men and issues for Harley.

1705   Travels throughout England for Harley July through November.

1706   Goes to Scotland September 13 to work for the union between England and Scotland, which are separate countries. Has been able to make new arrangements with his creditors and expects to be issued a Commission of Bankruptcy, which will protect him from future prosecutions.

1709   Publishes *History of the Union of Scotland and England*.

1713   Defoe arrested for debt March 23 and spends 11 days in prison; arrested for seditious libel April 11 and taken to Newgate where he spends a weekend. The charges are trumped up by an enemy who persuaded the government to prosecute him for three ironic pamphlets as if they were to be read literally. Committed to the Queen's Bench Prison for contempt of court on April 22 after publishing an outraged account of his arrest.

He publishes apologies in the April 28 and May 5 *Reviews*, pays a token fine, and is released.

1713–14   Defends the separate peace, the treaty, and Harley's policies.

1714   Queen Anne dies August 1. George I, Elector of Hanover and one of the Allies who refused to endorse the separate peace, becomes King of England. Defoe indicted September 3 for seditious libel for implying that one of George's regents was a Jacobite.

1715   In exchange for the end of the prosecution, begins to work for Secretary of State Townshend, primarily as a journalist, in November. Harley indicted for high treason and sent to the Tower. Defoe continues to defend him in print. Publishes *The Family Instructor*, the first of his conduct books and a popular book into the nineteenth century.

1717   Begins to write for Mist's *Weekly Journal*.

1719   *Robinson Crusoe* published in April. Four editions sell out before its sequel, *Farther Adventures of Robinson Crusoe*, is published in August.

1720   The South Sea Company stock increases astronomically in value and then falls (from a high of over £1,000 in June to £180 in September). *Memoirs of a Cavalier* and *Captain Singleton* published.

1722   Novels *Moll Flanders*, *A Journal of the Plague Year*, and *Colonel Jack* appear.

1722   Invests in land in Essex, begins farming, and tries to start a new brick and tile factory.

1724   Last novel, *The Fortunate Mistress*, or, as it is called today, *Roxana*, and the first volume of *A Tour thro' the Whole Island of Great Britain* published.

1724   Defoe's Colchester, Essex, partner, John Ward, begins court action against him for unpaid debts.

1725   First volume of *The Complete English Tradesman* published.

1726   Swift publishes *Gulliver's Travels* and Defoe the third volume of his *Tour thro' the Whole Island of Great Britain*.

1728   Mary Brooke and Elizabeth Stancliffe begin a suit against Defoe over an old debt. John Gay's *Beggar's Opera* is first performed January 29, and on May 18 the first edition of Alexander Pope's *Dunciad* appears. Defoe's *A Plan of the English Commerce* is published.

1730   Loses court case to Mary Brooke, who had charged that he had never paid a £400 debt and that it was now owed to the estate she had inherited. Goes into hiding to avoid imprisonment for debt.

1731 Dies April 24 of a lethargy, what is now called a stroke, in lodgings on Rope-Makers Alley in the City of London.

1731 Buried April 26 in Bunhill Fields, the famous cemetery for Dissenters.

1732 Mary Defoe is buried December 19 in Bunhill Fields.

Selected Bibliography

This bibliography does not include works excerpted in this volume.

BIOGRAPHICAL WORKS

Paula R. Backscheider, *Daniel Defoe: His Life* (Baltimore: Johns Hopkins UP, 1989), is the only full modern scholarly biography. James Sutherland, *Defoe* (1937; London: Methuen, 1950), is still a useful survey of Defoe's writing. Frank Bastian's somewhat speculative *Defoe's Early Life* (London: Macmillan, 1981) is a detailed look at Defoe's youth and gives a good picture of late seventeenth-century England. John Robert Moore's *Daniel Defoe: Citizen of the Modern World* (Bloomington: Indiana UP, 1958) was another pioneering life. Also of interest is George Chalmers, *The Life of Daniel De Foe* (London: John Stockdale, 1785; rev. and enl., 1790). All but a few of Defoe's letters are in George Healey, *The Letters of Daniel Defoe* (Oxford: Clarendon, 1955).

GENERAL STUDIES

Among the earliest ones are Theophilus Cibber and Robert Shiels, "Daniel De Foe," in *The Lives of the Poets of Great Britain and Ireland*, 4 vol. (London: R. Griffiths, 1753), and Sir Walter Scott, "Daniel De Foe," in *Miscellaneous Prose Works: Biographical Memoirs*, vol. 4 (Ediniburgh, 1827). The following are useful: Alan D. McKillop, "Daniel Defoe," in *The Early Masters of English Fiction* (Lawrence: U of Kansas P, 1956); Pat Rogers, *Defoe: The Critical Heritage* (London: Routledge & Kegan Paul, 1972); John J. Richetti, *Daniel Defoe* (Boston: Hall, 1987). Appropriate volumes of the *Dictionary of Literary Biography* (vol. 39, by Maximillian E. Novak; vol. 95, poetry, by Spiro Peterson; vol. 103, nonfiction prose, by Paula Backscheider) offer reliable general introductions and good bibliographies (Detroit: Gale, 1985–).

THEORETICAL STUDIES

Alkon, Paul. *Defoe and Fictional Time*. Athens: U of Georgia P, 1979.
Backscheider, Paula R. *A Being More Intense*. New York: AMS Press, 1984.
———. *Daniel Defoe: Ambition and Innovation*. Lexington: UP of Kentucky, 1986.
Baine, Rodney. *Daniel Defoe and the Supernatural*. Athens: U of Georgia P, 1979.
Bell, Ian A. *Defoe's Fiction*. Totowa: Barnes & Noble, 1985.
Blewett, David. *Defoe's Art of Fiction*. Toronto: U of Toronto P, 1979.
Earle, Peter. *The World of Defoe*. New York: Atheneum, 1977.
Novak, Maximillian E. *Defoe and the Nature of Man*. Oxford: Clarendon, 1963.
———. *Economics and the Fiction of Daniel Defoe*. Berkeley: U of California P, 1983.
———. *Realism, Myth, and History in Defoe's Fiction*. Lincoln: Nebraska UP, 1983.
Payne, William. *Mr. Review: Daniel Defoe as the Author of the Review*. New York: King's Crown, 1961.
Richetti, John. *Defoe's Narratives*. Oxford: Clarendon, 1975.
Rogers, Pat. "Defoe at Work: The Making of A *Tour thro' Great Britain*, Volume 1." *Bulletin of the New York Public Library* 78 (Summer 1975): 431–50.
———. *Eighteenth-Century Encounters*. Sussex: Harvester, 1985.
———. *Literature and Popular Culture in Eighteenth-Century England*. Totowa: Barnes & Noble, 1985.
Secord, Arthur. *Studies in the Narrative Method of Defoe*. Urbana: U of Illinois P, 1968.
Sill, Geoffrey. *Defoe and the Idea of Fiction*. Newark: U of Delaware P, 1983.
Starr, G.A. *Defoe and Casuistry*. Princeton: Princeton UP, 1971.
———. *Defoe and Spiritual Autobiography*. Princeton: Princeton UP, 1965.
Zimmerman, Everett. *Defoe and the Novel*. Berkeley: U of California P, 1975.

SIGNIFICANT CHAPTERS ON DEFOE

Damrosch, Leopold. *God's Plot and Man's Stories: Studies in the Fictional Imagination from Milton to Fielding.* Chicago: U of Chicago P, 1965.

Flynn, Carol H. *The Body in Swift and Defoe.* Cambridge: Cambridge UP, 1990.

Kay, Carol. *Political Constructions: Defoe, Richardson, and Sterne in Relation to Hobbes, Hume, and Burke.* Ithaca: Cornell UP, 1988.

McKeon, Michael. *The Origins of the English Novel, 1600–1740.* Baltimore: Johns Hopkins UP, 1987.

Marshall, David. *The Figure of Theater: Shaftesbury, Defoe, Adam Smith, and George Eliot.* New York: Columbia UP, 1986.

Paulson, Ronald. *Satire and the Novel in Eighteenth-Century England.* New Haven: Yale UP, 1967.

Price, Martin. *To the Palace of Wisdom: Studies in Order and Energy from Dryden to Blake.* Garden City: Doubleday, 1964.

Ray, William. *Story and History: Narrative Authority and Social Identity in the Eighteenth-Century French and English Novel.* New York: Basil Blackwell, 1990.

Spacks, Patricia Meyer. *Imagining a Self.* Cambridge: Harvard UP, 1976.

Van Ghent, Dorothy. *The English Novel: Form and Function.* New York: Rinehart, 1953.

Varey, Simon. *Space and the Eighteenth-Century English Novel.* Cambridge: Cambridge UP, 1990.

Watt, Ian. *The Rise of the Novel.* Berkeley: U of California P, 1957.

Weinstein, Arnold. *Fictions of the Self: 1550–1800.* Princeton: Princeton UP, 1981.

ARTICLES

Bastian, Frank. "Defoe's *Journal of the Plague Year* Reconsidered." *Review of English Studies* n.s. 16 (1965): 151–73.

Burke, John J. "Observing the Observer in Historical Fictions by Defoe." *Philological Quarterly* 61 (1982): 13–32.

Flanders, W. Austin. "Defoe's *Journal of the Plague Year* and the Modern Urban Experience," *Centennial Review* 16 (1972): 328–48.

Kay, Donald. "Defoe's Sense of History in A *Journal of the Plague Year.*" *Xavier University Studies* 9 (1970): 1–8.

Mayer, Robert. "The Reception of A *Journal of the Plague Year* and the Nexus of Fiction and History in the Novel." *ELH* 57 (1990): 529–56.

Novak, Maximillian E. "History, Ideology and the Method of Defoe's Historical Fiction." *Studies in the Eighteenth Century: Papers Presented at the Fourth David Nichol Smith Memorial Seminar.* Eds. R. F. Brissenden and J. C. Eade. Canberra: Australian National UP, 1979.

Rocks, James E. "Camus Reads Defoe: A *Journal of the Plague Year* as a Source of *The Plague.*" *Tulane Studies in English* 15 (1967): 81–87.

Schonhorn, Manuel. "Defoe's *Journal of the Plague Year:* Topography and Intention." *Review of English Studies* n.s. 19 (1968): 387–402.

Starr, G. A. "Defoe's Prose Style: 1. The Language of Interpretation." *Modern Philology* 71 (1974): 277–94.

PLAGUE STUDIES

Some excellent studies of plague around the time of A *Journal of the Plague Year* are Walter G. Bell, *The Great Plague in London in 1665* (London: John Lane, 1924); Charles F. Mullett, *The Bubonic Plague and England: An Essay in the History of Preventive Medicine* (Lexington: UP of Kentucky, 1956); and Paul Slack, *The Impact of Plague in Tudor and Stuart England* (London: Routledge & Kegan Paul, 1985) The notes written by Louis A. Landa in the Oxford edition of A *Journal of the Plague Year* include many citations to Defoe's and his contemporaries' medical sources (1969; Oxford: Oxford UP, 1990).